Human Resource Management

TENTH EDITION

Robert L. Mathis
University of Nebraska at Omaha

John H. Jackson
University of Wyoming

THOMSON
SOUTH-WESTERN

Australia · Canada · Mexico · Singapore · Spain · United Kingdom · United States

THOMSON

SOUTH-WESTERN

Human Resource Management, Tenth Edition
Robert L. Mathis and John H. Jackson

Publisher:
Melissa Acuña

Sr. Acquisitions Editor:
Charles E. McCormick, Jr.

Developmental Editor:
Mardell Toomey

Marketing Manager:
Larry Qualls

Sr. Production Editor:
Deanna Quinn

Manufacturing Coordinator:
Diane Lohman

Media Technology Editor:
Diane Van Bakel

Media Developmental Editor:
Chris Wittmer

Media Production Editor:
Amy Wilson

Cartoon Researcher:
Sam Marshall

Design Project Manager:
Michelle Kunkler

Internal and Cover Designer:
Ann Small/a small design studio, Cincinnati

Cover Image:
© PhotoDisc, Inc.

Production House/Compositor:
Shepherd, Inc

Printer:
R.R. Donnelley—Willard

COPYRIGHT © 2003
by South-Western, a division of
Thomson Learning. Thomson
Learning™ is a trademark used herein
under license.

Printed in the United States of America
2 3 4 5 05 04 03 02

For more information
contact South-Western,
5191 Natorp Boulevard,
Mason, Ohio 45040.
Or you can visit our Internet site at:
http://www.swcollege.com

Library of Congress Cataloging-in-
Publication Data

Mathis, Robert L.
    Human resource management/Robert L.
Mathis, John H. Jackson.—10th ed.
        p. cm
    Includes bibliographical references and
index.
    ISBN: 0-324-07151-5 (package)
    ISBN: 0-324-07152-3 (text)
    ISBN: 0-324-07153-1 (booklet)
    1. Personnel management.   I. Jackson,
John Harold.   II. Title.

HF5549 .M3349 2002
658.3—dc21   2002017683

TO

Jo Ann Mathis
who manages me

R. D. and M. M. Jackson
who were successful managers of people for many years

Contents in Brief

Contents

SECTION 2

Staffing the Organization

S E C T I O N 4

Compensating Human Resources

SECTION 5
Employee Relations and Global HR

Preface

"The future has suddenly and dramatically become the present."
—R. Babson

Organizations today face many challenges in the management of their human resources. Every week brings news media reports on organization downsizing, workforce diversity, shortages of skilled workers, and other concerns. The purpose of this book is to provide a current understanding of developments in the field of human resource (HR) management.

The authors of this book are gratified that this text is a leader in the field of HR management. The changes made in this edition are designed to keep it the standard against which other books in the field are compared. It is a standard for academics in educating students taking HR classes or those needing HR knowledge as part of other professional degree programs. It is a standard for HR professionals using it to review their HR knowledge in the pursuit of HR professional certifications.

The tenth edition of the book builds on successful past editions. At the same time, it incorporates a significant number of changes to maintain its leadership position. In the most thorough revision possible of this text, the authors evaluated every line and word of content from the previous edition, integrating valuable new information. Past users and readers will see that the tenth edition is the most current and readable HR text available.

There are a number of reasons for someone to read this book. Some readers will be current or future HR professionals, and for them, the book covers the body of HR knowledge faced in organizations regularly. However, other individuals will read the book while enrolled in HR or other management-related courses in a number of disciplines and fields. It is likely that these readers will not become HR generalists or specialists. But everyone who works in any organization will face HR issues and be confronted with HR management decisions with major consequences for every organization. Throughout the book, a feature entitled "Typical Division of HR Responsibilities" describes typical ways HR responsibilities are shared by HR specialists and operating managers and supervisors.

Another important audience for the book is composed of practicing HR professionals. Previous editions of the book aided hundreds of HR professionals in enhancing their knowledge and preparing for professional exams to become PHR or SPHR certified by the Human Resource Certification Institute (HRCI). This edition will continue to be valuable to HR professionals, and the authors made conscious efforts to provide content coverage of the topics in the HRCI certification exams. Specifically for those individuals, Appendix A reproduces the test specifications identified by HRCI when it released its most recent revised content outline.

In the Tenth Edition

This edition continues some features highly regarded in past editions, but readers will find some new ones as well. A few of the latter are noted next.

West Group HR Advisor on the Web

An important addition to the tenth edition is the West Group HR Advisor on the Web. As an industry leader in providing information to HR professionals, West Group produces and sells HR Advisor on the Web to thousands of HR practitioners. Through a cooperative arrangement, every instructor and purchaser of the new text will receive an individualized access code to all of the HR Advisor content at the West Group Web site. Details are in the booklet inside the front cover of the each copy of the tenth edition. On the HR Advisor readers will be able to read current analyses of HR issues, view sample HR policies in more than 70 areas, obtain compliance instructions, download numerous sample HR forms, and review background details on many topics that expand or supplement the coverage in the tenth edition. Also, individuals can subscribe to *HR Wire,* an Internet-provided newsletter that regularly covers current "hot topics," court decisions, and timely policy and practice information. To tie in the West Group content throughout the book, all chapters contain several specific West Group item notations as a margin feature, and directions for linking to the HR Advisor on the Web content in the designated area.

Internet

As the Internet becomes an increasingly valuable tool for HR professionals, it affects a number of HR activities. To incorporate more Internet links, this edition adds or expands several features. First, throughout the text the *Logging On* feature identifies Web sites that contain useful sources of HR information in specific content areas. Most of these links are new to the tenth edition, and each contains a specific World Wide Web address active at the publication time of this text. Second, within most chapters a new feature, e-HR, describes the impact of the Internet on how HR management is practiced or raises HR issues prompted by employee use of the Internet in organizations. Third, an end-of-chapter feature, *Using the Internet,* presents an exercise in which students respond to typical HR situations or managerial requests with the help of a designated Internet site. Finally, where appropriate, references from Web addresses are cited in the chapter notes.

Human Resource Management, Tenth Edition Web Site

At a dedicated Web site just for the tenth edition, instructors and students will find useful tools and additional resources to enrich and extend textbook presentations. Instructors will find downloadable ancillary materials. Students and other readers can locate other resources, such as quick links to a number of useful items, at ***http//mathis.swcollege.com.***

Included on the Web site are listings of HR literature, resources, and important organizations. Also, the Web site contains Web addresses for a variety of electronic newsletters from some leading consulting firms that provide HR content. Most of these newsletters can be subscribed to at no cost. Accessing these newsletters provides timely information on current HR events, court decisions, studies, and other areas.

Organization of the Tenth Edition

The organization of the tenth edition reflects significant changes from the previous edition. Throughout the text a number of key modifications include the following features.

HR Resources and Research Updated

To address the rapid changes within HR management, the authors used the most current references, with more than 90% of the references dated year 2000 or later. The few remaining references from the previous edition are classic research or conceptual articles, significant court decisions, or other timeless content. Interestingly, a comparative analysis of other HR text reveals that more than half of their resource citations were more than five years old when those books were released. The authors take pride in their efforts to include virtually all new resources and references to meet the commitment of providing the most current HR text.

HR's Strategic Contribution to Organizational Effectiveness

This text stresses how HR professionals and the activities they direct contribute to the strategic business success of organizations. The first chapter looks at the roles of HR management, particularly the importance of the *strategic* role of HR management. Chapter 2 addresses strategic human resource planning, the strategic factors affecting HR, how to evaluate the effectiveness of HR management, and the use of human resource information systems (HRIS).

Individual Performance and Employee Retention

In the competitive world of today, organizations require individuals who perform well and remain as employees. After a revised discussion of motivation, Chapter 3 contains extensive content on employee retention. No other general HR text provides comparable coverage of retention to that contained in the tenth edition.

Equal Employment and Affirmative Action

Major revisions made in Chapters 4 and 5 cover equal employment opportunity (EEO). As suggested by reviewers, Chapter 4 addresses the various laws, regulations, and court decisions that determine the legal framework of EEO. Because the issues of diversity and equal employment are so closely linked, Chapter 5 begins with a discussion of diversity and the importance of managing diversity as a critical part of HR management. This chapter also contains an updated look at various aspects of implementing equal employment, such as sexual harassment, age discrimination, and religious discrimination.

Staffing the Organization

Significant revisions to Chapter 6, Jobs and Human Resources, describe job design and redesign issues that impact organizations and the people working in them. Based on job design, the chapter then continues the useful coverage of job analysis and the task-based and competency approaches to job analysis.

Chapter 7 focuses on recruiting in tight labor markets. The difficulties of recruiting employees with scarce skills and new methods of attracting these individuals are discussed. Specifically, the chapter contains considerable new content on Internet recruiting. Strategic recruiting, including use of flexible staffing approaches, also is highlighted in Chapter 7. An expansion of the well-regarded coverage on selection in Chapter 8 encompasses the selection strategy choices that management must make. The revised discussion of psychological testing and interviewing approaches and techniques reflects current research and practices in HR management.

Training and HR Development

The revisions made to Chapter 9 on training are based on input from reviewers and assistance from Lisa Burke at Louisiana State University–Shreveport. The chapter now discusses the strategic role training plays in organizations and how training must be linked to business strategies and organizational competitiveness. Specific content on adult learning and newer training design and delivery means is provided. As the text addresses the growing use of *e*-learning, it includes why and how organizations move toward Web-based training. Chapter 10 on HR development looks at the means organizations use to expand the capabilities of their human resources. The chapter contains new content on succession planning and why it will grow in importance as a focus of HR management in the coming years. The chapter also discusses leadership and other management development approaches.

Performance Management

Chapter 11 expands the material on identifying and measuring employee performance, including additional information on multisource and 360 degree approaches as they become integral in many performance management systems. The chapter emphasizes performance management and the role of the performance appraisal process in enhancing the performance of human resources in organizations.

Compensating Human Resources

Compensation of human resources covers pay administration, incentives, and benefits. Chapters 12 and 13 include information on approaches such as broadbanding and competency-based pay to augment the well-regarded coverage of base compensation, pay-for-performance, and variable-pay programs already in those chapters. New coverage of variable-pay plans of various types has been added. Also, changes in content made in Chapter 14 on benefits highlight the growing cost concerns facing HR professionals and organizations.

Employee Relations

The discussion of employee relations addresses several areas, including health, safety, and security. The revisions to the coverage in Chapter 15 of health, safety, and security issues identify current health and safety issues and OSHA compliance requirements. The chapter offers new content on the prevention of workplace violence and the importance of workplace security. The various issues associated with employee rights and discipline, such as employment-at-will, privacy rights, and substance abuse are expanded in Chapter 16. It also looks at emerging issues such as electronic monitoring, privacy, and e-mail, and other employee-rights issues affected by technology.

Union-Management Relations

The changing role of unions in the U.S. economy is discussed in Chapter 17. In addition to covering the basic laws and regulations governing union-management relations in the United States, new material discusses reasons for the declining percentage of workers in unions and the challenges facing both unions and management.

Global HR Management

A significant change in this edition is the movement of the content on global HR management to be the final chapter. Contrary to what some may view as diminishing the importance of global HR, the authors constructed Chapter 18 as a "capstone" to emphasize how global forces affect the way in which HR management is practiced. Significantly revised global HR content addresses the expatriate selection and assignment process, as well as the repatriation process needed with global employees. Because all of the previously discussed HR activities must be addressed somewhat differently when global HR employees are managed, the authors responded to reviewers' suggestions to use the global HR content to conclude the book.

Chapter Features

Each chapter begins with specific learning objectives. Next, the *HR Insights* feature contains an example of an HR problem, situation, or practice in an actual organization, which illustrates some facet of that chapter's content. Each chapter also presents *HR Perspectives* vignettes that highlight HR management examples, ethical issues, and research studies. Additionally, new to this edition, many chapters contain *HR Practices* boxes, which offer suggestions on how to handle specific HR issues or situations, and the *e-HR* examples mentioned earlier. Both the *West Group* and the *Logging On* features provide linkages to additional material beyond the text content.

Following a point-by-point summary, the review and discussions questions link to the opening learning objectives. Key terms and concepts are listed, and a "Using the Internet" exercise is included. At the end of every chapter, a case presents a real-life problem or situation using actual organizations as examples. Finally, reference notes cite sources used in the chapter, with particular attention given to the inclusion of the most current references and research possible.

Supplements

Student Resource Guide
(ISBN 0-324-07156-6)

Designed from a student's perspective by Julie Woodard, SPHR, this useful study guide comes with all the tools necessary to maximize results in class and on exams. Chapter objectives and chapter outlines aid students in reviewing for exams. Study questions include matching (10–15 per chapter), true/false (15 per chapter), idea completion (5 per chapter), multiple choice (25 per chapter), and essay questions (3 per chapter). Answer keys are provided. Key issues are identified for each case presented in the text.

HR Management Electronic Review Guide (ISBN 0-324-18341-0)

A Web-based learning companion, the HR Management Electronic Review uses a question-and-feedback format to give individuals the opportunity to identify and review their professional knowledge of HR management content. Prepared by Julie Woodard, SPHR, and Alan Jaramillo, SPHR, the HR Management Professional Review provides a broad-based review of topics central to HR management. For individuals who will be taking tests over HR management content, a prologue of test-taking tips is included to ease exam anxiety and provide practical advice.

Videos (ISBN 0-538-89013-4)

A diverse selection of custom-produced, CNN news segments are available to introduce topics, supplement lecture material, and stimulate discussion. Companies, people, and events that are familiar to students illustrate human resource issues and offer insights into all phases of human resource management.

Instructor's Manual (ISBN 0-324-18531-6)

The instructor's manual, prepared by Cary Thorp, University of Nebraska–Lincoln, and Thomas R. Tudor, James Madison University, represents one of the most exciting and professionally useful instructor's aids available. Comprehensive teaching materials, including chapter overviews, chapter outlines, instructor's notes, and suggested answers to end-of-chapter Review and Discussion Questions and

Using the Internet exercises are provided for every chapter. A guide to the videos available for use in classes includes notes about how to introduce the videos to students, points to consider when viewing various segments, and questions for discussion.

Test Bank (ISBN 0-324-18532-4)

The test bank contains more than 1,500 test questions prepared by Roger Dean of Washington and Lee University. Multiple-choice, true/false, and essay questions are provided for every chapter. Answers are cross-referenced to pages in the textbook that pinpoint where relevant material can be found in the text. When the answer to a true/false question is false, feedback is provided to underscore the reason why.

The test bank is also available in a computerized Windows™-compatible format. Exam View (ISBN 0-324-17934-0) is a fully integrated software program that allows for test creation, delivery, and classroom management tools.

Transparency Acetates
(ISBN 0-324-07158-8)

Prepared by Cary Thorp, University of Nebraska–Lincoln, in conjunction with the instructor's manual, a full-color set of 120 transparency acetates is also available to instructors to enhance classroom presentations.

Instructor's Resource CD-ROM
(ISBN 0-324-07154-X)

The Instructor's Resource CD-ROM includes an electronic version of the instructor's manual, printed test bank and Exam View. In addition, it includes a comprehensive set of full-color PowerPoint presentation slides, prepared by Charlie T. Cook of The University of West Alabama.

Acknowledgments

Producing any book requires assistance from many others. The authors especially appreciated the contribution to the training chapter by Lisa A. Burke, Louisiana State University–Shreveport. The authors are especially grateful to those individuals who provided reviews and numerous helpful comments for the tenth edition. Including two reviewers who asked to remain anonymous, the following individuals did comprehensive reviews:

Enoch K. Beraho	*South Carolina State College*
Lisa A. Burke	*Louisiana State University–Shreveport*
Derek E. Crews	*Alderson-Broaddus College*
Rebby Denise Diehl	*Salt Lake Community College*
John Hannon	*University at Buffalo*
Michelle J. Jackson	*SPHR*
Avis L. Johnson	*University of Akron*
Gundars Kaupins	*Boise State University*
Brian Klaas	*University of South Carolina*
Daniel Lybrook	*Purdue University*
Jon Monat	*California State University, Long Beach*
Albert C. Smith, Jr.	*Radford University*
Cary Thorp	*University of Nebraska–Lincoln*
Dr. Linsey Craig Willis, SPHR	*Lynn University; Nova Southeastern University; Barry University*

Finally, some leading HR professionals provided ideas and assistance. Appreciation is expressed to Nicholas Dayan, SPHR; Jerry L. Sellentin, SPHR; and Raymond B. Weinberg, SPHR.

Those involved in changing messy scrawls into printed ideas deserve special recognition. At the top of that list is Jo Ann Mathis, whose guidance and prodding made this book better. Others who assisted with many critical details include Carolyn Foster and our copy editor, Cheryl Wilms. Also, Julie Woodard and Nealy Vicker provided valuable assistance.

The authors thank Charles McCormick, Jr., Senior Acquisitions Editor, and Mardell Toomey, Developmental Editor, for their guidance and involvement. We also appreciate the support of our Senior Production Editor, Deanna Quinn.

The authors feel confident that this edition will continue as a standard for the HR field. We believe it offers a relevant and interesting look at HR management, and we are optimistic that those who use the book will agree.

Robert L. Mathis, SPHR   John H. Jackson
Omaha, Nebraska   Laramie, Wyoming

Dr. Robert L. Mathis

Dr. Robert Mathis is Professor of Management at the University of Nebraska at Omaha (UNO). Born and raised in Texas, he received a B.B.A. and M.B.A. from Texas Tech University and a Ph.D. in Management and Organization from the University of Colorado. At UNO he has received the University's "Excellence in Teaching" award.

Dr. Mathis has co-authored several books and has published numerous articles covering a variety of topics over the last 25 years. On the professional level, Dr. Mathis has held numerous national offices in the Society for Human Resource Management and in other professional organizations, including the Academy of Management. He also has served as President of the Human Resource Certification Institute (HRCI) and is certified as a Senior Professional in Human Resources (SPHR) by HRCI.

He has had extensive consulting experiences with organizations of all sizes in a variety of areas. Firms assisted have been in telecommunications, telemarketing, financial, manufacturing, retail, health-care, and utility industries. He has extensive specialized consulting experience in establishing or revising compensation plans for small- and medium-sized firms. Internationally, Dr. Mathis has consulting and training experience with organizations in Australia, Lithuania, Romania, Moldova, and Taiwan.

Dr. John H. Jackson

Dr. John H. Jackson is Professor of Management at the University of Wyoming. Born in Alaska, he received his B.B.A. and M.B.A. from Texas Tech University. He then worked in the telecommunications industry in human resources management for several years. After leaving that industry, he completed his doctoral studies at the University of Colorado and received his Ph.D. in Management and Organization.

During his academic career, Dr. Jackson has authored four other college texts and over 50 articles and papers, including those appearing in *Academy of Management Review, Journal of Management, Human Resources Management,* and *Human Resources Planning.* He has consulted widely with a variety of organizations on HR and management development matters. During the past several years, Dr. Jackson has served as an expert witness in a number of HR-related cases.

At the University of Wyoming he served two terms as Department Head in the Department of Management and Marketing. Dr. Jackson has received teaching awards at Wyoming and was one of the first to work with two-way interactive television for MBA students in the state. In addition, he designed one of the first classes in the nation on *Business Environment and Natural Resources.* In addition to teaching, Dr. Jackson is president of Silverwood Ranches, Inc.

Nature of Human Resource Management

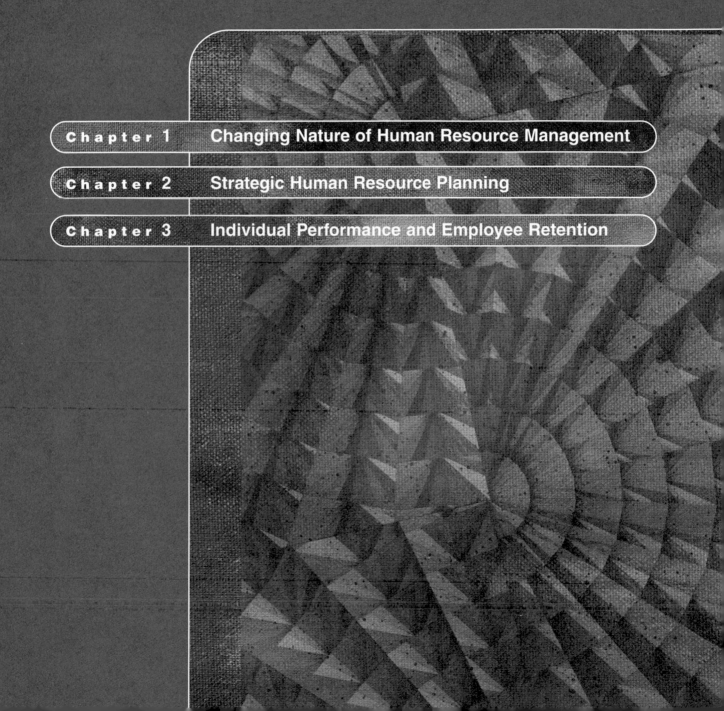

CHAPTER 1

Changing Nature of Human Resource Management

After you have read this chapter, you should be able to:

- Define HR management and explain why managers and HR staff must work together.

- List and define the seven categories of HR activities.

- Identify three challenges facing HR today.

- Describe the four roles of HR management.

- Discuss why ethical issues affect HR management.

People Can Be Problematic

As one manager put it, "People are a lot of trouble and they take a lot of time." He was correct. Yet many organizations have no choice but to hire employees and invest the time and trouble necessary to deal with their human resources.

Two examples show both the difficulty and the payoff of handling HR management issues well. The first is a look at a company on the rebound (ACNielsen), and the second is a summary of what we have learned from the wave of mergers and acquisitions over the last 10 years.

ACNielsen is a Samford, Connecticut-based market research firm that fell on hard times in the mid 1990s. The company lost hundreds of millions of dollars and client dissatisfaction was high. The situation was so bad that many were doubtful about turning around the firm's performance. But performance did improve, due in part to retaining valued employees and bringing in new talent to provide new insight and energy. Employee satisfaction, measured routinely by employee surveys, was low. The company executives realized they had to somehow engage the Nielsen workforce again. A new philosophy was adopted: Employees who have the necessary tools, appropriate leadership, and a positive work environment provide good customer service, which ultimately leads to profits.

A "business effectiveness survey" (BES) has been conducted each fall. The BES gives employees the opportunity to provide feedback to their managers, which the managers take very seriously. They should because 25% of their bonus pay is tied to their BES scores. Many positive outcomes have resulted from use of this survey: a reward system change, recognition awards, identification of necessary management competencies, ACNielsen University for training, and promotion from within, just to name a few. Employee retention has risen to 87% annually, and more than 90% of worldwide employees take the BES (up from 40%). BES ratings also have been used to remove managers who were unwilling to change. Overall, the firm's financial stability is improving, and motivated employees with the tools and training they need are making a big difference.

Another example of HR's importance can be found in the huge numbers of mergers and acquisitions in the past 10 years. Two companies that see opportunities for growth, market leadership, technological dominance, or just more profit by joining, frequently do so. Study after study shows that the results are often disappointing. One study showed that in the first year of mergers, the newly combined firms lose 10% of market value. Another study found that fully 50% of the merged firms failed to maintain book value two years later. The American Management Association reported only about 15% of corporate mergers and acquisitions achieve their financial objectives.

The factors most poorly handled are those that affect the employees of the organizations. Because of the unique pressures involved in a merger or acquisition, management is often stretched thin and inevitably focuses on the financial and legal aspects of operations. However, HR issues can make the combination successful or break it. Factors leading to poor organizational results frequently include: losing top talent, employee confusion that jeopardizes sales, internal operational paralysis causing missed deadlines, and customers who would rather not put up with problems caused by the merger/ acquisition.

Before, during, and after a merger or acquisition, HR issues can spell failure, and apparently do frequently.[1] Human resources *do* take time, but dealing with them successfully is the subject of this book.

> Motivated employees with the tools and training they need are making a big difference.

"The world economy is going through a seismic shift to intellectual capital from capital investment."

—**John Byrne**

For many organizations, talented employees are the cornerstone of a competitive advantage. If the organization competes based on new ideas, outstanding customer service, or quick, accurate decisions, having excellent employees is critical.[2] Of course, not every organization must compete on the basis of having the best employees, but even for those that do not, employees are a major source of performance, problems, growth, resistance, and lawsuits.

Humans are a necessary, varied, and sometimes problematic resource that most organizations must use to a greater or lesser degree. For example, customer relations management (CRM) is a business strategy to get, grow, and retain the right customers. CRM covers a wide range of approaches, including Web-based communications and other technological tools to provide excellent customer service.[3] One might think employees were the least important part of automated customer service, but even with all the technology, many companies are finding that part of what customers want is someone *human* to call and talk to at times. Dell computers, for example, allows a choice of Web-based, phone, or face-to-face customer contact. Further, customer loyalty is elusive without positive relations between customers and employees. If employees constantly "leave for greener pastures" who will build relationships with customers? The computer?[4]

Designing systems to effectively manage people with their needs, expectations, quirks, legal rights, and high potential is a challenge. Human Resource Management focuses on doing just that.

Nature of Human Resource Management

Human Resource (HR) management is a field that has evolved a great deal since its beginnings about 1900. It began as a primarily clerical operation concerned with payroll, employee records, and arranging community visits. The social legislation of the 1960s and 1970s forced dramatic changes. "Personnel departments," as they were called, became concerned with the legal ramifications of policies and procedures affecting employees. In the 1990s, globalization, competition, mergers, and acquisitions forced Human Resource departments to become more concerned with costs, planning, and the implications of various HR (human resources) strategies for both organizations and their employees.

Human Resource (HR) management The design of formal systems in an organization to ensure effective and efficient use of human talent to accomplish organizational goals.

Human Resource (HR) management is the design of formal systems in an organization to ensure effective and efficient use of human talent to accomplish organizational goals. Whether a big company with 10,000 employees or a small non-profit organization with 10 employees, those employees must be *paid,* which means an appropriate and legal compensation system is needed. Employees also must be recruited, selected, trained, and managed. Each of these activities requires thought and understanding about what will work well and what may not. Research on these issues and the knowledge from successful approaches form the basis for HR management. In an environment in which the workforce keeps changing, laws change, and the needs of the employer change too, HR management must continue to change and evolve. Understanding the challenges, problems, and trends helps those who must deal with such issues continue HR's evolution.

Who Is an HR Manager?

In a real sense *every* manager in an organization is an HR manager. Sales managers, head nurses, drafting supervisors, college deans, and accounting department supervisors all engage in HR management, and their effectiveness depends in part on the success of organizational HR systems. However, it is unrealistic to expect a nursing supervisor to know about the nuances of equal employment regulations, or how to design a compensation system. For that reason, larger organizations frequently have people in an HR department who specialize in these activities.

Cooperation between operating managers, such as those already mentioned, and the HR department is necessary for HR efforts to succeed. In many cases, the HR department designs processes and systems that the operating managers must help implement. The exact division of labor between the two varies from organization to organization. Throughout this book there will be suggestions as to how HR responsibilities in various areas typically are divided in organizations having specialized HR departments. The suggestions will appear as figures labeled *Typical Division of HR Responsibilities* such as in Figure 1-1. That figure shows how the responsibilities for interviewing applicants for a job might be divided between an HR department and the other managers in the organization.

HR in Small and Large Organizations

Not every organization is able to have an HR department. In a company with an owner and 10 employees, the owner usually takes care of HR issues. However, despite the obvious differences between large and small organizations, the same HR issues must be managed—as the HR Perspective box on the next page illustrates. At about 80–100 employees, organizations typically need to designate a person to specialize in HR management. Others are added only as the company gets much larger. Specifically what HR activities must be done in any organization regardless of its size are discussed in the next section.

Figure 1-1 ▶ **Typical Division of HR Responsibilities: Selection Interviewing**

HR Unit	Managers
• *Develops legal, effective interviewing techniques*	• *Advise HR of job openings*
• *Trains managers in conducting selection interviews*	• *Decide whether to do own final interviewing*
• *Conducts interviews and testing*	• *Receive interview training from HR unit*
• *Sends top three applicants to managers for final interview*	• *Do final interviewing and hiring where appropriate*
• *Checks references*	• *Review reference information*
• *Does final interviewing and hiring for certain job classifications*	• *Provide feedback to HR unit on hiring/rejection decisions*

HR problems and issues occur in organizations both large and small. However, the difference is often that harried owner/managers in small organizations have less time to deal with HR problems because they are doing everything else. For example, many small Internet companies have been so focused on survival they have paid little attention to issues such as sexual harassment, employee handbooks, and overtime pay. Even the most basic HR issues have been overlooked. New York-based Juno Online Services is facing lawsuits from two former employers alleging sexual harassment. It seemed more important to add another programmer than an HR person until something like that happened. "Once you get past 50 people, you can no longer handle things by intimate conversation," says the vice president of marketing for a San Francisco firm that grew from 12 to 119 employees in a short period.

A long-time Denver firm with about 20 employees that had competed successfully against Circuit City and Best Buy in the TV and appliance business, recently ended 59 years of family business because it was unable to keep enough good employees in a tight labor market. The key to the store's success had been extremely good service from knowledgeable, long-term employees. Three generations of the Valas family had been in the business that closed because of staffing difficulties.[5] This and countless other examples illustrate the impact of HR issues on small businesses.

HR Activities

HR management is composed of several groups of interlinked activities taking place within the context of the organization, represented by the inner rings in Figure 1-2. Additionally, all managers with HR responsibilities must consider external environmental forces—legal, political, economic, social, cultural, and technological—when addressing these activities. A brief overview of the seven HR activities follows:

- HR Planning and Analysis
- Equal Employment Opportunity
- Staffing
- HR Development
- Compensation and Benefits
- Health, Safety, and Security
- Employee and Labor/Management Relations

HR Planning and Analysis Through *HR planning,* managers attempt to anticipate forces that will influence the future supply of and demand for employees. Having adequate *human resource information systems (HRIS)* to provide accurate and timely information for HR planning is crucial. The importance of human resources in organizational competitiveness must be addressed as well. As part of maintaining organizational competitiveness, analysis and assessment of *HR effectiveness* must occur. Employees also must be appropriately motivated and be willing to stay with the organization for a reasonable time. These topics are examined in Chapters 2 and 3.

Figure 1-2 **HR Management Activities**

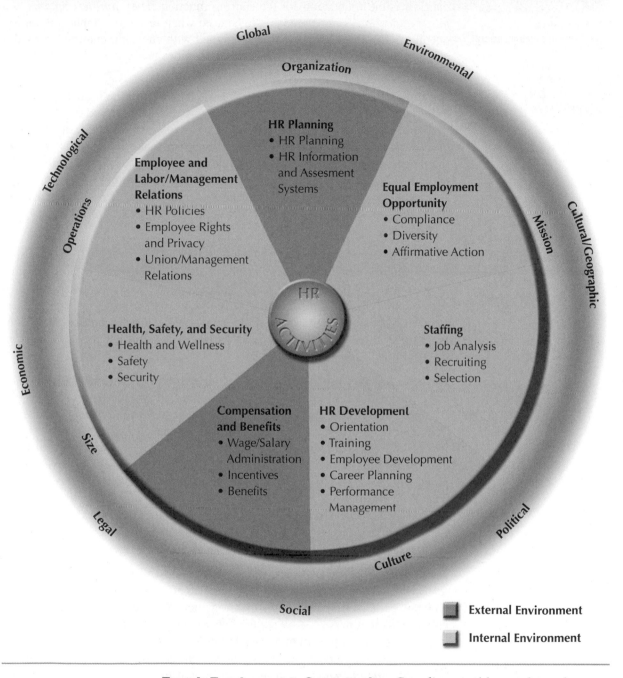

Equal Employment Opportunity *Compliance* with equal employment opportunity (EEO) laws and regulations affects all other HR activities and is integral to HR management. For instance, strategic HR plans must ensure sufficient availability of a *diversity* of individuals to meet *affirmative action* requirements. In addition, when recruiting, selecting, and training individuals, all managers must be aware of EEO requirements. The nature of EEO compliance is discussed in Chapters 4 and 5.

HR Functions
Lists activities within each HR function.
Custom Search:
☑ CHECKLISTS
Phrase: HR functions and activities

Staffing The aim of staffing is to provide an adequate supply of qualified individuals to fill the jobs in an organization. By studying what workers do, *job analysis* is the foundation for the staffing function. Then *job descriptions* and *job specifications* can be prepared to be used when *recruiting* applicants for job openings. The *selection* process is concerned with choosing qualified individuals to fill jobs in the organization. Staffing activities are discussed in Chapters 6, 7, and 8.

HR Development Beginning with the *orientation* of new employees, HR development also includes *job-skill training*. As jobs evolve and change, ongoing *retraining* is necessary to accommodate technological changes. Encouraging *development* of all employees, including supervisors and managers, is necessary to prepare organizations for future challenges. *Career planning* identifies paths and activities for individual employees as they develop within the organization. Assessing how employees perform their jobs is the focus of *performance management.* Activities associated with HR development are examined in Chapters 9, 10, and 11.

Compensation and Benefits Compensation rewards people for performing organizational work through *pay, incentives,* and *benefits.* Employers must develop and refine their basic *wage and salary* systems. Also, *incentive programs* such as gainsharing and productivity rewards are growing in usage. The rapid increase in the costs of *benefits,* especially health-care benefits, will continue to be a major issue. Compensation incentives, and benefits activities are discussed in Chapters 12, 13, and 14.

Health, Safety, and Security Ensuring the physical and mental health and safety of employees is vital. The Occupational Safety and Health Act of 1970 (OSHA) has made organizations more responsive to *health and safety* concerns. The traditional concern for *safety* has focused on eliminating accidents and injuries at work. Through a broader focus on *health,* HR management can assist employees with substance abuse and other problems through *employee assistance programs* (EAP) in order to retain otherwise satisfactory employees. *Health promotion* programs that promote healthy employee lifestyles are becoming more widespread. Additionally, workplace *security* has grown in importance, in response to the increasing number of acts of workplace violence. Health, safety, and security activities are examined in Chapter 15.

Employee and Labor/Management Relations The relationship between managers and their employees must be handled effectively if both the employees and the organization are to prosper together. Whether or not some of the employees are represented by a union, *employee rights* must be addressed. It is important to develop, communicate, and update HR *policies and procedures* so that managers and employees alike know what is expected. In some organizations, *union/management relations* must be addressed as well. Activities associated with employee and labor/management relations are discussed in Chapters 16 and 17.

Global HR The rapid pace at which organizations have "gone global" has greatly expanded HR issues with different cultures. International aspects of HR management are covered in Chapter 18.

HR Management Challenges

The environment faced by HR management is a challenging one. Some of the most significant changes facing HR management are as follows:

- Economic and technological changes
- Workforce availability and quality
- Growth in contingent workforce
- Demographics issues
- Work/family balancing
- Organizational restructuring and mergers/acquisitions

Economic and Technological Changes

Several economic changes have altered employment and occupational patterns in the United States. A major change is the shift of jobs from manufacturing and agriculture to service industries and telecommunications. This shift has meant that some organizations have reduced the number of employees, while others scramble to attract and retain employees with different capabilities than previously needed. Additionally, pressures from global competitors have forced many U.S. firms to close facilities, adapt their management practices, increase productivity, and decrease labor costs in order to become more competitive. Finally, the growth of information technology, particularly that linked to the Internet, has led to many changes throughout organizations of all types.

Technology-Caused Occupational Shifts Projections of the growth in some jobs and decline in others illustrate the current shifts occurring in the U.S. economy. Figure 1-3 on the next page lists occupations with both the largest number and percentage growth for the period ending in 2008. Most of the fastest-growing occupations percentage-wise are related to information technology. The increase in technology jobs is due to the rapid growth of information technology, such as databases, system design and analysis, and desktop publishing.

Global Competition A major factor affecting these shifts is economic globalization. Estimates are that more than 25% of all U.S. manufacturing workers hold jobs dependent on exporting goods to other countries, particularly with more highly skilled jobs in technology-driven industries. These jobs pay higher wages than most other manufacturing jobs. On the other hand, the less-skilled manufacturing assembly jobs have been shifting from the higher-wage, developed economies in the United States and Western Europe to developing countries in Eastern Europe, China, Thailand, Mexico, and the Philippines where wages are much lower. Information technology has extended global linkages, and production and transportation can be coordinated worldwide. Many manufacturing jobs in the United States have been replaced with jobs in information technology, financial services, health care, and retail services.

In summary, the U.S. economy has become predominately a service economy, and that shift is expected to continue. Approximately 80% of U.S. jobs are in service industries, and most new jobs created by the year 2008 also will be in services. It is estimated that manufacturing jobs will represent only 12% to 15% of all U.S. jobs by that date. Global and technological changes have not only

Logging On...

U.S. Bureau of Labor Statistics
This Web site contains data on workforce composition and trends from the U.S. Department of Labor, Bureau of Labor Statistics.

http://stats.bls.gov./sahome.html

Figure 1-3   *Jobs of the Future*

TOP FIVE TOTAL JOBS ADDED, 1998–2008

	Jobs Added	Percentage Growth
Systems Analyst	577,000	94%
Retail Salesperson	563,000	14
Cashier	556,000	17
General Manager	551,000	16
Truck Driver	493,000	17
Overall	20,300,000	14

TOP FIVE JOBS PERCENTAGE GROWTH, 1998–2008

	Jobs Added	Percentage Growth
Computer Engineer	323,000	108%
Computer Support Specialist	439,000	102
Systems Analyst	577,000	94
Database Administrator	67,000	77
Desktop Publishing Specialist	19,000	73
Overall	20,300,000	14

Source: U.S. Department of Labor, Bureau of Labor Statistics, 2001.

changed the workforce and the competition, they have changed the issues faced by HR management as well.[6]

Workforce Availability and Quality

In many parts of the United States today, significant workforce shortages exist due to an inadequate supply of workers with the skills needed to perform the jobs being added. It is not that there are too few people—only too few with the skills being demanded. In the last several years news reports have regularly described tight labor markets with unemployment rates in some locales below 3%. Also, industries and companies repeatedly report shortages of qualified, experienced workers. Consequently, HR professionals have faced greater pressures to retain, recruit, and train workers.

Even though more Americans are graduating from high school (84% over age 25 have high school diplomas) and from college (almost 26% over age 25 now have college degrees), employers are often concerned about the preparation and specific skills of new graduates.[7] Comparisons of international test results show that U.S. children perform slightly above average in math and science, but *well behind* some other directly competitive nations.[8] Also, graduates with degrees in computers, engineering and health sciences remain in short supply relative to the demand for them.

Unless major efforts are made to improve educational systems, especially those serving minorities, employers will be unable to find enough qualified workers for the growing number of "knowledge jobs." A number of employers are addressing the deficiencies that many employees have in basic literacy and mathematical skills by administering basic skills assessments to employees. Then they conduct basic mathematics and English skills training classes at workplace sites for employees with deficiencies. Some employers also sponsor programs to assist employees and their family members in obtaining general equivalency diplomas (GED). To address the skills deficiencies, HR management must do the following:

- Assess accurately the knowledge and skills of existing employees, as well as the knowledge and skills needed for specific jobs.
- Make training for future jobs and skills available for employees at all levels, not just managers and professionals.
- Increase the usage of new training methods, such as interactive videos, individualized computer training, and e-learning via the Internet.
- Become active partners with public school systems in upgrading the knowledge and skills of high school graduates.

Growth in Contingent Workforce

In the past, temporary workers were used for vacation relief, maternity leave, or workload peaks. Today "contingent workers" (temporary workers, independent contractors, leased employees, and part-timers) represent more than 20% of the workforce. Many employers operate with a core group of regular employees with critical skills and then expand and contract the workforce through the use of contingent workers.[9]

This practice requires determining staffing needs and deciding in advance which employees or positions should form the "core" and which should be more fluid. At one large firm, about 10% of the workforce is contingent now. The company sees using contingent employees as a way to stabilize the workforce. Instead of hiring regular workers when work loads increase and then terminating them when the work load decreases, the company relies more on temporary workers and independent contractors. Productivity is measured as output per hour. Thus, if employees are paid only when they are working (as contingents are), overall productivity often increases.[10]

The use of contingent workers has grown for many different reasons. During the 1970s and 1980s, courts made it more difficult for employers to fire regular workers, so employers hired more temps. Ironically, attempts to protect workers led to jobs that offered less security and often lower pay.[11]

Another reason for use of contingent workers is the possible reduced legal liability for employers. As more and more employment-related lawsuits are filed, some employers have become more wary about adding regular employees. Instead, by using contract workers supplied by others, employers face fewer employment legal issues regarding selection, discrimination, benefits, discipline, and termination.

The use of contingent workers is not without its problems, however. Microsoft employs over 40,000 people, with 5,000 to 6,000 as temps. Microsoft paid more than $97 million to "permatemps" to settle an eight-year suit over whether those individuals were really "independent contractors" or "employees." The courts held that the employees were not really temps and were really employees entitled to benefits under Microsoft's benefits plans.[12] The exact status of contingent workers can be an issue.

Further, not all contingent workers (or "flexible workforce" in the United Kingdom) want to be temporary employees.[13] In fact, recent research found 53% of workers holding contingent jobs would prefer regular jobs, but just 39% preferring the contingent arrangement.[14] Also, the National Labor Relations Board has held that temporary workers can join unions of regular employees where they are working, without permission of their employment agency or the client employer.[15]

Demographics and Diversity

The U.S. workforce has been changing dramatically. It is more diverse racially, women are in the labor force in much greater numbers than ever before, and the average age of the workforce is now considerably older than before. As a result of these demographic shifts, HR management in organizations has had to adapt to a more varied labor force both externally and internally.[16] For example, at Trident Manufacturing in Webster, New York, 14 different languages are spoken on the shop floor.[17]

Major changes in the demographics and diversity of the workforce are as follows:

- Minority racial and ethnic persons account for a growing percentage of the overall labor force, with the percentage of Latinos equal to or exceeding the number of African Americans. Immigrants will continue to expand this growth.
- A growing number of individuals characterize themselves as "multiracial" suggesting that the American "melting pot" is blurring racial/ethnic identities.
- Women constitute a growing percentage of the U.S. workforce, and a majority of women with smaller children are employed. A large percentage of the 3.67 million new moms are in the workforce (see Figure 1-4).
- The average age of the U.S. population and workforce is increasing, and a large number of those workers will be retiring from full-time employment in the next five to ten years.
- A significant number of individuals have disabilities, but they also represent a pool of highly motivated and capable individuals.

| Figure 1-4 | New Moms in the Workforce |

Level of education	Total	Percent in the workforce*	Percent working full-time	Percent working part-time
High school graduate	*1,034,000*	*58.4%*	*33.5%*	*17.0%*
At least one year of college	*1,844,000*	*67.9%*	*46.6%*	*19.1%*
Bachelor's degree	*627,000*	*66.5%*	*45.8%*	*19.9%*
Graduate or professional degree	*239,000*	*73.6%*	*63.2%*	*10.4%*

*Includes contingent workers and others counted in workforce

Source: U.S. Census Bureau, 2000.

Balancing Work and Family

For many workers in the United States, balancing the demands of family and work is a significant challenge. Although this balancing has always been a concern, the increased number of working women and dual-career couples has resulted in greater tensions for many workers. According to recent U.S. government data, families and households are composed as follows:

- Dual-career couples compose about 60% of all married couples, representing 30.3 million couples.
- Households headed by a single parent make up more than 25% of all families, with women heading most of these households. Single-parent households are less prevalent among whites than among other racial/ethnic groups.
- The number of households of married couples with no children living at home is growing and represents almost the same number of households as married couples with children.
- The "traditional family" where a male goes to work and the female stays home to raise children represents only 10% or less of today's U.S. households.
- Seventy percent of all women with children under age six are in the workforce, and 60% of all women with children under age three are working.
- Both men and women are marrying at later ages, with the median age of first marriage for men about 27 and for women about 24.

The decline of the traditional family and the increasing numbers of dual-career couples and working single parents place more stress on employees to balance family and work. To respond to pressures faced by employees, many employers have instituted various "family friendly" initiatives. Although important to both males and females, the reality is that family care for children and elderly relatives still is carried primarily by women. Thus, actions taken by employers to enable women to balance work and family responsibilities can be beneficial for both employee retention and organizational productivity.

Backlash Against Work/Family Programs Seemingly generous employer actions can also produce conflicts which employers must confront, such as a backlash against "family friendly" programs by single workers and those without children.[18] Because those programs often are geared to the needs of workers who are parents, those employees without children see such alternatives as flexible work schedules, job-sharing, time-off to attend children's school activities, and the like as excluding their time-off needs.[19] In some organizations single employees are often the ones who are asked to travel extensively or to take on additional responsibilities because "the other employees have families." Also, the extra efforts of employees without family responsibilities often do not carry extra compensation with them. One unnamed single male employee "invented" a seven-year old nephew who was fatherless and needed a male role model so the employee could take time off for his hobbies of biking and golf. Another single employee made up stories of the deteriorating health of her 70-year-old mother as a reason why she could not take a three-week job assignment out of town. Numerous other childless employees probably have had similar ideas.

Family/Work Issues

Ford Motor Company and the United Auto Workers recently announced a new program for child care and other family services at 30 cities around the country. The programs are in response to what employees have said they need. The program provides high quality child care available 24 hours per day, classes, wellness programs, and more.

Harley-Davidson's York, PA plant provides child care help for employees—75% of whom are men. Harley provides discounted slots in a nearby child-care facility. Round Mountain Gold Corporation provides child care, a general store, medical clinic and jobs for spouses of new employees in a remote location in Nevada. For employees the Federal National Mortgage Association in Washington, D.C., has a comprehensive elder-care program, including a geriatric social worker, opportunity to purchase discounted elder-care services, and long-term care insurance.

However, not all attempts to balance work and family have been successful. Five hotels in Atlanta led by Marriott opened "Atlanta Inn for Children," designed to dovetail with their employees' odd working hours. Four years later, however, only one-third of children in the center were from hotel industry employees. Because Industry employees represent 50 different cultures and speak 30 different languages, many were hesitant to go outside their extended families or neighborhoods to use paid child care. Further, 50 hours a week of child care costs $135 for an infant, and many hotel workers could not afford the price even with subsidies from employers. The director of the project says, "Atlanta taught us you can't carry debt service on a child-care project. The numbers just don't work."[20] All of these examples illustrate that work/family balance issues remain a challenge despite many attempts to deal with them.

The purpose of pointing out the backlash is that HR professionals must ensure that work/family programs are designed and implemented in a way that recognizes employees have "outside lives" and different values and needs.[21] Ignoring backlash may affect the working relationships of employees with and without family responsibilities. Also, as more employees have responsibilities for elderly family members, work/family programs must not be centered just on employees with children, as the HR Perspective illustrates.

Organizational Restructuring, Mergers/Acquisitions

Many organizations have restructured in the past few years in order to become more competitive. Also, mergers and acquisitions (M&A) of firms in the same industries have been made to ensure global competitiveness. The "mega-mergers" in the banking, petroleum, and telecommunications industries have been especially visible, but mergers and acquisitions in many other industries also have increased in recent years.

As part of these organizational changes, many organizations have "right-sized" by: (1) eliminating layers of managers, (2) closing facilities, (3) merging with other organizations, and (4) outplacing workers. A common transformation has been to flatten organizations by removing several layers of management in order to improve productivity, quality, and service while also reducing costs. As a result, jobs are redesigned and people affected. One of the challenges that HR management faces with organizational restructuring is dealing with the human consequences of change. The human cost associated with downsizing has been much discussed in the popular press: a survivor's mentality for those who remain, unfulfilled cost savings estimates, loss of loyalty, and many people looking for new jobs.

But three out of four mergers and acquisitions fail to achieve their financial and strategic objectives.[22] Many possible reasons explain why attempted M&As fail; and several of those reasons are in the HR arena. Unanticipated consequences of restructuring after an M&A often cause the need for more organizational restructuring later and a longer time frame for normal operations to resume.[23]

HR management can contribute to successful mergers and acquisitions. However, experience with the failures shows clearly what has to be done by HR managers for mergers to succeed is to ensure that different organizational cultures mesh. *Cultural compatibility* is the extent to which such factors as decision-making styles, levels of teamwork, information sharing philosophies, and the formality of the two organizations are similar. Human resource systems include those used to manage, motivate, and develop people. If all elements of a company's culture and HR systems are carefully analyzed, at least differences will be exposed and plans can be made to deal with them.[24] Some considerations here include:

HR—Mergers & Acquisitions
Describes common HR issues associated with mergers and acquisitions.
Custom Search:
☑ ANALYSIS
Phrase: Merger-related HR problems

- What kinds of behaviors are rewarded in each company?
- What skill areas are emphasized?
- How are development and career opportunities offered in each?
- How similar are the basic organizational attitudes and values?

Research sponsored by the Society for Human Resource Management found that for HR to provide good and useful input to M&A, it must be able to quickly evaluate the other company, understand the business and integration issues, and provide advice on employees' sensitivities, attitudes, and motivation/retention needs in both the parent and acquired organizations.[25] To illustrate, Cisco Systems had digested 51 companies in recent years. It successfully used acquisition to reshape itself and plug holes in its product lines. Even before Cisco signed an acquisition deal, a transition SWAT team would oversee every detail of the assimilation in order to reduce uncertainty so the newly acquired employees could continue to concentrate on their jobs. Not all Cisco acquisitions are flawless, but it has experienced fewer failures than normally occur.[26]

HR Management Roles

HR management professionals and their responsibilities, approaches, and credibility with upper management vary from organization to organization. In some, HR is a full, contributing partner to the mission and strategies of organizations. For example, in such a case senior executives would not even consider a merger without consulting HR on the issues just discussed. However, in other organizations HR remains more of a clerical and administrative operation limited primarily to doing payroll and benefits work. The difference between the two extremes has to do both with what upper management wants HR management in the organization to be, and with the competencies that HR staff have demonstrated. Thus, the amount of confidence senior management has in the HR staff varies. Figure 1-5 shows four different levels of HR roles. Each of these levels will be discussed next.

Figure 1-5 ▶ **Different Roles for HR Management**

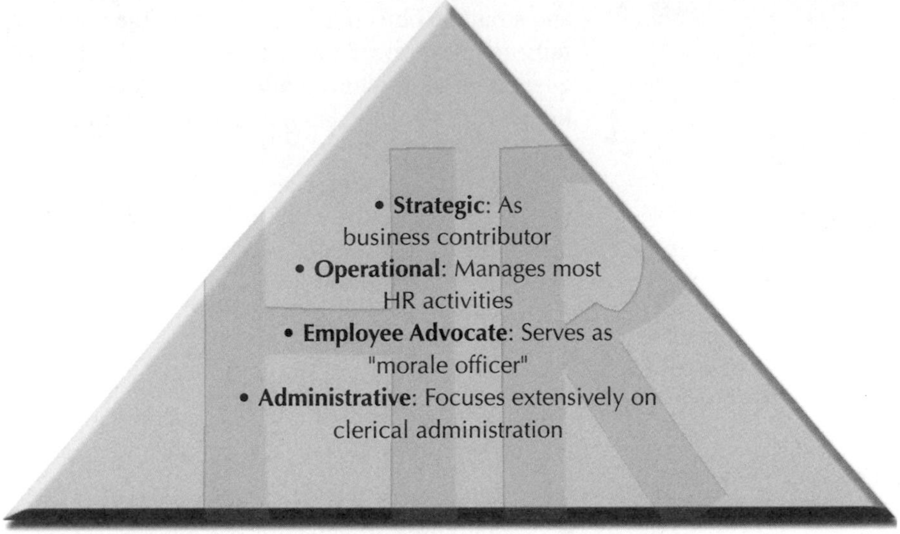

- **Strategic**: As
  business contributor
- **Operational**: Manages most
  HR activities
- **Employee Advocate**: Serves as
  "morale officer"
- **Administrative**: Focuses extensively on
  clerical administration

Administrative Role for HR

At the most basic level, the necessary HR activities in a company are handled by operating managers or "outsourced" under contract to specialized vendors. At this level HR management is mostly a clerical and administrative support operation. The organization may not even hire any HR employees directly, but "lease" them for a fee from an employee leasing firm that hires, pays, provides benefits, and dismisses when necessary.

More commonly, certain HR activities are done in-house and some are done under contract by another company or a consultant. Typical activities that are outsourced include employee assistance programs, pension administration, background/reference checks, benefits administration and training and development.

A recent survey looked at outsourcing of HR activities and found 70% of responding employers outsource some HR functions. That figure compares with 47% four years earlier. The larger the employer, the more likely it was to outsource. Employers that did not outsource cited philosophy, cost, loss of control, and privacy concerns as reasons for not outsourcing. Least frequently outsourced include HR information systems, compensation planning and administration, and handling family leave issues. Concern about the quality of the services they are receiving is the biggest reason employers select or change outsourcing vendors.[27]

Operating managers most often carry out HR activities in smaller organization. But as organizations grow and other issues consume their time, many managers find that the HR issues are ones they would most like to delegate to someone else.[28] Further, improvement in output is possible with investment of time in human resource issues, but extra time is the one commodity many operating managers do not have.[29]

To improve the administrative efficiency and responsiveness of HR to employees and managers, more HR functions are becoming available electronically

The Effect of "e"

The Web's emergence has been touted as nirvana for HR executives and professionals: "paperless" transactions, self-service for employees, recruiting by the Net, e-learning, and on and on. A senior vice president of HR at Wellpoint Health Networks notes HR services can be provided cheaper on the Web. "Why pay $4 per transaction when you can do it on the Web for $1?" he asks. A senior vice president at KPMG suggests, "I'd say the real big winners so far are recruiting, learning, corporate communications, collaboration, and transactions."

An executive at Resource Marketing tells the following story. The firm had planned an employment open house to bring in possible candidates for jobs, but the newspaper ad did not get in the paper on time. But the notice had been on the company's Web site and more than 100 people turned out–more candidates than they needed. In fact, it has been noted noted that when people come in for interviews, they have usually checked out the company Web site, which is the norm today.

But has "e-HR" actually delivered in all situations? The answer is both yes and no. It does seem to save time and some paperwork, but it also creates "Web work." The profusion of e-mail messages and more demands on HR from employees because of higher expectations are two examples.

A manager of professional training notes, "You need to focus on the goals, not the technology. It won't do much good to have a pretty picture if no one comes to look at it." CEOs want HR to tell them if they are getting the right people in the right jobs, and the Web in its current state may not do that completely. But "e-HR" appears to help HR with its administrative role.[30]

or done over the Internet. The e-HR discussion describes how e-HR is changing the administrative role of HR.

Employee Advocate Role for HR

Traditionally, HR has been viewed as the "employee advocate" in organizations. As the voice for employee concerns, HR professionals traditionally have been seen as "company morale officers" who do not understand the business realities of the organizations and do not contribute measurably to the strategic success of the business. Some have even suggested dismantling HR departments totally because under this role, they contribute little to the productivity and growth of organizations.

Despite this view, someone must be the "champion" for employees and employee issues. HR professionals spend considerable time on HR "crisis management" dealing with employee problems that are both work and nonwork related. Employee advocacy helps ensure fair and equitable treatment for employees regardless of personal background or circumstances. Some entity inside the organization must monitor employee situations and respond to employee complaints about unfair treatment or inappropriate actions. Otherwise, employers would face even more lawsuits and regulatory complaints than they do now.

As HR management changes, the need for HR to balance being the advocate for employees and being a business contributor becomes more evident. What this balancing means is that it is vital for HR professionals to represent employee issues and concerns in the organization. However, simply being an effective employee advocate is not sufficient. Ideally, HR professionals should be strategic contributors, operationally efficient, and cost-effective.

HR staff members find often themselves in an awkward spot in the organization when demands come both from executives and employees. However, it has been suggested that although HR executives are remarkably well-versed in HR expertise, they may lack sufficient knowledge of organizational products, services and major business issues. This limited knowledge may in some cases lead to HR managers advocating for employees against management. In the end, successful HR is part of management, and without that partnership, the employee advocate has limited effects on management decisions.[31]

Operational Role for HR

Typically the operational role requires HR professionals to identify and implement needed programs and policies in the organization in cooperation with operating managers. This role traditionally includes many of the HR activities mentioned earlier in the chapter. HR implements plans suggested by or developed in conjunction with other managers, as well as those identified by HR professionals. Even though priorities may change as labor markets and the economy change, in the operational role, HR managers devote time to a variety of basic HR concerns. Based on a survey of HR professionals, Figure 1-6 shows how HR's time typically is spent.

The operational HR role emphasizes support for the organization through adept handling of HR problems and issues. However, HR may not be heavily involved in strategic decision making in the organization.

Operational activities are tactical in nature. Compliance with equal employment opportunity and other laws are ensured, employment applications are processed, current openings are filled through interviews, supervisors are trained, safety problems are resolved, and wages and salaries are administered. Thus, various efforts performed typically are associated with coordinating the

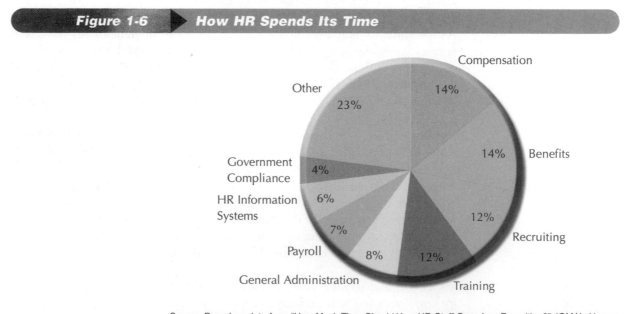

Figure 1-6 **How HR Spends Its Time**

Compensation 14%
Other 23%
Benefits 14%
Recruiting 12%
Training 12%
General Administration 8%
Payroll 7%
HR Information Systems 6%
Government Compliance 4%

Source: Based on data from "How Much Time Should Your HR Staff Spend on Recruiting?" *IOMA's Human Resources Department Management Report,* June 2000, p. 6.

Too Much Strategic Approach

The HR department at Unisys became more strategic and consultative, but many managers and employees did not like the new focus. In the process, Unisys lost sight of the operational basics. Certainly Unisys is not the only company to encounter these problems. Balancing the strategic role with employee services and advocacy requires a blend of efforts, not just one role.

At Unisys, the HR department had moved quickly in that direction, changing HR generalists into specialists. The HR staff had become so specialized that oper-ating managers were unable to find just one person to deal with multifaceted problems. An individual operating manager had to sort out who was the compensation specialist, the training person, or the employee relations expert and then bring them together to discuss a problem. Of course, it was not an effective way to provide good service to the customers HR had in the organization.

Unisys solved the problem by bringing back modern-day HR generalists who bring together all the specialized experts as needed to solve problems. To help service employee needs better, they put in place e-HR tools that provide a "one-stop shopping" access for all employees. An employee can use the Web site to enroll in training programs, change personal data, bid on open jobs in the company, and do skill assessments and career planning.

An HR spokesman notes that managers' and employees' impressions of HR are driven directly by how they experience the benefits and services that HR provides. Being a business partner means doing *both* strategic and operational work.[32]

management of HR activities with actions of managers and supervisors throughout organizations. This operational role is important, but if it is HR's only role, certain advantages may be lost for the organization.

Strategic Role for HR

For HR to play a strategic role it must focus on the longer-term implications of HR issues. How changing workforce demographics and workforce shortages will affect the organization, and what means will be used to address the shortages over time, are examples of the strategic role. A strategic role for HR is important, but it requires a high level of professional and business knowledge. The HR Perspective shows that the transition to a strategic role is not without difficulties.

The importance of the strategic role has been the subject of extensive discussion recently in the field, and those discussions have emphasized the need for HR management to become a greater strategic contributor to the success of organizations. Even organizations that are not-for-profit, such as governmental or social service entities, must manage their human resources in a "business-oriented" manner. Based upon the research and writings of a number of scholars, the role of HR as a *strategic business partner* has been stressed. The important components of that approach follow.

Enhancing Organizational Performance Organizational performance can be seen in how effectively the products or services of the organization are delivered to customers. The human resources in organizations are designers, producers, and deliverers of those services. Therefore, one goal of HR management is to establish activities that contribute to superior organizational performance. Only by doing so can HR professionals justify the claim that they contribute to the strategic success of organizations.

Involvement in Strategic Planning Integral to being a strategic partner is for HR to have "a seat at the table" when organizational strategic planning occurs. Strategically, then, human resources must be viewed in the same context as the financial, technological, and other resources that are managed in organizations. For instance, the strategic planning team at one consumer retailer was considering setting strategic goals to expand the number of stores by 25% and move geographically into new areas. The HR executive provided information on workforce availability and typical pay rates for each of the areas and recommended that the plans be scaled back due to tight labor markets for hiring employees at pay rates consistent with the financial plans being considered. This illustration of HR professionals participating in strategic planning is seen more frequently in organizations today than in the past.

Decision Making on Mergers, Acquisitions, and Downsizing In many industries today, organizations are merging with or acquiring other firms. In all of these mergers and acquisitions numerous HR issues are associated with combining organizational cultures and operations. If they are viewed as strategic contributors, HR professionals will participate in the discussions prior to top management making final decisions. For example, in one firm with 1,000 employees, the vice president of human resources spends one week in any firm that is proposed for merger or acquisition to determine whether the "corporate cultures" of the two entities are compatible. Two potential acquisitions that were viable financially were not made because he determined that the organizations would not mesh well and that some talented employees in both organizations probably would quit. In all industries, this level of involvement by HR professionals is unusual.

Redesigning Organizations and Work Processes In the strategic planning process, organization structure follows strategic planning. The implication of this concept is that changes in the organization structure and how work is divided into jobs are the vehicles through which the organization drives toward its strategic plans and goals. An understanding of strategic sources of competitive advantages for human resources must include analyses of the internal strengths and weaknesses of the human resources in an organization. Those in HR management must work with operating executives and managers to revise the organization and its components. HR managers should function in this way much as architects do when redesigning existing buildings.

Ensuring Financial Accountability for HR Results A final part of the HR management link to organizational performance is to demonstrate on a continuing basis that HR activities and efforts contribute to the financial results of the organization. Traditionally, HR was seen as activity-oriented, rather than concerned about the financial consequences of HR efforts. For instance, in one firm the HR director reported every month to senior management how many people were hired and how many had left the organization. However, the senior managers were becoming increasingly concerned about how long employment openings were vacant and the high turnover rate in customer service jobs. A new HR director conducted a study that documented the cost of losing customer service representatives. The HR director then requested funds to raise wages for customer service representatives and also implemented an incentive program for those employees.

Figure 1-7 ▶ *Overview of HR Management Roles*

	Administrative Role	Operational and Advocacy Roles	Strategic Role
Focus	Administrative processing and record keeping	Operational support Representing the employees	Organization-wide, global
Timing	Short term (less than 1 year)	Intermediate term (1–2 years)	Longer term (2–5 years)
Typical Activities	• Administering employee benefits • Conducting new employee orientations • Interpreting HR policies and procedures • Preparing equal employment reports	• Managing compensation programs • Recruiting and selecting for current openings • Conducting safety training • Resolving employee complaints • Representing employee concerns	• Assessing workforce trends and issues • Engaging in community workforce development planning • Assisting in organizational restructuring and downsizing • Advising on mergers or acquisitions • Planning compensation strategies

Also, a new customer service training program was developed. After one year the HR director was able to document a reduction of $150,000 in turnover and hiring costs for customer service representatives. This example illustrates that to be strategic contributors, HR professionals must measure what their activities produce as organizational results, specifically as a return on the investments in human resources. Figure 1-7 shows a summary of what is done in each of the HR roles in the organization and how all roles are important.

Ethics and HR

As the issues faced in HR management increase in number and complexity, so do the pressures and challenges of acting ethically. Ethical issues pose fundamental questions about fairness, justice, truthfulness, and social responsibility. Concerns arise about the ethical standards used by managers and employees, particularly those in business organizations.[33] But it appears that the concerns are well-founded. Some of the most frequent problems are cheating on expense accounts, paying or accepting bribes and kickbacks, forging signatures, and lying about sick leave.

What Is Ethical Behavior?

Ethics deals with what "ought" to be done. For the HR professional it is the way in which the manager *ought* to act relative to a given human resource issue. However, determining specific actions is not always easy. Ethical issues in management, including HR issues, have five dimensions:

- *Extended consequences:* Ethical decisions have consequences beyond the decisions themselves. Closing a plant and moving it to another location to avoid unionization of a workforce has an impact on the affected workers, their families, the community, and other businesses.
- *Multiple alternatives:* Various alternatives exist in most decision-making situations, so the issue may involve how far to "bend" rules. For example, deciding how much flexibility to offer employees with family problems, while denying other employees similar flexibility, may require considering various alternatives.
- *Mixed outcomes:* Decisions with ethical dimensions often involve weighing some beneficial outcomes against some negative ones. For example, preserving the jobs of some workers in a plant might require eliminating the jobs of others. The result would be a mix of negative and positive outcomes for the organization and the affected employees.
- *Uncertain consequences:* The consequences of decisions with ethical dimensions often are not known. Should employees' personal lifestyles or family situations eliminate them from promotion even though they clearly are the most qualified candidates?
- *Personal effects:* Ethical decisions often affect the personal lives of employees, their families, and others. Allowing foreign customers to dictate that they will not have a female or minority sales representative call on them may help with the business relationship short term, but what are the effects on the employees and future career opportunities?

Responding to Ethical Situations

To respond to situations with ethical elements, there are some guidelines to consider. Just complying with the laws does not guarantee ethical behavior. Laws and regulations cannot cover every situation HR professionals and employees will face. Instead, people must be guided by values and personal behavior "codes," including the following:

- Does the behavior or result meet all applicable *laws, regulations,* and *government codes?*
- Does the behavior or result achieved meet all *organizational standards* of ethical behavior?
- Does the behavior or result achieved meet *professional standards* of ethical behavior?

Ethical Issues in HR Management

HR professionals regularly are faced with ethical issues. To help HR professionals deal with ethical issues, the Society for Human Resource Management (SHRM) has developed a code of ethics for its members.

According to a study most employees surveyed indicated that they had seen unethical workplace conduct in the previous year. The most common unethical incidents by employees were lying to supervisors, employee drug or alcohol abuse, and falsification of records.[34] With HR management in an international environment, other ethical pressures arise. Such practices as gift giving and hir-

Logging On...

Society for Human Resource Management
This Web site contains the SHRM Code of Ethics and other information available through SHRM.

http://www.shrm.org

WEST GROUP
A THOMSON COMPANY

Ethics Policies
Highlights areas typically covered in employer ethics policies.
Custom Search:
☑ ANALYSIS
Phrase: Topics a handbook policy can cover

ing vary in other countries, and some of those practices would not be accepted as ethical in the United States. Consequently, all managers, including HR managers, must deal with ethical issues and be sensitive to how they interplay with HR activities. One way to address ethical issues in organizations is to conduct training of executives, managers, and employees. However, training of managers and employees in ethics compliance has not necessarily reduced employee misconduct.[35]

The complete study of ethics is philosophical, complex, and beyond the scope of this book. The intent here is to highlight ethical aspects of HR management. Various ethical issues in HR management are highlighted throughout the text as well.

HR Management Competencies and Careers

As HR management becomes more and more complex, greater demands are placed on individuals who make the HR field their career specialty. Although most readers of this book will not become HR managers, it is useful to know about the competencies required for effective HR management.

A wide variety of jobs can be performed in HR departments. As a firm grows large enough to need someone to focus primarily on HR activities, the role of the **HR generalist** emerges—that is, a person who has responsibility for performing a variety of HR activities. Further growth leads to adding **HR specialists** who have in-depth knowledge and expertise in a limited area. Intensive knowledge of an activity such as benefits, testing, training, or affirmative action compliance typifies the work of HR specialists.

HR generalist A person with responsibility for performing a variety of HR activities.

HR specialist A person with in-depth knowledge and expertise in a limited area of HR.

Changes in the HR field are leading to changes in the competencies and capabilities of individuals concentrating on HR management. The development of broader competencies by HR professionals will ensure that HR management plays a strategic role in organizations. The following sets of capabilities are important for HR professionals:

- Knowledge of business and organization
- Influence and change management
- Specific HR knowledge and expertise

Knowledge of Business and Organization

HR professionals must have knowledge of the organization and its strategies if they are to contribute strategically. This knowledge also means that they must have understanding of the financial, technological, and other facets of the industry and the organization. As illustration, in some organizations the top HR executive jobs are being filled by individuals who have been successful operations managers, but have never worked in HR. The thinking behind such a move is that good strategic business managers can rely on the HR specialists reporting to them, while bringing a performance-oriented, strategic view of HR management to the top of the organization. In other organizations, top HR managers have come up through HR specialties, and have demonstrated that they understand broader business and strategic realities, not just HR management functional issues.

Influence and Change Management

Another key capability that HR professionals need is to be able to influence others and to guide changes in organizations. Given the many HR-related changes affecting today's organizations, HR professionals must be able to influence others.

HR Specific Knowledge

The idea that "liking to work with people" is the major qualification necessary for success in HR is one of the greatest myths about the field. It ignores the technical knowledge and education needed. Depending on the job, HR professionals may need considerable knowledge about employment law, tax laws, finance, statistics, or information systems. In all cases, they need extensive knowledge about equal employment opportunity regulations and wage/hour regulations.

The body of knowledge of the HR field, as used by the Human Resource Certification Institute (HRCI), is contained in Appendix A. This outline reveals the breadth and depth of knowledge necessary for HR professionals. Additionally, those who want to succeed in the field must update their knowledge continually. Reading HR publications, such as those listed in Appendix B and on the Web site for this book, is one way to stay informed.

Professional Involvement The broad range of issues faced by HR professionals has made involvement in professional associations and organizations important. For HR generalists, the largest organization is the Society for Human Resource Management (SHRM). Public-sector HR professionals tend to be concentrated in the International Personnel Management Association (IPMA). Other major functional specialty HR organizations exist, such as the International Association for Human Resource Information Management (IHRIM), the World at Work Association, and the American Society for Training and Development (ASTD). A listing of major HR-related associations and organizations is contained in Appendix B.

Certification One of the characteristics of a professional field is having a means to certify the knowledge and competence of members of the profession. The CPA for accountants and the CLU for life insurance underwriters are well-known examples. The most well-known certification program for HR generalists is administered by the Human Resource Certification Institute (HRCI), which is affiliated with SHRM. More than 12,000 HR professionals annually have taken the HRCI exam.

Increasingly, employers hiring or promoting HR professionals are requesting certification as a "plus." HR professionals feel that HR certification gives them more credibility with corporate peers and senior managers. Certification by HRCI is available at two levels, and both levels have education and experience requirements.

Additional certification programs exist for both specialists and generalists sponsored by other organizations. For specialists, here are some of the most well-known programs:

- Certified Compensation Professional (CCP), sponsored by the World at Work Association
- Certified Employee Benefits Specialist (CEBS), sponsored by the International Foundation of Employee Benefits Plans

Logging On...

Human Resource Certification Institute
This site lists information on the HRCI certification process.

http://www.hrci.org

- Certified Benefits Professional (CBP), sponsored by World at Work Association
- Certified Safety Professional (CSP), sponsored by the Board of Certified Safety Professionals
- Occupational Health and Safety Technologist (OHST), given by the American Board of Industrial Hygiene and the Board of Certified Safety Professionals

The most prevalent specialist category is benefits specialist, followed by recruiting and training specialists, compensation specialists, and human resource information system (HRIS) specialists.[36]

Summary

- HR management is concerned with formal systems in organizations to ensure the effective and efficient use of human talent to accomplish organizational goals.
- The need for HR management occurs in all organizations, but larger ones are more likely to have a specialized HR function.
- HR challenges faced by managers and organizations include economic and technological changes, workforce availability and quality concerns, demographics, and organizational restructuring.
- HR management activities can be grouped as follows: HR planning, equal employment opportunity compliance, staffing, HR development, compensation and benefits, health, safety and security, and employee and labor/management relations.

- HR management must perform four roles: administrative, employee advocate, operational, and strategic.
- It is important for HR management to be a strategic business contributor in organizations.
- Outsourcing is being utilized more frequently than in past years.
- Ethical behavior is crucial in HR management, and a number of HR ethical issues are regularly being faced by HR professionals.
- HR as a career field requires maintaining current knowledge in HR management.
- Professional certification has grown in importance for HR generalists and specialists.

Review and Discussion Questions

1. Discuss the following statement: "In many ways, all managers are and must be HR managers."
2. What are the seven major sets of HR activities, and what activities fall within each set?
3. Identify how the HR challenges discussed in the chapter are evident in a current or past employer.
4. Why is it important for HR management to evolve from the administrative and operational roles to the strategic one?
5. Give some examples of how HR professionals must balance ethical demands made on them.

Terms to Know

Human Resource (HR) management   4
HR generalist   23

HR specialist   23

Professional Development in HR Management

Your organization is growing and as a result so is the HR department. You are currently the only HR generalist, and there are several specialists in other areas of HR. The Vice-President of Administration has asked you identify a professional development plan for the Human Resource department staff members. As part of this plan, it is important to identify the different types of professional certifications that are available in HR management that staff members could be offered the opportunity to obtain at company expense. Develop a table containing at least four different certifications, including the following information about each of the certifications:

- Name of the sponsoring organization
- Name and types of certification
- Web Site address for more information
- Cost and frequency of certification
- Nature of certification process

CASE

A Change in HR

A joint venture between General Electric and a Japanese company, GE Fanuc is a manufacturer of factory automation and control products. Headquartered in Virginia with 1,500 employees, the HR department primarily performed administrative support activities. But when Donald Borwhat, Jr., took over as Senior Vice President of Human Resources, he and his staff began by restructuring and decentralizing the HR entity so that each functional area of the company has an HR manager assigned to it. The HR managers were expected to be key contributors to their areas by becoming knowledgeable about the business issues faced by their business functional units. Today, HR managers participate in developing business strategies and ensure that human resource dimensions are considered. For instance, the HR manager for manufacturing has HR responsibilities for 600 employees. In that role she contributes to workflow, production, scheduling, and other manufacturing decisions. It also means that she is more accessible to and has more credibility with manufacturing workers, most of whom are hourly workers.

Making the transition in HR management required going from seven to three levels of management, greatly expanding the use of cross-functional work teams, and significantly increasing training. To ease employee and managerial anxieties about the changes, GE Fanuc promised that no employees would lose their jobs. Managers and supervisors affected by the elimination of levels were offered promotions, transfers to other jobs in GE Fanuc, or early retirement buyouts. Additionally, employees were promised profit sharing, which has resulted in up to three weeks additional pay in profit sharing bonuses in some years.

The test of the change is in the results. GE Fanuc's revenue is up almost 18%. More than 40 work teams meet regularly to discuss work goals, track their performance against established measures, and discuss problems and issues. Employee turnover is also extremely low in most areas.[37]

Questions

1. What possible problems do you see with this approach for HR management in other organizations?
2. Compare this approach to HR management with the involvement of HR in operations in a current or previous job you have had.

Notes

1. "Staging a Comeback," *Human Resource Executive,* May 15, 2001, 26–32; and Sylvia Devoge and Jeffrey Shiraki, "People Factors: The Missing Link in Merger Success," *Compensation and Benefit Management,* Winter 2000, 26–32.
2. Robert Wiseman, "Book Review of Rewarding Excellence, by Edward E. Lawler III," *Academy of Management Review,* 25 (2001), 135–138.
3. Kevin Ferguson, "Closer Than Ever," *Business Week,* May 21, 2001, 14–15.
4. Bob Thompson, "CRM and the Internet," *Business Week,* April 30, 2001, 67–86.
5. Stephanie Armour, "Start Ups Face Pent-up Personnel Items," *USA Today,* February 10, 2000, B1; and Kelly Pate, "Vala's Survives Several Tragedies . . . ," *Denver Post,* April 4, 2000, PC1.
6. Robert W. Thompson, "Tech Skills . . . Essential for Today's HR Professional," *HR News,* September 2000, 1–2.
7. "Census: Americans Graduating at Record Rates," *Omaha World Herald,* December 19, 2000, 8.
8. June Kronholz, "U.S. Students Backslide on International Retest," *The Wall Street Journal,* December 6, 2000, B2.
9. Michelle Conlin, "And Now, the Just-in-Time Employee," *Business Week,* August 28, 2000, 169.
10. "Part-Timers Raise Productivity," *IIE Solutions* (August 2000), 1.
11. David Wessel, "Temp Workers Have Lasting Effect," *The Wall Street Journal,* February 1, 2001, B1.
12. Judy Greenwald, "Microsoft Settles Temp Lawsuit," *Business Insurance,* December 18, 2000, 2; and Tom Porter, "How to Protect Your Company from Benefit Liability," *San Diego Business Journal,* November 6, 2000, 35.
13. Mary Mallon, "Managers and Professionals in the Contingent Workforce," *Human Resource Management Journal,* 1 (2000), 33–47.
14. "Contingent Workers," *Monthly Labor Review,* January 2000, 2.
15. Karyn Robinson, "Temp Workers Gain Union Access," *HR News,* October 2000, 1.
16. *The Wall Street Journal,* May 15, 2001, B1.
17. "Trident Precision Manufacturing Inc.," *Workindex.Com,* available at *http://www.workindex.com/PMR/ PMR-0104-3.asp.*
18. Amy Martinez, "Non-Parents Seek Fairness at Work," *Omaha World Herald,* April 29, 2001, 1G.
19. Sharon Leonard, "The Baby Gap," *HR Magazine,* June 2000, 368.
20. "Automakers, UAW Join Forces," *Bulletin to Management,* December 7, 2000, 390; Sue Shellenbarger, "Work and Family," *The Wall Street Journal,* July 21, 2000, B1; Simon Nadel, "Elder Care," *Bulletin to Management,* March 16, 2000, 87; and Ellen Graham, "Marriott's Bid . . . Get a Reality Check," *The Wall Street Journal,* February 2, 2000, B1.
21. Dawn Carlson and K. Michele Kacmar, "Work-Family Conflicts in the Organization," *Journal of Management* 26 (2000), 1031–1054.
22. Mitchell L. Marks and Philip H. Mirvis, "Making Mergers and Acquisitions Work: Strategic and Psychological Preparation," *Academy of Management Executive,* May 2001, 80–94.
23. Andreas Gerog Scherer, "Some Unanticipated Consequences of Organizational Restructuring," *Academy of Management Review,* 25 (2000), 735.
24. Stephan J. Wall, "Auditing the Intangibles," *The Right Communique,* Second Quarter 2001, 3–7.
25. Jeffrey A. Schmidt, "The Correct Spelling of M+A Begins with HR," *HR Magazine,* June 2001, 102.
26. Scott Thurm, "Joining the Fold," *The Wall Street Journal,* March 1, 2000, 1.
27. Maureen Minehan, "Big Jump in HR Outsourcing Found in New Survey," *HR Policies and Practices Update,* June 24, 2000, 7–8.
28. Steve Bates, "No Experience Necessary?" *HR Magazine,* November 2001, 34–41.
29. Bob Combs and Jeff Day, "Counting Human Input as Assets," *Bulletin to Management,* August 3, 2000, 1–2.
30. Tom Starner, "The Effect of 'e,'" *Human Resource Executive,* March 1, 2001, 44–51.
31. Frank Joss, "Eye on HR," *Human Resource Executive,* December 2000, 40–47.
32. Based on Jodi Spiegel Arthur, "Seeking Equilibrium," *Human Resource Executive,* May 15, 2001, 34–38.
33. Jim Kerstetter, "The Dark Side of the Valley," *Business Week,* July 17, 2000, 42.
34. "Ethics Policies Are Big with Employees," *Bulletin to Management,* June 29, 2000, 201–202.
35. "Ethics Programs Aren't Stemming Employee Misconduct a Study Indicates," *The Wall Street Journal,* May 11, 2000, 1.
36. "Human Resource Activities: Budgets and Staffs," *BNA Bulletin to Management,* June 28, 2001, S16–S17.
37. Adapted from Gillian Flynn, "Workforce 2000 Begins Here," *Workforce,* May 1997, 78–84; and Sylvia Devoge and Jeffrey Shiraki, "People Factors—The Missing Link in Merger Success," *Compensation and Benefits Review,* Winter 2000, 26–32.

CHAPTER 2

Strategic Human Resource Management

After you read this chapter, you should be able to:

- Discuss why human resources can be a core competency for organizations.

- Define HR planning, and outline the HR planning process.

- Specify four important HR benchmarking measures.

- Identify factors to be considered in forecasting the supply and demand for human resources in an organization.

- Discuss several ways to manage a surplus of human resources.

- Identify what a human resource information system (HRIS) is and why it is useful when doing HR planning.

Productivity and Changing Gears Fast

Consider the following two extremes. On a typical Saturday at Mitsukoshi department store in Tokyo, one clerk boxes and wraps the purchase, another takes the money, and a third rings up the sale, and a half dozen people are waiting in line for service. No one is complaining except the economists. Japan's workforce is diligent, dedicated, well-educated, and significantly less productive than in other countries. In fact, Japanese productivity is now twentieth among the 29 richest countries. Japan uses more employees to produce the same amount of goods and services than other countries, which is certainly part of the reason it has been in a decade-long economic slowdown.

At a sawmill in Dallas, Oregon, lasers scan incoming wooden logs, feed their shapes into a computer, and then in milliseconds compute the most efficient way to cut the logs with the least waste. In less time than it takes to read this sentence in goes a crooked, bumpy log and out comes a neat stack of 2 × 12 boards and narrower boards salvaged from narrower sides of the log. Using computers, lasers, and other new machines, the mill produces lumber with 20% fewer workers and 12% fewer trees than a decade ago, and the output per hour worked at the sawmill is much higher today.

What happened to the workers? Some are retired, some are in other jobs, some have been retrained. Oddly enough, changing productivity in companies sometimes requires both laying people off and hiring people at the same time. Consider Elcotel, a firm making pay phones. It discovered cellular phones were making pay phones irrelevant. So it closed a factory and eliminated 70 employees, most of them assembly workers. But at the same time the Sarasota, Florida, company hired engineers and software designers to develop cellular phone software. Both hiring and firing were necessary to follow management's strategy of building its technological division while reducing its manufacturing. The company notes it would have been impossible to train the $8/hour assemblers to be $100,000/year software engineers.

To add a final perspective on organizational strategic moves and human resource implications, consider the economic slide in 2001. When the economy dropped, companies that had been bragging about their flexibility to respond to sudden changes did so in different ways. Chipmaker Intel boosted spending on R & D saying it was the best time to get ahead of the competition. Tommy Hilfiger outsourced computer troubleshooting and e-mail systems. Microsoft used the slowdown to hire talented technology workers who were unemployed.

Some responses by employers to the economic slowdown were traditional: slashing advertising expenses, squeezing suppliers, delaying investment. But as noted, there were many new responses as well, because aggressive cost cutting does not always work to improve business results. In fact, a Mercer study of 800 companies that relied primarily on cost cutting found that 68% did not have profitable growth for the next five years.

Certainly companies remain wary of accumulating "corporate fat," and there is less guilt about layoffs today. Even changing the skill set of the employee group to meet competition is done differently—often by replacing the employees.

Planning for HR needs is different when competition is intense. Competition breeds productivity, and planning for productive employees requires HR professionals to know the strategic goals of the company and be prepared to take advantage of opportunities when they arise—like firms hiring even when sales are down—because it fits their long-term strategies to do so.[1]

> Changing productivity in companies sometimes requires both laying people off and hiring people at the same time.

"There is a growing recognition of the relationship between companies' overall strategies and their human resource practices."

—Charles Greer

Many factors determine whether an organization will be successful; human resources are only one of them. Competitiveness, ability to adapt to changes in the market, and many other issues are involved too. Effective management decides where the organization needs to go, how to get there, and then regularly evaluate to see whether the organization is on track. Strategic objectives, the external environment, internal business processes, and determining how effectiveness will be defined and measured are all issues in this process.

HR is (or should be) involved with all these points by identifying how it can aid in increasing organizational productivity, help deal effectively with foreign competition, or enhance innovativeness in the organization. This kind of thinking is indicative of strategic thinking.[2] **Strategic HR management** refers to organizational use of employees to gain or keep a competitive advantage against competitors. It does so through the HR department formally contributing to company-wide planning efforts, or by simply being knowledgeable about issues facing the organization.

The development of specific business strategies must be based on the areas of strength that an organization has. Referred to as *core competencies,* those strengths are the foundation for creating a competitive advantage for an organization. A **core competency** is a unique capability that creates high value and differentiates the organization from its competition. In some organizations, human resources can be a core competency.

Strategic Human Resource management
Organizational use of employees to gain or keep a competitive advantage against competitors.

Core competency
A unique capability that creates high value and that differentiates the organization from its competition.

Human Resources as a Core Competency

Certainly, many organizations have voiced the idea that their human resources differentiate them from their competitors. Organizations as widely diverse as Fed Ex, Nordstrom's Department Stores, and Dell Computers have focused on human resources as having special strategic value for the organization.

Some ways that human resources become a core competency are through attracting and retaining employees with unique professional and technical capabilities, investing in training and development of those employees, and compensating them in ways that retain and keep them competitive with their counterparts in other organizations. For example, smaller, community-oriented banks have picked up numerous small- and medium-sized commercial loan customers because they emphasize that "you can talk to the same person," rather than having to call an automated service center in another state. The focus is on their human resources as an advantage.

Organizational Strategies Based on Human Resources

Recognition has been growing that, under certain conditions, human resources contribute to a competitive advantage for organizations. Figure 2-1 shows some possible areas where human resources may become part of a core competency.

People can be an organizational core competency when they have special capabilities to make decisions and be innovative in ways that competitors cannot easily imitate.[3] Having those capabilities requires selection, training, and retention

Figure 2-1 ▶ **Possible HR Areas for Core Competencies**

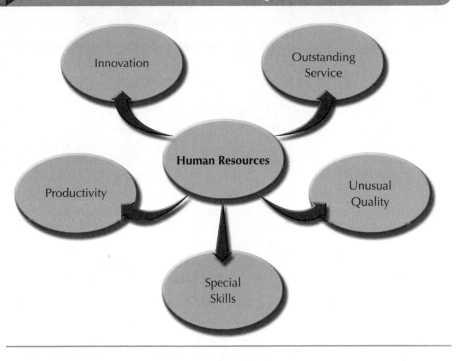

of good employees. An employee group without those special abilities would *not* be as strong a basis for competitive advantage.

Organizational culture The shared values and beliefs of a workforce.

The shared values and beliefs of a workforce is called **organizational culture**. For people to be a core competency managers must consider the culture of the organization because otherwise excellent strategies can be negated by a culture incompatible with those strategies. Further, the culture of the organization, as viewed by the people in it, affects attraction and retention of competent employees. Numerous examples can be given of key technical, professional, and administrative employees leaving firms because of corporate cultures that seem to devalue people and create barriers to the use of individual capabilities.[4]

Productivity as an HR-Based Strategy

The more productive an organization, the better its competitive advantage, because the costs to produce its goods and services are lower. Better productivity does not necessarily mean more is produced; perhaps fewer people (or less money or time) were used to produce the same amount. A useful way to measure the productivity of a workforce is the total cost of people per unit of output.

Productivity A measure of the quantity and quality of work done, considering the cost of the resources used.

In its most basic sense, **productivity** is a measure of the quantity and quality of work done, considering the cost of the resources used. It is also useful to view productivity as a ratio between inputs and outputs that indicates the *value added* by an organization or in an economy.

At the national level, high productivity leads to higher standards of living, as shown by the greater ability of a country to pay for what its citizens want. Increases in national wage levels (the cost of paying employees) without increases in national productivity lead to inflation, which results in an increase in costs and a decrease in purchasing power. Finally, as the opening example of Japan illustrates, lower rates of productivity make for higher labor costs and a less competitive position for a nation's products in the world marketplace.

Organizations and Productivity Productivity at the organizational level ultimately affects profitability and competitiveness in a for-profit organization, and total costs in a not-for-profit organization. Decisions made about the value of an organization often are based on the productivity of which it is capable.[5]

Perhaps none of the resources used for productivity in organizations are so closely scrutinized as the human resources. Many of the activities undertaken in an HR system are designed to affect individual or organizational productivity. Pay, appraisal systems, training, selection, job design, and compensation are HR activities directly concerned with productivity.

A useful way to measure organizational HR productivity is by considering **unit labor cost**, which is computed by dividing the average cost of workers by their average levels of output. Using unit labor costs, one can see that a company paying relatively high wages still can be economically competitive if it can also achieve an offsetting high productivity level. Low unit labor costs can be a basis for a strategy focusing on human resources.

Increasing Productivity U.S. firms have been on a decade-long crusade to improve organizational productivity. Much of the productivity improvement efforts have focused on their workforces.[6] The early stages included downsizing, reengineering jobs, increasing computer usage, and working employees harder and longer. These approaches have been useful in some firms.[7] Some ideas for the next round in productivity improvements include:

- *Outsourcing:* Contract with someone else to perform activities previously done by employees of the organization. For instance, if UPS can deliver products at a lower cost than a manufacturing company can ship them internally, then the firm could outsource shipping to UPS.
- *Making workers more efficient with capital equipment:* Typically the more spent on equipment per worker, the greater the output per worker.
- *Replacing workers with equipment:* Certain jobs are not done as well by humans. The jobs may be mindless, physically difficult, or require extreme precision. For example, a ditch usually is better dug by one person operating a backhoe than by several workers with shovels.
- *Helping workers work better:* Replace outmoded processes, methods, and rules. Also, find better ways of training people to work more efficiently.
- *Redesigning the work:* Some work can be redesigned to make it faster, easier, and possibly even more rewarding to employees. Such changes generally improve productivity.

Quality and Service as HR-Based Strategies

Both high-quality products, and/or extremely good service can be strategic competitive advantages that have HR dimensions. *Quality* of production must be considered as part of productivity, because one alternative might be to produce more products and services but of lower quality. At one time, American goods suffered as a result of this trade-off. W. Edwards Deming, an American quality expert, argued that getting the job done right the *first time*—through pride in

Unit labor cost Computed by dividing the average cost of workers by their average levels of output.

Figure 2-2 ▶ *Customer Service Dimensions*

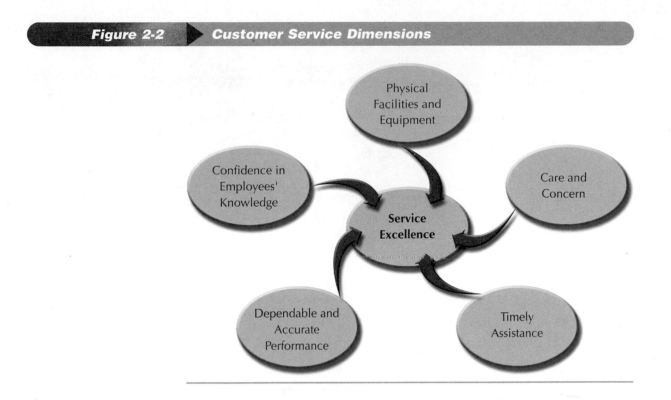

craftsmanship, excellent training, and an unwillingness to tolerate delays, defects, and mistakes—is essential to quality production.[8] However, attempts to improve quality have worked better for some firms than for others.[9]

Delivering excellent customer service is another approach to enhancing organizational competitive performance. Service begins with product design and includes interaction with customers, with the ultimate goal of meeting customers' needs. Some organizations do not produce products, only services. Estimates are that more the 75% of jobs in the U.S. economy are service jobs, including retail, banking, travel, and government, where service is the basis for productivity. Unfortunately, overall customer satisfaction has declined in the United States and other countries. The American Customer Satisfaction Index has revealed that in many U.S. industries, customers are growing more dissatisfied with the customer service they receive.[10]

Service excellence is difficult to define, but people know it when they see it. In many organizations, service quality is affected significantly by the individual employees who interact with customers. At least three of the five dimensions of service depicted in Figure 2-2 are HR related.

Linking HR Planning and Strategy for Competitive Advantage

Many think that organizations decide on strategies and then HR planning is done to supply the right number and kinds of employees. However, the relationship should go deeper. Figure 2-3 shows the relationship among the variables that determine the HR plans an organization will adopt. Business strategies affect HR plans. Consideration of human resource issues should be part of the initial input

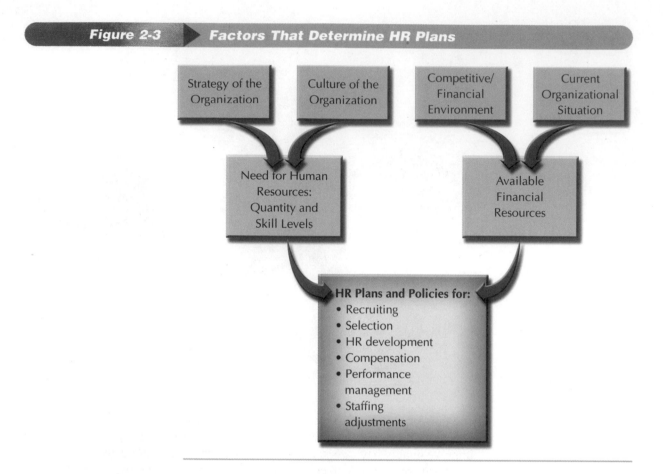

Figure 2-3 ▸ **Factors That Determine HR Plans**

Strategy of the Organization

Culture of the Organization

Competitive/ Financial Environment

Current Organizational Situation

Need for Human Resources: Quantity and Skill Levels

Available Financial Resources

HR Plans and Policies for:
- Recruiting
- Selection
- HR development
- Compensation
- Performance management
- Staffing adjustments

to the strategy formulation process. For example, it may be important to identify competitive advantage opportunities that fit the existing employees or assess strategic alternatives given the current capabilities of organizational human resources. HR professionals should be doing environmental scanning to know and pinpoint which skills are available and which are not. HR professionals also should be able to estimate lead times for adjusting to labor shortages or surpluses, because HR will be involved in implementing any strategies that affect people.[11]

To illustrate: A large bank wanted to become among the top 10 in size in the U.S. Its strategy included developing more global business and improving customer service. HR analyses turned up a basic deficiency in the workforce—they did not have the skills and knowledge necessary to carry out the strategy. In this case a series of training and development programs was designed and implemented to close the gap.

To describe the relationship between strategy and HR, two basic strategies can be identified: *cost-leadership* and *differentiation.* An example of a company following a cost-leadership strategy might be Wal-Mart, and of the differentiation strategy Intel or Microsoft. Figure 2-4 compares HR needs under each strategy and suggests the HR approaches that may be most appropriate. A cost-leadership strategy may be appropriate in a relatively stable business environment because it approaches competition on the basis of low price and high quality of product

Figure 2-4	▶ Linkage of Organizational and HR Strategies		
Organizational Strategy	**Strategic Focus**	**HR Strategy**	**HR Activities**
Cost Leadership	• *Efficiency* • *Stability* • *Cost Control*	• *Long HR planning horizon* • *Build skills in existing employee* • *Job and employee specialization efficiency*	• *Promote from within* • *Extensive training* • *Hire and train for specific capabilities*
Differentiation	• *Growth* • *Innovation* • *Decentralization*	• *Shorter HR planning horizon* • *Hire the HR capabilities needed* • *Broader, more flexible jobs and employees*	• *External staffing* • *Less training* • *Hire and train for broad competencies*

or service. The differentiation strategy is more appropriate in a more dynamic environment characterized by rapid change and requires continually finding new products and new markets. The two strategies may not be mutually exclusive, because it is possible for an organization to pursue one strategy in one product or service area and another with others.

The cost-leadership strategy requires an organization to "build" its own employees to fit its specialized needs. This approach needs a longer HR planning horizon. When specific skills are necessary for a new market or product, it may be more difficult to internally develop them quickly. However, with a differentiation strategy, responsiveness means that HR planning is likely to have a shorter time frame, and greater use of external sources, such as acquisition of another company with specialized employees, will be used to staff the organization.

Human Resource Planning

Human resource (HR) planning Process of analyzing and identifying the need for and availability of human resources so that the organization can meet its objectives.

The competitive organizational strategy of the firm derived with input from HR becomes the basis for **human resource (HR) planning**, which is the process of analyzing and identifying the need for and availability of human resources so that the organization can meet its objectives. This section discusses HR planning responsibilities, the importance of HR planning even in small businesses, and the HR planning process.

HR Planning Responsibilities

In most organizations that do HR planning, the top HR executive and subordinate staff specialists have most of the responsibilities for this planning. However, as Figure 2-5 indicates, other managers must provide information for the HR specialists to analyze. In turn, those managers need to receive data from the HR unit. Because top managers are responsible for overall strategic planning, they usually ask the HR unit to project the human resources needed to implement overall organizational goals.

Figure 2-5 ▶ Typical Division of HR Responsibilities: HR Planning

HR Unit	Managers
• Participates in strategic planning process for entire organization • Identifies HR strategies • Designs HR planning data systems • Compiles and analyzes data from managers on staffing needs • Implements HR plan as approved by top management	• Identify supply-and-demand needs for each division/department • Review/discuss HR planning information with HR specialists • Integrate HR plan with departmental plans • Monitor HR plan to identify changes needed • Review employee succession plans associated with HR plan

Small Business and HR Planning

The need for HR planning in larger organizations is clear because if some formal adjustments to changes are not made, people or even entire divisions might be working at cross-purposes with the rest of the company. However, in a smaller business, even though the owner/manager knows on a daily basis what is happening and what should be done, planning is still important.[12] Perhaps the most difficult area for planning in small business is family matters and succession.

Particular difficulties arise when a growing business is passed from one generation to another, resulting in a mix of family and nonfamily employees. Some family members may use employees as "pawns" in disagreements with other family members in the firm. Also, nonfamily employees may see different HR policies and rules used for family members.

Key to the successful transition of a business from one generation to another is having a clearly identified HR plan. In small businesses, such a plan includes incorporating key nonfamily members in HR planning efforts. Often, nonfamily members have important capabilities and expertise that family members do not possess.[13] Therefore, planning for the attraction and retention of these "outsiders" may be vital to the future success of smaller organizations.

Management succession is one of the top challenges faced by family-owned firms. It even may be that nonfamily members will assume top management leadership roles, with some or all family members who are owners serving on the board of directors, but not being active managers in the firm. Additionally, nonfamily executives may be the intermediaries who focus on the needs of the business when family member conflicts arise. Small businesses, depending on how small they are, may use the HR planning process that follows, but in very small organizations the process is much more intuitive and often done entirely by the top executives, who often are family members.

HR Planning Process

The steps in the HR planning process are shown in Figure 2-6. Notice that the HR planning process begins with considering the organizational objectives and strategies. Then both external and internal assessments of HR needs and supply sources must be done and forecasts developed. Key to assessing internal human

Figure 2-6 ▶ **HR Planning Process**

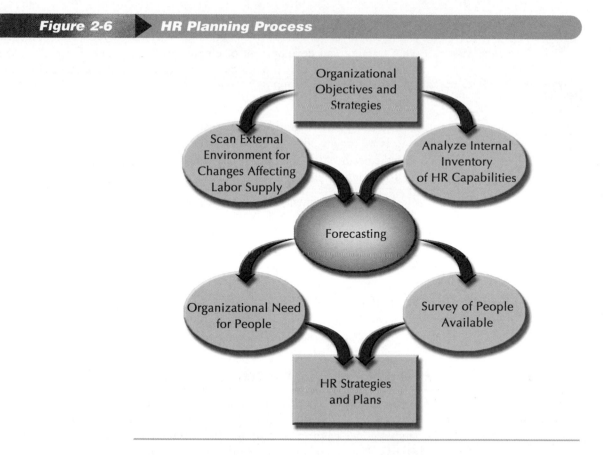

resources is having solid information accessible through a human resource information system (HRIS).

Once the assessments are complete, forecasts must be developed to identify the relationship between supply and demand for human resources. Management then formulates HR strategies and plans to address the imbalance, both short and long term.

HR strategies Means used to anticipate and manage the supply of and demand for human resources.

HR strategies are the means used to anticipate and manage the supply of and demand for human resources. These HR strategies provide overall direction for the ways in which HR activities will be developed and managed. Finally, specific HR plans are developed to provide more specific direction for the management of HR activities.

Developing the HR Plan The HR plan is guided by longer-term organizational plans. For example, in planning for human resources, an organization must consider the allocation of people to jobs over long periods of time, not just for the next month or even the next year. This level of planning requires knowledge of strategic expansions or reductions in operations and any technological changes that may affect the organization. On the basis of such analyses, plans can be made for shifting employees within the organization, laying off or otherwise cutting back the number of employees, retraining present employees, or increasing the number of employees in certain areas. Factors to consider include the current employees' knowledge, skills, and abilities in the organization and the expected vacancies resulting from retirements, promotions, transfers, or discharge.

HR Planning
Provides an overview of
key steps in HR planning.
Custom Search:
☑ ANALYSIS
Phrase: Virtues of
HR planning

In summary, the HR plan provides a road map for the future, identifying where employees are likely to be obtained, when employees will be needed, and what training and development of employees must occur. Through succession planning, employee career paths can be tailored to individual needs that are consistent with organizational requirements. Succession plans are discussed in more detail in Chapter 10.

Evaluating HR Planning The most telling evidence of successful HR planning is an organization in which the human resources are consistently aligned with the needs of the business over a period of time. If HR planning is done well, the following benefits should result:

- Upper management has a better view of the human resource dimensions of business decisions.
- HR costs may be lower because management can anticipate imbalances before they become expensive or unmanageable.
- More time is available to locate talent because needs are anticipated and identified before the actual staffing is required.
- Better opportunities exist to include members of protected groups in future growth plans to increase organizational diversity.
- Development of managers can be better planned.

Scanning the External Environment

Environmental scanning
Process of studying the
environment of the organization to pinpoint opportunities and threats.

At the heart of strategic planning is the knowledge gained from scanning the external environment for changes.[14] **Environmental scanning** is the process of studying the environment of the organization to pinpoint opportunities and threats. The external environment especially affects HR planning because each organization must draw from the same labor market that supplies all other employers. Indeed, one measure of organizational effectiveness is the ability of an organization to compete for a sufficient supply of human resources with the appropriate capabilities. To get a feel for the impact of environmental changes on businesses consider the following:

- The government has deregulated major sectors of the economy.
- During the past decade an uncertainty in energy prices brought new pressures on firms having major transportation/energy expenses.
- The globalization of markets and sources of supply has increased competition in many industries
- The composition of the workforce, along with its values, age, and working approaches, have changed.[15]

Environmental factors—government, economic conditions, geographic and competition issues, and workforce changes—all must be part of environmental scanning. Each is discussed.

Scanning Government Influences

A major element that affects labor supply and therefore HR planning is the government. Today, managers of HR activities are confronted with an expanding and often bewildering array of government regulations. As a result, HR planning must be done by individuals who understand the legal requirements of various government regulations, especially for firms operating globally. For example, in France the government has changed the length of the work week from 39 to 35 hours. This change has apparently led to more flexible work patterns, giving employers different staffing situations.[16]

Tax legislation at local, state, and federal levels also affects HR planning. Pension provisions and Social Security legislation may change retirement patterns and funding options. Elimination or expansion of tax benefits for job-training expenses might alter some job-training activities associated with work-force expansions. Employee benefits may be affected significantly by tax law changes. Tax credits for employee day care and financial aid for education may affect employer practices in recruiting and retaining workers. In summary, an organization must consider a wide variety of government policies, regulations, and laws during the HR planning process.

Economic Conditions

The general business cycle of recessions and economic booms also affects HR planning. Factors such as interest rates, inflation, and economic growth affect the availability of workers and should figure into organizational and HR plans and objectives. Decisions on wages, overtime, and hiring or laying off workers may be affected by economic conditions. For example, suppose economic conditions lead to a decrease in the unemployment rate. There is a considerable difference between finding qualified applicants in a 3% unemployment market and in a 7% unemployment market. In the 3% unemployment market, significantly fewer qualified applicants are likely to be available for any kind of position. Applicants still available may be less employable because they are less educated, less skilled, or unwilling to work. As the unemployment rate rises, the number of qualified people looking for work increases, making it easier to fill jobs.

Geographic and Competitive Concerns

Employers must consider the following geographic and competitive concerns in making HR plans, including other employers in the area, employee resistance to geographic relocation, direct competition in the industry, and the impact of international competition. The *net migration* into a particular region is important. For example, in the past decade, the population of U.S. cities in the South, Southwest, and West have grown rapidly and provided a ready source of labor.

Other employers in a geographic region can greatly expand or diminish the labor supply. If, for example, a large military facility closes or moves to another geographic location, a large supply of good civilian labor, previously employed by the military, may be available. In contrast, the opening of a new plant by another large employer may decrease the supply of potential employees in a labor market for some time.

Within the last decade, many workers, especially those with working spouses, have expressed an increasing reluctance to accept *geographic relocation* as a precondition of moving up in organizations. This trend has forced organizations to change their employee development policies and practices, as well as their HR plans.

Direct competitors are another important external force in HR planning. Failure to consider the competitive labor market and to offer pay scales and benefits competitive with those of organizations in the same general industry and geographic location may cost a company dearly in the long run. Underpaying or "undercompeting" may result in a much lower-quality workforce.

Finally, the impact of *international competition,* as well as numerous other external factors, must be considered as part of environmental scanning. Global competition for labor intensifies as global competitors shift jobs and workers around the world.

Workforce Composition

Changes in the composition of the workforce, combined with the use of different work patterns, have created workplaces and organizations that are notably different from those of a decade ago. Many organizations face major concerns about having sufficient workers with the necessary capabilities and the flexibility to expand and contract the workforce as needed. The use of part-time employees can add flexibility through temporary or more permanent arrangements. Figure 2-7 shows different types of part-time workers. To address those concerns, organizations are implementing "flexible staffing" arrangements that include temporary workers, independent contractors, job sharing, part-time, and outsourcing. These arrangements are used to meet workload fluctuations, replace an absent employee, work on a project with a definite end point, and as a way to "preview" whether an employee might work out well before formal hiring. For the results of a study on flexible staffing, see the HR Perspective. Whether to use flexible or alternative staffing, outsourcing, or some other method, is an example of the numerous decisions that need to be made in HR planning.

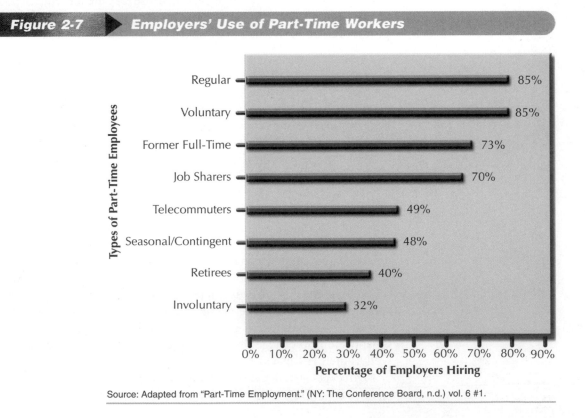

Figure 2-7 ▶ Employers' Use of Part-Time Workers

Types of Part-Time Employees	Percentage of Employers Hiring
Regular	85%
Voluntary	85%
Former Full-Time	73%
Job Sharers	70%
Telecommuters	49%
Seasonal/Contingent	48%
Retirees	40%
Involuntary	32%

Source: Adapted from "Part-Time Employment." (NY: The Conference Board, n.d.) vol. 6 #1.

Cynthia Gramm and John Schnell published a study in *Industrial and Labor Relations Review* that examined the use of flexible staffing arrangements. For their study, flexible staffing included temporary employees, independent contractors, and subcontracting with another business to do work normally done in-house. The researchers focused on the effects of these arrangements on the "core employees," the group of non-management employees making the company's product. Their sample consisted of data from 112 U.S. firms.

The study found that higher wages for core employees led to more subcontracting. The higher the cost to hire core employees, the more likely firms were to use flexible staffing arrangements. Through the use of flexible staffing, the findings showed that core employees gained stability in employment. If it was necessary to reduce employment, temporary employees were let go first.

Another finding from the study was that when a union was present, Gramm and Schnell noted subcontracting increased, but fewer of the other flexible staffing options were used. This may be because unions usually will not allow temporaries but cannot stop employers from subcontracting out certain work. Further, in companies with greater use of flexible work arrangements, job sharing was also more prevalent.

Clearly higher costs of core employees leads to more flexible arrangements, despite union concerns. However, the resulting advantages for the regular employees include a more secure job and more job sharing.[17]

Internal Assessment of the Organizational Workforce

Analyzing the jobs that will need to be done and the skills of people currently available to do them is the next part of HR planning. The needs of the organization must be compared against the labor supply available inside the organization.

Auditing Jobs and Skills

The starting point for evaluating internal strengths and weaknesses is an audit of the jobs currently being done in the organization. This comprehensive analysis of all current jobs provides a basis for forecasting what jobs will need to be done in the future. Much of the data to answer these questions should be available from existing staffing and organizational databases. The following questions are addressed during the internal assessment:

- What jobs exist now?
- How many individuals are performing each job?
- What are the reporting relationships of jobs?
- How essential is each job?
- What jobs will be needed to implement future organizational strategies?
- What are the characteristics of anticipated jobs?

Organizational Capabilities Inventory

As HR planners gain an understanding of the current and future jobs that will be necessary to carry out organizational plans, they can make a detailed audit of current employees and their capabilities. The basic source of data on employees is the HR records in the organization. By utilizing different databases in an

Using an Electronic Employee Profile

Micron Electronics Inc. is a provider of personal computers and services located in Nampa, Idaho. Micron redeploys 10 to 15 of its employees each month using software developed by Deploy Solutions Inc. of Westwood, Massachusetts. The software is designed to help a large employer keep track of its talent and reassign employees as necessary.

Before the software was available, like many companies, Micron did not look in-house to fill a job opening because it was too labor intensive and took a long time. Now if Micron needs an employee for an assignment in Germany, the HR staff can check the system to see which current employees can speak German. Participation in the system is voluntary for employees, and employee privacy is safeguarded.

The software uses "natural language processing" that goes beyond keyword searches and allows the software to point out less obvious matches. For example, it might identify a person who had hard-to-find skills, but who would need some training on some aspects of the job being filled. It might be easier to train for some skills than find someone with other scarce skills. Overall, Micron estimates the new system is 15 to 20 times faster than the old process and more accurate as well.[18]

HRIS, it is possible to identify the employees' knowledge, skills, and abilities (KSAs). Planners can use these inventories to determine long-range needs for recruiting, selection, and HR development. Also, that information can be the basis for determining which additional capabilities will be needed in the future workforce that may not currently exist. The HR Practice gives an example of this audit process.

Components of Organizational Capabilities Inventory An inventory of organizational capabilities may consist of the following elements:

- Individual employee demographics (age, length of service in the organization, time in present job)
- Individual career progression (jobs held, time in each job, promotions or other job changes, pay rates)
- Individual performance data (work accomplishment, growth in skills)

All the information that goes into an employee's skills inventory data bank may affect the employee's career. Therefore, the data and their use must meet the same standards of job-relatedness and nondiscrimination as when the employee was initially hired. Furthermore, security of such information ensures that sensitive information is available only to those who have specific use for it.

Using Organizational Inventory Data Managers and HR staff members can use data on individual employees to be aggregated into a profile of the current organizational workforce in total. This profile reveals many of the current strengths and deficiencies. The absence of some specialized expertise, such as advanced computer skills, may affect the ability of an organization to take advantage of new technological developments. Likewise, if a large group of experienced employees are all in the same age bracket, their eventual retirements might lead to future "gaps" in the organization. For example, in one case, eight skilled line workers in a small rural electric utility were due to retire within a three-year period. Yet it takes seven years of apprenticeship and on-the-job training for a person to be qualified for a senior skilled job within the utility. The company clearly needed to plan the most effective way to deal with this workforce situation.

It also can be helpful to plot charts giving an overview of the employee situation for each department in an organization, which may suggest where external candidates might be needed to fill future positions. Similarly, the charts may indicate where there is a reservoir of trained people that the employer can tap to meet future conditions. Increasingly, employers are making use of a computerized HRIS to compile such records.

Forecasting HR Supply and Demand

Forecasting
Use of information from the past and present to identify expected future conditions.

The information gathered from external environmental scanning and assessment of internal strengths and weaknesses is used to predict or *forecast* HR supply and demand in light of organizational objectives and strategies. **Forecasting** uses information from the past and present to identify expected future conditions. Projections for the future are, of course, subject to error.[19] Changes in the conditions on which the projections are based might even completely invalidate them, which is the chance forecasters take. Usually, though, experienced people are able to forecast with enough accuracy to benefit organizational long-range planning.

Forecasting Methods

Methods for forecasting human resources range from a manager's best guess to a rigorous and complex computer simulation. Simple assumptions may be sufficient in certain instances, but complex models may be necessary for others. It is beyond the scope of this text to discuss in detail the numerous methods of forecasting available, but a few of the more prominent ones will be highlighted. Forecasts may be either judgmental or mathematical methods, as Figure 2-8 on the next page indicates.

Despite the availability of sophisticated mathematical models and techniques, forecasting is still a combination of quantitative method and subjective judgment. The facts must be evaluated and weighed by knowledgeable individuals, such as managers and HR experts, who use the mathematical models as tools and make judgments to make decisions.

Judgmental methods regularly used include the following:

- *Estimates* can be either top-down or bottom-up, but essentially people who are in a position to know are asked, "How many people will you need next year?"
- *Rules of thumb* rely on general guidelines applied to a specific situation within the organization. For example, a guideline of "one operations manager per five reporting supervisors" aids in forecasting the number of supervisors needed in a division. However, it is important to adapt the guideline to recognize widely varying departmental needs.
- The *Delphi technique* uses input from a group of experts whose opinions of forecasted situations are sought. These expert opinions are then combined and returned to the experts for a second anonymous opinion. The process continues through several rounds until the experts essentially agree on a

Figure 2-8 ▶ **Forecasting Methods**

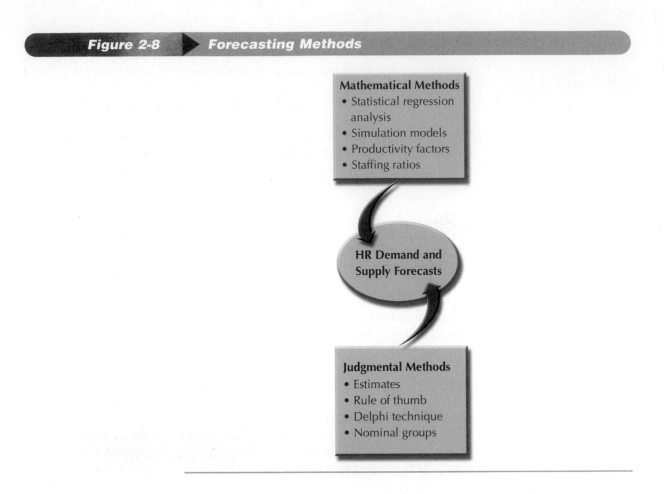

judgment. For example, this approach was used to forecast effects of technology on HR management and staffing needs.

- *Nominal groups,* unlike the Delphi method, require experts to meet face to face. Their ideas are usually generated independently at first, discussed as a group, and then compiled as a report.

Various mathematical methods, which vary in terms of sophistication and complexity, include the following:

- *Statistical regression analysis* makes a statistical comparison of past relationships among various factors. For example, a statistical relationship between gross sales and number of employees in a retail chain may be useful in forecasting the number of employees that will be needed if the retailer's sales increase 30%.
- *Simulation models* are representations of real situations in abstract form. For example, an econometric model of the growth in software usage would lead to forecasts of the need for software developers. Numerous simulations methods and techniques are available, but surveys reveal that the more complex simulation techniques are used by relatively few firms.
- *Productivity ratios* calculate the average number of units produced per employee. These averages can be applied to sales forecasts to determine the

number of employees needed. For example, a firm could forecast the number of needed sales representatives using these ratios.

- *Staffing ratios* can be used to estimate indirect labor. For example, if the company usually uses one clerical person for every 25 production employees, that ratio can be used to estimate the need for clerical employees.

Forecasting Periods

HR forecasting should be done over three planning periods: short, intermediate, and long ranges. The most commonly used planning period is *short range,* usually a period of six months to one year. This level of planning is routine in many organizations because few assumptions about the future are necessary for such short-range plans. These short-range forecasts offer the best estimates of the immediate HR needs of an organization. Intermediate and long-range forecasting are much more difficult processes. *Intermediate* plans usually project one to five years into the future, and *long-range* plans extend beyond five years.

Forecasting the Demand for Human Resources

The demand for employees can be calculated on an organization-wide basis and/or calculated based on the needs of individual units in the organization. For example, to forecast that the firm needs 125 new employees next year might mean less than to forecast that it needs 25 new people in sales and customer service, 45 in production, 20 in accounting, 5 in HR, and 30 in the warehouse. This unit breakdown obviously allows HR planners to better pinpoint the specific skills needed than the aggregate method does.

Forecasting human resources can be done using two frameworks. One approach considers specific openings that are likely to occur and uses that as the basis for planning. The openings (or demands) are created when employees leave a position because of promotions, transfers, and terminations. The analysis always begins with the top positions in the organization, because from there no promotions to a higher level are possible.

Based on this analysis, decision rules (or "fill rates") are developed for each job or level. For example, a decision rule for a financial institution might state that 50% of branch supervisor openings will be filled through promotions from customer service tellers, 25% through promotions from personal bankers, and 25% from new hires. But forecasters must be aware of chain effects throughout the organization, because as people are promoted, their previous positions become available. Continuing our example, forecasts for the need for customer service tellers and personal bankers would also have to be developed. The overall purpose of this analysis is to develop a forecast of the needs for human resources by number and type for the forecasted period.

Forecasting the Supply of Human Resources

Once human resources needs have been forecasted, then their availability must be identified. Forecasting the availability of human resources considers both *external* and *internal* supplies. Although the internal supply may be easier to calculate, it is important to calculate the external supply as accurately as possible.

External Supply The external supply of potential employees available to the organization needs to be estimated. Extensive use of government labor force

Forecasting
Identifies integrating information when doing forecasting.
Custom Search:
☑ ANALYSIS
Phrase: Integrating the information

population estimates, trends in the industry, and many more complex and inter-related factors must be considered, including the following:[20]

- Net migration into and out of the area
- Individuals entering and leaving the workforce
- Individuals graduating from schools and colleges
- Changing workforce composition and patterns
- Economic forecasts for the next few years
- Technological developments and shifts
- Actions of competing employers
- Government regulations and pressures
- Factors affecting persons entering and leaving the workforce

Internal Supply Figure 2-9 shows in general terms how the internal supply can be calculated. Estimating internal supply considers that employees move from their current jobs into others through promotions, lateral moves, and ter-minations. Also, it considers that the internal supply is influenced by training and development programs, transfer and promotion policies, and retirement poli-cies, among other factors.

Internally, *succession analysis* is one method used to forecast the supply of people for certain positions. It relies on *replacement charts,* which are succession

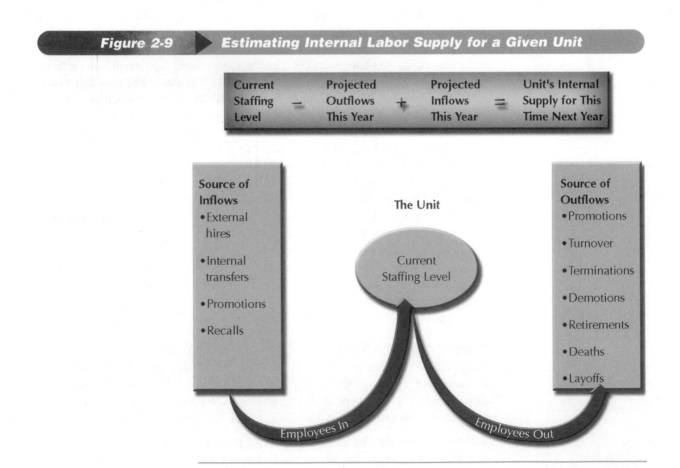

Figure 2-9 ▶ *Estimating Internal Labor Supply for a Given Unit*

| Current Staffing Level | − | Projected Outflows This Year | + | Projected Inflows This Year | = | Unit's Internal Supply for This Time Next Year |

Source of Inflows
- External hires
- Internal transfers
- Promotions
- Recalls

The Unit

Current Staffing Level

Source of Outflows
- Promotions
- Turnover
- Terminations
- Demotions
- Retirements
- Deaths
- Layoffs

Employees In   Employees Out

plans developed to identify potential personnel changes, select backup candidates, promote individuals, and keep track of attribution (resignations, retirements) for each department in an organization.

A *transition matrix,* or *Markov matrix,* can be used to model the internal flow of human resources. These matrices simply show as probabilities below average rates of historical movement from one job to another, as the example below shows.

	Exit	Manager	Supervisor	Line Worker
Manager	.15	.85	.00	.00
Supervisor	.10	.15	.70	.05
Line Worker	.20	.00	.15	.65

Looking at the simple transition matrix table for a line worker, there is a 20% probability of someone being gone in 12 months, a 0% probability of promotion to manager, a 15% probability of promotion to supervisor, and a 65% probability of someone staying a line worker next year. Such transition matrices form the bases for computer simulations of the internal flow of people through a large organization over time.

With all the data collected and forecasts done, an organization has the information it needs to develop an HR plan. Such a plan can be extremely sophisticated or rather rudimentary. Regardless of its degree of complexity, the ultimate purpose of the plan is to enable managers in the organization to match the available supply of labor with the forecasted demand based on the strategies of the organization. If the necessary skill levels do not exist in the present workforce, organizations can train employees in the new skills or undertake outside recruiting. Likewise, if the plan reveals that the firm employs too many people for its needs, a human resource surplus exists.

Managing Human Resource Surplus or Shortage

Planning is of little value if no subsequent action is taken. The action taken depends on the likelihood of a human resources surplus or shortage. A surplus of workers can be managed within an HR plan in a variety of ways. But regardless of the means, the actions are difficult because workforce reductions ultimately are necessary.

WARN Act
Identifies requirements for layoff advance notice.
Custom Search:
☑ ANALYSIS
Phrase: Giving advance notice

Workforce Reductions and the WARN Act
In this era of mergers, acquisitions, and downsizing, many workers have been laid off or had their jobs eliminated due to closing of selected offices, plants, and operations. To provide employees with sufficient notice, a federal law was passed, the Worker Adjustment and Retraining Notification (WARN) Act. This act requires employers to give a 60-day notice before a layoff or facility closing involving more than 50 people. However, part-time employees working fewer than 20 hours per week do not count toward the 50 employees. Also, seasonal employees do not have to receive WARN notification. The WARN Act also imposes stiff fines on employers who do not follow the required process and give proper notice.

Workforce Realignment

It has been called "downsizing," "rightsizing," "reduction in force" (RIF), and many other terms as well, but it almost always means cutting employees. "Layoffs" come in response to shortfall in demand for products, while "downsizing" involves job reductions based on a desire to operate more efficiently even when demand is strong.[21] Downsizing is a structural change that negates rehiring laid-off workers. However, workers who are laid off (but not as part of downsizing) may get their jobs back when demand picks up.[22]

The outcome of downsizing is a bit clearer after a decade of many examples and studies. Downsizing has worked for some firms, but it doesn't generate additional revenue. It only generates lower costs in the short term; "corporate liposuction" one observer calls it.[23] But when companies cannibalize the human resources they need to grow and innovate, disruption follows for some time.

Senior executives still see layoffs as their first line defense against an economic downturn, but some research suggests downsizing can hurt productivity by leaving "surviving" employees overburdened and demoralized.[24] Loss of employees may mean a loss of informal knowledge of how to handle specific problems and issues or respond to specific customers or suppliers. However focusing on trimming underperforming units or employees as part of a plan based on sound organizational strategies may make sense. Such a plan often includes cutting capital spending.[25]

Workforce realignment can occur in all forms as the HR Perspective illustrates. Some common problems include demoralized managers, lawsuits, sabotage, and a need for more security. Alternatives to layoffs should be examined first to avoid negative repercussions for organizations.

The Effects of Mergers and Acquisitions Another cause for downsizing has been the proliferation of mergers and acquisitions in many industries. One only has to look at the financial or telecommunications industry to see massive consolidation in the number of firms. Some mergers occurred between two huge firms, such as British Petroleum and Amoco or Norwest and Wells-Fargo banks, while others have been smaller mergers, such as the merger of two local hospitals. But a common result of most mergers and acquisitions (M&As) is an excess of employees once the firms have been combined.[26] The wave of M&A activity in the United States has often left the new, combined companies with redundant departments, plants, and people.[27] Because much of the rationale for combinations is financial, eliminating employees with overlapping responsibilities is a primary concern.

Corporations that are closing facilities or eliminating departments may need to offer financial transition arrangements. A **transition stay bonus** is extra payment for employees whose jobs are being eliminated, thereby motivating them to remain with the organization for a period of time.

Just as critical is the impact of job elimination on the remaining employees. An AMA survey found that in 69% of the surveyed firms, employee morale declined in the short term and 28% of the firms had longer-term declines in employee morale after downsizing. Additionally, resignations and employee turnover all increased substantially in the year following the downsizing.[28] These consequences of organizational restructuring are crucial challenges to be addressed by HR management.

Doing Layoffs and Downsizing Well . . . and Badly

During the economic downturn a few years ago, many companies resorted to layoffs and downsizing. Some tried innovative ways to lessen the pain, others were simply painfully and poorly done.

Better attempts included the following:

- Charles Schwab guaranteed a $7,500 bonus for any employee rehired within 18 months. Also, it asked 30% to 50% of its work-force to take (unpaid) days off *after* first slashing the pay of top managers.
- Cisco Systems gave employees a chance to forego a severance package and get instead one-third of a year's salary, all bene-fits, and stock option awards for working a year at a nonprofit group associated with Cisco. From there, employees would be rehired if business picked up.

- At Accenture employees were offered voluntary sabbaticals for 6 to 12 months. Employees could receive a small part of their salaries during such sabbaticals.
- Texas Instruments "loaned" employees to a vendor for as long as eight months, and in return, the vendor paid their salaries and agreed not to offer them jobs.
- Procter and Gamble offered a buyout package, in effect calling for volunteers. The firm felt the approach would help morale among remaining employees, but conceded it was a time-consuming process. The pack-age included severance pay, health care, outplacement assistance, and retraining reimbursement.

Layoffs that were handled less effectively included:

- Inacom told the company's 5,000 employees to call an 800 number. As they dialed in, a recorded voice told them they were out of work—effective immediately.
- Amazon.com used e-mail to layoff Seattle-area telecom-muters who could not come to a meeting in which job cuts were announced.
- Chrysler employees showed up for work only to find their ID badges no longer opened the security gates.

All of these examples illus-trate different ways to handle lay-offs and downsizing. Obviously, some employers handled staff cut-backs better than others.[29]

Managing Survivors of Downsizing A common myth is that those who are still around after downsizing in any of its many forms are so glad to have a job that they pose no problems to the organization. However, some observers draw an analogy between those who survive downsizing and those who survive wartime but experience guilt because they were spared while their friends were not. The result is that performance of the survivors and communications through-out the organization are adversely affected.[30]

The first major *reduction in force (RIF)* of workers ever undertaken in a firm is often a major jolt to the employees' view of the company. Bitterness, anger, disbe-lief, and shock all are common reactions. For those who survive the cuts, the pater-nalistic culture and image of the firm as a "lifetime" employer often is gone forever. Survivors need information about why the actions had to be taken, and what the future holds for them personally. The more that employees are involved in the regrouping, the more likely the transition is to be smooth. Managers, too, find down-sizing situations stressful and react negatively to having to be the bearers of bad news.

Downsizing Approaches

The need for downsizing has inspired various innovative ways of removing peo-ple from the payroll, sometimes on a massive scale. Several methods can be used when downsizing must occur: attrition, early retirement buyouts, and layoffs are the most common.

Attrition and Hiring Freezes *Attrition* occurs when individuals who quit, die, or retire are not replaced. With this approach, no one is cut out of a job, but those who remain must handle the same workload with fewer people. Unless turnover is high, attrition will eliminate only a relatively small number of employees in the short run. Therefore, employers may use a method that combines attrition with a freeze on hiring. This method is usually received with better employee understanding than many of the other methods.

Early Retirement Buyouts Early retirement is a means of encouraging more senior workers to leave the organization early. As an incentive, employers make additional payments to employees so that they will not be penalized too much economically until their pensions and Social Security benefits take effect. The financial incentives of such voluntary termination programs, or buyouts, entice employees to quit. They are widely viewed as ways to accomplish workforce reduction without resorting to layoffs and individual firings.[31]

Buyouts appeal to employers because they can reduce payroll costs significantly over time. Although it faces some up-front costs, the organization does not incur the continuing payroll costs. One hospital saved $2 for every $1 spent on early retirees. As noted, early retirement buyouts are viewed as a more humane way to reduce staff than terminating long-service, loyal employees. In addition, as long as buyouts are truly voluntary, the organization is less exposed to age discrimination suits. One drawback is that employees the company wishes would stay, as well as those it wishes would leave, can take advantage of the buyout.[32]

"Burns, you've done a good job downsizing,
but we've decided to outsource your function."

Layoffs Layoffs occur when employees are put on unpaid leaves of absence. If business improves for the employer, then employees can be called back to work. Layoffs may be an appropriate downsizing strategy during a temporary economic downturn in an industry. Nevertheless, careful planning of layoffs is essential. Managers must consider the following questions:

- How are decisions made about whom to lay off, using seniority or performance records?
- How will callbacks be made if all workers cannot be recalled at the same time?
- Will any benefits coverage be given workers who are laid off?
- If workers take other jobs, do they forfeit their callback rights?

Companies have no legal obligation to provide a financial cushion to laid-off employees; however, many do. When a provision exists for severance pay, the most common formula is one week's pay for every year of employment. Larger companies tend to be more generous. Loss of medical benefits is a major problem for laid-off employees, but under a federal law (COBRA), displaced workers can retain their medical group coverage for up to 18 months, and up to 36 months for dependents, if they pay the premiums themselves.

Logging On...

Right Management Consultants
This firm provides information, resources, and services assisting employers with outplacement and downsizing.

www.right.com

Outplacement Services

Outplacement is a group of services provided to displaced employees to give them support and assistance. It is most often used with those involuntarily removed because of performance problems or elimination of jobs. A variety of services may be available to displaced employees.[33] Outplacement services typically include personal career counseling, resume preparation and typing services, interviewing workshops, and referral assistance. Such services are generally provided by outside firms that specialize in outplacement assistance. Special severance pay arrangements also may be used. Firms commonly provide additional severance benefits and continue medical benefit coverage for a period of time at the same company-paid level as before. Other aids include retraining for different jobs, establishing on-site career centers, and contacting other employers for job placement opportunities.

In summary, a decade of experience with downsizing has led to some suggestions on how to deal with it if necessary, as follows:

- *Investigate alternatives to downsizing:* Given the potential problems of downsizing, alternatives should be seriously considered first.
- *Involve those people necessary for success in the planning for downsizing:* The downsizing process too frequently leaves out those who have to make the downsized organization operate.
- *Develop comprehensive communications plans:* Employees are entitled to advance notice so they can make plans.
- *Nurture the survivors:* Remaining employees may be confused about their future careers. These and other concerns obviously can have negative effects.
- *Outplacement pays off:* Helping separated employees find new work is good for the people and the reputation of the organization.

Assessing HR Effectiveness

Logging On...

HR Management.com
This site contains resource tools for HR professionals, including an HR legal section and many other HR-related links.

http://www.hrmgt.com

A long-standing myth perpetuates the notion that one cannot really measure what the HR function does. That myth has hurt HR departments in some cases, because it suggests that any value added by HR efforts is somehow "mystical" or "magical." That notion is, of course, untrue; HR—like marketing, legal, or finance—must be evaluated based on the value it adds to the organization. Even though defining and measuring HR effectiveness is not as straightforward as with some areas, it is part of HR planning.

Other departments, managers, and employees are the main "customers" for HR services. If those services are lacking, too expensive, or of poor quality, then the organization may have to consider outsourcing some HR activities.[34] HR can position itself as a partner in an organization, but only by demonstrating real links between what HR activities contribute and organizational results. To demonstrate to the rest of the organization that the HR unit is a partner with a positive influence on the bottom line of the business, HR professionals must be prepared to measure the results of HR activities. Then the HR unit must communicate that information to the rest of the organization. Measurement is a key to demonstrating the success of the HR activities. Figure 2-10 shows a general approach to evaluating the efficiency and effectiveness of HR activities.

Studies of large and medium-sized firms in the United States have found relationships between the best HR practices and reduced turnover and increased employee productivity. Further, those practices enhanced profitability and market value of the firms studied. A high-quality, highly motivated workforce is hard for competition to replicate.[35] Data to evaluate performance can come from several sources. Some of those sources are already available in most organizations, but some data may have to be collected from existing HR records, an HR audit, or HR research.

Assessing HR Effectiveness Using Records

With the proliferation of government regulations, the number of required HR records has expanded. Of course, the records are useful only if they are kept current and properly organized. Managers who must cope with the paperwork have not always accepted such record-keeping requirements easily. Also, many managers feel that HR records can be a source of trouble because they can be used to question past managerial actions.

Another view of HR record-keeping activities is that HR records serve as important documentation should legal challenges occur. Disciplinary actions, past performance appraisals, and other documents may provide the necessary "proof" that employers need to defend their actions as job-related and nondiscriminatory. Records and data also can be a crucial source of information for audit or assessment of unit effectiveness.

One valuable use of HR records is that they provide the basis for research into possible causes of HR problems. For example, HR records can identify units with high turnover or more disciplinary problems. Or, HR records on training can be compared to subsequent employee performance to justify additional training expenditures.

WEST GROUP
A THOMSON COMPANY

HR Effectiveness
Lists possible measures by HR area.
Custom Search:
☑ ANALYSIS
Phrase: Measures of HR effectiveness

Figure 2-10 ▶ Overview of the HR Evaluation Process

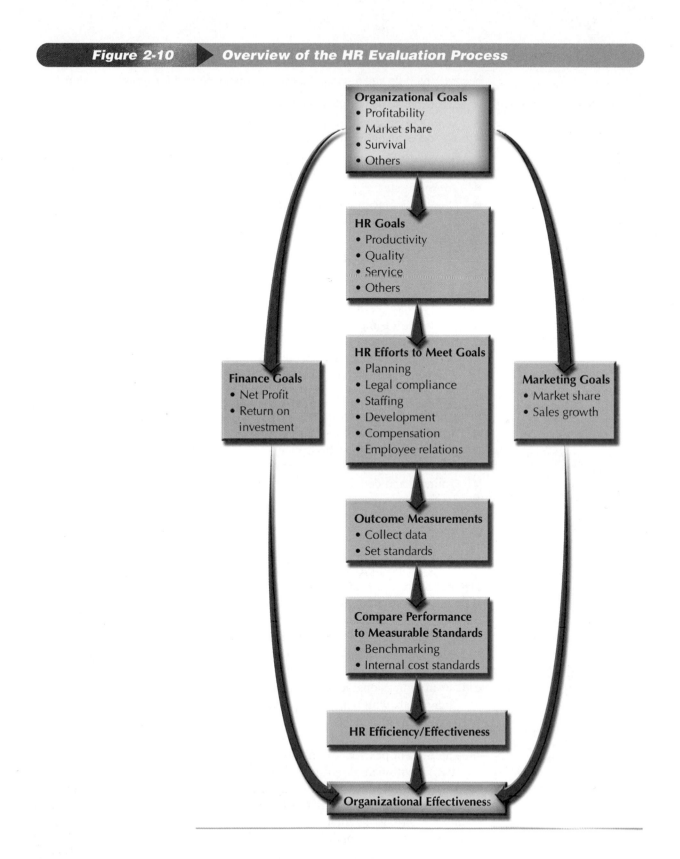

Some diagnostic measures from records can be used to check the effectiveness of the HR function. Note how each of the following measures requires accurate records and a comprehensive human resource information system:

- HR expense per employee
- Compensation as a percent of expenses
- HR department expense as a percent of total expenses
- Cost of hires
- Turnover rate
- Absence rate
- Workers' compensation cost per employee

HR Audit

One general means for assessing HR effectiveness is through an HR audit, similar to a financial audit. An **HR audit** is a formal research effort that evaluates the current state of HR management in an organization. These audits attempt to evaluate how well HR activities have been performed, so that management can identify areas for improvement.

An HR audit begins with a determination by management of the objectives for the HR area. The audit then compares the actual state of HR activities with these objectives, in such areas as:

- Legal compliance (EEO, OSHA, FSLA, Privacy, ERISA, FMLA)
- Current job descriptions and specifications
- Valid recruiting and selection processes
- Wage/salary and benefits systems
- Absenteeism and turnover control measures
- Training and development effort
- Performance management system
- Employee handbook policies
- Health, safety, and security issues

Using HR Research for Assessment

HR research is the analysis of data from HR records to determine the effectiveness of past and present HR practices. Research in general can be categorized as primary or secondary. In **primary research**, data are gathered firsthand for the specific project being conducted. Attitude surveys, questionnaires, interviews, and experiments are all primary research methods. **Secondary research** makes use of research data already gathered by others and reported in books, articles in professional journals, or other sources.

Individuals who plan to do primary research should decide first what they wish to study. Examples of primary research topics are causes of nursing employee turnover, employee attitudes about flextime, and the relationship of preemployment physical exams to workers' compensation claims.

HR practitioners do primary research when they conduct a pay survey on information technology jobs in other companies in their geographic area, or a study of turnover costs and reasons that employees in technical jobs leave more frequently during the first 24 to 30 months of employment. Thus, primary research has specific applications to resolving actual HR problems in particular organizations. Examples of primary research can be found in the *Academy of*

HR audit A formal research effort that evaluates the current state of HR management in an organization.

HR research The analysis of data from HR records to determine the effectiveness of past and present HR practices.

Primary research Research method in which data are gathered firsthand for the specific project being conducted.

Secondary research Research method using data already gathered by others and reported in books, articles in professional journals, or other sources.

Management Journal, Personnel Psychology, and the other research-oriented journals listed in Appendix B. The research studies described in these journals can offer HR professionals guidance on factors affecting HR issues and the impact of management approaches to HR.

Secondary research includes surveys done by various professional organizations can also provide useful perspectives. Some organizations, such as the Bureau of National Affairs and the Conference Board, sponsor surveys on HR practices in various communities, states, and regions. The results are distributed to participating organizations.

Finally, private management consulting firms and local colleges and universities can assist in HR research. These outside researchers may be more knowledgeable and unbiased than people inside the organization. Consultants skilled in questionnaire design and data analysis can give expert advice on HR research.

HR Performance and Benchmarking

Benchmarking Comparing specific measures of performance against data on those measures in other "best practice" organizations.

When information on HR performance has been gathered, it must be compared to a *standard,* which is a model or measure against which something is compared to determine its performance level. For example, it is meaningless to know that organizational turnover rate is 75% if the turnover rates at comparable organizations are unknown. One approach to assessing HR effectiveness is **benchmarking**, which compares specific measures of performance against data on those measures in other "best practices" organizations.[36] HR professionals interested in benchmarking try to locate organizations that do certain activities particularly well and thus become the "benchmarks." One means for obtaining benchmarking data is through telephone calls, which then may be followed up with questionnaires and site visits to benchmarking partners. The common benchmarked performance measures in HR management are:

- Total compensation as a percentage of net income before taxes
- Percent of management positions filled internally
- Dollar sales per employee
- Benefits as a percentage of payroll cost

Doing the Benchmarking Analysis

A useful way to analyze HR involves calculating ratios that can be compared from year to year, thus providing information about changes in HR operations. For example, one suggested series of ratios and measures is shown in Figure 2-11.

Effectiveness is best determined by comparing ratio measures with benchmarked national statistics. The comparisons should be tracked internally over time. For instance, the Society for Human Resource Management (SHRM) and the Saratoga Institute have developed benchmarks based on data from more than 500 companies, presented by industry and by organizational size. The Saratoga Institute in Santa Clara, California, surveys employers annually and compiles information that allows individual employers to compare HR costs against national figures.

Return on Investment (ROI) and Economic Value Added (EVA)

Return on investment (ROI) and economic value added (EVA) are two related approaches to measuring the contribution and cost of HR. Both calculations are a bit complex, so they are just highlighted here.

Logging On...

Saratoga Institute
This organization is well-known for its HR benchmarking data and studies.

www.saratogainstitute.com

Figure 2-11 **HR Business Performance Calculations**

HR Performance Area	Method of Calculation
1. CEO's priority numbers	Whatever CEO sees as linked to organizational strategic goals
2. Human value added	Revenue − Operating expense − *Pay and benefits* = Adjusted profit ÷ Full-time-equivalent employees
3. Return on human capital invested	Revenue − Operating expense − *Pay and benefits* = Adjusted profit ÷ Pay and benefits
4. Time to fill openings	Total calendar days from each requisition to accepted offer/Number of openings filled
5. Turnover cost	Cost to terminate + Cost to hire + Vacancy cost + *Productivity loss* = Total ÷ Employees lost
6. Volunteer turnover rate	Total voluntary employee separations ÷ Total employees
7. Return on training	(Dependent upon type of training done)
8. Cost per employee hired	Advertising expenses + Agency fees + Employee referral bonuses + HR recruiters pay and benefits + *10% misc. costs* = Total ÷ Total number of employees hired
9. Pay and benefits as % of operating expense	Total pay and benefits expenditures ÷ Total operating expenses
10. Healthcare costs per employee	Total healthcare benefits expenses ÷ Total number of employees

Source: Adapted from Jac Fitz-Enz, "Top 10 Calculations for Your HRIS," *HR Focus,* April 1998, S-3.

Return on investment (ROI) Calculation showing the value of expenditures for HR activities.

Return on investment (ROI) as a calculation shows the value of expenditures for HR activities. It can also be used to show how long it will take for the activities to pay for themselves. The following formula can be used to calculate the potential ROI for a new HR activity:

$$ROI = \frac{C}{A + B}$$

where:

A = Operating costs for a new or enhanced system for the time period
B = One-time cost of acquisition and implementation
C = Value of gains from productivity improvements for the time period

Economic value added (EVA) A firm's net operating profit after the cost of capital is deducted.

Economic value added (EVA) is a firm's net operating profit after the cost of capital is deducted. Cost of capital is the minimum rate of return demanded by shareholders. When a company is making more than the cost of capital, it is creating wealth for shareholders. An EVA approach requires that all policies, procedures, measures, and methods use cost of capital as a benchmark against which their return is judged. Human resource decisions can be subjected to the same analyses. Both of these methods are useful, and specific information on them is available from other sources.

Utility analysis Analysis in which economic or other statistical models are built to identify the costs and benefits associated with specific HR activities.

Utility or Cost/Benefit Analyses In **utility analysis**, economic or other statistical models are built to identify the costs and benefits associated with specific HR activities. These models generally contain equations that identify the relevant factors influencing the HR activity under study.

Human Resource Information Systems (HRIS)

Human resource information system (HRIS) An integrated system designed providing information used in HR decision making.

Computers have simplified the task of analyzing vast amounts of data, and they can be invaluable aids in HR management, from payroll processing to record retention. With computer hardware, software, and databases, organizations can keep records and information better, as well as retrieve them with greater ease. A **human resource information system (HRIS)** is an integrated system providing information used in HR decision making.

Purposes of an HRIS

An HRIS serves two major purposes in organizations. One relates to administrative and operational efficiency, the other to effectiveness. The first purpose of an HRIS is to improve the efficiency with which data on employees and HR activities are compiled. Many HR activities can be performed more efficiently and with less paperwork if automated, and better information is available, as the e-HR discussion on the next page shows.

The second purpose of an HRIS is more strategic and related to HR planning. Having accessible data enables HR planning and managerial decision making to be based to a greater degree on information rather than relying on managerial perceptions and intuition.

Uses of an HRIS

An HRIS has many uses in an organization. The most basic is the automation of payroll and benefit activities. With an HRIS, employees' time records are

Data Smart

The University of Minnesota at Rochester (UM/R) invested little on reporting HR matters. Even though such reports would be useful, the time and effort involved to obtain and analyze the data made the reports too expensive. At that time the university had seven different systems and databases handling HR information.

To build a better HRIS, these seven discrete sources were melded into a single "data warehouse" that was linked to reporting systems. Such systems are sold by companies such as Cognos, SAS Institute, Information Builders, Seagate, and Strategic Reporting.

At UM/R both the HR staff and managers can now access the data warehouse. For example they can generate a "payroll distribution report," which identifies salaries for every university employee and the different accounts from which they come. This categorization is important in universities because a researcher's salary may come partially from an academic depart-

ment and partially from various research grants.

Such a report formerly took 30 hours to generate. Now it can be done in minutes by the end users. The HR staff does not even have to get involved. The university on average can build reports in one-tenth the time previously taken without reliance on the IT department. In 95% of the cases, requested data can come from the data warehouse, truly a beneficial use for an HRIS.[37]

entered into the system, and the appropriate deductions and other individual adjustments are reflected in the final paychecks. As a result of HRIS development and implementation in many organizations, several payroll functions are being transferred from accounting departments to HR departments. Another common use of HRIS is EEO/Affirmative Action tracking. Beyond these basic activities, many other HR activities can benefit from use of an HRIS, as Figure 2-12 illustrates.

Designing and Implementing an HRIS

To design an effective HRIS, experts advise starting with questions about the data to be included. Questions that should be asked are the following:

- What information is available, and what information is needed about people in the organization?
- To what uses will the information be put?
- In what format should the output be presented to fit with other organizational records?
- Who needs the information?
- When and how often is it needed?

HRIS Checklist
Contains a checklist for determining HRIS priorities.
Custom Search:
☑ CHECKLIST
Phrase: HRIS automation

Answers to these questions help pinpoint the necessary hardware and software.[38] Experts recommend the formation of a *project team* be established and extensive planning be done. This team often includes representatives from several departments in the organization, including HR staff and management information specialists. The team serves as a steering committee to review user needs, identify desired capabilities of the system, solicit and examine bids from software and hardware vendors, and identify the implementation process required to install the system.[39]

Figure 2-12 **Uses of an HR Information System (HRIS)**

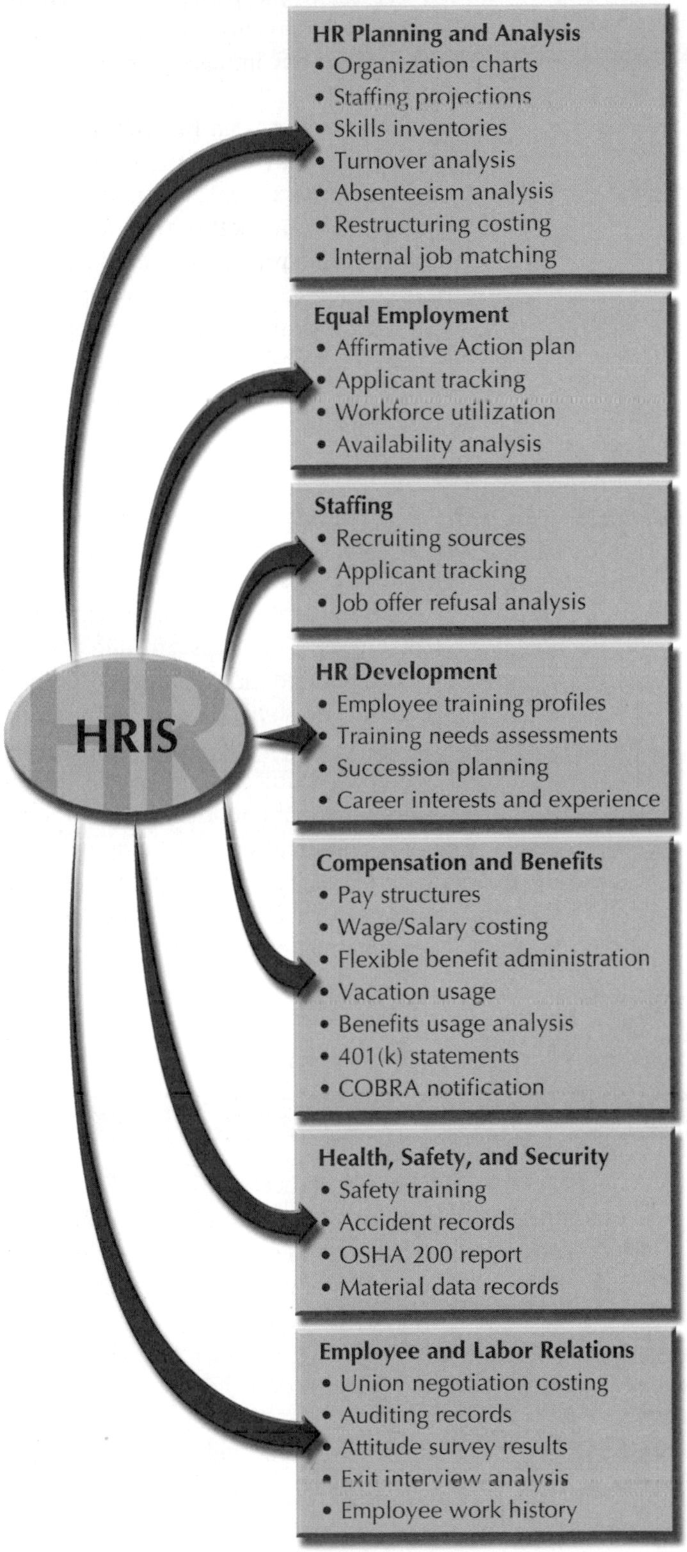

HR Planning and Analysis
- Organization charts
- Staffing projections
- Skills inventories
- Turnover analysis
- Absenteeism analysis
- Restructuring costing
- Internal job matching

Equal Employment
- Affirmative Action plan
- Applicant tracking
- Workforce utilization
- Availability analysis

Staffing
- Recruiting sources
- Applicant tracking
- Job offer refusal analysis

HR Development
- Employee training profiles
- Training needs assessments
- Succession planning
- Career interests and experience

Compensation and Benefits
- Pay structures
- Wage/Salary costing
- Flexible benefit administration
- Vacation usage
- Benefits usage analysis
- 401(k) statements
- COBRA notification

Health, Safety, and Security
- Safety training
- Accident records
- OSHA 200 report
- Material data records

Employee and Labor Relations
- Union negotiation costing
- Auditing records
- Attitude survey results
- Exit interview analysis
- Employee work history

HRIS

Intranet
An organizational network that operates over the Internet.

Extranet
An Internet-linked network that allows employees access to information provided by external entities.

Accessing the HRIS via Intranets and Extranets The dramatic increase in the use of the Internet is raising both possibilities and concerns for HR professionals, particularly when establishing intranets and extrancts. An **intranet** is an organizational network that operates over the Internet. The growth in the use of HR intranets for obtaining and disseminating HR information has been staggering.[40]

An **extranet** is an Internet-linked network that allows employees access to information provided by external entities. For instance, with an extranet, employees can access benefit information maintained by a third-party benefits administrator. In another situation employees can access their payroll information from a payroll service provider and submit their travel requests to an external travel service provider. For both extranets and intranets, security is necessary to prevent unauthorized or inappropriate access and usage.

Use of Web-based information systems has allowed the HR unit in organizations to become more administratively efficient and to be able to deal with more strategic and longer-term HR planning issues. Firms have used these Web-based HRIS options in four primary ways:

- *Bulletin boards:* Information on personnel policies, job posting, and training materials can be accessed by employees globally.
- *Data access:* Linked to databases, an extranet or intranet allows employees themselves to access benefit information such as sick leave usage or 401(k) balances. This frees up time for HR staff members who previously spent considerable time answering routine employee inquiries.
- *Employee self-service:* Many intranet uses incorporate employee self-service options whereby employees can access and update their own personnel records, change or enroll in employee benefits plans, and respond to employment opportunities in other locations. Obviously, maintaining security is critical when the employee self-service option is available.
- *Extended linkage:* Integrating extranets and intranets allows the databases of vendors of HR services and an employer to be linked so that data can be exchanged electronically. Also, employees can communicate directly from throughout the world to submit and retrieve personnel details.

Summary

- HR planning is tied to the broader process of strategic planning, beginning with identifying the philosophy and mission of the organization.
- Human resources can provide a core competency for the organization, which may represent unique capabilities of the organization.
- HR strategies are affected by the culture of the organization.
- Productivity at national, organizational, and individual levels is critical for organizational success.

- Service is critical to meeting customer expectations, and HR must support service through selection, training, and other activities.
- Different organizational strategies require different approaches to HR planning.
- HR planning involves analyzing and identifying the future needs for and availability of human resources for the organization. The HR unit has major responsibilities in HR planning, but managers must provide supportive information and input.

- When developing HR plans, it is important for managers to scan the external environment to identify the effects of governmental influences, economic conditions, geographic and competitive concerns, and workforce composition and patterns.
- Assessment of internal strengths and weaknesses as a part of HR planning requires that current jobs and employee capabilities be audited and organizational capabilities be inventoried.
- Information on past and present conditions is used to identify expected future conditions and forecast the supply and demand for human resources. This process can be carried out with a variety of methods and for differing periods of time.
- Management of HR surpluses may require downsizing. Attrition, layoffs, early retirement, and outplacement are commonly used.
- HR departments must set goals and measure effectiveness.

- Primary researchers gather data directly on issues, whereas secondary researchers use research done by others and reported elsewhere.
- HR audits can be used to gather comprehensive information on how well HR activities in an organization are being performed.
- Benchmarking allows an organization to compare its practices against "best practices" in different organizations.
- An HRIS is an integrated system designed to improve the efficiency with which HR data is compiled and to make HR records more useful as information sources.
- An HRIS offers a wide range of HR services, with payroll, benefits administration, and EEO/Affirmative Action tracking being the most prevalent.
- The growth of Web-based HRIS options means that training and security issues must be addressed.

Review and Discussion Questions

1. Describe some examples in your work experience of the human resources in an organization creating a competitive advantage and core competency.
2. Why must HR planning be seen as a process flowing from the organizational strategic plan?
3. How would you benchmark HR performance in a grocery retailer?
4. Why are the time frame and methods used to forecast supply and demand for human resources so important?
5. Assume that as a result of HR planning, a hospital identifies a shortage of physical therapists but a surplus of administrative workers. Discuss the actions that might be taken to address these problems, and explain why they must be approached carefully.
6. Describe the advantages and disadvantages of employees using a Web-based HRIS.

Terms to Know

strategic human resource management   30
core competency   30
organizational culture   31
productivity   31
unit labor cost   32
human resource (HR) planning   35
HR strategies   37

environmental scanning   38
forecasting   43
transition stay bonus   48
HR audit   54
HR research   54
primary research   54
secondary research   54

Using the Internet

Benchmarking HR Practices

As the Director of HR for your organization, you have been given a strategic assignment by the Chief Financial Officer (CFO). The CFO has asked you to do some research and identify what types of HR benchmarking tools exist and what are some of the areas of human resources that should be measured.

Complete the following two tasks using this Web site: *http://www.benchmarkingreports. com*
1. Identify the benchmarking reports available in the field of human resources.
2. Download the free executive summary report, "Developing Human Resources Measures," and identify the four areas of measurement.

CASE

Merging Incompatible Organizational Cultures

The number of mergers and acquisitions continues to increase, as does the evidence that merging two different organizational cultures is not easy. Also, many anticipated benefits of the mergers are not realized because of differing organizational and human resource cultures.

One example from the health-care industry illustrates the problems. Two large home health-care organizations, both headquartered in southern California, had been fierce competitors. Homedco and Abbey Healthcare Group decided that rather than continuing to compete, they could strengthen their market positions by merging to create one large firm, Apria Healthcare Group. Together, they planned to expand their home health services nationwide as the effects of managed care spread.

Yet several years later the stock value of Apria has declined significantly, and earnings have fallen. How far Apria declined was soon evident; when efforts began to find another company to take over the firm, few buyers were interested. What happened was primarily due to operational problems caused by the merger. Those issues had not been resolved because of internal conflict between the ex-Homedco and Abbey Healthcare executives and employees. Ultimately, the Board of Directors, which was evenly split, accepted the need to remove Timothy Aitken, former CEO of Abbey Healthcare, and have Jeremy Jones from Homedco as CEO.

It was obvious from the beginning that the organizational cultures were markedly different. Homedco had a more formalized structure with centralized decision making, whereas Abbey Healthcare had decentralized decision making, and branch managers had significant authority. Also, merging computer and billing systems by using the Abbey Healthcare system meant that employees from Homedco had to be trained, which did not happen fast enough. As a result, numerous billing errors and the resulting complaints and phone calls from unhappy customers overwhelmed Apria customer service departments.

To save costs and eliminate duplication of jobs, about 14% of the employees in the combined company lost jobs. But the greatest number of those cut were former Abbey employees. For those remaining, it appeared that most Homedco managers were not affected as much as the Abbey Healthcare managers. For instance, only 6 of the 21 regional mangers were formerly with Abbey Healthcare, which caused most of the best-performing Abbey sales representatives to quit.

Even changing some basic HR policies caused problems. For example, when Homedco HR policies were extended into Abbey offices, new dress code and time-recording procedures irritated many former Abbey workers. Consequently, a significant number of them left in the first year after the merger. The level of conflict was so severe that employees from one firm referred to those from the other company as "idiots" and refused to return phone calls from employees with the other firm. Instead of being a healthy merger, it turned into the "merger from hell."

Unfortunately, this situation is not unusual; other conflicting cultures have diminished the effective-ness of mergers in almost every industry. One instance is the merger of Daimler-Benz and Chrysler Corporation. During the first few years of the merger, the combined firm has lost profitability, significant staff departures have occurred, and employee morale has plunged as the firm has eliminated thousands of employees. In this case, as well as Apria, it is evident that human resource issues and organizational culture incompatibilities can destroy the value of mergers that appear to be logical from a broad business strategy perspective.[41]

Questions

1. Describe how analysis of human resource issues could have been beneficial prior to the Apria merger.
2. Given the problems in the examples cited in the case, what actions could be taken to create better organizational cultures?

Notes

1. Chikako Mogi, "Traditional Over-hiring by Japanese Questioned," *The Denver Post,* December 26, 2000, 2C; George Hager, "Sawmill Illustrates the Buzz about Productivity," *USA Today,* March 21, 2000, B1–2; Patrick Borta, "Zero-Sum Gain," *The Wall Street Journal,* March 13, 2001, 1A; and Del Jones, "Companies Change Gears Fast," *USA Today,* February 7, 2001, 1B.

2. Luis Gomez-Mejia, "Moving Forward," *HR News,* Spring 2000, 1–2.

3. Michael A. Hitt et. al., "Direct and Moderating Effects of Human Capital on Strategy and Performance in Professional Service Firms," *Academy of Management Journal,* 44 (2001), 13.

4. Daniel M. Cable et al., "The Source and Accuracy of Job Applicants' Beliefs About Organizational Culture," *Academy of Management Journal,* 43 (2000), 1076–1086.

5. Jennifer Reingold and Marcia Stepanek, "Why the Productivity Revolution Will Spread," *Business Week,* February 14, 2000, 112–118.

6. "Facts and Figures," *Bulletin to Management,* February 17, 2000, 53.

7. George Hager, *USA Today,* March 21, 2000, 1B.

8. "An Inside Job," *The Economist,* July 15, 2000, 61; and Jeffrey Garten, "The War for Better Quality Is Far from Won," *Business Week,* December 18, 2000, 32.

9. Thomas J. Douglas and William Q. Judge, Jr., "Total Quality Management Implementation and Competitive Advantage," *Academy of Management Journal,* 44 (2001), 158.

10. Diane Brady, "Why Service Stinks," *Business Week,* October 23, 2000, 118.

11. Charles Greer, *Strategic Human Resource Management,* 2nd ed. (Upper Saddle River, NJ: Prentice Hall, 2001).

12. Barbara J. Orsen et al., "Performance, Firm Size, and Problem Solving," *Journal of Small Business Management,* October 2000, 42.

13. Mark Gimern, "CEOs Who Manage Too Much," *Fortune,* September 4, 2000, 235–242.

14. Reginald M. Beal, "Competing Effectively: Environmental Scanning," *Journal of Small Business Management,* January 2000, 27.

15. Raymond Suutari, "Coping with Change," *CMA Management,* March 2000, 16.

16. Stephen Jefferys, "A 'Copernican Revolution' in French Industrial Relations: Are the Times a' Changing?", *British Journal of Industrial Relations,* June 2000, 241–260.

17. Based on Cynthia Gramm and John Schnell, "The Use of Flexible Staffing Arrangements in Core Production Jobs," *Industrial and Labor Relations Review,* 53 (2001), 245.

18. Adapted from "Electronic Employee Profiles Allow Redeployment of Talent," *Bulletin to Management,* August 10, 2000, 254.

19. Barry Gerhart et al., "Measurement Error in Research on Human

Resources," *Personnel Psychology,* 53 (2000), 803.

20. John Bound and Harry Holzer, "Demand Shifts, Population Adjustments, and Labor Market Outcomes," *Journal of Labor Economics,* January 2000, 20.

21. "The Skinny on Downsizing," *Business Week,* August 28, 2000, 38,

22. "The Strategic Difference Between Layoffs and Downsizing," *Bulletin to Management,* February 22, 2001, 61.

23. "Louis Lavelle, "Corporate Liposuction Can Have Nasty Side Effects," *Business Week,* July 17, 2000, 74–75.

24. Jon Hilsenrath, "Many Say Layoffs Hurt Companies More Than They Help," *The Wall Street Journal,* February 21, 2001, A2.

25. Charles Whalen, "Downsizing Spending," *Business Week,* September 11, 2000, 30.

26. Mitchell Lee Marks et. al., "Making Mergers and Acquisitions Work," *Academy of Management Executive,* May 2001, 80–94.

27. Joann S. Lublin, "Mergers Often Trigger Anxiety, Lower Morale," *The Wall Street Journal,* January 16, 2001, B1; and William McKinley and A. G. Scherer, "Some Unanticipated Consequences of Organizational Restructuring," *Academy of Management Review,* 25 (2000), 735–752.

28. "Corporate Job Creation, Job Elimination, and Downsizing," 1997 Survey, American Management Association, 1–8.

29. Charles Gasparino and Aaron Elstern, "Schwab Asks 30–50% of Work Force to Take Days Off," *The Wall Street Journal,* January 31, 2001, C1; Kemba Dunham, "Employees Seek Ways to Lure Back Workers When Times Improve," *The Wall Street Journal,* June 19, 2001, B1; Emily Nelson, "Job Cut Buyouts Favored by P & G Pose Problems," *The Wall Street Journal,* June 12, 2001, B1; and "Soothing the Sting," *Human Resource Executive,* June 1, 2001, 30.

30. Kembo J. Dunham, "The Kinder, Gentler Way to Lay Off Employees," *The Wall Street Journal,* March 13, 2001, B1.

31. Kerstin Isaksson and Gunn Johansson, "Adaptation to Continued Work and Early Retirement," *Journal of Occupational and Organizational Psychology,* June 2000, 241–256.

32. Daniel Feldman and Seongan Kim, "Bridge Employment During Retirement," *Human Resource Planning,* Spring 2000, 14–25.

33. Rachel Silverman, "Laid-Off Workers Find Job Search No Longer a Cinch," *The Wall Street Journal,* February 6, 2001, B1.

34. Brian S. Klaas, "HR Outsourcing and Its Impact: The Role of Transaction Costs," *Personnel Psychology,* 52 (1999), 113–136.

35. "HR Metric," *Bulletin to Management,* January 18, 2001, 20.

36. John Yuva, "Benchmarking for the Future," *Purchasing Today,* January 2001, 40–49.

37. Adapted from Tom Starner, "Data Smart," *Human Resource Executive,* May 15, 2001, 49.

38. "Information Systems," *Bulletin to Management,* February 8, 2001, 44.

39. "HRIS," *Bulletin to Management,* November 23, 2000, 372.

40. Tom Starner, "Building a Better Net," *Human Resource Executive,* May 15, 2001, 39.

41. Adapted from Rhonda L. Rundle, "Home Health Rivals Try Merger of Equals, Get Merger from Hell," *The Wall Street Journal,* February 26, 1999, A1; and Joann Müller, "Can This Man Save Chrysler?" *Business Week,* September 17, 2001, 86–94.

CHAPTER 3

Individual Performance and Retention

After you have read this chapter, you should be able to:

- Discuss how motivation is linked to individual performance.

- Identify the changing nature of the psychological contract.

- Describe several types of absenteeism and turnover.

- List the five major retention determinants and identify activities related to them.

- Outline the retention management process and how to measure and assess turnover.

▼ Employment Branding—Becoming an "Employer of Choice"

As the attraction and retention of talented individuals becomes more difficult, organizations recognize that how they are seen by potential and current employees is vital. Employers viewed as desirable organizations are better able to attract applicants for open jobs and to retain employees. However, organizations seen as less desirable may develop reputations in the community and industry that often make it harder to attract applicants and make it more likely that employees will leave. For instance, in one midwestern U.S. city a large employer's reputation for good pay and benefits was countered by its work demands that were seen as excessive by many employees. Frequent organizational restructurings resulted in people losing jobs at the same time new employees were being hired, only to have another restructuring occur six months later with more employees being terminated or transferred to other jobs. The end result at this employer was a lower flow of applicants and higher turnover rates than the averages in the city and the industry.

Unfortunately, this example may be more prevalent than expected. Right Management Consultants conducted an extensive study of a large number of employees identified as being the most valuable human resources in a wide range of companies. The researchers found that those employees basically gave their employers a C+ grade in a number of organizational areas. Firms in the study included both U.S. and international organizations, including ADP, Avis, Bethlehem Steel, Dupont, First Union, Thomson Learning, 3M, Union Pacific, New Zealand Post, Bumiputra-Commerce Bank, Semb Corp Industries, and Oracle.

The study also revealed that employees' views on such factors as organizational leadership, values, culture, work environment, and compensation/benefits affect the willingness of the individuals to continue current employment. If the most valued employees gave this type of rating, then the implications for the broader workforces cause even more concern.

The concept of *employment branding* has grown in recent years as a combination of HR and marketing. Organizations spend considerable effort trying to establish a brand image in the minds of consumers. Consider how the "identity" of a firm affects whether consumers even consider their products and services. Just think of the different images that Cadillac or Lexus creates in luxury cars, or Rolex or Timex creates in watches. Likewise, employers have "brands" in the minds of individuals. Therefore, a number of organizations have taken deliberate steps to become an "employer of choice" by developing and maintaining a highly positive employment image.

Those firms of choice often have been identified as *Fortune* magazine's "100 Best Companies to Work For." Included in the list are the Container Store (see case at end of chapter), Southwest Airlines, SAS Institute, Synovus Financial, Cisco Systems, Edward Jones, Continental Airlines, and Granite Rock, all consistently in the top 25. According to the selection committee compiling the list, the primary characteristic of the 100 firms on the list is having an organizational culture that commands respect and trust among their employees. Thus, a commitment to creating a positive employment brand pays off by being seen as "employers of choice" by potential and current employees.[1]

> Employers viewed as desirable organizations are better able to attract applicants for open jobs and to retain employees.

*"High performers are like frogs in a wheelbarrow—
they can jump out at any time."*

—McKinsey & Company study

In most organizations the performance of individual employees is a major determinant of organizational success. The opening discussion about employment branding and becoming an employer of choice emphasizes that how well employees perform their jobs significantly affects organizational productivity and performance.

Just as individuals in an organization can be a competitive advantage, they can also be a liability. When few employees know how to do their jobs, when people are constantly leaving the organization, and when those employees who do remain work ineffectively, the human resources are a competitive problem that puts the organization at a disadvantage. Individual performance, motivation, and employee retention are key for organizations to maximize the effectiveness of individual human resources, which is the focus of this chapter.

Individual Employee Performance

Many factors affect the performance of individual employees—their abilities, efforts expended, and the organizational support they receive. The HR unit in an organization exists in part to analyze and address these areas. Exactly what the role of the HR unit in an organization "should be" depends upon what upper management expects. As with any management function, HR management activities should be developed, evaluated, and changed as necessary so that they can contribute to the competitive performance of the organization and individuals at work.

Individual Performance Factors

The three major factors that affect how a given individual performs are illustrated in Figure 3-1. The factors are: (1) individual ability to do the work, (2) effort level expended, and (3) organizational support. The relationship of these factors is widely acknowledged in management literature as:

$$\text{Performance } (P) = \text{Ability } (A) \times \text{Effort } (E) \times \text{Support } (S)$$

Individual performance is enhanced to the degree that all three components are present with an individual employee. However, performance is diminished if any of these factors is reduced or absent. For instance, assume that several production workers have the abilities to do their jobs and work hard, but the organization provides outmoded equipment or the management style of supervisors causes negative reactions by the workers. Take another example of a customer service representative in a call center who has the abilities and an employer who provides excellent support. But the individual hates "being tied to a telephone cord" all day and is frequently absent because of the dislike of the job even though it pays well. In both cases individual performance is likely to be less than in situations where all three components are present. Individual motivation is often one of the missing variables, and an overview of motivation is presented next.

Figure 3-1 ▶ *Components of Individual Performance*

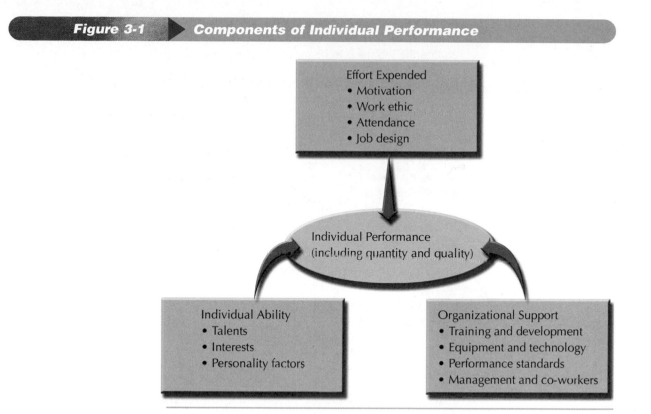

Individual Motivation

Motivation The desire within a person causing that person to act.

Motivation is the desire within a person causing that person to act. People usually act for one reason: to reach a goal. Thus, motivation is a goal-directed drive, and it seldom occurs in a void. The words *need, want, desire,* and *drive* are all similar to *motive,* from which the word *motivation* is derived. Understanding motivation is important because performance, reaction to compensation, and other HR concerns are affected by and influence motivation.

Approaches to understanding motivation vary because different theorists have developed their own views and models. Each approach has contributed to the understanding of human motivation and several are briefly highlighted next.

Maslow's Hierarchy of Needs One theory of human motivation developed by Abraham Maslow has received a great deal of exposure. In this theory, Maslow classified human needs into five categories that ascend in a definite order. Until the more basic needs are adequately fulfilled, a person will not strive to meet higher needs. Maslow's well-known hierarchy is composed of: (1) *physiological needs,* (2) *safety and security needs,* (3) *belonging and love needs,* (4) *esteem needs,* and (5) *self-actualization needs.*

An assumption often made by those using Maslow's hierarchy is that workers in modern, technologically advanced societies basically have satisfied their physiological, safety, and belonging needs. Therefore, they will be motivated by the needs for self-esteem and the esteem of others, and then self-actualization. Consequently, conditions to satisfy these needs should be present at work to enable the job itself to be meaningful and motivating.

Herzberg's Motivation/Hygiene Theory Frederick Herzberg's motivation/hygiene theory assumes that one group of factors, *motivators,* accounts for high levels of job satisfaction and motivation. However, *hygiene factors,* can cause dissatisfaction with work.

Motivators	**Hygiene Factors**
■ Achievement	■ Interpersonal relationships
■ Recognition	■ Company policy/administration
■ Work itself	■ Supervision
■ Responsibility	■ Salary
■ Advancement	■ Working conditions

The implication of Herzberg's research for management and HR practices is that even though managers carefully consider and address hygiene factors to avoid employee dissatisfaction, people may not be motivated to work harder. Herzberg suggests that only motivators cause employees to exert more effort and thereby enhance employee performance. However, subsequent research by others has questioned whether the two groups of factors are really as distinct as Herzberg outlined.

Equity as a Motivator People want to be treated fairly at work, which is referred to as equity in management literature.[2] **Equity** is defined as the perceived fairness of what the person does compared with what the person receives. *Inputs* are what a person brings to the organization, including educational level, age, experience, productivity, and other skills or efforts. The items received by a person, or the *outcomes,* are the rewards obtained in exchange for inputs. Outcomes include pay, benefits, recognition achievement, prestige, and any other rewards received. Note that an outcome can be either tangible (such as economic benefits) or intangible (such as recognition or achievement.)

The individual's view of fair value is critical to the relationship between performance and job satisfaction because one's sense of equity is an exchange and comparison process.[3] Assume an individual is an information technology (IT) specialist who exchanges talents and efforts (inputs) for the tangible and intangible rewards (outputs) the employer provides. To determine perceived equity the individual subconsciously compares talents, skills, and efforts to those of other IT specialists both internally and at other firms. That perception—correct or incorrect—significantly affects that person's valuation of the inputs and outcomes. A sense of inequity occurs when the comparison process results in an imbalance between inputs and outcomes.

One related theory by Lyman Porter and E. E. Lawler indicates that motivation is also influenced by people's expectations. If expectations are not met, people may feel that they have been unfairly treated and consequently become dissatisfied. Expectancy theory, discussed next, was developed to expand on these ideas.

Expectancy Theory This theory states that individuals base decisions about their behaviors on their expectations that one or another alternate behavior is

Equity The perceived fairness of what the person does compared with what the person receives.

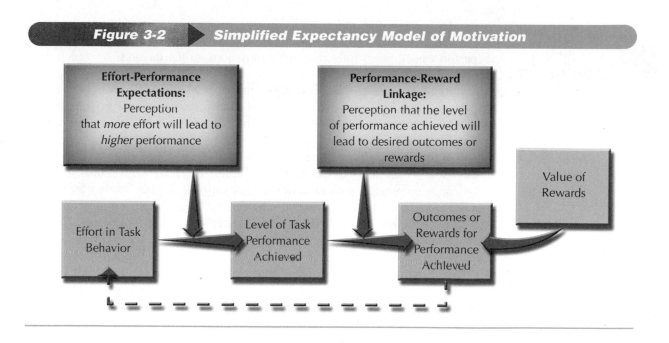

Figure 3-2 Simplified Expectancy Model of Motivation

Effort-Performance Expectations:
Perception that *more* effort will lead to *higher* performance

Performance-Reward Linkage:
Perception that the level of performance achieved will lead to desired outcomes or rewards

Value of Rewards

Effort in Task Behavior

Level of Task Performance Achieved

Outcomes or Rewards for Performance Achieved

more likely to lead to needed or desired outcomes. As Figure 3-2 depicts, the three crucial aspects of the behavior-outcome relationship are as follows:

- *Effort-Performance Expectations* refer to employees' beliefs that working harder will lead to performance. If people do not believe that working harder leads to performance, then their efforts may diminish.
- *Performance-Reward Linkage* considers individuals' expectations that high performance actually will lead to rewards. The performance-reward relationship indicates how instrumental or important effective performance is in producing desired results.
- *Value of Reward*s refers to how valuable the rewards are to the employee. One determinant of employees' willingness to exert effort is the degree to which they value the rewards offered by the organization.

This model of motivation suggests that individuals' levels of effort (motivation) are not simply functions of rewards. Employees must expect that they have the *ability to perform the task well;* they must feel that *high performance will result in receiving rewards;* and they must *value those rewards.* If all three conditions are met, employees will be motivated to exert greater effort.

Management Implications for Motivating Individual Performance

The concepts of equity and expectancy point out that motivation is complex and individualized, but managerial strategies and tactics must be comprehensive in order to address equity and expectations of individuals. For instance, managers must determine whether inadequate individual behavior is due to low effort-performance ties (ability), low performance-reward linkages (inconsistent reward policies), or low value (low desire for the rewards).

In the case of low effort-performance, managers may try training to improve the relationship and thus encourage high performance. In the case of low performance-reward links, managers must look to the methods by which they appraise and reward performance.

Finally, managers must investigate the desirability of the rewards given for performance. Even if skills and rewards for performance are both high, the employee may not value the rewards. The rewards must be based on what the employees value, not what the managers value.

Many organizations spend considerable money to "motivate" their employees using a wide range of tactics. For example, firms have motivational speakers to inspire employees, with some of the "motivational coaches" as they are called, commanding as much as $50,000 per speech. Other employers give T-shirts, mugs, books, and videos to employees as motivators. Such efforts are estimated to cost in excess of $3 billion per year, not including sales motivation rewards.[4] However, the effectiveness of these expenditures has been questioned, particularly given the short-term nature of many of these programs and rewards.

In summary, answering the question often asked by managers, "How do I motivate my employees?" requires managerial diagnoses of employees' efforts, abilities, and expectations. For that reason, the relationships between individuals and their organizations are an integral part of effective HR management.

Individual/Organizational Relationships

Various surveys have found that only about half of the workers in U.S. organizations are relatively satisfied with their jobs, a decline of 10% from five years previously. The biggest decline occurred with workers 45–54 years old. Even more concerning is that just 24% said they were committed to stay at least two years at their current employer. Also about one-fifth of employees in some surveys are so dissatisfied with their jobs that they negatively affect other employees.[5] Because the long-term economic health of most organizations depends on the efforts of employees with the appropriate capabilities and motivation to perform their jobs well, organizations that are successful over time demonstrate that individual relationships do matter and should be managed effectively.

The Psychological Contract

One concept that has been useful in discussing employees' relationships with organizations is that of a **psychological contract**, which refers to the unwritten expectations employees and employers have about the nature of their work relationships. Because the psychological contract is individual and subjective in nature, it focuses on expectations about "fairness" that may not be defined clearly by employees.

Psychological contract
The unwritten expectations employees and employers have about the nature of their work relationships.

Both tangible items (such as wages, benefits, employee productivity, and attendance) and intangible items (such as loyalty, fair treatment, and job security) are encompassed by psychological contracts between employers and employees. Many employers may attempt to detail their expectations through employee handbooks and policy manuals, but those materials are only part of the total "contractual" relationship.

Research on the Changing Psychological Contract

Numerous writers have highlighted changes in the nature of the psychological contract between employees and employers. Research includes documentation of the nature of the psychological contracts for the twenty-first century, such as a study conducted by Lester and Kickul and published in *Human Resource Planning.*

The research on psychological contracts identified what employees value most and how they respond when their expectations are and are not met. Using MBA students who were employed full-time, the researchers obtained survey responses from 268 individuals. The participants were employed in a wide range of occupational fields and had averaged 3.4 years with their employers. The survey questionnaire asked the individuals to provide details showing what psychological contract "obligations" were most important to them and how well their employers were fulfilling those obligations, as well as rating their job satisfaction and intentions to leave their current employers.

The results from analyses of the data revealed that both extrinsic and intrinsic outcomes were rated highly by the respondents. Extrinsic outcomes are such factors as competitive salary and health-care benefits, while intrinsic outcomes included honest communication, managerial support, and challenging work. Interestingly, eight of the ten most highly desired items were intrinsic in nature. Also, participants reported that they perceived a lack of competent management, which had the highest discrepancy between what employees valued and what employers provided.

The study found that discrepancies between what the individuals valued and the employers provided were related to lower job satisfaction and a higher intention to leave. Thus, the research confirmed what many would logically think, which is that individuals whose psychological contract "obligations" are not being satisfied by what their employers provide are more dissatisfied with their jobs and are more likely to leave.

The implications for organizations and HR professionals is that matching individuals' expectations before hiring is important. "Realistic job previews" give potential employees a sense of what the organization provides prior to hiring them. Also, the results of the study confirm the importance of competent management and managerial communication in contributing to employee satisfaction and retention. Finally, employees expect their employers to provide feedback on individual performance through performance appraisal systems and providing career development opportunities. Employers who understand the "new" psychological contracts expected by employees are more likely to have satisfied employees who stay longer.[6]

The Changing Psychological Contract At one time, employees exchanged their efforts and capabilities for a secure job that offered rising pay, good benefits, and career progression within the organization. But as organizations have downsized and cut workers who have given long and loyal service, a growing number of employees question whether they should be loyal to their employers. Closely related to the psychological contract is *psychological ownership.* When individuals feel that they have some control and perceived rights in the organization, they are more likely to be committed to the organization.[7] The HR Perspective discusses research on how employee expectations have changed in psychological contracts.

Rather than just paying employees to follow orders and put in time, increasingly employers are expecting employees to utilize their knowledge, skills, and abilities to accomplish organizational results. An effective psychological contract recognizes the following components:

Employers provide:	**Employees contribute:**
■ Competitive compensation and benefits	■ Continuous skill improvement and increased productivity
■ Career development opportunities	■ Reasonable time with organization
■ Flexibility to balance work and home life	■ Extra effort when needed

Two factors affecting the relationship between individuals and organizations are economic changes and the expectations of different generations of individuals. These factors affect the psychological contract in a number of ways.

Economic Changes The ebb and flow of the economy is a major factor affecting employee expectations. Just consider the "employment world" when the dot.com and technology boom was underway. Many individuals, especially younger ones with technology backgrounds, expected and demanded high starting salaries, hiring bonuses, stock options, relaxed and casual workplaces, and frequent career promotions or changes. However, when the dot.com bubble burst, these same individuals had to face a different job market and employers offering different rewards and job environments.[8]

Generational Differences Much has been written about the differing expectations of individuals in different generations. Many of these observations are anecdotal and give only generalizations about individuals in the various age groups. Some of the common generational labels are:

■ Matures (born before 1945)
■ Baby boomers (born 1945–1965)
■ Generation X (born 1966–1980)
■ Generation Y (born 1980–1990)

Rather than identifying the characteristics cited for each of these groups, it is most important here to emphasize that people's expectations differ between generations, as well as within these generation labels. For employers, the differing expectations present challenges. For instance, many of the baby boomers and matures are concerned about security and experience, whereas the younger generation Ys often are seen as the "why" generation who expect to be rewarded quickly, are very adaptable, and tend to be more questioning about why managers and organizations make the decisions they do.[9] Also, consider the dynamics of a mature manager directing generation X and Y individuals, or generation X managers supervising older, more experienced baby boomers. These generational differences are likely to continue to create challenges and conflicts in organizations because of the differing expectations that various individuals have.[10] One of the most noticeable differences is in loyalty to organizations.

Loyalty

Employees *do* believe in psychological contracts and hope their employers will honor that side of the "agreement." Many employees still want security and stability, interesting work, a supervisor they respect, and competitive pay and benefits. If these elements are not provided, employees may feel a diminished need to contribute to organizational performance. When organizations merge, lay off large numbers of employees, outsource work, and use large numbers of temporary and part-time workers, employees see fewer reasons to give their loyalty to employers in return for this loss of job security. This decline is evident in such firms as AT&T and Lucent, where significant staff cutbacks and declines in stock prices have demoralized many of the remaining staff members.[11] More employers are finding that in tight labor markets, turnover of key people occurs more frequently when employee loyalty is low, which in turn emphasizes the importance of a loyal and committed workforce.

Job Satisfaction and Organizational Commitment

Job satisfaction A positive emotional state resulting from evaluating one's job experience.

In its most basic sense, **job satisfaction** is a positive emotional state resulting from evaluating one's job experiences. Job *dis*satisfaction occurs when one's expectations are not met. For example, if an employee expects clean and safe working conditions on the job, then the employee is likely to be dissatisfied if the workplace is dirty and dangerous.

No simple formula can predict an individual employee's job satisfaction. Furthermore, the relationship between productivity and job satisfaction is not entirely clear. The critical factor is what employees expect from their jobs and what they receive as rewards from their jobs. Even though job satisfaction itself is important, perhaps the "bottom line" is the impact that job satisfaction has on organizational commitment, which affects employee turnover and organizational performance.[12] As Figure 3-3 depicts, the interaction of the individual and the job determines levels of job satisfaction/dissatisfaction and organizational commitment.

Organizational commitment The degree to which employees believe in and accept organizational goals and desire to remain with the organization.

Organizational commitment is the degree to which employees believe in and accept organizational goals and desire to remain with the organization. Various research studies have revealed that people who are relatively satisfied with their jobs will be somewhat more committed to the organization.

A logical extension of organizational commitment focuses specifically on *continuance commitment* factors, which suggests that decisions to remain with or leave an organization ultimately are reflected in employee absenteeism and turnover statistics. Individuals who are not as satisfied with their jobs or who are not as committed to the organization are more likely to withdraw from the organization, either occasionally through absenteeism or permanently through turnover.

Absenteeism

Absenteeism is expensive and costs an estimated $600 per employee per year. Total employer productivity losses due to absenteeism exceed $12 billion annually.[13] Being absent from work may seem like a small matter to an employee. But if a manager needs 12 people in a unit to get the work done, and four of the 12 are absent most of the time, the unit's work will probably not get done, or additional workers will have to be hired.

Absenteeism and Tardiness Policy
Contains a sample policy on absenteeism and tardiness control.
Custom Search:
☑ANALYSIS
Phrase: Employee absenteeism and tardiness

Types of Absenteeism Employees can be absent from work for several reasons. Clearly, some absenteeism is inevitable. Because illness, death in the family, and other personal reasons for absences are unavoidable and understandable, many employers have sick-leave policies that allow employees a certain number of paid absent days per year for these types of *involuntary* absenteeism. However,

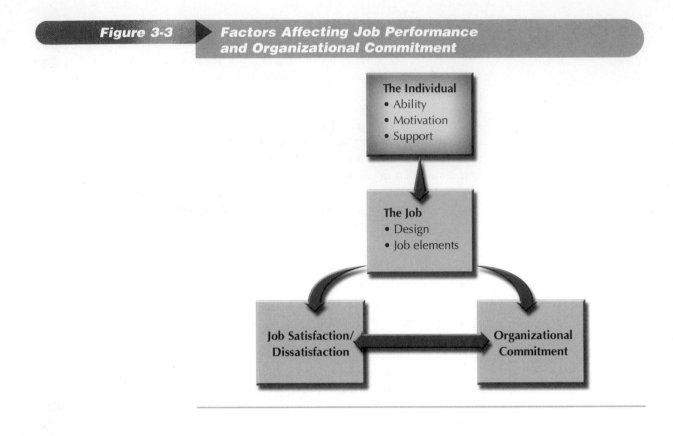

much absenteeism is avoidable, or *voluntary* absenteeism. Often, a relatively small number of individuals in the workplace are responsible for a disproportionate share of the total absenteeism in an organization. One study found that 41% of employees had 0–2 days of unscheduled absences, 43% of employees had 3–8 days, and 13% of employees had 9 or more days per year.[14]

That same study and others show the close linkage between absenteeism, job satisfaction, and organizational commitment. The study results indicate that how employees feel about their jobs and their employers affect unscheduled absenteeism. Employers with lower employee morale had significantly higher absenteeism rates. Figure 3-4 depicts common reasons for unscheduled absences.

Measuring Absenteeism Controlling or reducing absenteeism must begin with continuous monitoring of the absenteeism statistics in work units. Such monitoring helps managers pinpoint employees who are frequently absent and the departments that have excessive absenteeism. Various methods of measuring or computing absenteeism exist. One formula suggested by the U.S. Department of Labor for computing absenteeism rates is as follows:

$$\frac{\text{Number of person-days lost through job absence during period}}{(\text{Average number of employees}) \times (\text{Number of work days})} \times 100$$

(This rate also can be based on number of hours instead of number of days.)

Controlling Absenteeism Controlling voluntary absenteeism is easier if managers understand its causes more clearly. However, a variety of approaches

Figure 3-4 ▶ **Reasons for Unscheduled Absences**

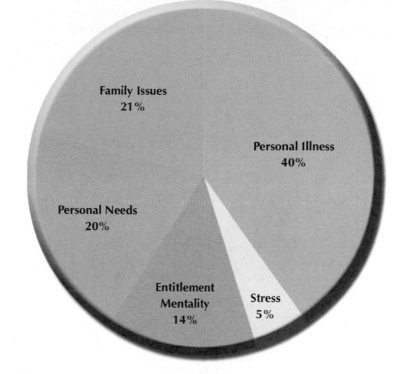

Source: Based on data from CCH Absenteeism Survey, *CCH Human Resources Management,* November 1, 2000.

can be used to reduce voluntary absenteeism. Organizational policies on absenteeism should be stated clearly in an employee handbook and stressed by supervisors and managers. The policies and rules an organization uses to govern absenteeism may provide a clue to the effectiveness of its absenteeism control efforts.[15] Absenteeism control options fall into several categories:

- *Disciplinary approach:* Many employers use a disciplinary approach. People who are absent the first time receive an oral warning, but subsequent absences bring written warnings, suspension, and finally dismissal.
- *Positive reinforcement:* Positive reinforcement includes such methods as giving employees cash, recognition, time off, or other rewards for meeting attendance standards. Offering rewards for good attendance, giving bonuses for missing fewer than a certain number of days, and "buying back" unused sick leave are all positive methods of reducing absenteeism.
- *Combination approach:* Combination approaches ideally reward desired behaviors and punish undesired behaviors. This "carrot and stick" approach uses policies and discipline to punish offenders and develops various programs and rewards for employees with outstanding attendance. One firm that has used attendance incentives effectively is Continental Airlines. As part of its "Go Forward" Program, employees with perfect attendance receive incentives of travel and other rewards.[16]

- *"No fault" absenteeism:* Here, the reasons for absences do not matter, but the employees must manage their time rather than having managers make decisions about excused and unexcused absences. Once absenteeism exceeds normal limits, then disciplinary action up to and including termination of employment can occur.[17] The advantages of the "no fault" approach are that all employees can be covered by it, and supervisors and HR staff do not have to judge whether absences count as excused or unexcused. Therefore, employees manage their own attendance except where extreme abuses occur.

- *Paid time-off (PTO) programs:* Some employers have a *paid time-off* (PTO) program in which vacation time, holidays, and sick leave for each employee are combined into a PTO account. Employees use days from their accounts at their discretion for illness, personal time, or vacation. If employees run out of days in their accounts, then they are not paid for any additional days missed. The PTO programs generally have reduced absenteeism, particularly one-day absences, but overall time away from work often increases because employees use all of "their" time off by taking unused days as vacation days.

The disciplinary approach is the most widely used means, with most employers using policies and punitive practices. However, one survey of employers found that the PTO programs appear to be the most effective in reducing absenteeism, even though only 21% of the firms have such an approach.[18]

Turnover

Like absenteeism, turnover is related to job satisfaction and organizational commitment. **Turnover** occurs when employees leave an organization and have to be replaced.

Many organizations have found that turnover is a costly problem, as documented by a number of studies. One study found that 45% of surveyed employers estimate annual turnover cost to exceed $10,000 per person. In the hotel/hospitality industry the average turnover cost of $4,100 per leaving employee costs a typical hotel $631,400 annually.[19] In many service industries the turnover rates and costs are very high. In the retail industry turnover of part-time workers averages 124% per year and 74% for full-time workers. In supermarkets the typical stay for an employee is only 97 days. Costing billions to the nation's grocers and other retailers, the costs per full-time employee leaving are estimated to be between $6,900 and $10,500, depending upon the type of retailer.[20] For higher-level executives and professionals, turnover costs can run as much as two times annual salary.

Types of Turnover Turnover is classified in a number of different ways. Each of the following classifications can be used and are not mutually exclusive.

- **Involuntary Turnover**
  Terminations for poor performance or work rule violations

- **Voluntary Turnover**
  Employee leaves by choice

Involuntary turnover is triggered by organizational policies, work rules, and performance standards that are not met by employees. Voluntary turnover can be caused by many factors, including career opportunities, pay, supervision, geography, and personal/family reasons. Voluntary turnover also appears to increase with the size of the organization, most likely due to the larger firms having more employees who may move, the more impersonal nature of organizations, and the "organizational bureaucracy" that is present in these organizations.

- **Functional Turnover**
  Lower-performing or disruptive employees leave

- **Dysfunctional Turnover**
  Key individuals and high performers leave at critical times

Not all turnover is negative for organizations because some workforce losses are desirable, especially if those workers who leave are lower-performing, less reliable individuals, or those who are disruptive to co-workers. Unfortunately for organizations, dysfunctional turnover occurs when key individuals leave, often at crucial work times. For example, a software project leader left in the midst of a system upgrade to take a promotion at another firm in the city, causing the system upgrade timeline to slip by two months due to the difficulty of replacing the project leader.

- **Uncontrollable Turnover**
  Occurs for reasons outside the impact of the employer

- **Controllable Turnover**
  Occurs due to factors that could be influenced by the employer

Many reasons employees quit cannot be controlled by the organization and include: (1) the employee moves out of the geographic area; (2) the employee decides to stay home for family reasons; (3) the employee's spouse is transferred; or (4) a student employee graduates from college. But, it is the controllable turnover that must be addressed. Organizations are better able to retain employees if they deal with the concerns of employees that are leading to turnover. Even though some turnover is inevitable, many employers today recognize that reducing turnover is crucial. The costs of turnover, including diminished organizational productivity, have led employers to direct considerable efforts on employee retention, which is the focus of the remainder of this chapter.

Retention of Human Resources

Retention of employees has become a primary concern in many organizations for several reasons. As a practical matter, with lower turnover, every individual who is retained means one less person to have to recruit, select, and train. Also, organizational and individual performance is enhanced by the continuity of employees who know their jobs, co-workers, organizational services and products, and the firm's customers. One survey of supervisors and workers found that losing high performers made it more difficult for organizations to reach their business goals.[21] Additionally, continuity of employees provides better "employee image" for attracting and retaining other individuals.

Importance of Retention

A survey of Chief Executive Officers found that they believe the greatest contribution to organizational success over the next five years will be to get and retain employee talent (26%). For example, one technology company with 5,000 employees, SAS Institute, determined that the turnover cost of their highly skilled employees averaged $60,000 per departure. By focusing on retention, the firm has had an attrition rate 17% below the industry average, meaning that 850 fewer employees had to be hired at an estimated "savings" of more than $50 million per year. SAS's focus on retention has allowed the organization to be more innovative with its retention programs. SAS also found that increased employee retention has contributed significantly to reaching its organizational goals.[22]

Retention as Management Concern Changes in economic conditions, along with the collapse of the dot.com employment bubble and slowing of the growth of technology firms, have led some to speculate that the emphasis on retention was a temporary concern. However, an updated McKinsey & Company survey found that 90% of those firms surveyed said it was more difficult to retain talented individuals than it was several years before.[23] Therefore, it is imperative that organizations and managers recognize that retention must be a continuing HR emphasis and a significant responsibility for all supervisors and managers.[24] Some firms, such as Mutual of Omaha, American Express, and others, conduct retention training for managers. Even more directly, firms evaluate managers and supervisors on retention as part of their performance reviews. Hartford Life Insurance and other firms tie managers' performance reviews and bonuses to the retention and attraction of employees. Also, more senior managers have stock options linked to employee retention.[25]

Retention Officer Some employers have placed such a high priority on employee retention that they have designated an individual as the retention officer for the firm. One estimate is that 10% of large U.S. firms have assigned at least one person to focus on retention.[26] Often an individual in the HR area is assigned a specific focus of retention to ensure that it receives high priority and the multifaceted efforts needed to increase employee retention.[27]

Why People Stay or Leave

Individuals stay or leave their jobs and organizations for many different reasons. Obviously, individuals who are terminated leave at the request of the organizations. But the bigger issue in many organizations is why employees voluntarily leave. One survey done by McKinsey & Company, a large international consulting firm, emphasized the importance of retention by concluding that employers face "a war for talent." The McKinsey studies done several years apart found that the most critical factors affecting the attraction and retention of managers and executives can be classified into three areas. The areas, key items, and percentage responses are listed next:[28]

Great Company	Great Job	Compensation and Lifestyle
■ Value and culture (58%)	■ Freedom and autonomy (56%)	■ Differentiated pay package (29%)
■ Well managed (50%)	■ Job has exciting challenges (51%)	■ High total compensation (23%)
■ Company has exciting challenges (38%)	■ Career advancement and growth (39%)	■ Geographic location (19%)
		■ Respect for lifestyle (12%)

Several different studies provide some consistent patterns and insights. Figure 3-5 contains data from a SHRM Retention Practices Survey. Notice that the first three factors with the highest percentages such as career opportunities, com-

Figure 3-5 ▶ **Most Common Reasons Employees Voluntarily Leave**

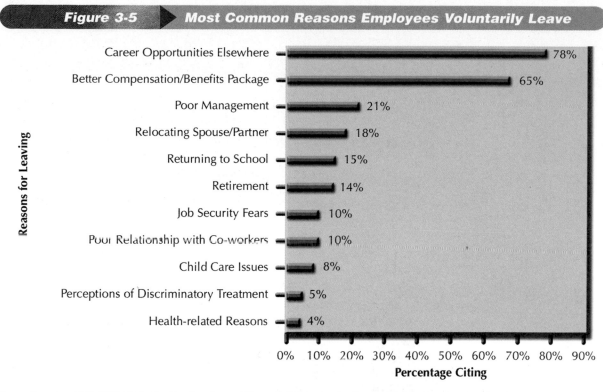

Source: Based on *2000 SHRM Retention Practices Survey* (Alexandria VA: Society for Human Resource Management, 2000). Used with permission.

petitive compensation/benefits, and poor management, are all items that are controllable in the sense that they are influenced by organizational policies and practices. Of the remaining areas cited, several of them are personal, less controllable by employers (relocation, returning to school, etc.).

Retention Determinants

It has been recognized by both employers and employees that some common areas affect employee retention. If certain organizational components are being provided, then other factors may affect retention. Surveys of employees consistently show that career opportunities and rewards are the two most important determinants of retention. Finally, job design/work factors and fair and supportive employee relationships with others inside the organization contribute to retention. How each set of components in Figure 3-6 affects employee retention is covered next.

Organizational Components

A number of organizational components influence individuals in their decisions to stay or leave their employers. Organizations that have positive, distinctive cultures and values have less turnover, as the opening discussion indicates.

Organizational culture
The shared values and beliefs of a workforce.

Organizational Culture and Values Organizational culture is a pattern of shared values and beliefs that provides organizational members meaning and rules for behavior. Numerous examples can be given of key technical, professional, and

Figure 3-6 ▶ **Retention Determinants**

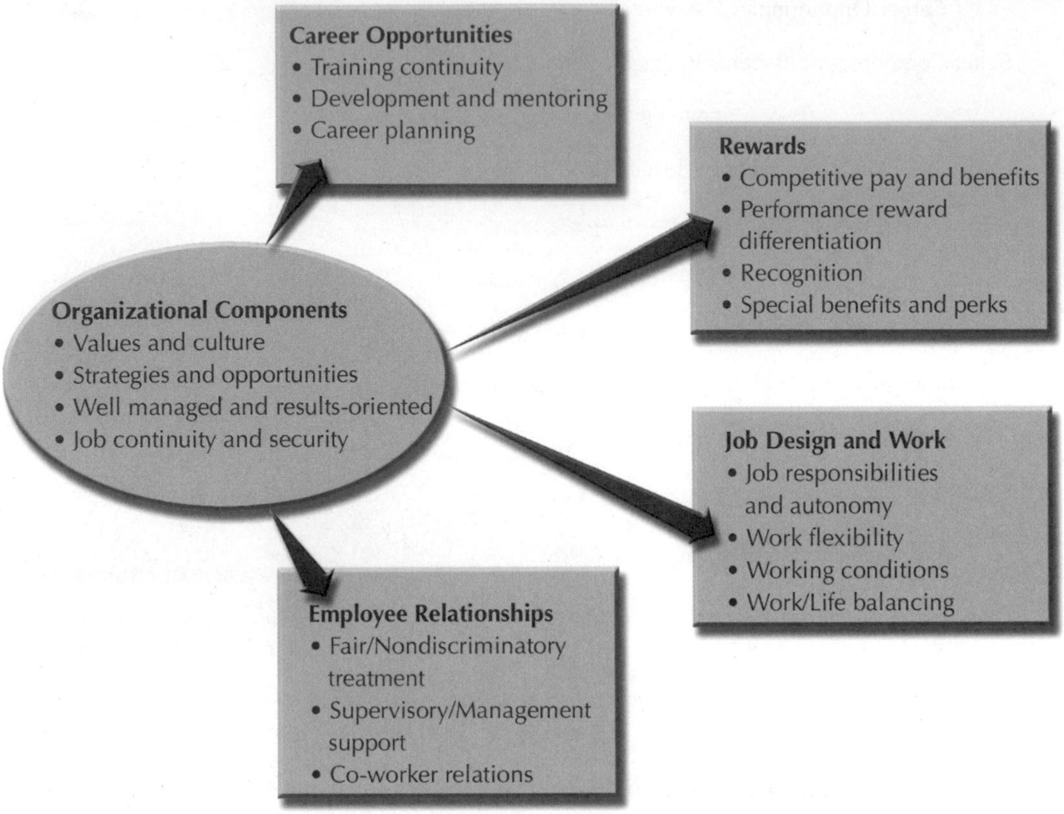

Career Opportunities
- Training continuity
- Development and mentoring
- Career planning

Rewards
- Competitive pay and benefits
- Performance reward differentiation
- Recognition
- Special benefits and perks

Organizational Components
- Values and culture
- Strategies and opportunities
- Well managed and results-oriented
- Job continuity and security

Job Design and Work
- Job responsibilities and autonomy
- Work flexibility
- Working conditions
- Work/Life balancing

Employee Relationships
- Fair/Nondiscriminatory treatment
- Supervisory/Management support
- Co-worker relations

administrative employees leaving firms because of corporate cultures that seem to devalue people and create barriers to the use of individual capabilities. In contrast, creating a culture that values people highly enables some corporations to successfully attract and retain employees.

One corporation well known for its culture and values is Southwest Airlines. The firm focuses considerable effort on instilling its values of customer service and employee involvement through its HR efforts. These efforts have yielded greater performance, retention of employees, and a reputation as an "employer of choice" in the airline industry. Even after the terrorist attacks in September 2001, Southwest was the only airline that did not cut staff and significantly reduce its flights. The genius of Southwest's culture, founding CEO Herb Kelleher, has repeatedly stated that showing respect for people is central to Southwest Airline's culture.[29]

One key organizational value that affects employee retention is *trust.* One study of more than 600 employees found that trust and organizational values were noted as factors that most influenced intentions by employees to stay with their current employers. Employees who believe that they can trust managers, co-workers, and the organizational justice systems are much less willing to leave their current employers.[30]

Organizational Strategies, Opportunities, and Management Other organizational components that affect employee retention are related to the strategies, opportunities, and management of the organization. In some organizations external events are seen as threatening, whereas others see changes as challenges requiring responses. The latter approach can be a source of competitive advantage, especially if an organization is in a growing, dynamic industry.

One factor affecting how employees view their organizations is the visionary quality of organizational leadership. Often such vision is demonstrated by having an identified strategic plan that guides the firm's response to changes. If a firm is not effectively managed, then employees maybe "turned off" by the ineffective responses and inefficiencies they deal with in their jobs. Organizations with clearly established goals that hold managers and employees accountable for accomplishing results are viewed as better places to work, especially by individuals wishing to progress both financially and careerwise.

Results of a number of surveys of employees, as shown in Figure 3-7, identified how well employers are meeting the five most desired organizational characteristics.

Job Continuity and Security Many individuals have seen a decline in job security over the past decade. All of the downsizings, layoffs, mergers and acquisitions, and organizational restructurings have affected employee loyalty and retention. Also as co-workers experience layoffs and job reductions, anxiety levels of the remaining employees rise.[31] Consequently, employees start thinking about leaving before they too get cut. On the other hand, organizations where job continuity and security is high tend to have higher retention rates.

Job insecurity concerns generally increase as workers become older because these individuals perceive they would have more difficulty in finding employment that provides comparable pay, benefits, and responsibilities. Even younger

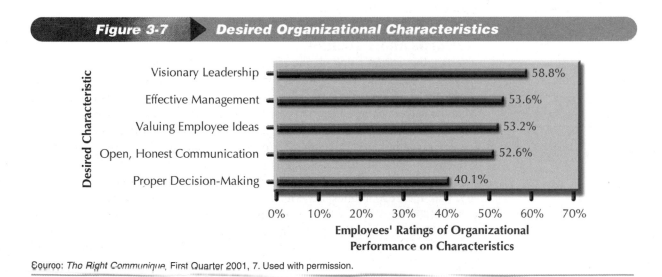

Figure 3-7 ▶ *Desired Organizational Characteristics*

Desired Characteristic

- Visionary Leadership — 58.8%
- Effective Management — 53.6%
- Valuing Employee Ideas — 53.2%
- Open, Honest Communication — 52.6%
- Proper Decision-Making — 40.1%

0% 10% 20% 30% 40% 50% 60% 70%

Employees' Ratings of Organizational Performance on Characteristics

Source: *The Right Communique*, First Quarter 2001, 7. Used with permission.

individuals have experienced some increase in job insecurity due to the decline in employment at some dot.com and high-technology companies.

AON Loyalty Institute
This Web site contains research and information on workplace loyalty.

www.aon.com

Organizational Career Opportunities

Surveys of workers in all types of jobs consistently indicate that organizational career development efforts can significantly affect employee retention. A Workforce Commitment Survey conducted annually by AON Consulting has found that *opportunities for personal growth* lead the reasons why individuals took their current jobs and why they stay there, which ranks ahead of compensation and work/family balance.[32] This factor is even more essential for technical professionals and those under age 30, for whom opportunities to develop skills and obtain promotions rank above compensation as a retention concern.[33]

Career Development Organizations address career opportunities and development in a number of ways. Tuition aid programs typically offered as benefits by many employers allow employees to pursue additional educational and training opportunities which may contribute to higher retention rates. However, just offering such a program is not sufficient. Organizations must also identify ways to use the employees' new knowledge and capabilities inside the organization. Otherwise, employees are more likely to take their new capabilities to another employer because they feel their increased "value" is not being recognized.[34] Overall, organizational career development efforts are designed to meet many employees' expectations that their employers are committed to keeping their knowledge, skills, and abilities current.

Career Planning Organizations also increase employee retention by having formal career planning efforts. Employees and their managers mutually discuss career opportunities within organizations and what career development activities will enhance employees' future growth. As discussed further in Chapter 10, career development and planning efforts often include mentoring programs whereby experienced managers and professionals serve as "career coaches" for younger or less-experienced employees.

Rewards and Retention

The tangible rewards that people receive for working come in the form of pay, incentives, and benefits. Numerous surveys and experiences of HR professionals reveal that one key to retention is to have *competitive compensation practices.* Many managers believe that money is the prime retention factor, 89% in one survey, and many employees cite better pay or higher compensation as a reason for leaving one employer for another.[35] However, the reality is a bit more complex.

Pay and benefits must be competitive, which means they must be "close" to what other employers are providing and what individuals believe to be consistent with their capabilities, experience, and performance. If compensation is not close, often defined as within 10% of the "market," then turnover is likely to be higher. This is especially true for individuals making lower rates of pay, such as those with less than $25,000 to $30,000 annual income. Simply put, their living costs and financial requirements mean that if these lower-paid workers can get $1 per hour more or get employer-paid family benefit coverage elsewhere, they are more likely to move. However, for more highly paid individuals, especially those paid $60,000 and higher, their retention is affected by having compensation relatively competitive. At that level, other considerations are more likely to enter into the decision to stay or leave. In fact, money may be why some people leave a job, but other factors may be why many stay.

Competitive Benefits Another compensation issue affecting employee retention is having competitive benefits programs. Offering health insurance, 401(k) retirement, tuition assistance, and many other benefits commonly offered by competing employers is vital. Burger King, Pizza Hut, and Taco Bell all have learned the importance of competitive benefits. By introducing new benefits, including 401(k) retirement plans, health insurance, and other benefits not previously provided, each of these fast-food firms has seen employee turnover decline significantly. All three firms attribute the enhanced benefits as contributing substantially to lower turnover rates. For instance, over several years Taco Bell's annual turnover rate fell from 243% to 144%.[36]

Employers also are learning that having some *benefits flexibility* aids retention.[37] When employees choose how much and what benefits they will have from a "cafeteria" of choices, given a set sum of money available from the employer, the employees can tailor the benefits to their needs. By giving employees greater choice, employees feel more "individual" and "in control," thus reducing their desire to move to another employer.[38]

Special Benefits and Perks A number of employers use a wide range of special benefits and perks to attract and retain employees. One large Seattle company has on-site recreation clubs, discount travel programs, day-care centers, and other resource benefits for employees. At other firms *concierge benefits* provide employees with assistance in personal matters at their places of work. Some of the coverage benefits offered at work have included dry cleaning pickup and dropoff, car maintenance services in company parking lots, coffee and latte kiosks, ATM machines in break rooms, along with many others.[39] By offering these special benefits and perks, employers hope to reduce the time employees spend after work on personal chores and to be seen as more desirable employers where individuals will remain for longer stays.

Performance and Compensation Many individuals expect their rewards to be differentiated from others based on performance. For instance, if an employee receives about the same pay increase and overall pay as others who have lower productivity, more absenteeism, and work fewer hours, then the result may be a feeling of "unfairness." This may prompt the individual to look for another job where compensation recognizes performance differences. The results of a survey on rewards at work found that individuals are more satisfied with the actual levels of their pay than the processes used to determine pay. That is why the performance management system and performance appraisal processes in organizations must be linked to compensation increases.[40]

To achieve greater performance links to organizational and individual performance, a growing number of private-sector firms are using variable pay and incentives programs. These programs in the form of cash bonuses or lump sum payments are one mechanism used to reward extra performance.

The growth of technology firms has highlighted another facet of performance differentiation—giving employees incentives in the form of stock options, organizational ownership, and other longer-term rewards. Yahoo, Amazon.com, and other technology firms have made extensive use of stock options for many employees.[41] However, the collapse of their stock prices in 2001 caused them to have to "reprice" or lower the levels at which the stock options were given, in order to retain employees.

Recognition Employee recognition as a form of reward can be both tangible and intangible. Tangible recognition comes in many forms, such as "employee of the month," perfect attendance, or other special awards.

Recognition also can be intangible and psychological in nature. Feedback from managers and supervisors that acknowledges extra effort and performance of individuals provides recognition, even though monetary rewards are not given. For instance, a franchise firm for the widely known KFC food chain uses both tangible and intangible recognition as part of employee retention efforts. Employees who receive recognition cards from either customers or co-workers can exchange them for movie tickets and other rewards. Also, managers have been trained to make special efforts to recognize employee performance and service.[42]

Job Design and Work

A fundamental factor affecting employee retention is the nature of the jobs and work done. First, retention is affected by the *selection process*. A number of organizations have found that high employee turnover rates in employees' first few months of employment often are linked to inadequate selection screening efforts. An example illustrates the importance of sound selection processes: A customer service call center experienced 89% annual turnover even though the firm paid above-market wages. Further analyses found that because many people hired did not have the proper KSAs for the jobs, the individuals left. Instituting new selection processes, including providing more realistic job previews to applicants and better selection efforts by HR staff members, led to reducing turnover to 24%. This reduction resulted in a savings of more than $1.3 million per year.[43]

Once individuals have been placed into jobs, several job/work factors affect retention. Because individuals spend significant time at work, they expect to work with modern equipment and technology and have good *working conditions,* given the nature of the work. Such factors as space, lighting, temperature, noise, layout, and other physical and environmental factors affect retention of employees.

Additionally, workers want a *safe work environment* where risks of accidents and injuries have been addressed. This is especially true for employers in such industries as manufacturing, agriculture, utilities, and transportation with higher safety risks than in many service industries and office environments.

Work Flexibility Flexibility in work schedules and how work is done has grown in importance.[44] Flexible HR policies such as casual dress also have been useful as retention aids. Studies demonstrate that work flexibility aids retention. As illustration, a two-year study of workplace flexibility found that 76% of managers and 80% of employees reported that flexible working relationships impacted retention positively. The study also found that work flexibility led to higher work quality and productivity.[45]

Work flexibility is particularly vital in the wake of organizational workload pressures that have increased due to organizational restructurings and "rightsizing." Approximately one-third of all U.S. employees surveyed said they often felt overworked or were "overloaded." Women more frequently cited being overworked, and managers and professionals indicated feeling more overworked than other occupational groups.[46] It is crucial that employers wishing to retain employees monitor the workloads placed on employees. If these demands become too great, then employees are more likely to change jobs to reduce their workloads.

The growth of technology, particularly the Internet, has added to work flexibility by permitting some work to be done from almost anywhere.[47] Although this capability is beneficial in some ways, it also means that many individuals spend significant time away from work or while traveling on business checking e-mail messages, reviewing reports, preparing presentations, and attending to other work-related tasks.

One way employers provide work flexibility is through *work scheduling alternatives.* These alternatives include telecommuting, whereby employees can work from home or other locations; alternative arrangements such as flextime, compressed workweeks (4 days/10 hours, 3 days/12 hours, etc.); and others discussed in detail in Chapter 6. The growth of work schedule flexibility is illustrated in Figure 3-8.

Work/Life Balancing One of the greatest benefits of work flexibility is that it meshes well with work/family efforts by employers. The changing demographics of the U.S. workforce highlighted in Chapter 1 is prompting many individuals to work harder at balancing work responsibilities, family needs, and personal life demands. With more single-parent families, dual-career couples with children, and workers' responsibilities for elderly relatives, balancing work and family roles may sometimes be incompatible.[48]

Figure 3-8 ▶ **Work Schedule Flexibility**

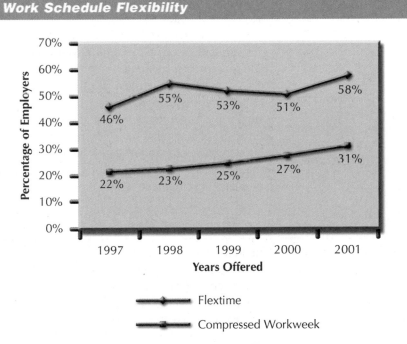

Source: Based on *2000 SHRM Retention Practices Survey* (Alexandria VA: Society for Human Resource Management, 2001). Used with permission.

Work/life programs offered by employers can include a wide range of items. Some include work/job options, such as flexible work scheduling, job sharing, or telecommuting, which are discussed in more detail in Chapter 6. Other components include flexible benefits, on-site fitness centers, child-care or elder-care assistance, and sick-leave policies. The purpose of all these offerings is to convey that employers recognize the challenges employees face when balancing work/life demands.[49]

The value of work/life programs has been documented by a number of employers. Ralston-Purina, a manufacturer of pet food and other products, with more than 20,000 employees, worked to reduce absenteeism and increase employee commitment to the firm. A revised time-off program and more flexible work arrangements have reduced absenteeism, unscheduled time off, and increased employee satisfaction with the company.[50]

Employee Relationships

A final set of factors found to affect retention is based on the relationships that employees have in organizations. Such areas as the reasonableness of HR policies, the fairness of disciplinary actions, and the means used to decide work assignments and opportunities all affect employee retention. If individuals feel that policies are unreasonably restrictive or applied inconsistently, then they may be more likely to look at jobs offered at other employers.

The increasing demographic diversity of U.S. workplaces makes *nondiscriminatory treatment* of all employees, regardless of gender, age, and other factors, particularly important. Organizational commitment and job satisfaction of ethnically diverse individuals are affected by perceived discriminatory treatment.[51] As discussed in detail in Chapter 5, a number of firms have recognized that proactive management of diversity issues results in greater retention of individuals of all backgrounds.[52]

Other concerns that affect employee retention are *supervisory/management support* and *co-worker relations.* Many individuals build close relationships with co-workers. In a survey of individuals of a variety of ages and working in a variety of industries, the most positively cited factor about going to work was the relationships with co-workers.[53] Coupled with co-worker relationships is having supportive supervisory and management relationships.[54] A supervisor builds positive relationships and aids retention by being fair and nondiscriminatory, allowing work flexibility and work/family balancing, giving employee feedback that recognizes employee efforts and performance, and supporting career planning and development for employees.

The Retention Management Process

In addition to identifying the determinants of retention, it is important that HR professionals and their organizations have processes in place to manage retention of employees. Left to chance or infrequent attention, employee retention is not as likely to be successful. That is why using the retention management process outlined in Figure 3-9 is important. Each phase of the process is discussed in the following sections.

Figure 3-9 ▶ **The Retention Management Process**

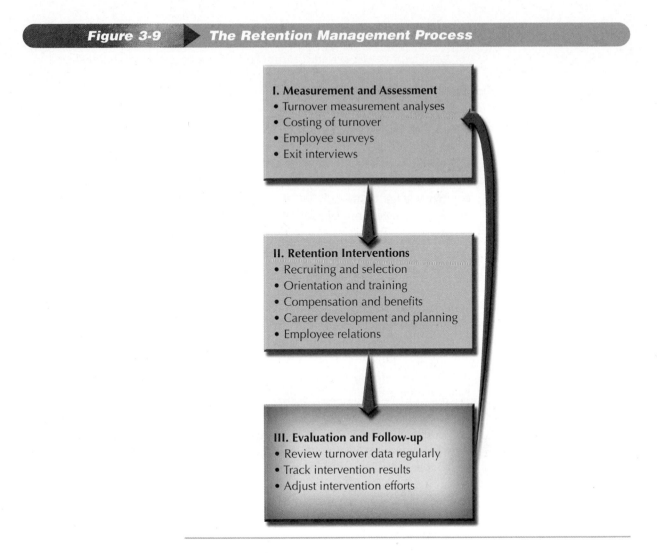

I. Measurement and Assessment
- Turnover measurement analyses
- Costing of turnover
- Employee surveys
- Exit interviews

II. Retention Interventions
- Recruiting and selection
- Orientation and training
- Compensation and benefits
- Career development and planning
- Employee relations

III. Evaluation and Follow-up
- Review turnover data regularly
- Track intervention results
- Adjust intervention efforts

Retention Measurement and Assessment

To ensure that appropriate actions are taken to enhance retention and reduce turnover, management decisions require data and analyses rather than subjective impressions, anecdotes of selected individual situations, or panic reactions to the loss of a few key people. Therefore, having several different types of measures and analyses is important.

Measuring Turnover The turnover rate for an organization can be computed in different ways. The following formula from the U.S. Department of Labor is widely used; in it *separation* means leaving the organization.

$$\frac{\text{Number of employee separations during the month}}{\text{Total number of employees at midmonth}} \times 100$$

Common turnover figures range from almost zero to more than 100% per year, with turnover rates varying among industries. Often a part of human resource information systems, turnover data can be gathered and analyzed in a number of ways, including the following:

- Jobs and job levels
- Departments, units, and location
- Reason for leaving
- Length of service
- Demographic characteristics
- Education and training
- Knowledge, skills, and abilities
- Performance ratings/levels

Several examples illustrate why detailed analyses of turnover are important. One manufacturing organization had a company-wide turnover rate that was not severe, but 80% of the turnover occurred within one department. This imbalance indicated that some action was needed to resolve problems in that unit. A health-care institution found that its greatest turnover in registered nurses occurred 24–36 months after hire, so the firm instituted a two-year employee recognition program and expanded the career development and training activities for employees with at least two years' service. In these example employers, the turnover rates declined as a result of the actions taken based on the turnover analyses done.

Costs of Turnover Determining turnover costs can be relatively simple or very complex, depending upon the nature of the efforts and data used. Figure 3-10 shows a simplified costing model. In that model if a job pays $20,000 (A) and benefits cost 40% (B), then the total annual cost for one employee is $28,000. Assuming 20 employees quit in the previous year (D) and that it takes three months for one employee to be fully productive, the calculation in (F) results in a per person turnover cost of $3,500. Overall, the annual turnover costs would be $70,000 for the 20 individuals who left. It should be noted that in spite of its conservative and simple nature, this model makes the point that turnover is

Figure 3-10 ▸ **Simplified Turnover Costing Model**

Job Title _____

A. Typical annual pay for job _____

B. Percentage of pay for benefits times (×) annual pay _____

C. Total employee annual cost (add A + B) _____

D. How many employees voluntarily quit in this job in the past 12 months? _____

E. How long does it take for one employee to become fully productive (in months)? _____

F. Per person turnover cost: (Multiply $E \div 12 \times C \times 50\%*$) _____

G. Annual turnover cost for this job: (Multiply $F \times D$) _____

* Assumes 50% productivity throughout the learning period (E).

costly. For instance, if the job is teller in a large bank where more than 150 people leave in a year, the conservative model results in turnover costs in excess of $500,000 per year.

More detailed and sophisticated turnover costing models consider a number of factors. Some of the most common areas considered include the following:[55]

- *Hiring costs:* Includes recruiting and advertising expenses, search fees, HR interviewer and staff time and salaries, employee referral fees, relocation and moving costs, supervisor and managerial time and salaries, employment testing costs, reference checking time, pre-employment medical expenses, etc.
- *Training costs:* Includes paid orientation time, training staff time and salaries, costs of training materials, supervisors' and managers' time and salaries, co-worker "coaching" time and salaries, etc.
- *Productivity costs:* Includes lost productivity due to "break-in" time of new employees, loss of customer contacts, unfamiliarity with organizational products and services, more time to use organizational resources and systems, etc.
- *Separation costs:* Includes HR staff and supervisor time and salaries to prevent separations, exit interview time, unemployment expenses, legal fees for separations challenged, etc.

Employee Surveys
Lists areas for including in employee surveys.
Custom Search:
☑ ANALYSIS
Phrase: Organizational effectiveness survey

Attitude survey One that focuses on employees' feelings and beliefs about their jobs and the organization.

Employee Surveys Employee surveys can be used to diagnose specific problem areas, identify employee needs or preferences, and reveal areas in which HR activities are well received or are viewed negatively. For example, questionnaires may be sent to employees to collect ideas for revising a performance appraisal system or to determine how satisfied employees are with their benefits programs. Regardless of the topic of the survey, obtaining employee input provides managers and HR professionals with data on the "retention climate" in an organization.

One specific type of survey used by many organizations is an **attitude survey** that focuses on employees' feelings and beliefs about their jobs and the organization. By serving as a means to obtain data on how employees view their jobs, their supervisors, their co-workers, and organizational policies and practices, these surveys can be starting points for reducing turnover and increasing employee retention for longer periods of time. Some employers conduct attitude surveys on a regularly scheduled basis (such as every year), while others do so intermittently. As the use of the Internet has spread, more organizations have begun conducting attitude surveys electronically.[56] The e-HR provides some examples.

Attitude surveys are developed by consulting firms, academicians, or others. They can also be custom-designed to address specific issues and concerns in an organization. But regardless of the type of surveys used, only surveys that are valid and reliable can measure attitudes accurately.[57] Often a "research" survey developed in-house is poorly structured, asks questions in a confusing manner, or leads employees to respond in ways that will give "favorable" results.

By asking employees to respond candidly to an attitude survey, management is building up employees' expectations that action will be taken on the concerns identified. Therefore, a crucial part of conducting an attitude survey is to provide feedback to those who participated in it. It is especially important that even negative survey results be communicated to avoid fostering the appearance of

Employee Surveys Online

With the growth of the Internet and computer technology in organizations in the past few years, employee surveying has evolved from primarily a paper-and-pencil process into one conducted largely online. Firms with limited employee Internet access usually still conduct surveys using paper-and-pencil methods. Larger firms are able to benefit from substantially reduced time for the collection, analyses, and dissemination of data from online surveys.

To begin, the survey goals and objectives must be clearly defined, the survey areas identified, and the survey design completed. After this point, the online process begins to differ from alternative survey methods.

Online surveys often are conducted with the assistance of outside consulting firms at any or all stages of the survey process. A dedicated Web page serves as a portal through which employees can access the survey. Access to the survey can be managed with varying levels of security.

Survey data will often be analyzed based on divisions, functions, locations, demographic variables, or any combination of these categories. For example, the survey results for "Southeast Region" might be accessed by age, gender, time on the job, or other demographic categories of interest.

A number of advantages can be realized through online surveys. First, surveys can be concurrently administered worldwide in a variety of languages, and online reminder messages to employees to encourage participation can be automatically generated. Additionally, data analysis and presentation of results are significantly faster than with paper-based surveys. Finally, survey results can be easily linked to other data (exit interviews, turnover statistics, etc.) so that feedback and action planning systems can be identified.

But two major disadvantages of online surveys are that some employees may not have online access, or they may perceive online surveys as less confidential than paper-based surveys.

One example of online surveying is illustrated by an employee survey done by Kenexa, a national consulting firm. The entire survey process was completed within a 12-week period, starting with survey design and ending with a detailed Power Point presentation of the consultants' analysis to executive management. Kenexa conducted an online survey that contained a core of 80 questions for a *Fortune* 500 company. The target population consisted of 21,000 employees and managers, 20,000 of whom had Web access and 1,000 of whom were surveyed by conventional paper-and-pencil means. The survey was sent out in English and in 14 additional European and Asian languages, and the overall response rate was 94%. After data was collected and analyzed, reports were generated. Because of a fairly complex matrix organization structure, the client required 2,500 manager reports and 200 executive summary analyses. All of the final analyses and reports were delivered online to individual managers to use for managerial and work team planning purposes.

As more employees at all levels become Web connected, online surveying is likely to grow. For information regarding any aspect of online surveys, see *www.kenexa.com*.[58]

hiding the results or placing blame. Generally, it is recommended that employee feedback be done through meetings with managers, supervisors, and employees; small groups encourage interaction and discussion.[59] This approach is consistent with the most common reason for conducting an attitude survey: to diagnose strengths and weaknesses so that actions can be taken to improve the HR activities in an organization.

Exit Interviews One widely used type of interview is the **exit interview**, in which individuals are asked to identify reasons for leaving the organization. One survey of employers found that 87% of them conduct exit interviews, and more than

Exit interview An interview in which individuals are asked to identify reasons for leaving the organization.

half have used the information gathered to make changes to aid retention.[60] A wide range of issues can be examined in exit interviews, as described in the HR Practice on the next page.

Retention Interventions

Based on what the measurement and assessment data reveal, a variety of HR interventions can be undertaken to improve retention. Turnover can be controlled and reduced in several ways.[61] During the *recruiting* process, the job should be outlined and a *realistic job preview* presented, so that the reality of the job matches the expectations of the new employee. By ensuring that the expectations of potential employees match what the organization is likely to offer, voluntary turnover may be reduced.

Another way to eliminate turnover is to improve the *selection process* in order to better match applicants to jobs. By fine-tuning the selection process and hiring people who will not have disciplinary or performance problems or whose work histories suggest higher turnover potential, employers can reduce turnover. Once selected, individuals who receive effective *orientation and training* are less likely to leave.

Other HR factors are important as well. *Compensation* is important because a competitive, fair, and equitable pay system can help reduce turnover. Inadequate benefits also may lead to voluntary turnover, especially if other employers offer significantly higher compensation levels for similar jobs. *Career development and planning* can help an organization keep employees. If individuals believe they have few opportunities for career development advancement, they are more likely to leave the organization. *Employee relations,* including fair/nondiscriminatory treatment and enforcement of HR policies, can enhance retention also.

Successful retention intervention efforts occurred at Deloitte & Touche, a national accounting and consulting firm. An HR study at the firm found that it was losing many talented women employees after several years of employment with the firm. Because the firm had invested significant time and funds in training and developing employees, a special program throughout Deloitte & Touche was established to focus on retaining all employees, especially women who had significantly higher turnover rates. Key portions of the program include workshops on "Men and Women as Colleagues," enhanced career mentoring programs, revised family/work policies and alternatives, and establishing a women's leadership program. Retention of all employees, including women, improved.[62]

Evaluation and Follow-Up

Once retention intervention efforts have been implemented, it is important that they be evaluated and appropriate follow-up and adjustments made. Regular *review of turnover data* can identify when turnover increases or decreases among different employees classified by length of service, education, department, gender, or other factors.

Tracking intervention results also should be part of evaluation efforts. Some firms may use pilot programs to see how turnover is affected before extending the changes to the entire organization. For instance, to test the impact of flextime scheduling on employee turnover, a firm might allow flexible scheduling in one

HR Practices

Conducting Exit Interviews

One of the more common tasks of HR staff members in organizations with significant turnover is conducting exit interviews. HR specialists, rather than department managers or supervisors, usually conduct exit interviews. One reason for using a skilled HR interviewer is the ability to gain useful information departing employees may not wish to share with managers and supervisors, particularly if it pertains to problems and issues with supervisors and managers.

Departing employees may be reluctant to divulge their real reasons for leaving because they may wish to return to the company some day. Also, they may fear that candid responses will hinder their chances of receiving favorable references. The following suggestions may be useful when conducting exit interviews:

- Decide who will conduct the exit interviews and when the discussions will occur. Usually they are done on the last day of the departing individual's employment.
- Develop a checklist or a set of standard questions so the information can be summarized. Typical areas covered include reasons for leaving, supervision, pay, training, best-liked and least-liked aspects of the job, and where the employee is moving and why the change occurred.
- Emphasize that the information provided by the departing employee will be treated confidentially, and will be summarized to use for making future improvements and changes in the organization.

- Regularly summarize the data by reasons for leaving, department, length of service, etc., in order to provide data for improving company retention efforts.
- If possible, contact the departing employee a month or so after departure. The "real reasons" for the departure may be voiced at that time. One major reason employees commonly give for leaving their jobs is an offer for more pay elsewhere. However, the pay increase may not be the only factor.
- Recognize that former employees may be more willing to provide information on questionnaires mailed to their homes or in telephone conversations conducted some time after they have left the organization.

department on a pilot basis. If the turnover rate of the employees in that department drops in comparison with the turnover in other departments still working set schedules, then the experimental pilot project may indicate that flexible scheduling can reduce turnover. Next, the firm might extend the use of flexible scheduling to other departments.

Summary

- Individual performance components include individual ability, effort expended, and organizational support.
- Motivation deals with the needs and desires of human behavior. Various theories of motivation have been developed.
- A psychological contract contains the unwritten expectations that employees and employers have about the nature of their work relationships.

Those contracts are changing along with employee loyalty to their employers.
- The interaction of individuals and their jobs affects both job satisfaction and organizational commitment.
- Absenteeism is expensive, but it can be controlled by discipline, positive reinforcement, or some combination of the two.

- Turnover is costly and can be classified in a number of different ways.
- Retention of employees is a major focus of HR efforts in organizations, as seen by use of retention measures and establishment of retention officers in some firms.
- The determinants of retention can be divided into five general categories, with the key organizational components being, organizational values and culture, strategies and management, and job continuity and security.
- Organizational career opportunities are frequently cited as crucial to employee retention.
- Rewards must be relatively competitive and different based on performance to enhance employee retention.

- The jobs and work done by employees impact retention, particularly if individuals are properly selected, work flexibility exists, and work/life balancing programs are offered.
- To enhance retention, employee relationships with managers and co-workers are important.
- Retention management should be seen as a process composed of measurement and assessment, interventions, and evaluation/follow-up.
- Turnover should be measured and its costs determined. Employee surveys and exit interviews aid assessing turnover also.
- HR interventions to reduce turnover can include a number of different HR activities. The efforts of those interventions should be evaluated and appropriate follow-up made.

Review and Discussion Questions

1. Using Figure 3-1, discuss how the three components of innate ability, effort expended, and organizational support have affected your performance in a current or past job.
2. Describe what your expectations are in a job and then discuss how well the employer is meeting your psychological contract expectations.
3. What actions would you take to reduce voluntary absenteeism and controllable turnover if you managed a restaurant?
4. Take each of the organizational determinants and describe how they have affected your decision to leave a previous job.
5. Discuss why it is important to identify turnover costs.

Terms to Know

motivation   69
equity   70
psychological contract   72
job satisfaction   75
organizational commitment   75

turnover   78
organizational culture   81
attitude survey   91
exit interview   92

Using the Internet

Determining Turnover Costs

As the HR Manager for your organization you have been asked to provide the senior management team with turnover costings for the highest turnover positions in the organization. You should show your calculations so they will better understand the process of how to calculate turnover and analyze the factors involved.

To complete this task, log on to *http://www. keepemployees.com/* This Web site assists organizations by providing tools and services in the area of retention management. Once you have logged on to this site, click on Est. Turnover Costs. After reading the page, click on *Automatically calculate your turnover costs.* Use the following information to calculate the turnover costs for each of the positions.

Machine Operator
Target Position: 250
# of Terminations: 85
Average Wage Rate: $11.50/ per hour
Cost of Benefits as a %: 28%
Turnover Cost as a %: 33%

Accountant
Target Position: 50
# of Terminations: 18
Average Wage Rate: $3,500/per month
Cost of Benefits as a %: 30%
Turnover Cost as a %: 100%

Vice President of Marketing
Target Position: 5
# of Terminations: 2
Average Wage Rate: $8,500/per month
Cost of Benefits as a %: 40%
Turnover Cost as a %: 350%

Address the following issues:

1. What is the cost of turnover for each of the positions, as well as the overall cost to the organization for employee turnover in these jobs?
2. List three areas you could address to reduce turnover costs.

CASE

Inside the Container Store

For several years in a row, the Container Store was rated at the top of *Fortune* magazine's "100 Best Companies to Work For." What makes a retailer that sells boxes, bags, packaging, shelving, and other goods a great place to work provides some ideas to other employers striving to improve individual performance and retention.

The basis for the Container Store's successful organizational efforts are summarized by the firm's CEO, Kip Tinedell, "A funny thing happens when you take the time to educate your employees, pay them well, and treat them as equals. You end up with extremely motivated and enthusiastic people."

The Container Store takes considerable time and effort to hire employees who "fit" the company's culture and values. This effort means additional recruiting and selection attention by HR staff and operating managers. The firm also pays higher wages than many retailers and offers a competitive benefits package. Incentive programs allow some hourly employees to earn up to $48,000, which may be close to store managers' starting rates.

The firm also spends considerable time training its employees, averaging more than 200 hours per year, compared to the seven hours of training typical at other retailers. Extensive use of internal promotions demonstrates the firm's commitment to providing career opportunities for employees.

At Container Store locations managers are expected to keep in constant communication with employees, help out in various jobs in the stores, and be more team leaders than "supervisors." Yearly, HR professionals have responsibilities in some areas of store operations, so that they maintain a sense of what employees and managers face daily and weekly.

All of these activities take considerable effort, but the payoffs make them worthwhile. Sales at the firm have increased 20–25% each year, and average dollars-per-customer has grown from $20 to almost $50. One HR measure, the employee turnover rate, has averaged 15–25% yearly, compared to the 100%-plus rate common in retail jobs. Obviously, the Container Store has the "right package" that enables its employees to be significant contributors to its success.[63]

Questions

1. Discuss how the culture of the Container Store is "made" by the HR activities and practices used.

2. Compare the culture at your present employer to the culture suggested by the examples at the Container Store. Then tell what recommendations you would make to the executives where you work.

Notes

1. "Employers Not Delivering Top Talent's Desired Brand, Survey Shows," *The Right Commique,* First Quarter 2001, 1+; Robert Levering and Milton Moskowita, "100 Best Companies to Work For," *Fortune,* January 8, 2001, 148–160; *www.fortune.com.*

2. For a review of research and methods used to measure equity, see Kerry S. Sauley and Arthur G. Bedeian, "Equity Sensitivity: Construction of a Measure and Examination of Its Psychometric Properties," *Journal of Management* 26 (2000), 885–910.

3. Edward L. Powers, "Employee Loyalty in the New Millennium," *S.A.M. Advanced Management Journal,* Summer 2000, 4–8.

4. Del Jones, "Firms Spend Billions to Fire Up Workers—With Little Luck," *USA Today,* May 10, 2001, 1A.

5. Shari Caudron, "The Myth of Job Happiness," *Workforce,* April 2001, 32–36; and "Jobs a Labor of Love? Not in U.S.," *Omaha World-Herald,* September 3, 2001, 3D.

6. Based on Scott W. Lester and Jill Kickul, "Psychological Contracts in the 21st Century," *Human Resource Planning* 24 (2001), 10–21.

7. Jon L. Pierce, Tatiana Kostova, and Kurt T. Dirks, "Toward a Theory of Psychological Ownership in Organizations," *Academy of Management Review,* 26 (2001), 298–310.

8. Joan Hamilton, "The Harder They Fall," *Business Week,* May 14, 2001, EB14–16.

9. "Generation Y Brings Challenges to Workplace," *Bulletin to Management,* May 10, 2001, 145.

10. James B. Lathrop, Jr., "Employers Can Expect Greater Conflict in Four-Generation Workforce," *HR News,* February 2001, 23.

11. Andrew Backover, "Loyalty Costs Employees of Struggling AT&T, Lucent," *USA Today,* February 2, 2001, 1B.

12. Daniel J. Koys, "The Effects of Employee Satisfaction, Organizational Citizenship Behavior, and Turnover on Organizational Effectiveness," *Personnel Psychology,* 54 (2001), 101–114.

13. "Cost of Lost Productivity During Absences Is Higher Than Cost of Benefits," *Bulletin to Management,* July 20, 2000, 27.

14. CCH Absenteeism Survey, *CCH Human Resource Management,* November 1, 2000.

15. Paul Falcone, "Tackling Excessive Absenteeism," *HR Magazine,* April 2000, 139–144.

16. Linda Micco, "Continental Soars from Worst to First by Engaging Employees at Every Turn," *Bulletin to Management,* November 30, 2000, S1.

17. "Link Absenteeism and Benefits and Help Cut Costs," *HR Focus,* April 2000, 5–6.

18. CCH Absenteeism Survey.

19. Carla Joinson, "Capturing Turnover Costs," *HR Magazine,* July 2000, 107–109.

20. "Employee Turnover," *The Economist,* July 15, 2000, 64–65; and "Turnover Costs," *The Wall Street Journal,* August 29, 2000, B12.

21. "Everyone Feels Loss When Top Performers Leave the Job," *Working Age,* May/June 2000, 5.

22. Shannon Reilly and Keith Simmons, "What Are CEO's Thinking?" *USA Today,* May 3, 2001, 1B; and "Enough About Amenities. . . ." *Bulletin to Management,* August 2, 2001, S1.

23. Elizabeth L. Axelrod, Helen Handfield-Jones, and Timothy Welsh, "War for Talent, Part Two," *The McKinsey Quarterly,* 2001, available at *www.mckinsey.com.*

24. Beverly Kaye and Sharon Jordan-Evans, "Retention: Tag, You're It," *Training & Development,* April 2000, 29–35.

25. Stephanie Armour, "Bosses Held Liable for Keeping Workers," *USA Today,* April 12, 2000, 1B.

26. JoAnn S. Lublin, "In Hot Demand, Retention Czars Face Tough Job," *The Wall Street Journal,* September 12, 2000, B1+.

27. Jodi Spiegel Arthur, "Title Wave," *Human Resource Executive,* October 2, 2000, 115–118.

28. *War for Talent* (New York: McKinsey & Company, 1998).

29. Michelle Conlin, "Where Layoffs Are A Last Resort," *Business Week,* October 8, 2001, 42; and Katrina Boroker, "The Chairman of the Board Looks Back," *Fortune,* May 28, 2001, 63–76.

30. "Survey Says That Trust Is the Basis for Employee Retention," *HR Focus,* February 2001, 8; and Pam Withers, "Retention Strategies that Respond to Worker Values," *Workforce,* July 2001, 37–41.

31. "Steve Gibbons," "Down to a System: Keeping Employee Morale and Retention High," *The Journal of Quality and Participation,* March/April 2000, 20–22.

32. *United States @Work,* AON Consulting, 2000, available at *www.aon.com.*

33. "Survey Finds Top-Performing Employees Want Opportunities for Advancement and Skill Development," *Watson-Wyatt Worldwide Global News & Issues,* December

18, 2000, available at *www.watson-wyatt.com.*

34. Maureen Hannay and Melissa Northam, "Low-Cost Strategies for Employee Retention," *Compensation and Benefits Review,* July/August 2000, 65–72.

35. Hara Marks, "Money—That's Not What They Want," *HR-eSource,* May 7, 2001.

36. Devon Spurgeon, "Fast-Food Industry Pitches 'Burger Flipping' as Career," *The Wall Street Journal,* May 29, 2001, B1.

37. David Kelly, "When It Comes to Benefits, One Size Does Not Fit All," *HR-esource,* May 14, 2001, available at *www.hr-esource.com.*

38. Christopher Ryan, "Employee Retention: What Can the Benefits Professional Do?" *Employee Benefits Journal,* December 2000, 18–22.

39. Lore Lawrence, "Companies Still Offering Perks, But HR's Taking Another Look," *Human Resource Executive, HR News,* June 2001, 4; and Ann Vincola, "Helping Employees Balance Work-Life Issues," *Workspan,* June 2001, 27–33.

40. Paul W. Mulvey, Gerald Ledford, and Peter V. LeBlanc, "Records of Work," *World at Work Journal,* Third Quarter 2000, 9.

41. Jeremy Handel, "Give Them Equity and They Will Come," *Workspan,* September 2000, 39–42.

42. Adrian Gostick, "They Do Recognition Right," *Workspan,* October 2000, 34–36.

43. Rodney K. Platt, "Taking Care of Turnover," *Workspan,* February 2001, 39–40.

44. Crayton Harrison, "Flexible Programs Help Companies Maintain Talent," *Dallas Morning News,* April 1, 2001, 11L.

45. Margaret M. Clark, "More Companies Offering Flextime," *HR News,* June 2001, 1+.

46. Ellen Galinsky, Stacy S. Kim, and James T. Bond, *Feeling Overworked: When Work Becomes a Burden* (New York: Families and Work Institute, 2001).

47. Judy Meleliat, "Shaping Up with a Total Web Workout," *Workspan,* March 2001, 17–20.

48. Jeffrey R. Edwards and Nancy P. Rothbard, "Mechanisms Linking Work and Family: Clarifying the Relationship Between Work and Family Constructs," *Academy of Management Review,* 25 (2000), 178–199.

49. Daniel B. Moskowitz, "Care Package," *Human Resource Executive,* May 1, 2001, 1, 30–36.

50. Barbara Parus, "Lives in the Balance," *Workspan,* June 2000, 53–55.

51. Ellen A. Ersher, Elisa J. Grant-Vallore, and Stewart I. Donaldson, "Effects of Perceived Discrimination on Job Satisfaction, Organizational Commitment, Organizational Citizenship Behavior, and Grievances," *Human Resource Development Quarterly,* 12 (2001), 53–72.

52. "Diversity: A 'New' Tool for Retention," *HR Focus,* June 2000, 1+.

53. "Worker Dissatisfaction Rising, Studies Indicate," *Omaha World-Herald,* May 20, 2001, 5G.

54. Paul R. Bernthal and Richard S. Wellins, *Retaining Talent: A Bench-marking Study* (Pittsburgh, PA: Development Dimensions International, 2001).

55. Wayne F. Cascio, *Costing Human Resources* (Cincinnati: South-Western Publishing, 2000), 73–75.

56. Kwan Jee, "Best Practices of Web-Based Employee Opinion Surveys." *The Next Frontier,* September 2001, 13–15.

57. For information on attitude surveys, see David W. Bracken, "Designing and Using Organizational Surveys," *Personnel Psychology* 53 (2000), 206–209.

58. Based on information provided by Ted Hill, *www.Kenaxa.com.*

59. Kevin Sheridan, "Making the Most of Your Post-Survey Action Planning and Communications Process," *New Solutions,* Winter/Spring 2001, 3.

60. *SHRM Retention Practices Survey* (Alexandria VA: Society for Human Resource Management, 2000), 10.

61. D. Mitchell, "How to Reduce the High Cost of Turnover," available at *http://www.ijob.com/news,* October 30, 2000.

62. Charlene Marmer Solomon, "Cracks in the Glass Ceiling," *Workforce,* September 2000, 86–94.

63. Based on Jennifer K. Laabs, "Thinking Outside the Box at the Container Store," *Workforce,* March 2001, 34–38; "The Right Package," *Human Resource Executive,* December 2000, 34–38; and Daniel Roth, "My Job at the Container Store," *Fortune,* January 10, 2000, 74–78.

Staffing the Organization

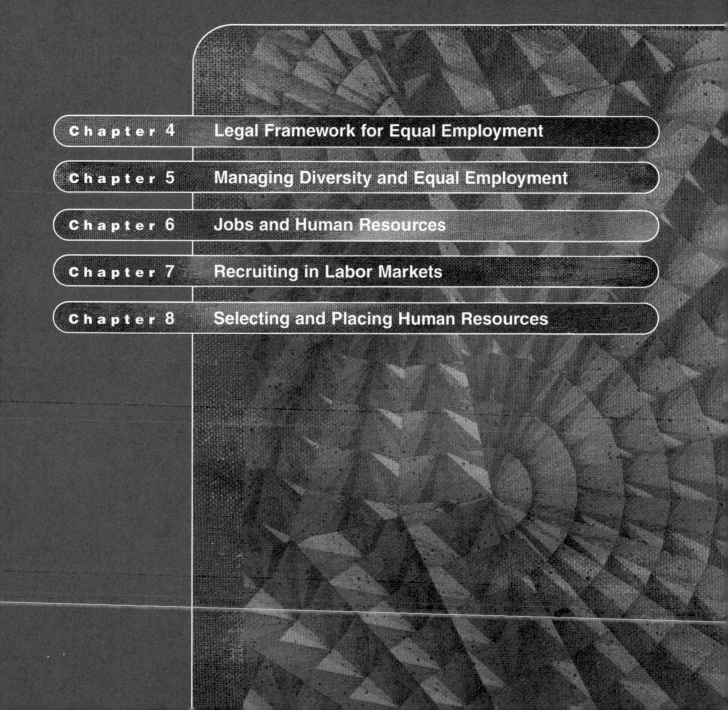

CHAPTER 4

Legal Framework
for Equal Employment

After you have read this chapter, you should be able to:

- Differentiate among diversity management, equal employment opportunity (EEO), and affirmative action.

- Discuss the key provisions of the Civil Rights Act of 1964, Title VII, and define five basic EEO concepts.

- Give examples of three sex-based discrimination issues.

- Discuss the major requirements of the Americans with Disabilities Act.

- Describe four other types of EEO discrimination.

- Discuss the two general approaches for complying with the 1978 Uniform Guidelines on Employee Selection Procedures.

- Define *validity* and *reliability*, and explain three approaches to validating employment requirements.

- Identify typical EEO record-keeping requirements and those records used in the EEO investigative process.

Discrimination Is Expensive

Over the past 40 years, numerous laws designed to eliminate illegal employment discrimination have been enacted. Even so, some employers continue to engage in discriminatory practices, sometimes through ignorance and sometimes intentionally, that lead to large fines and settlements. Some examples show just how expensive illegal employment discrimination can be.

Race Discrimination

Several large corporations have faced sizable settlements in race discrimination cases. For instance, Interstate Brands Corporation, the largest baker in the United States, makes Wonder Bread, Twinkies, and Hostess Cupcakes. However, African American employees won big dough from Interstate in the form of $131 million in compensatory and punitive damages for racial discrimination.

In Texas, Premier Operator Services was found to have engaged in national origin discrimination by having an English-only policy for employees. Employees who were not Hispanic were subjected to less severe monitoring and disciplinary procedures. Having won the lawsuit,13 Hispanic employees split the $710,000 awarded by a court decision.

Sex Discrimination and Sexual Harassment

Women have won large settlements for illegal sex discrimination and sexual harassment. CBS Broadcasting settled several lawsuits by agreeing to pay $8 million to more than 200 women working in six of its television stations. According to the charges, female technicians were subjected to discriminating practices in pay, assignment of overtime, promotions, and training.

A restaurant in Chicago was ordered to pay $3.25 million to four female restaurant employees. The employees claimed that they endured sexual harassment so severe that they had often hidden in the women's restroom. The restaurant is appealing the findings of the case.

Smith & Associates, a Massachusetts firm, was ordered to pay $250,000 to a woman as a result of a sexual harassment lawsuit. The woman was fired after she ended a consensual relationship with the President of the firm and began a new relationship with someone else.

Age Discrimination

Some employers have paid for discriminating against individuals over age 40, who are protected by the federal and state age discrimination laws. Nestle USA was ordered by a California jury to pay an older former employee $5.16 million. The individual who had worked as a financial manager was repeatedly passed over for promotions that went to younger employees.

Storage Technology Corporation, a Colorado-based firm, paid $5 million to settle age discrimination charges. About 400 employees were laid off, and the plaintiffs charged that the firm targeted employees over 40 in order to save money in wages and benefits.

Disabilities Discrimination

Individuals with disabilities also have won substantial judgments for discrimination related to disabilities. For instance, American Airlines resolved a disabilities complaint by paying $1.7 million to 99 individuals denied ramp jobs due to disabilities they had.

The North Kansas City Fire Department settled a complaint of an applicant by paying him $60,000. The applicant was rejected for a firefighter paramedic job because he had insulin-dependent diabetes.

All of these cases emphasize that the costs of illegal employment discrimination can be significant. Therefore, employers of all sizes must be familiar with EEO laws and regulations and ensure that their practices are nondiscriminatory.[1]

> Employers of all sizes must be familiar with EEO laws and regulations and ensure that their practices are nondiscriminatory.

> *"All progress is precarious, and the solution of one problem brings us face to face with another problem."*
>
> **—Martin Luther King**

As the opening examples illustrate, employers of all sizes in various industries have incurred significant costs for violating federal, state, and local laws and regulations prohibiting illegal employment-related discrimination. The major purpose of this chapter to review what employers should do to comply with Equal Employment Opportunity (EEO) laws, regulations, and requirements. Once the legal framework from this chapter has been established, the next chapter turns to managing diversity within the organization.

Diversity, Equal Employment, and Affirmative Action

Diversity The differences among people.

The changing composition of the workforce in the United States and other countries is evident in a variety of ways in almost all organizations. Based on both apparent and less obvious characteristics, the diversity in the workforce in many organizations continues to grow. The concept of **diversity** recognizes that there are differences among people. To assist in identifying the issues involved in workplace diversity, it is critical to clarify the terminology that is often used.

Figure 4-1 shows that diversity management is the broadest level, whereby organizations have taken initiatives and made efforts that value all people equally, regardless of their differences. More on diversity management is discussed in the next chapter. As the figure shows, organizations can also address diversity issues in more restricted ways: equal employment opportunity and affirmative action. These levels are discussed next.

Equal Employment Opportunity

Equal employment opportunity (EEO) Individuals should have equal treatment in all employment-related actions.

Equal employment opportunity (EEO) is a broad concept holding that individuals should have equal treatment in all employment-related actions. Individuals who are covered under equal employment laws are protected from illegal discrimination.

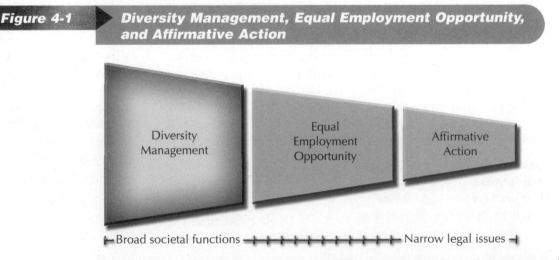

Figure 4-1 **Diversity Management, Equal Employment Opportunity, and Affirmative Action**

Diversity Management

Equal Employment Opportunity

Affirmative Action

├─ Broad societal functions ─┼┼┼┼┼┼┼┼┼┼┼┼─ Narrow legal issues ─┤

Illegal Discrimination The word *discrimination* simply means recognizing differences among items or people. For example, employers must discriminate (choose) among applicants for a job on the basis of job requirements and candidates' qualifications. However, discrimination can be illegal in employment-related situations in which either (1) different standards are used to judge different individuals, or (2) the same standard is used, but it is not related to the individuals' jobs.

Protected Class Various laws have been passed to protect individuals who share certain characteristics, such as race, age, or gender. Those having the designated characteristics are referred to as a **protected class,** which is composed of individuals who fall within a group identified for protection under equal employment laws and regulations. The following bases for protection have been identified by various federal, state, and/or local laws:

1

- Race, ethnic origin, color (African Americans, Hispanic Americans, Native Americans, Asian Americans)
- Sex/Gender (women, including those who are pregnant)
- Age (individuals over 40)
- Individuals with disabilities (physical or mental)
- Military experience (Vietnam-era veterans)
- Religion (special beliefs and practices)
- Marital status (some states)   *not federal*
- Sexual orientation (some states and cities)

Affirmative Action

Affirmative action occurs when employers identify problem areas, set goals, and take positive steps to enhance opportunities for protected-class members. Affirmative action focuses on hiring, training, and promoting of protected-class members where they are *underrepresented* in an organization in relation to their availability in the labor markets from which recruiting occurs. Sometimes employers have instituted affirmative action voluntarily, but many times employers have been required to do so because they are government contractors with more than 50 employees and over $50,000 in government contracts annually. The details of complying with affirmative action regulations are discussed in this chapter.

Affirmative Action and Reverse Discrimination When employment regulations are discussed, probably the most volatile issue concerns the view that affirmative action leads to *quotas* or *preferential selection*. At the heart of the conflict is the employers' role in selecting, training, and promoting protected-class members when they are underrepresented in various jobs in an organization. Those who are not members of any protected class have claimed **reverse discrimination**, which may exist when a person is denied an opportunity because of preferences given to a member of a protected class who may be less qualified.

Specifically, some critics charge that white males are at a disadvantage today, even though they traditionally have held many of the better jobs. These critics say that white males are having to "pay for the sins of their fathers." To illustrate, in a Florida county a white fire department employee was not selected for one of the lieutenant positions, despite outstanding performance ratings and qualifications. Instead the county chose protected-class individuals using a selection system that allowed consideration of race. Also, a county official indicated that the county wanted to continue to consider race or color as a basis for promotion as part of affirmative action efforts. The court ruled that the white individual had been discriminated against because of his race, which was illegal, and the county was ordered to take action to remedy the "reverse discrimination."[2]

Court Decisions and Legislation on Affirmative Action Increasingly, court decisions and legislative efforts have focused on restricting the use of affirmative action. Federal court decisions have addressed admission standards at various universities, including the University of Texas and the University of Michigan. The University of Texas Law School used separate admissions committees to evaluate minority and nonminority applicants. The suit was brought by Cheryl Hopwood and three other white students who were denied admission to the law school, even though they had test scores and grade point averages significantly higher than those of a majority of African Americans and Hispanic Americans who were admitted. Clarifying an earlier case, *Bakke v. University of California*,[3] the Fifth Circuit Court of Appeals in *Hopwood v. State of Texas* ruled:

> *The use of race in admissions for diversity in higher education contradicts, rather than furthers, the aims of equal protection. Diversity fosters, rather than minimizes, the use of race. It treats minorities as a group, rather than as individuals. It may further remedial purposes, but just as likely, may promote improper racial stereotypes, thus fueling racial hostility.*[4]

Affirmative action as a concept is under attack by courts and employers, as well as by males and non-minorities. However, the consequence of implementing such decisions must be considered as well. For instance, in California, the use of affirmative action for determining admission to universities in that state has been restricted. As a result, the numbers of African American and Hispanic students have declined dramatically, but the number of Asian-American students has increased significantly.[5] Whether that trend continues will depend on future decisions by the U.S. Supreme Court and the results of presidential and congressional elections.

The authors of this text believe that whether one supports or opposes affirmative action, it is important to understand why its supporters believe that it is needed and why its opponents believe it should be discontinued. More on the debate over affirmative action is contained in the next chapter.

Major Equal Employment Laws and Concepts

Even if an organization has little regard for the principles of diversity, it must follow federal, state, and local EEO laws and some affirmative action regulations to avoid costly penalties. Numerous federal, state, and local laws address equal employment opportunity concerns, as shown in Appendix C. Some laws have a general civil rights emphasis, while others address specific EEO issues and concerns. An overview of the major laws, regulations, and concepts follows next.

Civil Rights Act of 1964, Title VII

Although the first civil rights act was passed in 1866, it was not until the passage of the Civil Rights Act of 1964 that the keystone of antidiscrimination employment legislation was put into place. The Equal Employment Opportunity Commission (EEOC) was established to enforce the provisions of Title VII, the portion of the act that deals with employment.

Title VII Coverage Title VII, as amended by the Equal Employment Opportunity Act of 1972, covers most employers in the United States. Any organization meeting one of the criteria in the following list is subject to rules and regulations that specific government agencies have established to administer the act:

- All private employers of 15 or more persons who are employed 20 or more weeks per year
- All educational institutions, public and private
- State and local governments
- Public and private employment agencies
- Labor unions with 15 or more members
- Joint labor/management committees for apprenticeships and training

There are a number of basic concepts that were identified in the Civil Rights Act of 1964, Title VII. The concepts depicted in Figure 4-2 are the bases for court decisions, regulations, and in other laws discussed later in the chapter.

Business Necessity and Job Relatedness As has been emphasized by both regulations and a variety of court decisions, employers are expected to use job-related employment practices. In a Michigan case, a federal court ruled that a staffing agency was discriminating by filling job requests from employers with

Equal Employment Advisory Council
This Web site is for a non-profit association focused on equal employment opportunities.

http://www.eeac.org/

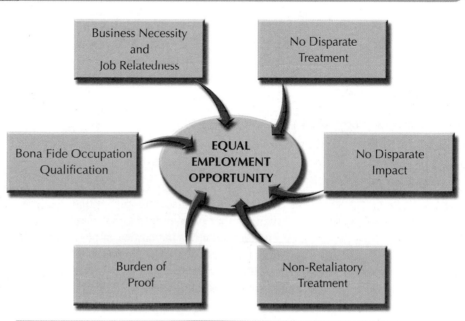

Figure 4-2 ▸ *Concepts Resulting in Equal Employment Opportunity*

such limitations as "males only," "no applicants with accents," and "no Detroit residents." The court ruled that such criteria were not job-related and little business necessity could be shown for these illegal requests being made by employers using the staffing service.[6]

A **business necessity** is a practice necessary for safe and efficient organizational operations. Business necessity has been the subject of numerous court decisions. Educational requirements often are based on business necessity. However, an employer who requires a minimum level of education, such as a high school diploma, must be able to defend the requirement as essential to the performance of the job. For instance, equating a degree or diploma with the possession of math or reading abilities is considered questionable.

Bona Fide Occupational Qualification (BFOQ) Title VII of the 1964 Civil Rights Act specifically states that employers may discriminate on the basis of sex, religion, or national origin if the characteristic can be justified as a "bona fide occupational qualification reasonably necessary to the normal operation of the particular business or enterprise."[7] Thus, a **bona fide occupational qualification (BFOQ)** is a legitimate reason why an employer can exclude persons on otherwise illegal bases of consideration. What constitutes a BFOQ has been subject to different interpretations in various courts across the country. Legal uses of BFOQs have been found for hiring Asian waiters in a Chinese restaurant or Catholics to serve in certain religious-based positions in Catholic churches.

Disparate Treatment and Disparate Impact It would seem that the motives or intentions of the employer might enter into the determination of whether discrimination has occurred—but they do not. The outcome of the employer's actions, not the intent, is considered by the regulatory agencies or courts when deciding whether or not illegal discrimination has occurred. Two concepts used to activate this principle are disparate treatment and disparate impact.

Disparate treatment occurs when protected-class members are treated differently from others. For example, if female applicants must take a special skills test not given to male applicants, then disparate treatment may be occurring. If disparate treatment has occurred, the courts generally have said that intentional discrimination exists.

Disparate impact occurs when substantial underrepresentation of protected-class members results from employment decisions that work to their disadvantage. The landmark case that established the importance of disparate impact as a legal foundation of EEO law is *Griggs v. Duke Power* (1971).[8] The decision of the U.S. Supreme Court established two major points:

1. It is not enough to show a lack of discriminatory intent if the employment tool results in a disparate impact that discriminates against one group more than another or continues a past pattern of discrimination.
2. The employer has the burden of proving that an employment requirement is directly job related as a "business necessity." Consequently, the intelligence test and high school diploma requirements of Duke Power were ruled not to be related to the job.

Based on this and a number of other decisions, it is clear that employers covered by Title VII must be able to document through numerical calculations and

---

Business necessity
A practice necessary for safe and efficient organizational operations.

Bona fide occupational qualification (BFOQ)
Characteristic providing a legitimate reason why an employer can exclude persons on otherwise illegal bases of consideration.

Disparate treatment
Situation that exists when protected-class members are treated differently from others.

Disparate impact Occurs when substantial underrepresentation of protected-class members results from employment decisions that work to their disadvantage.

statistical analyses that disparate treatment and disparate impact have not occurred. How to make these calculations is discussed later in this chapter.

Burden of Proof Another legal issue that arises when discrimination is alleged is the determination of which party has the *burden of proof.* At issue is what individuals who are filing suit against employers must prove in order to establish that illegal discrimination has occurred. Building on an earlier case, *McDonnell Douglas v. Green,* the U.S. Supreme Court in *Reeves v. Sanderson Plumbing Products* ruled that circumstantial evidence can shift the burden of proof to the employer.[9]

Based on the evolution of court decisions, current laws and regulations state that the plaintiff charging discrimination: (1) must be a *protected-class member,* and (2) must prove that *disparate impact* or *disparate treatment* existed. Once a court rules that a *prima facie* (preliminary), case has been made, the burden of proof shifts to the employer. The employer then must show that the bases for making employment-related decisions were specifically job related and consistent with considerations of business necessity.

Retaliation Employers are prohibited by EEO laws from retaliating against individuals who file discrimination charges. **Retaliation** occurs when employers take punitive actions against individuals who exercise their legal rights. For example, a construction company was ruled to have engaged in retaliation when an employee who filed a discrimination complaint had work hours reduced, resulting in a loss of pay, and no other employees' work hours were reduced.[10]

Retaliation Punitive actions taken by employers against individuals who exercise their legal rights.

Civil Rights Act of 1991

The Civil Rights Act of 1991 requires employers to show that an employment practice is *job related for the position* and is consistent with *business necessity.* The act clarifies that the plaintiffs bringing the discrimination charges must identify the particular employer practice being challenged and must show only that protected-class status played *some factor.* For employers, this requirement means that an individual's race, color, religion, sex, or national origin *must play no factor* in their employment practices.

Compensatory/Punitive Damages and Jury Trials One major impact of the 1991 act is that it allows victims of discrimination on the basis of sex, religion, or disability to receive both compensatory and punitive damages in cases of intentional discrimination. Compensatory damages typically include payments for emotional pain and suffering, loss of enjoyment of life, mental anguish, or inconvenience. However, limits were set on the amount of compensatory and punitive damages. Additionally, the 1991 act allows jury trials to determine the liability for and the amount of compensatory and punitive damages, subject to the caps just mentioned, instead of being decided by judges.

Other Provisions of the 1991 Act The Civil Rights Act of 1991 addressed a variety of other issues. Briefly, some of the key issues and the provisions of the act are as follows:

- *Race Norming:* The act prohibited adjustment of employment test scores or use of alternative scoring mechanisms on the basis of the race or gender of test takers. The concern addressed by this provision is the use of different passing or cutoff scores for protected-class members than for those individuals in nonprotected classes.

- *International Employees:* The act extended coverage of U.S. EEO laws to U.S. citizens working abroad, except where local laws or customs conflict.
- *Government Employee Rights:* Congress extended EEO law coverage to employees of the Senate, presidential appointments, and previously excluded state government employees.

Affirmative Action Regulations

The changing laws over the last 30 years have forced employers to address additional areas of potential discrimination. Several acts and regulations apply specifically to government contractors. These acts and regulations specify a minimum number of employees and size of government contracts. The requirements primarily come from federal Executive Orders 11246, 11375, and 11478. Many states have similar requirements for firms with state government contracts.

WEST GROUP
A THOMSON COMPANY
Executive Order 11246
Outlines government contractor record-keeping requirements.
Custom Search:
☑ ANALYSIS
Phrase: AA programs

Affirmative action plan (AAP) Formal document that an employer compiles annually for submission to enforcement agencies.

Executive Orders 11246, 11375, and 11478 Numerous executive orders require that employers holding federal government contracts not discriminate on the basis of race, color, religion, national origin, or sex. An *Executive Order* is issued by the President of the United States to provide direction to government departments on a specific area. The Office of Federal Contract Compliance Programs (OFCCP) in the U.S. Department of Labor has responsibility for enforcing nondiscrimination in government contracts.[11]

Affirmative Action Plans (AAPs) Federal, state, and local regulations require many government contractors to compile affirmative action plans (AAPs) to report on the composition of their workforces. An **affirmative action plan (AAP)** is a formal document that an employer compiles annually for submission to enforcement agencies. Generally, contractors with at least 50 employees and $50,000 in government contracts annually must submit these plans. Courts have noted that any employer may have a *voluntary* AAP, although employers *must* have such a plan if they are government contractors. Some courts have ordered employers that are not government contractors to submit required AAPs because of past discriminatory practices and violations of laws.

Contents of an Affirmative Action Plan The contents of an AAP and the policies flowing from it must be available for review by managers and supervisors within the organization. Plans vary in length; some are long and require extensive staff time to prepare. Figure 4-3 depicts the phases in the development of an AAP.[12]

A crucial but time-consuming phase is the second one in which two different types of analyses and comparisons are done. The **availability analysis** identifies the number of protected-class members available to work in the appropriate labor markets in given jobs. This analysis can be developed with data from a state labor department, the U.S. Census Bureau, and other sources. Another major section of an AAP is the **utilization analysis**, which identifies the number of protected-class members employed and the types of jobs they hold in an organization.[13]

Availability analysis
An analysis that identifies the number of protected-class members available to work in the appropriate labor markets in given jobs.

Utilization analysis
An analysis that identifies the number of protected-class members employed and the types of jobs they hold in an organization.

One of the difficulties in conducting the analyses is how to report and count individuals who are multiracial or multiethnic. Under long-standing regulations, a multiracial person such as Tiger Woods would be reported in two or more

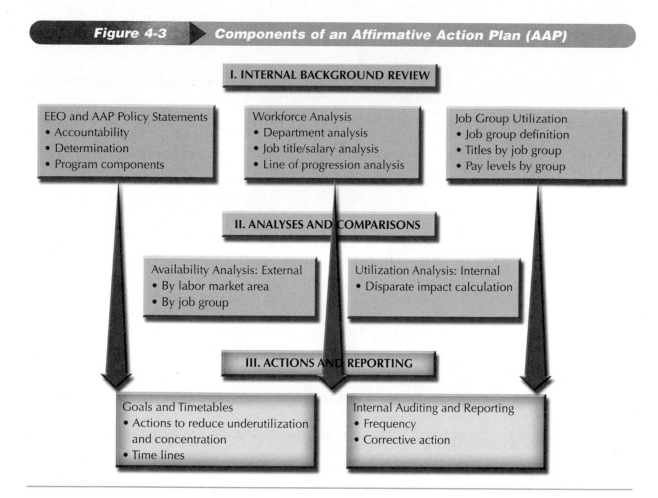

Figure 4-3   *Components of an Affirmative Action Plan (AAP)*

I. INTERNAL BACKGROUND REVIEW

EEO and AAP Policy Statements
- Accountability
- Determination
- Program components

Workforce Analysis
- Department analysis
- Job title/salary analysis
- Line of progression analysis

Job Group Utilization
- Job group definition
- Titles by job group
- Pay levels by group

II. ANALYSES AND COMPARISONS

Availability Analysis: External
- By labor market area
- By job group

Utilization Analysis: Internal
- Disparate impact calculation

III. ACTIONS AND REPORTING

Goals and Timetables
- Actions to reduce underutilization and concentration
- Time lines

Internal Auditing and Reporting
- Frequency
- Corrective action

categories. The enforcement agencies have recognized such concerns and are expected to develop new reporting categories and guidelines within the next two years.

Once all of the data have been analyzed and compared, then *underutilization* statistics must be calculated by comparing the workforce analyses with the utilization analysis. It is useful to think of this stage as a comparison of whether the internal workforce is a "representative sampling" of the available external labor force from which employees are hired.

Using the underutilization data, *goals and timetables* for reducing the underutilization of protected-class individuals must then be identified. Actions that will be taken to recruit, hire, promote, and train more protected-class individuals are described. Also, the AAP must be updated and reviewed each year to reflect changes in the utilization and availability of protected-class members. If an audit of an AAP is done by the OFCCP, the employer must be prepared to provide additional details and documentation.

Laws on Sex/Gender Discrimination

A number of laws and regulations address discrimination on the bases of sex/gender. Historically, women experienced employment discrimination in a variety of ways. The inclusion of sex as a basis for protected-class status in Title VII of the 1964 Civil Rights Act has led to various areas of protection for women.

Pregnancy Discrimination The Pregnancy Discrimination Act (PDA) of 1978 requires that any employer with 15 or more employees treat maternity leave the same as other personal or medical leaves. Closely related to the PDA is the Family and Medical Leave Act (FMLA) of 1993, which requires that individuals be given up to 12 weeks of family leave without pay and also requires that those taking family leave be allowed to return to jobs (see Chapter 14 for details). The FMLA applies to both men and women.

In court cases it generally has been ruled that the PDA requires employers to treat pregnant employees the same as nonpregnant employees with similar abilities or inabilities. Therefore, an employer was ruled to have acted properly when terminating a pregnant employee for excessive absenteeism due to pregnancy-related illnesses because the employee was not treated differently than other employees with absenteeism problems.[14] However, in another case, a dental employee who was fired five days after she told her manager that she was pregnant was awarded $18,460 by a court decision that ruled her employer violated the PDA.[15]

Two other areas somewhat related to pregnancy and motherhood also have been subjects of legal and regulatory action. The U.S. Equal Employment Commission has ruled that denial of health insurance coverage for prescription contraceptives under employer-provided health plans violates the PDA. A result of this ruling is that employers who have changed their health insurance plans to offer contraceptive coverage may face increases in benefit costs.[16]

A number of states have passed laws that guarantee breast-feeding rights at work for new mothers. Although attempts have been to enact such legislation at the federal level, that legislation has not been enacted yet.

Equal Pay and Pay Equity The Equal Pay Act of 1963 requires employers to pay similar wage rates for similar work without regard to gender. A *common core of tasks* must be similar, but tasks performed only intermittently or infrequently do not make jobs different enough to justify significantly different wages.[17] Differences in pay may be allowed because of: (1) differences in seniority, (2) differences in performance, (3) differences in quality and/or quantity of production, and (4) factors other than sex, such as skill, effort, and working conditions. For example, a university was found to have violated the Equal Pay Act by paying a female professor a starting salary lower than salaries paid to male professors with similar responsibilities. In fact, the court found that the woman professor taught larger classes and had more total students than some of the male faculty members.[18]

Pay equity Similarity in pay for jobs requiring comparable levels of knowledge, skill, and ability, even if actual job duties differ significantly.

Another pay-related theory is **pay equity**, which is that the pay for jobs requiring comparable levels of knowledge, skill, and ability should be similar, even if actual duties differ significantly. This theory has also been called *comparable worth* in earlier cases. But except where state laws have mandated pay equity for public-sector employees, U.S. federal courts generally have ruled that the existence of pay differences between jobs held by women and jobs held by men is not sufficient to prove that illegal discrimination has occurred.

A major reason for the development of the pay equity idea is the continuing gap between the earnings of women and men. For instance, in 1980, the average

Research on Pay Differences by Gender and Race

The persistent gap between the median pay levels of men and women, and between whites and nonwhites has been a concern for years. However, some research has shown that as education increases, the pay differential decreases. Other studies have shown the gap to remain, depending upon the individuals' field of work.

To evaluate pay differences among holders of masters of business administration (MBA) degrees, Dreher and Cox utilized data for MBA graduates at nine universities. The respondents were asked to provide career and compensation history details. Only responses from those holding full-time jobs were used, in order to limit the impact on the study of those who were not working, were working part-time, or were self-employed. The remaining 758 full-time responses allowed for more accurate comparisons to be made. Reflecting the enrollment patterns in MBA programs, the study had more responses from men (73%) and nonminorities (64%).

Statistical analyses using various methods led to some interesting results published in *The Regional Economist*. One finding was that white male individuals who changed companies received about $15,000 per year more than those who had stayed with just one employer. The difference was even greater when race or gender was considered. Another part of the study asked respondents about pay expectations and satisfaction. The study results found that white females with MBAs had somewhat lower pay expectations than their white male counterparts, but no statistically significant differences separated minority female and male expectations and satisfaction.

In discussing the study, the authors indicate that some of the compensation differences between males and females and minorities and non-minorities can be explained by the dynamics of the labor markets, and the willingness of individuals, particularly white males, to change jobs and companies. Although the study did not address why white males seem to be more willing to change jobs and companies more often, it is an issue sure to be examined by employers and researchers in the future.[19]

annual pay of full-time women workers was 60% of that of full-time men workers. By 2001, the reported rate of 72% showed some progress.[20] More in-depth data and research studies have shown that when education and experience differences of men and women are considered, women earn about 90% of what comparable men workers earn.[21] Another interesting reason for the pay differential, job mobility and changing employers, is explored in the HR Perspective.

Sexual Harassment Regulations and Cases The Equal Employment Opportunity Commission (EEOC) has issued guidelines designed to curtail sexual harassment. **Sexual harassment** refers to actions that are sexually directed, are unwanted, and subject the worker to adverse employment conditions or create a hostile work environment. Sexual harassment can occur between a boss and a subordinate, among co-workers, and when non-employees have business contacts with employees.

According to EEOC statistics, more than 90% of sexual harassment charges filed involve harassment of women by men. However, some sexual harassment cases have been filed by men against women managers and supervisors, and for same-sex harassment. An in-depth discussion of prevention and investigation of sexual harassment complaints is contained in Chapter 5.

Sexual harassment
Actions that are sexually directed, are unwanted, and subject the worker to adverse employment conditions or create a hostile work environment.

Figure 4-4 ▶ **Major Sections of the Americans with Disabilities Act**

Title I	Title II	Title III	Title IV	Title V
Employment Provisions	**Public Participation and Service**	**Public Access**	**Telecommunications**	**Administration and Enforcement**
Prohibits employment-related discrimination against persons with disabilities	*Prohibits discrimination related to participation of disabled persons in government programs and for public transportation*	*Ensures accessibility of public and commercial facilities*	*Requires provision of telecommunications capabilities and television closed captions for persons with hearing and speech disabilities*	*Describes administrative and enforcement provisions and lists who is not covered by ADA*

Americans with Disabilities Act (ADA)

The passage of the Americans with Disabilities Act (ADA) in 1990 expanded the scope and impact of laws and regulations on discrimination against individuals with disabilities. The ADA affects more than just employment matters, as Figure 4-4 shows. All employers with 15 or more employees are covered by the provisions of the ADA, which are enforced by the EEOC, and it applies to private employers, employment agencies, and labor unions. A U.S. Supreme Court decision ruled that state government employees are not covered by the ADA, which means that those employees cannot sue in federal courts for redress and damages.[22] However, they still may bring suits under state laws in state courts.

Who Is Disabled? As defined by the ADA, a **disabled person** is someone who has a physical or mental impairment that substantially limits that person in some major life activities, who has a record of such an impairment, or who is regarded as having such an impairment. In spite of the EEOC guidelines, some confusion still remains as to who is disabled. Court decisions have found individuals who have high blood pressure, epilepsy, allergies, obesity, and color blindness to be disabled. For example, another high-profile U.S. Supreme Court case involving professional golfer Casey Martin resulted in the decision that Martin, who suffers from a severe circulatory disorder in his legs, must be allowed to ride a golf cart while competing in PGA tournaments.[23] Some guidance on disability status was provided by a U.S. Supreme Court case involving United Airlines. Two pilots sued claiming they were disabled because they wore glasses to correct their nearsightedness, but their uncorrected vision was too low to meet United's requirements for pilots. The Supreme Court ruled in favor of United Airlines when it stated that the means used to mitigate an individual's physical or mental impairments, such as corrective eyeglasses or controlling medications, must be considered when determining if someone is disabled as defined by the ADA.[24]

Mental Disabilities A growing area of concern under the ADA is individuals with mental disabilities. A mental illness is often more difficult to diagnose than a physical disability. Employers must be careful when considering "emotional"

Disabled person Someone who has a physical or mental impairment that substantially limits life activities, who has a record of such an impairment, or who is regarded as having such an impairment.

WEST GROUP
A THOMSON COMPANY

ADA Covered Disabilities
Identifies disabilities covered by ADA and court decisions.
Custom Search:
☑ ANALYSIS
Phrase: What is a disability

or "mental health" factors when making employment-related decisions. However, employers must not stereotype individuals with mental disabilities, but base their evaluation on sound medical information.[25]

Life-Threatening Illnesses In recent years, the types of disabilities covered by various local, state, and federal acts prohibiting discrimination have been expanded. The most feared contagious disease is acquired immunodeficiency syndrome (AIDS). A U.S. Supreme Court decision ruled that individuals infected with human immunodeficiency virus (HIV), not just those with AIDS, have a disability covered by the ADA.[26]

ADA and Job Requirements The ADA contains a number of specific requirements that deal with employment of individuals with disabilities. The major ones are discussed next.

Discrimination is prohibited against individuals with disabilities who can perform **essential job functions**—the fundamental job duties of the employment position that an individual with a disability holds or desires. These functions do not include marginal functions of the position. For persons with disabilities, employers must make a **reasonable accommodation,** which is a modification or adjustment to a job or work environment that enables a qualified individual with a disability to have equal employment opportunity. EEOC guidelines encourage an interactive process between employers and individuals to determine what appropriate reasonable accommodations are, rather than the employer solely making that judgment.[27]

Reasonable accommodation is restricted to actions that do not place an "undue hardship" on an employer. An **undue hardship** is a significant difficulty or expense imposed on an employer in making an accommodation for individuals with disabilities. The ADA offers only general guidelines in determining when an accommodation becomes unreasonable and places undue hardship on an employer. However, most accommodation expenditures by employers have been relatively inexpensive. More information on reasonable accommodations is given in Chapter 5.

ADA Restrictions and Medical Information The ADA contains restrictions on obtaining and retaining medically related information on applicants and employees. One restriction is that the ADA prohibits employers from rejecting an individual because of a disability and from asking job applicants any question relative to current or past medical history until a conditional job offer is made. The HR Practice on the next page discusses how employment applications and interview questions should be handled to comply with the ADA restrictions. The ADA also prohibits the use of preemployment medical exams, except for drug tests, until a job has been conditionally offered.

An additional requirement of the ADA is that all medically related information be maintained in files separated from the general personnel files. The medical files must have security and limited access procedures identified.

Age Discrimination in Employment Act (ADEA)

The Age Discrimination in Employment Act of 1967, amended in 1978 and 1986, prohibits discrimination in compensation terms, conditions, or privileges of employment against all individuals age 40 or older working for employers having 20 or more workers. However, the U.S. Supreme Court has ruled that

Essential job functions
Fundamental duties of a job.

Reasonable accommodation A modification or adjustment to a job or work environment for a qualified individual with a disability.

Undue hardship Significant difficulty or expense imposed on an employer when making an accommodation for individuals with disabilities.

Logging On...

Administration on Aging
Provides information on aging and age discrimination from government agencies, association, and organizations.

http://www.aoa.dhhs.gov

The ADA and the Employment Process

The ADA prohibits asking job applicants any questions relative to past or current medical or health history until a conditional job offer is made, with the condition often being passing of a physical exam or medical background check. Any physical or medical requirements must be related to the specific job for which the applicant is being considered. Consequently, HR practitioners have had to monitor their employment processes to ensure that they do not violate requirements in the ADA. Two specific areas that are affected are employment applications and interviews.

On employment applications, medically related questions should be limited. Therefore, questions about past workers' compensation claims or injuries violate the ADA restrictions. Also, any other medical history questions should not be included on the initial application form. Instead, it is recommended that a question such as the following be used:

> "Can you perform the essential functions of the job for which you are applying with or without accommodation? Please describe any accommodations needed."

Court decisions have made it clear that employers are not expected to be clairvoyant and guess at the need for accommodations. By asking this question, employers can obtain useful information to determine whether or even what reasonable accommodations can be made. However, the employer is not required to make the specific accommodations requested by the applicant, only to make a reasonable effort to develop accommodations.

Several examples of questions that should and should not be asked in employment interviews are shown in the chart below.

As is evident, the questions that should be asked are specifically job-related and address essential job functions. Also, even if the applicant reveals a medical condition or disability in answering questions, any use of that information must be in a job-related context and linked to identifying possible reasonable accommodations.

⊗ DO NOT ASK	✔ DO ASK
• Do you have any physical or mental disabilities? • Why are you using crutches, and how did you become injured? • How many times were you absent due to illness in the past two years? • Have you been treated for any of the following medical conditions? • Have you ever filed for or collected workers' compensation?	• How would you perform the essential tasks of the job for which you have applied? • If hired, which tasks outlined in the job description that you reviewed would be more enjoyable and most difficult? • Describe your attendance record on your last job. • Describe any problems you would have reaching the top of a six-foot filing cabinet. • What did your prior job duties consist of, and which ones were the most challenging?

state employees may not sue state government employers in federal courts because the ADEA is a federal law.[28]

The act does not apply if age is a job-related occupational qualification and prohibitions against age discrimination do not apply when an individual is disciplined or discharged for good cause, such as poor job performance. But targeting older workers for replacement is illegal. One case involving a Florida supermarket found age discrimination because a district manager fired or demoted five older managers and replaced them with younger, less experienced individuals. The district manager even had commented that he preferred "younger, aggressive men" to receive promotions to store managers.[29]

Immigration Reform and Control Acts (IRCA)

Race is often a factor in discrimination on the basis of national origin. The Immigration Reform and Control Acts (IRCA) and later revisions passed made it illegal for an employer to discriminate in recruiting, hiring, disciplining, or terminating employees based on an individual's national origin or citizenship. In addition, the IRCA requires that employers who knowingly hire illegal aliens be penalized. Employers must ask for proof of identity, such as a driver's license with a picture, Social Security card, birth certificate, immigration permit, or other documents. The required I-9 form must be completed by all new employees within 72 hours.

Recent revisions to the IRCA changed some of the restrictions on the entry of immigrants to work in U.S. organizations, particularly those organizations with high-technology and other "scarce skill" areas. The number of immigrants allowed legal entry was increased, and categories for entry visas were revised.

Other Types of Discrimination

Several other types of discrimination have been identified as illegal. A growing number of issues in the area of religious discrimination require attention by employers.

Religious Discrimination Title VII of the Civil Rights Act identifies discrimination on the basis of religion as illegal. However, religious schools and institutions can use religion as a bona fide occupational qualification (BFOQ) for employment practices on a limited scale. Also, the employers must make *reasonable accommodation* efforts regarding an employee's religious beliefs.

A major guide in this area was established by the U.S. Supreme Court in *TWA v. Hardison.* In that case, the Supreme Court ruled that an employer is required to make reasonable accommodation of an employee's religious beliefs. Because TWA had done so, the ruling denied Hardison's discrimination charges.[30] In a more recent case, a Muslim plumber was fired for leaving his job early on Fridays to attend Islamic prayer services. The individual was awarded more than $100,000 for being discriminated against for his religion, especially since his employer made no efforts to make reasonable accommodations.[31]

Genetic Bias Regulations Somewhat related to medical disabilities is the emerging area of workplace genetic bias. As medical research has revealed the human genome, medical tests have been developed that can identify an individual's genetic "markers" for various diseases. Whether these tests should be used and how they are used raises ethical issues, as the HR Perspective discusses.

Appearance and Weight Discrimination Several EEO cases have been filed concerning the physical appearance of employees. Court decisions consistently have allowed employers to have dress codes as long as they are applied uniformly. For example, requiring a dress code for women but not for men has been ruled to be discriminatory. Also, employers should be cautious when enforcing dress standards for women employees who are members of certain religions that prescribe appropriate and inappropriate dress and appearance

HR Perspectives

Ethical Issues with Genetic Testing

Advances in biological and medical research have resulted in the ability of employers to obtain information on the genetic makeup of applicants and employees. However, being able to get such information raises ethical issues about balancing employee privacy rights with legitimate employer concerns.

Some large companies currently have used genetic tests and many more have considered their use in the future. However, the general public disapproves strongly of their use, as shown in a poll in which 80% of those surveyed said employers and insurance companies should not have access to genetic testing data.

Employers that use genetic screening tests do so for two primary reasons. First, genetic testing may be used to make workers aware of genetic problems that may exist, so that medical treatment can begin. However, some employers may use this information to terminate employees who may make extensive use of health insurance benefits, thus raising the employers' benefits costs and utilization rates. A major railroad, Burlington Northern Santa Fe had to publicly apologize to employees for secretly subjecting employees to genetic testing to determine if employees were genetically predisposed to carpal-tunnel syndrome.

The second reason is the most controversial: to exclude individuals from certain jobs if they have genetic conditions that increase their health risks. Because people cannot change their genetic makeup, the potential for discrimination based, for example, on race or sex is real. For example, a study reprinted in *The Journal of the American Medical Association* reported that almost 60% of women with a family history suggesting risks for breast or ovarian cancer refused to take genetic tests because of concerns about the use of the information by their employers or insurance companies.

To address such concerns, laws to prohibit discrimination based on genetic information and to protect the privacy of that information have been passed in 22 states including Arizona, California, Connecticut, Florida, and others. Federal legislation also has been proposed.

But in the private sector employers increasingly must make decisions about obtaining and using genetic testing details on employees. The ethics of employers using genetic testing are likely to grow as even more sophisticated genetic technology explores and maps the human genome.[32]

standards. Other individuals have brought cases of employment discrimination based on height or weight discrimination. The crucial factor that employers must consider is that any weight or height requirements be job-related, such that excess weight hampers individuals' job performance.[33]

Cases also have addressed the issue of beards, mustaches, and hair length and style. Because African American men are more likely than white males to suffer from a skin disease that is worsened by shaving, they have filed suits challenging policies prohibiting beards or long sideburns. Generally, courts have ruled for employers in such cases, except where certain religious standards expect men to have beards and facial hair.

Sexual Orientation Recent battles in a number of states and communities illustrate the depth of emotions that accompany discussions of "gay rights." Some states and cities have passed laws prohibiting discrimination based on sexual orientation or lifestyle. Even the issue of benefits coverage for "domestic partners," whether heterosexual or homosexual, has been the subject of state and city legislation. At the federal level no laws of a similar nature have been passed. Whether gay men and lesbians have rights under the equal protection amendment to the U.S. Constitution has not been decided by the U.S. Supreme Court.

Veterans' Employment Rights The employment rights of military veterans and reservists have been addressed several times. The two most important laws are: (1) Vietnam-Era Veterans Readjustment Act of 1974, and (2) Uniformed Services Employment and Reemployment Rights Act of 1994. Under the Uniformed Services Employment and Reemployment Rights Act of 1994, employees are required to notify their employers of military service obligations. Employees serving in the military must be provided leaves of absence and have reemployment rights for up to five years. Other provisions protect the right to benefits of employees called to military duty.

Seniority and Discrimination Conflicts between EEO regulations and organizational practices giving preference to employees on the basis of seniority represent another problem area. Employers, especially those with union contracts, frequently make layoff, promotion, and internal transfer decisions by giving employees with longer service first consideration. However, the use of seniority often means disparate impact on protected-class members, who may be the workers most recently hired. The result of this system is that protected-class members who have obtained jobs through an affirmative action program are at a disadvantage because of their low levels of seniority. They may find themselves "last hired, first fired" or "last hired, last promoted." In most cases, the courts have held that a valid seniority system does not violate rights based on protected-class status.[34] However, in a few cases, gender, racial, disability, or age considerations have been given precedence over seniority.

Conviction and Arrest Records Court decisions consistently have ruled that using records of arrests, rather than records of convictions, has a disparate impact on some racial and ethnic minority groups protected by Title VII. An arrest, unlike a conviction, does not imply guilt. Statistics indicate that in some geographic areas, the arrest rates for members of some minority groups are higher than for non-minorities.

Generally, courts have held that conviction records may be used in determining employability if the offense is job related. For example, a bank could use an applicant's conviction for embezzlement as a valid basis for rejection. Some courts have held that only job-related convictions occurring within the most recent five to seven years may be considered. Consequently, employers inquiring about convictions often add a phrase such as "indication of a conviction will not be an absolute bar to employment."

Pre-employment vs. After-Hire Inquiries

Figure 4-5 lists pre-employment inquiries and identifies whether they may or may not be discriminatory. The pre-employment inquiries labeled in the figure as "may be discriminatory" have been so designated because of findings in a variety of court cases. Those labeled "may not be discriminatory" are practices that are legal, but only if they reflect a business necessity or are job related.

Once an employer tells an applicant he or she is hired (the "point of hire"), inquiries that were prohibited earlier may be made. After hiring, medical examination forms, group insurance cards, and other enrollment cards containing inquiries related directly or indirectly to sex, age, or other bases may be requested.

Figure 4-5 **Guidelines to Lawful and Unlawful Pre-employment Inquiries**

Subject of Inquiry	It May Not Be Discriminatory to Inquire About	It May Be Discriminatory to Inquire About
1. Name	a. Whether applicant has ever worked under a different name	a. The original name of an applicant whose name has been legally changed b. The ethnic association of applicant's name
2. Age	a. If applicant is over the age of 18 b. If applicant is under the age of 18 or 21 if job related (i.e., selling liquor in retail store)	a. Date of birth b. Date of high school graduation
3. Residence	a. Applicant's place of residence b. Alternate contact information	a. Previous addresses b. Birthplace of applicant or applicant's parents c. Length of current and previous addresses
4. Race or Color		a. Applicant's race or color of applicant's skin
5. National Origin and Ancestry		a. Applicant's lineage, ancestry, national origin, parentage, or nationality b. Nationality of applicant's parents or spouse
6. Sex and Family Composition		a. Sex of applicant b. Marital status c. Dependents of applicant or child-care arrangements d. Who to contact in case of emergency
7. Creed or Religion		a. Applicant's religious affiliation b. Church, parish, mosque, synagogue c. Holidays observed
8. Citizenship	a. Whether the applicant is a U.S. citizen or has current permit/visa to work in U.S.	a. Whether applicant is a citizen of a country other than the U.S. b. Date of citizenship
9. Language	a. Language applicant speaks and/or writes fluently, if job related	a. Applicant's native tongue b. Language commonly used at home

(Continued on next page)

Figure 4-5 ▶ **Continued**

Subject of Inquiry	It May Not Be Discriminatory to Inquire About	It May Be Discriminatory to Inquire About
10. References	a. Names of persons willing to provide professional and/or character references for applicant b. Previous work contacts	a. Name of applicant's religious leader b. Political affiliation and contacts
11. Relatives	a. Names of relatives already employed by the employer	a. Name and/or address of any relative of applicant b. Whom to contact in case of emergency
12. Organizations	a. Applicant's membership in any professional, service, or trade organization	a. All clubs or social organizations to which applicant belongs
13. Arrest Record and Convictions	a. Convictions, if related to job performance (disclaimer should accompany)	a. Number and kinds of arrests b. Convictions unless related to job performance
14. Photographs		a. Photograph with application, with resume, or before hiring
15. Height and Weight		a. Any inquiry into height and weight of applicant except where a BFOQ
16. Physical Limitations	a. Whether applicant has the ability to perform job-related functions with or without accommodation	a. The nature or severity of an illness or person's physical condition b. Whether applicant has ever filed workers' compensation claim c. Any recent or past operations or surgery and dates
17. Education	a. Training applicant has received if related to the job b. Highest level of education attained, if validated that having certain educational background (e.g., high school diploma or college degree) is necessary to perform the specific job	a. Date of high school graduation
18. Military	a. Branch of the military applicant served in and ranks attained b. Type of education or training received in military	a. Type of military discharge b. Military service records
19. Financial Status		a. Applicant's debts or assets b. Garnishments

Figure 4-6 ▶ *Equal Employment Charges by Type*

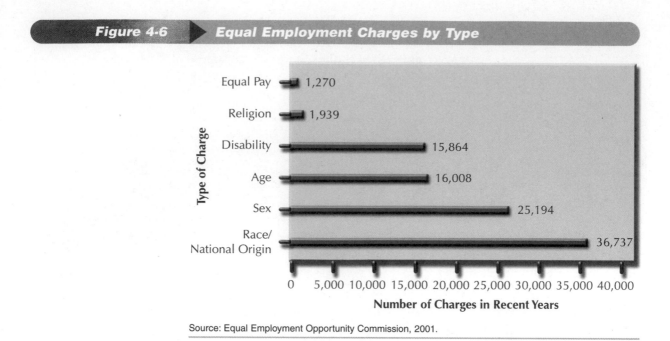

Source: Equal Employment Opportunity Commission, 2001.

Enforcement Agencies

Government agencies at several levels can investigate illegal discriminatory practices. At the federal level, the two most prominent agencies are the Equal Employment Opportunity Commission and the Office of Federal Contract Compliance Programs.

Equal Employment Opportunity Commission (EEOC)

The EEOC has enforcement authority for charges brought under a number of federal laws. As Figure 4-6 shows, the greatest number of equal employment charges are based on race/national origin and sex discrimination.

Office of Federal Contract Compliance Programs (OFCCP)

While the EEOC is an independent agency, the OFCCP is part of the Department of Labor and ensures that federal contractors and subcontractors have nondiscriminatory practices. A major thrust of OFCCP efforts is to require that covered employers take affirmative action to counter prior discriminatory practices.

State and Local Enforcement Agencies

In addition to federal laws and orders, many states and municipalities have passed their own laws prohibiting discrimination on a variety of bases, and state and local enforcement bodies have been established. However, state and local laws sometimes provide greater remedies, require different actions, or prohibit discrimination in areas beyond those addressed by federal law.

Evolving Nature of EEO Enforcement

Enforcement of EEO laws and regulations must be seen as an evolving concept that is inconsistent and confusing at times. The court system is left to resolve the disputes and issue interpretations of the laws. The courts, especially the lower courts, have issued conflicting rulings and interpretations. The ultimate interpretation often has rested on decisions by the U.S. Supreme Court, although those rulings, too, have been interpreted differently.

Controversial Use of "Testers" Beginning several years ago, the EEOC started using "matched-pair" testers who posed as interested applicants for jobs to determine whether employers would discriminate in their treatments of the individuals. One tester might be white and the other African American, for instance. The two individuals apply for a job and then compare their treatment. These testers can then testify in court as to their differential treatment if necessary.

The use of testers has outraged employers, whose argument is that because the testers are not truly applicants, they should not be able to file charges. In one case a U.S. circuit court allowed testers to provide evidence and sue employers for what they believe to be disparate treatment and illegal discrimination. However, other lower courts have ruled against the use of testers.[35] Consequently, the ultimate legality of the use of testers is likely to be decided by the U.S. Supreme Court.

Uniform Guidelines on Employee Selection Procedures

The Uniform Guidelines on Employee Selection Procedures apply to the federal EEOC, the U.S. Department of Labor's OFCCP, the U.S. Department of Justice, and the federal Office of Personnel Management. These guidelines affect virtually all phases of HR management, not just to the initial hiring process. Two major compliance approaches are identified by the guidelines: (1) no disparate impact, and (2) job-related validation.

"No Disparate Impact" Approach

Generally, the most important issue regarding discrimination in organizations is the *effect* of employment policies and procedures, regardless of employer *intent*. *Disparate impact* occurs when a substantial underrepresentation of protected-class members is evident in employment decisions. The Uniform Guidelines identify one approach in the following statement: "These guidelines do not require a user to conduct validity studies of selection procedures where no adverse impact results."[36]

4/5ths rule Rule stating that discrimination generally is considered to occur if the selection rate for a protected group is less than 80% (4/5ths) of the selection rate for the majority group or less than 80% of the group's representation in the relevant labor market.

Under the guidelines, disparate impact is determined with the **4/5ths rule.** If the selection rate for a protected group is less than 80% (4/5ths) of the selection rate for the majority group or less than 80% of the group's representation in the relevant labor market, discrimination exists. Thus, the guidelines have attempted to define discrimination in statistical terms. Disparate impact can be checked both internally and externally.

Internal Checking disparate impact internally compares the treatment received by protected-class members with that received by nonprotected-group members. HR activities for which internal disparate impact can be checked most frequently include the following:

- Candidates selected for interviews of those recruited
- Pass rates for various selection tests
- Performance appraisal ratings as they affect pay increases
- Promotions, demotions, and terminations
- Individuals identified for layoffs

Figure 4-7 ▶ **Internal Disparate Impact**

Female applicants = 25% selected for jobs
Male applicants   = 45% selected for jobs

Disparate Impact Determination

- Male selection rate of 45% × 4/5ths rule (80%) = 36%
- Compared to female selection rate   = 25%

Therefore: Disparate impact exists because female selection rate is lower than
            4/5ths rule.

As shown in Figure 4-7, both men and women were interviewed for jobs at a firm. Of the men who applied, 45% were hired; of the women who applied, 25% were hired. The selection rate for women of 25% is less than 80% (4/5ths) of the selection rate for men (45% × 4/5 = 36%). Consequently, the company's selection process does have "disparate impact" internally.

The practical meaning of these calculations is that statistically women have a lesser chance of being selected for jobs than men do, so much so that illegal discrimination exists unless the firm can demonstrate that its selection activities are specifically job-related.

External Employers can check for disparate impact externally by comparing the percentage of employed workers in a protected class in the organization with the percentage of protected-class members in the relevant labor market. The relevant labor market consists of the areas where the firm recruits workers, not just where those employed live. External comparisons can also consider the percentage of protected-class members who are recruited and who apply for jobs to ensure that the employer has drawn a "representative sample" from the relevant labor market. Although employers are not required to maintain exact proportionate equality, they must be "close." Courts have applied statistical analyses to determine if any disparities that exist are too high.

To illustrate external disparate impact, impact analyses for a sample metropolitan area is contained in Figure 4-8. Using data from that figure, assume Acme Company has 500 employees, 50 of whom are Black/African American and 75 are Hispanic/Latino. To determine if the company has external disparate impact, the following comparisons would be made.

Protected Class	Acme Co., % of total employees	4/5ths of population (from Figure 4-7)	Disparate Impact
Black/ African American	10%	13.6%	Yes
Hispanic/ Latino	15%	14.4%	No

Therefore, external disparate impact exists for Black/African American individuals because Acme has fewer of those employees than the 4/5ths threshold

Figure 4-8 **External Disparate Impact**

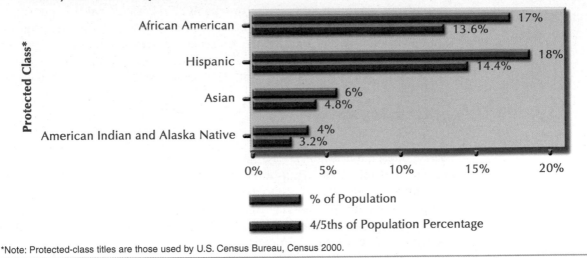

Valleyville Area = Population 250,000

*Note: Protected-class titles are those used by U.S. Census Bureau, Census 2000.

of 13.6% However, because Acme has 15% Hispanic/Latino employees, but the 4/5ths threshold is 14.4%, there is not disparate impact for this group.

The preceding example illustrates one way external disparate impact can be determined. Although some methodological problems have been identified in the use of the 4/5ths rule, nevertheless the 4/5ths rule is a yardstick against which employers can measure the extent of disparate impact on protected-class members.[37] In reality, statistical comparisons for disparate-impact determination may use more complex methods. Knowing how to do such calculations is necessary for HR professionals because external disparate impact must be computed and reported in Affirmative Action Plans that government contractors submit to governmental agencies.

Job-Related Validation Approach

Under the job-related validation approach virtually every factor used to make employment-related decisions—recruiting, selection, promotion, termination, discipline, and performance appraisal—must be shown to be specifically job related. Hence, the concept of validity affects many of the common tools used to make HR decisions.

Validity Extent to which a test actually measures what it says it measures.

Validity is simply the extent to which a test actually measures what it says it measures. The concept relates to inferences made from tests. For instance, it may be valid to assume that performance on a mechanical knowledge test may predict performance of a machinist in a manufacturing plant. However, it is probably invalid to assume these same test scores measure general intelligence or promotability for a manufacturing sales representative.

Employment "test" Any employment procedure used as the basis for making an employment-related decision.

An **employment "test"** is any employment procedure used as the basis for making an employment-related decision. For instance, for a general intelligence test to be valid, it must actually measure intelligence, not just a person's vocabulary. An employment test that is valid must measure the person's ability to perform the job for which he or she is being hired.

Reliability Consistency
with which a test mea-
sures an item.

The ideal condition for employment-related tests is to be both valid and reliable. **Reliability** refers to the consistency with which a test measures an item.
For a test to be reliable, an individual's score should be about the same every
time the individual takes that test (allowing for the effects of practice). Unless a
test measures a factor consistently (or reliably), it is of little value in predicting
job performance. Reliability can be measured by several different statistical methodologies. The most frequent ones are test-retest, alternate forms, and
internal-consistency estimates. A more detailed methodological discussion is
beyond the scope of this text; those interested can consult appropriate references.[38]

Validity and Equal Employment

If a charge of discrimination is brought against an employer on the basis of disparate impact, a *prima facie* case must be established. The employer then must
be able to demonstrate that its employment procedures are valid, which means
to demonstrate that they relate to the job and the requirements of the job. A key
element in establishing job-relatedness is to conduct a *job analysis* to identify
the *knowledge, skills, and abilities (KSAs)* and other characteristics needed to
perform a job satisfactorily. A detailed analysis of the job provides the foundation for linking the KSAs to job requirements and job performance, as Chapter 6
discusses. Using an invalid instrument to select, place, or promote an employee
has never been a good management practice, regardless of its legality.

In one sense, then, current requirements have done management a favor by
forcing employers to do what they should have been doing previously—using
job-related employment procedures. The 1978 Uniform Selection Guidelines
recognize validation strategies measuring three types of validity:

1. Content validity
2. Criterion-related validity (concurrent and predictive)
3. Construct validity

Content Validity

Content validity Validity
measured by use of a log-
ical, nonstatistical method
to identify the KSAs and
other characteristics necessary to perform a job.

Content validity is a logical, nonstatistical method used to identify the KSAs
and other characteristics necessary to perform a job. A test has content validity
if it reflects an actual sample of the work done on the job in question. For example, an arithmetic test for a retail cashier might contain problems about determining amounts for refunds, purchases, and merchandise exchanges. Content
validity is especially useful if the workforce is not large enough to allow other,
more statistical approaches.

A content validity study begins with a comprehensive job analysis to identify what is done on a job and what KSAs are used. Then managers, supervisors,
and HR specialists must identify the most important KSAs needed for the job.
Finally, a test is devised to determine if individuals have the necessary KSAs.
The "test" may be an interview question about previous supervisory experience,
or an ability test in which someone types a letter using a word-processing software program, or a knowledge test about consumer credit regulations.

Many practitioners and specialists see content validity as a commonsense
way to validate staffing requirements, and as more realistic than statistically-
oriented methods. Consequently, content validity approaches are growing in use.

Criterion-Related Validity

Criterion-related validity
Validity measured by a procedure that uses a test as the predictor of how well an individual will perform on the job.

Employment tests of any kind attempt to predict how well an individual will perform on the job. In measuring **criterion-related validity,** a test is the *predictor* and the desired KSAs and measures for job performance are the *criterion variables.* Job analysis determines as exactly as possible what KSAs and behaviors are needed for each task in the job. Tests (predictors) are then devised and used to measure different dimensions of the criterion-related variables. Examples of "tests" are: (1) having a college degree, (2) scoring a required number of words per minute on a typing test, or (3) having five years of banking experience. These predictors are then validated against criteria used to measure job performance, such as performance appraisals, sales records, and absenteeism rates. If the predictors satisfactorily predict job performance behavior, they are legally acceptable and useful.

Correlation coefficient
Index number giving the relationship between a predictor and a criterion variable.

A simple analogy is to think of two circles, one labeled *predictor* and the other *criterion variable.* The criterion-related approach to validity attempts to see how much the two circles overlap. The more overlap, the better the performance of the predictor. The degree of overlap is described by a **correlation coefficient,** which is an index number giving the relationship between a predictor and a criterion variable. These coefficients can range from –1.0 to +1.0. A correlation coefficient of +.80 indicates that the test is a good predictor, whereas a –.25 correlation coefficient indicates that the test is a poor predictor. Thus, a high correlation suggests that the test can differentiate between the better-performing employees and those with poor performance records.

There are two different approaches to criterion-related validity. *Concurrent validity* is an "at-the-same-time" approach, while *predictive validity* is a "before-the-fact" approach. Figure 4-9 on the next page depicts both approaches.

Concurrent validity Measured when an employer tests current employees and correlates the scores with their performance ratings.

Concurrent Validity *Concurrent* means "at the same time." As shown in Figure 4-9 when an employer measures **concurrent validity,** a test is given to current employees and the scores are correlated with their performance ratings, determined by such measures as accident rates, absenteeism records, and supervisory performance appraisals. The reason it is called *concurrent* is because the job performance measures and the test scores are available at the same time (concurrently) rather than subject to a time lag as in the predictive validity approach.

A drawback of the concurrent validity approach is that employees who have not performed satisfactorily on the job are probably no longer with the firm and therefore cannot be tested, while extremely good employees may have been promoted or may have left the organization for better jobs. Also, any learning that has taken place on the job may influence test scores, presenting another problem.

Predictive validity Measured when test results of applicants are compared with subsequent job performance.

Predictive Validity To measure **predictive validity,** test results of applicants are compared with their subsequent job performance. (See Figure 4-9.) Success on the job is measured by such factors as absenteeism, accidents, errors, and performance appraisals. If those employees who had one year of experience at the time of hire demonstrate better performance than those without such experience, as calculated by statistical comparisons, then the experience requirement is considered a valid predictor of performance and may be used in hiring future employees.

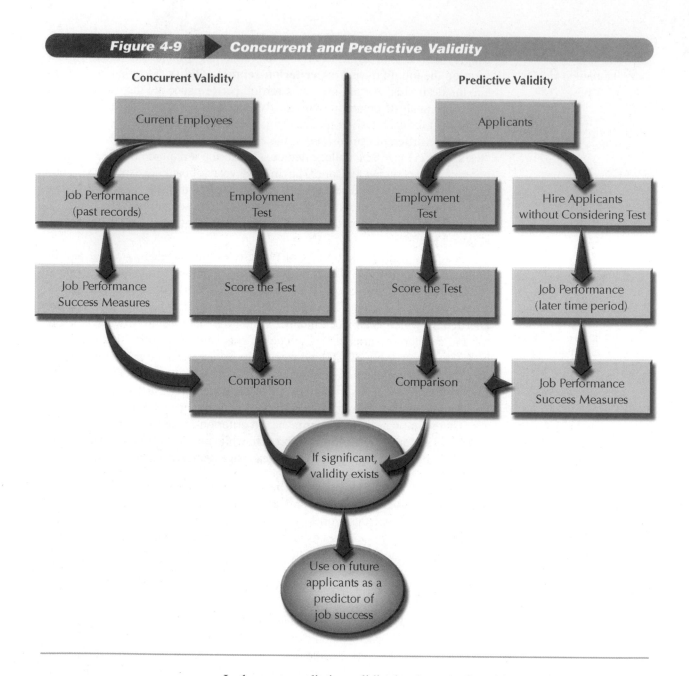

Figure 4-9 ▶ Concurrent and Predictive Validity

In the past, predictive validity has been preferred by the EEOC because it is presumed to be most closely tied to job performance. However, predictive validity requires: (1) a fairly large number of people (usually at least 30), and (2) a time gap between the test and the performance (usually one year). As a result, predictive validity is not useful in many situations. Because of these and other problems, other types of validity are more popular.

Construct validity Validity showing a relationship between an abstract characteristic and job performance.

Construct Validity

Construct validity shows a relationship between an abstract characteristic inferred from research and job performance. Researchers who study behavior have given various personality characteristics names, such as *introversion,* *aggression,* and *dominance.* These are called *constructs.* Other common constructs for which tests have been devised include *creativity, leadership potential,* and *interpersonal sensitivity.* Because a hypothetical construct is used as a predictor in establishing this type of validity, personality tests and tests that measure other such constructs are more likely to be questioned for their legality and usefulness than other measures of validity. Consequently, construct validity is used less frequently in employment situations than the other types of validity.

Elements of EEO Compliance

Employers must comply with a variety of EEO regulations and guidelines. To do so, management should have an EEO policy statement and maintain all required EEO-related records.

EEO Policy Statement

It is crucial that all employers have a written EEO policy statement. This policy should be widely communicated by posting it on bulletin boards, printing it in employee handbooks, reproducing it in organizational newsletters, and reinforcing it in training programs. The contents of the policy should clearly state the organizational commitment to equal employment, and incorporate the listing of the appropriate protected classes.

EEO Records

All employers with 15 or more employees are required to keep certain records that can be requested by the Equal Employment Opportunity Commission (EEOC), the Office of Federal Contract Compliance Programs (OFCCP), or other state and local enforcement agencies. Under various laws, employers also are required to post an "officially approved notice" in a prominent place where employees can see it. This notice states that the employer is an equal opportunity employer and does not discriminate.

EEO Records Retention All employment records must be maintained as required by the EEOC. Such records include application forms and records concerning hiring, promotion, demotion, transfer, layoff, termination, rates of pay or other terms of compensation, and selection for training and apprenticeship. Even application forms or test papers completed by unsuccessful applicants may be requested. The length of time documents must be kept varies, but generally *three years is recommended as a minimum.* Complete records are necessary to enable an employer to respond should a charge of discrimination be made.

EEO-1 Form
Provides a copy of the EEO-1 form.
Custom Search:
☑ FORMS
Phrase: EEO-1

Annual Reporting Form The basic report that must be filed with the EEOC is the annual report form EEO-1. The following employers must file this report:

- All employers with 100 or more employees, except state and local governments
- Subsidiaries of other companies where total employees equal 100
- Federal contractors with at least 50 employees and contracts of $50,000 or more
- Financial institutions with at least 50 employees in which government funds are held or saving bonds are issued

The annual report must be filed by March 31 for the preceding year. The form requires employment data by job category, classified according to various protected classes.

Applicant Flow Data Under EEO laws and regulations, employers may be required to show that they do not discriminate in the recruiting and selection of members of protected classes. Because collection of racial data on application blanks and other pre-employment records is not permitted, the EEOC allows employers to use a "visual" survey or a separate *applicant flow form* that is not used in the selection process. This form is filled out voluntarily by the applicant, and the data must be maintained separately from other selection-related materials. These analyses may be useful in showing whether an employer has underutilized a protected class because of an inadequate applicant flow of protected-class members, in spite of special efforts to recruit them. Also, these data are reported as part of Affirmative Action Plans that are filed with the OFCCP.

EEOC Compliance Investigation Process

When a discrimination complaint is received by the EEOC or a similar agency, it must be processed. To handle a growing number of complaints, the EEOC has instituted a system that categorizes complaints into three categories: *priority, needing further investigation,* and *immediate dismissal.* If the EEOC decides to pursue a complaint, it uses the process outlined here.

Compliance Investigative Stages In a typical situation, an EEO complaint goes through several stages before the compliance process is completed. First, the charges are filed by an individual, a group of individuals, or their representative. A charge must be filed within 180 days of when the alleged discriminatory action occurred. Then the EEOC staff reviews the specifics of the charges to determine if it has *jurisdiction,* which means that the agency is authorized to investigate that type of charge. If jurisdiction exists, a notice of the charge must be served on the employer within 10 days after the filing; the employer is asked to respond. Following the charge notification, the EEOC's major effort turns to investigating the complaint.

During the investigation, the EEOC may interview the complainants, other employees, company managers, and supervisors. Also, it can request additional records and documents from the employer. Assuming that sufficient cause is found that alleged discrimination occurred, the next stage involves mediation efforts by the agency and the employer. **Mediation** is a dispute resolution process by which a third party assists negotiators in reaching a settlement. The EEOC has found that use of mediation has reduced its backlog of EEO complaints and has resulted in faster resolution of complaints. More than 90% of employers using mediation said they would use it in future cases.[39]

If the employer agrees that discrimination has occurred and accepts the proposed settlement, then the employer posts a notice of relief within the company and takes the agreed-on actions. If the employer objects to the charge and rejects conciliation, the EEOC can file suit or issue a **right-to-sue letter** to the complainant. The letter notifies the complainant that he or she has 90 days in which to file a personal suit in federal court.

In the court litigation stage, a legal trial takes place in the appropriate state or federal court. At that point, both sides retain lawyers and rely on the court to

Logging On...

U.S. Equal Employment Opportunity Commission
The commission's website provides information about its purpose, facts about employment discrimination, enforcement statistics, and details on technical assistance programs.

http://www.eeoc.gov

Mediation Process by which a third party assists negotiators in reaching a settlement.

Right-to-sue letter A letter issued by the EEOC that notifies a complainant that he or she has 90 days in which to file a personal suit in federal court.

Figure 4-10 ► *Stages in Responding to EEO Complaints*

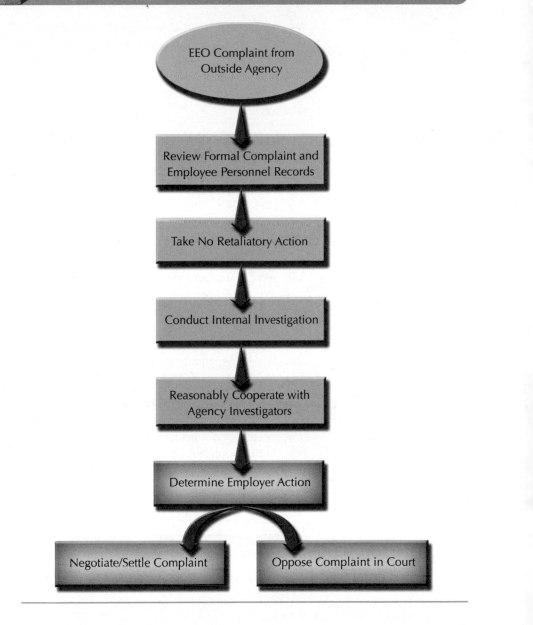

render a decision. The Civil Rights Act of 1991 provides for jury trials in most EEO cases. If either party disagrees with the court ruling, either can file appeals with a higher court. The U.S. Supreme Court becomes the ultimate adjudication body.

Employer Responses to EEO Complaints

The general steps in responding effectively to an EEO complaint are outlined in Figure 4-10 and discussed next. Many problems and expenses associated with EEO complaints can be controlled by employers who vigorously investigate their employees' discrimination complaints before they are taken to outside agencies. An internal employee complaint system and prompt, thorough

responses to problem situations are essential tools in reducing EEO charges and in remedying illegal discriminatory actions.

Review Claim and Employee's Personnel File By reviewing the claim, the HR staff can determine which individuals and agencies are handling the investigation. Also, any personnel files on the employees involved should be reviewed to determine the nature and adequacy of internal documentation. For many employers, contacting outside legal counsel at this point also may be advisable.

Take No Retaliatory Action It is crucial that no retaliatory actions, even snide remarks, be used against individuals filing EEO complaints. The HR staff also should notify relevant managers and supervisors of the complaint, instructing them to refrain from any retaliatory actions, such as changing job assignments or work schedules unnecessarily. However, appropriate disciplinary action that is work-related still can be administered.

Conduct Internal Investigation A thorough internal investigation of the facts and circumstances of the claim should be conducted. Some firms use outside legal counsel to conduct these investigations in order to obtain a more objective view. Once the investigative data have been obtained, then a decision about the strength or weakness of the employer's case should be determined. If the case is weak, possible settlement discussions may begin with the enforcement agency representatives. However, if the employer believes that a strong case exists, then the employer likely will draft a response stating the relevant facts and reasons why the employer does not believe the complaint is valid.

Determine Whether to Negotiate, Settle, or Oppose Complaint Once the agency investigation has been completed, the employer will be notified of the results. Also, the remedies proposed by the agency investigators will be identified. At that point, the HR staff, outside legal counsel, and senior managers often meet to decide whether to settle the complaint, negotiate different terms of the settlement, or to oppose the charges and begin court proceedings.

Summary

- Diversity is a broad concept that recognizes differences among people; equal employment opportunity (EEO) holds that individuals should have equal treatment in all employment-related actions.
- Affirmative action requires employers to identify problem areas in the employment of protected-class members and to set goals and take steps to overcome them, but concerns have been raised about "reverse discrimination."
- The 1964 Civil Rights Act, Title VII, was the first significant equal employment law. The Civil Rights Act of 1991 both altered and expanded on the 1964 provisions.

- Employers must be able to defend their management practices based on *bona fide* occupational qualifications (BFOQ), business necessity, and job relatedness.
- Disparate treatment occurs when protected-class members are treated differently from others, regardless of discriminatory intent.
- Disparate impact occurs when employment decisions work to the disadvantage of members of protected classes, regardless of discriminatory intent.
- Employers have the burden of proof once a *prima facie* case of discrimination has been

- shown, and they should take care to avoid retaliation against individuals who exercise their rights.
- Many employers are required to develop affirmative action plans (AAPs) that identify problem areas in the employment of protected-class members and initiate goals and steps to overcome those problems.
- Laws on sex/gender discrimination have addressed issues regarding pregnancy discrimination, unequal pay for similar jobs, and sexual harassment.
- The Americans with Disabilities Act (ADA) requires that most employers identify the essential functions of jobs and make reasonable accommodation for individuals with disabilities, unless undue hardship results.
- Age discrimination against persons over age 40 is illegal, based on the Age Discrimination in Employment Acts.
- The Immigration Reform and Control Acts identify employment regulations affecting workers from other countries.
- A number of other concerns have been addressed by laws, including discrimination based on religion, genetic bias, appearance and weight, sexual orientation, and others.
- The Equal Employment Opportunity Commission (EEOC) and the Office of Federal Contract Compliance Programs (OFCCP) are the major federal equal employment enforcement agencies.

- The 1978 Uniform Guidelines on Employee Selection Procedures are used by enforcement agencies to examine recruiting, hiring, promotion, and many other employment practices. Two alternative compliance approaches are identified: (1) no disparate impact, and (2) job-related validation.
- Job-related validation requires that tests measure what they are supposed to measure (validity) in a consistent manner (reliability).
- Disparate impact can be determined through the use of the 4/5ths rule.
- One of the three types of validity, content-validity, uses a sample of the actual work to be performed.
- The two criterion-related strategies measure concurrent validity and predictive validity. Predictive validity involves a "before-the-fact" measure, whereas concurrent validity involves a comparison of tests and criteria measures available at the same time.
- Construct validity involves the relationship between a measure of an abstract characteristic, such as intelligence, and job performance.
- Implementation of equal employment opportunity requires appropriate record keeping, such as completing the annual report (EEO-1), and keeping applicant flow data.

Review and Discussion Questions

1. If you were asked by an employer to review an employment decision to determine if discrimination had occurred, what factors would you consider, and how would you evaluate them?
2. Why is the Civil Rights Act of 1964, Title VII, such a significant law?
3. Based on your experiences, identify examples of sex discrimination in jobs.
4. The Americans with Disabilities Act contains several key terms. Define the following: (a) *essential job function,* (b) *reasonable accommodation,* and (c) *undue hardship.*

5. Respond to the following comment made by the president of a company: "It's getting so that you can't ask anybody anything personal."
6. Why is the job-related validation approach considered more business-oriented than the no-disparate-impact approach in complying with the 1978 Uniform Guidelines on Employee Selection Procedures?
7. Explain what validity is and why the content validity approach is growing in use compared with the criterion-related and construct validity approaches.
8. What process would be followed if you filed a discrimination complaint against a former employer?

Using the Internet

Recruiting Individuals with Disabilities

You are an HR Recruiter who has just been promoted to HR Manager, so you are training your replacement for the position of Recruiter. You have been recruiting for a highly technical engineering position within your organization. You have had many applicants apply for the position, but you have narrowed it down to two qualified applicants. One of the two qualified applicants has a disability. You decide this situation is ideal for the new recruiter to learn and deal with the Americans with Disabilities Act. You have decided to take this opportunity to make sure the new recruiter understands compliance requirements of the act and how those requirements might be applied in this situation. To help this new recruiter, consult the U.S. Department of Justice, American with Disabilities Act Web site, found at:

http://www.usdoj.gov/crt/ada/adhom1.htm.
Please prepare answers to the following questions.

- What practices and activities are covered by the employment and nondiscrimination requirements?
- What is a "reasonable accommodation"?
- Does an employer have to give preference to a qualified applicant with a disability over another qualified applicant?

Race Discrimination Costs Coca-Cola

Recently Coca-Cola paid $192.5 million to settle race discrimination charges, which is one of the largest penalties for race discrimination ever paid. Originally brought by eight current and former African American employees, the charges were expanded to become a class action lawsuit covering more than 2,000 individuals.

The plaintiffs charged that Coke used discriminatory practices in determining pay, performance evaluations, and promotions. Statistics cited by the employees who worked for Coke from 1995 until the case was filed seemed to support the allegations of racial disparities. For instance, at Coke's headquarters in Atlanta, Georgia, the median salary for African American employees was $36,000, compared with $65,000 for white employees working there. In addition, it was likely that the differences in performance evaluations between African American and white employees had an impact in the promotions received by minority employees. Consequently, the plaintiffs alleged that African American employees composed a significantly lower percentage of managers and executives than was found to exist when the labor force demographics in the area were compared.

Settlement of the cases included both monetary and non-monetary aspects. In settling the lawsuit, the $192.5 million was to be divided whereby the employees in the class action received $92.4 million, their attorneys received $20.6 million, $43.5 million was to be used to ensure future salary comparability between white and nonwhite employees, and $36 million was to be used for diversity programs.

As part of the settlement, Coca-Cola agreed to establish a seven-person task force, composed of individuals outside the firm, to oversee future diversity efforts. The task force was given responsibilities for conducting a review of all of Coke's employment processes, and the company had to implement the recommendations of the task force except in unusual circumstances. Also, managerial diversity goals were established and reported annually to the firm's board of directors, which also has to have its membership become more diverse.

But Coke's problems may not be over, because some of the plaintiffs have filed a separate $1.5 billion racial bias suit. Others in the class group have refused to sign the agreement, and have hired high-profile attorneys to sue Coke for additional damages. Thus, the ultimate costs to Coca-Cola in terms of its reputation, as well as financial and managerial consequences, are likely to be significantly more than the dollars paid in the settlement.[40]

Questions

1. Describe how the legal concepts of disparate impact and disparate treatment may have been used by the plaintiffs in this case.
2. Discuss some of the likely effects of the lawsuit and its consequences on the management of human resources at Coca-Cola.

1. Daniel Machalaba, "Norfolk Southern Set to Pay $28 Million to Black Workers in Race-Bias Lawsuit," *The Wall Street Journal,* January 10, 2001, B13; "Bakery Workers Awarded $131 Million on Race Bias Claims," *Fair Employment Practices,* August 17, 2000, 99; "Firm Ordered to Pay $710,000 in English-only Lawsuit, *Fair Employment Practices,* October 12, 2000, 128; "CBS Will Pay $8 Million in Settlement of Female TV Technicians' Bias Claims," *Fair Employment Practices,* November 9, 2000, 135–136; *Anderson v. Stefani Management Services,* N.D. Ill., 99-D5410, November 15, 2000; "Around the States," *Fair Employment Practices,* February 15, 2001; "President Can Be Held Individually Liable for Harassment of Former Paramour," *Fair Employment Practices,* January 4, 2001; "American Airlines Will Pay $1.7 Million," *Fair Employment Practices,* August 17, 2000; Age Discrimination Claim Nets President $6 Million," available at *www.hrcomply. com,* February 21, 2001; and "$5 Million Age Bias Settlement," *Fair Employment Practices,* February 3, 2000, 17.

2. *Bass v. Board of County Commissioners,* 11th Ct. U.S., 99-10579, February 21, 2001.

3. *Bakke v. the University of California,* 438 U.S. 193 (1978).

4. *Hopwood v. State of Texas,* 78 F.3d 932 (1996).

5. *http://allpolitics.com/1998/04/01/ap/affirmative.action/.*

6. "Court Orders Michigan Employment Agency to End Wholesale Discrimination," *The Wall Street Journal,* May 2, 2000, A1.

7. Civil Rights Act of 1964, Title VII, sec. 703a.

8. *Griggs v. Duke Power Co.,* 401 U.S. 424 (1971).

9. *Reeves v. Sanderson Plumbing Products, Inc.,* 530 U.S. 99-536, June 12, 2000.

10. *O'Neal v. Ferguson Construction Co.,* 10th Ct. U.S. 99-2037, January 24, 2001.

11. For details, see *www.dol.gov/ofccp.*

12. In depicting the components of AAPs, the authors acknowledge the assistance of Raymond B. Weinberg, SPHR, CCP; and Kathleen Shotkoski, SPHR, of Omaha, NE.

13. Reginald E. Jones and Dara L. Dehaven, "OFCCP's Revised 60-2 Regulations," *Legal Report,* January/February 2001, 1–4.

14. *Arimindo v. Padlocker, Inc.,* 11th Cir, 99-4144, April 20, 2000.

15. "Additional Pregnancy Bias Rulings," *Fair Employment Practices,* March 9, 2000, 78.

16. "EEOC Ruling on Contraceptives May Be Costly for Employers," *HR Executive,* February 2001, 10+.

17. "Comparing Apples and Apples, Plaintiffs Must Cut to the Core," *Bulletin to Management,* January 11, 2001, 14.

18. *Ryduchowski v. Port Authority of NY and NJ,* 2d Cir, 99-7397, February 8, 2000; and *EEOC v. Eastern Michigan University,* E.D. Michigan, 98-71806, September 3, 1999.

19. Adapted from George F. Dreher and Taylor H. Cox, Jr., "Labor Market Mobility and Cash Compensation: The Moderating Effects of Race and Gender," *Academy of Management Journal,* 43(2000), 890–900.

20. U.S. Census Bureau, 2001.

21. Howard J. Well, "The Gender Wage Gap and Wage Discrimination: Illusion or Reality?" *The Regional Economist,* October 2000, available at *www.stls.org/publications.*

22. *Board of Trustees of University of Alabama v. Garrett,* February 21, 2001.

23. *PGA Tour v. Martin,* 00-24, 2001, WL 567717, May 29, 2001.

24. *Sutton v. United Airlines, Inc.,* 9 AD Cases 673, 1999.

25. Jonathan A. Segal, "I'm Depressed—Accommodate Me," *HR Magazine,* February 2001, 139–148.

26. *Bragdon v. Abbott,* U.S. S.Ct. No. 97-156, June 25, 1998.

27. "Employers' ADA Obligations to Engage in Interactive Process," *Fair Employment Practices,* September 14, 2000, 114.

28. *Kimel v. Florida, Board of Regents,* U.S. S.Ct., 98-791, 2000.

29. "Firing Line Reveals Age Discrimination," *Workforce,* February 2000, 28.

30. *TransWorld Airlines v. Hardison,* 432 U.S. 63 (1977).

31. *Ansari v. Ray and Claude Goodwin, Inc.,* MD, Fla, 3:98-C-1052-J-20C, March 29, 2000.

32. Based on Jeanne Cummings and Glenn Simpson, "Bush Readies Plan for Legislation To Prevent Genetic Discrimination." *The Wall Street Journal,* June 25, 2001, B2; Andrew R. McIlvaine, "Under the Microscope," *Human Resource Executive,* January 2000, 90–94; and Grace Shim, "BN Apologizes for Genetic Testing," *Omaha World-Herald,* March 9, 2001, 21+.

33. R. K. Miller, "Weighty Issues," *Human Resource Executive,* May 2001, 50–54.

34. "Accommodations Under ADA Take Back Seat to Contracts," *Bulletin to Management,* January 18, 2001, 22.

35. *Kyles v. J.K. Guardian Service,* 7th Cir, 98–3652, July 5, 2000; and *EEOC v. K & J Management,* N.D. Ill., 99-C8116, June 7, 2000.

36. "Adoption by Four Agencies of Uniform Guideline on Employee Selection Procedures, (1978)," *Federal Register,* August 15, 1978, Part IV, 38295-38309.

37. Scott B. Morris and Russell E. Lobsenz, "Significance Tests and Confidence Intervals for the Adverse Impact Ratio," *Personnel Psychology* 53 (2000), 89–111.

38. For example, see Herbert G. Heneman, Robert Heneman, and Timothy A. Judge, *Staffing Organizations,* 3 ed. (New York: McGraw-Hill-Irwin, 2000).

39. "Mediation, Small Business Initiative Cited in FY 2000 Report," *Fair Labor Practices,* February 1, 2001, 16.

40. Based on "Coca-Cola Litigants Request Settlement Delay," *HR Comply, available at http://216.133.243. 67/newsletter,* March 21, 2001; Joshua M. Javits, "It's the Real Thing: $192.5 Million," *Legal Report,* March–April 2001 1; Theresa Howard, "Coke Settles Bias Lawsuit for $192.5 M," *USA Today,* November 17, 2000, 1B; and Coca Cola Agrees to pay $192.5 Million," *Fair Employment Practices,* November 23, 2000, 141.

CHAPTER 5

Managing Diversity and Equal Employment

After you have read this chapter, you should be able to:

- Define *diversity management*, and discuss why it is important.

- Discuss several arguments supporting and opposing affirmative action.

- Identify why racial/ethnic diversity is likely to grow in organizations.

- Describe how women are affected by work/family and job assignment issues in organizations.

- Discuss the two types of sexual harassment and how employers should respond to complaints.

- Identify two means organizations are using to deal with the aging of their workforces.

- Discuss how reasonable accommodation is made when managing individuals with disabilities and differing religious beliefs.

Booming Hispanic Workforce and Diversity Issues

As the population of the United States has grown, its composition has changed and become more diverse. Especially over the decade from 1990 to 2000, the greatest growth throughout the United States of any ethnic group occurred in the Hispanic population. According to the 2000 U.S. census, the number of individuals identifying themselves as being of Hispanic origin grew by 58%, compared to a 13% growth rate for the U.S. population as a whole. As a result, the 35.3 million Hispanic Americans compose about the same percentage of the U.S. population as African Americans. Also, the Hispanic population is widely dispersed throughout the U.S., even though higher concentrations of Hispanics exist in California, Arizona, New Mexico, Texas, and Florida.

Employers large and small are recognizing that their Hispanic employees represent a significant talent pool that will be a growing part of the future workforce. But with this growth comes increasing HR challenges for organizations of all sizes and types. Surveys of Hispanic employees consistently reveal that many non-Hispanic managers and employers have negative stereotypical images of Hispanics. This translates into Hispanics feeling that they do not have access to the same opportunities that white and even African American employees have. The stereotyping leads to denial of employment opportunities, diminished promotional possibilities, and greater disciplinary disparity between Hispanics and non-Hispanics.

Fortunately, a number of employers have recognized that Hispanics are important in their workforces. Some examples follow:

- A number of firms such as PriceWaterhouseCoopers and the Gap actively recruit at college campuses that have large numbers of Hispanic students in order to demonstrate that Hispanics are welcome and have good career opportunities.
- Such firms as K-Mart advertise for employees in Hispanic publications and post job openings on Spanish language online job sites.
- Organizations with large Hispanic customer bases have found that having employees with Spanish fluency means being able to respond to Spanish-speaking customers more effectively.
- Employers with a large number of Hispanic workers have Hispanic HR staff members who serve as translators when conducting new employee orientations, safety meetings, and job training programs. That means those with limited English skills are given information needed for them to be productive employees.
- Firms such as American Airlines have encouraged managers and employees in Tucson, Arizona, Miami, Florida, and other cities to become active in community affairs, such as Hispanic Chambers of Commerce, school partnerships, and community groups. One side effect of such involvement is that these firms get a greater number of Hispanic applicants and Hispanic employee referrals for job openings.

The diversity of the workforce provides both opportunities and challenges. Enlightened employers are tapping the growing pool of Hispanic workers, as well as ensuring that all individuals regardless of their backgrounds and differences are viewed as valuable human resources.[1]

The diversity of the workforce provides both opportunities and challenges.

"If you think diversity is all about race and gender, you have not been keeping up. The new diversity is about differences of all kinds."

—**Eric Watson**

Diversity The differences among people.

Two key words that describe what is happening in the U.S. population and workforce are *change* and *diversity*. Change is seen in the shifting makeup of the U.S. population. **Diversity** is about the differences among people, but there is some controversy over what diversity means.[2] As used by most employers and enforcement agencies, the concept of diversity typically includes the dimensions depicted in Figure 5-1.

Any of these dimensions can create conflicts among people at work, but they can also bring the advantages of different ideas and viewpoints. As organizations and managers have more diverse individuals in the workplace, they are finding that diversity is a strategic HR consideration.

Managing Diversity

Diversity is seen in demographic differences in the workforce. The U.S. workforce is more diverse racially, women are in the labor force in much greater numbers than ever before, and the average age of the workforce is now considerably older than before. As a result of these and other demographic shifts, HR management in organizations has had to adapt to a more diverse labor force both externally and internally. Among the problems to be addressed as part of managing diversity is to deal with a number of concerns often cited by protected group individuals as well as others. Two common concerns are *perceived hostile organizational cultures* and *stereotyping*.

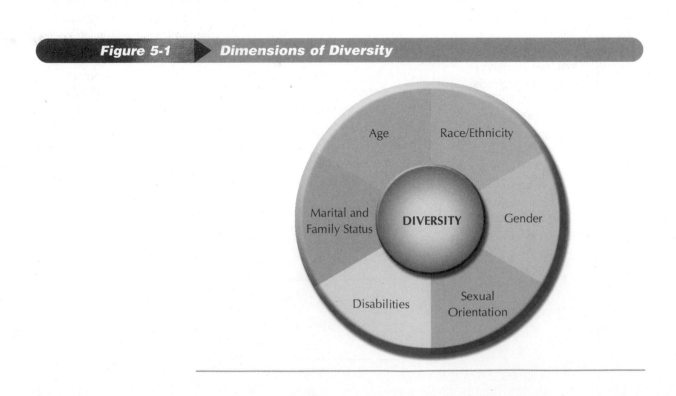

Figure 5-1 **Dimensions of Diversity**

Many protected group persons perceive that they work in organizational cultures that are hostile to them. For instance, the perceptions are striking when racial/ethnic minorities are interviewed. Over a 20-year period, 75% to 85% of African American workers surveyed consistently indicated a belief that people of color had to perform better than whites to get ahead.[3] Studies of the perceptions of women workers have revealed similar beliefs.

The primary way to overcome these perceptions is to have an active diversity management program. Only by working to create a culture that is inclusive can organizational cultures be seen as less hostile by racial/ethnic minorities, women, older workers, those with disabilities, as well as those who are white, male, and younger.

Another concern often voiced by people of color is the stereotyping that occurs. Often these stereotypes are based on previous negative experiences and limited recent contacts with people in a certain group. The result of stereotyping in workplaces is to create conflicts between groups of people and to lead to less workplace interaction and cooperation, which is why managing diversity is so important.

Approaches to Managing Diversity

Organizations can approach the management of diversity from several different perspectives. As Figure 5-2 shows, the continuum can run from resistance to creation of an inclusive diversity culture. The increasing diversity of the workforce available, combined with growing shortages of workers in many occupations and industries, has forced more employers to recognize that diversity must be

Figure 5-2 ▶ *Continuum of Diversity Approaches*

	Resistance	Fairness	Access-Legitimacy	Diversity Culture
Viewpoint	*Diversity not important and does not affect management*	*Diversity creates conflicts and problems*	*Diversity provides opportunities for employers and organizations*	*Diversity culture permeates organization*
Action	• *Resistant to change* • *Denial of problems*	• *Diversity training* • *Affirmative Action compliance* • *Focus on protected groups*	• *Build "diversity acceptance" culture* • *Reduce conflicts in multicultural workforce*	• *Proactive efforts on diversity* • *Employees are seen as resources*
Consequences	• *Protect status quo* • *Increased possible legal liabilities*	• *Discrimination addressed through internal responses* • *Minimize legal exposure*	• *All employees are valuable to recruit and retain* • *Acceptance leads to internal problem-solving*	• *Effective relations among all employees* • *Diversity access throughout organization*

Source: Adapted from ideas suggested by Stella M. Nkomo and Ellen Ernst Kossek, "Managing Diversity," in Ellen Ernst Kossek and Richard N. Block, *Managing Human Resources in the 21st Century* (Cincinnati: Thomson Learning, 2000), Chapter 9; and Parshotam Dass and Barbara Parker, "Strategies for Managing Human Resource Diversity," *Academy of Management Executive,* May 1999, 68–80.

Research on Racial Diversity and Organizational Performance

The importance of "valuing diversity" has been stated often by both employers and employees. However, relatively few studies have empirically examined how diversity in organizations is linked to organizational performance.

Orlando Richard focused on racial diversity and the productivity and performance of firms in the banking industry in a study presented in the *Academy of Management Journal.* Richard used data that all banks are required to report to government regulators, which is also available in reports accessible to others. He used a sample of banks from California, Kentucky, and North Carolina in order to get data from banks in states having varying degrees of diversity and financial growth.

Using the government listing he contacted HR managers at each of the banks and asked them to complete a written questionnaire on each firm's workforce composition and approach to diversity. A total of 63 banks were represented in the survey responses, which were then compared to data on the performance of each of the banks. Firm performance measures used included asset growth and employee productivity. This productivity was calculated by determining a bank's net income to the number of employees, return on equity, and survey responses regarding marketing, growth, and profitability.

Once Richard statistically analyzed all the data, he found that banks having growth strategies that had high racial diversity had higher productivity. However, little statistical evidence supported the connection between just having racial diversity and higher bank performance.

The major implication of the study is that racial diversity can affect productivity, which can affect organizational performance if the firm has growth as a strategy. However, for banks where growth is not as important, the increased employee productivity does not necessarily lead to better overall bank financial performance. In summary, racial diversity can make a difference in organizational performance if a firm values growth, but if it does not stress growth, then the advantages of racial diversity are diminished.[4]

addressed. Further, the increasing prevalence of protected group members filing legal complaints has increased the legal liabilities faced by employers who resist diversity and engage in discriminatory employment practices. Therefore, organizations large and small see important reasons for proactively addressing diversity issues. These employers experience significant benefits because of their diversity efforts, including those described next.

Diversity and Organizational Performance A number of organizations have found that because they serve a diverse set of customers, there are significant business reasons for having a diverse workforce.[5] The employees have greater cultural understanding of how products and services can be viewed and accepted by different groups. The value of diversity is reinforced by a survey that found a majority of both HR professionals and job seekers believes diversity initiatives have made organizations more successful.[6] For example, Charles Schwab & Co. has identified ethnic groups for marketing its financial services. Schwab has an online Spanish language Web site that is generating about 10,000 hits per week. Also, the firm has targeted Chinese Americans for a major marketing effort by opening 14 Chinese-language offices in major cities such as New York City and San Francisco.[7]

Even though many organizations have instituted diversity programs, most of them have not documented how diversity efforts affect organizational perfor-

mance. However, some research sheds light on how diversity is linked to organizational performance as the HR Perspective on the opposite page describes.

Recruiting and Retention A second reason for diversity efforts is that they aid in recruiting and retaining workers from diverse backgrounds. Not surprisingly, people of different backgrounds prefer to work in an organization where there are others "like" them. Support for the important role that diversity plays in recruiting and retention comes from a study of 750 diverse professional job holders. That study found that one-third of minority and female job candidates will rule out an employer because of perceived lack of diversity.[8]

Diverse Thinking and Problem Solving Another advantage of embracing diversity is to get more diverse thinking and problem solving. Groups containing people with widely varying backgrounds are more likely to see factors and issues differently and consider a greater range of decision alternatives. One example illustrates this point. A group of managers were planning the introduction of a new telecommunications service. By having African American and Hispanic employees who come from less affluent economic backgrounds as part of the planning, the firm developed multitier pricing and service plans that would appeal to low and moderate income consumers, not just the more affluent ones.

Reduction in Discrimination Complaints and Costs Even if all the advantages of diversity are ignored, efforts that ensure compliance with EEO laws and regulations can reduce the time and legal costs associated with discrimination complaints. Legal experts and others have noticed that when employers tolerate incidents of discrimination or other inappropriate actions to individuals based on "being different," then isolated incidents spread to become bigger organizational issues.[9]

Diversity Management Programs and Activities

A wide variety of programs and activities have been used in organizations as part of diversity management efforts. Figure 5-3 on the next page shows common components of diversity management efforts. For diversity to succeed, the most crucial component is for diversity to be seen as a commitment throughout the organization, beginning with top management.[10] Diversity results must be measured and management accountability for achieving these results must be emphasized and rewarded. Once management accountability for diversity results has been established, then a number of different activities can be implemented as part of a diversity management program, including diversity training.

Diversity Training

There are a number of different goals for diversity training.[11] One prevalent goal is to minimize discrimination and harassment lawsuits. But other goals focus on improving acceptance and understanding of people with different backgrounds, experiences, capabilities, and lifestyles.

Components of Diversity Training

Approaches to training vary, but often include at least three components. *Legal awareness* is the first and most common component of diversity training. Here

Figure 5-3 ▶ **Common Diversity Management Components**

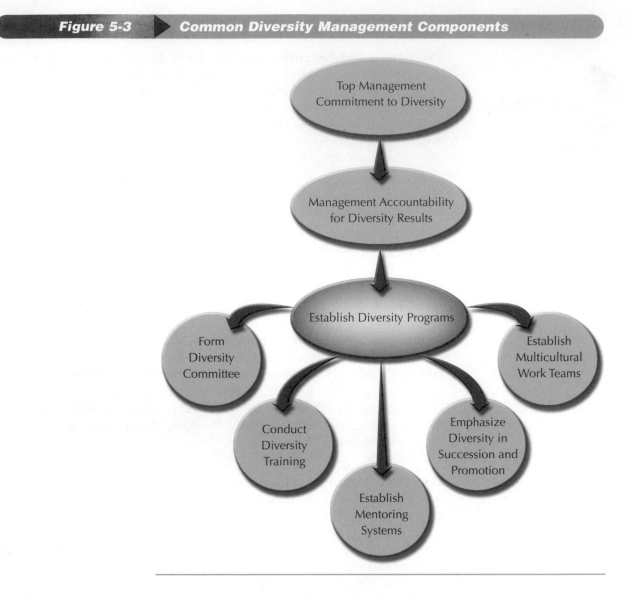

the training focuses on the legal implications of discrimination. A limited approach to diversity training stops with these legal "do's and don'ts."

By introducing *cultural awareness,* employers hope to build greater understanding of the differences among people. Cultural awareness training assists all participants to see and accept the differences in people with widely varying cultural backgrounds.

The third component of diversity training—*sensitivity training*—is more difficult. The aim here is to "sensitize" people to the differences among them and how their words and behaviors are seen by others. Some diversity training includes exercises containing examples of harassment and other behaviors.

Effects of Diversity Training

The effects of diversity training are viewed as mixed by both organizations and participants. Relatively few studies have been done on the effectiveness of diver-

Logging On...

The Diversity Training Group
Describes diversity training materials and resources.

http://diversitydtg.com/

sity training expenditures, other than asking participants how they felt about the training. There is some concern that the programs may be interesting or entertaining, but may not produce longer-term changes in people's attitudes and behaviors toward others with characteristics different from their own.

Mixed reviews about the effectiveness of diversity training suggest that either the programs or how they are implemented are suspect. Two common complaints are:

1. Diversity training tends to draw attention to differences, building walls rather than breaking them down.
2. Much of the content in diversity training is viewed as "politically correct," which blames majority individuals, particularly white males, for past wrongs.

Some argue that diversity training more often than not has failed, pointing out that it does not reduce discrimination and harassment complaints. Rather than reducing conflict, in a number of situations diversity training has heightened hostility and conflicts.[12] In a number of firms it has produced divisive effects, and has not taught the behaviors needed for employees to get along in a diverse workplace.

This last point, focusing on behaviors, seems to hold the most promise for making diversity training more effective. For instance, dealing with cultural diversity as part of training efforts for sales representatives and managers has produced positive results.[13] Teaching appropriate behaviors and skills in relationships with others is more likely to produce satisfactory results than focusing just on attitudes and beliefs among diverse employees.

Backlash Against Diversity Efforts

The negative consequences of diversity training manifest themselves more broadly in a backlash against diversity efforts. This backlash takes two main forms. First, and somewhat surprisingly, the individuals in protected groups, such as women and racial minorities, sometimes see the diversity efforts as inadequate and nothing but "corporate public relations." Thus, it appears that by establishing diversity programs, employers are raising the expectation levels of protected group individuals, but the programs are not meeting these expectations.[14] This failure can result in further disillusionment and more negativity toward the organization by those who would initially appear to benefit the most from such programs.

On the other side, a number of those individuals who are not in protected groups, primarily white males, believes the emphasis on diversity sets them up as scapegoats for the societal problems created by increasing diversity. Surveys of white males frequently show hostility and anger at diversity efforts. Those programs are widely perceived as only benefitting women and minorities and taking away opportunities for men and non-minorities.[15] This resentment and hostility is usually directed at affirmative action programs that employers have instituted.

Affirmative Action and Diversity Efforts

Affirmative action began as a requirement for federal government contractors to document the inclusion of women and racial minorities in the workforce. As part

Diversity Training
Contains ten diversity tips and links to diversity management and training information.
Custom Search:
☑ ANALYSIS
Phrase: Consider diversity training

HR Perspectives

Affirmative Action Is Needed

1. Affirmative action is needed to overcome past injustices or eliminate the effects of those injustices. Proponents of affirmative action believe it is necessary because women and racial minorities in particular, have long been subjected to unfair employment treatment by being relegated to lower positions (such as clerical and low-paying jobs), being discriminated against for promotions, and being disciplined more often. Without affirmative action, the inequities will continue to exist for individuals who are not white males.

2. Affirmative action creates more equality for all persons, even if temporary injustice to some individuals may result. White males in particular may be disadvantaged temporarily in order for affirmative action to create broader opportunities for all.

Proponents argue for programs to enable women, minorities, and other protected group members to be competitive with males and non-minorities. Otherwise, they will never "catch up."

3. Raising the employment level of protected group members will benefit U.S. society in the long run. Statistics consistently indicate that the greatest percentage of those in lower socioeconomic groups belong to protected groups. As affirmative action assists these minorities, it addresses socioeconomic disparities. Without affirmative action, proponents argue that many in the U.S. will be permanently economically disadvantaged. When economic levels are low, other social ills proliferate, such as single-parent families, crime, drug use, and educational disparities.

4. Properly used, affirmative action does not discriminate against males or non-minorities. An affirmative action plan should have a deadline for accomplishing its long-term goals, but individuals must meet the basic qualifications for jobs. Once all of these job criteria are established, qualified women or minorities should be chosen. In this way, those not selected are discriminated against only in the sense that they did not get the jobs.

5. Goals indicate progress needed, not quotas. Proponents of affirmative action also stress that affirmative action involves *goals* not *quotas.* The difference is that quotas are specific, required numbers, whereas goals are targets for "good faith" efforts to ensure that protected-group individuals truly are given consideration in employment-related decisions.

of those government regulations, covered employers must submit plans describing their attempts to narrow the gaps between the composition of their workforces and that of labor markets where they obtain employees. A practical concern with affirmative action efforts is how to "count" individuals with a multiracial background, such as the famous golfer Tiger Woods, whose father is African American and mother is Asian American. In fact, in the 2000 U.S. Census almost 7 million people classified themselves as multiracial, and in California almost 5% of the population classified themselves as being of two or more races.[16]

By setting *goals, targets,* and *time tables* as part of affirmative action efforts, employers specify how many of which types of individuals they hope to have in their workforce in the future. By specifying these goals the employers say they are trying to "appropriately include protected group members" or "ensure a balanced and representative workforce." These phrases and others like them commonly are used to describe the thrust of affirmative action.

However, critics of affirmative action say that regardless of the language used, subsequent actions lead to the use of *preferential selection* for protected

Eliminate Affirmative Action

1. Affirmative action penalizes individuals (males and non-minorities) even though they have not been guilty of practicing discrimination. Opponents argue that affirmative action is unfair to "innocent victims"—males and non-minorities. These individuals had nothing to do with past discrimination or disparate impact and were not even present at the time. Thus, opponents of affirmative action wonder why these individuals should have to pay for the remediation of past discriminatory actions.

2. Creating preferences for certain groups results in reverse discrimination. Those opposed to affirmative action believe that discriminating *for* someone means discriminating *against* someone else. If equality is the ultimate aim, then discriminating for or against anyone on any basis other than the knowl-edge, skills, and abilities needed to perform jobs is wrong. Thus, discrimination in reverse is counter to creating a truly equal society.

3. Affirmative action results in greater polarization and separatism along gender and racial lines. The opponents of affirmative action believe that it establishes two groups: 1) women, minorities, and others in protected groups, and 2) everyone else. For any job, a person will clearly fall into one group or the other. Thus, affirmative action results in males and non-minorities being affected negatively because of their gender or race. Consequently, they become bitter against the protected groups, leading to greater racism, prejudice, and societal conflicts.

4. Affirmative action stigmatizes those it is designed to help. Because affirmative action has come to be viewed by some people as placing unqualified protected group members in jobs, it reinforces the beliefs held by some that women and minorities would not have succeeded on their own efforts. Thus, women or minority members who have responsible positions are there only because of who they are, not because of what they can do and have done. Additionally, when protected-group individuals perform poorly in jobs because they do not have the knowledge, skills, and abilities needed, the result is to reinforce gender or racial/ethnic stereotypes.

5. Goals become quotas by forcing employers to "play by the numbers." Opponents of affirmative action state that regardless of the language used, when goals or targets are set, they become quotas to be met. Otherwise employers are subjected to legal actions and condemnation.

---

group members over equally qualified white males and others not covered by the EEO regulations. The result is *reverse discrimination* whereby a person is refused employment opportunities because of being the "wrong" race, sex, age, or other classification.

Supporters have offered many reasons why affirmative action is necessary and important, while opponents argue against it. The reasons given by both sides are highlighted in the HR Perspective debate. Readers can examine the points in the debate to compare with their personal views of affirmative action.

Affirmative Action and Court Decisions As the composition of U.S. courts has changed, judicial views of affirmative action have changed also. Many of these decisions have been close votes in the courts, especially at the U.S. Supreme Court. Obviously as judges are appointed who are either more favorable or more skeptical of affirmative action, the legal status of affirmative action might change.

The HR Perspective on the next page describes one case that captures the contentious issues associated with affirmative action. In the five-plus years the case has been proceeding through the various federal courts, affirmative action has been both upheld and rejected. The ultimate decision rests with the U.S. Supreme Court.

Logging On...

The Affirmative Action and Diversity Project
Discusses differing opinions about affirmative action and its economic and cultural aspects

http://racerelations.about.com

Ethical and Legal Aspects of Affirmative Action

Many of the landmark cases dealing with affirmative have involved universities. The purpose of this HR Perspective is to give the key facts of a case involving the admission standards at the University of Michigan that has reached the U.S. Supreme Court. This case is highlighted because it clearly shows why affirmative action has become such a volatile issue.

The University of Michigan established a plan to increase social diversity of its student body by adopting the Michigan Mandate in 1987. This plan had a goal of increasing minority enrollment at the university from 13.5% to at least 25% in 10 years. By ensuring that more racial/ethnic minority individuals were admitted, the hope was to have a diverse student body and to increase college education opportunities for groups traditionally having lower rates of higher education degrees and opportunities.

The case began when two Michigan residents, Jennifer Gratz and Patrick Hamacher, applied for admission to the University of Michigan. Both students are white and had excellent academic records, were active in their respective schools, and had scored well on the ACT admissions test. For instance, Gratz had a 3.9 grade point average (GPA) and an ACT score of 25, and Hamacher had a 3.4 GPA and an ACT score of 28. However, both were rejected because the university also considered race as another criterion when determining admission. In fact, the university used a chart that showed that a minority student with a GPA of 3.0 and an ACT score of 18 would be accepted, but a white student with a GPA of 3.6 and an ACT score of 21 would be rejected. Applicants also could be deferred for admission depending upon the number of other admission slots filled. Clearly, different standards were being used, with the university's justification being to ensure racial diversity and access for minority students. The President of the University of Michigan defended the university's system by stating:

> The numbers make it sound like all we're interested in are digits. Our belief is this is the only way we can achieve diversity and remain highly selective. This (diversity) strikes at the very heart of what it means to be a great public university.[17]

How do you view the conflicting ethical and legal issues associated with affirmative action in this case?

Regardless of the viewpoints held about affirmative action, diversity is a reality that is a strategic HR concern to be addressed in all organizations. Also, despite the differing philosophical views of affirmative action, there are still a large number of EEO regulations and laws that exist. HR professionals must ensure that their organizations comply with EEO requirements for different protected groups. The following sections examine the nature, issues, and HR practices to be addressed in managing diversity and equal employment on the bases of race/national origin, sex/gender, disabilities, age, and others.

EEO Issues and Race, National Origin, and Citizenship

The original purpose of the Civil Rights Act of 1964 was to address race and national origin discrimination. This concern continues to be important today, and employers must be aware of practices that may be discriminatory on the basis of race, national origin, and citizenship.

Racial/Ethnic Demographics

Data from the U.S. 2000 census reveals that the racial/ethnic mix of the U.S. population continues to shift. As Figure 5-4 shows, the white population has

Figure 5-4 ▶ *Racial/Ethnic Composition of U.S. Population, 2000*

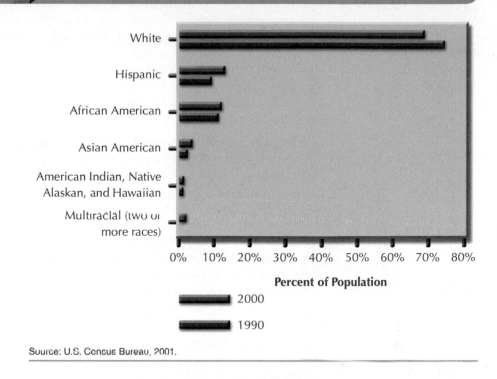

Percent of Population

2000

1990

Source: U.S. Census Bureau, 2001.

declined from 76% of the workforce in 1980 to about 69% in 2000. The greatest growth has been in the Hispanic population, as pointed out in the chapter opening discussion. Even more telling, almost 40% of all children are non-white, which is significant because they will be the workforce of the future.

Immigrants and Foreign-Born Worker Requirements

Much of the growth in the various racial and ethnic groups is due to immigration from other countries. Approximately 800,000–900,000 immigrants are arriving annually in the United States. These immigrants come into the country as temporary workers, visitors, students, illegals, or for other reasons. Recent statistics indicate that for many types of jobs, particularly the lower-skilled jobs in such areas as hospitality and agricultural businesses, workers with limited educational skills are coming from Mexico, Sudan, the Balkan countries, and poorer Latin American and Asian countries.

On the other hand, about one-fourth of all immigrants and foreign workers are college graduates. Increasingly, people with advanced degrees in science and engineering being hired by U.S. firms are foreign-born. For instance, many software firms are relying on individuals from India and other Asian countries for programmers and technology experts.[18] Because many employers have faced shortages of highly skilled workers, they consistently have lobbied to be able to "import" more workers to fill their jobs. As a result of their efforts, the American Competitiveness and Workforce Improvement Act was passed that increases the number of visas for highly skilled workers.

Visas and Documentation Requirements The increasing number of foreign-born workers means that employers must comply with the provisions of the Immigration Reform Control Acts. Employers are required to obtain and inspect I-9 forms, verification documents such as birth certificates, passports, visas, and work permits. A number of different types of visas can be obtained by individuals entering the United States. The visa category of highly skilled workers where shortages have been documented is called the H1-B. Other widely used categories are the J-series visas used by foreign college students.

Bilingual Employees and English-Only Requirements

As the diversity of the workforce has increased, more employees have language skills beyond English. Interestingly, some employers have attempted to restrict the use of foreign languages, while other employers have recognized that bilingual employees have valuable skills.

English-Only Requirements A number of employers have policies requiring that employees speak only English at work. Employers with these policies contend that the policies are necessary for valid business purposes. For instance, a manufacturer has a requirement that all employees working with dangerous chemicals use English in order to communicate hazardous situations to other workers and to be able to read chemical labels. The EEOC has issued guidelines clearly stating that employers may require workers to speak only English at certain times or in certain situations, but the business necessity of the requirements must be justified.[19]

Bilingual Employees A growing number of employers have found it beneficial to have bilingual employees so that foreign-language customers can contact someone speaking their languages. Some employers do not pay bilingual employees extra, believing that paying for the jobs being done is more appropriate than paying individuals for language skills that are used infrequently on the job. Other employers pay "language premiums" if employees must speak to customers in another language. For instance, MCI-WorldCom pays workers in some locations a 10% bonus if they are required to use a foreign language a majority of the time with customers. Regardless of the policies used, the reality is that language issues must be dealt with as part of managing a racially and ethnically diverse workforce.

Racial/Ethnic Harassment The area of harassment is such a concern that the EEOC has issued guidelines on racial/ethnic harassment. It is recommended that employers adopt policies against harassment of any type, including ethnic jokes, vulgar epithets, racial slurs, or physical actions. The advantage of taking quick remedial action is shown in a case in which an employee filed suit against Delta Airlines because co-workers told racist jokes and hung nooses in his workplace. However, each time any employee, including this plaintiff, reported an incident, Delta was able to show that management acted quickly by conducting an investigation and took corrective and disciplinary actions against the offending employees. Following the management actions, no further incidents occurred, so the court ruled for Delta Airlines in this particular case.[20]

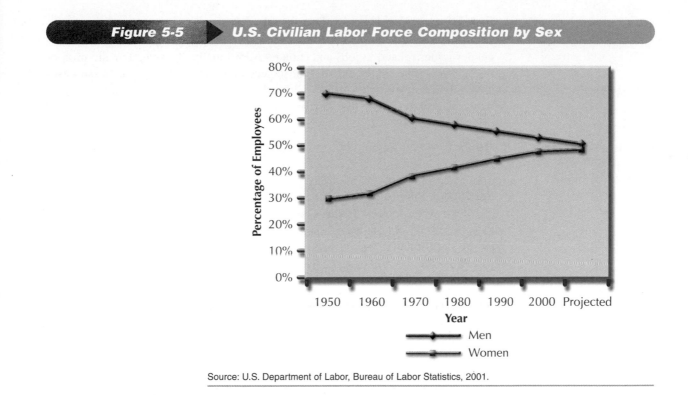

Figure 5-5 ▸ **U.S. Civilian Labor Force Composition by Sex**

── Men
── Women

Source: U.S. Department of Labor, Bureau of Labor Statistics, 2001.

Sex/Gender Issues in Equal Employment

The influx of women into the workforce has major social, economic, and organizational consequences. As Figure 5-5 shows, the percentage of the total U.S. civilian workforce has increased dramatically since 1950, to where women comprise almost half of today's workers.

A major reason for the increasing share of women in the workforce is that more women with children are working than in previous decades. About 76% of women ages 25–54 are in the workforce. Further, about half of all currently working women are single, separated, divorced, widowed, or otherwise single heads of households. Consequently, they are "primary" income earners, not co-income providers, who often must balance family and work responsibilities.

As part of managing diversity, it is important that employers take steps to have policies compatible with workers who are pregnant or are new parents. Due to the Pregnancy Discrimination Act discussed in Chapter 4, employers must not discriminate against pregnant women when making selection, promotion, training, or other employment-related decisions. The Family and Medical Leave Act (FMLA) requirements also affect the management of pregnant workers and new parents. This act applies to both female and male employees who are new parents, either through adoptions or natural births. Many employers have policies allowing new mothers to nurse or use breast pumps during business hours away from their worksites.[21]

Sex Discrimination in Jobs and Careers

The growth in the number of women in the workforce has led to more sex/gender issues related to jobs and careers. Additionally, the selection and promotion criteria that employers use can discriminate against women. Some cases have found that women were not allowed to enter certain jobs or job fields. Particularly problematic is the use of marital or family status as a basis for not selecting women.

Nepotism Practice of allowing relatives to work for the same employer.

Nepotism Many employers have policies that restrict or prohibit **nepotism,** the practice of allowing relatives to work for the same employer. Other firms require only that relatives not work directly for or with each other or be placed in a position where potential collusion or conflicts could occur. The policies most frequently cover spouses, brothers, sisters, mothers, fathers, sons, and daughters. Generally, employer anti-nepotism policies have been upheld by courts, in spite of the concern that they tend to discriminate against women more than men (because women tend to be denied employment or leave employers more often as a result of marriage to other employees).

Job Assignments and "Nontraditional Jobs" One result of the increasing number of women in the workforce is the movement of women into jobs traditionally held by men. The U.S. Department of Labor defines nontraditional occupations for women as those in which women comprise 25% or less of the total number employed.[22]

Figure 5-6 shows some of the typically male-dominated occupations in which women comprise relatively few of those employed. Even though the nature of the work and working conditions may contribute some to this pattern, many of these jobs pay well, and more women would enter these occupations if greater efforts were made by employers.

The right of employers to reassign women from hazardous jobs to ones that may be lower paying because of health-related concerns is another issue.

Figure 5-6	**Nontraditional Occupations for Women in 2000**		
Occupation	Employed: Both Sexes (numbers in thousands)	Employed: Female (numbers in thousands)	Percent Female
Welders and cutters	594	29	4.9
Truck drivers	3,088	145	4.7
Airplane pilots and navigators	129	5	3.9
Construction laborers	1,015	38	3.7
Firefighting and fire prevention occupations	248	9	3.6
Excavating and loading machine operators	98	3	3.1
Tool and die makers	121	3	2.7
Operating engineers	253	4	1.7
Crane and tower operators	70	1	1.4
Motion picture projectionists	7	0	<1.0

Source: "Nontraditional Occupations for Women in 2000," U.S. Department of Labor, Women's Bureau, 2001, available at *www.dol.gov/dol/wb.*

Employers' fears about higher health insurance costs, and even possible lawsuits involving such problems as birth defects caused by damage sustained during pregnancy, have led some employers to institute reproductive and fetal protection policies. However, the U.S. Supreme Court has ruled such policies are illegal. Also, having different job conditions for men and women usually is held to be discriminatory. In a related area, a U.S. district court case found that the exclusion of prescription contraceptions from an employer's benefits plan constitutes sex discrimination.[23]

The Glass Ceiling For years, women's groups have alleged that women in workplaces encounter a **glass ceiling,** which refers to discriminatory practices that have prevented women and other protected-class members from advancing to executive-level jobs. The extent of the problem is seen in the results of a survey of 825 large firms, in which women accounted for only 3.9% of the highest-paid executives, and only 1% of the firms had a female CEO.[24] Similar problems exist for racial/minority individuals as well.[25] In conjunction with the Civil Rights Act of 1991, a Glass Ceiling Commission conducted a study on how to shatter the glass ceiling encountered by women and other protected-class members. A number of recommendations were included in the commission's report.[26]

Glass ceiling Discriminatory practices that have prevented women and other protected-class members from advancing to executive-level jobs

"Glass Walls" and "Glass Elevator" A related problem is that women have tended to advance to senior management in a limited number of support areas, such as HR and corporate communications. Because jobs in these "supporting" areas tend to pay less than jobs in sales, marketing, operations, or finance, the overall impact is to reduce women's career progression and income. Limits that keep women from progressing only in certain fields have been referred to as "glass walls" or "glass elevators."

Breaking the Glass A growing number of employers have recognized that "breaking the glass," whether ceilings, walls, or elevators, is good business. Some of the most common means used to "break the glass" are as follows:

- Establishing formal mentoring programs for women and racial/ethnic individuals.
- Providing career rotation opportunities into operations, marketing, and sales for individuals who have shown talent in accounting, human resources, and other areas.[27]
- Increasing top management and Board of Directors membership to include women and individuals of color.
- Establishing clear goals for retention and progression of protected-class individuals and holding managers accountable for achieving these goals.
- Allowing for alternative work arrangements for employees, particularly those balancing work/family responsibilities.

Sexual Harassment and Workplace Relationships

As more women have entered the workforce, more men and women work together in teams and on projects. Consequently, more employers are becoming concerned about the close personal relationships that do develop at work.

Consensual Relationships and Romance at Work

When work-based friendships lead to romance and off-the-job sexual relationships, managers and employers face a dilemma: Should they "monitor" these relationships in order to protect the firm from potential legal complaints, but thereby "meddling" in employees' private, off-the-job lives? Or do they simply ignore such relationships and the potential problems they present? One study found that the way a romance relationship is viewed affects the actions that may be taken.[28] For instance, if a relationship is clearly consensual, or if it involves a supervisor-subordinate relationship, then the actions taken may be different.

The greatest concerns are romantic relationships between supervisors and subordinates, because the harassment of subordinates by supervisors is the most frequent type of sexual harassment situation. Some employers have addressed the issue of workplace romances by establishing policies permitting workplace romances, as shown by a study that over 70% of surveyed firms had such a policy.[29] Those policies often describe "appropriate" workplace behaviors or may require disclosure to the HR department. Employment attorneys generally recommend that the HR manager remind both parties in workplace romances of the company policy on sexual harassment and encourage either party to contact the HR department should the relationship cool and become one involving unwanted and unwelcome attentions. Also, the HR manager always should document that such conversations occurred.

WEST GROUP
A THOMSON COMPANY

Consensual Romantic Relationships
Sample policy on consensual romantic relationships.
Custom Search:
☑ ANALYSIS
Phrase: Romantic or sexual relationships

Nature of Sexual Harassment

Sexual harassment is a significant concern in many organizations and can occur by men harassing women, women harassing men, or same sex harassment. As shown by Figure 5-7, individuals in different roles can be sexual harassers.

Most frequently, sexual harassment occurs by a male in a supervisory or managerial position who harasses women within his "power structure." How-

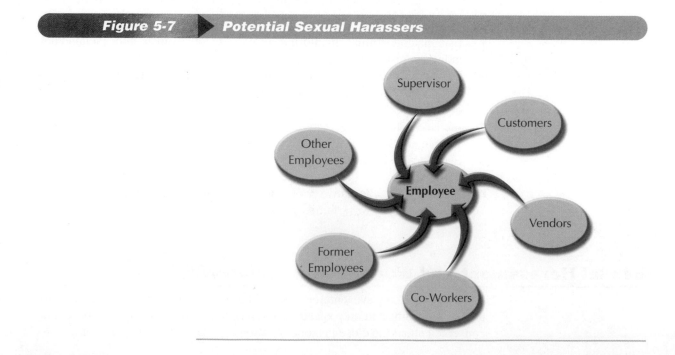

Figure 5-7 ▶ **Potential Sexual Harassers**

ever, women managers have been found guilty of sexually harassing male employees. Also, same sex harassment has occurred.

Third parties who are not employees also have been found to be harassers.[30] From a vending machine sales driver to a board member in a rural cooperative, employees have won sexual harassment complaints against their employers who took no action against the third party causing the harassment. Even customer service representatives and food servers have won sexual harassment complaints because their employers refused to protect the employees from regular sexual harassment by aggressive customers.

Types of Sexual Harassment Two basic types of sexual harassment have been defined by EEOC regulations and a large number of court cases. The two types are defined as follows:

1. *Quid pro quo* is harassment in which employment outcomes are linked to the individual granting sexual favors.
2. *Hostile environment* harassment exists when an individual's work performance or psychological well-being is unreasonably affected by intimidating or offensive working conditions.

In the *quid pro quo* type, an employee may be told he or she may get promoted, receive a special raise, or be given a desirable work assignment, but only if the employee submits to granting some sexual favors to the supervisor. Unfortunately, *hostile environment* harassment is much more prevalent, partially because the standards and consequences are more varied. Actual case situations illustrate how the hostile environment standard has been used.

- The male manager at a fast-food franchise restaurant in Maryland was found guilty of sexual harassment when he repeatedly made sexual jokes and discussed sexual behavior with two younger female employees. When they complained to the manager's boss, no action was taken, and the harassment increased.[31]
- A female sales representative filed a sexual harassment charge that a male manager used offensive language, told derogatory jokes, and distributed sexually explicit materials at sales meetings. Following her complaint, the firm required the manager to take an unpaid three-month leave and have additional management training. Interestingly, the court ruled that the alleged name-calling and offensive language was not offensive because the woman used such language regularly. Ultimately the court ruled against the woman's sexual harassment complaint.[32]

These cases and many others have revealed that commenting on dress or appearance, telling jokes that are suggestive or sexual in nature, allowing revealing photos and posters to be on display, or making continual requests to get together after work can lead to the creation of a hostile work environment. As computer and Internet technology has spread, the number of electronic sexual harassment cases has grown, as the e-HR on the next page describes.

Regardless of the type of sexual harassment, it is apparent that sexual harassment has significant consequences on the organization, other employees, and especially those harassed. Follow-up interviews and research with victims of sexual harassment reveal that the harassment has both job-related and psychological effects.[34] Also, harassment even has a ripple effect on others who fear

Quid pro quo Sexual harassment in which employment outcomes are linked to the individual granting sexual favors.

Hostile environment Sexual harassment where an individual's work performance or psychological well-being is unreasonably affected by intimidating or offensive working conditions.

Sexual Harassment Becomes Electronic

Much has been made of the advantages of the Internet and its positive effects on HR management. However, electronic information technology is also creating new problems for HR managers as well because sexual harassment occurs in e-mails and Internet access systems.

Cyber sexual harassment is a growing concern, as evidenced by a survey of HR professionals, which found 31% of them had dealt with situations involving sexually harassing e-mails at work. This cyber sexual harassment occurs in a variety of forms. It may be an employee forwarding a joke with sexual content received from a friend outside the company. Or it may be an employee repeatedly asking another employee to meet for lunch or a date.

Another more troublesome form is employees who access pornographic Web sites at work, and then share some contents with other employees. Even something such as an employee who has a screen saver of his wife in a revealing outfit or an actress dressed in a bikini has led to complaints by other employees.

Many employers have developed policies addressing inappropriate use of e-mail and company computer systems. According to one study, 85% of employers had policies on electronic technology usage. Many policies have "zero-tolerance," whereby disciplinary action occurs regardless of the proclaimed innocence of the employee.

More serious situations have led to employee terminations, as evidenced by some examples. Blue Cross & Blue Shield of Michigan fired seven employees for sending pornographic e-mails. Dow Chemical disciplined more than 200 employees and fired 50 of them for having e-mailed pornographic images and other inappropriate materials using the company information system. A well-publicized case occurred at the *New York Times* where 20 employees were fired for sending offensive and inappropriate e-mails—many of the individuals repeatedly doing so.

HR managers are handling cyber sexual harassment in a number of ways. First, having a policy is important, but it is even more crucial to train all employees on sexual harassment and electronic usage policies. Additionally, many employers have placed "scanners" on their e-mail and Web sites that screen for inappropriate words and images. Offending employees receive the warnings and disciplinary actions associated with "flagged" items.

As with other types of sexual harassment, investigation and prompt action are essential. Investigations often follow "electronic trails." Some employers also have required individual employees who are accessing child or violent pornographic Web sites to either resign or enter clinical treatment programs to avoid termination. As with all sexual harassment situations, HR professionals should document the incidents, their investigative efforts, and the actions taken to prevent further cyber sexual harassment.[33]

being harassed or view their employer more negatively if prompt, remedial actions do not occur. Thus, how employers respond to sexual harassment complaints is crucial for both legal reasons and employee morale.

Changing Legal Standards on Sexual Harassment

Several years ago the U.S. Supreme Court issued rulings in three different cases that significantly clarified both the legal aspects of when sexual harassment occurs and what actions employers should take to reduce their liabilities if sexual harassment claims are filed.[35] As Figure 5-8 indicates, if the employee suffered any tangible employment action (such as being denied raises, being terminated, or being refused access to training) because of the sexual harassment, then the employer is liable. However, even if the employee suffered no tangible

Figure 5-8 ▶ *Sexual Harassment Liability Determination*

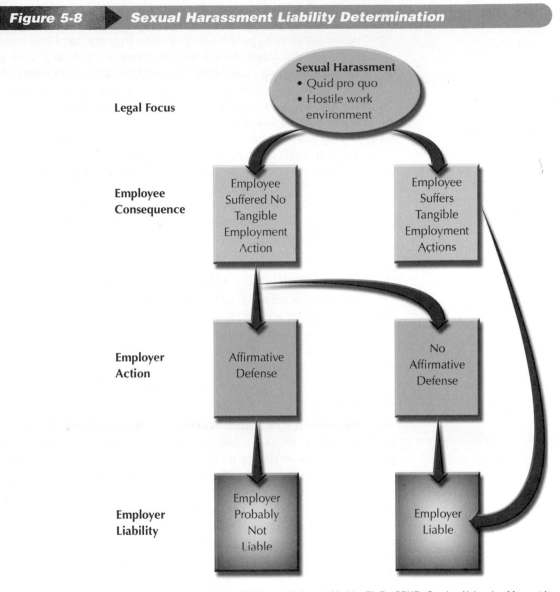

Source: Virginia Collins, Ph.D., SPHR, and Robert L. Mathis, Ph.D., SPHR, Omaha, Nebraska. May not be reproduced without permission.

employment action, and the employer has not produced an affirmative defense, then employer liability still exists.

Only if the employer can produce evidence of an affirmative defense in which the employer took reasonable care to prohibit sexual harassment does the employer have the possibility of avoiding liability. Components of ensuring reasonable care include the following:

- Establishing a sexual harassment policy
- Communicating the policy regularly
- Training employees and managers on avoiding sexual harassment
- Investigating and taking action when complaints are voiced

Age Issues and Diversity Management

Most of the developed countries are experiencing an aging of their populations, including Australia, Japan, most European countries, and the United States. The aging of the population means many "mature workers" in organizations.

As more older workers with a lifetime of experience and skills retire, HR will face significant challenges in replacing them with workers having the capabilities and work ethic that characterize many mature workers. But, many older workers stay active in the workforce. For instance, more than half of both men and women workers over 70 are employed part-time. Also, full-time workforce participation does not drop significantly until age 65, especially for women.[36]

Employment discrimination against individuals age 40 and older is prohibited by the Age Discrimination in Employment Act (ADEA), as mentioned in the previous chapter. Employers must be aware of a number of legal issues associated with managing older workers.

Job Opportunities for Older Employees

One issue that has led to age discrimination charges is labeling older workers as "overqualified" for jobs or promotions. In a number of cases, courts have ruled that the term *overqualified* may have been used as a code word for workers being too old, thus causing them not to be considered for employment. Also, selection and promotion practices must be "age-neutral." Research has found that older workers face substantial barriers to entry in a number of occupations, especially those requiring significant amounts of training.[37]

Age Discrimination and Workforce Reductions In the past decade, early retirement programs and organizational downsizing have been used by many employers to reduce their employment costs. Illegal age discrimination sometimes occurs when an individual over the age of 40 is forced into retirement or is denied employment or promotion on the basis of age. If disparate impact or treatment for those over 40 exists, age discrimination occurs.

Numerous lawsuits under the ADEA have been filed involving workers over 40 who were forced to take "voluntary retirement" when organizational restructuring or workforce reduction programs were implemented. In one case 26 employees at a power plant won a lawsuit because a workforce reduction resulted in 36 of the 39 laid-off employees being over age 40. Thus, the process for deciding who to lay off was ruled to be age biased.[38] However, terminations based on documented performance deficiencies not related to age are perfectly legal. Additionally, in the case of older employees, care must be taken that references to age ("old Fred" or "need younger blood") in conversations are not used.

Older Workers Benefit Protection Act (OWBPA) The Older Workers Benefit Protection Act (OWBPA) of 1990 was passed to amend the ADEA to ensure that equal treatment for older workers occurs in early retirement or severance situations. Additionally, guidelines issued by the EEOC are designed to ensure that older workers are protected when early retirement and downsizing programs include severance agreements and employee waivers.[39]

Attracting, Retaining, and Managing Older Workers To counter significant staffing difficulties many employers are attracting older persons to

WEST GROUP
A THOMSON COMPANY

Older Workers' Benefit Protection Act
Outlines OWBPA provisions on early incentives.
Custom Search:
☑ ANALYSIS
Phrase: Voluntary early retirement incentive

return to the workforce through the use of part-time and other scheduling options. According to the U.S. Bureau of Labor Statistics, during the past decade the number of older workers holding part-time jobs has been increasing.[40] A change in Social Security regulations has allowed individuals over age 65 to earn more per year without affecting their Social Security payments. As a result, it is likely that the number of older workers interested in working part-time will increase, and that they will work more hours than previously.

Another strategy used by employers to retain the talents of older workers is **phased retirement** whereby employees reduce their workloads and pay. This option is growing in use as a way to allow older workers with significant knowledge and experience to have more personal flexibility, while the organization retains them for their valuable capabilities. Some firms also rehire their retirees as part-time workers, independent contractors, or consultants. One survey found that more than 60% of surveyed organizations are using such means.[41]

Phased retirement
Approach in which employees reduce their workloads and pay.

Individuals with Disabilities in the Workforce

Employers looking for workers with the knowledge, skills, and abilities to perform jobs often have neglected a significant source—individuals with physical or mental disabilities. At least 55 million Americans with disabilities are covered by the Americans with Disabilities Act (ADA), but only 25% of them are currently employed. Estimates are that as many as 10 million of these individuals could be added to the workforce if appropriate accommodations were made by employers. Figure 5-9 shows the results of a survey of 1,400 employers conducted by the Society for Human Resource Management on the employment barriers faced by people with disabilities.

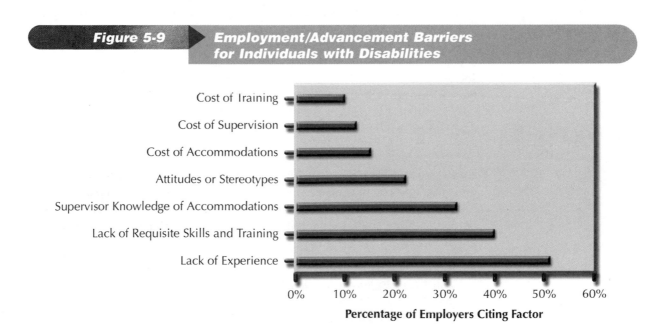

Figure 5-9 **Employment/Advancement Barriers for Individuals with Disabilities**

Percentage of Employers Citing Factor

Source: Based on data in *SHRM/Cornell University Survey on Implementation of the Employment Provisions of the ADA,* (Alexandria, VA: Society for Human Resource Management, 2001).

The number of complaints filed under the ADA has skyrocketed in recent years. According to statistics from the EEOC, over 125,000 disability discrimination complaints were filed in the first several years the act was in effect.[42] Fortunately for employers, only 48% of those complaints resulted in a finding of "reasonable cause" of discrimination, leading to further compliance actions or lawsuits. Over half of all complaints had to do with discharge of employees with disabilities or employees who became disabled. Another 25% dealt with failure to provide reasonable accommodation.

Reasonable Accommodations

At the heart of employing individuals with disabilities is for employers to make reasonable accommodations in several areas. First, architectural barriers should not prohibit disabled individuals' access to work areas or restrooms. A second area of reasonable accommodation is the assignment of work tasks. Satisfying this requirement may mean modifying jobs, work area layouts, work schedules, or providing special equipment.[43]

Recruiting Individuals with Disabilities Some companies have specifically targeted these individuals as employees. Some examples include the following:[44]

- Proctor & Gamble formed a special recruiting team to identify individuals with severe disabilities and how they can be employed.
- Microsoft hired summer interns with disabilities and made a video featuring Microsoft employees with disabilities. Also, as part of its diversity efforts, the video is shown as part of orientation training to all new employees in order to reinforce Microsoft's commitment to those with disabilities.

Key to making reasonable accommodations is to identify the essential job functions and then determine which accommodations are reasonable so that the individual can perform the core job duties. Fortunately for employers, most accommodations made are relatively inexpensive. According to data from the Job Accommodation Network, half of all employer accommodations cost less than $500, with about 20% costing little or nothing.[45] Employers who show a positive interest in making accommodations are more likely to provide encouragement to individuals with disabilities that they will receive appropriate considerations for employment opportunities.[46]

Employees Who Develop Disabilities For many employers the impact of the ADA has been the greatest on handling employees who develop disabilities, not just dealing with applicants with disabilities. As the workforce ages, it is likely that more employees are likely to develop disabilities in some of the following ways:

- An accounting managers suffers a heart attack and must limit how much she can travel to conduct audits at company locations throughout the United States.

Logging On...

The Job Accommodation Network
Provides information about the ADA, job accommodations, and the employability of people with disabilities.

http://janweb.icdi.wvu.edu/

- A utility repair worker suffers a back injury while on vacation skiing, and is restricted from climbing ladders and poles or lifting items weighing more than 10 pounds.
- An office employee is involved in a severe car accident, resulting in neck injuries that constrain how much time he can sit at computer terminals doing data input.

These and countless other examples illustrate that employers must develop responses for handling accommodation requests from individuals who have been satisfactory employees without disabilities, but now must be considered for accommodations if they are to be able to continue working. Handled inappropriately, these individuals are likely to file ADA complaints with the EEOC or private lawsuits.

Sometimes employees can be shifted to other jobs where their disabilities do not affect them as much. For instance, the utility was able to move the injured worker to a dispatcher job inside, so that climbing and lifting were unnecessary. But the problem for employers is what to do with the next utility worker who develops back problems and a dispatcher's job is not available. Even if the accommodations are just for one employee, the reactions of co-workers must be considered.[47]

Individuals with Mental Disabilities More ADA complaints are being filed by individuals who have or claim to have mental disabilities. About 16% of all ADA claims are based on psychiatric or mental illness.[48] The cases that have been filed have ranged from individuals with a medical history of paranoid schizophrenia or clinical depression to individuals who claim that job stress has affected their marriage or sex life. Regardless of the nature of employees' claims, it is important that employers respond to such claims properly by obtaining medical verifications for claims of mental illnesses and considering accommodation requests for mental disabilities in the same manner as physical disabilities requests.

Individuals with Life-Threatening Illnesses

Individuals with life-threatening illnesses have been determined by the U.S. Supreme Court to be covered by the ADA. Individuals with leukemia, cancer, or AIDS are all considered as having disabilities, and employers must respond to them appropriately or face charges of discrimination.

Unfortunately, employers and employees often react with fear about working with an AIDS victim or others with life-threatening illness. Nevertheless, if an employer does have an employee with a life-threatening illness, it may be that educating other employees is more appropriate than terminating the victim's employment. A medical leave of absence (without pay if that is the general policy) can be used to assist the afflicted employee during medical treatments. Also, employees who indicate that they will not work with an afflicted victim should be told that their refusal to work is not protected by law, and that they could be subject to disciplinary action up to and including discharge.

Religion and Spirituality in Workplaces

Diversity is also found in the religious beliefs and degrees of spirituality that employees bring to work. Title VII of the Civil Rights Act of 1964 prohibits discrimination at work on the basis of religion; also, employers are prohibited from discriminating against employees for their religious beliefs and practices. Such considerations have become even more important since the September 2001 attacks in protecting Muslim individuals from discrimination and harassment.

Managing Religious Diversity in Workplaces

Employers increasingly are having to balance the rights of employees with differing religious beliefs. One way is to make reasonable accommodation of employees' religious beliefs in making work assignments and setting work schedules because many religions have differing days of worship and holidays.[49] For example, some firms in California have established "holiday swapping pools," whereby Christian employees can work during Passover, or Ramadan, or Chinese New Year, and employees from other religions work Christmas. Other firms allow employees a set number of days off for holidays without specifying the holidays in company personnel policies.[50]

Another potential area for conflict between employer policies and employees' religious practices is in the area of dress and appearance. Some religions have standards about the appropriate attire for women. Also, some religions expect men to have beards and facial hair. For instance, a Muslim worker at Federal Express received $70,000 in back pay and damages because the company's policy of prohibiting beards violated the worker's religious standards. Also, Federal Express agreed to conduct training for managers on religious tolerance.[51]

Another issue relates to religious expression. In the last several years, employees in several cases have sued employers for prohibiting them from expressing their religious beliefs at work. In one case, an individual won a court case because the employer would not let him pray during his work breaks and co-workers harassed him and wiped their shoes on his prayer rug.[52] In other cases, employers have had to take action because of the complaints by other workers that employees were aggressively "pushing" their religious views at work, thus creating a "hostile environment."[53]

Individuals with Differing Lifestyles and Sexual Orientations

As if demographic diversity did not place pressure enough on managers and organizations, individuals in the workforce today have widely varying lifestyles that can have work-related consequences. Legislative efforts have been made to protect individuals with differing lifestyles or sexual orientations from employment discrimination, though at present only a few cities and states have passed such laws.[54]

One specific issue that some employers have had to address is that of transgendered individuals who have had or are undergoing sex change surgery. Regarding transsexuals (individuals who have had sex-change surgery), federal court cases and the EEOC have ruled that sex discrimination under Title VII applies to a person's gender at birth. Thus, it does not apply to the new gender of those who have had gender-altering operations. The HR Practice discusses those issues and how they can be addressed by employers.

HR Practices

Transgendered Employees: When Individuals Change Sex

An increasing number of HR practitioners and operating managers are encountering an issue that formerly was less common: what to do when employees change their sex or gender identity. According to the Transgender Education Association, about 1,000 people undergo sex-change surgery each year. As a result, a number of lawsuits have been filed by persons claiming discrimination as they changed genders. A bank was even sued by a male customer who was denied a request for a loan while attired in a dress.

From a legal standpoint, for decades the federal law has been that the gender you are at birth is what you are under the law. However, a number of local governments have included transsexuals in their antidiscrimination statutes, including Boulder, Colorado; Madison, Wisconsin; Atlanta, Georgia; and Portland, Oregon. Also, the state of Minnesota covers transsexuals in its human rights laws. Additionally, a number of companies apply their EEO policies to transsexuals, including Lucent Technologies, Apple Computer, Xerox, and others.

Assume you are the HR manager who must decide how to respond when an employee indicates he or she is undergoing gender transformation treatment or is "more comfortable" as a different sex. For example, a male accounting employee at a midwestern manufacturing firm told the firm's HR director that he was undergoing sexual transformation treatment and surgery. He said that beginning the next month he would be wearing women's attire to work, wanted to be called by his feminine name, and planned to use the women's restroom.

This example raises a number of HR issues:

- *Clarification of HR policies:* Access to company benefits plans for transgender treatments and surgeries must be clarified. Also, the "restroom issue" often is the most sensitive. At some firms, the policy is that whatever restroom the individual wishes to use, that is the one that is acceptable. However, other firms, such as a Minnesota publishing company, have established a policy that requires employees to use the facilities consistent with their anatomical make-up. In some situations this latter policy has been challenged in courts, and the verdicts have varied from jurisdiction to jurisdiction.

- *Reactions of co-workers:* It is crucial to ensure that acceptance of the change is communicated to co-workers and that the employer will not tolerate snide remarks or harassment of the transgendered individuals.

- *Continuing acceptance:* If an employer believes that every individual who is a satisfactorily performing worker is important to retain, then keeping the talents of an individual who decides to change gender is just as important as retaining any other employee. Attention should be given to working with managers and supervisors to ensure that the "new" individual is evaluated fairly and not discriminated against in work assignments, raises, training, or promotions.[55]

Summary

- Diversity management is concerned with organizational efforts to ensure that all people are valued regardless of their differences.
- Efforts to value diversity can enhance organizational performance, aid in employee attraction and retention, encourage more varied decision-making, and reduce discrimination.
- Diversity training has had limited success, possibly because it too often has focused on beliefs rather than behaviors.
- Affirmative action has been intensely litigated, and the debate continues today.
- Discrimination on the basis of race and national origin is illegal and employers must be prepared

to deal with language issues and racial harassment as part of effectively managing racial/ethnic diversity.

- As more women have entered the workforce, sex/gender issues in equal employment have included discrimination in jobs and careers and sexual harassment, which takes two forms: (a) *quid pro quo,* and (b) hostile environment.
- Employers should develop policies on sexual harassment, have identifiable complaint procedures, train all employees on what constitutes sexual harassment, promptly investigate complaints, and take action when sexual harassment is found to have occurred.
- Aging of the U.S. workforce has led to more concerns about age discrimination, especially in the form of forced retirements and terminations.

- Employers are recognizing the value of attracting and retaining older workers through greater use of part-time work and phased retirement programs.
- Individuals with disabilities represent a significant number of current and potential employees and the definition of who is disabled has expanded in recent years.
- Employers are making reasonable accommodations for individuals with disabilities, including those with mental or life-threatening illnesses.
- Reasonable accommodation is a strategy that can be used to deal with the religious diversity of employees.
- Managing diversity means ensuring that individuals with differing lifestyles and sexual orientations are treated with respect at work.

Review and Discussion Questions

1. Discuss the following statement: "U.S. organizations must adjust to diversity if they are to be effective in managing the workforce of the present and future."
2. Regarding the affirmative action debate, why do you support or oppose affirmative action?
3. Assume your firm was hiring some workers from other countries, what would be some key issues to consider?
4. Give some illustrations of how women have been affected by discrimination in job assignments and career decisions in organizations where you have worked.

5. Cite examples that you have experienced or observed of the two types of sexual harassment in employment situations.
6. Discuss the following comment: "The combination of the aging of the workforce and shortages of qualified workers in many jobs is changing the meaning of 'retirement'."
7. How should an HR manager decide what, if any, reasonable accommodations in work policies and work schedules should be made for an employee who developed AIDS and another one who is Muslim?

Terms to Know

diversity   138
nepotism   150
glass ceiling   151

quid pro quo   153
hostile environment   153
phased retirement   157

Developing Diversity Training

As the Training and Development Manager, one of your key objectives this year is to initiate a company-wide diversity program. The entire Training and Development department is very interested in the prospect, but you have yet to convince the senior management group of the need for such a company initiative. You are responsible for presenting your ideas to them to get funding for such a program. But for these executives you need to put your case in business terms.

Using the Web site *http://www.diversityworld.com/* and the article on the site called "Workforce Diversity," gather information about the following two questions which are going to be the focus in your presentation to the senior management group.

Questions
1. How would you define "workforce diversity" as part of policy and program efforts?
2. Be ready to discuss the factors that lead companies to diversify their workforce.

Construction Industry Confronts Diversity

The construction industry is a major employer in many states and communities throughout the United States. Unfortunately, another common characteristic of the construction industry is a high number of work-related accidents and injuries. Increasingly the employees in the construction industry are individuals for whom English is not their primary language, and a number of construction site accidents have been attributed to the lack of English language skills of some construction workers. For instance, it has been estimated that 40% of work-related accidents in the Houston, Texas, area involve Hispanic workers. Some specific examples illustrate the concerns:

- A worker demolishing a building in New York City was hit and killed by a demolition boom. He left the machine on and pushed the wrong boom control pedal. Even though a safety instruction manual was available in English, the worker spoke and understood only Polish.
- A Hispanic worker was killed when the window-washing lift he was on fell 30 feet because the lift platform had not been locked properly. None of the safety instructions and warnings were in Spanish.

Even if injuries or deaths do not result, the diversity of workers on many construction sites means many different languages are being used by employees, with English fluency less common than might be desirable. Assume that workers from Croatia, Mexico, Sudan, and Laos are all working on the same construction project. How would a supervisor who speaks only English communicate with them?

Fortunately, some progressive construction firms have recognized that the diversity of workers presents some opportunities for building better workplaces. By working with construction unions, some employers have developed English training programs for workers that are offered to non-English-speaking employees. Other employers have translated their safety training materials into Spanish or other languages. Also, greater use of pictures and diagrams rather than written instructions has helped with safer operation of equipment and machinery. Some construction firms have conducted basic foreign language classes for English-speaking supervisors and managers. Still other employers have conducted diversity training in order to reduce conflicts among the different racial/ethnic groups and to promote better working relationships and greater understanding. This training also has helped reduce the number of racial harassment complaints and lawsuits.

The major benefit of these efforts is that the number of work-related accidents at construction sites has declined some. Another benefit is that whenever employees receive training in their own languages and/or their boss makes some effort to speak the native language of construction workers,

employee morale appears to increase and turnover tends to decline. Thus it appears that addressing diversity issues pays off for construction employers.[56]

Questions

1. As the HR manager, how would you begin development of a diversity effort for a construction firm?
2. Discuss the difficulties in dealing with employees from a number of different racial/ethnic groups when developing and conducting safety training.

Notes

1. Stephanie Armour, "Welcome Mat Rolls Out for Hispanic Workers," *USA Today,* April 12, 2001, 1B; Carol Patton, "When Worlds Collide," *HR Executive,* December 2000, 50–56; and Carla Joinson, "Strength in Numbers," *HR Magazine,* November 2000, 43–49.
2. Alison Wellner, "How Do You Spell Diversity?" *Training,* April 2000, 34–38.
3. Robert L. Grossman, "Race in the Workplace," *HR Magazine,* March 2000, 41–45.
4. Based on Orlando C. Richard, "Racial Diversity, Business Strategy, and Firm Performance: A Resource-Based View," *Academy of Management Journal* 43 (2000), 164–177.
5. Pepi Sappal, "Dare to Be Different," *Global HR,* May 2001, 16–19.
6. Based on data in SHRM/Career Journal.com "Impact of Diversity, Initiatives Poll," October 2000, available at *www.shrm.org.*
7. Louise Lee, "Speaking the Customer's Language—Literally," *Business Week,* September 25, 2000, 178.
8. *Diversity Recruitment Report 2001,* 2001 available at *www.wetfeet. com;* and "Change Your Perspective, Attract a More Diverse Workforce," newsletter, March 31, 2001, available at *www.hr-esource.com.*

9. "Assessing, Solving Issues of Color Reveal Gray Areas," *Bulletin to Management,* July 27, 2000, 239.
10. Jacqueline A. Gilbert and John M. Ivancevich, "Valuing Diversity: A Tale of Two Organizations," *Academy of Management Executive,* February 2000, 93–105.
11. Lorraine Gutierrez, Jan Kruzich, Teresa Jones, and Nora Coronado, "Identifying Goals and Outcome Measures for Diversity Training," *Administration in Social Work* 24 (2000), 53–71.
12. Andrew R. McIlvaine, "Hostile Environments," *Human Resource Executive,* December 2000, 71–75.
13. Victoria D. Bush and Thomas N. Ingram, "Building and Assessing Cultural Diversity Skills: Implications for Sales Training," *Industrial Marketing Management,* January 2001, 65–76.
14. *SHRM/Fortune Impact of Diversity Initiatives on Bottom Line* (Alexandria VA: Society for Human Resource Management, 2001.)
15. Vidu Soni, "A Twenty-First Century Perception for Diversity in the Public Sector," *Public Administration Review,* September/October 2000, 395–408.
16. U.S. Census Bureau, 2000 Census, as released in 2001.

17. Based on *Gratz v. Bollinger,* 97-75231 (E.D. Mich.), as appealed 99a-0295 (6th Ct), April 4, 2001; and Carol Morello, "A New Battleground for Affirmative Action," *USA Today,* November 28, 1997, 10A.
18. "The Uses of Strangers," *The Economist,* March 31, 2001, 26–28.
19. T. Shawn Taylor, "A New Language Barrier," *Chicago Tribune,* June 10, 2001, G-1.
20. *Hollins v. Delta Airlines,* 99-4072 (10th Circuit), January 29, 2001.
21. Cheryl Dore, "Room for Mom," *Human Resource Executive,* March 15, 2001, 42–47; and Diane Brady, "Give Nursing Moms a Break," *Business Week,* August 6, 2001, 70.
22. "Nontraditional Occupations for Women in 2000," U.S. Department of Labor, Women's Bureau, 2001, available at *www.dol.gov/dol/wb.*
23. *Erickson v. Bartell Drug Co.* C00-1213L. (2001) WL 649651.
24. Louis Lavelle, "For Female CEOs, It's Stingy at the Top," *Business Week,* April 23, 2001, 70–71.
25. Eric Raimy, "Cultural Captives," *Human Resource Executive,* June 1, 2001, 53–55.
26. Glass Ceiling Commission, *A Solid Investment: Making Use of the Nation's Human Capital* (Washington, DC: U.S. Department of Labor, 1995).

27. "Managers and Diversity," *Omaha World-Herald,* April 22, 2001, 1G.

28. Charles A. Pierce, Herman Agunis, and Susan K. R. Adams, "Effects of a Dissolved Workplace Romance and Rater Characteristics on Responses to a Sexual Harassment Accusation," *Academy of Management Journal* 43 (2000), 869–880.

29. Allison Bloom, "Love Is in the Air," *MSN Careers,* February 23, 2001.

30. Gillian Flynn, "Third-Party Sexual Harassment: Commonplace and Laden with Liability," *Workforce,* November 2000, 88–92.

31. *EEOC v. R&R Ventures,* 00-1702 (4th Circuit), April 2, 2001.

32.. "Courts Consider What Constitutes a Hostile Work Environment," *Fair Employment Practices,* August 31, 2000, 108.

33. Karyn-Siobhan Robinson, "Cybersex Permeates the Workplace," *HR News,* April 2001, 10; and "Companies Crack Down," *The Wall Street Journal,* September 21, 1999, A1.

34. Libert J. Munson, Charles Hulin, and Fritz Drasgow, "Longitudinal Analysis of Dispositional Influences and Sexual Harassment: Effects on Job and Psychological Outcomes," *Personnel Psychology* 53 (2000), 21–46.

35. *Burlington Industries v. Ellerth,* U.S. S.Ct. No. 97-569, June 26, 1998; *Faragher v. Boca Raton,* U.S. S.Ct. No. 97-282, June 26, 1998; and *Oncale v. Sundowner Offshore Services,* U.S. S.Ct. No. 96-568, March 4, 1998.

36. Patrick J. Pursell, "Older Workers: Employment and Retirement Trends," *Monthly Labor Review,* October 2000, 22.

37. Barry T. Hirsch, David A. MacPherson, and Melissa A. Hardy, "Occupational Age Structure and Access for Older Workers," *Industrial & Labor Relations Review* 53 (2000), 401–418.

38. *Meacham v. Knolls Atomic Power Lab,* ND.NY, 97-CV-0012, July 26, 2000.

39. Darryl Van Duch, "New EEOC Rules Target 'Won't Sue' Severance Pledges," *The National Law Journal,* March 5, 2001, 1.

40. Patrick J. Pursell, "Older Workers: Employment and Retirement Trends," *Monthly Labor Review,* October 2000, 19–31.

41. Stephanie Armour "More Firms Ask Retirees to Remain," *USA Today,* January 4, 2001, 1B.

42. Susan J. Wells, "Is the ADA Working?" *HR Magazine,* April 2001, 38–46.

43. Kathryn Tyler, "Looking for a Few Good Workers?" *HR Magazine,* December 2000, 129–134.

44. Daniel B. Moskowitz, "Accessing the Disabled," *Human Resource Executive,* February 2001, 70–73.

45. "No Room for Narrow Minds in Tight Labor Market," *Bulletin to Management,* February 15, 2001, 70–73.

46. David C. Baldridge and John F. Veiga, "Toward a Greater Understanding of the Willingness to Request an Accommodation," *Academy of Management Review* 26 (2001), 85–99.

47 Adrienne Coella, "Co-Worker Distributive Fairness Judgments of Workplace Accommodation of Employees with Disabilities," *Academy of Management Review,* 26 (2001), 100–116.

48. Julie Forster, "When Workers Just Can't Cope," *Business Week,* October 30, 2000, 100–102.

49. Karen C. Cash and George R. Gray, " A Framework for Accommodating Religion and Spirituality at Work," *Academy of Management Executive,* August 2000, 131.

50. Phaedra Brotherton, "Religious Diversity Initiatives Foster Respect and Understanding," *Mosaics,* March/April 2001, 1+; and "Office Tolerance," *The Wall Street Journal,* May 1, 2001, B10.

51. "FedEx Delivers Agreement on Employees' Beards," *Omaha World-Herald,* June 20, 2001, 11.

52. Marc Adams, "Showing Good Faith Toward Muslims," *HR Magazine,* November 2000, 53–64.

53. Bob Calandra, "From On High," *Human Resource Executive,* January 2001, 95–98.

54. Maureen Minehan, "Transgendered Employees Winning Protection," available at *http://hr-esource.com,* August 20, 2001.

55. Based on R. K. Miller, "About Face," *HR Executive,* January 2001, 85–88; and "More Transsexuals . . ." *HR Comply,* February 2001, available at *http://216:133.243.67newsletter.*

56. Based on Mike Florey, "Solving the Language Barrier," *Occupational Health and Safety,* January 2001, 37–38; and Tina Kelley "Foreign Languages Often Form Construction Barriers," *Omaha World-Herald,* February 27, 2000, 17G.

CHAPTER 6

Jobs

After you have read this chapter, you should be able to:

- Discuss workflow analysis and business process re-engineering as approaches to organizational work.

- Explain how changing job characteristics can be used to improve jobs.

- Indicate how job analysis has both legal and behavioral aspects.

- List and explain four job analysis methods.

- Identify the five steps in conducting a job analysis.

- Write a job description and the job specifications for it.

- Compare the task-based approach and the competency approach of job analysis.

Companies compete by providing goods and services when demanded. Jobs in the United States have taken on a new dimension as late night and weekend demand for goods and services has increased. Someone has to be there to run the business if demand is 24 hours a day and 7 days a week, , , , so jobs are created and people hired to fill a 24/7 need.

How did this "non-standard" demand come about? At the Home Depot store in Brooklyn, New York, many shift workers stop by after work, so the store provides kitchen and bathroom designers who work until 1 A.M. to provide for the shift workers' business. The Web has affected the 24/7 situation too. Stock trading is now available 24 hours. Night time in America is when customers from Sydney, Australia, call for help with problems in software sold by U.S. firms. Nights and weekends are also the times busy people answer personal e-mail, pay bills, and deal with banking problems.

For decades many nurses, security guards, police officers, factory workers, and others have known evening, late night, and weekend work, but now stockbrokers, contractors, retailers, account representatives, and software consultants, among others, are on 24/7. So are many restaurant employees, taxi drivers, and delivery people.

How many employees have jobs that require nontraditional time scheduling is difficult to determine exactly; the U.S. government does not directly gather information on that point. According to the Bureau of Labor Statistics, just 10% of the 90 million full-time employees in the U.S. work nights. However, that figure does not include part-time, temporary, or flextime employees, nor does it consider weekend work.

According to a University of Maryland sociologist, Harriet Presser, estimates are that close to 66% of American employees (about 75 million) work outside the traditional 8–5 Monday through Friday schedule. Her five-year study of 3,475 married couples helped identify some of the problems created by changes as we move toward more 24/7 work.

Professor Presser speculates that sleep deprivation, impact on a family's social life, and lack of time alone as a couple may contribute to higher divorce rates among parents who work nonstandard hours. Problems identified by other researchers include more forced overtime and limited available overnight child-care service. For example, an individual spent 10 years rotating every 12 to 18 months from day, to evening, and then to night shifts as a data processing supervisor for an insurance company. Communication with her husband (who was a day worker) was difficult. She missed her kids' games and school events and would even wake up and not know what time of day it was.

When a Florida manufacturer of electronic filters had to go to 24/7 production to meet demand, employees had a say in designing the schedule. With employee input, the company finally went to a 12-hour shift schedule that involved severe lifestyle changes, but having a role in picking it eased the change for many employees.[1]

Employers have work they need to have done around the clock and on all days. Employees need jobs, and the ways those jobs are constructed affect them. Consequently, the importance of balancing employer and employee needs is a challenge increasingly being faced in today's workforce.

> Someone has to be there to run the business if demand is 24 hours a day and 7 days a week

"That is not in my job description."

—A disgruntled employee

The work that needs to be done in an organization, and how it gets done matters to both employers and employees. Important elements for *employers* are: (1) having work done properly that will lead to organization goals; (2) making sure that work is logically organized into jobs that can be compensated fairly; and (3) having work that people are willing (even eager) to do. Important factors for *employees* are: (1) having a clear understanding of what is expected in the job; (2) doing tasks they personally enjoy; (3) being rewarded appropriately for their work; and (4) having a sense that what they do is important and respected.

HR Management and Jobs

Several areas associated with jobs involve human resources professionals. The issues surrounding jobs and various approaches that can be used to address the issues are shown in Figure 6-1. But seldom does one design all the jobs in an organization from scratch. Jobs grow in number, evolve, and then disappear as the organization changes. So as a practical matter, the concerns with jobs are typically redesign and re-engineering of existing jobs. This chapter addresses the issues in Figure 6-1 in its look at jobs in organizations.

Dividing Work into Jobs

One way to visualize an organization is as an entity that takes inputs from the surrounding environment and through some kind of "work" turns those inputs into goods or services. The work may be done by humans, machines, or both.[2] But the entire amount of work to be done must be divided up so that it can be coordinated in some logical way.

Figure 6-2 shows how organizational values, strategies, and customer needs influence the work the organization has to do.[3] **Work** is effort directed toward producing or accomplishing results. A **job** is a grouping of tasks, duties, and responsibilities that constitutes the total work assignment for employees. These tasks, duties, and responsibilities may change over time and therefore the job

Work Effort directed toward producing or accomplishing results.

Job Grouping of tasks, duties, and responsibilities that constitutes the total work assignment for employees.

Figure 6-1	Job Issues and HR Approaches	
Issue	**Approaches**
• *Dividing up organizational work into jobs*	• *Work flow analysis and "re-engineering" jobs*
• *Improving existing jobs for people and productivity*	• *Job design/or redesign*
• *Using group inputs/effort in certain jobs*	• *Alternative scheduling*
• *Identifying what people are doing in specific jobs currently*	• *Teams*
	• *Job analysis*
• *Recording job tasks and the characteristics of the person necessary to do the job*	• *Job descriptions*
	• *Job specifications*
	• *Competency identification*

Section 2   Staffing the Organization

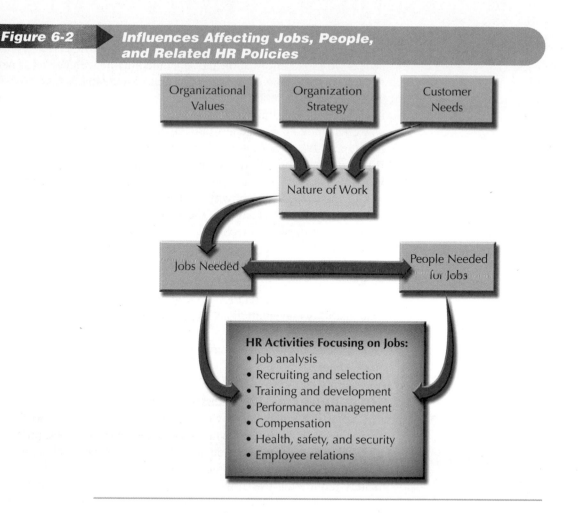

may change. Ideally, when all the jobs are added together they should equal the amount of work that the organization needs to have done—no more, no less.

Workflow Analysis

Workflow analysis
A study of the way work (inputs, activities, and outputs) moves through an organization.

Workflow analysis studies the way work moves through the organization and usually begins with an examination of the desired and actual *outputs* (goods and services) in terms of both quantity and quality. Then the *activities* (tasks and jobs) that lead to the outputs are evaluated to see if they can achieve the desired outputs. Finally the *inputs* (people, material, information, data, equipment, etc.) must be assessed to determine if these inputs make the outputs and activities more efficient and better.

For instance, in an electric utility company, if a customer calls with a service outage problem, a customer service representative typically takes the information and enters it into a database. Then in the operations department, a dispatcher accesses the database to schedule a line technician to repair the problem and the customer is called and notified about the timing of the repair. The line technician also must receive instructions from a supervisor, who gets the information on workload and locations from the dispatcher.

Using a workflow analysis it can be understood that there are too many steps involving too many different jobs in this process. Therefore, the utility implemented a new customer information system and combined the dispatching function with customer service. The redesign permitted the customer service representatives to access workload information and schedule the line technicians as part of the initial consumer phone calls, except in unusual situations. The redesign required redefining tasks, duties, and responsibilities of several jobs. To implement the new jobs required training the customer service representatives in dispatching, as well as moving dispatchers into the customer service department and training them in all facets of customer service. The result was a more responsive workflow for customers, more efficient scheduling of line technicians, and broader jobs for customer service representatives.

In another example of why workflow analysis may be needed consider how secretarial jobs are changing. The number of secretaries has declined sharply over the last decade as technology has changed. For instance, the demand for typists has dropped as more managers compose their own memos and reports on e-mail. Also voice mail has reduced the need for someone taking messages, and copying and filing are done in many organizations through office service centers, not by individual secretaries. Current office support functions require greater responsibility and entail more coordination and authority. The job titles are more likely to be "administrative coordinator" or "administrative assistant" to reflect these changes, and organizations will need to analyze the workflow to adjust to those changes.

Re-engineering Business Processes

After workflow analysis provides an understanding of how work is being done, re-engineering generates the needed changes in the business processes. The purpose of business process re-engineering is to improve such activities as product development, customer service, and service delivery. Re-engineering may ultimately require the use of work teams, training employees to do more than one job, and reorganizing operations, workflow, and offices to simplify and speed work. It focuses on work and jobs and how they need to evolve to improve customer service.

Re-engineering consists of three phases:

1. *Rethink.* Examine how the current organization of work and jobs affects customer satisfaction and service.
2. *Redesign.* Analyze how jobs are put together, the workflow, and results achieved; then redesign as necessary.
3. *Retool.* Look at new technologies (equipment, computers, software, etc.) as opportunities to improve product and service quality and customer satisfaction.

Re-engineering of the work to be done is one source of change in jobs. There are other pressures affecting jobs in the future. The HR Perspective looks at predictions from futurists on how jobs may have to change in the years to come as a result of changes in the people who do them.

Developing Jobs for Individuals and Teams

Individual responses to jobs vary because a job may be motivating to one person but not to someone else. Also, depending on how jobs are designed, they may provide more or less opportunity for employees to satisfy their job-related needs.

Jobs in the Future

Some futuristic views of the upcoming workplace and workforce suggest the following changes may occur:

- Technology will play an even more important role in new jobs. Business will be conducted anytime, day or night.
- Many workers may choose to work weekends, but attend to such personal activities as golf or going shopping during the week when these venues are less crowded.
- Balancing work and family life will be even more important. Women's share of all levels of the workforce will continue to grow as glass ceilings are shattered by women with degrees.

As a result, employees will demand even more flexibility from employers in their job schedules.

- Teen and retiree entrepreneurship will increase. Many young people who have seen their parents "downsized" will not want to work for corporations but will set up shop for themselves. Further, a huge wave of retired baby boomers will provide another source for entrepreneurs.
- "Occupational synthesis" will bring big salaries for some currently lower-paying jobs. For example, scarcity of public school teachers may result in more teachers managing aides

and others who work with students.

- Auto mechanics who combine knowledge of computerized automobile functions and traditional mechanical skills are becoming half mechanics, half information technology specialists. Such combination jobs are already paying as much as $150,000 annually.
- Employees will be more isolated in their high-tech jobs. Digital communication and telecommuting are replacing face-to-face interactions in many situations, causing social disconnection for some.[4]

For example, a sales job may furnish a good opportunity to satisfy social needs, whereas a training assignment may satisfy a person's need to develop expertise in a specific area. A job that gives little autonomy may not satisfy an individual's need to be creative or innovative.

Job design Organizing tasks, duties, and responsibilities into a productive unit of work.

Designing or redesigning jobs encompasses many factors. **Job design** refers to organizing tasks, duties, and responsibilities into a productive unit of work. It addresses the content of jobs and the effect of jobs on employees. Identifying the components of a given job is an integral part of job design. Currently, job design is receiving greater attention for three major reasons:

- Job design can influence *performance* in certain jobs, especially those where employee motivation can make a substantial difference. Lower costs through reduced turnover and absenteeism also are related to good job design.
- Job design can affect *job satisfaction*. Because people are more satisfied with certain job configurations than with others, identifying what makes a "good" job becomes critical.
- Job design can affect both *physical and mental health*. Problems such as hearing loss, backache, and leg pain sometimes can be traced directly to job design, as can stress, high blood pressure, and heart disease.

Not everyone would enjoy being a physician, an engineer, or a dishwasher. But certain people like and do well at each of those jobs.[5] The person/job fit is a simple but important concept that involves matching characteristics of people with characteristics of jobs. Obviously, if a person does not fit a job, either the person can be changed or replaced, or the job can be altered. In the past, it was much more common to try to make the "round" person fit the "square" job. However, successfully reshaping people is not easy to do. By redesigning jobs, the person/job fit may be improved more easily.

Nature of Job Design

One tactic for designing or redesigning jobs is to simplify the job tasks and responsibilities. Job simplification may be appropriate when a job is to be staffed with entry-level employees. However, making a job too simple may result in a boring job that appeals to few, causing high turnover. There are several approaches useful as part of job design.

Job Enlargement and Job Enrichment Attempts to alleviate some of the problems encountered in excessive job simplification fall under the general headings of job enlargement and job enrichment. **Job enlargement** involves broadening the scope of a job by expanding the number of different tasks to be performed. **Job enrichment** is increasing the depth of a job by adding responsibility for planning, organizing, controlling, or evaluating the job. A manager might enrich a job by promoting variety, requiring more skill and responsibility, providing more autonomy, and adding opportunities for personal growth. Giving an employee more planning and controlling responsibilities over the tasks to be done also enriches. However, simply adding more similar tasks does not enrich the job. Some examples of job enrichment include:

- Giving a person an entire job rather than just a piece of the work.
- Giving more freedom and authority so the employee can perform the job as he or she sees fit.
- Increasing a person's accountability for work by reducing external control.
- Expanding assignments so employees can learn to do new tasks and develop new areas of expertise.
- Giving feedback reports directly to employees rather than to management only.

Job Rotation One technique that can break the monotony of an otherwise simple, routine job is **job rotation,** which is the process of shifting a person from job to job. For example, one week on the auto assembly line, a worker attaches doors to the rest of the body assembly. The next week, he attaches bumpers. The third week he puts in seat assemblies, then rotates back to doors again the following week. Job rotation need not be done on a weekly basis. A worker could spend one-third of a day on each job or one entire day, instead of a week, on each job. However, some argue that job rotation does little in the long run because rotating a person from one boring job to another may help somewhat initially, but the jobs are still perceived as boring. The advantage is that job rotation develops an employee's capabilities for doing several different jobs.

Characteristics of Jobs

The job characteristics model developed by Hackman and Oldham identifies five important design characteristics of jobs. Figure 6-3 shows that *skill variety, task*

Job enlargement Broadening the scope of a job by expanding the number of different tasks to be performed.

Job enrichment Increasing the depth of a job by adding the responsibility for planning, organizing, controlling, and evaluating the job.

Job rotation The process of shifting a person from job to job.

Figure 6-3 | **Job Characteristics Model**

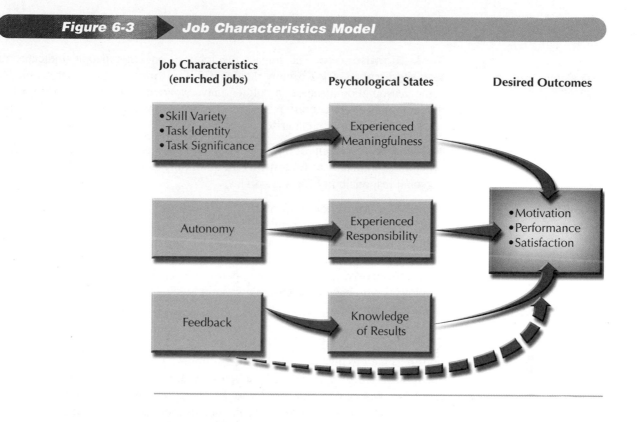

**Job Characteristics
(enriched jobs)**

Psychological States

Desired Outcomes

- Skill Variety
- Task Identity
- Task Significance

Experienced
Meaningfulness

Autonomy

Experienced
Responsibility

- Motivation
- Performance
- Satisfaction

Feedback

Knowledge
of Results

---

identity, and *task significance* affect the meaningfulness of work. *Autonomy* stimulates responsibility, and *feedback* provides knowledge of results. Each aspect can make a job better for the job holder to the degree that each is present.

Skill Variety The extent to which the work requires several different activities for successful completion indicates its **skill variety.** For example, lower skill variety exists when an assembly-line worker performs the same two tasks repetitively. The more skills involved, the more meaningful the work is. Skill variety is not to be confused with "multi-tasking," which is doing several tasks at the same time with computers, telephones, personal organizers, and other gadgets. The price of multi-tasking may be to never get away from the job—not a "better" outcome for everyone.[6]

Task Identity The extent to which the job includes a "whole" identifiable unit of work that is carried out from start to finish and that results in a visible outcome is its **task identity.** For example, one corporation changed its customer service processes so that when a customer calls with a problem, one employee, called a Customer Care Advocate, handles most or all facets of the problem from maintenance to repair. As a result, more than 40% of customer problems are resolved by one person while the customer is still on the line. Previously, less than 1% of the customer problems were resolved immediately because the customer service representative had to complete paperwork and forward it to operations, which then followed a number of separate steps using different people to resolve problems. In the current system, the Customer Care Advocate follows

Skill variety The extent to which the work requires several different activities for successful completion.

Task identity The extent to which the job includes a "whole" identifiable unit of work that is carried out from start to finish and that results in a visible outcome.

the problem from start to finish, solving the "whole" problem, not just a part of it, which makes the job more meaningful.

Task Significance The impact the job has on other people indicates its **task significance.** A job is more meaningful if it is important to other people for some reason. For instance, a soldier may experience more fulfillment when defending his or her country from a real threat than when merely training to stay ready in case such a threat arises.

Autonomy The extent of individual freedom and discretion in the work and its scheduling indicates **autonomy.** More autonomy leads to a greater feeling of personal responsibility for the work.

Feedback The amount of information employees receive about how well or how poorly they have performed is **feedback.** The advantage of feedback is that it helps employees to understand the effectiveness of their performance and contributes to their overall knowledge about the work. At one firm, feedback reports from customers who contact the company with problems are given directly to the employees who handle the customers' complaints, instead of being given only to the department manager.

Consequences of Job Design

Jobs designed to take advantage of these important job characteristics are more likely to be positively received by employees. Job characteristics can help distinguish between "good" and "bad" jobs. Many approaches to enhancing productivity and quality reflect efforts to expand one or more of the job characteristics.

Because of the effects of job design on performance, employee satisfaction, health, and other factors, organizations are changing or have already changed the design of some jobs.[7] Work can be designed in inefficient ways so that employees struggle to accomplish tasks and take too long to do so. In some organizations employees themselves contribute good ideas and then make the changes to succeed as the HR Perspective describes.[7]

Using Teams in Jobs

Typically, a job is thought of as something done by one person. However, jobs may be designed for teams, where it is appropriate. In an attempt to make jobs more meaningful and take advantage of the increased productivity and commitment that can follow, more organizations are using teams of employees instead of individuals for jobs. Some firms have gone as far as dropping such terms as *workers* and *employees,* replacing them with *teammates, crew members, associates,* and other titles that emphasize teamwork.

Special-Purpose Teams Organizations use several types of teams that function outside the scope of members' normal jobs and meet from time to time. One is the **special-purpose team,** which is formed to address specific problems, improve work processes, and enhance the overall quality of products and services. Often, these teams are a mixture of employees, supervisors, and managers. Another kind of team is the **quality circle,** a small group of employees who monitor productivity and quality and suggest solutions to problems. Organizations must take care to ensure that such teams do not violate federal labor

---

Task significance The impact the job has on other people.

Autonomy The extent of individual freedom and discretion in the work and its scheduling.

Feedback The amount of information received about how well or how poorly one has performed.

Special-purpose team Organizational team formed to address specific problems, improve work processes, and enhance product and service quality.

Quality circle Small group of employees who monitor productivity and quality and suggest solutions to problems.

Research on "Crafting" a Job

Even though managers like to think they "design" jobs in some rational fashion, employees over time play a major role in shaping the tasks and social relationships that compose their jobs. Amy Wrzesniewski and Jane Dutton looked at previous research in the *Academy of Management Review* and proposed a model of "job crafting" by employees. Job crafting is the change that individuals make in their job tasks and their relationships with others at work. By changing their jobs to better fit their own motivations, job crafting by employees creates different jobs that fit them and their work better in some way.

The job-crafting process is neither inherently good nor bad. In some cases it results in better goal achievement for the organiza-

tion, but in others it does not. Not all employees change their jobs by changing their tasks, by working with other people, or by taking on more or less responsibility. But many do, and indeed it may be a way in which people who work in jobs with little autonomy or authority have made their jobs tolerable for generations.

A specific example from one of the different groups the researchers considered was a hospital cleaning staff. By crafting their jobs differently, some of the cleaners experienced the *meaning of their jobs* differently. Cleaners who did craft their jobs added tasks and timed when they did their tasks to fit well with the work flow in their units. As a result, they saw themselves as an important

part of the patient care in the hospital, even though they were not doctors or nurses. Other cleaners did no crafting and simply saw their work as cleaning, and themselves as cleaners with work to do. The crafters communicated with patients, visitors, and nurses, which contributed to a work unit that functioned more smoothly.

The researchers also identified similar crafting by hairdressers, engineers, restaurant kitchen employees, and information technicians. As changes in organizations become more pervasive, employees' abilities to understand their roles in the work process and to craft jobs to organizational changes may be a strategic advantage for organizations that can foster such behaviors.[8]

---

laws. In a number of court cases, teams selected by and dominated by managers have been ruled to violate provisions of the National Labor Relations Act.

Production cells Groupings of workers who produce entire products or components.

Production Cells Another way work is restructured is through the use of production cells. As used in a number of manufacturing operations, **production cells** are groupings of workers who make components or entire products. As many as fifty employees and as few as two can be grouped into a production cell, and each cell has all necessary machines and equipment. The cells ultimately replace the assembly line as the primary means of production.

Self-directed work team One composed of individuals assigned a cluster of tasks, duties, and responsibilities to be accomplished.

Self-Directed Work Teams The **self-directed work team** is composed of individuals who are assigned a cluster of tasks, duties, and responsibilities to be accomplished. Unlike special-purpose teams, these teams become the regular entities in which team members work.

An interesting challenge for self-directed work teams involves the emergence or development of team leaders. This role differs from the traditional role played by supervisors or managers. Rather than giving orders, the team leader becomes a facilitator to assist the team, mediate and resolve conflicts among team members, and interact with other teams and managers in other parts of the organization. Shared leadership may be necessary, whereby team members rotate leadership for different phases of projects in which special expertise may

Figure 6-4 ▸ **Shamrock Team**

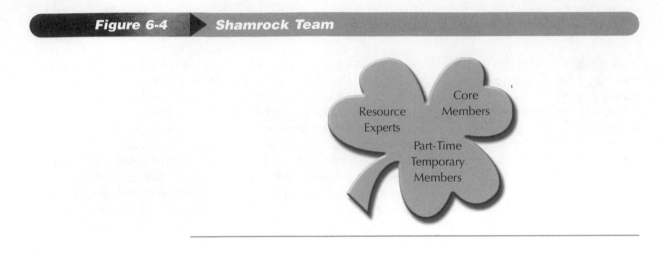

be beneficial. Certain characteristics contribute to the successful use of self-directed work teams in the United States:

- *Teams value and endorse dissent.* The effective use of self-directed work teams requires that conflict and dissent be recognized and addressed.[9] Contrary to what some might believe, suppressing dissent and conflict to preserve harmony ultimately becomes destructive to the effective operations of the team.

- *Teams use "shamrock" structures and have some variation in membership.* As Figure 6-4 shows, a **shamrock team** is composed of a core of members, resource experts who join the team as appropriate, and part-time/temporary members as needed. The presence of core members provides stability, but the infusion of the resource experts and part-time/temporary members provides renewal and change to the team.

- *Teams have authority to make decisions.* For self-directed work teams to be effective, they must be allowed to function with sufficient authority to make decisions about team activities and operations. As transition to self-directed work teams occurs, significant efforts are necessary to define the areas, scope of authority, and goals of the teams.

Shamrock team One composed of a core of members, resource experts who join the team as appropriate, and part-time/temporary members as needed.

Advantages and Disadvantages of Team Jobs

Doing work with teams has been a popular form of job redesign for the last decade. Improved productivity, increased employee involvement, more widespread employee learning, and greater employee ownership of problems are among the potential benefits. Some organizations have found favorable results with *transnational* teams as the challenges of managing across borders become more common and complex. Even *virtual teams* linked primarily through advanced technology can contribute despite geographical dispersion of essential employees.

But not every use of teams as a part of job design has been successful. In some cases employers find that teams work better with employees who are "group oriented," than with more individualistically-focused workers. Further, much work does not really need a team, but many companies have used teamwork without much thought. Too often, *teamwork* can be a buzzword or "feel-good" device that may actually get in the way of good decisions. Another problem is how to measure the performance of teams.[10] Finally, compensating individual team members so that they see themselves as a team rather than just a group of individuals is another issue not adequately addressed in many team-oriented situations.

Other Job Design Issues: Work Schedules and Locations

Jobs consist of the tasks an employee does, the relationships required on the job, the tools one works with, and many other elements as well. Two of these important elements are when and how the work is scheduled, and where an employee is located when working.

Work Schedules

The traditional work schedule, in which employees work full time, eight hours a day, five days a week at the employer's place of operations, is in transition. Organizations have been experimenting with many different possibilities for change: the 4-day, 40-hour week; the 4-day, 32-hour week; the 3-day week; and flexible scheduling. Many employers have adopted some flexibility in work schedules and locations. These alternative work schedules allow organizations to make better use of workers by matching work demands to work hours.[11] Workers also are better able to balance their work and family responsibilities.[12]

Flextime Scheduling arrangement in which employees work a set number of hours per day but vary starting and ending times.

One type of schedule redesign is **flextime**, in which employees work a set number of hours per day but vary starting and ending times. The traditional starting and ending times of the eight-hour work shift can vary up to one or more hours at the beginning and end of the normal workday. Flextime allows management to relax some of the traditional "time clock" control of employees. Generally, use of flextime has resulted in higher employee morale, reduced absenteeism, and lower employee turnover.[13] However, some problems must be addressed when flextime is used, particularly if unionized workers are involved.

Compressed workweek One in which a full week's work is accomplished in fewer than five days.

Another way to change work patterns is with the **compressed workweek**, in which a full week's work is accomplished in fewer than five days. Compression simply alters the number of hours per day per employee, usually resulting in longer working times each day and a decreased number of days worked per week.

More than 25% of the full-time workforce varies their work hours from the "traditional" model, more than double the rate in 1985 the first year data was collected by the U.S. Bureau of Labor Statistics. About 17% of workers have alternative shifts in the form of evening or night shifts.[14]

Work and Job Stress The pressures of modern life, coupled with the demands of a job, can lead to emotional imbalances that are collectively labeled *stress*. Not all stress is unpleasant. To be alive means to respond to the stress of achievement and the excitement of a challenge. In fact, evidence indicates that people *need* a certain amount of stimulation, and that monotony can bring on some of the same problems as overwork. The term *stress* usually refers to excessive stress.

Evidence of stress can be seen everywhere, from the 35-year-old executive who suddenly dies of a heart attack to the dependable worker who unexpectedly commits suicide. Several studies show that some people who abuse alcohol and/or drugs do so to help reduce stress.[15] The main causes of job-related stress appear to be time pressure, fear of losing a job, deadlines, and fragmented work. Such stress can even result in "desk rage" in the form of shouting matches, fistfights, and even bloodshed.[16]

Regardless of the reasons, when an emotional problem (stress-related or otherwise) becomes so severe that it disrupts an employee's ability to function normally, the employee should be directed to appropriate professionals for help. Because emotional problems are difficult to diagnose, supervisors and managers should not become involved in the diagnosis. For example, if a worker is emotionally upset because of marital difficulties, a supervisor should not give advice. Instead, the employee should be referred to an Employee Assistance Program staffed by professionals.

Shift Work Using an eight-hour standard, the 24-hour day can be divided into three "shifts." Many organizations need 24-hour coverage and therefore schedule three shifts each day. Many employers provide some form of additional pay for working evening or night shifts. The average shift differential is about 50¢ per hour.[17] Also, shift work has long been known to cause difficulties for many people with families. Twelve-hour shifts, which some employees choose, involve significant life changes for many too.

Alternative Physical Work Locations

A growing number of employers are allowing workers to use widely different working locations. Some employees work partly at home and partly at an office, while others share office space with other "office nomads." According to data from governmental statistics for a recent year, more than 21 million U.S. workers worked at home for some or all of the time.

Telecommuting is the process of going to work via electronic computing and telecommunications equipment. Many U.S. employers have telecommuting employees or are experimenting with them,[18] including such firms as American Express, Travelers Insurance, and J.C. Penney Co. Other types of nontraditional work arrangements have been labeled in various ways.

Another physical work arrangement is *hoteling,* in which workers check in with an office concierge, carry their own nameplates with them, and are assigned to work cubicles or small offices. A worker uses the assigned office for a day or more, but other workers may use the same office in later days and weeks.

Other employees have *virtual offices,* which means that their offices are wherever they are, whenever they are there.[19] An office could be a customer's project room, an airport conference room, a work suite in a hotel resort, a business-class seat on an international airline flight, or even a rental car.

The shift to such arrangements means employees work anywhere, anytime, and are judged more on results than on "putting in time." Greater trust, less direct supervision, and more self-scheduling are all job characteristics of those with virtual offices and other less traditional arrangements. However, there is some evidence that such arrangements are beginning to lose favor with employers, as they feel it causes resentment with office bound employees and weakens loyalty.[20] Health and safety risks at home and different benefits for contingent and "virtual" workers also raise concerns. Another concern comes from evidence that telecommuting managers do not advance as quickly as office-based executives.

Telecommuting Process of going to work via electronic computing and telecommunications equipment.

WEST GROUP
A THOMSON COMPANY

Telecommuting
Describes considerations when developing a telecommuting policy.
Custom Search:
☑ ANALYSIS
Phrase: Preparing a telecommuting policy

The Nature of Job Analysis

Job analysis Systematic way to gather and analyze information about the content, context, and the human requirements of jobs.

The most basic building block of HR management, **job analysis**, is a systematic way to gather and analyze information about the content, context, and human requirement of jobs. Figure 6-5 shows job analysis in perspective.

Much of the current interest in analyzing jobs stems from the importance assigned to the activity by federal and state courts. The legal defensibility of an employer's recruiting and selection procedures, performance appraisal system, employee disciplinary actions, and pay practices rests in part on the foundation of job analysis. In a number of court cases, the rulings went against employers because judges viewed their HR processes and practices as insufficiently job related. The importance of using job analysis to document HR activities must be emphasized.

It is useful to clarify the differences between job design and job analysis. Job design attempts to develop jobs that fit effectively into the flow of the organizational work that needs to be done. The more narrow focus of job analysis centers on gathering data in a formal and systematic way about what people do in their jobs.

Figure 6-5 ▶ **Job Analysis in Perspective**

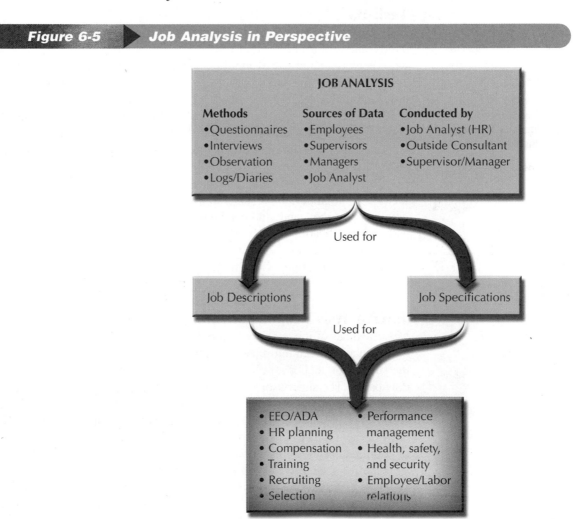

Job analysis involves collecting information on the characteristics of a job that differentiate it from other jobs. Information that can be helpful in making the distinction includes the following:

- Work activities and behaviors
- Interactions with others
- Performance standards
- Financial and budgeting impact
- Machines and equipment used
- Working conditions
- Supervision given and received
- Knowledge, skills, and abilities needed

The information generated by job analysis may be useful in redesigning jobs, but its primary purpose is to capture a clear understanding of what is done on a job and what capabilities are needed to do it as designed. Documents that summarize the elements identified during a job analysis are job descriptions and job specifications.

Task-Based Job Analysis

Task A distinct, identifiable work activity composed of motions.

Duty A larger work segment composed of several tasks that are performed by an individual.

Responsibilities Obligations to perform certain tasks and duties.

Task-based job analysis is the most common form and focuses on the tasks, duties, and responsibilities performed in a job. A **task** is a distinct, identifiable work activity composed of motions, whereas a **duty** is a larger work segment composed of several tasks that are performed by an individual. Because both tasks and duties describe activities, it is not always easy or necessary to distinguish between the two. For example, if one of the employment supervisor's duties is to interview applicants, one task associated with that duty would be asking questions. **Responsibilities** are obligations to perform certain tasks and duties.

The process of analyzing jobs in organizations requires planning of several factors. Some important considerations include how job analysis is to be done, who provides data, and who conducts and uses the data so that job descriptions and job specifications can be prepared and reviewed. In its most fundamental form, job analysis provides the information necessary to develop job descriptions and specifications. Once those are prepared, a wide range of HR activities follows.

Job Analysis Responsibilities

Most methods of job analysis require that a knowledgeable person describe what occurs in a job. Such information can be provided by the employee doing the job, the supervisor, and/or a trained job analyst. Each source is useful, but each has drawbacks. The supervisor seems to be the best source of information on what should be done, but employees often know more about what actually is done. However, both may lack the knowledge needed to complete a job analysis and draw the appropriate conclusions from it. Thus, job analysis requires a high degree of coordination and cooperation between the HR unit and operating managers.

The responsibility for job analysis depends on who can best perform various aspects of the process. Figure 6-6 shows a typical division of responsibilities in organizations with an HR unit. In larger companies, the HR unit supervises the process to maintain its integrity and writes the job descriptions and

Figure 6-6 ▶ **Typical Division of HR Responsibilities: Job Analysis**

HR Unit	Managers
• *Coordinates job analysis procedures*	• *Complete or assist in completing job analysis*
• *Writes job descriptions and specifications for review by managers*	*information*
	• *Review and maintain accuracy of job descriptions/job specifications*
• *Periodically reviews job descriptions and specifications*	
• *Reviews managerial input to ensure accuracy*	• *Request new analysis as jobs change*
• *May seek assistance from outside experts for difficult or unusual analyses*	• *Identify performance standards based on job analysis information*

specifications for uniformity. The managers review the efforts of the HR unit to ensure accuracy and completeness. They also may request reanalysis when jobs change significantly. In small organizations, managers perform all the work activities identified in Figure 6-6.

Stages in the Job Analysis Process

The process of job analysis must be conducted in a logical manner, following appropriate management and professional psychometric practices. Therefore, analysts usually follow a multistage process, regardless of the specific job analysis methods used. The stages for a typical job analysis, as outlined next, may vary somewhat with the number of jobs included.

Planning the Job Analysis

A crucial aspect of the job analysis process is the planning done before gathering data from managers and employees. Probably the most important consideration is to identify the objectives of the job analysis. Maybe it is just to update job descriptions. Or it may include revising the compensation programs in the organization. Another objective could be to redesign certain jobs in a department or division of the organization. Also, it could be to change the structure in parts of the organization to align it better with business strategies.

Whatever the purpose identified, it is vital to obtain top management support. The backing of senior managers is essential as issues arise regarding changes in jobs or the organizational structure. Support from the highest levels of management also helps when managerial and employee anxieties and resistance arise.

Preparing and Introducing the Job Analysis

Preparation for job analysis begins by identifying the jobs under review. For example, are the jobs to be analyzed hourly jobs, clerical jobs, all jobs in one division, or all jobs in the entire organization? This phase identifies those who will be involved in conducting the job analysis and the methods to be used. It also specifies how current incumbents and managers will participate in the process and how many employees' jobs will be considered.

Another task in the identification phase requires reviewing existing documentation. Existing job descriptions, organization charts, previous job analysis information, and other industry-related resources can contribute to the review. Having details from this review may save time and effort later in the process.

A crucial step is to communicate and explain the process to managers, affected employees, and other concerned people, such as union stewards. Explanations should address the natural concerns and anxieties people have when someone closely scrutinizes their jobs. Items to be covered often include the purpose of the job analysis, the steps involved, the time schedule, how managers and employees will participate, who is doing the analysis, and whom to contact as questions arise. When employees are represented by a union, it is essential that union representatives be included in reviewing the job descriptions and specifications to lessen the possibility of future conflicts.

Conducting the Job Analysis

With the preparation completed, the job analysis can be conducted. The methods selected will determine the timeline for the project. Sufficient time should be allotted for obtaining the information from employees and managers. If questionnaires are used, it is often helpful to have employees return them to supervisors or managers for review before giving them back to those conducting the job analysis. The questionnaire should be accompanied by a letter explaining the process and instructions for completing and returning the job analysis questionnaires.

Once data from job analysis are compiled, the information should be sorted by job, organizational unit, and the job family. This step allows for comparison of data from similar jobs throughout the organization. The data also should be reviewed for completeness, with follow-up as needed in the form of additional interviews or questions to be answered by managers and/or employees.

Developing Job Descriptions and Job Specifications

At this stage the job analysts prepare draft job descriptions and job specifications. A later section in this chapter provides details on how to write job descriptions and job specifications. Although drafts should be relatively complete at this point, analysts and managers can use them to identify areas that need additional clarification.

Generally, organizations find that having managers and employees write job descriptions is not recommended for several reasons. First, it reduces the consistency in format and details, both of which are important given the legal consequences of job descriptions. Second, managers and employees vary in their writing skills. Also, they may write the job descriptions and job specifications to reflect what they do and what their personal qualifications are, not what the job requires.

Completed drafts should be reviewed by managers and supervisors. Whether employees review the drafts or wait to receive the final job descriptions is often determined by the managerial style of the supervisors/managers and the culture of the organization regarding employee participation and communication. When finished, the HR department distributes job descriptions to managers, supervisors, and employees. Each supervisor or manager then should review the completed description with individual employees to ensure understanding and

agreement on the content that will be linked to performance appraisals, as well as to all other HR activities.

Maintaining and Updating Job Descriptions and Job Specifications

Once job descriptions and specifications have been completed and reviewed by all appropriate individuals, a system must be developed for keeping them current. Someone in the HR department usually has responsibility for ensuring that job descriptions and specifications stay current. Employees performing the jobs and their managers play a crucial role because, as those closest to the jobs, they know when changes occur. One effective way to ensure that appropriate reviews occur is to use job descriptions and job specifications in other HR activities. For example, each time a vacancy occurs, the job description and specifications should be reviewed and revised as appropriate *before* recruiting and selection efforts begin. Similarly, in some organizations, managers review the job description during each performance appraisal interview. This review enables the job holder and the supervisor to discuss whether the job description still describes the actual job adequately or whether it needs to be revised. In addition, a comprehensive and systematic review may be done during HR planning efforts. For many organizations, a complete review once every three years, or as technology shifts occur, and more frequently when organization changes are made. Figure 6-7 on the next page summarizes the job analysis process.

Job Analysis Methods

Job-Analysis.NETwork
This Web site has resources for conducting a job analysis, including different types of methods, legal issues, questionnaires, and job descriptions.

http://www.job-analysis.net

Job analysis information about what people are doing in their jobs can be gathered in a variety of ways. One consideration is who is to conduct the job analysis. Most frequently, a member of the HR staff coordinates this effort. Depending on which of the methods discussed next is used, others who often participate are managers, supervisors, and employees doing the jobs. For more complex analyses, industrial engineers may conduct time and motion studies. Another consideration is the method to be used. Common methods are observations, interviews, questionnaires, and specialized methods of analysis. The use of a combination of these approaches depends on the situation and the organization. Each of these methods is discussed next.

Observation

With the observation method, a manager, job analyst, or industrial engineer observes the individual performing the job and takes notes to describe the tasks and duties performed. Observation may be continuous or based on intermittent sampling. Use of the observation method is limited because many jobs do not have complete and easily observed job duties or complete job cycles. Thus, observation may be more useful for repetitive jobs and in conjunction with other methods.

Work Sampling As a type of observation, work sampling does not require attention to each detailed action throughout an entire work cycle. Instead, a manager can determine the content and pace of a typical workday through statistical sampling of certain actions rather than through continuous observation and

Figure 6-7 ▶ **Stages in the Job Analysis Process**

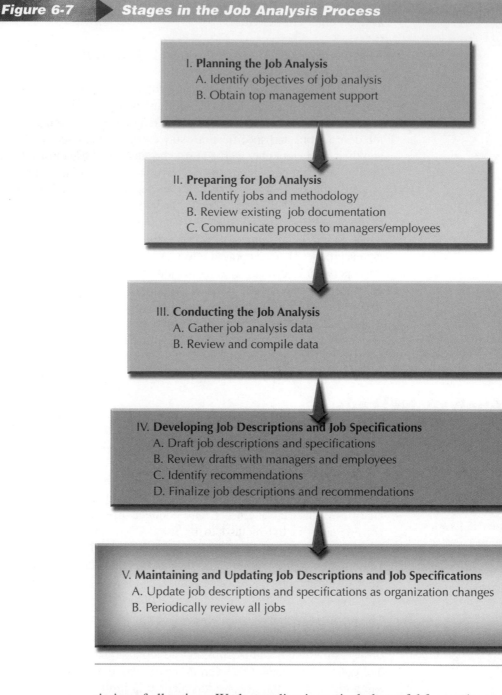

I. **Planning the Job Analysis**
   A. Identify objectives of job analysis
   B. Obtain top management support

II. **Preparing for Job Analysis**
   A. Identify jobs and methodology
   B. Review existing job documentation
   C. Communicate process to managers/employees

III. **Conducting the Job Analysis**
   A. Gather job analysis data
   B. Review and compile data

IV. **Developing Job Descriptions and Job Specifications**
   A. Draft job descriptions and specifications
   B. Review drafts with managers and employees
   C. Identify recommendations
   D. Finalize job descriptions and recommendations

V. **Maintaining and Updating Job Descriptions and Job Specifications**
   A. Update job descriptions and specifications as organization changes
   B. Periodically review all jobs

timing of all actions. Work sampling is particularly useful for routine and repetitive jobs.

Employee Diary/Log Another method requires that employees "observe" their own performances by keeping a diary/log of their job duties, noting how frequently they are performed and the time required for each duty. Although this approach sometimes generates useful information, it may be burdensome for employees to compile an accurate log. Also, employees sometimes perceive this approach as creating needless documentation that detracts from the performance of their work.

Interviewing

The interview method of gathering information requires that a manager or HR specialist visit each job site and talk with the employees performing each job. A standardized interview form is used most often to record the information. Frequently, both the employee and the employee's supervisor must be interviewed to obtain a complete understanding of the job. In some situations, such as team-directed jobs, group interviews also can be used, typically involving experienced job incumbents and/or supervisors. It usually requires the presence of a representative from the HR department as a mediator. For certain difficult-to-define jobs, group interviews are probably most appropriate.

The interview method can be quite time consuming, especially if the interviewer talks with two or three employees doing each job. Professional and managerial jobs often are more complicated to analyze and usually require longer interviews. For these reasons, combining the interview with one of the other methods is suggested.

Questionnaires

The questionnaire is a widely used method of gathering data on jobs. A survey instrument is developed and given to employees and managers to complete. The typical job questionnaire often covers the areas shown in Figure 6-8.

The questionnaire method offers a major advantage in that information on a large number of jobs can be collected inexpensively in a relatively short period of time. However the questionnaire method assumes that employees can accurately analyze and communicate information about their jobs. Employees may vary in their perceptions of the jobs, and even in their literacy. For these reasons, the questionnaire method used in combination with interviews and observations allows analysts to clarify and verify the questionnaire information.

One type of questionnaire sometimes used is a *checklist*. Checklists differ from the open-ended questionnaire and offer a simplified way for employees to

Figure 6-8	Typical Areas Covered in a Job Analysis Questionnaire

Duties and Percent of Time Spent on Each
- *Regular duties*
- *Special duties performed less frequently*

Supervision
- *Supervision given to others*
- *Supervision received from the boss*

Decisions Made
- *Records and reports repaired*
- *Materials and equipment used*
- *Financial/budget responsibilities*

Contact with Other People
- *Internal contacts*
- *External contacts*

Physical Dimensions
- *Physical demands*
- *Working conditions*

Job-Holder Characteristics
- *Knowledge*
- *Skills*
- *Abilities*
- *Training needed*

give information. An obvious difficulty with the checklist is constructing it, which can be a complicated and detailed process.

Specialized Job Analysis Methods

Several job analysis methods are built on the questionnaire approach. Some of these methods are described next.

Position Analysis Questionnaire (PAQ) The PAQ is a specialized questionnaire method incorporating checklists. Each job is analyzed on 27 dimensions composed of 187 "elements." The PAQ comprises a number of divisions, with each division containing numerous job elements. The divisions include:

- *Information input:* Where and how does the worker get information to do the job?
- *Mental process:* What levels of reasoning are necessary on the job?
- *Work output:* What physical activities are performed?
- *Relationships with others:* What relationships are required while performing the job?
- *Job context:* What working conditions and social contexts are involved?
- *Other:* What else is relevant to the job?

The PAQ focuses on "worker-oriented" elements that describe behaviors necessary to do the job, rather than on "job-oriented" elements that describe the technical aspects of the work. Although its complexity may deter many potential users, the PAQ is easily quantified and can be used to conduct validity studies on selection tests. It also may contribute to internal pay fairness because it considers the varying demands of different jobs.

Managerial Job Analysis Because managerial jobs differ in character from jobs with clearly observable routines and procedures, some specialized methods have evolved for their analysis. One of the most well-known and widely used methods was developed at a computer company and is labeled the Management Position Description Questionnaire (MPDQ). Composed of more than 200 statements, the MPDQ examines a variety of managerial dimensions, including decision making and supervising.

Computerized Job Analysis

With the expansion of information technology, researchers have developed computerized job analysis systems. These systems all have several common characteristics, including the way they are administered. First, analysts compose task statements that relate to all jobs. They are then distributed as questionnaires that list the task statements. Next, employee responses on computer-scanable documents are fed into computer-based scoring and reporting services capable of recording, analyzing, and reporting thousands of pieces of information about any job.

An important feature of computerized job analysis is the specificity of data that can be gathered. All of this specific data is compiled into a job analysis database. As a result, a computerized job analysis system often can reduce the time and effort involved in writing job descriptions. These systems store banks of job duty statements that relate to each of the task and scope statements of the questionnaires.

Logging On...

PAQ Services, Inc.
Information on position analysis questionnaires for management and administrative positions is provided.

http://www.paq.com

O*Net

O*Net is a database compiled by the U.S. Department of Labor to provide basic occupational data to anyone who is interested. Certainly job analysts and others who write job descriptions and specifications find this a useful source.

Information on O*Net covers more than 950 occupations based on the Standard Occupational Classification (SOC) developed by the government. The database is largely from data supplied by analysts using the *Dictionary of Occupational Titles (DOT)*.

HR can use this source to develop job descriptions, define

job-specific employee success factors, and for many other uses related to training, recruiting, and selection. The framework that organizes the data is called the "Content Model." It describes five domains:

- Experience requirements
- Worker requirements
- Occupational requirements
- Occupation-specific information
- Occupational characteristics

These domains consider the main aspects of work from descriptions of the worker to requirements of the work.

O*Net also provides extensive linkages to additional resources on workplace issues. All government agencies are moving toward using this system because the coding structure has been aligned with the Standard Occupational Classification (SOC). It represents a valuable and time-saving resource for job analysis and for writing good descriptions and specifications. It can be accessed at *http://www.onetcenter.org/rd/ index.html.*

Job Analysis and the U.S. Department of Labor

A variety of resources related to job analysis are available from the U.S. Department of Labor (DOL). The resources have been developed and used over many years by various entities with the DOL, primarily the Employment and Training Administration.

Functional Job Analysis (FJA) This method is a comprehensive approach to job analysis. FJA considers: (1) goals of the organization, (2) what workers do to achieve those goals in their jobs, (3) level and orientation of what workers do, (4) performance standards, and (5) training content. A functional definition of what is done in a job can be generated by examining the three components of *data, people,* and *things.* The levels of these components are used to identify and compare important elements of jobs given in the *Dictionary of Occupational Titles (DOT),* a standardized data source provided by the federal government.

Dictionary of Occupational Titles (DOT) Functional job analysis, as captured in the *DOT,* is a valuable source of job information, regardless of the job analysis method used. The *DOT* describes a wide range of jobs. A manager or HR specialist confronted with preparing a large number of job descriptions can use the *DOT* as a starting point. The job description from the *DOT* can then be modified to fit the particular organizational situation. However, the *DOT* is a rather old resource, which increasingly is being replaced in use by O*Net. More information on O*Net is available in the e-HR discussion.

O*Net Online The DOL has made a major commitment to provide useable information on skills, abilities, knowledge, work activities, and interests associated with a wide range of jobs and occupations. This information is available online and can be used to develop job descriptions, job specifications, and career opportunity information. O*Net transforms mountains of data into precise, focused, information that anyone can understand and use.

Combination Methods

There are a number of different ways to obtain and analyze information about a job. Therefore, in dealing with issues that may end up in court, HR specialists and others doing job analysis must carefully document all of the steps taken. Each of the methods has strengths and weaknesses, and a combination of methods generally is preferred over one method alone.

Behavioral Aspects of Job Analysis

A detailed examination of jobs, although necessary, can be a demanding and threatening experience for both managers and employees, in part because job analysis can identify the difference between what currently is being performed in a job and what *should* be done. Job analysis involves determining what the "core" job is. This determination may require discussion with managers about the design of the job. Often the content of a job may reflect the desires and skills of the incumbent employee. For example, in one firm a woman promoted to office manager continued to spend considerable time opening and sorting the mail because she had done that duty in her old job. Yet her duties of supervising the work of the eight clerical employees meant she should have been delegating mail duties to one of the clerks. Her manager indicated that opening and sorting mail was not one of the top five tasks of her new job as reflected in the job description. The manager also met with the employee to discuss what it meant to be a supervisor and what duties should receive more emphasis.

Job "Inflation"

Employees and managers also have some tendency to inflate the importance and significance of their jobs. Because job analysis information is used for compensation purposes, both managers and employees hope that "puffing up" their jobs will result in higher pay levels.

Titles of jobs often get inflated too, and some HR specialists believe the problem continues to grow.[21] Some firms give fancy titles in place of pay raises, while others do it to keep well-paid employees from leaving for "status" reasons.[22] Some industries, such as banking and entertainment, are well known for their title inflation. For instance, banking and financial institutions use officer designations to enhance status. In one small midwestern bank, an employee who had three years' experience as a teller was "promoted" with no pay increase to Second Vice President and Senior Customer Service Coordinator. She basically became the lead teller when her supervisor was out of the bank and now could sign a few customer account forms.

Managerial Straitjacket

Through the information developed in a job analysis, the job description is supposed to capture the nature of a job. However, if it fails—if some portions of the job are mistakenly left out of the description—some employees may use any omission to limit managerial flexibility. The resulting attitude, "It's not in my job description," puts a straitjacket on a manager. In some organizations with unionized workforces, very restrictive job descriptions exist.

Because of such difficulties, the final statement in many job descriptions is a *miscellaneous clause,* which consists of a phrase similar to "Performs other duties as needed upon request by immediate supervisor." This statement covers unusual situations that may occur in an employee's job. However, duties covered by this phrase cannot be considered essential functions under the Americans with Disabilities Act (ADA).

Current Incumbent Emphasis

As suggested earlier, it is important that a job analysis and the resulting job description and job specifications should not describe just what the person currently doing the job does and what his or her qualifications are. The person may have unique capabilities and the ability to expand the scope of the job to assume more responsibilities. The company would have difficulty finding someone exactly like that individual if he or she left. Consequently, it is useful to focus on the *core* jobs and *necessary* KSAs by determining what the jobs would be if the current incumbents quit or were no longer available to do the jobs.

Employee Anxieties

One fear that employees may have concerns the purpose of a detailed investigation of their job. Perhaps they feel such a detailed look means someone thinks they have been done something wrong. The attitude behind such a fear might be, " As long as no one knows precisely what I am supposed to be doing, I am safe."

"Productivity is up nine per cent since I made everyone a vice-president."

Also, some employees may fear that an analysis of their jobs will put a "straitjacket" on them, limiting their creativity and flexibility by formalizing their duties. However, analyzing a job does not necessarily limit job scope or depth. In fact, having a well-written, well-communicated job description can assist employees by clarifying their roles and the expectations within those roles. One effective way to handle anxieties is to involve the employees in the revision process.

Legal Aspects of Job Analysis

The previous chapters on equal employment laws, regulations, and court cases emphasize that legal compliance must focus on the jobs that individuals perform. The 1978 Uniform Selection Guidelines make it clear that HR requirements must be tied to specific job-related factors if employers are to defend their actions as a business necessity.

Job Analysis and the Americans with Disabilities Act (ADA)

HR managers and their organizations must identify job activities and then document the steps taken to identify job responsibilities.[23] One result of the ADA is increased emphasis by employers on conducting job analysis, as well as developing and maintaining current and accurate job descriptions and job specifications.

Essential job functions
Fundamental duties of a job.

Marginal functions
Duties that are part of a job but are incidental or ancillary to the purpose and nature of a job.

The ADA requires that organizations identify the **essential job functions,** which are the fundamental duties of a job. The term *essential functions* does not include the marginal functions of the positions. **Marginal functions** are those duties that are part of a job but are incidental or ancillary to the purpose and nature of a job. Figure 6-9 shows three major considerations used in determining essential functions and marginal functions.[24] Job analysts, HR staff members, and operating managers must evaluate and make decisions when the information on the three considerations is not clear.

An important part of job analysis is to obtain information about what duties are being performed and what percentage of time is devoted to each duty. As the ADA suggests, the percentage of time spent on a duty generally indicates its relative importance. How often the duties are performed also becomes important. If duties are regularly performed daily, weekly, and/or monthly, they are more likely to be seen as essential. However, a task performed only infrequently or

Figure 6-9	Determining Essential and Marginal Functions	
Considerations	**Essential Functions**	**Marginal Functions**
Percentage of time spent	• *Significant time spent: often 20% of time or more*	• *Generally less than 10% of time*
Frequency	• *Performed regularly: daily, weekly, monthly*	• *Performed infrequently or when substituting in part of another job*
Importance	• *Task has consequences to other parts of job and other jobs.*	• *Task is unrelated to job and has little consequence if not performed.*

when helping another worker on a totally unrelated job more likely falls in the marginal category.[25]

Another consideration is the ease or difficulty involved in assigning a duty to be performed by someone else, or in a different job. For instance, assume an assembler of electronic components places the completed parts in a bin next to the work area. At the end of each day, the bin of completed parts must be carried to another room for use in final assembly of a product. Carrying the bin to the other room probably would be defined as a marginal task, because assigning someone else to carry it would not likely create major workflow problems with other jobs and workers.

Job analysis also can identify the physical demands of jobs. An understanding of the skills and capabilities used on a job is critical. For example, a customer service representative must be able to hear well enough to take customer orders. However, hearing may be less essential for a heavy equipment operator in a quarry.

Job Analysis and Wage/Hour Regulations

Typically, job analysis identifies the percentage of time spent on each duty in a job. This information helps determine whether someone should be classified as exempt or nonexempt under the wage/hour laws.

As will be noted in the compensation chapter, the federal Fair Labor Standards Act (FLSA) and most state wage/hour laws indicate that the percentage of time employees spend on manual, routine, or clerical duties affects whether they must be paid overtime for hours worked in excess of 40 per week. To be exempt from overtime, the employees must perform their *primary duties* as executive, administrative, or professional employees. *Primary* has been interpreted to mean occurring at least 50% of the time. Additionally, the exemption regulations state that no more than 20% (40% in retail settings) of the time can be spent on manual, routine, or clerical duties.

Other legal-compliance efforts, such as those involving workplace safety and health, can also be aided through the data provided by job analysis. In summary, it is extremely difficult for an employer to have a legal staffing system without performing job analysis. Truly, job analysis is the most basic HR activity.

Job Descriptions and Job Specifications

The output from analysis of a job is used to develop a job description and its job specifications. Together, they summarize job analysis information in a readable format and provide the basis for defensible job-related actions. They also identify individual jobs for employees by providing documentation from management.

In most cases, the job description and job specifications are combined into one document that contains several different sections. A **job description** identifies the tasks, duties, and responsibilities of a job. It describes what is done, why it is done, where it is done, and briefly, how it is done. Then, **performance standards** can flow directly from a job description and indicate what the job accomplishes and how performance is measured in key areas of the job description.[26] The reason for including the performance standards is clear. If employees know what is expected and how performance is to be measured, they have a much better chance of performing satisfactorily. Figure 6-10 shows job description duty

Job description Identification of the tasks, duties, and responsibilities of a job.

Performance standards Indicators of what the job accomplishes and how performance is measured in key areas of the job description.

Figure 6-10

**Sample Job Duty Statements
and Performance Standards**

Job Title: Customer Response Representative
Supervisor: Customer Response Supervisor

Duty	Performance Standards
Discusses nonpayment of bills with customers and notifies them of nonpayment disconnecting of service.	• *Flags accounts within two days that are not to be disconnected according to discussions with Local Manager.* • *Mails notices to cable television customers to be received at least five days prior to disconnection date.* • *Determines which accounts require credit deposit, based on prior payment history.* • *Calmly discusses the nonpayment status of the account, along with options for reconnection with customers.* • *Disconnects and reconnects long distance calling cards for nonpayments with 100% accuracy.*
Receives and records trouble reports from customers on mechanized trouble-reporting system for telephone or proper form for cable television. Dispatches reports to appropriate personnel.	• *Completes all required trouble information on the trouble-reporting system accurately with no more than five errors annually.* • *Dispatches trouble ticket information to voice mail with 100% accuracy.* • *Tests line if needed or as requested by technician for telephone troubles.*

statements and some performance standards used for a customer response representative in a telecommunications firm.

Unfortunately, performance standards often are omitted from job descriptions. Even if performance standards have been identified and matched to job descriptions, they may not be communicated to employees if the job descriptions are not provided to employees, but used only as tools by the HR department and managers. Such an approach limits the value of job descriptions.

While the job description describes activities to be done, the **job specifications** list the knowledge, skills, and abilities an individual needs to perform a job satisfactorily. Knowledge, skills, and abilities (KSAs) include education, experience, work skill requirements, personal abilities, and mental and physical requirements. Job specifications for a data entry operator might include a required educational level, a certain number of months of experience, a typing ability of 60 words per minute, a high degree of visual concentration, and ability to work under time pressure. It is important to note that accurate job specifications identify what KSAs a person needs to do the job, not necessarily what qualifications the current employee possesses.

Job specifications The knowledge, skills, and abilities (KSAs) an individual needs to perform a job satisfactorily.

Job Description Components

A typical job description contains several major parts. Overviews of the most common components are presented next.

Identification The first part of the job description is the identification section, in which the job title, reporting relationships, department, location, and date of analysis may be given. Usually, it is advisable to note other information that is useful in tracking jobs and employees through human resource information systems (HRIS). Additional items commonly noted in the identification section are:

- Job code
- Pay grade
- Exempt/nonexempt status under Fair Labor Standards Act (FLSA)
- EEOC Classification (from EEO-1 form)

General Summary The second part, the general summary, is a concise statement of the general responsibilities and components that make the job different from others. One HR specialist has characterized the general summary statement as follows: "In thirty words or less, describe the essence of the job."

Essential Functions and Duties The third part of the typical job description lists the essential functions and duties. It contains clear, precise statements on the major tasks, duties, and responsibilities performed. Writing this section is the most time-consuming aspect of preparing job descriptions.

Job Specifications The next portion of the job description gives the qualifications needed to perform the job satisfactorily. The job specifications typically are stated as: (1) knowledge, skills, and abilities (KSAs), (2) education and experience, and (3) physical requirements and/or working conditions. The components of the job specifications provide information necessary to determine what accommodations might and might not be possible under Americans with Disabilities Act (ADA) regulations.[27]

Disclaimer and Approvals The final section on many job descriptions contains approval signatures by appropriate managers and a legal disclaimer. This disclaimer allows employers to change employees' job duties or request employees to perform duties not listed, so that the job description is not viewed as a "contract" between the employer and the employee. Figure 6-11 on the next page shows a sample job description and contains job specifications also.

The Competency Approach to Job Analysis

More and more often, commentators and writers address the notion that the nature of jobs and work is changing so much that the concept of a "job" may be obsolete for many people. In some high-technology industries, employees work in cross-functional project teams and shift from project to project. Organizations in these industries focus less on performing specific tasks and duties and more on fulfilling responsibilities and attaining results. For example, a project team of eight employees developing software to allow various credit cards to be used with ATMs worldwide will work on many different tasks, some individually and

Figure 6-11 **Sample Job Description and Specifications**

JOB TITLE: Compensation Manager

SUPERVISOR'S TITLE: Vice President of Human Resources

DEPARTMENT: Human Resources

JOB CODE: _____

GRADE: _____

FLSA STATUS: _____Exempt_____

EEOC CLASS: _____O/M_____

General Summary: Responsible for the design and administration of all cash compensation programs, ensures proper consideration of the relationship of compensation to performance of each employee, and provides consultation on compensation administration to managers and supervisors.

Essential Duties and Responsibilities:

1. Prepares and maintains job descriptions for all jobs and periodically reviews and updates them. Responds to questions from employees and supervisors regarding job descriptions. (25%)
2. Ensures that Company compensation rates are in line with pay structures. Obtains or conducts pay surveys as necessary and presents recommendations on pay structures on an annual basis. (20%)
3. Develops and administers the performance appraisal program and monitors the use of the performance appraisal instruments to ensure the integrity of the system and its proper use. (20%)
4. Directs the job evaluation process by coordinating committee activities and resolves disputes over job values. Conducts initial evaluation of new jobs prior to hiring and assigns jobs to pay ranges. (15%)
5. Researches and provides recommendations on executive compensation issues. Assists in the development and oversees the administration of all annual bonus payments for senior managers and executives. (15%)
6. Coordinates the development of an integrated HR information system and interfaces with the Management Information Systems Department to achieve departmental goals for information needs. (5%)
7. Performs related duties as assigned or as the situation dictates.

Required Knowledge, Skills, and Abilities:

1. Knowledge of compensation and HR management practices and approaches.
2. Knowledge of effective job analysis methods and survey development and interpretation practices and principles.
3. Knowledge of performance management program design and administration.
4. Knowledge of federal and state wage and hour regulations.
5. Skill in writing job descriptions, memorandums, letters, and proposals.
6. Skill in use of word processing, spreadsheet, and database software.
7. Ability to make presentations to groups on compensation policies and practices.
8. Ability to plan and prioritize work.

Education and Experience:

This position requires the equivalent of a college degree in Business Administration, Psychology, or a related field plus 3–5 years experience in HR management, 2–3 of which should include compensation administration experience. An advanced degree in Industrial Psychology, Business Administration, or HR Management is preferred, but not required.

Physical Requirements	Rarely (0–12%)	Occasionally (12–33%)	Frequently (34–66%)	Regularly (67–100%)
Seeing: Must be able to read reports and use computer				X
Hearing: Must be able to hear well enough to communicate with coworkers				X
Standing/Walking	X			
Climbing/Stooping/Kneeling	X			
Lifting/Pulling/Pushing	X			
Fingering/Grasping/Feeling: Must be able to write, type, and use phone system				X

Working Conditions: Normal office working conditions with the absence of disagreeable elements.

Note: The statements herein are intended to describe the general nature and level of work being performed by employees, and are not to be construed as an exhaustive list of responsibilities, duties, and skills required of personnel so classified. Furthermore, they do not establish a contract for employment and are subject to change at the discretion of the employer.

Figure 6-12 ▶ **Examples of Competencies**

- *Customer focus*
- *Team orientation*
- *Technical expertise*
- *Results orientation*
- *Leadership*
- *Innovation*
- *Adaptability*
- *Decisiveness*

some with other team members. When that project is finished those employees will move to other projects, possibly with other employers. Such shifts may happen several times per year. Therefore, the basis for recruiting, selecting, and compensating these individuals is their competence and capabilities, not just what they do. Writing an accurate job description for such a job would be difficult or even impossible.

In many industries traditional jobs will continue to exist. Studying these jobs and their work consequences is relatively easy because of the repetitiveness of the work and the limited number of tasks each worker performs, so the task-based approach to job analysis is appropriate.

Clearly, studying the two different types of jobs—lower-skilled ones and more varied, highly technical ones—requires different approaches. Focusing on the competencies that individuals need to perform jobs, rather than on the tasks, duties, and responsibilities composing a job emphasizes how significantly people's capabilities influence organizational performance. Instead of thinking of individuals having jobs that are relatively stable and can be written up into typical job descriptions, it may be more relevant to focus on the competencies used.

Competencies Basic characteristics that can be linked to enhanced performance by individuals or teams.

Competencies are basic characteristics that can be linked to enhanced performance by individuals or teams. Figure 6-12 shows examples of commonly identified competencies.

A growing number of organizations use some facets of competency analysis. The three primary reasons organizations use a competency approach are: (1) to communicate valued behaviors throughout the organization; (2) to raise the competency levels of the organization; and (3) to emphasize the capabilities of people to enhance organizational competitive advantage.

Competency Analysis Methodology

Unlike the traditional approach to analyzing jobs, which identifies the tasks, duties, knowledge, and skills associated with a job, the competency approach considers how the knowledge and skills are used. The competency approach also attempts to identify the hidden factors that are often critical to superior performance. For instance, many supervisors talk about employees' attitudes, but they have difficulty identifying what they mean by *attitude*. The competency approach uses some methodologies to help supervisors articulate examples of what they mean by attitude and how those factors affect performance.

One method used to determine competencies is *behavioral event interviews*. This process involves the following steps:

1. A team of senior managers identifies future performance results areas critical to the business and strategic plans of the organization. These concepts may be broader than those used in the past.

Logging On...

Job and Competency Analysis
This Web site provides an integrated job and competency analysis tool to be used in job design and evaluation.

http://www.claytonwallis.com/cxomf.htm

2. Panel groups are assembled, composed of individuals knowledgeable about the jobs in the company. This group can include both high- and low-performing employees, supervisors, managers, trainers, and others.
3. A facilitator from HR or an outside consultant interviews the panel members to get specific examples of job behaviors and actual occurrences on the jobs. During the interview the individuals are also asked about their thoughts and feelings during each of the described events.
4. Using the behavioral events, the facilitator develops detailed descriptions of each of the competencies. Descriptive phases provide clarity and specifics so that employees, supervisors, managers, and others in the organization have a clearer understanding of the competencies associated with individual jobs.
5. The competencies are rated and levels needed to meet them are identified. Then the competencies are specified for each of the jobs.
6. Finally, standards of performance are identified and tied to the jobs. Appropriate selection screening, training, and compensation processes that focus on competencies must be developed and implemented.

Possible Legal Problems with the Competency Approach

Traditional task-based job analysis provides a rational basis for such activities as compensation, selection, and training, all of which are subject to legal action by employees if they believe they are being wronged in some way. The traditional job analysis approach has been used successfully to substantiate employment decisions. Currently, there is little legal precedent regarding competency analysis, which leaves it open to legal challenge as not being as job-related as the traditional approach.[28]

Summary

- Work is organized into jobs for people to do. Workflow analysis and business process re-engineering are two approaches used to check how well this has been done.
- Job design is involved with developing jobs that people like to do. It may include simplification, rotation, enlargement, or enrichment.
- Designing jobs so that they incorporate skill variety, task identity and significance, autonomy, and feedback can make for jobs people are more likely to prefer.
- "Crafting" jobs is another way of allowing employees to participate in the design of their jobs, while using team design is another option.
- Job analysis is a systematic investigation of the tasks, duties, and responsibilities necessary to do a job.

- Task-based job analysis focuses on the tasks, duties, and responsibilities associated with jobs.
- The end products of job analysis are job descriptions, which identify the tasks, duties, and responsibilities in jobs, and job specifications, which list the knowledge, skills, and abilities (KSAs) needed to perform a job satisfactorily.
- Job analysis information is useful in most HR activities, such as human resource planning, recruiting and selection, compensation, training and development, performance appraisal, safety and health, and union relations.
- Legal compliance in HR must be based on job analysis. The Americans with Disabilities Act (ADA) has increased the importance of job analysis and its components.

- Behavioral factors, including creating a managerial straitjacket and employee anxieties, must be considered when conducting a job analysis.
- Methods of gathering job analysis information include observation, interviews, questionnaires, some specialized methods, and computer job analysis. In practice, a combination of methods is often used.
- The process of conducting a job analysis has the following steps:
  1. Planning the job analysis
  2. Preparing and communicating the job analysis
  3. Conducting the job analysis
  4. Developing job descriptions and job specifications
  5. Maintaining and updating job descriptions and job specifications
- When writing job descriptions and job specifications, the essential job functions and KSAs should be described clearly.
- One approach to job analysis identifies competencies, which are the basic characteristics linked to the performance of individuals or teams.
- Once competencies have been identified, they can be used for HR selection, development, compensation, and performance management.

Review and Discussion Questions

1. Explain both workflow analysis and business process re-engineering as approaches to work redesign.
2. Pick a job and discuss which of the job characteristics in Figure 6-3 would improve it most.
3. Discuss why the Americans with Disabilities Act (ADA) has heightened the importance of job analysis activities.
4. Describe three task-based methods of analyzing jobs, including some advantages and disadvantages of each method.
5. Explain how you would conduct a job analysis in a company that had never had job descriptions.
6. Discuss how you would train someone to write job descriptions and job specifications for a small bank.
7. Why is competency-based job analysis more difficult to conduct than the traditional task-based approach?

Terms to Know

Computer Programmer Job Description

As the Human Resources Specialist, it is your job to make sure all of the job documentation is updated on a regular basis and that current job descriptions are on file. Most of the managers do not complete job questionnaires or update their job descriptions, so it is a difficult task to keep job descriptions current and consistent across all departments.

Recently, the IT manager asked for your assistance with a new position she is creating. The position is for a computer programmer, but this programmer would be functioning at a more complex level than current programmers in her department. She has asked you to create a job description for this new job that will be providing support to the whole organization. The following are a few key descriptive words given you to assist with your task.

- Complex programming
- Written and oral communication
- Critical analysis
- Use of equipment
- Mathematical calculations
- Reasoning

To write your description for the computer programmer position based on your conversation with the IT manager and the list of descriptive words she has given you, use the descriptions and O*Net, *http://online.onetcenter.org*.

1. At that website go to *Find Occupations* and search for computer programmers.
2. Identify three important KSA statements listed for the job.
3. Finally, write a job description that contains: (a) a summary statement, (b) the main job functions, and (c) three each of the KSAs that best match the concerns of the IT manager.

Airline Mechanic's Job

Even with higher salaries, the number of airline mechanics has been declining and airlines are having a difficult time hiring enough mechanics. Why this is occurring can be seen by looking at the job. Whether it is diagnosing bad wiring at 3 A.M., squeezing into fuel tanks, or replacing antennas 60 feet off the ground, an aircraft mechanic's job takes place in less than ideal circumstances. The individual works weekends, holidays, and late night shifts, which is when most airline maintenance is done. The pay is about $57,000 per year for a job that certainly affects airline passengers and their lives. Mechanics are invisible to most customers, but their work is the backbone of flying.

"Aviation mechanics think they are perceived as the underbelly of the aviation industry," says the Deputy Director of the International Association of Machinists. The FAA is studying the effects of fatigue and shift work to see whether duty rules are needed for mechanics. The agency does not even limit the number of hours a mechanic can work as it does with airline pilots.

The number of mechanics licenses issued has dropped by two-thirds in nine years from over 24,000 per year in the early '90s to almost 8,000 per year now. Further adding to the problem are large numbers of mid-career mechanics switching to other jobs. Mechanics are leaving the airlines in record numbers for better mechanics jobs as in power plants, electronics firms, the railroad and auto industries, and even amusement parks. If attrition does not slow and more new mechanics are not trained, the results will be more flight delays, late packages, and aircraft sitting on the ground, says a highly placed official.[29]

Questions

1. Excluding any pay problems, how could the airline mechanics job be redesigned?
2. Considering both the task-based and competency approaches, identify several tasks and several competencies in order to illustrate the differences in approaches.

Notes

1. The following is adapted from Laura Bird, "The New 24/7 Work Cycle," *The Wall Street Journal,* September 20, 2000, B1; Julie Cook, "Out of the Dark," *Human Resource Executive,* January 2001, 80–85; and Sue Shellenbarger, "Work and Family," *The Wall Street Journal,* September 20, 2000, B1.
2. Robert Hof, "Look, Ma, No Humans," *Business Week,* November 20, 2000, EB 132.
3. Bob Cardy, "Considering the Source," *HR News,* Spring 2000, 10–11.
4. Based on John A. Challenger, "24 Trends Reshaping the Workplace," *The Futurist* 34 (September 2000), 35; Sue Shellenbarger, "More Relaxed Boomers, Fewer Workplace Frills . . . ," *The Wall Street Journal,* December 20, 2001, B1; and Robert Taylor, "A US Policy Vacuum," *Financial Times,* October 20, 2000, 11.
5. A. E. M. Van Vianen, "Person-Organization Fit: The Match Between Newcomers' and Recruiters' Preferences for Organizational Cultures," *Personnel Psychology* 53 (2000), 113–149.
6. Maria Puente, "Multi-Tasking to the MAX?" *USA Today,* April 25, 2000, 10.
7. Eric Raimy, "Back to the Table," *Human Resource Executive,* March 2001, 1.
8. Adapted from Amy Wrzesniewski and Jane Dutton, "Crafting a Job: Revisioning Employees as Active Crafters of Their Work," *Academy of Management Review* 26 (2001), 179–201.
9. Greg Stewart and Murry Barrick, "Team Structure and Performance," *Academy of Management Journal* 43 (2000), 135.
10. Bradley L. Kirkman, Paul E. Tesluk, and Benson Rosen, "Assessing the Incremental Validity of Team Consensus Ratings . . ." *Personnel Psychology* 54 (2001), 645–667.
11. Sue Shellenbarger, "Flexible Scheduling Works Best If It Serves Both Boss and Worker," *The Wall Street Journal,* January 17, 2001, B1.
12. Marisa DiNatale, "Characteristics of and Preference for Alternative Work Arrangements," *Monthly Labor Review,* March 2001, 28–49.
13. Sara Gale, "Formalized Flextime," *Workforce,* February 2001, 39–42.
14. Thomas Beers, "Flexible Schedules and Shift Work," *Monthly Labor Review,* June 2000, 33–40.
15. D. J. Dwyer and M. L. Fox, "The Moderating Role of Hostility in the Relationship Between Enriched Jobs and Health," *Academy of Management Journal,* 43 (2000), 1086–1096.
16. Carol Hymowitz, "Can Workplace Stress Get Worse?" *The Wall Street Journal,* January 16, 2001, B1.
17. "Survey Spotlights Shiftwork Practices," *Occupational Hazards,* October 2000, 56.
18. Susan J. Wells, "Making Telecommuting Work," *HR Magazine,* October 2001, 34–45.
19. Jeremy Handel, "Virtually Speaking," *WorkSpan,* September 2000, 55–57.
20. Kemba Dunham, "Telecommuter's Lament," *The Wall Street Journal,* October 31, 2000, B1.
21. Tammy Joyner, "Staff, Let's Play the Name Game," *Omaha World-Herald,* July 1, 2001, 1G.
22. Charlotte Garvey, "Getting a Grip on Titles," *HR Magazine,* December 2000, 113–117.
23. Don Caruth and Gail Handlogten, "Avoiding HR Lawsuits," *Credit Union Executive,* November–December 2001, 25.
24. Matthew Miklave and A. Jonathan Trafimow, "Expect to See Your Words on Tomorrow's Front Page," *Workforce,* June 2000, 180.
25. Stephen Sonneberg, "Mental Disabilities in the Workplace," *Workforce,* June 2000, 143.
26. Joanne Wojcik, "Focus on Performance," *Business Insurance,* July 10, 2000, 20.
27. Peter Petesch, "Popping the Disability-Related Question," *HR Magazine,* November 2000, 161.
28. Carla Joinson, "Refocusing Job Descriptions," *HR Magazine,* January 2001, 67–72.
29. Based on Marilyn Adams, "Airlines Grapple with Shortage of Mechanics," *USA Today,* October 17, 2000, 1B.

CHAPTER 7

Recruiting in Labor Markets

After you have read this chapter, you should be able to:

- Identify different ways that labor markets can be identified and approached.

- Describe the phases in strategic recruiting and decisions made in each phase.

- Discuss the advantages and disadvantages of internal vs. external recruiting.

- Identify three internal sources for recruiting and issues associated with their use.

- Discuss why Internet recruiting has grown and how employers are conducting it.

- List and briefly discuss five external recruiting sources.

- Discuss three factors to consider when evaluating recruiting efforts.

Where Are the Workers We Need?

Even during times of economic slowdown, as well as prosperity, shortages of sufficient qualified workers have existed in specific industries in the U.S. economy. Some examples illustrate the challenges faced by various employers.

Trucking companies have faced serious shortages for drivers, particularly those who drive long distances, and spend many nights away from home. According to the American Trucking Association, the number of trucks on the road has increased by 25% in the past five years. To find drivers, many trucking firms have full-time recruiters on staff, whose jobs are to recruit drivers from other companies. To attract drivers, USA Trucking, Werner Trucking, and other firms provide truckers electronic logs and e-mail access, subsidize phone cards for calling home, supply newer trucks with more comfortable amenities, and raise pay. Some firms combat the shortage by using immigrant drivers from Poland, Bosnia, Mexico, and other countries, but safety and law enforcement officials have expressed concerns about the qualifications of some of the immigrants hired.

The food-service industry also has been suffering from worker shortages. With more and more Americans eating out, staffing jobs from the counter workers and cooks to food servers and restaurant managers presents a challenge. For instance, many fast-food firms have boosted pay, added part-time benefits, offered tuition aid grants, and used hiring bonuses of up to $500 just to recruit entry-level workers. Recruiting fast-food restaurant managers is just as difficult because of the work demands of six-day 55-hour workweeks, trying to hire and train staff, and dealing with operational issues.

In the information technology (IT) arena, some talent shortages persist despite the demise of a number of dot.com companies over the past few years. Yet small and large employers alike are still expanding the use of information technology, and shortages of programmers, systems analysts, software engineers, and telecommunications network technicians remain in certain areas. Some estimate the current shortage at more than 800,000 qualified IT workers, a number that will continue to increase over the next five years. Some employers fill their shortage of IT workers by recruiting younger students to work part-time. High-schoolers, college freshmen, and sophomores have been hired by some employers. Hiring workers from other countries and outsourcing programming to workers in India or Russia also have been used.

Teacher shortages are another area of concern. As more teachers retire, the supply of new teachers has been diminishing. Particularly in the math, science, and technology areas, teachers find their skills are in high demand in private industry, which offers higher pay levels. In extreme cases, school systems have set up student loan payoffs, provide subsidized housing for teachers, and recruit "second career" individuals who have no teaching experience just to fill classroom jobs.

In summary, a significant HR challenge likely to continue over the next decade is: finding, recruiting, hiring, and keeping good workers with the capabilities needed for jobs to be performed well. Answering the question, "Where are the workers?" will require both managerial and HR efforts.[1]

> A significant HR challenge likely to continue over the next decade is: finding, recruiting, hiring, and keeping good workers. . . .

"Ability will never catch up with the demand for it."

—Malcolm Forbes

Recruiting The process of generating a pool of qualified applicants for organizational jobs.

The staffing process matches people with jobs through recruiting and selection. This chapter examines recruiting, and the next examines selection. **Recruiting** is the process of generating a pool of qualified applicants for organizational jobs. If the number of available candidates only equals the number of people to be hired, no real selection is required—the choice has already been made. The organization must either leave some openings unfilled or take all the candidates.

Various employers have faced shortages of workers who have the appropriate knowledge, skills, and abilities (KSAs), as the chapter opener indicates. However, because business cycles go up and down, the demand for labor changes and the number of people looking for work changes. Because staffing takes place in labor markets, learning some basics about labor markets aids understanding of recruiting.

Labor Markets

Labor markets The external supply pool from which organizations attract employees.

Labor markets are the external supply pool from which employers attract employees. To understand where recruiting takes place, the sources of employees can be thought of as a funnel (Figure 7-1), in which the broad scope of markets narrow progressively to the point of selection and job offers. Of course, if the selected candidate rejects the offer, then HR staff members must move back up the funnel to the applicant pool to other candidates, and in extreme cases to reopen the recruiting process. It is important for recruiting efforts to address a number of specific issues that affect employers in today's labor markets.

Labor Market Components

Labor force population All individuals who are available for selection if all possible recruitment strategies are used.

The broadest labor market component is the **labor force population** made up of all individuals who are available for selection if all possible recruitment strategies are used. This large number of potential applicants may be reached using many different recruiting methods—for example, newspaper ads, Internet, colleges, world-of-mouth, etc. Each recruiting method will reach different segments of the labor force population.

Applicant population A subset of the labor force population that is available for selection using a particular recruiting approach.

The **applicant population** is a subset of the labor force population that is available for selection using a particular recruiting approach. For example, an organization might limit its recruiting for management trainees to MBA graduates from major universities. This recruiting method results in a different group of applicants from those who might apply if the employer advertises openings for management trainees on a local radio station or posts a listing on an Internet jobs board.

At least four recruiting decisions affect reaching the applicant population:

- *Recruiting method:* Advertising medium chosen, including use of employment agencies.
- *Recruiting message:* What is said about the job and how it is said.
- *Applicant qualifications required:* Education level and amount of experience necessary.
- *Administrative procedures:* When recruiting is done, applicant follow-up, and use of previous applicant files.

Figure 7-1 ▶ **Labor Market Components**

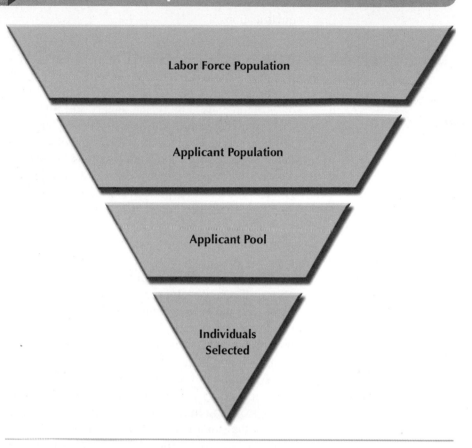

In tight labor markets, many employers try to expand the applicant population in a number of ways. For instance, *welfare-to-work* programs have been used to expand the applicant population for jobs requiring lower KSAs. These programs have generated numerous success stories from firms such as Sprint, United Airlines, and Marriott Corporation. Another way that employers expand the applicant population is to consider *ex-convicts*. Care in evaluating the individuals and ensuring appropriate placements given their backgrounds and capabilities is needed, but giving individuals second chances has paid off in some situations for both small and large employers.[2]

Applicant pool All persons who are actually evaluated for selection.

The **applicant pool** consists of all persons who are actually evaluated for selection. Many factors can affect the size of the applicant pool. For example, the reputation of the organization and industry as a place to work, the screening efforts of the organization, and the information available all may affect the applicant population. Assuming a suitable candidate can be found, the organization then selects the individual and makes the job offer.

Labor Markets and Recruiting Issues

Throughout all of the labor market components from the labor force population through the applicant pool, the supply of and demand for workers in various labor markets substantially affect the staffing strategies of organizations. An organization can use a number of different ways to identify labor markets, including by geographic area, industry and occupation, and education/technical qualifications.

Geographic Labor Markets One common way to classify labor markets is based on geographic location. Some markets are local, some area or regional, and others national. International labor markets also can be tapped, as the HR Perspective describes. Local and area labor markets vary significantly in terms of workforce availability and quality. For instance, the state of Iowa did a study and found that even if Iowa retained every high school graduate, ten years later it still would be short workers for many jobs because of the aging populations in many Iowa counties. In some locations in Iowa and other states, a shortage of workers has cause employers to close operations and relocate to areas with greater numbers of potential workers. Therefore, state agencies and Iowa employers have developed an aggressive campaign to "import" workers. Efforts have included recruiting native Iowans to return to the state, encouraging foreign immigrants to move to Iowa, and encouraging graduates of Iowa high schools and colleges to remain in the state.[3]

Changes in a geographic labor market may force changes in recruiting efforts. If a new major employer locates in a regional labor market, then other employers may see a decline in their numbers of applicants. For instance, some employers, particularly smaller manufacturing firms, had to raise their wages to prevent turnover of existing workers following the opening of large automobile manufacturing plants in South Carolina, Tennessee, Kentucky, and Alabama.

Attempting to recruit locally or in a limited geographic area for a job market that is really national likely will result in disappointing applicant rates. For example, trying to recruit a senior merchandising manager for a catalog retailer only in the small town where the firm is located is not likely to be successful. Conversely, it may not be necessary to recruit nationally for workers to fill administrative support jobs.

Industry and Occupational Labor Markets Labor markets also can be classified by industry and occupation. As the chapter opener describes, the demand for truck drivers, hotel workers, teachers, and others has been strong, creating tight labor markets in those industries.

Occupational labor markets are based on the KSAs required for the jobs. Examples include physical therapists, HR managers, engineers, accountants, welders, and bank tellers. One occupational area of extreme volatility in the past several years is composed of information technology jobs

The *information technology* labor market, as noted earlier, has fluctuated from being extremely tight due to Y-2K software conversion needs and the explosive growth of dot.com firms, to rather soft after many dot.coms failed. Longer-term forecasts indicate that the shortage of IT workers is expected to continue both in the United States and globally.[4] The greatest shortages are anticipated in Unix, Java, and C++ programmers, Internet and Web design specialists, and network technical professionals. To counter the shortage of IT workers, firms have resorted to a wide range of recruiting efforts, from employee referrals, signing and hiring bonuses, to more creative measures, some of which are described elsewhere in this chapter.

Logging On...

Job Web
This Web site offers a job outlook section containing a special report about labor markets and jobs. Also, it contains information on career fairs, starting salaries, and researching potential employers.

http://www.jobweb.com

Tapping the Global Labor Market

The shortages of workers in certain industries in the United States has led U.S. employers to tap global labor markets to fill jobs ranging from ski instructors to software programmers. Some examples illustrate.

Skiing is a major industry in Colorado, and the ski resorts at Vail, Aspen, Copper Mountain, Keystone, and other areas have gone global to find bus drivers, ski instructors, housekeepers, and other resort workers. Colorado recruiters have traveled to Australia and New Zealand to hire more than 300 employees, who receive wages significantly higher than those paid in New Zealand or Australian dollars. These and other hotels in Colorado have recruited housekeeping staff, food servers, spa assistants, and front desk clerks from Croatia, Poland, Jamaica, Sudan, and the Philippines. Beyond Colorado, some hotels throughout the U.S. are hiring workers from other countries. For instance, forty percent of workers at the Wyndham Anatole hotel in Dallas do not speak English as a first language. In Salt Lake City, 60 Bosnian refugees work in jobs at the Doubletree Hotel.

Information technology (IT) firms recruit and hire significant numbers of foreign workers. India has been a prime source for computer programmers and software engineers for firms such as Texas Instruments, Microsoft, and many smaller IT employers. Manufacturers, meat packing firms, and construction roofing companies use workers from Mexico, Haiti, Honduras, and other Latin American countries, as well as workers from Sudan, Laos, Albania, and Romania.

Even U.S. school systems have recruited globally to fill teacher and educational aide jobs left vacant by increasing numbers of retirements of experienced teachers. Public school systems in Illinois, North Carolina, Georgia, California, and Texas have recruited teachers from Australia, Canada, Jamaica, Chile, England, and Ghana. As a side benefit of recruiting teachers globally, U.S. students receive greater exposure to international cultures.

Employers must comply with U.S. immigration laws and visa requirements in recruiting and hiring international workers. But many employers aid foreign workers in complying with the requirements by sponsoring them and providing travel and housing assistance.[5]

Educational and Technical Qualifications Another way to look at labor markets closely is by considering education and technical qualifications. Employers may need individuals with specific licenses, certifications, or educational attainment levels. For instance, a shortage of business professors with Ph.D.s is forecasted to affect many colleges and universities in the next few years due to the retirement of many "baby boomers" from faculty positions. Other examples have been shortages of certified auto mechanics, heating and air-conditioning technicians, and network certified computer specialists.

Strategic Approach to Recruiting

A strategic approach to recruiting becomes more important as labor markets shift and become more competitive. As discussed in Chapter 2, strategic HR planning efforts help to align HR strategies with organizational goals and plans. Therefore, it is important that recruiting be a part of strategic HR Planning. Walgreens, the drugstore chain, had to cut back its expansion plans to open new stores because of a shortage of trained pharmacists. This example illustrates how HR planning and recruiting issues affect organizational strategic plans.[6]

Figure 7-2   Strategic Recruiting Stages

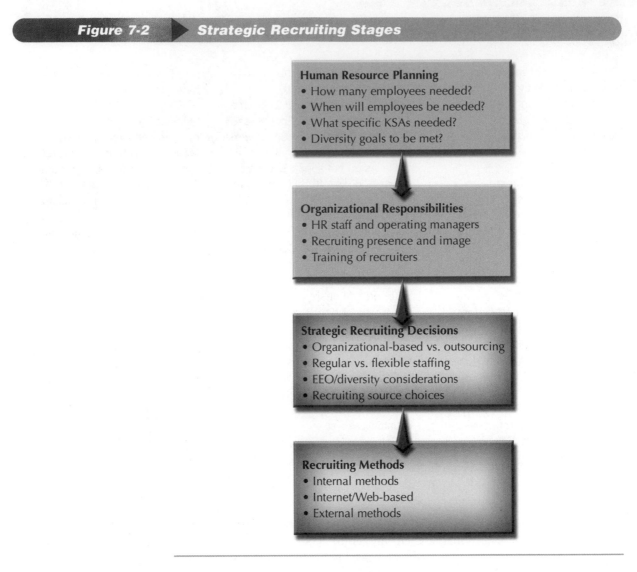

Human Resource Planning
- How many employees needed?
- When will employees be needed?
- What specific KSAs needed?
- Diversity goals to be met?

Organizational Responsibilities
- HR staff and operating managers
- Recruiting presence and image
- Training of recruiters

Strategic Recruiting Decisions
- Organizational-based vs. outsourcing
- Regular vs. flexible staffing
- EEO/diversity considerations
- Recruiting source choices

Recruiting Methods
- Internal methods
- Internet/Web-based
- External methods

The decisions made about recruiting dictate not only the kinds and numbers of applicants, but also how difficult or successful recruiting efforts may be. Figure 7-2 shows an overview of the strategic recruiting stages.

Even during periods of reduced hiring, implementing long-range plans means keeping in contact with outside recruiting sources to maintain visibility while also maintaining employee recruiting channels in the organization. These activities allow management to match recruiting activity with organizational and human resource plans.

Organizational Recruiting Activities

In most organizations, HR staff members handle the bulk of recruiting efforts. Figure 7-3 shows a typical distribution of recruiting responsibilities between the HR department and managers in all but the smallest organizations.

Use of HR staff to recruit is common for all but hard-to-fill specialized openings and executive management jobs. For such jobs, employers frequently

Figure 7-3 ▸ **Typical Division of HR Responsibilities: Recruiting**

HR Unit	Managers
• Forecasts recruiting needs.	• Anticipate needs for employees to fill vacancies.
• Prepares copy for recruiting adds and campaigns.	• Determine KSAs needed from applicants.
• Plans and conducts recruiting efforts.	• Assist in recruiting effort with information about job requirements.
• Audits and evaluates all recruiting activities.	• Review success/failure of recruiting activities.

contact search firms specializing in specific areas, such as information technology, physician recruitment, or industry sales representatives. Because these search firms typically charge fees of 20% to 30% of the annual salary of the person recruited, many employers use their own HR staff to do as much recruiting as possible.

Recruiting Image One critical factor related to recruiting is portraying a positive image of the employer. As mentioned in Chapter 3 on retention, how the "employment brand" of the organization is viewed by both employees and outsiders is crucial to attracting applicants and retaining employees, who also may describe the organization in positive or negative terms to others.

The recruiting image of an industry and an employer can significantly affect whether individuals ever consider a firm and submit applications. For example, a study of the fast-food industry found that the product image and reputation of a firm affects the attractiveness of the firm as a potential employer of both teenagers and retirees. The retirees generally perceived the work at fast-food firms as being more demanding than did teenagers, which would affect the desire of older workers to apply for employment.[7] This study and other indicators reveal that recruiting should be seen as part of organizational marketing efforts and linked to the overall image and reputation of the organization and its industry.

Recruiting Presence Being seen as an employer with jobs available that is looking for qualified candidates contributes to a positive recruiting image. Recruiting efforts may be viewed as either continuous or intensive. *Continuous* efforts to recruit offer the advantage of keeping the employer in the recruiting market. For example, with college recruiting some organizations may find it advantageous to have a recruiter on a given campus each year. Those employers that visit a campus only occasionally are less likely to build a following in that school over time.

Intensive recruiting may take the form of a vigorous recruiting campaign aimed at hiring a given number of employees, usually within a short period of time. Such efforts may be the result of failure in the HR planning system to identify needs in advance or to recognize drastic changes in workforce needs due to unexpected workloads.

Training of Recruiters Another part of effective recruiting is training recruiters. In addition to training recruiters on interviewing techniques and communication skills, it is crucial that they know the types of actions that violate EEO regulations and how to be sensitive to diversity issues with applicants. Such training often includes interview do's and don'ts and appropriate language to use with applicants. Racist, sexist, and other inappropriate remarks hurt the image of the employer and may result in legal complaints. For instance, a male college recruiter regularly asked female candidates about their marital status, and if they were single and attractive, he later called applicants and asked them for dates. Only after two students complained to the university placement office did the employer learn of the recruiter's misconduct.

Incidents such as these reinforce the importance of employers monitoring recruiters' behaviors and actions. Some employers send follow-up surveys to interviewees asking about the effectiveness of the recruiters and the image the candidates have of the employers as a result of their recruiting contacts.

Strategic Recruiting Decisions

Based on the recruiting needs identified as part of HR planning, a number of recruiting decisions must be made. The most important ones are discussed next.

Organizational-Based vs. Outsourcing

An initial and basic decision is whether recruiting will be done by HR staff and/or other organizational employees. Otherwise, outsourcing of some or most recruiting can be done. It need not be an "either-or" decision where all recruiting is done by organizational staff or external resources are used exclusively.

Because recruiting can be a time-consuming process, given all the other responsibilities of HR staff and other managers in organizations, outsourcing of recruiting is a way to both decrease the number of HR staff needed and to free up time for HR staff members. Outsourcing of recruiting can be done in a number of ways. For example, Dole Foods outsources such functions as placing advertisements, initial screening of resumes, and initial phone contacts with potential applicants. Once those activities are done, then Dole's HR staff take over the rest of the recruiting activities.[8]

A common means of outsourcing is use of search firms and employment agencies who are retained to recruit candidates. Also, employers who list or advertise openings externally frequently are contacted by search firms who have possible candidates for referral. Some HR professionals maintain policies that discourage use of such calls, while others welcome the additional availability of candidates, even though the search firm earns a fee if the referred candidate is selected.

Professional Employer Organizations and Employee Leasing A specific type of outsourcing uses professional employer organizations (PEOs) and employee leasing. This approach has grown rapidly in recent years. Some sources estimate that more than 2 million individuals are employed by PEOs doing employee leasing.[9]

The employee leasing process is simple: An employer signs an agreement with the PEO, after which the existing staff is hired by the leasing firm and leased back to the company. For a fee, a small business owner or operator turns the staff over to the leasing company, which then writes the paychecks, pays the taxes, prepares and implements HR policies, and keeps all the required records.[10]

Logging On...

Professional Employers Organizations
This is an informational website about PEOs and contains a directory of PEOs.

http://www.peo.com/peo/

Research on Small Businesses and PEOs

The rapid growth of PEOs has occurred primarily with smaller organizations in many industries. Klaas, McClendon, and Gainey conducted a study of how satisfied these employers were with the use of PEOs and reported the results in *Entrepreneurship Theory and Practice.* More than 600 customers of PEOs throughout the U.S. responded to a mail survey. The organizations from varying industries typically had fewer than 100 employees.

The results of the study found that the clients of the PEOs were satisfied with the services and costs of their PEOs. One finding was that firms with higher overall satisfaction with PEOs also had higher growth rates in revenues, one of the benefits often attributed to using PEOs. By not having to deal with HR concerns and issues outsourced to PEOs, managers of smaller organizations can focus on operations, marketing, and other business areas.

The study also found that having clear and specific contracts and a good relationship with a PEO's client services representatives contribute to client satisfaction with PEOs. By having a well-written contract and being able to discuss issues with a PEO representative meant problems could be resolved more easily, thus enhancing client satisfaction. It seems that PEOs may represent a viable staffing alternative for many smaller employers.[11]

One advantage for employees of leasing companies is that they may receive better benefits than they otherwise would get in many small businesses.

All this service comes at a cost. Leasing companies often charge employers between 4% and 6% of employees' monthly salaries. Thus, while leasing may save employers money on benefits and HR administration, it may also increase total costs of payroll. The HR Perspective describes a study of small firms and PEOs.

Regular vs. Flexible Staffing

Another decision affects how much recruiting will be done to fill staffing needs with regular full-time and part-time employees. Decisions as to who should be recruited hinge on whether to seek traditional employees or use more flexible approaches, which might include temporaries or independent contractors. A number of employers feel that the cost of keeping a regular workforce has become excessive and grows worse due to increasing government-mandated costs. However, not just the money is at issue. The number of governmental regulations also constrain the employment relationship, making many employers reluctant to hire new employees.

Flexible staffing Use of recruiting sources and workers who are not traditional employees.

Flexible staffing makes use of recruiting sources and workers who are not traditional employees. Using flexible staffing arrangements allows an employer to avoid some of the cost of full-time benefits such as vacation pay and pension plans, as well as to recruit in a somewhat different market. These arrangements use temporary workers, independent contractors, and employee leasing.

Temporary Workers Employers who use temporary employees can hire their own temporary staff or use agencies supplying temporary workers. Such firms supply workers on a rate-per-day or per-week basis. Originally developed to provide clerical and office workers to employers, agencies now provide workers in many other areas. The use of temporary workers may make sense for an organization if its work is subject to seasonal or other fluctuations. Hiring regular employees to meet peak employment needs would require that the employer find some tasks to keep employees busy during less active periods or resort to layoffs.

Some employers hire temporary workers as a way for individuals to move into full-time, regular employment. After 90 days or some other period as a "temp," better-performing workers may move to regular positions when they become available. This "try before you buy" approach is potentially beneficial both to employers and employees. However, most temporary service firms bill client companies a placement charge if a temporary worker is hired full-time within a certain time period—usually 90 days.

Independent contractors
Workers who perform specific services on a contract basis.

Independent Contractors Some firms employ **independent contractors**, who are workers that perform specific services on a contract basis. However, those contractors must be independent as determined by a 20-item test used by the U.S. Internal Revenue Service and the U.S. Department of Labor, which is discussed in greater detail in Chapter 12. Independent contractors are used in a number of areas, including building maintenance, security, and advertising/public relations. Some estimates indicate that employers get significant savings by using independent contractors because benefits do not have to be provided.

Recruiting and EEO/Diversity Considerations

As Figure 7-4 indicates, a number of factors go into ensuring that recruiting decisions meet diversity considerations. Recruiting as a key employment-related activity is subject to various legal considerations especially equal employment laws and regulations. As part of legal compliance in the recruiting process, organizations must work to reduce external disparate impact, or underrepresentation of protected-class members compared to the labor markets utilized by the employer. If disparate impact exists, then the employer may need to make special efforts to persuade protected-class individuals to apply for jobs. For employers with affirmative action plans (AAPs), special ways to reduce disparate impact will be identified as goals listed in those plans. Some employers that emphasize internal recruiting should take actions to obtain protected-class applicants externally if disparate impact exists in the current workforce. When the organization has an underrepresentation of a particular protected class, word-of-mouth referral has been considered a violation of Title VII of the Civil Rights Act, 1964, because it continues a past pattern of discrimination.[12]

Employment Advertising Employers covered by equal employment regulations must exercise care when preparing employment advertisements. The Equal Employment Opportunity Commission guidelines state that no direct or indirect references that have gender or age connotations are permitted. Some examples of likely impermissible terminology include the following: "young and enthusiastic," "recent college graduate," "Christian values," and "journeyman lineman."

Additionally, employment advertisements should indicate that the employer has a policy of complying with equal employment regulations. Typically, advertisements should contain a general phrase, such as Equal Opportunity Employer, or more specific designations, such as EEO/M-F/AA/ADA. Employers demonstrate inclusive recruiting by having diverse individuals represented in company

Figure 7-4 ▶ *Recruiting and Diversity Considerations*

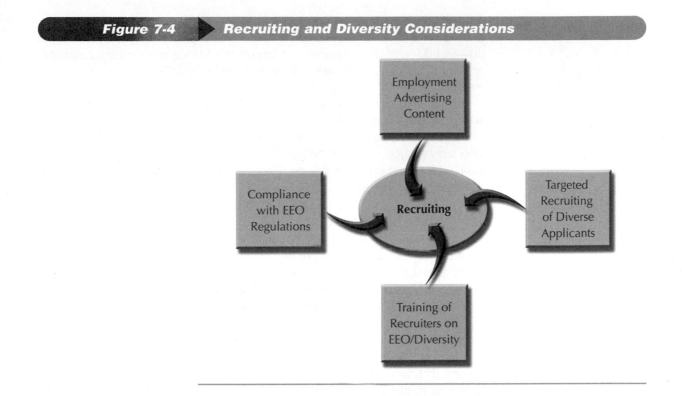

materials, advertisements, and as recruiters. For instance, Microsoft, Prudential Insurance, Bristol Myers, and other firms have found that having diversity visible in recruiting efforts has aided them in recruiting more individuals from a greater variety of backgrounds.[13]

Recruiting Diverse Workers The growing difficulty that many employers have had in attracting and retaining workers has led them to recruit workers from diverse backgrounds.[14] Three specific groups that have been attracted into the workforce effectively by some employers are individuals over 55 years of age, persons with disabilities, and members of racial/ethnic minorities.

When discussing the recruitment of older workers, the first task is to identify which individuals are included in this group.[15] Senior and experienced individuals may include the following:

- *Midlife career changers:* Those who are burned out in their jobs and career fields and leave voluntarily to try new fields.
- *Displaced older workers:* Those who have worked but have been displaced, often involuntarily, through job reductions or plant closings.
- *Retirees:* Those who took early retirement buyouts or formally retired from prior jobs.

Individuals with disabilities provide a potential pool of recruits numbering more than 40 million individuals. Jobs must be such that accommodation can be made for people with disabilities. Not every disability lends itself to every job for accommodations. However, in many cases changes in job duties, work stations, and equipment might result in a job that a person with a disability can do—and do well. For example, a Marriott Worldwide reservations center has special monitors and software that can be used by visually impaired individuals who take customer calls and make hotel reservations.[16]

Employers that do business with federal and state governments must have affirmative action plans (AAPs), as discussed in Chapter 4. Consequently, those employers face pressures to increase proportionately the number of employees who are women or are racial/ethnic minorities. These pressures often are stronger for managerial, professional, and technical jobs than for unskilled, clerical, and blue-collar jobs.

Recruiting Source Choices: Internal vs. External

Recruiting strategy and policy decisions entail identifying where to recruit, whom to recruit, and how recruiting will be done. One of the first decisions determines the extent to which internal or external sources and methods will be used. Both promoting from within the organization (internal recruitment) or hiring from outside the organization (external recruitment) to fill openings come with associated advantages and disadvantages. Figure 7-5 shows some of the major advantages and disadvantages of internal versus external recruiting.

Most employers combine the use of internal and external methods. Organizations that face a rapidly changing competitive environment and conditions may need to place a heavier emphasis on external sources in addition to developing internal sources. However, for those organizations existing in environments that change slowly, promotion from within may be more suitable.

Once the various recruiting policy decisions have been addressed, then the actual recruiting methods can be identified and used. These include internal and external sources, as well as, Internet/Web-based approaches.

Figure 7-5 ▶ **Advantages and Disadvantages of Internal and External Recruiting Sources**

Recruiting Source	Advantages	Disadvantages
Internal	• *Morale of promotee* • *Better assessment of abilities* • *Lower cost for some jobs* • *Motivator for good performance* • *Causes a succession of promotions* • *Have to hire only at entry level*	• *Inbreeding* • *Possible morale problems of those not promoted* • *"Political" infighting for promotions* • *Need for management development program*
External	• *New "blood" brings new perspectives* • *Cheaper and faster than training professionals* • *No group of political supporters in organization already* • *May bring new industry insights*	• *May not select someone who will "fit" the job or organization* • *May cause morale problems for internal candidates not selected* • *Longer "adjustment" or orientation time*

Figure 7-6 ▶ ***Internal Recruiting Methods***

- *Organizational databases*
- *Job posting system*
- *Promotion and transfers*

- *Current employee referrals*
- *Re-recruiting former employees*

Internal Recruiting

Pursuing internal recruiting with the advantages mentioned earlier means using various sources developed and managed inside the organization. Figure 7-6 depicts the common internal recruiting methods.

Internal Recruiting Processes

Within the organization tapping into databases, job postings, promotions, and transfers provide the means that allow current employees to move to other jobs. The design of these processes outline ways for employees to "surface" and be considered for openings as they occur. Filling openings internally may add motivation for employees to stay and grow in the organization rather than pursuing career opportunities elsewhere.

Organizational Databases The increased use of human resource information systems (HRIS) allows HR staff members to maintain background and KSA information on existing employees. As openings arise, HR employment specialists can access databases by entering job requirements and then receive a listing of current employees meeting the job requirement. Various types of employment software sort employee data by occupational fields, education, areas of career interests, previous work histories, and other factors. For instance, if a firm has an opening for someone with an MBA and marketing experience, the key words *MBA* and *marketing* can be entered in a search field, and the program displays a list of all current employees with these two items identified in their employee profiles.

The advantage of such databases is that they can be linked to other HR activities. As Chapter 3 noted, opportunities for career development and advancement are major reasons why individuals stay or leave their employers. With databases, internal opportunities for individuals can be identified. Employee profiles are continually updated to include such items as additional training or education completed, special projects worked on, and career plans and desires noted during performance appraisal and career mentoring discussions.

Job Posting The major means for recruiting employees for other jobs within the organization is **job posting**, a system in which the employer provides notices of job openings and employees respond by applying for specific openings. Without some sort of job posting system, it is difficult for many employees to find out what jobs are open elsewhere in the organization. The organization can notify employees of job vacancies in a number of ways, including posting notices on bulletin boards, using employee newsletters, and sending out e-mails to managers and employees. But posting job openings on company intranet and Internet Web sites has grown in use. In a unionized organization, job posting and bidding can be quite formal because the procedures often are spelled out in labor

Job posting A system in which the employer provides notices of job openings and employees respond to apply.

Job Posting
Contains overview and
sample job posting policy.
Custom Search:
☑ ANALYSIS
Phrase: Posted jobs

agreements. Seniority lists may be used by organizations that make promotions based strictly on seniority, so candidates are considered for promotions in the order of seniority.

Regardless of the means used, the purpose of the job posting system is to provide employees more opportunities to move within the organization. When establishing and managing a job posting system, a number of answers to many potential questions must be addressed:

- What happens if no qualified candidates respond to postings?
- Must employees inform their supervisors that they are posting for another job?
- Are there restrictions on how long an employee must stay in a job before posting for another one?
- How much notice should an employee be required to give before transferring to a new department?
- When should job notices not be posted?

Job posting systems can be ineffective if handled improperly. Jobs generally are posted before any external recruiting is done. The organization must allow a reasonable period of time for present employees to check notices of available jobs before it considers external applicants. When employees' bids are turned down, they should have discussions with their supervisors or someone in the HR area regarding the knowledge, skills, and abilities (KSAs) they need in order to improve their opportunities in the future.

Promotions and Job Transfers Many organizations choose to fill vacancies through promotions or transfers from within whenever possible. Although most often successful, promotions and transfers from within have some drawbacks as well. The person's performance on one job may not be a good predictor of performance on another, because different skills may be required on the new job. For example, not every high-performing worker makes a successful supervisor. In most supervisory jobs, an ability to accomplish the work through others requires skills in influencing and dealing with people and those skills may not have been a factor in non-supervisory jobs.

As employees transfer to or are promoted to other jobs, individuals must be recruited to fill their vacated jobs. Planning on how to fill those openings should occur prior to job transfers or promotions, not afterwards. It is clear that people in organizations with fewer levels may have less frequent chances for promotion. Also, in most organizations, promotions may not be an effective way to speed the movement of protected-class individuals up through the organization if that is an organizational concern.

Employee-Focused Recruiting

One reliable source of potential recruits is suggestions from current or former employees. Because current and former employees are familiar with the employer, their references often are high-potential candidates, because most employees usually do not refer individuals who are likely to be unqualified or make the employees look bad. Also, follow-up with former employees is likely to be done only with persons who were solid employees previously.

Current Employee Referrals A reliable source of people to fill vacancies is composed of acquaintances, friends, and family members of employees. The current employees can acquaint potential applicants with the advantages of a job with the company, furnish letters of introduction, and encourage them to apply. However, using only word-of-mouth or current employee referrals can violate equal employment regulations if protected-class individuals are underrepresented in the current organizational workforce. Therefore, some external recruiting might be necessary to avoid legal problems in this area.

Utilizing this source is usually one of the most effective methods of recruiting because many qualified people can be reached at a low cost. In an organization with numerous employees, this approach can develop quite a large pool of potential employees. Some studies have found that new workers recruited through current employee referrals have longer tenure with organizations than those from other recruiting sources. According to a study by the Employment Management Association, referral programs cost an average of $500 per salaried employee hired and $70 per hourly employee hired, whereas print advertising costs $2,884 per salaried employee hired and $726 per hourly employee hired.[17]

Tight labor markets in many geographic areas and certain occupational fields prompted many employers to establish employee referral incentive programs. One study found that mid-sized and larger employers are much more likely to use employee referral bonuses.[18] Some referral programs provide different amounts for hard-to-fill jobs compared to basic referrals for common openings.

Re-Recruiting Former Employees and Applicants Former employees and former applicants represent another source for recruitment. Both cases offer a time-saving advantage, because something is already known about the potential employees.[19] Known as *re-recruiting* because the individuals previously were successfully recruited, former employees are considered an internal source in the sense that they have ties to the employer and may be called "boomerangers" because they left and came back. Individuals who left for other jobs might be willing to return because the other job and employers turned out to be less attractive than initially thought. For example, Accenture, a consulting firm, was able to attract more than 100 people who had left in the prior two years by contacting them and offering them "loyalty grants." Firms such as Accenture, Microsoft, and others also have established "alumni reunions" to keep in touch with individuals who have left, which also allows the firm to re-recruit individuals as appropriate openings arise.[20]

Key issues in the decision to re-recruit someone include the reasons why the individual left originally and if performance and capabilities were solid. Another potential source of applicants can be found in the organizational files or an applicant database. Although not entirely an internal source, those who have previously applied for jobs can be recontacted, which can be a quick and inexpensive way to fill an unexpected opening. For instance, one firm that needed two cost accountants immediately contacted qualified previous applicants and was able to hire those individuals who were disenchanted with their current jobs at other companies.

Internet Recruiting

Organizations first started using computers as a recruiting tool by advertising jobs on a bulletin board service from which prospective applicants would contact employers. Then some companies began to take e-mail applications. Today the Internet has become a primary means for employers to search for job candidates and for applicants to look for jobs. The explosive growth in Internet use is a key reason. Estimates are that there are more than 160 million Internet users in the U.S. and 1.2 billion worldwide. In the U.S. it is estimated that 74% of those with Internet access, aged 18 years or older, annually use the Internet as part of job searching.[21] As Figure 7-7 indicates, Internet users tap the Internet to search for jobs almost as frequently as reading newspaper classified ads. Also many of these Internet users post or submit resumes on the Internet.

HR professionals and recruiters are using the Internet regularly also. When HR recruiters were asked what sources generate more new hires, 77% of those responding indicated Internet job postings, compared with 17.5% citing newspaper ads.[22] Various surveys found that 80% to 90% of employers use the Internet for recruiting. As many as 100,000 recruiting Web sites are available to employers and job candidates on which to post jobs and review resumes of various types. But the explosive growth of Internet recruiting also means that HR professionals can be overwhelmed by the breadth and scope of Internet recruiting.

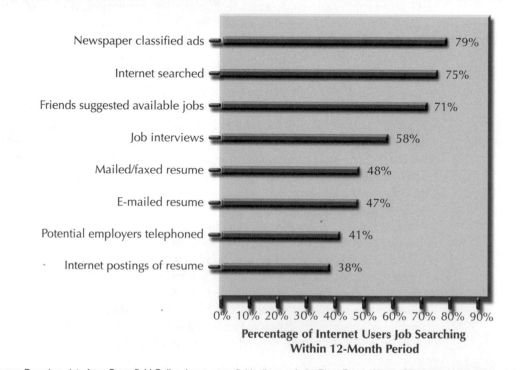

Figure 7-7 ▶ **Job Searching Means**

Job Searching Means	Percentage
Newspaper classified ads	79%
Internet searched	75%
Friends suggested available jobs	71%
Job interviews	58%
Mailed/faxed resume	48%
E-mailed resume	47%
Potential employers telephoned	41%
Internet postings of resume	38%

Percentage of Internet Users Job Searching Within 12-Month Period

Source: Based on data from Greenfield Online (*www.greenfieldonline.com*), 21 River Road, Wilton, CT 06897. Used with permission.

E-Recruiting Methods

Several different methods are used for Internet recruiting. The most commons ones are job boards, professional/career Web sites, and employer Web sites.

Job Boards Numerous job boards, such as *www.monster.com* and *www.hotjobs.com*, provide places for employers to post jobs or search for candidates. Another prevalent one is America's Job Bank, operated in conjunction with the U.S. Department of Labor and state job services.

Even though job boards provide access to numerous candidates, many individuals accessing the sites are "job lookers" who are not serious about changing jobs, but checking out compensation levels and what job availability exists in their areas of interest. One estimate is that about one-third of all visitors to the job boards are just browsing, not seriously considering changing employment.[23] Despite these concerns, HR recruiters find the general job boards useful for generating applicant responses. Also, a recruiter for a firm can pretend to be an applicant in order to check out what other employers are looking for in similar job candidates and competitor compensation information in order to maintain recruiting competitiveness.[24]

Professional/Career Web Sites Many professional associations have employment sections at their Web sites. As illustration, for HR jobs see *www.shrm.org* or *www.astd.org*. A number of private corporations maintain specialized career or industry Web sites in order to focus on IT, telecommunications, engineering, physician, or other areas. Using these more targeted Web sites limits somewhat the recruiters' search time and efforts. Also, posting jobs on such Web sites is likely to target applicants specifically interested in the job field and may reduce the number of less-qualified applicants who actually apply.

Employer Web Sites Aside from the popularity of job boards and other job sites, many employers have found their Web sites to be more effective and efficient when recruiting candidates.[25] Numerous employers have included employment and career information as part of their organizational Web sites. On many of these sites, job seekers are encouraged to e-mail resumes or complete on-line applications. The e-HR discussion on the next page provides suggestions on preparing on-line job listings in order to attract more and better candidates.

It is important that the recruiting and employment portions of employer Web sites be seen as part of the employer's marketing efforts. Therefore, the employment sections of organizational Web sites must be shaped to market jobs and careers effectively.[26] Also, the Web site should market the employer by outlining information on the organization, its products and services, organizational and industry growth potential, and organizational operations. Unfortunately, many employers' Web sites do not incorporate career and employment information effectively. For example, a study of *Fortune 500* company Web sites found that 21% of the career sites were difficult to navigate, and another 40% of them had inconsistent uses of icons and links.[27]

Advantages of Internet Recruiting

Employers have found a number of advantages in using Internet recruiting. A primary one is that many employers have realized cost savings using Internet recruiting compared to other sources such as newspaper advertising, employment

Job Boards

For a listing of some of the common ones, see this text's dedicated Web site,

http:mathis.swcollege.com

WEST GROUP
A THOMSON COMPANY

Effective Recruiting Web Site
Describes results of Internet recruiting survey and tips for success.
Custom Search:
☑ ANALYSIS
Phrase: Recruiting site needs

Effective On-Line Job Postings

The rapid growth of the Internet for recruiting has changed the way many organizations find applicants. Instead of using newspaper ads as a primary source for recruiting, on-line job posting is an integral part of most recruiting efforts. However, developing effective on-line job announcements is not simply putting a newspaper ad into an electronic form. Some of the suggestions for preparing effective on-line job postings include:

- *Make the posting appealing.* It must "grab" people's interest, so use some graphics, company logo, and other simple art work to make the posting stand out.
- *Make it readable.* Use easy-to-read language and avoid too many abbreviations and jargon not easily recognizable by applicants. Also, do not use all capital or bolded letters, which look too dense.
- *Recognize that shorter is better.* Too many employers start on-line ads with 50 to 60-word paragraphs on the company

and general descriptive words that are overused, such as "challenging," "progressive," etc.

- *Start with clear job title and overview.* The job title and brief description of job responsibilities determine whether anything else is read. These items are like the headline and first paragraph of a news article. If they are not interesting, the rest of the details will not be read.
- *Describe the employer concisely.* A brief description of the employer, especially the division and location of the job, should provide information and create interest in the organization.
- *State necessary qualifications clearly.* Carefully and accurately described qualifications let exceptional candidates know that the qualifications are not too low, which might discourage them from applying. Likewise, "puffing up" qualifications may eliminate candidates who see the job as above their capabilities.

- *Provide salary and benefits information.* A job posting should provide a salary range and emphasize competitive benefits, especially by noting any special benefits available. However, no benefits summary should look like a "laundry list."
- *How to apply.* Automatic links to e-mail or to an employment application should allow an applicant to click to apply. As back-up, fax number and mailing address information should be provided along with a contact name or code number. Generally, phone numbers are recommended only if the employer wishes to field telephone inquiries, which may be numerous in some cases, but desirable in others.

To see effective and ineffective on-line job postings, go to some of the job boards and employer Web sites. Then rate them on how well they meet the suggestions listed here.

---

agencies and search firms, and other external sources. Some employers experience savings from several hundred dollars per hire to as high as $4,000 to $6,000 for senior professional and management jobs.[28]

Internet recruiting also can save considerable *time*. Applicants can respond quickly to job postings by sending e-mails, rather than using "snail mail." Recruiters can respond to qualified candidates more quickly and establish times for interviews or request additional candidate information.

An expanded pool of applicants can be generated using Internet recruiting. In fact, a large number of candidates may see any given job listing, although exposure depends on which Internet sources are used. One side benefit of the Internet is that jobs literally are posted globally, so potential applicants in other geographic areas and countries can view job openings posted on the Web.

Disadvantages of Internet Recruiting

The positives associated with Internet recruiting come with a number of disadvantages. By getting broader exposure, employers also may get more unqualified applicants. A survey of HR recruiters found that one-third of them felt Internet recruiting created additional work for HR staff members.[29] More resumes must be reviewed, more e-mails dealt with, and specialized applicant tracking software may be needed to handle the increase in applicants caused in many Internet recruiting efforts. A related concern is that many individuals who access job sites are just browsers who may submit resumes just to see what happens, but who are not seriously looking for new jobs.

Another issue with Internet recruiting is that applicants may have limited Internet access, especially individuals from lower socio-economic groups and certain racial/ethnic minority groups. Data from a U.S. Department of Labor study identified a "digital divide," whereby fewer Hispanic and African American job seekers have Internet access at home or not at all.[30] Consequently, employers using Internet recruiting may not be reaching as diverse a recruitment pool as might be desired. Even in the face of these disadvantages, it is likely that Internet recruiting will continue to grow in usage. Employers and job seekers alike are seeing e-recruiting as a major part of external recruiting.

External Recruiting

Many different external sources are available for recruiting. In some tight labor markets multiple sources and methods may be used to attract candidates for the variety of jobs available in organizations. Some of the more prominent methods are highlighted next.

College and University Recruiting

At the college or university level, the recruitment of students is a significant source for entry-level professional and technical employees. Most colleges and universities maintain career placement offices in which employers and applicants can meet. However, some interesting and unique problems exist, as shown in the HR Perspective on the next page.

The major determinants affecting an employer's selection of colleges and universities at which to conduct interviews are:

- Current and anticipated job openings
- College reputation
- Experiences with placement offices and previous graduates
- Organizational budget constraints
- Cost of available talent and typical salaries
- Market competition

College recruiting can be expensive; therefore, an organization should determine if the jobs it is trying to fill really require persons with college degrees. A great many jobs do not; yet many employers insist on filling them with college graduates. The result may be employees who must be paid more and who are likely to leave if the jobs are not sufficiently challenging.

College recruiters often report being impressed with the quality and capabilities of many of the students they interview on campuses. However, some students do not create positive impressions. Various HR professionals have reported "horror stories" from student interviews. If you are a college student, do not do what some of these students did!

- Discussed adult entertainment and pornography films during the interview

- Wore swimming trunks, T-shirt, no socks, and loafers to an on-campus interview
- Brought sack lunch and ate it during the interview
- Asked the receptionist for money to pay for parking
- Came to the interview drunk
- Asked the interviewer about his religious views
- Requested information on airplanes and aerospace jobs from an accounting firm recruiter

Fortunately, most college students approach interviews professionally. Most college and university placement offices have brochures containing guidelines for going to an interview. The greatest complaint that most recruiters have is not dealing with weird behavior, but that students often do not familiarize themselves with the employer *prior* to arriving for an interview. Because many employers have Web sites, such information usually is easily accessible.[31]

There is a great deal of competition for the top students in many college and university programs. However, less competition exists for those students with less impressive records. Attributes that recruiters seem to value most highly in college graduates—poise, oral and written communication skills, personality, and appearance—all typically are mentioned ahead of grade point average (GPA). However, for many employers, a high GPA is a major criterion when considering candidates for jobs during on-campus interviews. Top graduates in difficult-to-fill specialties sometimes receive signing bonuses from employers in some job specialties.

A number of factors determine success in college recruiting. Some employers actively build continuing relationships with individual faculty members and career staff at designated colleges and universities. A continuing presence on campus through providing guest speakers to classes and student groups increases the contacts for an employer. The important point to stress is that those employers who show continuing presence and support on a campus are more likely to see better college recruiting results.[32]

Such efforts also allow employers to attract students in high-demand specialties to accept internships or part-time jobs while they complete their degrees. One area where this approach is being used extensively is to fill IT jobs. In fact, the shortage of IT workers has led to recruiting younger applicants, which raises concerns about students dropping out of school to "earn big bucks" and not completing their degrees at all or taking much longer to do so.[33]

School Recruiting

High schools or vocational/technical schools may be a good source of new employees for some organizations. Many schools have a centralized guidance or placement office. Promotional brochures that acquaint students with starting jobs

WEST GROUP
A THOMSON COMPANY

College and University Recruiting
Suggests ideas for effective college recruiting.
Custom Search:
☑ ANALYSIS
Phrase: College recruiting efforts

and career opportunities can be distributed to counselors, librarians, or others. Participating in career days and giving tours of the company to school groups are other ways of maintaining good contact with school sources. Cooperative programs in which students work part-time and receive some school credits also may be useful in generating qualified future applicants for full-time positions.

Until recently, students not going on to college received little guidance or training on finding jobs after high school. However, the number of "partnerships" with schools through "school to work" programs have grown. Companies are entering the classroom not only to recruit, but to tutor students in skills such as the reading and math needed for work. Internships during the summer and work/school programs also are being widely used.

Employers involved in HR planning recognize that attracting students with capabilities may need to begin in high school. For example, GE, Bell Atlantic, IBM, and other corporations fund programs to encourage students with science and math skills to participate in engineering internships during summers. These and other employers target racial minority youth in high schools to provide career encouragement, summer internships, and mentoring programs. In addition to fulfilling some social responsibilities, the organizations hope to generate employment interest from the students they assist, which may help fill future openings.

Labor Unions

Labor unions are a source of certain types of workers. In some industries, such as construction, unions have traditionally supplied workers to employers. A labor pool is generally available through a union, and workers can be dispatched to particular jobs to meet the needs of the employers.

In some instances, the union can control or influence recruiting and staffing needs. An organization with a strong union may have less flexibility than a nonunion company in deciding who will be hired and where that person will be placed. Unions also can work to an employer's advantage through apprenticeship and cooperative staffing programs, as they do in the building and printing industries.

Employment Agencies and Search Firms

Every state in the United States has its own state-sponsored employment agency. These agencies operate branch offices in many cities throughout the states and do not charge fees to applicants or employers.

Private employment agencies also operate in most cities. For a fee collected from either the employee or the employer, these agencies do some preliminary screening and put the organization in touch with applicants. Private employment agencies differ considerably in the level of service, costs, policies, and types of applicants they provide. Employers can reduce the range of possible problems from these sources by giving complete job descriptions and specifications on jobs to be filled.

Some employment agencies focus their efforts on executive, managerial, and professional positions. These executive search firms are split into two groups: (1) contingency firms that charge a fee only after a candidate has been hired by a client company, and (2) retainer firms that charge a client a set fee whether or not the contracted search is successful. Most of the larger firms work on a retainer basis.

WEST GROUP
A THOMSON COMPANY
Apprenticeships
Discusses how to establish and administer apprenticeship programs.
Custom Search:
☑ ANALYSIS
Phrase: Administering apprenticeship programs

The fees charged by executive search firms may be 30% or more of the employee's first-year salary. Most employers pay the fees, but in some circumstances the employees pay the fees. For placing someone in a high-level executive job, a search firm may receive $300,000 or more, counting travel expenses, and the placement fees. The size of the fees and the aggressiveness with which some firms pursue candidates for openings have led to such firms being called *headhunters*. However, search firms are ethically bound not to approach employees of client companies in their search efforts for another client.

Competitive Sources

Other sources for recruiting include professional and trade associations, trade publications, and competitors. Many professional societies and trade associations publish newsletters or magazines and have Web sites containing job ads. Such sources may be useful for recruiting specialized professionals needed in an industry.

Some employers have extended recruiting to customers. Retailers such as Target, Home Depot, Best Buy, and others have aggressive programs to recruit employees in stores. Customers at these firms can receive applications blanks, apply on-line using in-store kiosks, or schedule interviews with managers or HR staff members while in the stores. Other firms have included employment announcements when sending out customer bills or newsletters.

Media Sources

Media sources such as newspapers, magazines, television, radio, and billboards are widely used. Some firms have used direct mail by purchasing lists of individuals in certain fields or industries. Whatever medium is used, it should be tied to the relevant labor market and provide sufficient information on the company and the job. Figure 7-8 shows information a good recruiting advertisement should include. Notice that desired qualifications, details on the job and application process, and an overview of the organization are all important.

Evaluating Ads HR recruiters should measure the responses they generate in order to evaluate the effectiveness of various media. The easiest way to track responses to an ad is to use different contact names, addresses, or phone number codes. Then the employer can note the source of the advertisement each time an applicant response is received.

Although the total number of responses should be tracked, judging the success of an ad only by this number is a mistake. For example, it is better to have 10 responses with two qualified applicants than 30 responses with only one qualified applicant. Therefore, after the individuals are hired, follow-up should be done to see which sources produced employees who stayed longer and performed better.

Job Fairs and Special Events

Employers in tight labor markets or needing to fill a large number of jobs quickly have used job fairs and special recruiting events. Job fairs also have been held by economic development entities, employer associations, HR associations, and other community groups in order to assist bringing employers and potential job candidates together. For instance, to fill jobs in one metropolitan area the local SHRM chapter annually sponsors a job fair at which 75–125 employers

Figure 7-8 ▶ **What to Include in an Effective Recruiting Ad**

EMPLOYMENT OPPORTUNITY

Information on the Job and Process of Application
- Job title and responsibilities
- Location of job
- Starting pay range
- Closing date for application
- Whether or not to submit a resume and cover letter
- Whether calls are invited
- Where to mail application or resume

Candidate Desired Qualifications
- Years of experience
- Three to five key characteristics of successful candidates

Information on the Organization
- That it is an EEO employer
- Its primary business

can meet applicants. Publicity in the city draws more than 1,000 potential recruits. One cautionary note: Some employers at this and other job fairs may see current employees "shopping" for jobs at other employers.

Some firms also establish special events such as open houses, sponsor community events at which recruiters try to obtain applications from attendees, and use other means to recruit individuals. For instance, "drive-through" job fairs at shopping malls have been used by employers in a number of communities. At one such job fair, interested persons can drive up to a tent outside the mall and pick up applications from a "menu board" of employers, then park and interview in the tent with recruiters if time allows.

Creative Recruiting Methods

In tight labor markets and industries with significant shortages of qualified applicants, employers turn to more creative recruiting methods. Regardless of the methods used, the goal is to generate a pool of qualified applicants so that the jobs in organizations are filled in a timely manner. Some methods may be more effective at recruiting for certain jobs than others. To illustrate, some examples include the following:

- Using a plane towing an advertising banner over beach areas
- Advertising jobs on local movie theater screens as part of the pre-show entertainment
- Holding raffles for employees who refer candidates, with cars and trips being prizes
- Offering free rock concert tickets to the first 20 applicants hired
- Setting up recruiting tables at bowling alleys, minor league baseball games, or stock car races
- Recruiting younger technical employees at video game parlors

- Sponsoring book fairs in order to recruit publishing company sales representatives
- As part of U.S. military recruiting, employers guarantee enlistees jobs after completing military service
- Parking motor homes—all set up for interviews, testing, and hiring—in parking lots at the malls with signs saying, "Want a job? Apply here."

Recruiting Evaluation

In order to determine how effective various recruiting sources and methods have been, it is important to evaluate recruiting efforts. The primary way to find out whether recruiting efforts are cost effective is to conduct formal analyses as part of recruiting evaluation.

Evaluating Recruiting Costs and Benefits

Because recruiting activities are important, the costs and benefits associated with them should be analyzed. When doing a cost-benefit analysis to evaluate recruiting efforts, costs may include both direct costs (advertising, recruiters' salaries, travel, agency fees, telephone) and the indirect costs (involvement of operating managers, public relations, image). Cost-benefit information on each recruiting source can be calculated. Comparing the length of time applicants from each source stay in the organization with the cost of hiring from that source offers a useful perspective also.

Evaluating Time Required to Fill Openings

The length of time it takes to fill openings is one of the most common means of evaluating recruiting efforts. If openings are not filled quickly with qualified candidates, the work and productivity of the organization likely suffer. Generally speaking, it is useful to calculate the average amount of time it takes from contact to hire for each source of applicants, because some sources may produce recruits faster than others.

Evaluating Recruiting Quantity and Quality

As additional means of evaluating recruiting, organizations can see how their recruiting efforts compare with past patterns and with the recruiting performance of other organizations. Certain measures of recruiting effectiveness are quite useful in indicating whether sufficient numbers of the targeted applicant population group are being attracted. Information on job performance, absenteeism, cost of training, and turnover by recruiting source helps to adjust future recruiting. For example, some companies find that recruiting at certain colleges or universities furnishes stable, high performers, whereas other schools provide employees who are more prone to leave the organization. General areas for evaluating recruiting include the following:

- *Quantity of applicants:* Because the goal of a good recruiting program is to generate a large pool of applicants from which to choose, quantity is a natural place to begin evaluation. Is it sufficient to fill job vacancies?

- *EEO goals met:* The recruiting program is the key activity used to meet goals for hiring protected-class individuals. It is especially relevant when a company is engaged in affirmative action to meet such goals. Does recruiting provide qualified applicants with an appropriate mix of protected-class individuals?
- *Quality of applicants:* In addition to quantity, the issue arises as to whether or not the qualifications of the applicant pool are sufficient to fill the job openings. Do the applicants meet job specifications, and do they perform the jobs well after hire?

Yield ratios A comparison of the number of applicants at one stage of the recruiting process to the number at the next stage.

Yield Ratios One means for evaluating recruiting efforts is to determine **yield ratios**, which compare the number of applicants at one stage of the recruiting process to the number at another stage. The result is a tool for approximating the necessary size of the initial applicant pool. It is useful to visualize the yield ratios as a pyramid, whereby the employer starts with a broad base of applicants that progressively narrows. As Figure 7-9 depicts, to end up with 5 hires for the job in question, the company must begin with 100 applicants in the pool, as long as yield ratios remain as shown.

A different approach to using yield ratios suggests that over time, organizations can develop ranges for crucial ratios. When a given indicator ratio falls

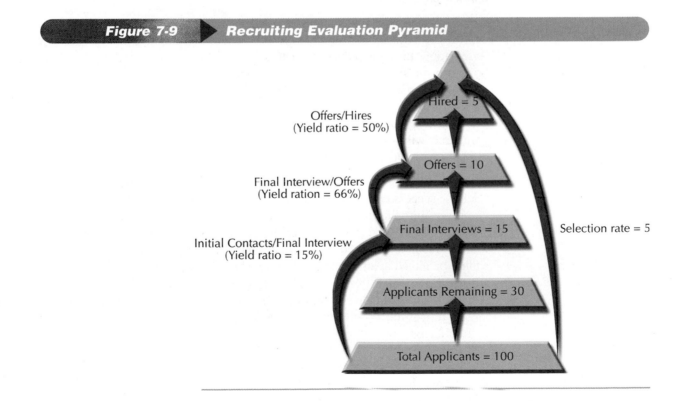

Figure 7-9   **Recruiting Evaluation Pyramid**

Offers/Hires
(Yield ratio = 50%)

Hired = 5

Final Interview/Offers
(Yield ration = 66%)

Offers = 10

Initial Contacts/Final Interview
(Yield ratio = 15%)

Final Interviews = 15

Selection rate = 5

Applicants Remaining = 30

Total Applicants = 100

outside that range, it may indicate problems in the recruiting process. For example, in college recruiting the following ratios might be useful:

$$\frac{\text{College seniors given second interview}}{\text{Total number of seniors interviewed}} = \text{Range of } 30 - 50\%$$

$$\frac{\text{Number who accept offer}}{\text{Number invited to the company to visit}} = \text{Range of } 50 - 70\%$$

$$\frac{\text{Number who were hired}}{\text{Number offered a job}} = \text{Range of } 70 - 80\%$$

$$\frac{\text{Number finally hired}}{\text{Total number interviewed on campus}} = \text{Range of } 10 - 20\%$$

Selection rate The percentage hired from a given group of candidates.

Selection Rate Another useful calculation is to determine the **selection rate**, which is the percentage hired from a given group of candidates. It equals the number hired divided by the number of applicants; for example, a rate of 30% would indicate that 3 out of 10 applicants were hired. The percentage typically goes down as unemployment rates in the job market decrease, because fewer qualified candidates typically are available. The selection rate is also affected by the validity of the selection process. A relatively unsophisticated selection program might pick 8 out of 10 applicants for the job. Four of those might turn out to be good employees. A more valid selection process might pick 5 out of 10 applicants but all perform well.

Acceptance Rate Calculating the acceptance rate helps identify how successful the organization is at hiring the candidates that it wants to employ. After going through all the effort to screen, interview, and make job offers, hopefully most candidates accept job offers. If not, then HR might want to look at reasons why managers and HR staff cannot "close the deal." It is common for HR staff members to track the reasons candidates turn down job offers, the rejection rate, in order to learn how competitive the employer is compared with other employers and what factors are causing candidates to choose employment elsewhere.

Success Base Rate A longer-term measure of recruiting effectiveness is to track the success rate of applicants. This rate indicates whether the quality of the employees hired results in employees who perform well and have low turnover. For example, assume that if 10 people were hired at random, one would expect four of them to be good employees. Thus, a successful recruiting program should be aimed at attracting the 4 in 10 who are capable of doing well on this particular job. Realistically, no recruiting program will attract only the 4 in 10 who will succeed. However, efforts to make the recruiting program attract the largest proportion of those in the base rate group can make recruiting efforts more effective.

The success base rate can be determined by comparing the number of past applicants who have become successful employees using historical data within the organization. Also, it can be compared to the success rates of other employers in the area or industry using benchmarking data.

Increasing Recruiting Effectiveness

The efforts to evaluate recruiting should be used to make recruiting activities more effective. Using the data to target different applicant pools, tap broader labor markets, utilize different recruiting methods, improve internal handling and interviewing of applicants, and train recruiters and managers all can increase recruiting effectiveness. Other beneficial activities include:

- *Applicant tracking systems* to collect data on applicants and provide various analyses.[34]
- *Realistic job previews* that provide job candidates accurate details about the organization and the job. (See Chapter 8 for more details.)
- *Responsive recruitment process* in which applicants receive timely responses, get feedback on the process when promised, and are treated with consideration.

Another key way to increase recruiting effectiveness rests on the recruiters themselves. The reactions of candidates to those involved in the recruiting process can turn off recruits or create excitement. A number of studies on the reactions of applicants to recruiters has revealed that recruiters who are knowledgeable about the jobs and their employers and who treat applicants with respect and enthusiasm are viewed more positively.[35] This positive image is more likely to result in more applicants pursuing employment opportunities with an employer, which is vital in the labor markets faced by many organizations today.

Summary

- Recruiting is the process of generating a pool of qualified applicants for organizational jobs through a series of activities.
- Recruiting must be viewed strategically, and discussions should be held about the relevant labor markets in which to recruit.
- The components of labor markets are labor force population, applicant population, and applicant pool.
- Labor markets can be categorized by geographic industry, occupations, and qualifications.
- A strategic approach to recruiting begins with human resource planning and decisions about organizational recruiting responsibilities.
- Employers must make decisions about organizational-based versus outsourcing of recruiting, such as flexible staffing.
- Efforts should be made to recruit a diverse workforce, including older workers, individuals with disabilities, women, and racial/ethnic minority individuals.

- The decision to use internal or external sources should consider both the advantages and disadvantages of each source.
- The most common methods of internal recruiting are job posting, current employee referrals, and re-recruiting former employees.
- Internet recruiting has grown in use through job boards and various Web sites.
- Internet recruiting can save costs and time, but also can generate more unqualified applicants and frequently may not reach certain groups of potential applicants.
- The most common external recruiting sources include colleges and universities, schools, labor unions, employment agencies, and media sources.
- Recruiting efforts should be evaluated to assess how effectively they are being performed.
- Recruiting evaluation typically includes examining the costs and benefits of various recruiting sources, tracking the time to fill openings, and evaluating applicant quality and quantity.

1. What labor markets could be considered when recruiting to fill openings for a sales representative's job for a pharmaceutical manufacturer?
2. Discuss what strategic recruiting considerations should be addressed by HR executives at a mid-sized bank with locations in several cities. Give examples and be specific.
3. Discuss the advantages and disadvantages of recruiting internally versus externally.
4. What internal sources for recruiting have you seen work effectively and ineffectively? Why?
5. Discuss some ways firms can make Internet recruiting more effective.
6. Assume you had to recruit restaurant employees in a tight labor market. What external and creative methods could be used?
7. What factors should be considered in evaluating the recruiting efforts of a regional discount retailer with 80–100 stores in a geographic arca?

Terms to Know

recruiting   202
labor markets   202
labor force population   202
applicant population   202
applicant pool   203

flexible staffing   209
independent contractors   210
job posting   213
yield ratios   225
selection rate   226

Using the Internet

Recruiting Physical Therapists

As the HR Manager you are in charge of recruiting for your health-care organization. An executive has asked you to work with her on recruiting two new Physical Therapists for your Dallas, Texas-based hospital. She will supply you with the job description and requirements for the job. The hospital is short-staffed in this area and just lost another physical therapist, so it is important that you begin immediately.

Address the Following Issues:
- Identify three of the Web sites you found to be most useful in your search and why they were useful.
- Identify two sites that were more difficult to use and why they did not assist in your search.
- Research and list some of the surrounding hospitals and labor markets and competitors recruiting for physical therapists.
- Write a one-page description of your recruiting plan to fill these openings and which sites you will recommend using now and in the future.

Recruiting for the Ritz-Carlton

When a new Ritz-Carlton hotel in Washington, D.C., was preparing to open, recruiting to fill all of the positions was a major challenge for the hotel's Human Resources Director, Marie Minarich. Positions in housekeeping, front desk, banquet, security, maintenance, and guest services all had to be filled.

Both conventional and creative recruiting approaches were used to generate several thousand applicants. As the hotel was being built, signs were put on the building indicating the opening date and how to apply for jobs. As the opening got closer, some newspaper ads were placed, but no Internet or radio ads were used.

Additionally, Ritz-Carlton mangers and staff made it a point to hand out business cards and "service praise" cards to employees at other restaurants and hotels in the months and weeks before the peak hiring was to occur. Those individuals were encouraged to apply at Ritz-Carlton, and many of those receiving the cards showed up at a two-day job fair held by Ritz-Carlton.

The job fair was the major source for recruits, generating 2,300 applicants in two days. To generate more applicants at the job fair, Ritz-Carlton recruiters handed out job fair invitations at subway stations the mornings of the job fair. During the job fair, refreshments were served by employees of other Ritz-Carlton hotels in the area. To keep with the upscale theme of Ritz-Carlton, musicians played at the fair.

Once applicants arrived at the job fair, they completed application blanks and were asked several preliminary screening interview questions. Those who passed the screening interview were then scheduled for more in-depth 1½-hour interviews consisting of 55 questions. More than 150 in-depth interviews were conducted at the job fair, and about 300 more were scheduled when the applicants' schedules allowed. The result of all of these efforts was that Minarich and the HR staff filled the needed positions for the opening of the hotel.[36]

Questions

1. Describe why a strategic approach to recruiting was crucial at the Ritz-Carlton.

2. Why were the conventional recruiting approaches less important than the creative methods in generating a large number of applicants at one time?

Notes

1. Based on Sherry Kuczynski, "While Supplies Last," *HR Magazine,* June 2000, 36–44; Grace Shim, "Shortage of Truckers Leads Some Firms to Bend Rules," *Omaha World-Herald,* July 15, 2000, 13; Benard Wysocki, "When It Is the Job from Hell, Recruiting Is Rough," *The Wall Street Journal,* July 10, 2001, B1+; and Barbara Kantrowitz and Pat Wingert, "Teachers Wanted," *Newsweek,* October 2, 2000, 37–42.

2. Mark Talge, "With Unemployment Low, a New Group Is in Demand: Ex-Cons," *The Wall Street Journal,* April 24, 2000, A1+.

3. "Iowa—the Future's Foreign," *The Economist,* September 16, 2000, 36; and "Immigration Foes Take Aim at Vilsack," *Omaha World-Herald,* August 21, 2001, A14.

4. Sean Kelly, "IT Labor Shortage Continues," *Communications News,* May 2001, 8.

5. Based on Laura Parker, "USA Just Wouldn't Work Without Immigrant Labor," *USA Today,* July 23, 2001, 1A++; Jason Blevins, "Resorts Look Down Under for Hires," *The Denver Post,* August 20, 2000, I2; Amy Borus, "Workers of the World: Welcome," *Business Week,* November 20, 2000, 129–132; and Tamara Henry, "Teacher Shortage Gets Foreign Aid," *USA Today,* July 16, 2001, 6D.

6. "Walgreen's Expansion Plans Stymied by Lack of Pharmacists," *Chicago Tribune,* May 15, 2000.

7. Scott Highhouse et al., "Assessing Company Employment Image: An Example in the Fast-Food Industry," *Personnel Psychology,* 52 (1999), 151–172.

8. Jennifer Laabs, "Are You Ready to Outsource Staffing?" *Workforce,* April 2000, 56–60.

9. "Outsourcing HR," *Industry Week,* May 15, 2000, 71.

10. Dave Anderson, "A PEO Can Be Good for Business," *Financial Executive,* September–October 2000, 52–57.

11. Brian Klaas, John McClendon, and Thomas Gainey, "Managing HR in the Small and Medium Enterprise: The Impact of Professional Employer Organizations," *Entrepreneurship Theory and Practice* 25 (2000), 107–124.

12. "Are Your Recruiting Methods Discriminatory?" *Workforce,* May 2000, 105–106.

13. Ruth E. Thaler-Carter, "Diversify Your Recruitment Advertising," *HR Magazine,* June 2001, 92–100.

14. Dennis Doverspike, Mary Anne Taylor, Kenneth S. Schultz, and Patrick F. McKay, "Responding to the Challenge of a Changing Workforce: Recruiting Nontraditional Demographic Groups," *Public Personnel Management,* 29 (2000), 445–457.

15. Dayton Fandray, "Gray Matter," *Workforce,* July 2000, 26–32.

16. Kathryn Tyler, "Looking for a Few Good Workers," *HR Magazine,* December 2000, 129–134.

17. Carrall Lachnit, "Employee Referral Saves Times, Saves Money, Delivers Quality," *HR Magazine,* June 2001, 67–72.

18. Thomas G. Moehrle, "The Cost and Incidence of Referral, Hiring, and Retention Bonuses," *Compensation and Working Conditions,* Winter 2000, 37–42.

19. Carolyn Hirschman, "Reserve Space for Rehires," *HR Magazine,* January 2000, 58–64.

20. Rachael Emma Silverman, "Alumni Reunions," *The Wall Street Journal,* January 2, 2001, B14.

21. John R. Hall, "Recruiting Via the Internet," *Air Conditioning, Heating, & Refrigeration News,* April 9, 2001, 26.

22. *Internet Recruiting Newsletter,* available at *www.recruitersnetwork.com,* March 9, 2001.

23. Kate Dale, "Making the Net Work," *HR World,* May–June 2000, 32–36.

24. Bill Leonard, "Online and Overwhelmed," *HR Magazine,* August 2000, 37–42.

25. C. Glenn Pearce and Tracy L. Tuten, "Internet Recruiting in the Banking Industry," *Business Communications Quarterly,* March 2001, 9–18.

26. Peter Cappelli, "Making the Most of Online Recruiting," *Harvard Business Review,* March 2001, 139–146.

27. *Benchmarks in Online Recruiting: Maximizing Corporate Site Effectiveness* (Fitzwilliam, NH: Kennedy Information Research Group, 2001).

28. Skip Corsini, "Wired to Hire," *Training,* June 2001, 50–54.

29. "Online Recruiting: What Works, What Doesn't," *HR Focus,* March 2000, 1+.

30. Peter Kuhn and Mikal Skuiterud, "Job Search Methods: Internet versus Traditional," *Monthly Labor Review,* October 2000, 3–11.

31. "College Recruiters See It All," *Human Resources Report,* February 7, 2000, 119.

32. Sandra Grabczynski, "Nab New Grads by Building Relationships with Colleges," *Workforce,* May 2000, 98–103.

33. "Promising Students Noticed, Courted Earlier for Top Jobs," *Bulletin to Management,* August 16, 2001, 263; and Robert J. Grossman, "Robbing the Cradle?" *HR Magazine,* September 2000, 40–45.

34. William Dickmeyer, "Applicant Tracking Reports Make Data Meaningful," *Workforce,* February 2001, 65–67.

35. James A. Breaugh and Mary Starke, "Research on Employee Recruitment," *Journal of Management,* 26 (2000), 405–424.

36. Based on "All Is Fair in Talent War for Filling Jobs in New Hotel," *Bulletin to Management,* September 7, 2000, 286.

CHAPTER 8

Selecting and Placing Human Resources

After you have read this chapter, you should be able to:

- Describe why selection and placement must consider both person-job and person-organization fit.

- Diagram the sequence of a typical selection process.

- Identify three types of selection tests and legal concerns about their uses.

- Discuss several types of selection interviews and some key considerations when conducting these interviews.

- Explain how legal concerns affect background investigations of applicants and use of medical examinations in the selection process.

Selection at Home Depot

Home Depot, the large national retailer, hires more than 100,000 people per year to staff new stores and replace employees who leave, receive promotions, or get transfers. To handle this volume of applicants, Home Depot uses a customized, automated system based on electronic technology. However, the initial impetus to develop the Job Performance Program (JPP), its automated hiring and promotion system, was not to create a more efficient selection process. Instead, it grew out of a settlement of a sex-discrimination class action lawsuit. Home Depot settled the lawsuit by paying $65 million to women who claimed that they were guided into lower-paying jobs and denied promotions. As part of the settlement, the company agreed to establish a selection process to ensure that all applicants were fairly considered for openings whenever and wherever they occurred.

Home Depot spent more than $10 million to develop and implement the JPP. Electronic kiosks stand in Home Depot stores to pre-screen applicants for jobs. Individuals, including current employees, can apply for jobs at the in store kiosks or by calling a toll-free phone number. Individuals then may complete an electronic application and take an on-line basic skills test that takes 40–90 minutes, depending on the jobs being considered. The JPP system prints out test results and identifies suggested questions for managers to use when conducting in-person interviews on candidates getting satisfactory scores on the automated tests.

Managers, applicants, and current employees interested in job changes have all benefited from the new selection system. The benefits include less time, more targeted assessments, and greater availability of opportunities for current employees.

Specifically for current employees, the JPP has been useful for providing promotion placement opportunities. Employees can register for future jobs of interest and update their personal profile information. The system then can identify how the individual's future job interests do and do not match the qualifications of the individual. For example, individuals interested in becoming assistant managers can learn that sales associate experience is required. Therefore, cashiers interested in becoming assistant managers may want to get sales associate experience as part of longer-term career progression.

Home Depot has benefited from the new selection process in several ways. For instance, individuals hired using the JPP have been found to have higher product knowledge and receive higher performance ratings than employees hired under the old system. Automating much of the "paper flow" has saved Home Depot more than $132 per applicant by transferring JPP data on hired individuals into the firm's payroll and human resource information systems (HRIS), saving countless hours of data entry.

On a broader scale, the new system helped to increase the number of female and minority mangers by about 30%. Also, Home Depot has experienced lower turnover rates for individuals screened through the JPP than what previously occurred under the old process. In summary, what started out to be a response to a lawsuit led to significant positive results for building Home Depot for the future.[1]

> Managers, applicants, and current employees interested in job changes have all benefited from the new selection system.

"Selecting qualified employees is like putting money in the bank."

—John Boudreau

Selection decisions are an important part of successful HR management. Some even would argue that these decisions are the most important part. Organizational performance improvement for an employer may come from changes in incentive pay plans, improved training, or better job design; but unless the employer begins with the necessary people with the appropriate capabilities in place, those results may not occur.

Selection and Placement

Selection Process of choosing individuals who have needed qualifications to fill jobs in an organization.

Selection is the process of choosing individuals who have needed qualifications to fill jobs in an organization. Without qualified employees, an organization is less likely to succeed. Organizations on average reject a high percentage of applicants. In some situations about five out of six applicants for jobs are rejected. Perhaps the best perspective on selection and placement comes from two HR truisms that clearly identify the importance of effective employment selection.

- *"Good training will not make up for bad selection."* When the right people with the appropriate capabilities are not selected for jobs, employers have difficulty later trying to train those individuals.
- *"Hire hard, manage easy."* The amount of time and effort spent in selecting the right people for jobs may make managing them as employees much less difficult because more problems will be eliminated.

Selection Responsibilities

Organizations vary in how they allocate selection responsibilities between HR specialists and managers. Until the impact of EEO regulations became widespread, selection often was carried out in an unplanned manner in many organizations. The need to meet EEO requirements has forced organizations to plan better in this regard. Still, in some organizations, each department screens and hires its own employees. Many managers insist on selecting their own people because they are sure no one else can choose employees for them as well as they can themselves. This practice is particularly prevalent in smaller firms. But the validity and fairness of such an approach may be questionable.

Other organizations have the HR unit do the initial screening of the candidates, while managers or supervisors make the final selection. As a rule, the higher the position being filled, the greater the likelihood that the ultimate hiring decisions will be made by operating managers rather than HR specialists. Typical selection responsibilities are shown in Figure 8-1.

Selection responsibilities are affected by the existence of a central employment office, which usually is part of an HR department. In smaller organizations, especially in those with fewer than 100 employees, a full-time employment specialist or unit may be impractical. But for larger employers, centralizing employment within one unit may be appropriate for several reasons:

- It is easier for applicants to have only one place in which to apply for jobs.
- Contact with outside applicant sources is easier because those contacts can be handled through one central location.

Logging On...

HR-Guide.com
This Web site is a guide to the selection process and includes information on methods, laws, best practices, tests, and software programs that can be used for selection.

http://www.hr-guide.com/selection.htm

Figure 8-1

Typical Division of HR Responsibilities: Selection

HR Unit	Managers
• Provides initial reception for applicants	• Requisition employees with specific qualifications to fill jobs
• Conducts initial screening interview	• Participate in selection process as appropriate
• Administers appropriate employment tests	• Interview final candidates
• Obtains background and reference information and arranges for the employment physical examination, if used	• Make final selection decision, subject to advice of HR specialists
• Refers top candidates to managers for final selection	• Provide follow-up information on the suitability of selected individuals
• Evaluates success of selection process	

- Managers can concentrate on their operating responsibilities rather than on time-consuming interviewing and selection efforts.
- Selection costs may be cut by avoiding duplication of effort.
- People well-trained in EEO regulations handle a major part of the process to reduce future lawsuits and the costs associated with them.

The employment function in any organization may be concerned with some or all of the following activities: (1) receiving applications, (2) interviewing applicants, (3) administering tests to applicants, (4) conducting background investigations, (5) arranging for physical examinations, (6) placing and assigning new employees, (7) coordinating follow-up of these employees, (8) exit interviewing of departing employees, and (9) maintaining appropriate records and reports.

Placement

Placement Fitting a person to the right job.

The ultimate purpose of selection is **placement,** or fitting a person to the right job. More than anything else, placement of human resources should be seen as a matching process. How well an employee is matched to a job affects the amount and quality of the employee's work. This matching also directly affects training and operating costs. Individuals who are unable to produce the expected amount and quality of work can cost an organization a great deal of money and time.

Person-Job Fit Selection and placement entail much more than just choosing the best available person. Selecting the appropriate capabilities and talents—which come packaged in a human being—attempts to "fit" what the applicant can and wants to do with what the organization needs. The task is further complicated by the difficulty in discerning exactly what the applicant really can and wants to do, as well as other intangible factors that may affect the fit.

Person-job fit Matching the KSAs of people with the characteristics of jobs.

Selection and placement activities typically focus on applicants' knowledge, skills, and abilities (KSAs). The **person-job fit** is a simple but important concept that involves matching the KSAs of people with the characteristics of jobs. Obviously, without a good fit between the KSAs of the person and the demands of the job, the likelihood of lower employee performance, higher turnover and

Figure 8-2   *Person-Organization Fit*

Individual
- Goals
- Values
- Interests
- Expectations
- KSAs

Organization
- Objectives and strategies
- Values
- Culture
- Structure and management
- Rewards

absenteeism, and other HR problems increases. Much of selection is concerned with gathering needed information on the applicants' KSAs through application forms, resumes, interviews, tests, and other means.

Having the needed KSAs is important for an employee to do a job well. Specific KSAs may be used to hire people for a given job: math skills, ability to weld, or a knowledge of spreadsheets. Job analysis can provide the basis for identifying KSAs needed in a job if it is done properly. People already in jobs can help identify the most important KSAs for success as part of job analysis. This is suitable especially in the following placement situations:

- KSAs brought to jobs are more critical than what is learned on the jobs.
- Jobs change infrequently and employees are closely monitored against well-established performance standards.
- The needed KSAs are observable, clearly identified, and closely linked to task performance on the jobs.

Person-Organization Fit In addition to matching individuals to jobs, employers also increasingly try to determine the congruence between individuals and organizational factors to achieve **person-organization fit,** as Figure 8-2 depicts.

Person-organization fit is important when general factors of job success are as important as specific KSAs. For example, if an employer hires at the entry level and promotes from within for most jobs, specific KSAs might be less important than general cognitive and problem-solving abilities and work ethic. Ability to learn allows a person to grasp new information and make good decisions based on that job knowledge. Work ethic might include thoroughness, responsibility, and an organized approach to the job. Person-organization fit is used in the following placement situations:

Person-organization fit
The congruence between individuals and organizational factors.

Research on Person-Job and Person-Organization Fit

The importance of both person-job and person-organization fit was examined in two different research studies by Amy L. Kristof-Brown published in *Personnel Psychology*. She based her research on the fact that traditionally recruiters have focused on person-job fit using KSAs, and only recently have recruiters considered person-organization fit as well.

In the first study recruiters from financial and IT consulting organizations, viewed videotaped mock interviews of MBA students and reviewed their resumes. After viewing the interviews, the recruiters were questioned about which applicants best fit the identified job. This study revealed that all of the recruiters evaluated applicants' KSAs, which indicated a focus on person-job fit.

The second study used different recruiters from some of the same consulting companies. These recruiters conducted in-person interviews with the mock applicants. Then they were asked to identify one "successful" and one "unsuccessful" applicant based on the interviews. The recruiters completed a survey on person-organization fit, as well as on person-job fit characteristics.

The results of the second study indicated that person-job fit was still the most important decision concern for the recruiters, but person-organization factors, such as personality characteristics and values, played some role in selection decisions.

Taken together, the results of the studies reveal that initial selection decisions based on interviews and resumes still focus heavily on identifiable KSAs, so person-job fit is the primary concern. However, person-organization fit is a likely determinant later using other selection activities.[2]

- Organization culture is unique and teamwork is highly valued.
- Employees work independently and have considerable judgment and discretion in doing their work.
- Most KSAs can be learned on the job if the person has basic cognitive abilities, work ethic, and other capabilities.
- Jobs and the organization change often and employee adaptability and creativity are expected.

Determining person-organization fit may require use of multiple selection means and take considerable time and effort. Multiple in-depth interviews, use of extensive ability, aptitude, and psychological tests, and involvement of several levels of managers and employees are just some ways of ensuring person-organization fit.[3] The HR Perspectives describes research on person-job and person-organization fit.

Criteria, Predictors, and Job Performance

Whether an employer uses specific KSAs or the more general approach, effective selection of employees involves using criteria and predictors of job performance. At the heart of an effective selection system is knowledge of what constitutes appropriate job performance and what employee characteristics are associated with that performance. First, an employer defines employee success (performance), and then, using that definition as a basis, determines the employee specifications required to achieve success. A **selection criterion** is a characteristic that a person must have to do the job successfully. A pre-existing ability is often a selection criterion. Figure 8-3 shows that ability, motivation,

Selection criterion
Characteristic that a person must have to do a job successfully.

Figure 8-3 | *Job Performance, Selection Criteria, and Predictors*

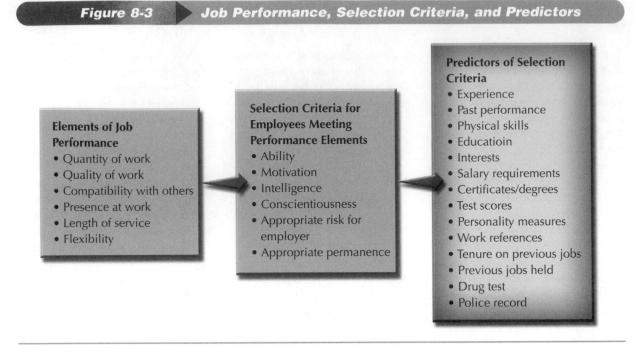

Elements of Job Performance
- Quantity of work
- Quality of work
- Compatibility with others
- Presence at work
- Length of service
- Flexibility

Selection Criteria for Employees Meeting Performance Elements
- Ability
- Motivation
- Intelligence
- Conscientiousness
- Appropriate risk for employer
- Appropriate permanence

Predictors of Selection Criteria
- Experience
- Past performance
- Physical skills
- Educatioin
- Interests
- Salary requirements
- Certificates/degrees
- Test scores
- Personality measures
- Work references
- Tenure on previous jobs
- Previous jobs held
- Drug test
- Police record

intelligence, conscientiousness, appropriate risk, and permanence might be good selection criteria for many jobs.

To predict whether a selection criterion (such as "motivation" or "ability") is present, employers try to identify predictors as measurable indicators of selection criteria. For example, in Figure 8-3 three good predictors for some criteria might be individual interests, salary requirements, and tenure on previous jobs.

The information gathered about an applicant should be focused on finding predictors of the likelihood that the applicant will be able to perform the job well. Predictors can take many forms, but any selection tool used (for example, application form, test, interview, education requirements, or years of experience required) should be used only if it is a valid predictor of job performance. Using invalid predictors can result in selecting the "wrong" candidate and rejecting the "right" one.

Validity In selection, validity is the correlation between a predictor and job performance. As mentioned in Chapter 4 validity occurs to the extent that a predictor actually predicts what it is supposed to predict. Validity depends on the situation in which the selection device is being used. For example, a psychological test designed to predict aptitude for child-care jobs might not be valid in predicting sales aptitudes for marketing representative jobs.

Reliability Reliability of a predictor is the extent to which it repeatedly produces the same results, over time. For example, if the same person took a test in December and scored 75, but upon taking it in March scored significantly higher, the test may not be reliable. Thus, reliability has to do with the consistency of predictors in selection.

Combining Predictors

If an employer chooses to use only one predictor (for example, a test) to select who will be hired, the decision is straightforward. If the test is valid and encompasses a major dimension of a job, and the applicant does well on the test, he or she can be hired. In this single-predictor approach, selection accuracy depends on how valid that single predictor is at predicting performance.

When using several predictors, all must be met. For example, when requiring 3 years of experience, having a college degree, and attaining a certain score on an aptitude test, qualified candidates are those who possess all of those criteria.

When using more than one predictor, they must be combined in some way.[4] Two different approaches for combining predictors are:

- *Multiple hurdles:* A minimum cutoff is set on each predictor, and each minimum level must be "passed." For example, in order to be hired a candidate for a sales representative job must achieve a minimum education level, a certain score on a sales aptitude test, and a minimum score on a structured interview.
- *Compensatory approach:* In this approach, scores from individual predictors are added together and combined into an overall score, thus allowing a higher score on one predictor to offset or compensate for a lower score on another. The combined index takes into consideration performance on all predictors.

The Selection Process

Most organizations take steps to process applicants for jobs. Variations on the basic process depend on organizational size, nature of jobs to be filled, number of people to be selected, the use of electronic technology, and other factors. This process can take place in a day or over a much longer period of time. If the applicant is processed in one day, the employer usually checks references after selection. One or more phases of the process may be omitted or the order changed, depending on the employer. Figure 8-4 on the next page represents a selection process typical in many organizations.

Legal Concerns in the Selection Process

Selection is subject to a number of legal concerns, especially all the equal employment opportunity (EEO) regulations and laws covered in previous chapters. Throughout the selection process, application forms, interviews, tests, background investigations, and any other selection activities must be conducted in a nondiscriminatory manner. Also, applicants not hired should be rejected only for job-related reasons, not based on protected-class or personal factors, which are illegal. For instance because of religious policies against premarital sex, a parochial school refused continued employment to a single female who was pregnant. However, the woman won her lawsuit because the school's policy was not enforced against men also.[5]

A different legal area concerns information about union activities or affiliation. The National Labor Relations Board has ruled that inquiring about union-related information or excluding applicants with union backgrounds violates federal labor laws.[6]

Logging On...

Uniform Guidelines.com
This Web site is a free site on the use of selection procedures and tests to ensure compliance with federal laws.

http://www.uniformguidelines.com.

Figure 8-4 ▶ **Selection Process Flowchart**

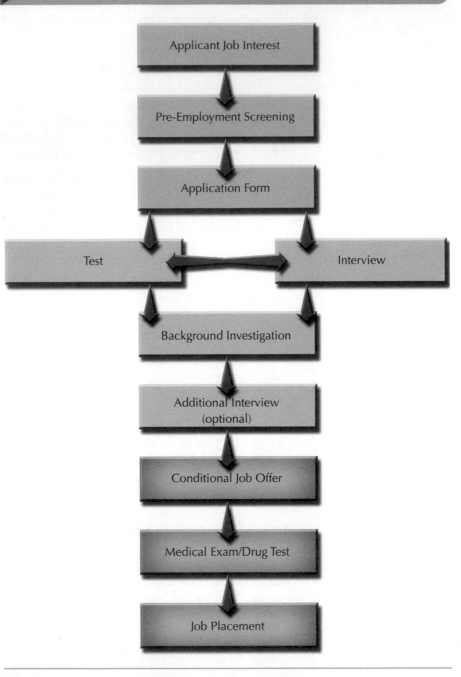

Defining Who Is an Applicant It is increasingly important for employers to carefully define exactly who is an applicant because many employers are required to do applicant tracking and reporting as part of equal employment and affirmative action plans. Also, it is important because of "scams" involving individuals who try to apply for jobs, but their primary purpose is to then file lawsuits. Without clear definition of who is an applicant, all individuals who submit unsolicited resumes, respond electronically to Web site employment postings, and persons who walk in to apply for jobs might have to be counted as "applicants." Several means are used to narrow who is defined as an applicant, not just someone expressing interest in employment. Common ones are shown in Figure 8-5.

The use of these policies may vary by organization and by the tightness of the labor market. For instance, a general recommendation is that applications be accepted only for existing openings. However, a bank that has high turnover in tellers may decide to accept applications at any time for teller candidates, even though it currently has no openings, because the bank is likely to need tellers in the next few months. Those applying can then be contacted when openings occur.

In some organizations, someone in the employment office or in the HR department conducts a brief interview, often called an initial screening or a job preview/interest screen, to see if the individual expressing interest in employment is likely to match any jobs available in the organization. Assuming that the individual meets the minimum qualifications, the individual is then given an application form and becomes counted as an "applicant"

Applicant Flow Documentation One interesting point to remember is that many employers must collect data on the race, sex, and other demographics on applicants to fulfill EEO reporting requirements. As discussed in Chapter 4, many employers use an applicant flow form for applicants to provide EEOC reporting data separately. It is important that this form be filed separately and not be used in any other HR selection activities, or the employers may be accused of using applicant information inappropriately. Because completing the forms is

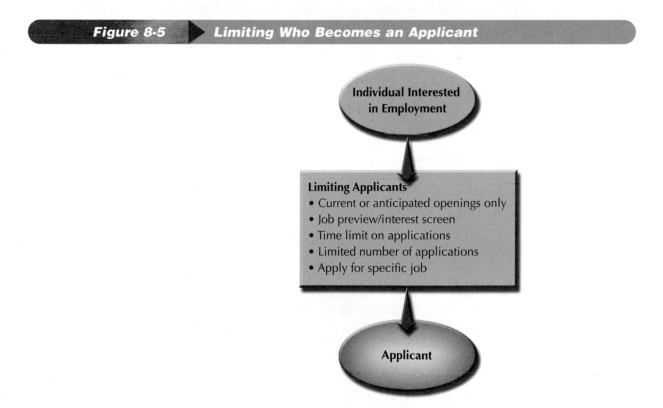

Figure 8-5 ▶ *Limiting Who Becomes an Applicant*

Individual Interested in Employment

Limiting Applicants
• Current or anticipated openings only
• Job preview/interest screen
• Time limit on applications
• Limited number of applications
• Apply for specific job

Applicant

voluntary, employers can demonstrate that they tried to obtain the data even if the individuals do not return the form.

The Office of Federal Contract Compliance Programs (OFCCP) has established requirements about who is considered an applicant.[7] However, those regulations do not adequately consider the impact of the Internet as a source of applicant flow. Some firms respond to electronically submitted resumes and applications by sending an applicant flow form along with acknowledgment that the resumes or applications have been received.

Applicant Job Interest

Individuals desiring employment can indicate interest in employment in a number of ways. Traditionally, individuals have submitted resumes by mail/fax or applied in person at an employer's location. But with the growth in Internet recruiting, many individuals complete applications online or submit resumes electronically.

Regardless of how individuals express interest in employment, the selection process has an important public relations dimension. Discriminatory hiring practices, impolite interviewers, unnecessarily long waits, unreturned telephone inquiries, inappropriate testing procedures, and lack of follow-up responses can produce unfavorable impressions of an employer. Job applicants' perceptions of the organization, and even about the products or services it offers, will be influenced by how they are treated.

Realistic Job Previews Most job seekers appear to know little about organizations prior to applying for jobs. Consequently, job seekers tend to give considerable weight to the information received from prospective employers in the recruiting/selection process when making decisions of whether or not to accept jobs. For applicants, information on pay, nature of the work, geographic location, and opportunity for promotion is useful. Unfortunately, some employers oversell their jobs in recruiting advertisements, making them appear better than they really are.

Realistic job preview (RJP) The process through which a job applicant receives an accurate picture of a job.

Through the process of a **realistic job preview (RJP),** job applicants are provided with an accurate picture of a job, including the "organizational realities" of a job, so that applicants can more accurately evaluate their own job expectations. With an RJP, the organization hopes to prevent unrealistic expectations, which helps reduce employee disenchantment and ultimately employee dissatisfaction and turnover. A review of research on RJPs found that they tend to be effective in that regard.[8]

Pre-Employment Screening

Many employers conduct pre-employment screening in order to determine if applicants meet the minimum qualifications for open jobs. For example, one firm that hires security guards and armored-car drivers uses a pre-screening interview to verify whether an applicant meets the minimum qualifications of having a valid driver's license, being free of any criminal convictions in the past seven years, and having been trained to use a pistol. Because these minimum standards are required, it would be a waste of time for any applicant who could not meet them to fill out an application form. Other areas typically covered by other employers include types of available jobs, applicants' pay expectations, job location, and travel requirements.

Electronic Screening Pre-employment screening done electronically has increased dramatically in the past few years. One type of screening uses computer software to scan resumes or applications submitted electronically for key words.[9] Hundreds of large companies use types of "text searching" or artificial-intelligence (AI) software to scan, score, and track resumes of applicants. For example, the financial firm Charles Schwab streamlined its application process whereby individuals can complete applications electronically. The applicants' qualifications then are compared to job profiles in order to determine which candidates are likely to be successful, and those candidates are contacted for interviews. The system allows Schwab to cut its average time to fill jobs by seven days.[10]

Other pre-employment screening systems incorporate some application profiling and skills or other tests, as the opening discussion on Home Depot illustrates. One industry heavily using electronic screening is customer call centers. In one system, individuals complete on-line applications at kiosks in the firm's employment office or over the Internet. The program then presents four customer service situations to the individual who is asked to respond to statements concerning those situations. Those seen as better candidates based on their responses then proceed into other phases of the selection process. The company recoups the cost of $20 to $25 per applicant many times over due to the shortened selection process that focuses time and efforts on candidates identified as less likely to turnover and more likely to meet the positive profile requirements.[11]

Regardless of the electronic pre-employment systems used, the screening analyses must be job-related, without using age, gender, or other data as screening criteria. Otherwise, potential illegal discrimination complaints could not be defended well.

Application Forms

Application forms are widely used and can take many different formats. Properly prepared, the application form serves four purposes:

- It is a record of the applicant's desire to obtain a position.
- It provides the interviewer with a profile of the applicant that can be used in the interview.
- It is a basic employee record for applicants who are hired.
- It can be used for research on the effectiveness of the selection process.

Many employers use only one application form, but others need several. For example, a hospital might need one form for nurses and medical technicians, another form for clerical and office employees, another for managers and supervisors, and another for support persons in housekeeping and food-service areas.

Application Disclaimers and Notices Application forms need disclaimers and notices so that appropriate legal protections are stated by employers. Recommended disclosures and notices appearing on applications include:

- *Employment-at-will:* Indicates the right of the employer or applicant to terminate the employment relationship at any time with or without notice or cause (where applicable by state law).
- *Reference contacts:* Requests permission to contact references listed by applicants.

- *Employment testing:* Notifies applicants of required drug tests, physical exams, or other tests.
- *Application time limit:* Indicates how long applications are active (typically six months) and that individuals must reactivate applications after that period.
- *Information falsification:* Conveys to an applicant signing the form that falsification of application information is grounds for termination.

Immigration Forms The Immigration Reform and Control Act (IRCA) of 1986, as revised in 1990, requires that within 72 hours of hiring, an employer must determine whether a job applicant is a U.S. citizen, registered alien, or illegal alien. Those applicants not eligible to work in this country must not be hired. Employers use the I-9 form to identify the status of potential employees. Employers have a responsibility that documents submitted by new employees, such as U.S. passports, birth certificates, original Social Security cards, and driver's licenses, appear to be genuine. Also, employers who hire employees on special visas must maintain appropriate documentation and records.[12]

EEO Considerations and Application Forms An organization should retain all applications and hiring-related documents and records for *three years*. Guidelines from the EEOC and court decisions require that the data requested on application forms must be job related. Employers of all types should review their application forms. According to a review of 41 state government on-line employment applications, all but one had at least one inadvisable question, with an average of four on each form.[13] Illegal questions typically found on application forms ask for the following:

- Marital status
- Height/weight
- Number and ages of dependents
- Information on spouse
- Date of high school graduation
- Contact in case of emergency

Concern about such questions stems from their potential disparate impact on some protected groups. For example, the question about dependents can be used to identify women with small children, who may not be hired because of a manager's perception that they will have more absences than women without small children. The high school graduation date more closely identifies a person's age, which can be used to discriminate against individuals over 40. Or, the question about emergency contact might reveal marital status or other protected personal information. Figure 8-6 shows a sample application form that avoids some of these problems.

Resumes as Applications One of the most common methods applicants use to provide background information is through resumes. Technically, a resume used in place of an application form must be treated by an employer as an application form for EEO purposes. Consequently, even if an applicant's resume voluntarily furnishes some information that cannot be legally obtained, the employer should not use that information during the selection process.[14]

Figure 8-6   **Sample Application Form**

Application for Employment
An Equal Opportunity Employer*

Today's Date _____

Personal Information   Please Print or Type

Name (Last) (First) (Full Middle Name)	Social Security Number
Current Address City State Zip Code	Phone Number ( )
What position are you applying for?	Date available for employment?	e-mail address

Are you willing to relocate? ☐ Yes ☐ No	Are you willing to travel if required? ☐ Yes ☐ No	Any restrictions on hours, weekends, or overtime? If yes, explain.
Have you ever been employed by this Company or any of its subsidiaries before? ☐ Yes ☐ No		Indicate Location and Dates
Can you, after employment, submit verification of your legal right to work in the United States? ☐ Yes ☐ No	Have you ever been convicted of a felony? ☐ Yes ☐ No	Convictions will not automatically disqualify job candidates. The seriousness of the crime and date of conviction will be considered.

Performance of Job Functions

Are you able to perform all the functions of the job for which you are applying, with or without accommodation?

☐ Yes, without accommodation   ☐ Yes, with accommodation   ☐ No

If you indicated you can perform all the functions with an accommodation, please explain how you would perform the tasks and with what accommodation.

Education

School level	School Name & Address	No. of Years Attended	Did You Graduate?	Course of Study
High School				
Vo-Tech, Business or Trade School				
College				
Graduate School				

Personal Driving Record

This section is to be completed ONLY if the operation of a motor vehicle will be required in the course of the applicant's employment

How long have you been a licensed driver?	Driver's license number	Expiration date	Issuing state

List any other state(s) in which you have had a driver's license(s) in the past:

Within the past five years have you had a vehicle accident? ☐ Yes ☐ No	Been convicted of reckless or drunken driving? ☐ Yes ☐ No	If yes, give dates:	Been cited for moving violations? If yes, give dates: ☐ Yes ☐ No
Has your driver's license ever been revoked or suspended? If yes, explain: ☐ Yes ☐ No		Is your driver's license restricted? If yes, explain: ☐ Yes ☐ No	

*We are an Equal Opportunity Employer. We do not discriminate on the basis of race, religion, color, gender, age, national origin or disability.

Reviewing Application Forms and Resumes

The information on application forms and resumes must be reviewed and screened. Some commonly used ways that experienced HR professionals "read between the lines" on applications include the following:

- *Gaps in employment:* Applicants show dates of employment, but gaps in time periods may appear. These gaps may indicate jobs held that individuals did not want to report, being imprisoned, or other reasons. However, gaps for medical or family reasons may be legitimate and should not disqualify applicants.

- *Education completion:* Careful reading of an application or resume may reveal that the individual attended a college, but did not graduate because a degree and graduation date are not noted.

- *Responsibility and job levels:* Typically job responsibilities and types of jobs held may provide useful information on the suitability of candidates. If an individual is applying for management jobs but no previous management experience is shown, or if the individual has had significantly more responsibilities and has applied for a lower-level job, the change in responsibility levels may indicate an underqualified or overqualified individual whose salary expectations may be unrealistically high.

- *Qualifications and accomplishments:* Details on specific qualifications and accomplishments in previous jobs may aid the HR person in identifying which applicants come closest to matching the KSAs for the job. These candidates are then identified as the first ones to move to the next phase of the selection process.

The HR Practice contains some suggestions useful when reviewing applications forms and resumes. Some employers require that all who submit resumes complete an application form as well. Individuals who mail in resumes may be sent thank-you letters and application forms to be completed and returned. Appendix D contains some suggestions on resume preparation.

Biodata and Weighted Application Forms One method that has been devised to gather and use application information is through the use of biodata and weighted application forms. To develop these types of forms, it is necessary to develop questions that can be asked legally and are weighted to differentiate between satisfactory and poor-performing employees. An employer then can evaluate and compare applicants' responses numerically to a valid, job-related set of inquiries.[15] This approach is at the heart of many of the electronic pre-employment screening systems used by Home Depot and other employers. However several problems are associated with biodata and weighted application forms.[16] Consequently, although these types of forms are mentioned frequently in academic studies, they are not as widely used by employers.

A number of federal, state, and local governmental employers rate training and experience on applications and resumes. The submitted applications and resumes are examined using checklists, and candidates are ranked using the results in order to determine those to be interviewed or tested.

Selection Testing

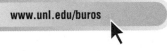
According to the Uniform Selection Guidelines issued by the EEOC, any employment requirement is a "test." The focus in this section is on specific tests because a number of employers feel that formal tests can be of great benefit in the selection process when properly used and administered. One survey showed that 69% of employers use some type of pre-employment testing. Most entry-level applicants (92%) are tested in some way, but just one half of all executives receive some types of testing.[17]

A number of different types of tests are used as part of the selection process. Figure 8-7 on the next page shows some of these types based on a survey of 283 organizations. A look at the most common types of tests follows, except for drug screening tests, which are discussed later in the chapter.

Ability Tests

Tests that assess an individual's ability to perform in a specific manner are grouped as ability tests. Sometimes further differentiated into *aptitude* and *achievement* tests, each of the several types of ability tests is briefly examined next.

Cognitive ability tests measure an individual's thinking, memory, reasoning, and verbal and mathematical abilities. Tests such as these can be used to test applicants' basic knowledge of terminology and concepts, word fluency, spatial orientation, comprehension and retention span, and general and conceptual reasoning. The Wonderlic Personnel Test and the General Aptitude Test Battery (GATB) are two widely used tests of this type. The important consideration when

"I see...so, the gaps in your employment correspond to each of your alien abductions?"

Source: *The Wall Street Journal.*

Figure 8-7 ▶ *Types of Pre-Employment Testing Used*

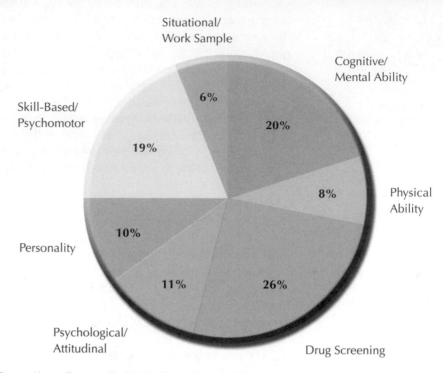

Source: *Human Resource Executive* by Human Resource Executive. Copyright 2000 by L R P PUBNS. Reproduced with permission of L R P PUBNS in the format Textbook via Copyright Clearance Center.

using cognitive ability tests is to ensure that the cognitive concepts tested are clearly job-related. For example, giving a sales clerk applicant a basic mathematics test may be useful to determine the individual's ability to make change and determine customers' bills when both purchases and returns are being handled.

Physical ability tests measure individual abilities such as strength, endurance, and muscular movement. At an electric utility, line workers regularly must lift and carry equipment, climb ladders, and perform other physical tasks. Testing applicants' mobility, strength, and other physical attributes is job-related. A type of physical ability test, *functional capacity testing,* measures such areas as range of motion, strength and posture, cardiovascular fitness, and other facets.[18] As noted later, care should be taken to limit physical ability testing until after a conditional job offer is made in order to avoid violating the provisions of the Americans with Disabilities Act (ADA).

Different skill-based tests can be used, including **psychomotor tests** that measure a person's dexterity, hand-eye coordination, arm-hand steadiness, and other factors. Such tests as the MacQuarie Test for Mechanical Ability can measure manual dexterity for assembly-line workers and others using psychomotor skills regularly.

Many organizations use situational or **work sample tests,** which require an applicant to perform a simulated job task that is part of the target job. Having an applicant for a financial analyst's job prepare a computer spreadsheet is one such test. Requiring a person applying for a truck driver's job to back a truck to a

Physical ability tests Tests that measure individual abilities such as strength, endurance, and muscular movement.

Psychomotor tests Tests that measure dexterity, hand-eye coordination, arm-hand steadiness, and other factors.

Work sample tests Tests that require an applicant to perform a simulated job task.

loading dock is another. An "in-basket" test is a work sample test in which a job candidate is asked to respond to memos in a hypothetical in-basket that are typical of the problems faced by people holding that job. The key for any work sample test is the behavioral consistency between the criteria of the job and the requirements for the test.

Assessment Centers An assessment center is composed of a series of evaluative exercises and tests used for selection and development. Most often used in the selection process when filling managerial openings, an assessment center uses multiple exercises and multiple raters. In one assessment center, candidates go through a comprehensive interview, pencil-and-paper test, individual and group simulations, and work exercises. The candidates' performances are then evaluated by a panel of trained raters. It is crucial to any assessment center that the tests and exercises reflect the job content and types of problems faced on the jobs for which individuals are being screened.

Psychological Testing
This Web site from a firm offering pre-employment testing lists assessment and other development tools.

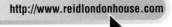

http://www.reidlondonhouse.com

Personality Tests

Personality is a unique blend of individual characteristics that affect interaction with the environment and help define a person. Of the many different types of personality tests, one of the most widely known and used is the Minnesota Multiphasic Personality Inventory (MMPI). It was originally developed to diagnose major psychological disorders and has become widely used as a selection test. From this and many other personality tests, an extensive number of personality characteristics can be identified and used. The Myers-Briggs test is another widely used test of this type.

The multitude of different personality traits has long frustrated psychologists, who have argued that there is a relatively small number of underlying *major* traits. The most widely accepted approach to these underlying personality traits (although not the only one) is often referred to as the "Big Five" personality traits. The Big Five that can be considered generally useful predictors of training success and job performance are shown in Figure 8-8 on the next page.

Of the Big Five, conscientiousness has been found to be related to job success across most organizations and occupations. Extroversion has been found to predict success in jobs requiring social interaction, such as many sales jobs. The usefulness of the other three varies depending on the kind of jobs and organizations. When used in selection, psychological or personality testing requires that a solid job-related link be made.

Honesty/Integrity Testing

Different types of tests are being used by employers to assess the honesty and integrity of applicants and employees. They include standardized honesty/integrity tests and polygraphs. Both are controversial.

Employers use these tests for several reasons. Firms such as retailers use honesty tests to screen out potentially dishonest individuals and decrease the incidence of employee theft. These firms believe that giving honesty tests not only helps them to screen out potentially dishonest individuals, but also sends a message to applicants and employees alike that dishonesty will not be tolerated.

Two types of tests assess honesty and integrity of individuals. *Overt integrity tests* inquire specifically about individual honesty and attitudes and

Figure 8-8 ▶ **Big Five Personality Characteristics**

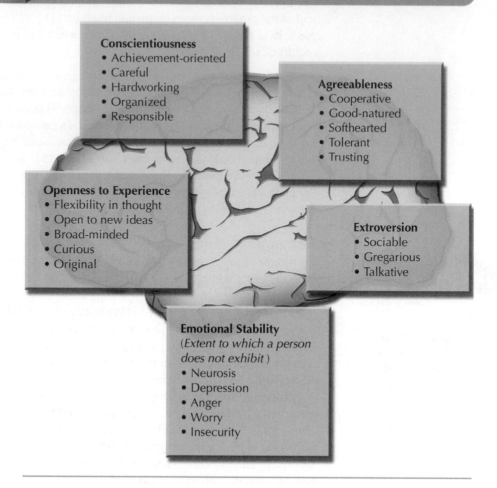

behavior regarding theft. Samples of such overt questions on some of these tests might include:

- Would you tell your boss if you knew another employee was stealing from the company?
- Is it okay to borrow company equipment to use at home if the property is always returned?
- Have you ever told a lie?
- Have you ever wished you were physically more attractive?

The other type, *personality-oriented integrity* tests, uses psychological concepts such as dependability, respect for authority, and others. Analyses of these dimensions are used to identify individuals whose psychological "profile" indicates greater or lesser integrity orientations.

Honesty/integrity tests may be valid as broad screening devices for organizations if used properly. However, it is important that the tests be chosen, used, and evaluated to ensure that they are and remain valid and reliable. They should be used as one piece of the selection process along with applications, interviews, and other data.[19] One documented concern about integrity tests is the "fake-ability" of the tests. Research indicates that the ability of the test takers to "fake" honesty and pass integrity tests is higher with overt tests than personality tests.[20] Also, the use of these tests can have a negative public relations impact on applicants. A final concern is that the types of questions asked may constitute invasion of individual privacy.

Polygraphs and the Employee Polygraph Protection Act The polygraph, more generally and incorrectly referred to as the "lie detector," is a mechanical device that measures a person's galvanic skin response, heart rate, and breathing rate. The theory behind the polygraph is that if a person answers incorrectly, the body's physiological responses will "reveal" the falsification through the polygraph's recording mechanisms. As a result of concerns, Congress passed the Employee Polygraph Protection Act, which prohibits polygraph use for pre-employment screening purposes by most employers. However, federal, state, and local government agencies are exempt from the act. Also exempted are certain private-sector employers such as security companies and pharmaceutical companies. The act does allow employers to continue to use polygraphs as part of internal investigations of theft or losses. But the polygraph test should be taken voluntarily, and the employee should be allowed to end the test at any time.

Controversial and Questionable Tests

Some questionable tests sometimes are used in employee selection. But experts warn of the legal and ethical problems in using these techniques for employee selection. For instance, graphology and psychics have been used by various employers.

- *Graphology* (handwriting analysis): This type of "test" uses an "analysis" of an individual's handwriting. Such characteristics as how people dot an *i* or cross a *t*, whether they write with a left or right slant, and the size and boldness of the letters they form supposedly tell graphologists about the individuals' personalities and their suitability for employment. It is popular in France, Israel, and several other countries, but is used on a limited basis in the United States. However, formal scientific evaluations of graphology are not easily found. Its value as a personality predictor is somewhat questionable and may not be easily validated as job-related.
- *Psychics:* Similarly, some firms use psychics to help select managerial talent. The psychics are supposedly able to determine if a person is suited for a job both intellectually and emotionally. However, most businesses would not want anyone to know that they used "psychic advisers."

Testing Considerations and Concerns

Selection testing can provide useful insights on the abilities and characteristics of applicants that may not be determined through interviews or other means. Person-job fit can be enhanced through ability and other tests focusing on specific KSAs. Tests are particularly beneficial in obtaining information to determine person-organization fit, so that a good match occurs between applicants' values, expectations, and capabilities and organizational values, culture, and management issues.

However, testing must be used carefully and appropriately. Too often, tests are used for automatic disqualification or acceptance, rather than as additional information to be evaluated and compared with other sources of information such as interviews and background investigations. Also, concerns exist about the negative reactions that some applicants have to certain types of tests, such as honesty/integrity and personality tests. Depending upon the tests used, testing costs can be significant, which must be balanced with the consequences of making "bad hires." Finally, selection testing can and has raised legal concerns and liability for employers.

Legal Concerns and Selection Testing Employers must continue to emphasize that selection tests used must be job-related and nondiscriminatory to protected-class members. Several court cases have ruled that some tests used by employers, particularly psychological personality tests, are illegally discriminatory. For example, Rent-A-Center paid $2.1 million to settle a class action lawsuit that alleged that required psychological tests, the MMPI and the Bernreiter Personality Inventory, violated the Americans with Disabilities Act.[21] In another case, a general knowledge test used by shipping firms and longshore unions was found to discriminate against minority applicants who applied for dock shipping jobs because the failure rates for Hispanic, Asian, and African American applicants was significantly higher.[22] In summary, the role of testing in the selection process must be kept in perspective because tests represent only one possible data source, and they must be used appropriately and legally.

Selection Interviewing

Selection interviewing of job applicants is done to both obtain additional information and to clarify information gathered throughout the selection process. Typically, interviews are conducted at two levels: first in the HR department as an initial interview, and then second as an in-depth interview often involving HR staff members and operating supervisors and managers in the departments where the individuals will work.

In both interviews, but particularly the in-depth interview, information from various sources is pulled together in order to identify conflicting information that may have emerged from tests, application forms, and references. As a result, the interviewer must obtain as much pertinent information about the applicant as possible during the limited interview time and evaluate this information against job standards.

An interviewer making a hiring recommendation must be able to identify the factors determining that decision. Lawyers recommend the following in order to minimize EEO concerns with interviewing:

- Identify objective criteria related to the job to be sought in the interview.
- Specify decision-making criteria used.
- Provide multiple levels of review for difficult or controversial decisions.
- Use structured interviews, with the same questions asked of all those interviewed for a specific job.

As Figure 8-9 shows, there are a number of different types of interviews. They range from the structured to unstructured and vary in terms of effectiveness. Each of the types is discussed next.

Figure 8-9 ▸ Types of Selection Interviews

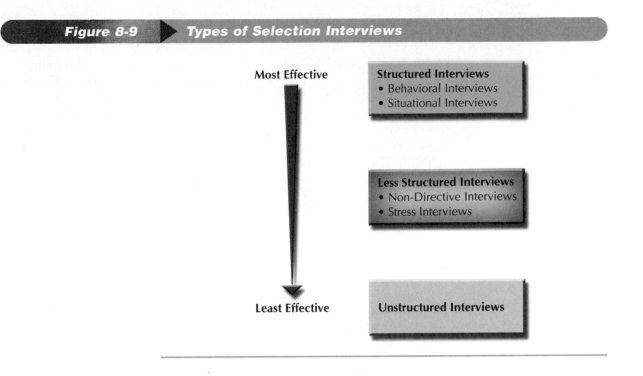

Most Effective

Structured Interviews
- Behavioral Interviews
- Situational Interviews

Less Structured Interviews
- Non-Directive Interviews
- Stress Interviews

Least Effective

Unstructured Interviews

Structured Interviews

Structured interview
Interview that uses a set of standardized questions asked of all job applicants.

A **structured interview** uses a set of standardized questions asked of all applicants. The interviewer asks every applicant the same basic questions, so that comparisons among applicants can more easily be made. This type of interview allows an interviewer to prepare job-related questions in advance and then complete a standardized interviewee evaluation form that provides documentation indicating why one applicant was selected over another. Sample questions that might be asked of all applicants for a retail sales clerk opening are as follows:

- I noticed on your application that you were previously employed with _____. How did you get a job there?
- Tell me about your responsibilities and duties with _____.
- Describe a time you were frustrated as a customer because of the way a store clerk treated you. What do you think should have been done?
- How many hours can you work a week without your school work and/or personal life being negatively affected?

The structured interview is especially useful in the initial screening because of the large number of applicants in this step of the selection process. Even for more in-depth interviews, the structured interview does not have to be rigid. The predetermined questions should be asked in a logical manner, but interviewers can avoid reading the questions word for word down the list. Also, the applicants should be allowed adequate opportunity to explain their answers, and each interviewer should probe until he or she fully understands applicants' responses.

Research on interviews consistently finds the structured interview to be more reliable and valid than other approaches.[23] This format for the interview ensures that a given interviewer has similar information on each candidate. Also, when several interviewers ask the same questions of applicants, there is greater consistency in the subsequent evaluation of candidates by different interviewers.

Behavioral Interview More and more interviewers are using an experienced-based type of structured interview. In the **behavioral interview** applicants are asked to give specific examples of how they have performed a certain task or handled a problem in the past. The notion that past behaviors are good predictors of future actions provides the logic behind behavioral interviews. Learning about how candidates describe their previous behaviors helps determine which applicants may be best suited for current jobs.[24] For example, applicants might be asked the following questions:

- How did you handle a situation that had no rules or guidelines for employee discipline?
- Why did you choose that approach?
- How did your supervisor react?
- How was the situation finally resolved?

The results of behavioral interviews can be scored like any other type of structured interview using predetermined dimensions and then compared to interviewer judgments. Also, behavioral interviews generally provide better validity than general structured interviews or less structured methods.[25]

Situational Interview The **situational interview** is a type of structured interview that is composed of questions about how applicants might handle specific job situations. Interview questions are based on job analysis and checked by experts in the job so they will be content valid. For some situational interviews, job experts also rate responses to the questions to facilitate ranking candidates. The interviewer can code the suitability of the answer, assign point values, and add up the total number of points an interviewee received. Some organizations also use creative interviewing tactics along with situational interviewing questions, as the HR Perspectives indicates.

Less Structured Interviews

Unfortunately, too many interviews occur unplanned and without any structure. Often, these interviews are conducted by operating managers or supervisors who have had little training on interviewing do's and don'ts. The unstructured interview occurs when the interviewer "wings it," asking such questions as "Tell me about yourself," that have no direct purpose identified.

Nondirective Interview The **nondirective interview** uses questions that are developed from the answers to previous questions. The interviewer asks general questions designed to prompt the applicant to discuss herself or himself. The interviewer then picks up on an idea in the applicant's response to shape the next question. For example, if the applicant says, "One aspect that I enjoyed in my last job was my supervisor," the interviewer might ask, "What type of supervisor do you most enjoy working with?"

As with any less structured interview, difficulties with a nondirective interview include keeping it job related and obtaining comparable data on various applicants. Many nondirective interviews are only semiorganized; the result is that a combination of general and specific questions is asked in no set order, and

---

Behavioral interview
Interview in which applicants give specific examples of how they have performed a certain task or handled a problem in the past.

Situational interview A structured interview composed of questions about how applicants might handle specific job situations.

Nondirective interview
Interview that uses questions that are developed from the answers to previous questions.

Creative Interviewing Tactics

Interviewers handling selection activities at some employers are using logic questions, brain teasers, and other problems to determine applicants' problem-solving skills and creative-thinking abilities. Examples of such questions by Microsoft, Zefer Internet, and other technology companies include:

- How many gallons of white paint are sold in the U.S. every year?
- If you were a car, what kind and color would you be?

- Using a box of Lego blocks, build whatever you want in five minutes and then we will discuss it.
- If you have two pitchers of colored water and you have to put them together in a single pitcher and then separate them, how would you do it?

Although these questions may seem cute or intriguing by interviewers and applicants, the reality is that their purpose and nature must be linked to job characteristics. For example, the house paint

question is used to determine how a candidate logically solves problems and what information would be needed to give an estimate. (The correct answer is 100 million gallons.) Such a question might be especially relevant for a marketing research job or one requiring research and analytical skills. From a legal standpoint, employers should document the purpose and nature of such exercises or questions, how they are job-related, and what answers are acceptable and unacceptable.[26]

---

different questions are asked of different applicants for the same job. Comparing and ranking candidates is more open to subjective judgments and legal challenges under this format.

Stress interview Interview designed to create anxiety and put pressure on an applicant to see how the person responds.

Stress Interview The **stress interview** is a special type of interview designed to create anxiety and put pressure on the applicant to see how the person responds. In a stress interview, the interviewer assumes an extremely aggressive and insulting posture. Those who use this approach often justify its use with individuals who will encounter high degrees of stress on the job, such as a consumer-complaint clerk in a department store or an air traffic controller.

However, the stress interview is a high-risk approach for an employer. The typical applicant is already somewhat anxious in any interview, and the stress interview can easily generate a poor image of the interviewer and the employer. Consequently, an applicant that the organization wishes to hire might turn down the job offer. Even so, many interviewers deliberately put applicants under stress.

Who Does Interviews?

Interviews can be done individually, by several individuals in sequence, or by panels or teams of interviewers. For some jobs, such as entry-level, lesser skilled jobs, applicants are interviewed by an HR representative alone. Other jobs are filled using multiple interviews, beginning with an HR interviewer, followed by interviews conducted by appropriate supervisors and managers. Then a selection decision is made based on discussions by those who have conducted the interviews. When an interviewee must see several people, often many of the interviews are redundant and therefore unnecessarily time consuming.

Panel interview Interview in which several interviewers interview the candidate at the same time.

In a **panel interview**, several interviewers interview the candidate at the same time. All the interviewers hear the same responses. For example, to select a new marketing manager in a distribution firm, three vice presidents interviewed the top two candidates after the Vice President of Sales had conducted individual interviews to identify the two finalists. On the negative side, without planning by the panel of interviewers, an unstructured interview can result. Also, applicants are frequently uncomfortable with the group interview format.

The prevalence of work teams, as described in Chapter 6, has increased the use of **team interviews,** in which applicants are interviewed by the "team members" with whom they will work. To be successful, team members may be involved in selecting their co-workers. However, a good deal of training is required to make sure that teams understand the selection process, interviewing, and legal constraints. Further, a selection procedure in which the team votes for the top choice may be inappropriate; usually the decision should be made by consensus, which may take longer.

Team interview Interview in which applicants are interviewed by the team members with whom they will work.

Video Interviewing A number of employers use video interviewing to augment or replace in-depth telephone interviews.[27] Applicants are asked to go to video conferencing facilities scheduled by the employer. At the designated time, the applicant and those conducting the interview are video linked. The greatest use of video interviewing is done by large corporations, executive recruiting firms, and colleges and university placement offices, who offer such facilities to aid both students and employers.[28]

Savings on time and travel costs are an advantage of video interviewing. Often, the video interviews are used to narrow a pool of candidates down to two or three finalists who then are interviewed in person. Video technology using the Internet and digital cameras presents additional interviewing options to employers as well.

Effective Interviewing

WEST GROUP
A THOMSON COMPANY

Interviewing
Suggests effective employment interviewing tips.
Custom Search:
☑ ANALYSIS
Phrase: Interviewing tips

Many people think that the ability to interview is an innate talent, but this contention is difficult to support. Just because someone is personable and likes to talk is no guarantee that the person will be a good interviewer. Interviewing skills are developed through training. There have been a number of suggestions developed to make interviewing more effective. Several key ones commonly cited are as follows:

- *Planning the interview* is important. Interviewers should review pre-employment screening information, the application or resume, and the appropriate job description before beginning the interview and then identify specific areas for questioning during the interview.
- *Controlling the interview* includes knowing in advance what information must be collected, systematically collecting it, and stopping when that information has been collected. But, effective interviewers should talk no more than about 25% of the time in an in-depth interview.
- The *questioning techniques* an interviewer uses can and do significantly affect the type and quality of the information obtained.[29] Describe, who, what, when, why, tell me, how, and which are all good ways to begin questions that will produce longer and more informative answers. Figure 8-10 lists questions often used in selection interviews.

Figure 8-10 ▶ **Common Selection Interview Questions**

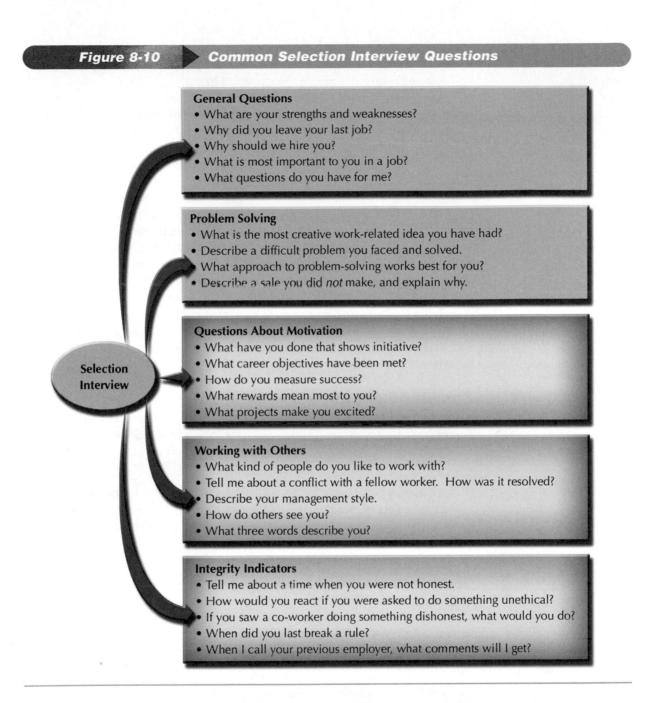

General Questions
- What are your strengths and weaknesses?
- Why did you leave your last job?
- Why should we hire you?
- What is most important to you in a job?
- What questions do you have for me?

Problem Solving
- What is the most creative work-related idea you have had?
- Describe a difficult problem you faced and solved.
- What approach to problem-solving works best for you?
- Describe a sale you did *not* make, and explain why.

Questions About Motivation
- What have you done that shows initiative?
- What career objectives have been met?
- How do you measure success?
- What rewards mean most to you?
- What projects make you excited?

Working with Others
- What kind of people do you like to work with?
- Tell me about a conflict with a fellow worker. How was it resolved?
- Describe your management style.
- How do others see you?
- What three words describe you?

Integrity Indicators
- Tell me about a time when you were not honest.
- How would you react if you were asked to do something unethical?
- If you saw a co-worker doing something dishonest, what would you do?
- When did you last break a rule?
- When I call your previous employer, what comments will I get?

Selection
Interview

Certain kinds of questions should be avoided in selection interviews:

- *Yes/No questions:* Unless verifying specific information, it is best to avoid questions that can be answered "Yes" or "No." For example, "Did you have good attendance on your last job?" The answer will probably be "yes."
- *Obvious questions:* An obvious question is one for which the interviewer already has the answer and the applicant knows it.
- *Questions that rarely produce a true answer:* An example is, "How did you get along with your co-workers?" The likely answer is, "Just fine."

- *Leading questions:* A leading question is one to which the answer is obvious from the way that the question is asked. For example, "How do you like working with other people?" Answer: "I like it."
- *Illegal questions:* Questions that involve information such as race, age, gender, national origin, marital status, and number of children are illegal. They are just as inappropriate in the interview as on the application form.
- *Questions that are not job related:* All questions asked should be directly related to the job for which the interviewee has applied.

Avoid Listening Responses Effective interviewers avoid listening responses, such as nodding, pausing, making casual remarks, echoing, and mirroring. A friendly but neutral demeanor is appropriate. Listening responses are an essential part of everyday, normal conversation, but they may unintentionally provide feedback to the applicant. Applicants may try to please interviewers and look to the interviewers' listening responses for cues. Even though the listening responses may be subtle, they do provide information to applicants.

However, by giving no response to applicants' answers, interviewers may present the appearance of boredom or inattention. Therefore, interviewers should make a neutral comment, acknowledge the response, or use a reply, such as "That is interesting and useful information."

Problems in the Interview

Operating managers and supervisors most often use poor interviewing techniques because they do not interview often or lack training. Some common problems encountered in the interview are highlighted next.

Snap Judgments Unfortunately, many interviewers make a decision on the job suitability of applicants within the first two to four minutes of the interview and spend the balance of the interview looking for evidence to support it. This impression may be based on a review of an individual's application blank or on more subjective factors such as dress or appearance. Ideally, the interviewer should collect all the information possible on an applicant before making a judgment.

Negative Emphasis As might be expected, unfavorable information about an applicant is the biggest factor considered in interviewers' decisions about overall suitability. Unfavorable information is given roughly twice the weight of favorable information. Often, a single negative characteristic may bar an individual from being accepted, whereas no amount of positive characteristics will guarantee a candidate's acceptance.

Halo Effect Interviewers should try to avoid the halo effect, which occurs when an interviewer allows a prominent characteristic to overshadow other evidence. The *halo effect* is present if an interviewer lets a candidate's accomplishments in athletics overshadow other characteristics, which leads the interviewer to hire the applicant because "athletes make good salespeople." *Devil's horns* (a reverse halo effect), such as inappropriate dress or a low grade point average, may affect an interviewer as well.

Biases and Stereotyping Personal biases and stereotyping of applicants should be avoided in interviews. The "similarity" bias occurs because interviewers tend to favor or select people they perceive to be similar to themselves.

Job Interview Tales

Some amusing, unbelievable, and even inappropriate actions by both interviewers and applicants occur during job interviews.[30] The following examples of poor interviewing behaviors and responses *are not* recommended for future use!

Interviewers: Surveys and reports of college students found that some interviewers act in strange or inappropriate ways:

- Interviewers asked the following questions:
  - "How many girlfriends do you have?"
  - "What method of birth control do you use?"
  - "Would you like to see my appendectomy scar?"
  - "What do your mother and father do for a living?"
  - "What will your boyfriend think of you working long hours?"

- Interviewer talked on the phone while applicant answered questions.
- Interviewer asked applicant to guess his nationality.
- Interviewer watched CNN on television over applicant's shoulder during the interview.

Interviewees: Some applicants obviously are not acquainted with acceptable interview behavior and responses

- Applicant showed up in torn camouflage pants, T-shirt, and hiking boots for secretarial job interview.
- The graduate came to the interview wearing sunglasses and eating a hamburger and fries.
- Applicant put his head down on the interviewer's desk and complained of studying all night.
- Female applicant for office job wore bare midriff shirt, expos-

ing multiple tattoos on her stomach.
- Applicant vomited in interviewer's trash can because he said he had been drinking for several hours before the interview.
- Interviewees made the following statements:
  - "Do I have to come to work before 9:00 A.M., because I work nights as a stripper?"
  - "My previous supervisor didn't like me—just like at my last three other companies."
  - "I haven't job hopped [four jobs in past year] because I was fired from all of them."
  - "I don't need to answer questions about my job history. Just read my resume."

This similarity can be in age, race, sex, previous work experiences, personal background, or other factors. Also, as workforce demographics shift, interviewers should avoid stereotyping individuals because of demographic characteristics and differences.

Cultural Noise The interviewer must learn to recognize and handle cultural noise, which comes from responses the applicant believes are socially acceptable rather than factual. An interviewer can handle cultural noise by not encouraging it. If the interviewer supports cultural noise, the applicant will take the cue and continue those kinds of answers. Instead, the applicant can be made aware that the interviewer is not being taken in and interviewer control over the interview re-established. As the HR Perspective illustrates, interview problems exist with both interviewers and applicants.

Reliability and Validity of Interviews

Virtually all employers use interviews as part of the employment process. Therefore, interviews must be reliable, exhibiting a consistency in the ability of interviewers to pick the same capabilities again and again in applicants. Some interviewers may be better than others at selecting individuals who will perform well. A high *intra*rater reliability (the same interviewer) can be demonstrated, but only moderate-to-low *inter*rater reliability (different interviewers), is generally shown. Interrater reliability liability becomes important when each of several interviewers is each selecting employees from a pool of applicants, or if the employer uses team or panel interviews with multiple interviewers.

The interview is popular with employers because it has high "face validity," because it seems valid to employers and they like it. In the case of interviews the assumption often made is that if someone interviews well and the information obtained in the interview is useful, then the individual will perform well on the job.

However, research over several decades consistently confirms that the interview is not an especially valid predictor of job performance and success, particularly when using unstructured interviews. An especially problematic issue occurs when interviewers make judgments about applicants' personality characteristics based on interviewing questions.[31] But use of structured interviews can increase validity of selection interviewing.

Background Investigation

Background investigation may take place either before or after the in-depth interview. It costs the organization some time and money, but it generally proves beneficial when making selection decisions. Background references can be obtained from several sources. Some information tends to be useful and relevant, depending on the jobs for which applicants are being considered. Figure 8-11 shows the most commonly used reference checking sources.

Personal references, such as those from relatives, clergy, or friends, often are of little value, and should not even be used. No applicant asks somebody who would give a negative response to write a recommendation. Instead, greater reliance should be placed on work-related references from previous employers and supervisors.

Figure 8-11 ▶ **Background Investigation Sources**

Source: Based on Pinkerton, *Top Security Threats and Management Issues Facing Corporate America Year 2001 Survey of Fortune 1000 Companies.* Used with permission.

Falsification of Background Information

The value of background investigation efforts is evident when applicants who misrepresent their qualifications and backgrounds are revealed. According to various employers, estimates are that about one-third of all applications and resumes contain "factual misstatements" or "significant omissions." The most common false information given is length of prior employment, past salary, criminal record, and former job title.

Additionally, many universities report that inquiries on graduates and former students often reveal that the individuals never graduated. Some did not even attend the university. Another type of credential fraud uses the mail-order "degree mill." To enhance their chances of employment, individuals purchase unaccredited degrees from organizations that grant them for a fee—as one advertisement puts it, "with no exams, no studying, no classes."

The only way for employers to protect themselves from resume fraud and false credentials is to request verification from applicants either before or after hire. If hired, the employee can be terminated for falsifying employment information. It is unwise for employers to assume that "someone else has already checked." Too often, that assumption has been proved wrong.

Reference Checking Methods

Several methods of obtaining reference information are available to an employer, with telephoning a reference the most commonly used method. To conduct a telephone reference check many experts recommend using a form. Typically, such forms focus on factual verification of information given by the applicant, such as employment dates, salary history, type of job responsibilities, and attendance record. Other questions often include reasons for leaving the previous job, the individual's manner of working with supervisors and other employees, and other less factual information. Naturally, many firms will provide only factual information. But the use of the form can provide evidence that a diligent effort was made.

Written methods of reference checking are also used whereby some organizations send preprinted reference forms to individuals giving references for applicants. These forms often contain a release statement signed by the applicant, so that those providing the reference can see that they have been released from liability on the information they furnish. Specific or general letters of reference also are requested by some employers or provided by applicants.

Outsourcing of reference checking is growing. Employers contract with a third-party vendor to conduct reference checks and access specialized databases. Often these outside firms have special expertise and staff trained in conducting investigations. Also, using these firms can offer some limited legal protection to employers.[32] As the e-HR discussion on the next page indicates, a growing number of employers use Internet sources to conduct background investigations.

Legal Constraints on Background Investigations

Various federal and state laws protect the rights of individuals whose backgrounds may be investigated during pre-employment screening. An employer's most important action when conducting background investigations is to obtain signed releases by applicants giving the employers permission to conduct background investigations.

Web-Based Background Checks

Some employers use outside firms to conduct background investigations. One survey of several hundred employers found that about two-thirds use outside investigative vendors. The growth of the Internet makes it even easier to contract with outside sources. Vendors provide their services to employers who have applicants complete a form. This form can either be faxed or e-mailed to the vendor. Most frequently faxing is used because

it provides a bit more security when sent to secure, dedicated fax machines. The vendor taps databases containing criminal, credit, and other data on individuals. The vendor then e-mails back the investigative report to a designated HR staff member at the employer. Financial institutions, governmental entities, public schools, retailers, and many other employers are using these services.

Some banks, child-care agencies, school systems, and other employers are using electronic fingerprint investigation services. Prior to a final offer, fingerprints of candidates are screened through the Federal Bureau of Investigation's database. Newer technology allows for electronic fingerprint images to be obtained and transmitted instead of using the messy, ink-based method.[33]

States vary in what they allow employers to investigate. In some states, employers can request information from law enforcement agencies on any applicant. One study found that all local government employers conducted criminal background checks on applicants for public safety jobs, and 50% of them conducted criminal background checks on all prospective employees.[34]

WEST GROUP
A THOMSON COMPANY

Fair Credit Reporting Act
Discusses provisions of the act and the use of consumer reports in employment decisions.
Custom Search:
☑ ANALYSIS
Phrase: Using consumer reports

Fair Credit Reporting Act Many employers check applicants' credit histories. The logic is that individuals' with poor credit histories may signal irresponsibility. This assumption may be questioned, however, and firms that check applicants' credit records must comply with the federal Fair Credit Reporting Act. This act basically requires disclosing that a credit check is being made, obtaining written consent from the person being checked, and furnishing the applicant a copy of the report. Some state laws also prohibit employers from getting certain credit information.

Credit history checking should be done on applicants for jobs in which use, access, or management of money is an essential job function. Commonly, financial institutions check credit histories on loan officers or tellers, and retailers conduct credit checks on cashiers and managerial staff.

Giving References on Former Employees In a number of court cases, individuals sued their former employers for slander, libel, or defamation of character as a result of what the employers said to other potential employers that prevented the individuals from obtaining jobs. Because of such problems, lawyers advise organizations who are asked about former employees to give out only name, employment date, and title; many organizations have adopted policies restricting the release of reference information.

Under the Federal Privacy Act of 1974, a governmental employer must have a signed release from a person before it can give information about that person to someone else. The recommendation is that all employers obtain a signed release from individuals during exit interviews authorizing the employer to provide reference information in the future.

Clearly, employers are in a difficult position. Because of threats of lawsuits, they must obtain information on potential employees but are unwilling to give out information in return. To address these concerns, 35 states have laws that protect employers from civil liability when giving reference information in good faith that is objective and factual in nature.[35]

Risks of Negligent Hiring The costs of failing to check references may be high. Some organizations have become targets of lawsuits that charge them with negligence in hiring workers who have committed violent acts on the job. Lawyers say that an employer's liability hinges on how well it investigates an applicant's background. Prior convictions and frequent moves or gaps in employment should be cues for further inquiry. Details provided on the application form by the applicant should be investigated to the greatest extent possible, so the employer can show that due diligence was exercised.[36] Also, employers should document their efforts to check background information by noting who was contacted, when, and what information was or was not provided. This documentation can aid in countering negligent hiring claims.

Medical Examinations and Inquiries

Medical information on applicants may be used to determine the individual's physical and mental capability for performing jobs. Physical standards for jobs should be realistic, justifiable, and geared to the job requirements. Workers with disabilities can perform satisfactorily in many jobs. However, in many places, they are rejected because of their disabilities, rather than being screened and placed in appropriate jobs.

ADA and Medical Inquiries The Americans with Disabilities Act (ADA) prohibits the use of pre-employment medical exams, except for drug tests, until a job has been conditionally offered. Also, the ADA prohibits a company from rejecting an individual because of a disability and from asking job applicants any question relative to current or past medical history until a conditional job offer is made.[37] Assuming a conditional offer of employment is made, then some organizations ask applicants to complete a pre-employment health checklist or are given a physical examination paid for by the employer.

Drug Testing Drug testing may be a part of a medical exam, or it may be done separately. Using drug testing as a part of the selection process has increased in the past few years, although some employers facing tight labor markets have discontinued drug testing. If used, employers should remember that the accuracy of drug tests varies according to the type of test used, the item tested, and the quality of the laboratory where the test samples are sent. Because of the potential impact of prescription drugs on test results, applicants should complete a detailed questionnaire on this matter before the testing. If an individual tests positive for drug use, then a second, more detailed analysis should be administered by an independent medical laboratory. Whether urine, blood, saliva, or hair samples are used, the process of obtaining, labeling, and transferring the samples to the testing lab should be outlined clearly and definite policies and procedures established.

Genetic Testing Another controversial area of medical testing is genetic testing. Employers that use genetic screening tests do so for several reasons. First, the tests may link workplace health hazards and individuals with certain genetic characteristics. Second, genetic testing may be used to make workers aware of genetic problems that could occur in certain work situations. The third use is the most controversial: to exclude individuals from certain jobs if they have genetic conditions that increase their health risks. Because people cannot change their genetic makeup, the potential for illegal discrimination based, for example, on race or sex is real. As mentioned in Chapter 4, the Equal Employment Opportunity Commission (EEOC) proposed guidelines and a number of states have passed laws prohibiting genetic discrimination or limiting genetic testing.[38]

Making the Job Offer

The final step of the selection process is making a job offer. Often extended over the phone, many job offers are formalized in letters and sent to applicants. It is important that the offer document be reviewed by legal counsel and that the terms and conditions of employment be clearly identified. Care should be taken to avoid vague, general statements and promises about bonuses, work schedules, or other matters that might change later. These documents also should provide for the individuals to sign an acceptance of the offer and return it to the employer, who should place it in the individual's personnel files.

Relocation Assistance

Employers may provide relocation assistance for selected individuals who live away from the new job site. Such relocation assistance often includes sales of existing homes, moving expenses, house-hunting trip costs, automobile transportation, and new home mortgage assistance. Regardless of the type of relocation assistance, the nature and extent of relocation assistance sets a tone for the way new employees view their new jobs. Such assistance also aids in the adjustment of the employees' family members. Relocation assistance enables new employees to become more productive more quickly in their new locations.[39]

Summary

- Selection is a process that matches individuals and their qualifications to jobs in an organization.
- Placement of people increasingly considers both person-job fit and person-organization fit.
- Predictors linked to criteria are used to identify job applicants more likely than others to perform jobs successfully.
- The selection process—from applicant interest through pre-employment screening, application, testing interviewing, and background investigations—must be handled by trained, knowledgeable individuals.
- A growing number of employers use electronic pre-employment screening.
- Application forms must meet EEO guidelines and ask only for job-related information.

- Selection tests include ability, assessment centers, personality, honesty/integrity, and other more controversial types.
- Structured interviews, including behavioral and situational ones, are more effective and face fewer EEO compliance concerns than nondirective and unstructured interviews.
- Interviews can be conducted individually, by multiple individuals, and by video technology. Regardless of the method, effective interviewing questioning techniques should be used.
- Background investigations can be conducted in a variety of areas. However, care must be taken when either requesting or giving reference information to avoid potential legal concerns such as negligent hiring, libel, and slander.

- Medical examinations may be an appropriate part of the selection process for some employers, but only after a conditional job offer has been made.

- Drug testing has grown in use as a pre-employment screening device in spite of some problems and concerns associated with it.

Review and Discussion Questions

1. Respond to the following statement: "Even though it is easier to determine person-job fit, effective selection and placement must integrate person-organization fit considerations."
2. You are the manager of a new customer-service center to employ 300 people. What phases would you use to select your new employees?
3. Develop a structured interview for hiring assistant managers for a large retail supermarket chain.
4. Some employers use personality tests more frequently for selecting employees. What are the pro's and con's associated with these types of tests?
5. Why have background investigations, including medical exams and drug tests, become so prevalent in many employer selection processes?

Terms to Know

selection   234
placement   235
person-job fit   235
person-organization fit   236
selection criteria   237
realistic job preview (RJP)   242
cognitive ability tests   247
physical ability tests   248
psychomotor tests   248

work sample tests   248
structured interview   253
behavioral interview   254
situational interview   254
nondirective interview   254
stress interview   255
panel interview   255
team interview   256

Using the Internet

Preparing for a Behavioral Interview

The accounting department has traditionally hired accountants, but because of recent increases in department turnover, the Accounting Manager is concerned that the right candidates are not being hired. As the Human Resources Specialist, you have been asked to assist with developing a behavioral interview guide for the accountant position. Three main skills have been identified on which the candidate shall be selected: *leadership skills, interpersonal skills,* and *communication skills.* These capabilities are in addition to several technical skills and qualifications required of an accountant. Using the following Web site for assistance, write several behavioral interview questions for the Accounting Manager to use in the upcoming interviews: *http://www.job-interview.net/Interviewgen.htm*. Look under *Interviews by Job.*

Improving Selection in Smaller Companies

The cost of making bad decisions when selecting new employees is leading employers of all sizes to review their selection processes. Some smaller companies have taken specific steps to improve their selection practices.

Jellyvision, a firm that develops computer games, requires applicants to go through an "audition" process. The purpose of the audition is to ensure that applicants understand the culture of the firm and what is required to succeed. Applicants for jobs using writing skills sometimes complete 50-page written exercises. Prior to being hired, even the HR Director had to complete a take-home HR test that required 15 hours, in order to make sure she could handle the work demands and expectations of senior managers at Jellyvision.

At City Garage, a Texas-based auto service chain with 200 employees, selection traditionally was handled by individual store managers who administered a paper-and-pencil test and conducted one interview. But high turnover rates made it clear that a new selection process was needed. Therefore, the firm changed to a process using an application, followed by a background check. Then individuals still seen as viable candidates take a ten-minute on-line test that focuses on personality characteristics such as dominance, influence, steadiness, and compliance. Answers on the test are analyzed and then interviews are conducted that focus on work capabilities and personality issues such as conflict, lack of patience, and others. Finally, those applicants still considered for employment several days later go through an all-day series of interviews with several levels of managers. Even though this extensive process may appear costly and time-consuming, the firm reports lower turnover and fewer problems with new employees as a result.[40]

Questions

1. Discuss the advantages of the selection efforts used in these two firms.
2. What would be some drawbacks in using these processes, especially in larger firms?

Notes

1. Adapted from Linda Micco, "Electronic Applications Yield Better Hiring Decisions," *Bulletin to Management,* June 29, 2000, 207; and Cora Daniels, "To Hire a Lumber Expert, Click Here," *Fortune,* April 3, 2000, 267–269.
2. Adapted from Amy L. Kristof-Brown, "Perceived Applicant Fit: Distinguishing Between Recruiters' Perceptions of Person-Job and Person-Organization Fit," *Personnel Psychology,* 53 (2000), 643–672.
3. Stephanie Armour, "Job Seekers Get Put Through the Wringer," *The USA Today,* August 17, 2001, 1B+.
4. For more details, see Herbert G. Heneman III, Timothy A. Judge, and Robert L. Heneman, *Staffing Organizations* (Middleton WI: Mendota House, Irwin McGraw-Hill, 2000), 553–558.
5. "Employee Virtue Rules," *The Wall Street Journal,* February 1, 2000, A1.
6. *Mainline Contracting Corp.,* 333 NLRB, 120, August 2, 2001.
7. "Revising the Definition of Applicant," *HR News,* January 2002, 2; and *Federal Register,* November 13, 2000, 68023–68024.
8. Jean M Philips, "Effects of Realistic Job Previews on Multiple Organizational Outcomes," *Academy of Management Journal* 41 (1998), 673–690; and Peter W. Horn, et al., "An Exploratory Investigation into Theoretical Mechanisms Underlying Realistic Job Previews," *Personnel Psychology* 51 (1998), 421.
9. Jim Meade, "Where Did They Go?" *HR Magazine,* September 2000, 81–84.
10. "Shorter Job Applications Streamline Hiring Process," *Bulletin to Management,* June 22, 2000, 198.
11. John F. Bonfatti, "Calling for Help," *Human Resource Executive,* April 2001, 54–56.
12. Lynda S. Zengerle and Irene M. Ricio, "Admit One," *HR Magazine,* August 2000, 149–158.
13. J. Craig Wallace, Mary G. Tye, and Stephen J. Vodanovich, "Applying for Jobs Online: Examining the Legality of Internet-Based Forms," *Public Personnel Management,* 29 (2000), 497–504.

14. Nancy Hatch Woodward, "The Function of Forms," *HR Magazine,* January 2000, 67–73.

15. Herschel N. Chart, et al., "Measuring Service Orientation with Biodata, *Journal of Managerial Issues* 12 (2000), 109–120; and Michael K. Mount, L. A. Witt, and Murray R. Barrick, "Incremental Validity of Empirically Keyed Biodata Scales over GMA and the Five Factor Personality Constructs," *Personnel Psychology,* 53 (2000), 299–323.

16. J. E. Harvey-Cook, "Biodata in Professional-Entry Selection," *Journal of Occupational & Organizational Psychology,* 73 (2000), 103–119.

17. Linda A. Jones, "Most Companies Employ Pre-Employment Testing Methods," *Human Resource Executive,* January 2001, 37.

18. Craig S. Philson, "Functional Capacity Testing," *Occupational Health and Safety,* January 2000, 78–84.

19. James E. Wanek, "Integrity and Honesty Testing," *International Journal of Selection and Assessment,* 7 (1999), 183–195.

20. George M. Alliger and Stephen A. Dwight, "A Meta-Analytical Investigation of the Susceptibility of Integrity Tests to Faking and Coaching," *Educational & Psychological Measurement,* 60 (2000), 59–73.

21. "Rent-A-Center to Pay $2.1 Million," *Bulletin to Management,* July 20, 2000, 89.

22. *Equal Employment Opportunity Commission v. Pacific Maritime Commission,* CD-CA, CV 00-01516 DT JWJ, February 22, 2000.

23. Timothy A. Judge, "The Employment Interview: A Review of Recent Research and Recommendations for Future Research," *Human Resource Management,* 10 (2000), 383–407.

24. "Interview Questions That Hit the Mark," *Harvard Management Update,* March 2001, 9.

25. Yoau Ganzach, et al., "Making Decisions from an Interview: Expert Measurement and Mechanical Combination," *Personnel Psychology,* 53 (2000), 1–20; and Allen Huffcutt, *et al,* "Comparison of Situational and Behavior Description Interview Questions for Higher-Level Positions" *Personnel Psychology* 54 (2001), 619–644.

26. Based on Martha Frase-Blunt, "Games Interviewers Play," *HR Magazine,* January 2001, 106–114; and Diane E. Lewis, "Brainteasers Join Interviews in Hiring," *Omaha World-Herald,* February 2, 2000, 1G

27. David Kelly, "Can Video Conferencing Help HR Get the Picture?" *www.hr-esource.com,* July 16, 2001.

28. Mike Frost, "Video Interviewing," *HR Magazine,* August 2001, 93–98.

29. Stanley M. Slowik, "Objective Pre-Employment Interviewing: Balancing Recruitment, Selection, and Retention Goals," *Public Personnel Management,* 30 (2001), 77–94.

30. Based on "In Bad Taste," *The Wall Street Journal,* May 8, 2001, B12; and personal reports by interviewers to the authors.

31. Murray R. Barrick, Gregory Patton, and Shanna N. Haugland, "Accuracy of Interviewer Judgments of Job Applicant Personality Traits," *Personnel Psychology,* 53 (2000), 925–945.

32. Charlotte Garvey, "Outsourcing Background Checks," *HR Magazine,* March 2001, 95–104.

33. Based on Vikas Bajaj, "Technology Speeds Background Checks," *Omaha-World Herald,* April 16, 2001, IG.

34. Mary L. Connerly, et al., "Criminal Background Checks for Prospective and Current Employees: Current Practices Among Municipal Agencies," *Public Personnel Management,* 30 (2001), 173–183.

35. Carolyn Hirschman, "Laws Protect Reference Checks," *HR Magazine,* June 2000, 91.

36. Merry Mayer, "Background Checks in Focus," *HR Magazine,* January 2002, 59–62.

37. Peter J. Petesch, "Popping the Disability-Related Question," *HR Magazine,* November 2000, 161–172.

38. Steve Bates, "Science Friction," *HR Magazine,* July 2001, 35–44.

39. Thomas Philbin, "Give Your Movers a Performance Review," *HR Magazine,* January 2001, 81–84.

40. Adapted from "Slow and Steady Helps Employer Win Hiring Race," *Bulletin to Management,* February 3, 2000, 38; and Gilbert Nicholson, "Automated Assessment for Better Hires," *Workforce,* December 2000, 102–107.

Training and Developing Human Resources

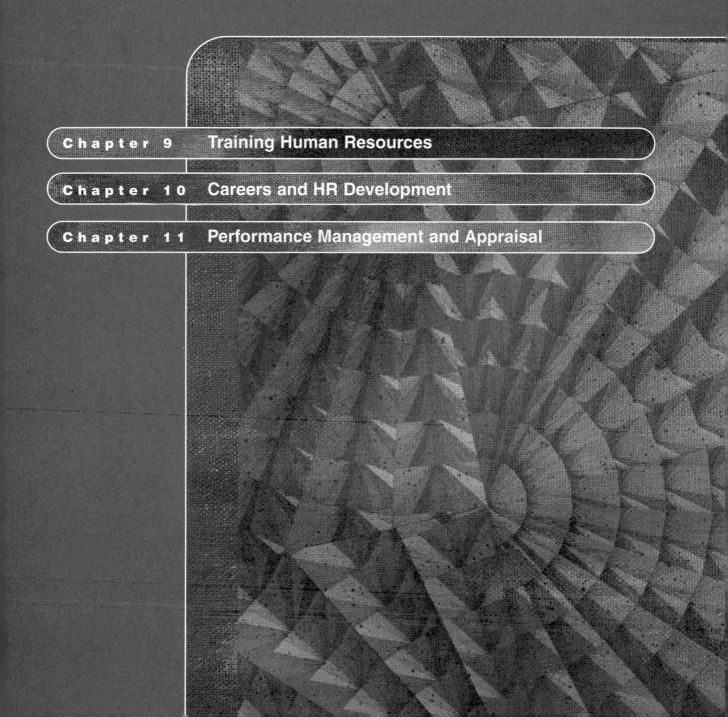

CHAPTER 9

Training Human Resources

After you have read this chapter, you should be able to:

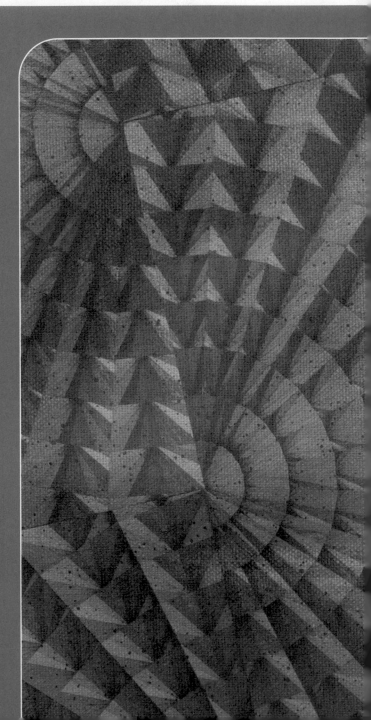

- Define training and discuss why a strategic approach is important.

- Discuss the four phases of the training process.

- Identify three types of analyses used to determine training needs.

- Describe internal, external, and e-learning as training delivery approaches.

- Give an example for each of the four levels of training evaluation.

Cisco Systems and E-Learning

To cope with competitive and technological changes, more organizations are recognizing that training through e-learning is critical to future organizational success. To find a firm that understands the importance of training and learning, look no farther than Cisco Systems and its use of e-learning. E-learning (electronic learning) is using the Internet and internal information technology systems to provide training on-line. As a staunch supporter of technology, John Chambers, CEO at Cisco, identified electronic learning as a strategic initiative for his firm.

Chambers believes that information technology is changing how employers and educational institutions teach, students and employees learn, and corporations keep their human capital current and cutting-edge. Therefore, Cisco uses Web-based training as an integral tool to make employees more productive because it is available anytime and anywhere. Also, as more firms turn to e-learning, more Cisco networking servers and routers will be needed.

The Internet Learning Solutions Group (ILSG) coordinates the Cisco e-learning push. ILSG was created to respond to Chambers' challenge to make Cisco a leader in e-learning. All of the firm's training activities, including various Web-based training efforts, had to be identified. At the same time, the ILSG pinpointed and began developing e-learning support tools, such as video servers, templates for content development, and virtual classrooms.

A primary step was to create the Field E-Learning Connection, a learning portal with 8,000 learning resources available to field sales employees. Such resources included online learning content, PowerPoint presentations, class schedules, white papers, listings of materials, books, and videos, and other items.

Several years later the Connection boasts a 95% utilization rate by the members of Cisco's global salesforce. The Connection contains "learning roadmaps" covering the jobs of everyone in the field sales organization. The roadmaps cover sales, systems, engineering, and account management jobs.

With the Field Sales Connection operational, the ILSG built a Partner-E-Learning Connection. This Partner Connection targets the 40,000-plus firms that sell Cisco's products and services in 130 countries worldwide.

The strategic commitment by Cisco to e-learning has paid off in a number of ways. First, it has focused Cisco's training efforts on getting employees and partners to needed levels of competencies more quickly by using a variety of training resources, including e-learning, formal training courses, attending industry seminars, and other more traditional means.

Second, e-learning has resulted in better pass rates by e-learners for certification tests than by classroom-trained individuals. Another major benefit that produces huge cost savings for Cisco is that the e-learners are not away at training as much. At Cisco, e-learning allows employees to do e-learning while at their desks. (Some employees put yellow police tape on their doors or cubicles when they are busy with online e-learning activities to avoid being interrupted.) Even assembly-line workers have used e-learning, resulting in savings of more than $4 million per year in improved productivity.[1]

> To cope with competitive and technological changes, more organizations are recognizing that training through e-learning is critical to future organizational success.

> *"Training is something we hope to integrate into every manager's mindset."*
>
> —Chris Landauer

The competitive pressures facing organizations today require employees whose knowledge and ideas are current, and whose skills and abilities can deliver results. As organizations compete and change, training becomes even more critical than before. Employees who must adapt to the myriad of changes facing organizations must be trained continually in order to maintain and update their capabilities. Also, managers must have training and development to enhance their leadership skills and abilities. In a number of situations, employers have documented that effective training produces productivity gains that more than offset the cost of the training.

The Nature of Training

Training A process whereby people acquire capabilities to aid in the achievement of organizational goals.

Training is a process whereby people acquire capabilities to aid in the achievement of organizational goals. Because this process is tied to a variety of organizational purposes, training can be viewed either narrowly or broadly. In a limited sense, training provides employees with specific, identifiable knowledge and skills for use in their present jobs. Sometimes a distinction is drawn between *training* and *development,* with development being broader in scope and focusing on individuals gaining new capabilities useful for both present and future jobs. Development is discussed in the next chapter, while training is the focus of this chapter.

The Context of Training

Contemporary training in organizations has evolved significantly over the past decade. The changes have been reflected in a number of ways that are discussed next.[2]

Organizational Competitiveness and Training More employers are recognizing that training their human resources is vital. Currently, U.S. employers spend at least $60 billion annually on training. For many employers, training expenditures average at least 1½ to 2% of payroll expenses, and run $677 per eligible employee according to a study by the American Society of Training & Development (ASTD). However, organizations that see training as especially crucial to business competitiveness average $1,665 in training expenditures per eligible employee.[3]

General Electric, Sun Microsystems, Motorola, Marriott, Cisco, FedEx, and Texas Instruments all emphasize the importance of training employees and managers. These companies and others recognize that training and HR development efforts are integral to competitive business success. For example, consider the telecommunications industry today compared to five years ago, with all of the new technologies, wireless services, and competitive shifts. Without continual training, organizations may not have staff members with the KSAs needed to compete effectively.

Training also assists organizational competitiveness by aiding in the retention of employees. As emphasized in Chapter 3, a primary reason why many

Logging On...

American Society for Training and Development
This Web site on training and development contains information on articles, research, education seminars, and conferences.

http://www.astd.org/

individuals stay or leave organizations is career training and development opportunities. Employers that invest in training and developing their employees do so as part of retention efforts.

Something else is changing as well. An old axiom in HR management traditionally has been, "When times get tough, training is the first expenditure cut." But a growing number of employers have recognized that training is not just a cost; it is an investment in the human capital of the organization that benefits the entire organization in the longer term. Although training expenditures may decline some as organizational cost-cutting occurs, in more progressive organizations seldom are all training efforts eliminated. In some firms training for selected groups, such as sales representatives, actually may be increased in tough times in order to help generate more sales revenues.

Training as a Revenue Source Some organizations have identified that training can be a source of business revenues. For instance, Motorola, Microsoft, Ceridian, Cisco, and other technology firms bundle training as part of sales packages of products and services for customers. Manufacturers of industrial equipment also offer customer training on machine upgrades and new features. Customers of many of these firms pay for training either by course, participant, or as part of equipment or software purchases. Not only are the costs of the trainers' salaries, travel, and other expenses covered, the suppliers make a profit on the training through the fees paid by customers.

As a side benefit of such training, customer satisfaction and loyalty increase if customers know how to use the products and services purchased.[4] Thus, this training aids with customer retention and enhances future sales revenues.

Integration of Job Performance, Training, and Learning Job performance, training, and employee learning must be integrated to be effective. First, because training interventions progressively move "closer to the job" in order to achieve "real-time" learning, the linkage between training and job performance is vital. Consider the following organizational example. U.S. Air Force flight-line personnel must undergo regular safety training. However, the days of sending them to a conference room where they watch a one-hour video tape on safety are gone. Instead, such training is conducted out on the flight line with the actual equipment (i.e., a real context, with real tools and equipment, and real people), without moving personnel to an artificial learning environment. Trainees can watch the trainer put on the necessary gear in the proper manner, attempt to replicate the actions themselves, and receive real-time feedback in an actual work setting.

Second, organizations are seeking more authentic (and hence more effective) training experiences for their trainees, using real business problems to advance employee learning. Rather than separating the training experience from actual job performance context, trainers who incorporate everyday business issues as learning examples increase the realism of training exercises and scenarios. General Electric has used this method for years. As part of GE's management training, managers are given actual business problems to solve, and they must present their solutions to organizational business leaders. It is yet another way that the lines between training, learning, and job performance merge.

Logging On...

International Society for Performance Improvement
This professional organization focuses on improving productivity and performance in the workplace.

http://www.ispi.org

Training and Performance Consulting

Training must be linked to enhancing organizational performance. This occurs most effectively when a performance consulting approach is used. **Performance consulting** is a process in which a trainer (either internal or external to the organization) and the organizational client work together to boost workplace performance in support of business goals.

As Figure 9-1 depicts, performance consulting compares desired and actual organizational results with desired and actual employee performance. Once these comparisons are made, then performance consulting takes a multifaceted approach to performance issues.[5] It does so by:

- Focusing on identifying and addressing *root causes* of performance problems.
- Recognizing that the *interaction of individual and organizational factors* influences employee performance.
- Documenting the *actions and accomplishments* of high performers and comparing them with actions of more typical performers.[6]

Regardless of whether the trainer is internal to the firm or an outside training consultant, a performance consulting approach sees that training cannot automatically solve every employee performance problem. Instead, training must be viewed as one piece of a larger "bundled solution." For instance, some employee performance issues might be resolved by creating a training program for employees, while other situations might call for compensation or job design changes.

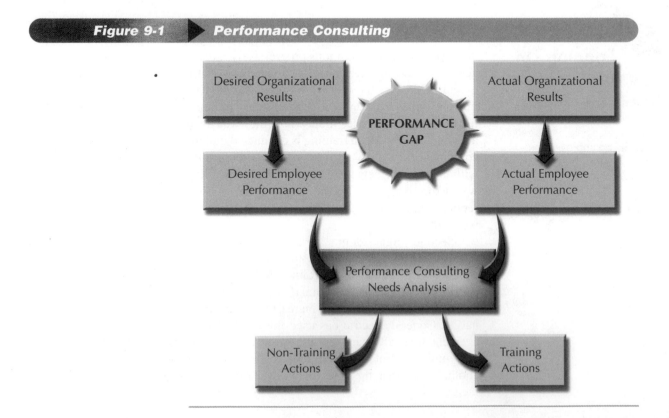

Figure 9-1 Performance Consulting

The following scenario illustrates the performance consulting approach. Assume you are the HR training specialist in a large pharmaceutical firm, and the marketing manager for the Midwestern sales region contacts you about creating a training program for sales representatives. Over the last six months, the manager has noticed that new account sales are down and asks you to develop a new customized training program on assertive communications and selling skills for the sales representatives.

Instead of just developing a training program, use of performance consulting means gathering more information in order to identify: (1) the root causes of the recent new account sales slump in the Midwest region, (2) the various individual salesperson and organizational factors contributing to this slump, and (3) the primary reasons for the gap between high-performance salespeople and lower-performance salespeople in this specific region. Obtaining all of this information helps in determining whether *any training* (much less assertive communications skills training) will play a role in the integrative performance improvement solution. Perhaps recent changes in the sales incentive compensation plan has resulted in emphasis on existing accounts or maybe changes in sales territory assignments have caused problems. Whatever the causes, a tailored and comprehensive performance consulting approach is needed to get to the root of the sales decline.

Integrating Training Responsibilities

One of the most important implications resulting from the performance consulting approach is that HR staff members and trainers work as partners with operating managers to integrate training that bolsters both individual employee and organizational performance. A typical division of training responsibilities is shown in Figure 9-2. The HR unit serves as a source of expert training assistance and coordination. The unit often operates with a more long-range view of employee training and development for the entire organization than do individual operating managers. The difference is especially true at lower levels in the organization.

Managers are likely to be the best source of technical information used in skills training. They also are in a better position to decide when employees need training or retraining. Their close and continual interaction with employees puts

| Figure 9-2 | **Typical Division of HR Responsibilities: Training** |

HR Unit	Managers
• *Prepares skill-training materials*	• *Provide technical information*
• *Coordinates training efforts*	• *Monitor training needs*
• *Conducts or arranges for off-the-job training*	• *Conduct and monitor continuing on-the-job training*
• *Coordinates career plans and employee development efforts*	• *Continually discuss employees' growth and future potential*
• *Provides input and expertise for organizational development*	• *Participate in organizational change efforts*

managers in the most appropriate place to determine and discuss employee career possibilities and plans with individual employees. Therefore, a "training partnership" between the HR staff members and operating managers is important.

Chief Learning Officers

To emphasize the importance of training, a number of organizations have created positions entitled *Chief Learning Officer* (CLO) or *Chief Knowledge Officer* (CKO). However, note that the CLO role is not just an inflated new title for a Training Director.[7] Instead, the CLO functions as a strategic leader who links learning and knowledge through training for individual employees and the organization to strategic business capabilities needed throughout the organization. According to the president of Motorola University, CLOs must demonstrate a high comfort level in working with boards of directors and the top management team, a track record of success in running some type of business unit, and an understanding of adult learning technologies and processes.[8] If these exist, then CLOs are more likely to take part in developing a strategic training plan for their organizations.

Strategic Training

Training adds value to an organization by linking training strategy to organizational objectives, goals, and business strategies. *Strategic training* focuses on efforts that develop competencies, value, and competitive advantages for the organization. This basically means that training and learning interventions must be based on organizational strategic plans and HR planning efforts. Strategic training also implies that HR and training professionals need to be involved in organizational change and strategic planning in order to develop training plans and activities that support top management's strategic decisions. Thus, effective training helps the firm create competitive advantage.

As illustrated in Figure 9-3, training is strategic when it: (1) develops essential worker capabilities, (2) encourages adaptability to change, (3) promotes ongoing learning in the organization, (4) creates and disseminates new knowledge throughout the organization, and (5) facilitates communication and focus.[9] Consider an example of a group of managers attending a training session where the firm's hottest new products are being discussed, and the managers develop some creative ways to reach target audiences who would benefit from these new products.

Figure 9-3 ▶ **Linking Business and Training Strategies**

Strategic Training
- Develops employee capabilities
- Encourages change
- Promotes continuous learning
- Creates/shares new knowledge
- Facilitates communication

Business Strategies

Training Strategies and Activities

Source: Based on ideas from Lisa A. Burke and Joseph V. Wilson III.

Linking Training to Business Strategies

To understand how to link training and business strategies, it is useful to understand some basic business strategy concepts. A *low-cost leader business strategy* attempts to increase market share by focusing on the low cost of the firm's products or services, compared to competitors (e.g., Wal-Mart, Bic pens, Southwest Airlines). In contrast, firms with a *differentiation business strategy* try to make their products or services different from others in the industry in terms of quality, exceptional service, new technology, or perceived distinctiveness (e.g., Maytag products, Mercedes autos, Rolex watches).

The primary implications of organizational business strategies for the firm's training efforts emphasize the need for training programs and activities to support the firm's business strategy.[10] For instance, if a company is trying to distinguish itself from its competition based on customer service quality, then significant customer service training is needed to support the firm's strategic thrust. However, if another firm differentiates itself from competitors with products or services that customers perceive as distinctive and unique, then training resources should be shifted to keeping employees abreast of the latest advertising and marketing ideas. For instance, an exclusive jewelry store selling Rolex watches and expensive jewelry must ensure that its employees are trained on all of the models, features, and operations of such items. Also, training in dress, appearance, communications, and special customer relations skills also support the firm's business strategies. These scenarios are just two brief examples of how training must parallel business strategies.

Developing a Strategic Training Plan

The framework for developing a strategic training plan contains four major stages. Each is highlighted next.

1. *Strategize:* HR and training managers must first work with management to determine how training will link strategically to the strategic business plan, with an eye toward employee and organizational performance improvement.
2. *Plan:* Planning must occur in order to deliver training that will provide positive results for the organization and its employees. As part of planning, the objectives and expectations of training should be identified and specific, measurable learning objectives created in order to track the effectiveness of the training.
3. *Organize:* Then, the training must be organized by deciding how training will occur, obtaining the resources needed, and developing the training interventions. All these activities culminate in the actual training.
4. *Justify:* Finally, measuring and evaluating the extent to which training meets the objectives set will legitimize training efforts. Past mistakes in training can be explicitly identified in this phase. Learning from these mistakes provides an effective way to improve future training.

The benefits of strategic training are numerous. First, it enables HR and training professionals to get intimately involved with the business, partner with operating managers to help solve their problems, and make significant contributions to organizational results. Strategic training also may prevent HR professionals and trainers from chasing fads or the hottest or latest type of training gimmick. Additionally, a strategic training mindset also reduces the

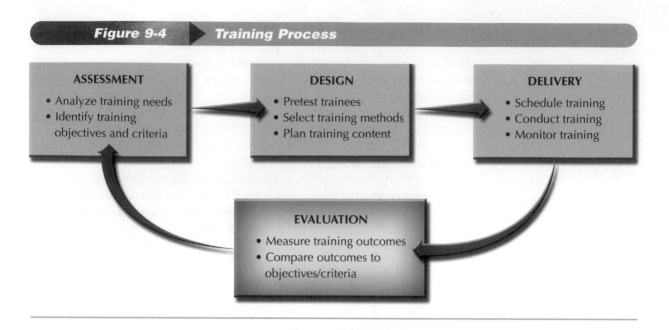

Figure 9-4 ▶ **Training Process**

ASSESSMENT
- Analyze training needs
- Identify training objectives and criteria

DESIGN
- Pretest trainees
- Select training methods
- Plan training content

DELIVERY
- Schedule training
- Conduct training
- Monitor training

EVALUATION
- Measure training outcomes
- Compare outcomes to objectives/criteria

likelihood of thinking that training can solve most employee or organizational problems. As in the earlier situation where the marketing manager was convinced his employees needed assertive communications skills training, it is not uncommon for operating managers, HR professionals, and trainers to react to problems by saying, "I need a training program on X." With a strategic training focus, the response is more likely to be an assessment of such requests to determine what training and/or non-training approaches might address the performance issues.

The value of strategic training can be seen in the example of Walt Disney World. It has established specific strategic training plans. Implementing these training plans results in a distinct and noted competitive advantage for Disney. For example, at the Disney Institute, employees (called Cast Members) gain critical experience from the perspective of their Guests. As a part of training for individuals taking hotel reservations, those employees stay at a resort as guests to gain greater understanding of what they are selling and experience the services themselves.[11]

The Training Process

Effective implementation of strategic training requires use of a systematic training process. Figure 9-4 depicts the four phases of the training process: assessment, design, delivery, and evaluation. Using such a process reduces the likelihood that unplanned, uncoordinated, and haphazard training efforts will occur. A discussion of each phase of the training process follows next.

Training Needs Assessment

Training is designed to help the organization accomplish its objectives. Therefore, assessing organizational training needs represents the diagnostic phase of setting training objectives. This assessment considers employee and organizational performance issues to determine if training can help. Using the perfor-

Figure 9-5	Sources of Training Needs Assessment

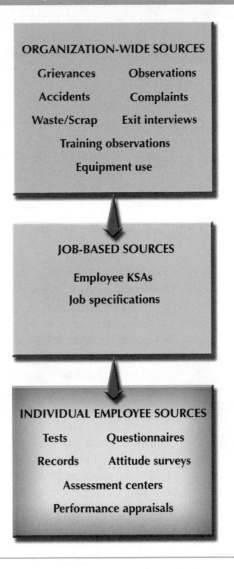

mance consulting approach mentioned earlier, it is important that non-training factors be considered also, such as compensation, organization structure, job design, and physical work settings. When training needs are identified, the assessment efforts then specify the objectives to be accomplished.[12] For instance, looking at the performance of clerks in a billing department, a manager identifies problems with their data-entry and keyboard abilities and believes that they would benefit from instruction in these areas. As part of assessment, the clerks take a keyboard data-entry test to measure their current skills. Then the manager might establish an objective of increasing the clerks' keyboard entry speed to 60 words per minute without errors. The number of words per minute without errors is the criterion against which training success can be measured, and it represents the way in which the objective is made specific. Figure 9-5 shows the three sources of training needs assessment analyses.

Organizational Analyses

Training needs can be diagnosed through organizational analyses. An important part of organizational strategic HR planning is the identification of the knowledge, skills, and abilities (KSAs) that will be needed in the future as both jobs and the organization change. Both internal and external forces will influence training and must be considered when doing organizational analyses. For instance, the problems posed by the technical obsolescence of current employees and an insufficiently educated labor pool from which to draw new workers should be confronted before those training needs become critical.

One important source for organizational analyses comes from various operational measures of organizational performance. On a continuing basis, detailed analyses of HR data reveal training weaknesses. Departments or areas with high turnover, high absenteeism, low performance, or other deficiencies can be pinpointed. Following an analysis of such problems, training objectives can be developed.

Job/Task Analyses

The second way to diagnose training needs is through analyses of the jobs and tasks performed in those jobs. By comparing the requirements of jobs with the knowledge, skills, and abilities of employees, training needs can be identified. As an example, at a manufacturing firm analyses identified the tasks to be performed by engineers who served as technical instructors for other employees. By listing the tasks required of a technical instructor, management established a program to teach specific instruction skills; thus the engineers were able to become more successful instructors.

Individual Analyses

The third means of diagnosing training needs focuses on individuals and how they perform their jobs. The use of performance appraisal data in making these individual analyses is the most common approach. In some instances, a good HR information system can be used to identify individuals who require training in specific areas. To assess training needs through the performance appraisal process, an employee's performance inadequacies first must be determined in a formal review. Then some type of training can be designed to help the employee overcome the weaknesses.

Another way of assessing individual training needs is to survey both managerial and nonmanagerial employees about what training is needed. Such a survey also can be useful in building support for training from those who will be trained because they had input on identifying their training needs.[13] A training needs survey can take the form of questionnaires or interviews with supervisors and employees on an individual or group basis. The purpose is to gather information on problems perceived by the individuals involved. In addition to performance appraisals and training surveys, the following sources are useful for individual analyses:

- Questionnaires
- Job knowledge tools
- Skill tests

- Attitude surveys
- Records of critical incidents
- Individual assessment tests

WEST GROUP
A THOMSON COMPANY

Training Needs
Provides checklist of areas for identifying training needs.
Custom Search:
☑ CHECKLIST
Phrase: Training needs checklist

Establishing Training Objectives and Priorities

Once training needs have been identified using appropriate analyses, then training objectives and priorities must be established by identifying a *gap analysis,* which indicates the distance between where an organization is with its employee capabilities and where it needs to be. Training objectives and priorities are set to close the gap. Three types of training objectives can be set:

- *Knowledge:* Impart cognitive information and details to trainees.
- *Skill:* Develop behavior changes in how jobs and task requirements are performed.
- *Attitude:* Create interest in and awareness of the importance of training.

The success of training should be measured in terms of the objectives set. Useful objectives are measurable. For example, an objective for a new sales clerk might be to "demonstrate the ability to explain the function of each product in the department within two weeks." This objective serves as a check on internalization, or whether the person really learned and is able to use the training.

Because training seldom is an unlimited budget item and because organizations have multiple training needs, prioritization is necessary. Ideally, management ranks training needs based on organizational objectives. Conducting the training most needed to improve the performance of the organization will produce visible results more quickly.

Training Design

Once training objectives have been determined, training design can be done. Whether job-specific or broader in nature, training must be designed to address the assessed needs. Effective training design considers learning concepts, legal issues, and different approaches to training.

Learning: The Focus of Training

Working in organizations should be a continual learning process, and learning is the focus of all training activities. Different approaches are possible, but learning is a complex psychological process that is not fully understood by practitioners or research psychologists. As depicted in Figure 9-6 on the next page, there are three primary considerations when designing training: (1) determining learner readiness, (2) understanding different learning styles, and (3) designing training for transfer. Each of these elements must be considered in order for the training design to mesh together.[14]

Learner Readiness

For training to be successful, learners must be ready to learn. This readiness means they must have the basic skills necessary for learning, the motivation to learn, and possess self-efficacy.

Ability to Learn Learners must possess basic skills, such as fundamental reading and math proficiency, and sufficient cognitive abilities. Companies may discover that some workers lack the requisite skills to comprehend their training effectively. For example, the firearms manufacturer Smith and Wesson initiated

Figure 9-6 ▶ **Elements of Training Design**

a five-year intensive remedial skills training effort after finding that some of their production operators lacked basic reading and math skills. But this is not just one company's problem. Data from surveys of various firms show about 38% of job applicants lack the necessary reading, writing, and math skills to do the jobs they seek.[15] Employers attempting to deal with the lack of basic employee skills can approach the problem in several ways:

1. Offer remedial training to people in their current workforce who need it.
2. Hire workers they know are deficient and then implement specific workplace training.
3. Work with schools to help better educate people for jobs.

Motivation to Learn A person's desire to learn training content is referred to as motivation to learn and is influenced by multiple factors. For example, the extent to which a student taking a college course is motivated to learn the course content is influenced by several variables. That student might desire to learn the content because of personal career interests and values, degree plan requirements and area of study, the positive value the student has on getting an A in the course, or simply due to personal expectations of doing well in school. However, the student's motivation level also may be influenced by the instructor's motivation and ability, friends' encouragements to do well, classmates' motivation levels, the physical classroom environment, and the training methods used.

Self-efficacy A person's belief that he/she can successfully learn the training program content.

Self-Efficacy Learners must also possess **self-efficacy,** which refers to a person's belief that he/she can successfully learn the training program content. For learners to be ready and receptive to the training content, they must feel like they can learn it. As an example, some college students' levels of self-efficacy diminish in advanced quantitative or statistics courses when they do not feel ade-

Research on Age Differences and Technology Training

Technology is now a part of many jobs. Many current workers are having to learn and use new technology, including computer hardware and software. But how individuals of different ages learn and use technology varies.

To investigate age differences in the adoption and use of technology, Morris and Venkatesh studied individuals learning a new software system. In this study, published in *Personnel Psychology*, shifting to the new software system was voluntary; individual workers could continue to use the old system or convert to the new system. After a year, management would decide whether or not to require conversion to the new software system.

More than 100 customer account representatives in a financial accounting firm participated in a two-day training session on the new software. Methods used included lectures, hands-on use, and interactive usage assisted by trainers. Sessions contained about 25 participants each. In the week following the training, the firm's IT support staff was available to answer trainees' questions and solve problems.

The researchers gathered demographic data on the trainees, including their ages. The results indicated clear age differences in the adoption and use of the new software in the workplace. Younger workers (under 40) initially had more positive attitudes toward the new software. However, older workers (over 40) were more likely to seek support and opinions of friends and co-workers to form their attitudes toward the new system. Also, the ease or difficulty of using the new technology was a much greater concern to the older workers. These differences in attitudes carried over to the usage rates of the new software in the short-term.

The researchers concluded that training of older adults in technology may require greater attention to explaining the need for changes and building older trainees' confidence in their abilities to learn new technology. However, younger adults' willingness to try new technology likely has evolved out of their earlier exposure to computers and technology. Consequently, a variety of training designs and delivery considerations must be assessed when developing training for adults of varying ages.[16]

---

quately able to grasp the material. These perceptions may have nothing to do with their actual ability to learn, but rather reflect the way they see themselves and their abilities. Instructors and trainers must help in these instances to appropriately boost trainee confidence. For instance, people with a low level of belief that they can accomplish something may benefit from one-on-one training. The HR Perspective discusses research on how age differences affect workers being introduced to new software.

Learning Styles

In designing training interventions, trainers also should consider individual learning styles. For example, *auditory* learners are ones who learn best by listening to someone else tell them about the training content. Others are *tactile* learners who must "get their hands on" and use the training resources. Still others are *visual* learners who think in pictures and figures and need to see the purpose and process of the training. Trainers who address all of these styles by using multiple training methods can design more effective interventions.

Training many different people from diverse backgrounds poses a significant challenge in today's work organizations. In addition to cultural, gender, and race/ethnicity diversity considerations, research reveals that adult learning presents some special issues. For instance, assume a firm is training a group of

Logging On...

Learnativity.com
This Web site on adult learning contains articles and other readings on adult learning, training, and evaluation, as well as frequently asked questions about training resources.

http://www.learnativity.com

Adult Learning
Describes eight keys for effective adult learning.
Custom Search:
☑ ANALYSIS
Phrase: Keys to adult learning

thirty customer service representatives, ten of whom are under age 25 who are highly computer and Internet literate, and the remainder of the individuals are older and are not as computer proficient. Certainly, the training design must consider that all the trainees are adults, but they come with widely varying learning styles, experiences, and anxieties.[17]

Adult Learning The classic work of Malcolm Knowles on adult learning suggests five principles for designing training for adults. This and subsequent work by others suggest that adults:[18]

1. Have the need to know why they are learning something.
2. Have a need to be self-directed.
3. Bring more work-related experiences into the learning process.
4. Enter into a learning experience with a problem-centered approach to learning.
5. Are motivated to learn by both extrinsic and intrinsic factors.

Adult learners in work organizations present different issues for training design based on Knowles's principles. For instance, trainers cannot expect to do a "brain dump" of material without giving trainees the context or bigger picture of why participants need the training information. This concept is referred to as *whole learning* or *Gestalt learning.* As applied to job training, this means that instructions should be divided into small elements *after* employees have had the opportunity to see how all the elements fit together.

Adult learners should be encouraged to bring work-related problems to training as a way to make the material more relevant to them. Effective training should involve participants in learning by actively engaging them in the learning and problem-solving process. **Active practice** occurs when trainees perform job-related tasks and duties during training. It is more effective than simply reading or passively listening. Assume a person is being trained as a customer service representative. After being given some basic selling instructions and product details, the trainee calls a customer and uses the knowledge received. Active practice can be structured in two ways. The first, **spaced practice,** occurs when several practice sessions are spaced over a period of hours or days. The other, **massed practice,** occurs when a person performs all of the practice at once. Spaced practice works better for some kinds of learning, whereas for other kinds of tasks, such as memorizing tasks, massed practice is usually more effective. Imagine the difficulty in trying to memorize the list of model options for a dishwasher one model per day for 20 days as an appliance distribution salesperson? By the time the last option was learned, the person likely would have forgotten the first one.

Active practice The performance of job-related tasks and duties by trainees during training.

Spaced practice Several practice sessions spaced over a period of hours or days.

Massed practice The performance of all of the practice at once.

Behavior modeling
Copying someone else's behavior.

Behavior Modeling The most elementary way in which people learn—and one of the best—is **behavior modeling,** or copying someone else's behavior. The use of behavior modeling is particularly appropriate for skill training in which the trainees must use both knowledge and practice. For example, a new supervisor receives mentoring and training on how to handle disciplinary discussions with employees by observing as the HR director or department manager deals with such problems. Behavior modeling is used extensively as the primary means for training supervisors and managers in interpersonal skills. It can aid in the transfer and usage of those skills by the trained supervisors.[19] Fortunately or unfortunately, many supervisors and managers end up modeling the behavior they see their bosses use. For that reason, effective training should include good examples of how to handle interpersonal and other issues and problems.

Reinforcement People tend to repeat responses that give them some type of positive reward and avoid actions associated with negative consequences.

Immediate confirmation The concept that people learn best if reinforcement and feedback is given after training.

Reinforcement and Immediate Confirmation The concept of **reinforcement** is based on the *law of effect,* which states that people tend to repeat responses that give them some type of positive reward and avoid actions associated with negative consequences. Closely related is another learning concept called **immediate confirmation**: people learn best if reinforcement and feedback is given as soon as possible after training. Immediate confirmation corrects errors that, if made throughout the training, might establish an undesirable pattern that would need to be unlearned. It also aids with the transfer of training to the actual work done.

Transfer of Training

Finally, trainers should design training interventions for the highest possible transfer of training. This transfer occurs when trainees actually use on the job what they learned in training. Estimates of transfer in corporate training are fairly dismal. Organizations with 100 or more employees collectively spend about $60 billion on training each year, but of that total amount, only about $6 billion, or 10%, is thought to result in effective training transfer.[20]

Effective transfer of training meets two conditions. First, the trainees can take the material learned in training and apply it to the job context in which they work. Second, employees maintain their use of the learned material over time.

A number of methods can increase the transfer of training.[21] Offering trainees an overview of the training content and process prior to the actual training seems to help with both short-term and longer-term training transfer.[22] One specific way to aid transfer of training to job situations is to ensure that the training mirrors the job context as much as possible. For example, training managers to be better interviewers should include role playing with "applicants" who respond in the same way that real applicants would.

Types of Training

Training can be designed to meet a number of different objectives and can be classified in various ways. Some common groupings include the following:

- *Required and regular training:* Complies with various mandated legal requirements (e.g., Occupational Safety, EEO) and serves as training for all employees (new employee orientation)
- *Job/technical training:* Enables employees to perform their jobs, tasks, and responsibilities well (e.g., product knowledge, technical processes and procedures, customer relations)
- *Interpersonal and problem-solving training:* Addresses both operational and interpersonal problems and seeks improve organizational working relationships (e.g., interpersonal communication, managerial/supervisory skills, conflict resolution)
- *Developmental and innovative training:* Provides a long-term focus to enhance individual and organizational capabilities for the future (e.g., business practices, executive development, organizational change)

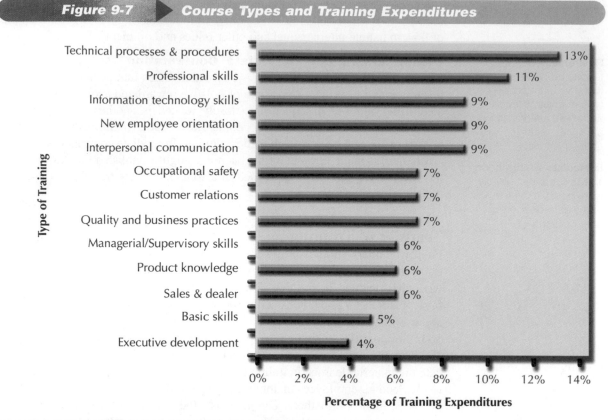

Figure 9-7 ▶ *Course Types and Training Expenditures*

Type of Training

- Technical processes & procedures — 13%
- Professional skills — 11%
- Information technology skills — 9%
- New employee orientation — 9%
- Interpersonal communication — 9%
- Occupational safety — 7%
- Customer relations — 7%
- Quality and business practices — 7%
- Managerial/Supervisory skills — 6%
- Product knowledge — 6%
- Sales & dealer — 6%
- Basic skills — 5%
- Executive development — 4%

0% 2% 4% 6% 8% 10% 12% 14%

Percentage of Training Expenditures

Source: Mark E. Van Buren, ASTD State of the Industry Report, 2001 (Alexandria, VA: ASTD, 2001), 13. Used with permission.

Figure 9-7 shows some of the different types of training identified during a recent survey by ASTD. The amount of each type of training varies by organization, depending upon its strategic plans, resources, and identified needs.

Orientation: Training for New Employees The most important and widely conducted type of regular training is done for new employees. **Orientation** is the planned introduction of new employees to their jobs, co-workers, and the organization, and is offered by most employers. It requires cooperation between individuals in the HR unit and other managers and supervisors. In a small organization without an HR department, the new employee's supervisor or manager usually assumes most of the responsibility for orientation. In large organizations, managers and supervisors, as well as the HR department, generally work as a team to orient new employees.

Effective orientation achieves several key purposes:

- Establishes a favorable employee impression of the organization and the job
- Provides organization and job information
- Enhances interpersonal acceptance by co-workers
- Accelerates socialization and integration of the new employee into the organization
- Ensures employee performance and productivity begin more quickly

Orientation The planned introduction of new employees to their jobs, co-workers, and the organization.

HR Practices

Effective New Employee Orientation

Effective new employee orientation requires planning and preparation. Unfortunately, orientation often is conducted rather haphazardly. In order to make orientation more effective, the following suggestions may be useful:

- *Prepare for new employees:* New employees must feel that they belong and are important to the organization. Both the supervisor and the HR unit should be prepared to give each new employee this perception. Further, co-workers should be prepared for a new employee's arrival. The manager or supervisor should discuss the purpose of hiring the new worker with all current employees before the arrival of the new worker.

- *Consider "buddy" mentors:* Some organizations use co-workers or peers to serve as buddies or mentors as part of the new employees' orientation. It is particularly useful to involve more experienced and higher-performing individuals who can serve as role models for new employees.

- *Use an orientation checklist:* An orientation checklist can be used by HR department representatives, the new employee's supervisor, or both to cover what the new employee needs to know now. Many employers have new employees sign the checklist to verify that they have been told of pertinent rules and procedures.

- *Cover needed information:* It is important to give employees information on the policies, work rules, and benefits of the company. Policies about sick leave, tardiness, absenteeism, vacations, benefits, hospitalization, parking, and safety rules must be made known to every new employee. Also, the employee's supervisor or manager should describe the routine of a normal workday for the employee the first morning.

- *Present orientation information effectively:* Managers and HR representatives should determine the most appropriate ways to present orientation information. Employees will retain more of the orientation information if it is presented in a manner that encourages them to learn. In addition to the videotapes, movies, slides, and charts, self-paced orientation available electronically can be used.

- *Avoid information overload:* One common failing of many orientation programs is information overload. New workers presented with too many facts may ignore important details or inaccurately recall much of the information.

- *Evaluate and follow-up:* An HR representative or manager can evaluate the effectiveness of the orientation by conducting follow-up interviews with new employees a few weeks or months after the orientation. Employee questionnaires also can be used. Unfortunately, it appears that most employers do limited or no evaluation of the effectiveness of orientation.

Effective orientation efforts also contribute to both short-term and longer success. The HR Practice contains some suggestions on how to make employee orientation more effective. Some research studies and employer surveys report that the socialization of new employees and their initial commitment to the organization are positively affected by orientation.[23] This socialization enhances the "person-organization fit," which also reinforces the positive views of the jobs, co-workers, and the organization.[24] Another value of orientation is that employers have found that higher employee retention rates result when new employees receive effective orientation. This form of training also contributes to overall organizational performance when employees more quickly feel a part of the organization and can begin contributing to organizational work efforts.

One way to expand the efficiency of orientation is through use of electronic orientation. A number of employers place general employee orientation information on company intranets or corporate Web sites. New employees can log on and go through much of the general material on organizational history, structure, products and services, mission statements, and other background information instead of sitting in a classroom where the information is delivered in person or by videotape. Then more specific questions and concerns can be addressed by HR staff and others after employees review the Web-based information. Unfortunately, many new employee orientation sessions come across as boring, irrelevant, and a waste of time by both new employees and their department supervisors and managers.

Legal Issues and Training A number of legal issues must be considered when designing and delivering training. A primary concern centers on the criteria and practices used to select individuals for inclusion in training programs, making sure those criteria are job related and do not unfairly restrict the participation of protected-class members. Failure to accommodate the participation of individuals with disabilities in training also exposes organizations to EEO lawsuits.

Another contemporary issue is the use of *training contracts* whereby employers require employees participating in expensive training to sign such contracts in order to protect the costs and time invested in specialized employee training. For instance, a telecommunications firm paid $77,000 to train four network technicians and certify them in specialized equipment. The firm required that the technicians sign training contracts whereby one-fourth of the cost would be forgiven each year the employee stayed with the organization following the training. A technician who left sooner would be liable to the firm for the unforgiven balance. Health care organizations, IT firms, and other employers also use training contracts.

Training Delivery

Once training has been designed, then the actual delivery of training can begin. It is generally recommended that the training be pilot-tested or conducted on a trial basis in order to ensure that the training meets the needs identified and that the design is appropriate. Regardless of the type of training done, a number of different training approaches and methods can be used. The growth of training technology continues to expand the available choices.

Regardless of the approaches used, a variety of considerations must be balanced when selecting training methods. The common variables considered are:

- Nature of training
- Subject matter
- Number of trainees
- Individual vs. team
- Self-paced vs. guided

- Training resources
- Costs
- Geographic locations
- Time allotted
- Completion timeline

To illustrate, a large firm with many new hires may be able to conduct employee orientation using the Internet, videotapes, and specific HR staff members. However, a small firm with few new hires may have an HR staff member meet individually for several hours with the new hires. Or, supervisory training for a medium-sized company with three locations in a geographic area may bring supervisors together for a two-day workshop once a quarter. However, a large, global firm may use Web-based courses to reach supervisors throughout the world, with content available in several languages. Frequently, training is conducted internally, but other types of training make use of external or technological training resources.

Internal Training

Training internally generally applies to specific aspects of the job. It is also popular because it saves the cost of sending employees away for training and often avoids the cost of outside trainers. Often, skills-based, technical training is conducted inside organizations. Due to rapid changes in technology, the building and updating of technical skills have become crucial training needs. Basic technical skills training is also being mandated by federal regulations in areas where the Occupational Safety and Health Administration (OSHA), the Environmental Protection Agency (EPA), and other agencies have regulations.

Informal training Training that occurs through interactions and feedback among employees.

Informal Training One internal source of training that has grown is **informal training,** which occurs through interactions and feedback among employees. Much of what employees know about their jobs they learn informally from asking questions and getting advice from other employees and their supervisors, rather than from formal training programs.

On-the-Job Training (OJT) The most common type of training at all levels in an organization is *on-the-job training* (OJT). Different from informal training that often occurs spontaneously, OJT should be planned. The supervisor or manager conducting the training must be able to both teach and show the employees what to do. Based on a special guided form of training known as *job instruction training* (JIT), on-the-job training is most effective if a logical progression of stages is used, as shown in Figure 9-8.

On-the-job training is by far the most commonly used form of training because it is flexible and relevant to what employees do. However, OJT has some problems as well. Often, those doing the training may have no experience in training, no time to do it, and no desire to participate. Under such conditions, learners essentially are on their own, and training likely will not be effective. Another problem is that OJT can disrupt regular work. Unfortunately, OJT can amount to no training at all in some circumstances, especially if the trainers simply abandon the trainees to learn the job alone. Also, bad habits or incorrect information from the supervisor or manager can be transferred to the trainees. On the other hand, well-planned and well-executed OJT can be very effective.

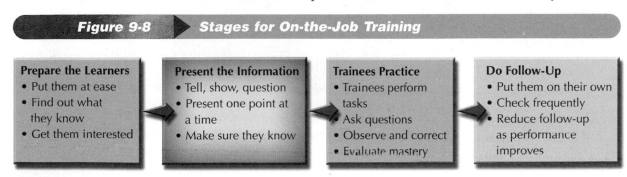

Figure 9-8   Stages for On-the-Job Training

Prepare the Learners	**Present the Information**	**Trainees Practice**	**Do Follow-Up**
• Put them at ease	• Tell, show, question	• Trainees perform tasks	• Put them on their own
• Find out what they know	• Present one point at a time	• Ask questions	• Check frequently
• Get them interested	• Make sure they know	• Observe and correct	• Reduce follow-up as performance improves
		• Evaluate mastery	

External Training

External training is used extensively by organizations of all sizes. Large organizations use external training in the absence of needed internal training capabilities or when many people need to be trained quickly. External training may be the best option for training in smaller firms due to limitations in the size of their HR staffs and in the number of employees who may need various types of specialized training. Whatever the size of the organization, external training occurs for several reasons:

- It may be less expensive for an employer to have an outside trainer conduct training in areas where internal training resources are limited.
- The organization may have insufficient time to develop internal training materials.
- The HR staff may not have the necessary level of expertise for the subject matter in which training is needed.
- There are advantages to having employees interact with managers and peers in other companies in training programs held externally.

Outsourcing of Training Many employers of all sizes outsource training to external training firms, consultants, and other entities. According to data from ASTD, approximately 20% of training expenditures go to outside training sources. Interestingly, over a recent three-year period, the outsourcing of training has declined some, especially in firms with fewer than 500 employees.[26] The reasons for the decline may be cost concerns, greater emphasis on internal linking of training to organizational strategies, or others.

A popular route for some employers is to use vendors and suppliers to train employees. Several computer software vendors offer employees technical certifications on their software. For example, being a Microsoft Certified Product Specialist gives employees credentials that show their level of technical expertise. The certifications also provide employees items to put on their resumes should they decide to change jobs. These certifications also benefit employers, who can use the certifications as job specifications for hiring and promotion purposes.

Many suppliers, including software providers, also have users' conferences where employees from a number of employers receive detailed training on using the software and new features being added. Some vendors conduct the training inside the organization as well if sufficient numbers of employees are to be trained.

Government-Supported Job Training Federal, state, and local governments provide a wide range of external training assistance. Government programs on both the state and federal levels provide training support to employers who hire new workers, particularly those who are long-term unemployed or have been receiving welfare benefits. The Workforce Investment Partnership Act (WIPA) provides states block grant programs that target adult education, disadvantaged youth, and family literacy. Employers hiring and training individuals who meet the WIPA criteria receive tax credits and other assistance for six months or more, depending upon the program regulations.

At state and local levels, employers who add to their workforces can take advantage of a number of programs that provide funding assistance to offset training costs. As examples, a number of states offer workforce training assistance for employers. Georgia's Quick Start, Texas's Smart Jobs, and Alabama's

Logging On...

Quick Start: Georgia Department of Technical and Adult Learning
The economic development Web site of the Georgia Department of Technical and Adult Learning describes training services for new or expanding businesses.

http://www.dtae.org/quickstart/qs.html

Partnership programs are three of the more well-known training support efforts. Often these programs are linked with two-year and four-year colleges throughout the states.

E-Learning: Training On-line

e-learning The use of the Internet or an organizational intranet to conduct training on-line.

E-learning is defined as the use of the Internet or an organizational intranet to conduct training on-line. Many people possess a familiarity with the Internet, which has so dramatically altered the way people do business, locate information, and communicate. An intranet is similar to the Internet, but it is a private organizational network behind "firewall" software that restricts access to authorized users, including employees participating in e-learning.

The explosive growth in the use of the Internet changes many aspects of how training is done in organizations. As more and more employees use computers and have access to Internet portals, their employers look at the World Wide Web as a means for distributing training to employees located in widely dispersed locations and jobs. For those who do not have computers a number of employers, such as Ford Motor, Olin Corporation, and Delta Airlines, had programs that provided computers free or at significant cost savings.

The growth of e-learning is seen in a number of statistics. One study forecasted that U.S. spending on e-learning is increasing 400% every three years and is expected to total about $15 billion by 2004. Adding in global employers raises this figure even higher.[27] Another indicator comes from ASTD, which found that the firms surveyed delivered about 8.4% of their training through e-learning. Even though e-learning has leveled off some in smaller companies, larger companies continue to make the most use of e-learning—almost 14% of their training is done using e-learning. This higher percentage is understandable because larger firms have more resources, and they also benefit most from the savings in distribution and travel costs due to the economies of scale provided by e-learning. For example, Delta Airlines uses on-line delivery to provide government-required training to about 70% of its workforce. Previously the courses were paper-based and took 6–8 hours. E-learning training now allows employees to complete the training in an hour, with course participation and test results being tracked online. Significant cost savings for Delta have resulted because the training takes less work time and most employees no longer have to travel to centralized training facilities.[28]

Developing E-Learning E-learning does not simply mean putting existing training courses and materials on a Web site. Rather than being adopted just for its "gee-whiz" effect, e-learning is meant to meet strategic training needs.[29] Certain criteria to consider before adopting e-learning include the following.

WEST GROUP
A THOMSON COMPANY
e-Learning
Describes factors affecting employee acceptance of and satisfaction with e-learning.
Custom Search:
☑ NEWS
Phrase: Employees and e-learning

- Sufficient top management support and funding are committed to developing and implementing e-learning.
- Managers and HR professionals must be "retrained" to accept the idea that training is being decentralized and individualized.
- Current training methods (compared to e-learning) are not adequately meeting organizational training needs.
- Potential learners are adequately computer literate and have ready access to computers and the Internet.

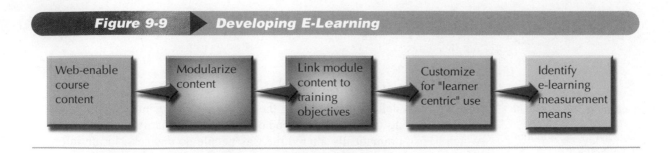

Figure 9-9 ▶ *Developing E-Learning*

Web-enable course content → Modularize content → Link module content to training objectives → Customize for "learner centric" use → Identify e-learning measurement means

- Trainees attending pre-scheduled training programs are geographically separated, and travel time and costs are concerns.
- Sufficient numbers of trainees exist and many trainees are self-motivated enough to direct their own learning.

As Figure 9-9 indicates, e-learning can be developed following several steps. First, training content must be Web enabled, meaning it is converted to electronic form. Consequently, the framework, presentation, and flow of the content must also be seen in light of electronic delivery, and rarely does it occur without glitches.[30] For instance, it is insufficient to put current PowerPoint presentations on-line and call it a training course.

Modularizing of content permits trainees to complete segments of training materials, rather than sitting for several hours at a time to complete an entire course. Once modules are developed, then the e-learning must be made "learner centric," which means that users can customize their learning. For instance, rather than taking an entire module or course, an employee wanting to learn one segment could access that information specifically.

Finally, e-learning should be measured, usage tracked, and training evaluated to see whether it meets the objectives set. To establish and implement e-learning requires considerable investment in resources and time by HR and training staff, managers, and employees, and the return on that investment should be assessed.[31] Often, employers turn to outside consultants and firms specializing in e-learning for assistance. Frequently, application service providers (ASPs) are used to facilitate and implement e-learning for individual employers.[32]

Advantages and Disadvantages of E-Learning The rapid growth of e-learning makes the Internet or an intranet a viable means for delivering training content. A study of 700 e-learners found that 62% had positive experiences with on-line learning, but only 38% indicated they preferred e-learning to classroom training.[33] These findings support the view that e-learning has both advantages and disadvantages that must be considered. In addition to concerns about employee access to and desire to use e-learning, some employers worry that trainees will use e-learning to complete courses quickly but will not retain and use much of their learning.[34]

In sum, e-learning is the latest development in the evolution of training delivery. However, some of the biggest obstacles will continue to be keeping up with the rapid change in technological innovation, knowing when and how much to invest, and dealing with employee and manager resistance to change.[35] Undoubtedly, e-learning will have a major impact on HR and training, but there

Figure 9-10 ▶ Advantages and Disadvantages of E-Learning

Advantages	Disadvantages
• Self-paced; trainees can proceed on their own time	• May cause trainee anxiety
• Is interactive, tapping multiple trainee senses	• Not all trainees may be ready for e-learning
• Allows for consistency in the delivery of training	• Not all trainees may have easy and uninterrupted access to computers
• Enables scoring of exercises/assessments and the appropriate feedback	• Not appropriate for all training content (e.g., leadership, cultural change)
• Incorporates built-in guidance and help for trainees to use when needed	• Requires significant upfront cost and investment
• Is relatively easy for trainers to update content	• No significantly greater learning evidenced in research studies
• Can be used to enhance instructor-led training	• Requires significant top management support to be successful

Source: Developed by Lisa A. Burke and Robert L. Mathis.

are not "ten easy steps" to make e-learning successful.[36] Figure 9-10 presents a balanced list of e-learning's most commonly cited advantages and disadvantages.

Training Methods

Whether delivered internally, externally, or through e-learning, appropriate training methods must be chosen. The following overview classifies common training methods into several major groups. Some methods are used more frequently for job-based training. Others are utilized more for human resource development, as discussed in the next chapter.

Cooperative Training Cooperative training methods mix classroom training and on-the-job experiences. This training takes several forms. One method, generally referred to as *school-to-work* transition, helps individuals move into jobs while still in school or upon completion of formal schooling.

A form of cooperative training called *internships* usually combines job training with classroom instruction schools, colleges, and universities. Internships offer advantages to both employers and interns. Interns get "real-world" exposure, a line on their resumes, and a chance to examine a possible employer closely. Employers who hire interns get a cost-effective source that includes a chance to see an intern at work before making a final hiring decision.

Another form of cooperative training used by employers, trade unions, and government agencies is *apprentice training*. An apprenticeship program provides an employee with on-the-job experience under the guidance of a skilled and certified worker. Certain requirements for training, equipment, time length, and proficiency levels may be monitored by a unit of the U.S. Department of Labor. Apprenticeships, train people for jobs in skilled crafts, such as carpentry, plumbing, photoengraving, typesetting, and welding. Apprenticeships usually last two to five years, depending on the occupation. During this time the apprentice usually receives lower wages than the certified individual.

Instructor-Led Classroom and Conference Training Instructor-led training is still the most prevalent method for training. Employer-conducted short courses, lectures, and meetings usually consist of classroom training, whereas numerous employee development courses offered by professional organizations, trade associations, and educational institutions are examples of conference training. A particularly important aspect of classroom training is to recognize that adults in classroom training have different expectations and learning styles than do younger students. A number of large firms have established their own "universities" to offer classroom and other training as part of curricula for employees.[37] Because these corporate universities generally offer both training and development courses, they are discussed in the next chapter.

Distance Training/Learning A growing number of college and university classes use some form of Internet-based course support. Blackboard and WebCT, two of the more popular support packages that thousands of college professors use to make their lecture content available to students, enable virtual chat and electronic file exchange among course participants. They also enhance instructor-student contact. Many large employers, as well as colleges and universities use interactive two-way television to present classes. The medium allows an instructor in one place to see and respond to a "class" in any number of other locations. With a fully configured system, employees can take courses from anywhere in the world.

Technology and Training The explosive growth in information technology in the past few years has revolutionized the way in which all individuals work, including how they are trained.[38] Today, computer-based training involves a wide array of multimedia technologies—including sound, motion (video and animation), graphics, and hypertext—to tap multiple learner senses. Video streaming allows video clips of training materials to be stored on a firm's network server. Employees then can access the material using the firm's intranet.

Computer-supported simulations within organizational training can replicate the psychological and behavioral requirements of a task, often in addition to providing some amount of physical resemblance to the trainee's work environment. From highly complicated flight-pilot simulators replicating difficult landing scenarios, to training that helps medical trainees learn to sew sutures, simulations allow for safe training when the risks associated with failure are high. Also virtual reality creates an artificial environment for trainees so they can participate in the training. For example, virtual reality is used in some military operations training and in the robotic manufacturing of electronic equipment.

Additionally, the new technologies incorporated into training delivery also affect the design, administration, and support of training. For example, companies invest in electronic registration and record-keeping systems that allow trainers to register participants, record exam results, and monitor learning progress.

Generally speaking, what is occurring is a movement from technology taking center stage in training to "technology in the background," whereby technology becomes embedded in learning and training.[39] As learning and work merge even closer in the future, technology is likely to integrate seamlessly into

Logging On...

Blackboard.com
Blackboard is a Web site that offers a complete set of software products and services for e-education development.

http://www.blackboard.com

more employees' work environment. This integration will allow employees to spend less time in the future learning how to use technology, and more time on the desired learning content.

Evaluation of Training

Evaluation of training compares the post-training results to the objectives expected by managers, trainers, and trainees. Too often, training is conducted with little thought of measuring and evaluating it later to see how well it worked. Because training is both time-consuming and costly, evaluation should be done.

Levels of Evaluation

It is best to consider how training is to be evaluated before it begins. Donald L. Kirkpatrick identified four levels at which training can be evaluated.[40] As Figure 9-11 shows, evaluating training becomes successively more difficult as evaluation moves from reaction to learning to behavior, and then to results measures. But the training that affects behavior and results instead of reaction and learning-level evaluations provides greater value.

Reaction Organizations evaluate the reaction level of trainees by conducting interviews or by administering questionnaires to the trainees. Assume that

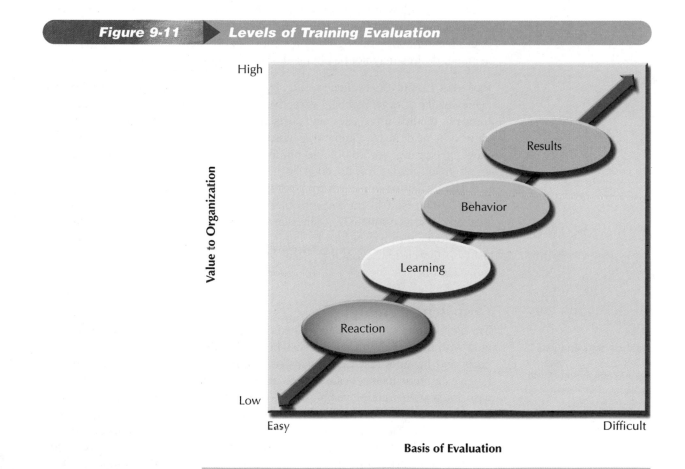

Figure 9-11 ▶ **Levels of Training Evaluation**

30 managers attend a two-day workshop on effective interviewing skills. A reaction-level measure could be gathered by having the managers complete a survey that asked them to rate the value of the training, the style of the instructors, and the usefulness of the training to them. However, immediate reactions may measure only how much the people liked the training rather than how it benefited them or it affected how they conduct interviews.

Learning Learning levels can be evaluated by measuring how well trainees have learned facts, ideas, concepts, theories, and attitudes. Tests on the training material are commonly used for evaluating learning and can be given both before and after training to compare scores. If test scores indicate learning problems, then instructors get feedback and courses are redesigned so that the content can be delivered more effectively. Of course, learning enough to pass a test does not guarantee that trainees will remember the training content months later or will change job behaviors.

Behavior Evaluating training at the behavioral level means: (1) measuring the effect of training on job performance through interviews of trainees and their co-workers, and (2) observing job performance. For instance, a behavioral evaluation of the managers who participated in the interviewing workshop might be done by observing them conducting actual interviews of applicants for jobs in their departments. If the managers asked questions as they were trained and used appropriate follow-up questions, then behavioral indicators of the interviewing training could be obtained. However, behaviors are more difficult to measure than reaction and learning. Even if behaviors do change, the results that management desires may not be obtained.

Results Employers evaluate results by measuring the effect of training on the achievement of organizational objectives. Because results such as productivity, turnover, quality, time, sales, and costs are relatively concrete, this type of evaluation can be done by comparing records before and after training. For the interviewing training, records of the number of individuals hired to the offers of employment made prior to and after the training could be gathered.

The difficulty with measuring results is pinpointing whether changes were actually the result of training or other factors of major impact. For example, managers who completed the interviewing training program can be measured on employee turnover before and after the training. But turnover is also dependent on the current economic situation, the demand for products, and many other factors.

Cost-Benefit Analyses

Cost-benefit analysis
Comparison of costs and benefits associated with training.

Training results can also be examined on the basis of costs and benefits associated with the training through a **cost-benefit analysis**. Figure 9-12 shows some costs and benefits that may result from training. Even though some benefits (such as attitude changes) are hard to quantify, comparison of costs and benefits associated with training remains a way to determine whether training is cost effective.[41] For example, one firm evaluated a traditional safety training program and found that the program did not lead to a reduction in accidents. Therefore, the training was redesigned and better safety practices resulted. However, careful measurement of both the costs and the benefits may be difficult.

Figure 9-12 ▶ Balancing Costs and Benefits of Training

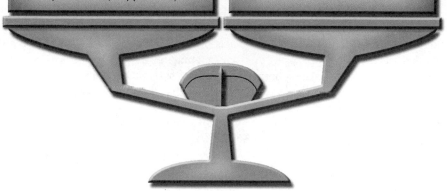

Typical Costs
- Trainer's salary and time
- Trainees' salaries and time
- Materials for training
- Expenses for trainer and trainees
- Cost of facilities and equipment
- Lost productivity (opportunity cost)

Typical Benefits
- Increase in production
- Reduction in errors and accidents
- Reduction in turnover
- Less supervision necessary
- Ability to use new capabilities
- Attitude changes

ROI of Training
Explains methods for determining the return on investment (ROI) of training expenditures.
Custom Search:
☑ ANALYSIS
Phrase: Calculate training return

Return on Investment (ROI)

In organizations training often is expected to produce a return on investment (ROI), as the HR Perspective on the next page indicates. Unfortunately, in too many circumstances, training is justified because someone liked it, rather than based on resource accountability.[42] Firms that measure ROI on training include Lens Crafters, Sears, and Apple Computers.[43]

Benchmarking Training

Rather than evaluating training internally, some organizations use benchmark measures of training that are compared from one organization to others. To do benchmarking, HR professionals in an organization gather data on training and compare them to data on training at other organizations in the industry and of their size. Comparison data are available through the American Society of Training and Development (ASTD) and its Benchmarking Service. This service has training-related data from more than 1,000 participating employers who complete detailed questionnaires annually. Training also can be benchmarked against data from the American Productivity and Quality Center and the Saratoga Institute.[44]

Evaluation Designs

Even if benchmarking data are not available, internal evaluation of training programs can be designed in a number of ways. The rigor of the three designs discussed next increases with each level.

Post-Measure The most obvious way to evaluate training effectiveness is to determine after the training whether the individuals can perform the way management wants them to perform. Assume that a customer service manager

Measuring the Value Added by Training

Many organizations make large expenditures on training, but whether those outlays produce value remains questionable. Methods for quantifying training's return on investment are illustrated by those used at Verizon, the large telecommunications firm. Toni Hodges, a manager of measurement and evaluation for Verizon's Workforce Development Division, actively measures the value added by her training division. She has spent as much as $5,000 when conducting an ROI study on training, but with Verizon's 240,000 employees, this expense would soon become unreasonable if Hodges were to complete such a study for every training intervention at Verizon. So Hodges has

conducted what she calls "ROE analyses" to help assess a training program's "return on expectations."

Before the beginning of a training program, Hodges conducts an interview with a key executive associated with the learning effort (i.e., usually a company vice president who is financially accountable for the project). Using this information and other assessment data, she and her staff establish specific learning objectives for a training program.

Once the training program has been completed, she again interviews the executive and quantifies the results of training. For example, if employees waste less time after attending a time management workshop, Hodges asks

the senior manager to assign a monetary value to that time. She then uses that data as "reasonable evidence" in an ROI calculation.

Hodges warns against conducting these interviews arbitrarily, and stresses that it takes a capable facilitator to obtain the necessary information from the senior managers. She finds it interesting that each time she conducts both return on expectations (ROE) and return on investment ROI, analyses, the results are compatible. Regardless of whether evaluation efforts use ROI, ROE, or some other methods, the important goal of measuring the value added by training is being met.[45]

has 20 representatives who need to improve their data entry speeds. After a one-day training session, they take a test to measure their speeds. If the representatives can all type the required speed after training, was the training beneficial? It is a difficult to say; perhaps most of them could have done as well before training. Test results do not always clearly indicate whether the typing speed is a result of the training or could have been achieved without training.

Pre-/Post-Measure By designing the evaluation differently, the issue of pre-test skill levels could have been considered. If the manager had measured the data entry speed before and after training, she could have known whether the training made any difference. However, a question remains. Was a change in speed a response to the training, or did these employees simply work faster because they knew they were being tested? People often perform better when they know their efforts are being evaluated.

Pre-/Post-Measure with Control Group Another evaluation design can address this problem. In addition to the 20 representatives who will be trained, a manager can test another group of representatives who will not be trained to see if they do as well as those who are to be trained. This second group is called a *control group*. After training, if the trained representatives work significantly faster than those who were not trained, the manager can be reasonably sure that the training was effective.

Other designs also can be used, but these three are the most common ones. When possible, the pre-/post-measure or pre-/post-measure with control group design should be used, because each provides a much stronger evaluation than the post-measure design alone.

Summary

- Training is a learning process whereby people acquire capabilities to aid in the achievement of organizational goals.
- The integration of learning, training, and job performance enhances organizational competitiveness.
- Performance consulting compares desired and actual results in order to identify both needed training and non-training actions.
- A strategic approach to training links organizational strategies and HR planning to training efforts.
- The training process contains four phases: assessment, design, delivery, and evaluation.
- Assessment of training needs can be done using organizational, job/task, and individual analyses in order to set training objectives.
- Training design must consider learner readiness, the learning environment, legal issues, and training transfer.
- Basic learning considerations that guide training design should include trainees' ability and motivation to learn, and adult learning styles and concepts.
- Orientation as a kind of training is designed to help new employees learn about their jobs.
- Training can be delivered internally in the organization and done formally, informally, or on the job.
- External training delivery may include use of outside sources, including government training programs.
- E-learning is training conducted using the Internet or an intranet, and its development must consider both advantages and disadvantages.
- Common training methods available include cooperative programs, classroom and conference training, and distance learning.
- Various organizations are taking advantage of training that uses technology such as multimedia, video streaming, simulation, and virtual reality.
- Evaluation of training can be done at four levels: reaction, learning, behavior, and results.
- Training evaluation may include cost-benefit analyses, return on investment, and benchmarking.
- A pre-/post-measure with control group design is the most rigorous training evaluation design, but others can be used as well.

Review and Discussion Questions

1. Discuss the following comment: "Training must be a strategic imperative in today's organization, not just a cost to be cut back when times get tough."
2. Using orientation of new employees as an example, identify the four phases of the training process.
3. Assume that you want to identify training needs for a group of sales employees in a luxury-oriented jewelry store. What would you do?
4. Develop a chart that compares the advantages and disadvantages of internal, external, and e-learning as means of training delivery.
5. What methods and measures would you use to evaluate training of bank tellers on customer service communications skills.

training   272

performance consulting   274

self-efficacy   282

active practice   284

spaced practice   284

massed practice   284

behavior modeling   284

reinforcement   285

immediate confirmation   285

orientation   286

informal training   289

e-learning   291

cost-benefit analysis   296

Using the Internet

Planning for E-Learning

As the Training Manager for your organization you are planning to launch an e-learning initiative for your corporate headquarters in the next fiscal year. To receive funding for this initiative you have been asked to put together a presentation to the President/CEO, Senior Vice Presidents, and the Board of Directors on e-learning and the needs assessment for phase one of the process. The presentation is an attempt to educate them on e-learning and should include the following:

- Key advantages of e-learning for the learners and trainers
- Concerns and problems with e-learning
- Plan for starting e-learning project to include communications about e-learning, managing e-learning projects, and managing the risks associated with e-learning.

Prepare this information as a presentation and use the following Web site to gather the information: *http://www.e-learninghub.com*

CASE

Hotels Link Training and Customer Service

Hotels, particularly upscale, luxury ones, focus on providing high-quality service to their guests. Hotel executives have learned that high-quality service is usually what determines if guests will return to upscale resorts, even more so than price. Consequently, having a well-trained hotel staff is crucial to delivering the premium service guests expect.

The importance of training to deliver this service can be seen in several examples. At the Broadmoor Hotel in Colorado Springs with 1,600 employees, developing and conducting training for all employees is a priority. Beginning with extensive new employee orientation and training, employees learn how to greet guests, resolve problems, and respond to guests' requests. The value of this training is that when hotel guests fill out comments cards, many of

them convey positive comments on the personalized service provided, a desire to return in the future, or other indications of the success of training at the Broadmoor.

Other upscale hotels and resorts see training as crucial as well. Rockresorts, which owns luxury properties in the United States and Caribbean, averages $1,000 in training expenditures per staff member, or 400% greater than the industry average. One program is a three-day training session for all 1,400 of Rockresorts employees. The objectives of this program include improving customer service, identifying ideas for improvements, and instilling customer service confidence in employees. Based on the results from employees who have completed the training, the objectives are being met. One indicator is an increase in the scores and comments on customer surveys and response cards. Another benefit of the training is that it appears to have aided in employee retention, particularly in the first year of employees' service.

The Starwood collection of hotels (St. Regis, Westin, Sheraton, Four Points, W Hotels) sees a specific focus on training as a contributor to competitive success. To increase the sales of beverages at the Starwood hotels and restaurants, a corporate initiative called "WineBuzz" was developed. With the specific goal of increasing wine sales through the Starwood hotel properties, Starwood executives recognized that guests purchasing wine expected to be served by knowledgeable, well-trained employees. Because serving beer is much different from serving wine, particularly given the different varieties and styles of wine, a training program on wine types and how to serve them was developed. A part of the training was Wine Camp, where food and beverage staff members from Starwood Hotels attended a multi-day session in Napa Valley, California. The 22 attendees from throughout the U.S. toured wineries, learned about viniculture and the different types of grapes used to produce different wines, and the wine production process. The trainees practiced opening bottles, discussing the merits of various grapes and wines, and other skills. Also, the Wine Camp contained "train-the-trainer" content, because the 22 attendees were then expected to conduct regional training sessions at Starwood hotels in their regional areas.

From these examples, it is evident that these hotels are investing in training. The payoffs of the training are likely to be seen in more satisfied guests, better-performing employees, and increased organizational revenues and profits.[46]

Questions

1. Discuss how these hotels are using a strategic and performance consulting approach to developing training efforts.
2. Identify how the effectiveness of Starwood's WineBuzz program might be measured several years later.

Notes

1. Based on Patricia A. Galagan, "Mission E-Possible: The Cisco E-Learning Story," *Training & Development*, February 2001, 46–56.
2. The authors acknowledge the assistance and contribution of Lisa A. Burke, PhD, SPHR in structuring the chapter and providing content in several sections.
3. ASTD Press Release, March 26, 2001. Available from *www.astd.org*.
4. Eric Krell, "Training Earns Its Keep," *Training*, April 2001, 68–74.
5. For example, see James Robinson, *The Evolving Performance Consultant Job* (Pittsburg, PA: Partners in Charge, Inc., 2000).
6. Michael Wykes, J. March-Swets, and L. Rynbrandt, "Performance Analysis: Field Operations Management," in J. Phillips, Ed., *In Action: Performance Consulting and Analysis* (Alexandria, VA: American Society of Training and Development, 2000), 135–153.
7. Dede Bonner, "Enter the Chief Knowledge Officer," *Training & Development*, February 2000, 36–40.
8. Timothy Baldwin and Camden Danielson, "Building a Learning Strategy at the Top: Interviews with Ten of America's CLOs," *Business Horizons*, June 2000, 5–14.
9. Joseph Wilson, "Strategic Training: Creating Advantage and Value," in Lisa A. Burke, ed., *High-Impact Training Solutions* (Westport, CT: Quorum Publishers, 2001).
10. Ramon Valle, et al., "Business Strategy, Work Processes, and Human Resource Training: Are They Congruent?" *Journal of Organizational Behavior*, 21 (2000), 283–297.
11. Richard Chang, "Tuning into Organizational Performance," *Training & Development*, May 2001, 104–111.
12. Elwood F. Holton III, Reid A. Bates, and Sharon S. Naquin, "Large-Scale Performance-Driven Training Needs Assessment: A Case Study," *Public Personnel Management*, 29 (2000), 249–267.
13. Marilyn J. Woods, "Interpersonal Communication for Police Officers: Using Needs Assessment to Prepare for Skeptical Trainees," *Business Communication Quarterly*, December 2000, 40–48.
14. Based on concepts and models suggested by Lisa A. Burke, PhD, SPHR.
15. Dannah Baynton, "America's $60 Billion Problem," *Training*, May 2001, 50–56.
16. Based on Michael G. Morris and Viswanath Venkatesh, "Age Differences in Technology Adoption Decisions: Implications for a Changing Workforce," *Personnel Psychology*, 53 (2000), 375–403.

17. Jennifer J. Salopek, "The Young and the Rest of Us," *Training & Development,* February 2000, 26–30.

18. Shawn B. Merriam and Rosemary Caffarella, *Learning in Adulthood: A Comprehensive Guide,* 2nd ed. (San Francisco: Jossey-Bass, 1999).

19. Gary L. May and William M. Kahnweiler, "The Effect of a Mastery Practice Design on Learning and Transfer in Behavior Modeling Training," *Personnel Psychology,* 53 (2000), 353–373.

20. Kathryn Tyler, "Hold On to What You've Learned," *HR Magazine,* May 2000, 94–102.

21. For a detailed discussion on transfer of training, see Raymond A. Noe, *Employee Training & Development* (New York: Irwin McGraw-Hill, 1999), 109–128.

22. Marvin L. Schroth, "The Effects of Type and Amount of Pre-training on Transfer in Concept Formation," *The Journal of General Psychology,* 127 (2000), 261.

23. Howard J. Klein and Natasha A. Weaver, "The Effectiveness of an Organizational-Level Orientation Training Program in the Socialization of New Hires," *Personnel Psychology* 53 (2000), 47–66.

24. Daniel M. Cable and Charles K. Parsons, "Socialization Tactics and Person-Organization Fit," *Personnel Psychology* 54 (2001), 1.

25. Charlotte Garvey, "The Whirlwind of a New Job," *HR Magazine,* June 2001, 111–118, and Linda Micco, "Giving Front-Line Hires the Full Story Up Front," *Bulletin to Management,* August 2, 2001, 247.

26. Mark E. Van Buren, *ASTD State of the Industry Report, 2001* (Alexandria VA: American Society of Training and Development, 2001), 11–12.

27. Rob Eure, "On the Job: Corporate E-Learning Makes Training Available Anytime, Anywhere," *The Wall Street Journal,* March 12, 2001, R33.

28. Ellene Zimmerman, "Better Training Is Just a Click Away," *Workforce,* January 2001, 36–42.

29. Patricia A. Galagan, "The E-Learning Revolution," *Training & Development,* December 2000, 24–30.

30. John V. Moran, "Top Ten E-Learning Myths," *Training & Development,* September 2000, 32–33.

31. "How to Illustrate Potential for Saving with E-Learning," *Bulletin to Management,* August 2, 2001, 244.

32. Kathryn Tyler, "E-Learning: Not Just for E-Normous Companies Anymore," *HR Magazine,* May 2001, 82–88.

33. Paula Santonocito, "Employees and E-Learning: Increasing Acceptance and Satisfaction," available from *www.hr-esource,* August 6, 2001.

34. Kenneth G. Brown, "Using Computers to Deliver Training," *Personnel Psychology* 54 (2001), 271–296.

35. "Lessons of a Virtual Timetable," *The Economist,* February 17, 2001, 69–71.

36. Albert A. Vicene, "Ten Observations on E-Learning and Leadership Development," *Human Resource Planning,* April 2000, 34–46.

37. Godfrey Golzen, "Real-Life Classes," *HR World,* November/December 2000, 27–30.

38. For a more detailed review of training technology, see Larry A. Pace, "Technological Advancements in Training Design, Delivery, Support and Administration," in Lisa A. Burke, ed., *High-Impact Training Solutions* (Westport, CT: Quorum Publishers, 2001).

39. H. W. Hodgins, *Into the Future: A Vision Paper,* American Society for Training & Development and the National Governor's Association Commission on Technology and Adult Learning (Washington, DC: American Society for Training & Development, 2000.)

40. Donald L. Kirkpatrick, *Evaluating Training Programs: The Four Levels,* (New York: Barrett-Kohler, 1998).

41. Robert W. Rowden, "A Practical Guide to Assessing the Value of Training in Your Company," *National Productivity Review,* Autumn 2000, 9–13.

42. Ben Worthen, "Measuring the ROI of Training," *CIO,* February 15, 2001, 128–136.

43. Amy Purcell, "20/20 ROI," *Training & Development,* July 2000, 28–33.

44. For information on each of these sources, go to the following Web sites: *www.astd.org, www.apqc.org, www.saratogainstitute.com.*

45. Based on Donna Goldwasser, "Beyond ROI," *Training,* January 2001, 82–90.

46. Based on Bill Kelley, "Refresher Course," *Human Resource Executive,* May 15, 2001, 59–64; and Jennifer J. Salopek, "Grape Expectations," *Training & Development,* August 2000, 52–57.

CHAPTER 10

Careers and HR Development

After you have read this chapter, you should be able to:

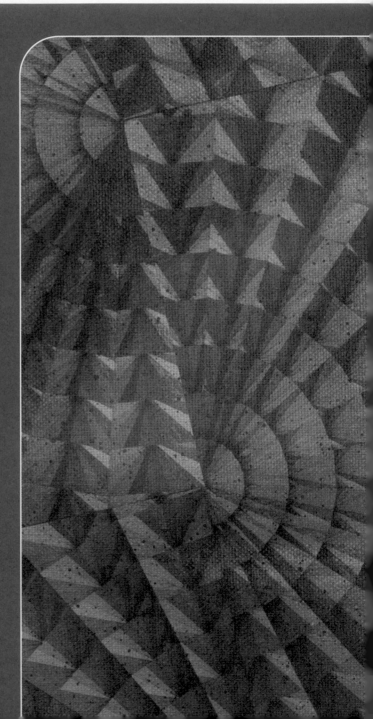

- Differentiate between organization-centered and individual-centered career planning.

- Discuss several career issues that organizations and employees face.

- Define *human resource development,* and describe the development process.

- Discuss specific advantages and problems associated with assessment centers.

- Identify four on-the-job and four off-the-job development methods.

Evolution of Career Development

The old model of a career where a person worked his or her way up the ladder in one organization is becoming rarer. Smaller, flatter companies provide less room to move up, and various signs indicate that the patterns of individuals' work lives are indeed changing in many areas: more freelancing, more working at home, more frequent job changes, more opportunity but less security. All of these job factors have affected the careers of individuals. Rather than letting jobs define their lives, more people set goals for the type of lives they want and then use jobs to meet those goals.

There are several reasons behind this shift. One reason is that U.S. workers in high-demand fields often dictate their own circumstances to some extent. The average 32-year-old in the U.S. has already worked for seven different firms. However, other workers change jobs infrequently. Physicians, teachers, economists, and others do not change jobs as frequently as others.

A very different trend is the insecurity caused by layoffs and downsizings. A greater number of older male American workers express fear of losing their jobs. This situation is not just a U.S.

phenomenon—a *Sarariman* in Japan, who typically has worked for one Japanese company his entire life, now is experiencing similar job insecurity. As a result, careers for many individuals contain both more flexibility and more insecurity.

Career issues also are affecting organizations and employees worldwide. In Europe, efforts to keep the traditional career system of job security are becoming more costly. European governments are facing pressures by employers to dismantle outmoded labor rules that make eliminating employees difficult, while also facing pressures by workers to alleviate high unemployment rates.

Another career-related change in the U.S. is overwork. The average middle-income couple with children now works 3,335 hours a year—eight weeks more than 20 years ago—due mainly to more women with small children who are now in the workforce. But working such schedules is often expected if one wishes to have career success.

The overriding career lesson in all of the shifts for individuals is clear: Educate yourself and do not

stop. Today, to be one of the 20% who are less skilled is a big disadvantage—U.S. high school grads earn 71% less than college grads. The need for re-education extends even into the middle and late stages of work life.

For employers, career issues have changed too. The best people will not go to workplaces viewed as undesirable because they do not have to do so. Employers must focus on core competencies. Successful employers look within their own ranks and identify those key employees with the competencies they need. Then, they focus on retaining and developing these talented workers by providing coaching, mentoring, and appropriate assignments.

In summary, employers in many developed countries increasingly are offering a deal to employees (usually implicit) that: "We may have to let you go in the interest of organizational flexibility, *but* we will help you develop the marketable skills you may need to find another job." Yes, careers are different and still evolving, but that evolution puts a premium on career development by both the employers and the employees.[1]

> Rather than letting jobs define their lives, more people set goals for the types of lives they want and then use jobs to meet those goals.

*"Nothing is more important than growing your 'A' players
and promptly dealing with your 'C' players."*

—Richard Brown

When organizational strategies involve endless organizational restructurings and downsizing, it is difficult to know what a career is, much less how to develop one. Further, some employers wonder why they should worry about career "development" for employees when the future likely holds fewer internal promotion opportunities and more movement in and out of organizations by individuals. Even though these views may seem extreme, employee development has changed recently in three significant ways:

1. The middle-management "ladder" in organizations now includes more horizontal rather than upward moves.
2. Many firms target their efforts to ensure that their businesses focus on core competencies.
3. The growth of project-based work makes careers a series of projects, not just steps upward in a given organization.

Traditionally, career development efforts targeted managerial personnel to look beyond their current jobs and to prepare them for a variety of future jobs in the organization. But development for all employees, not just managers, is necessary for organizations to have the needed human resource capabilities for future growth and change.

Career Planning
Describes career planning and development program at Dupont Corporation.
Custom Search:
☑ ANALYSIS
Phrase: Career movement

Mergers, acquisitions, restructurings, and layoffs all have influenced the way people and organizations look at careers and development. In the "new career," the individual—not the organization—manages his or her own development. Such self-development consists of personal educational experiences, training, organizational experiences, projects, and even changes in occupational fields. Under this system, the individual defines career success, which may or may not coincide with the organizational view of success.

Organizations promote this "self-reliance" as the basis for career development by telling employees they should focus on creating employability for themselves in the uncertain future. However, employability also must be defined in such a way that gives it value for the employing organization. It is a dilemma of sorts that if employers give employees unrestricted access to development opportunities, employers may not be able to retain talent in today's highly competitive labor markets.

Indeed, in some industries, changing jobs and companies every year or two is becoming more the norm than the exception. Valuable employees, deluged with job offers, change jobs at a rate much higher than in the past. Also, some individuals exhibit more loyalty to their careers than to an employer. Even though attempts to limit employees' abilities to change jobs through use of employment agreements containing noncompetition clauses put some restrictions on job hoppers, these clauses must be enforced in court, taking time and organizational resources.[2] All of these factors and more are changing how careers are defined and viewed.

Careers

Career The series of work-related positions a person occupies throughout life.

A **career** is the series of work-related positions a person occupies throughout life. People pursue careers to satisfy deeply individual needs. At one time, identifying with one employer seemed to fulfill many of those needs. Now, the distinction between the way individuals and organizations view careers is significantly different.

Employers that fail to help employees focus their careers in areas that benefit the organization experience shortages of employees who believe themselves to be ready to assume new jobs and responsibilities. From the viewpoint of individuals, failure to achieve psychological success or a feeling of pride and accomplishment in their careers may cause them to change careers, look outside work for "life success," or simply be unhappy. Effective career planning considers both organization-centered and individual-centered perspectives. Figure 10-1 summarizes the perspectives and interaction between the organizational and individual approaches to career planning. A look at each follows next.

Organization-Centered Career Planning

Organization-centered career planning Career planning that focuses on jobs and on identifying career paths that provide for the logical progression of people between jobs in an organization.

Organization-centered career planning focuses on jobs and on identifying career paths that provide for the logical progression of people between jobs in an organization. Individuals follow these paths as they advance in certain organizational units. For example, a person might enter the sales department as a sales representative, then be promoted to account director, to sales manager, and finally to vice president of sales.

Top management is responsible for developing career planning programs. A good program identifies career paths and includes performance appraisal, development, opportunities for transfer and promotion, and some planning for succession. To communicate with employees about opportunities and to help with planning, employers frequently use career workshops, a career "center" or newsletter, and career counseling. As the HR Perspective indicates, individual

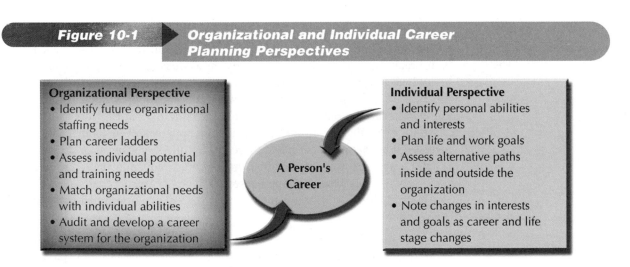

Figure 10-1 Organizational and Individual Career Planning Perspectives

Organizational Perspective
- Identify future organizational staffing needs
- Plan career ladders
- Assess individual potential and training needs
- Match organizational needs with individual abilities
- Audit and develop a career system for the organization

A Person's Career

Individual Perspective
- Identify personal abilities and interests
- Plan life and work goals
- Assess alternative paths inside and outside the organization
- Note changes in interests and goals as career and life stage changes

Career Changes at Sears Credit

A major reorganization at Sears Credit resulted in nine units expanding, 50 units closing, and a voluntary retirement plan that greatly reduced the total number of employees. All these actions were taken to implement major changes in the business itself, but they also caused significant career dislocations for the remaining employees. Duties in most jobs were altered, which meant that previous career paths no longer existed, and the previously prepared succession plans became obsolete. Some of the changes in the jobs required identifying specific competencies for success that included factors such as: business

knowledge, contribution to financial results, leadership, customer focus, individual effectiveness, and associate development.

Management at Sears Credit emphasized that employees had to take greater personal responsibility for managing their careers, because managers would no longer be the ones who determined what employees' careers would be. Instead, the managers would become career coaches. To aid employees in developing their career plans, workshops were offered to explain individual self-assessment activities and the new career development planning process. Managers also took semi-

nars on career coaching skills. Once individual employees had identified their career goals, a database was developed that could be used to match employee interests to specific jobs. Lateral job transfers were encouraged to help individual employees develop broader ranges of capabilities.

At Sears Credit the entire process for career planning shifted from a passive one where employees "received" career planning, to an active one requiring employees to take responsibility for their own career development. Consequently, the career planning roles for both managers and employees changed.[3]

managers frequently must play the role of coach and counselor in their direct contact with individual employees and within an HR-designed career management system.[4]

Organizational retrenchment and downsizing have changed career plans for many people. More and more individuals have had to face "career transitions"—in other words, they must find jobs.

Individual-Centered Career Planning

Individual-centered career planning Career planning that focuses on individuals' careers rather than on organizational needs.

Individual-centered career planning focuses on an individual's career rather than organizational needs. It is done by employees themselves analyzing their individual goals and skills. Such efforts might consider situations both inside and outside the organization that could expand a person's career. Even though individuals are the only ones who know for certain what they consider a successful career, that definition is not always apparent even to the individuals involved. For example, few college students enrolled in business programs know exactly what they want to do upon graduation. Frequently they can eliminate some types of jobs, but might be interested in any of many other options.

For individuals to manage their careers several activities must happen:

- *Self-assessment.* Individuals need to think about what interests them, what they do not like, what they do well, and their strengths and weaknesses. Career advisors use a number of tools to help people understand themselves.[5] Common professional tests may include the *Strong Vocational Interest Inventory* to determine preferences among occupations, or the *Allport-Vernon-Lindzey Study of Values* to identify a person's dominant values.

■ *Feedback on reality.* Employees need feedback on how well they are doing, how their bosses see their capabilities, and where they fit in organizational plans for the future. One source of this information should occur through performance appraisal feedback.

■ *Setting career goals.* Deciding on a desired path, setting some timetables, and writing down these items all set the stage for a person to pursue the career of choice. These goals are supported by short-term plans for the individual to get the experience or training necessary to move forward toward the career goals.

How People Choose Careers

Four general individual characteristics affect how people make career choices:

■ *Interests:* People tend to pursue careers that they believe match their interests. But over time, interests change for many people, and career decisions eventually are made based on special skills, abilities, and which career paths are realistic for them.

■ *Self-image:* A career is an extension of a person's self-image, as well as a molder of it. People follow careers they can "see" themselves doing and avoid those that do not fit with the perceptions of their talents, motives, and values.

■ *Personality:* This factor includes an employee's personal orientation (for example, if the employee is realistic, enterprising, or artistic) and personal needs (including affiliation, power, and achievement needs). Individuals with certain personality types gravitate to different clusters of occupations.

■ *Social backgrounds:* Socioeconomic status and the educational level and occupation of a person's parents are also factors included in this category. Children of a physician or a welder know from their parents what those jobs are like and may either seek or reject them based on how they view the parents' jobs.

Less is known about how and why people choose specific organizations than about why they choose specific careers. One obvious factor is timing—the availability of a job when the person is looking for work. The amount of information available about alternatives is an important factor as well. Beyond these issues, people seem to pick an organization on the basis of a "fit" between the climate of the organization as they perceive it and their own personal characteristics, interests, and needs.

General Career Progression

The typical career of many individuals today probably includes different positions, transitions, and organizations—more so than in the past, when employees were less mobile and organizations more stable as long-term employers. A typical U.S. worker holds seven jobs between ages 18 and 32, with most of those job changes occurring at earlier ages rather than later. However the median years of time spent with one employer has changed little over the last two decades, as Figure 10-2 on the next page indicates. Therefore, it is useful to think about general patterns in people's lives and the effects on their careers.

Many theorists in adult development describe the first half of life as the young adult's quest for competence and a way to make a mark in the world.

Figure 10-2 ▶ **Length of Employee Tenure with an Employer**

Source: U.S. Department of Labor, Bureau of Labor Statistics, 2001.

According to this view, a person attains happiness during this time primarily through achievement and the acquisition of capabilities. The second half of life is different. Once the adult starts to measure time from the expected end of his or her life rather than from the beginning, the need for competence and acquisition changes to the need for integrity, values, and well-being. For many people internal values take precedence over external scorecards or accomplishments such as wealth and job title status. In addition, mature adults already possess certain skills, so their focus may shift to other interests. Career-ending concerns reflect additional shifts also. Figure 10-3 shows a model identifying general career and life periods.

Contained within this life pattern is the idea that careers and lives are not predictably linear but cyclical.[6] Individuals experience periods of high stability, followed by transition periods with less stability, and by inevitable discoveries, disappointments, and triumphs. These cycles of structure and transition occur throughout individuals' lives and careers. This cyclical view may be an especially useful

Figure 10-3 ▶ General Career Periods

Career Stage	Early Career	Mid-Career	Late Career	Career End
Age Group:	*20 years*	*30–40 years*	*50 years*	*60–70 years*
Needs:	*Identifying interests, exploring several jobs*	*Advancing in career; lifestyle may limit options, growth, contribution*	*Updating skills; settled in, leader, opinions valued*	*Planning for retirement, examining nonwork interests*
Concerns:	*External rewards, acquiring more capabilities*	*Values, contribution, integrity, well-being*	*Mentoring, disengaging, organization continuance*	*Retirement, part-time employment*

perspective for those individuals affected by downsizing or early career plateaus in large organizations. Such a perspective argues for the importance of flexibility in an individual's career. It also emphasizes the importance of individuals continuing to acquire more and diverse knowledge, skills, and abilities.

Career Transitions and HR

Three career transitions are of special interests to HR: organizational entry and socialization, transfers and promotions, and job loss.[7] Starting as a new employee can be overwhelming. "Entry Shock" is especially difficult for younger new hires who find the work world very different from school. Entry shock includes the following concerns:

- *Supervisors:* The boss/employee relationship is different from student/teacher.
- *Feedback:* In school, feedback is frequent and quantitative; not so at work in most jobs.
- *Time:* School has short (quarter/semester) time cycles, while time horizons are longer at work.
- *The work:* Problems are more tightly defined at school, while at work the logistical and political aspects of solving problems are more uncertain.

Transfers and promotions offer opportunities for employees to develop and often bring pay increases. However, unlike new hires, the employee is often expected to perform well immediately, which may not be realistic. International transfers cause even more difficulties than in-country transfers for many.

Job loss has been most associated with downsizing, mergers, and acquisitions. Losing a job is a stressful event in one's career, frequently causing depression, anxiety, and nervousness. The financial implications and the effects on family can be extreme as well. Yet the potential for job loss continues to increase and should be considered in career decision making.

Late Career/Retirement Issues

Research about late careers provides insight into successful use of people toward the ends of their careers.[8] Phased-in retirement, consulting arrangements, and callback of some retirees as needed all act as means for gradual disengagement between the organization and individual.

Whether retirement comes at age 50 or 70, it can require a major adjustment for many people. Some common emotional adjustments faced by retirees include:

- *Self-management:* The person must adjust to being totally self-directed after retirement. In retirement, no supervisor or work agenda dictates what to do and when to do it.
- *Need to belong:* When a person retires, he or she is no longer a member of the work group that took up so much time and formed an important social structure for so many years. What takes its place is often unknown when someone retires.
- *Pride in achievement:* Achievement reinforces self-esteem and often centers around work. In retirement, past achievements quickly wear thin as a source of self-esteem.

- *Territoriality:* Personal "turf," in the form of office, company, and title, is removed in retirement. Other ways to satisfy territorial and status needs must be found.
- *Goals:* Organizations provide directions for many goals of individuals. Some people may be unprepared to set their own goals when they retire.

Of course, from the standpoint of the organization, retirement represents an orderly way to move people out at the ends of their careers. However, in an attempt to be mindful of the problems that retirement poses for some individuals, some organizations are experimenting with phased retirement through gradually reduced workweeks and increased vacation time. These and other pre-retirement and post-retirement programs aid in the transition of individuals to a useful retirement and may keep experienced people available to the organization for a longer time.

The phenomenon of "forced" early retirement is often seen as a result of downsizings and organizational restructurings that have required thousands of individuals, including many managers and professionals, to determine what is important to them while still active and healthy. As a result, some of the "younger retirees" begin second careers rather than focusing primarily on leisure activities or travel.

Special Career Issues for Organizations and Employees

Although the goals and perspectives in career planning may differ for organizations and employees, three issues can be problematic for both, perhaps for different reasons. Those are career plateaus (or the lack of opportunity to move up), dealing with technical professionals who do not want to go into management, and dual-career couples.

Career Plateaus

Those who do not job hop may face another problem: career plateaus. As the baby-boomer generation reaches midlife, and as large employers cut back on their workforces, increasing numbers of employees find themselves at a career plateau where they are "stuck" at a career level. This plateauing may seem a sign of failure to some people, and plateaued employees can cause problems for employers if their frustrations affect their job performance.

Many workers define career success in terms of upward mobility. However, as the opportunities to move up decrease, some employers try to convince employees they can find happiness in lateral movement. Such moves can be reasonable if employees learn new skills that increase individual marketability in case of future layoffs, termination, or organizational restructurings.

One strategy of retooling to get off career plateaus is through taking seminars and university courses. This approach may reveal new opportunities for plateaued employees. Rotating workers to other departments is another way to deal with career plateaus. A computer chip manufacturer instituted a formal "poaching" program that encouraged managers to recruit employees from other departments, thereby giving employees greater opportunities to experience new challenges without having to leave the employer.[9] Some plateaued individuals change careers and go into other lines of work altogether.[10]

Logging On...

Career Builder
On this Web site you can post a job, search for a job, research employers, take online workshops on interviewing, and receive career coaching and counseling.

www.careerbuilder.com

| | | | | Toward End |
Beginning	Expanding	Changing	Mid-Career	of Career
Spend several years at large company to learn skills and build network	*Begin networking to develop broader skills and make contacts; establish good reputation*	*Change industries, or go to work for smaller companies; start a company*	*Refresh skills; take a sabbatical; go back to school; gain experience in nonprofit organizations*	*Move to appealing projects as a temporary employee or subcontractor*

Figure 10-4 ▶ The "Portable" Career Path

Figure 10-4 shows a "portable" career path that can include such major changes. In summary, plateaued employees present a particular challenge for employers. If plateaued employees become negative they can affect morale, but they also represent valuable resources that are not being well used.

Technical and Professional Workers

Technical and professional workers, such as engineers, scientists, physical therapists, IT systems experts, and others, present a special challenge for organizations.[11] Many of these individuals want to stay in their technical areas rather than enter management; yet advancement in many organizations frequently requires a move into management. Most of these people like the idea of the responsibility and opportunity associated with advancement, but they do not want to leave the professional and technical puzzles and problems at which they excel.

The *dual-career ladder* is an attempt to solve this problem. As shown in Figure 10-5 on the next page, a person can advance up either the management ladder or a corresponding ladder on the technical/professional side. Dual-career paths have been used at IBM, Union Carbide, and AT&T/Bell Labs for years and are now used at many other firms. They are most common in technology-driven industries such as pharmaceuticals, chemicals, computers, and electronics.[12] For instance, a telecommunications firm created a dual-career ladder in its data processing department to reward talented technical people who do not want to move into management. Different tracks, each with attractive job titles and pay opportunities, are provided.[13]

Unfortunately, the technical/professional ladder sometimes leads to an image of "second-class citizenship" within the organization. For a second or third career track to be taken seriously, management must apply standards as rigorous as those applied to management promotions.

Dual-Career Couples

As the number of women in the workforce, particularly in professional careers, continues of increase, so does the number of dual-career couples. The U.S. Bureau of Labor Statistics estimates that 81% of all couples are dual-career couples. Marriages in which both mates are managers, professionals, or technicians doubled over the past two decades. Leading geographic areas of growth in the number of dual-career couples are the U.S. West coast states, Denver, Chicago,

Figure 10-5 ▶ **Dual-Career Path for Engineers**

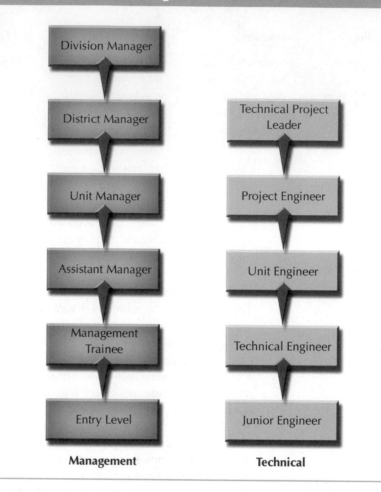

Management	Technical
Division Manager	
District Manager	Technical Project Leader
Unit Manager	Project Engineer
Assistant Manager	Unit Engineer
Management Trainee	Technical Engineer
Entry Level	Junior Engineer

New York, and the Washington, D.C.–Baltimore area. Problem areas for dual-career couples include retirement, transfer, and family issues.

It is important that the career development problems of dual-career couples be recognized as early as possible, especially if they involve transfer of locations. Early planning by employees and their supervisors can prevent crises from occurring. Whenever possible, having both partners involved in planning, even when one is not employed by the company, has been found to enhance the success of such efforts.

For dual-career couples with children, family issues may conflict with career progression. Thus, in job transfer situations, one partner's flexibility may depend on what is "best" for the family. Companies may consider part-time work, flextime, and work-at-home arrangements as possible options, especially for parents with younger children.

Recruitment Problems with Dual-Career Couples Recruiting a member of a dual-career couple may mean having an equally attractive job available for the candidate's partner at the new location. Dual-career couples may lose some income when relocating; thus they often have higher expectations, request more help, and expect higher salaries in such situations.

Relocation of Dual-Career Couples Traditionally, employees accepted transfers as part of upward mobility in organizations. However, for some dual-career couples the mobility required because of one partner's transfer often interferes with the other's career. In addition having two careers, dual-career couples often have established support networks of co-workers, friends, and business contacts to cope with both their careers and personal lives. Relocating one partner in a dual-career couple may mean upsetting this carefully constructed network for the other person or creating a "commuting" relationship.[14]

In a company without a partner-assistance program, an employee may be hesitant to request such services or may turn down the relocation. Because the dual-career family has not been the norm for very long, traditional role expectations remain. In some cases, male employees may fear they will appear "unmanly" should their partners refuse to defer in support of career changes. On the other hand, some female employees may feel guilty about violating the traditional concept of male career dominance when the female moves and a male must quit his job to follow.

When revising HR policies on employee relocation assistance, the following approaches address the dual-career concerns:

- Paying employment agency fees for the relocating partner
- Paying for a designated number of trips for the partner to look for a job in the proposed new location
- Helping the partner find a job within the same company or in another division or subsidiary of the company
- Developing computerized job banks to share with other companies in the area that list partners available for job openings.

Developing Human Resources

Development Efforts to improve employees' ability to handle a variety of assignments.

Development represents efforts to improve employees' ability to handle a variety of assignments and to cultivate capabilities beyond those required by the current job. Development benefits both organizations and individuals. Employees and managers with appropriate experiences and abilities may enhance organizational competitiveness and the ability to adapt to a changing environment. In the development process, individuals' careers also may evolve and gain new or different focus.[15]

Development differs from training. It is possible to train most people to run a copy machine, answer customer service questions, drive a truck, operate a computer, or assemble a radio. However, development in areas such as judgment, responsibility, decision making, and communications presents a bigger challenge. These areas may or may not develop through life experiences by individuals. A planned system of development experiences for all employees, not just managers, can help expand the overall level of capabilities in an organization. Figure 10-6 on the next page profiles development and compares it to training.

At the organizational level of analysis, executives craft the broader organizational strategies as well as establish a system for developing the people to manage and achieve those identified strategies. Development must be tied to this strategic planning because the firm needs to develop those talents to carry out the plans. The successful CEO plans employee and managerial succession on several levels and in several different pathways as part of that development.

Logging On...

Training and Development Community Center
This Web site provides over 300 Web site links for training and development.

http://www.tcm.com/trdev/

Figure 10-6   Development vs. Training

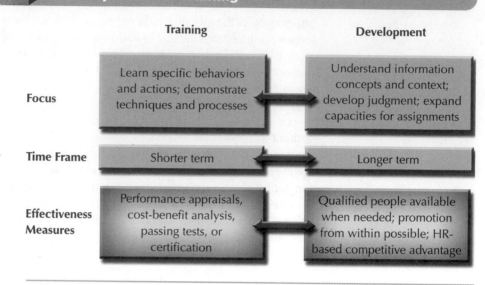

Currently, more jobs take on the characteristics of *knowledge work.* Such workers combine mastery of technical expertise with the ability to work in teams, form relationships with customers, and analyze their own practices. The practice of management involves guiding and integrating increasingly autonomous, highly skilled people.

The HR Development Process

Development starts with the HR plans of an organization because these plans analyze, forecast, and identify current and future organizational needs for human resources. Also, HR planning anticipates the movement of people in the organization due to retirements, promotions, and transfers. Also, it helps identify the capabilities needed by the organization in the future and the development necessary for people to be available to meet those needs.

In Figure 10-7 illustrating the HR development process, HR plans first identify necessary capabilities of individuals. Such capabilities can of course, influence planning in return. The specific abilities needed also influence decisions about promotions and the leadership succession process with in the organization. Those decisions influence—and are influenced by—an assessment of the development needs in the organization. Two categories of development planning follow from this needs assessment: organizational and individual. Finally, the success of the developmental process must be evaluated and necessary changes made as appropriate.

Make or Buy?

To some extent, employers face a "make-or-buy" choice: Develop competitive human resources, or "buy" them already developed from somewhere else. Current trends indicate that technical and professional people usually are hired based on the amount of skill development already achieved, rather than on their ability to learn or their behavioral traits. Many organizations show an apparent

preference to buy rather than "make" scarce employees in today's labor market. However, buying rather than developing human resource capabilities may not contribute to a strategy of sustained competitive advantage through human resources. As in finance, the make-or-buy decision can be quantified and calculated when some assumptions are made.[16]

Developing Specific Capabilities

Exactly what kind of development a given individual might need to expand his or her capabilities depends on both the person and the capabilities needed. However, some important and common management capabilities often include action orientation, quality decision making, ethical values, and technical skills.

For high demand tech specialties (tech support, database administrator, network designer, etc.) certain non-technical abilities must be developed as well:[17]

- Ability to work under pressure
- Ability to work independently
- Ability to solve problems quickly
- Ability to use past knowledge in a new situation

Team building, developing subordinates, directing others, and dealing with uncertainty are equally important but much less commonly developed capabilities for successful managers.

Development frequently includes judgment and responsibility. How to develop an "action orientation" or the "ability to work under pressure" must be addressed by organizations. These skills cannot successfully be taught in a course and not everyone will develop these abilities. As a result, development is less certain and less well-defined than training.

One point is clear about development, however. In studies that asked employees what they want out of their jobs, training and development ranked at or near the top. Because the assets of individuals are their knowledge, skills, and abilities (KSAs), many people view the development of their KSAs as an important part of their organizational package.[18]

Lifelong Learning

Learning and development are not one-time occurrences. For most people, lifelong learning and development are much more likely and desirable. For many professionals, lifelong learning may mean continuing education requirements to keep certified. For example, lawyers, CPAs, teachers, dentists, and others must complete continuing education requirements in most states to keep their licenses to practice.[19] For semiskilled employees, learning and development may involve training to expand existing skills and prepare for different jobs, promotions, or even for new jobs after retirement.[20]

Assistance from employers for needed lifelong development typically comes through programs at work, including tuition reimbursement. However, much of lifelong learning is voluntary, takes place outside work hours, and is not always formal.[21] Although it might may have no immediate relevance to a person's current job, learning often can enhance confidence, ideas, or enthusiasm of individuals.

Redevelopment

Whether due to a desire for career change or because the employer needs different capabilities, people may shift jobs in mid-life or mid-career. Redeveloping or re-training people in the capabilities they need is logical and important. In the last decade the number of college enrollees over the age of 35 has increased more than 25%.[22] But going back to college is only one way to redevelop individuals. Some companies offer redevelopment programs in order to recruit expe-

Etiquette and More

What is the minimum level individuals representing firms should have in the way of courtesy, table manners, and social skills? Also, how does a company develop those social skills in employees? Many employers have dealt with this sort of problem, but professional sports teams face the challenge on a greater scale, given the numbers, the backgrounds, and the far-reaching influence of today's high-profile athletes.

More professional sports teams are offering player development programs to protect their multimillion-dollar investments. For instance, the National Basketball Association holds a rookie semi-

nar on potential temptations such as groupies, gambling, and drugs. Similarly, major league baseball offers a course to players coming into the big leagues. However, the Texas Rangers baseball club has taken both of those ideas quite a bit further, to help players both enjoy their playing days and avoid trouble. The Rangers' Career Development Program uses role playing, lectures, and guest speakers and covers everything from AIDS to etiquette in six days before spring training. The ball club feels such development of its players is beneficial because, as the Rangers' Director of Player Development notes, "These play-

ers don't understand what they're getting into." Rangers' players consistently give the development program high marks. If nothing else, it gets across to *most* players accustomed to scratching and spitting in public that they are judged on how they look, speak, eat, and act.

But it is not just athletes who lack social skills. Many firms are discovering that their young, new hires are relatively unaware of social niceties. More and more companies send young hires to "Manners Camp" or bring in etiquette trainers for half-day training courses.[23]

---

rienced workers from other fields. For example, firms needing truck drivers, reporters, and IT workers sponsor second-career programs.[24] Public-sector employers have been using redevelopment as a recruiting tool as well.

Development Needs Analyses

As with training, employee development begins with analyses of the needs of both the organization and individuals. Even though evidence indicates that this analysis of an individual's development needs frequently receives insufficient attention, some industries are using innovative methods, as the HR Perspective shows.

Either the company or the individual can analyze what a given person needs by way of development. The goal, of course, is to identify strengths and weaknesses. Methods used by organizations to assess development needs include use of assessment centers, psychological testing, and performance appraisals.

Assessment Centers

Assessment center
A collection of instruments and exercises designed to diagnose individuals' development needs.

Assessment centers are collections of instruments and exercises designed to diagnose an individual's development needs. Organizational leadership uses assessment centers for both developing and selecting managers. Many types of large organizations, such as police departments, use assessment centers.

In a typical assessment-center experience, an individual spends two or three days away from the job, performing many activities. These activities might include role playing, pencil-and-paper tests, cases, leaderless group discussions, computer-based simulations, management games, and peer evaluations. Frequently, in-basket exercises are used also, in which the individual handles typical problems coming across a manager's desk.[25] For the most part, the exercises represent situations that require the use of managerial skills and behaviors. During the exercises, several specially trained judges observe the participants.

Assessment centers provide an excellent means for determining management potential. Management and participants often praise assessment centers because they are more likely to overcome many of the biases inherent in interview situations, supervisor ratings, and written tests. Experience shows that key variables such as leadership, initiative, and supervisory skills cannot be measured with paper-and-pencil tests alone. Assessment centers also offer the advantage of helping identify employees with potential in large organizations. Supervisors may nominate people for the assessment center, or employees may volunteer. For talented people, the opportunity to volunteer is invaluable because supervisors may not recognize their potential interests and capabilities.

Assessment centers also can raise concerns. Some managers may use an assessment center as a way to avoid difficult promotion decisions. Suppose a plant supervisor has personally decided that an employee is not qualified for promotion. Rather than be straightforward and inform the employee, the supervisor sends the employee to the assessment center, hoping the report will show that the employee is unqualified for promotion. Problems between the employee and the supervisor may worsen if the employee earns a positive report. Using the assessment center for this purpose does not aid the development of the employee and is not recommended.

Psychological Testing

Psychological pencil-and-paper tests have been used for several years to determine employees' development potential and needs. Intelligence tests, verbal and mathematical reasoning tests, and personality tests are often used. Even a test that supposedly assesses common sense is available.[26] Such testing can furnish useful information on individuals about such factors as motivation, reasoning abilities, leadership style, interpersonal response traits, and job preferences.

The biggest problem with psychological testing lies in interpretation, because untrained managers, supervisors, and workers usually cannot accurately interpret test results. After a professional reports test-taker scores to someone in the organization, untrained managers may attach their own meanings to the results. Also, some psychological tests are of limited validity, and test-takers can easily fake desirable responses. Thus, psychological testing is appropriate only when the testing and feedback process is closely supervised by a qualified professional.

Performance Appraisals

Well-done performance appraisals can be a source of development information. Performance data on productivity, employee relations, job knowledge, and other relevant dimensions can be gathered in this way. As noted in Chapter 11, appraisals designed for development purposes may be more useful in aiding individual employee development than appraisals designed strictly for administrative purposes.

Succession Planning

Succession planning
Process of identifying a longer-term plan for the orderly replacement of key employees.

Planning for the succession of key executives, managers, and other employees is an important part of HR development. **Succession planning** is a process of identifying a longer-term plan for the orderly replacement of key employees. The need to replace key employees results from promotions, transfers, retirements, deaths, disability, departures, or other reasons. Succession planning often focuses on top management, such as ensuring a CEO successor. (See the HR Perspective). However, limiting succession planning just to top executive jobs is one of the greatest mistakes made.[28] For instance, identifying successors for accounting managers, marketing directors, admissions supervisors, IT technicians, physical therapists, and other key jobs is just as crucial as succession planning for the top executive jobs in a health-care institution.

Succession in Small and Closely Held Organizations

Succession planning can be especially important in small and medium-sized firms, but studies show that few of these firms formalize any succession plans. In fact, 58% of respondents in one study named lack of succession planning as the biggest threat facing small businesses.[29] In closely held family firms (those that are not publicly traded on stock exchanges), many CEOs plan to pass the business on to a family member. Most of these firms would benefit from advance planning for orderly succession. Addressing development needs of the successor also helps to avoid a host of potential problems for both the organization and family member relationships.

Succession Planning Process

Whether in small or large firms, succession planning is linked to strategic HR planning.[30] Both the quantity and capabilities of potential successors must be linked to organizational strategies and HR plans. For example, a retailer whose

Figure 10-8 ▶ *Succession Planning Process*

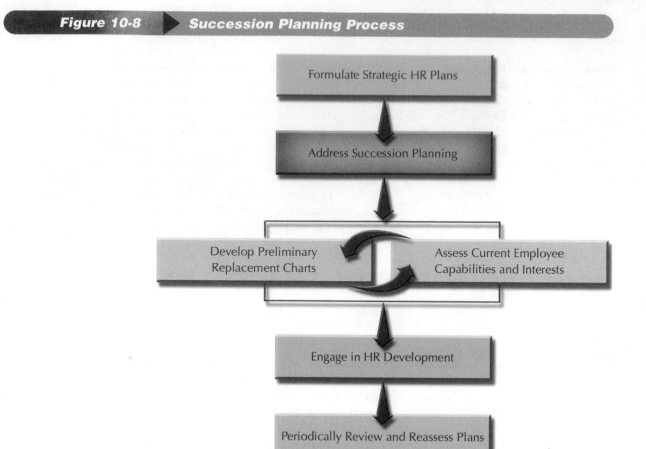

key merchandising managers are likely to retire soon must consider the implications for future merchandising and store expansion plans, particularly if the firm plans to enter or withdraw from offering certain lines of goods. Based on these broader planning efforts, the succession planning process shown in Figure 10-8 is recommended.

Two coordinated activities begin the actual succession planning process. First, the development of preliminary replacement charts ensures that the right individuals with sufficient capabilities and experience to perform the targeted jobs are available at the right time. Replacement charts (similar to depth charts used by football teams) both show the backup "players" at each position and identify positions without a current qualified backup. The charts identify who could take over key jobs if someone leaves, retires, dies unexpectedly, or otherwise creates a vacancy.

In conjunction with developing replacement charts, assessing the capabilities of current employees and their career interests allows companies to create career development plans for employees. As mentioned earlier, managers may perform these assessments based on performance appraisals and other information. Organizations also use psychological tests, assessment centers, or other individual assessment means to identify individual development needs and pos-

Logging On...

Business Decisions
This Web site provides an overview of succession planning.

http://www.businessdecisions.com/succession.asp

sible career moves for employees. Then HR efforts to develop the capabilities of the individuals facilitate orderly and planned successions. Finally, as with most planning efforts, periodic review and reassessment both organization-wide and with individuals ensures that the succession plan remains current and aligned with organizational strategies and HR plans.

Choosing a Development Approach

Common development approaches can be categorized under two major headings— job-site development and off-site development. Both are appropriate in developing managers and other employees. Investing in human intellectual capital, whether at work or off the job, becomes imperative for organizations as "knowledge work" aspects increase for almost all employers. Yet identifying exactly the right mix and approaches for development needs remains an art rather than a science.[31]

Development Approaches: Job-Site Methods

A number of job-site development methods are available. However, all too often unplanned and perhaps useless activities pass as development on the job. To ensure that the desired development actually occurs, managers must plan and coordinate development efforts, and several means can be used.

Coaching Training and feedback given to employees by immediate supervisors.

Coaching The oldest on-the-job development technique is **coaching**, which is the training and feedback given to employees by immediate supervisors. Coaching involves a continual process of learning by doing. For effective coaching, a healthy and open relationship must exist between employees and their supervisors or managers. Many firms conduct formal training courses to improve the coaching skills of their managers and supervisors. For instance, the Men's Warehouse uses off-site meetings of the management group as a vehicle for development. In this model, development cascades down a hierarchy in which people at each level are responsible for developing those below. These managerial meetings of the whole company impart selling skills and product and market knowledge.[32]

Unfortunately, organizations may be tempted to implement coaching without any planning at all. Even someone who is good at a job or a particular part of a job will not necessarily be able to coach someone else to do it well. The "coaches" can easily fall short in guiding learners systematically, even if they know which experiences are best. Sometimes, too, doing a full day's work takes priority over learning and coaching. Also, the intellectual component of many skills might be better learned from a book or course before coaching occurs. Sometimes "executive" coaches, hired either by individual executives or employers, work with individual managers and executives. These outside coaches provide critiques and advice to the individuals.

Committee Assignments/Meetings Assigning promising employees to important committees may broaden their experiences and can help them understand the personalities, issues, and processes governing the organization. For instance, employees on a safety committee can gain a greater understanding of safety management, which would aid them to become supervisors. They may also experience the problems involved in maintaining employee safety

Logging On...

Coaching
This Web site provides information about a firm that specializes in coaching techniques and describes its approach to coaching.

http://www.refocusinc.com/
services.htm#coaching

awareness. However, managers need to guard against committee assignments that turn into time-wasting activities.

Job rotation The process of shifting an employee from job to job.

Job Rotation The process of shifting an employee from job to job is **job rotation**. In some organizations, job rotation is unplanned. However, other organizations follow elaborate charts and schedules, precisely planning a rotation program for each employee. Regardless of the approach, job rotation is widely used as a development technique.[33] For example, a promising young manager may spend three months in the plant, three months in corporate planning, and three months in purchasing. When properly handled, such job rotation fosters a greater understanding of the organization.

When opportunities for promotion are scarce, job rotation through use of lateral transfers may be beneficial in rekindling enthusiasm and developing employees' talents. The best lateral moves do one or more of the following:

- Move the person into the core business.
- Provide closer contact with customers.
- Teach new skills or perspectives.

Despite its benefits, job rotation can be expensive. Furthermore, a substantial amount of time is taken when trainees change positions, because they must become acquainted with different people and techniques in each new unit.

"Assistant-to" Positions Some firms create "assistant-to" positions, which are staff positions immediately under a manager. Through such jobs, trainees can work with outstanding managers they might not otherwise have met. Some organizations set up "junior boards of directors" or "management cabinets" to which trainees may be appointed. These assignments provide useful experiences if they present challenging or interesting assignments to trainees.

On-line Development Technology is here to stay and provides an appropriate tool for development.[34] On-line development can take many forms, such as video conferencing, live chat, document sharing, streamlining video and audio, Web-based courses, and more. HR staff members can facilitate on-line development by providing a "learning portal," which is a centralized Web site for news, information, course listings, and materials.[35]

On-line development allows participation in courses previously out of reach due to geographic, travel, or cost considerations. Also, costs can be spread over a larger number of people, and virtual reality and other technological tools can be used to make more presentation interesting. Travel can be eliminated as well. However, because of time needed to develop materials or perhaps because it is not seen as clearly appropriate for development efforts, on-line development is not widely used.[36]

Corporate Universities/Career Development Centers Large organizations may use a "corporate university" as a way to develop managers or other employees. Corporate universities take various forms. Sometimes regarded as little more than fancy packaging for company training, they often do not provide a degree, accreditation, or graduation in the traditional sense.[37] However, partnerships between companies and traditional universities continue to evolve and change.

Figure 10-9 | Possible Means Used in a Learning Organization

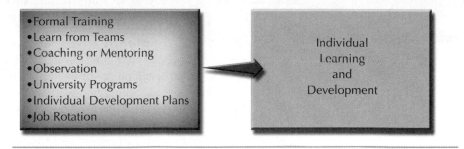

- Formal Training
- Learn from Teams
- Coaching or Mentoring
- Observation
- University Programs
- Individual Development Plans
- Job Rotation

Individual Learning and Development

Career development centers often are set up to coordinate both in-house programs and those provided by outsourced suppliers. They may include assessment data for individuals, career goals and strategies, coaching, seminars, and on-line approaches.[38]

"Learning Organization" Knowledge-based organizations that deal primarily with ideas and information must have employees who are expert on one or more conceptual tasks. These employees continuously learn and solve problems in their areas of expertise. Such a situation requires an "organizational learning capacity" based on a culture of problem solving and learning new ways not previously used.

A "learning organization" is difficult to describe, except to say that development occurs through shared information, culture, leadership that values learning, and employees who want to learn and develop new skills. Such a mindset is probably difficult to introduce into an organization where it does not exist. But where it does exist, it represents the ultimate potential for development. It remains a theoretical and somewhat idealistic model in HR development. Figure 10-9 depicts some means that might be used in a learning organization.

Development Approaches: Off-Site Methods

Off-the-job development techniques give individuals opportunities to get away from the job and concentrate solely on what is to be learned. Moreover, contact with others who are concerned with somewhat different problems and come from different organizations may provide employees with new and different perspectives. Various off-site methods are used.

Classroom Courses and Degrees Most off-the-job development programs include some classroom instruction. Most people are familiar with classroom training, which gives it the advantage of being widely accepted. But the lecture system sometimes used in classroom instruction encourages passive listening and reduced learner participation, which is a distinct disadvantage. Sometimes trainees have little opportunity to question, clarify, and discuss the lecture material. The effectiveness of classroom instruction depends on multiple factors: group size, trainees' abilities, instructors' capabilities and styles, and subject matter.

Organizations often send employees to externally sponsored seminars or professional courses, such as those offered by the American Management

Logging On...

Development Sources
Information on management development sources is available at this Web site.

http://www.tregistry.com/ama.htm

Association. Many organizations also encourage continuing education by reimbursing employees for the costs of college tuition courses.[39] Such programs provide incentive for employees to study for advanced degrees, such as MBAs, through evening and weekend classes, outside of their regular workdays.

Human Relations Training This type of training attempts to prepare supervisors to deal with "people problems" brought to them by their employees. The training focuses on the development of the human relations skills a person needs to work well with others. Most human relations programs typically are aimed at new or relatively inexperienced first-line supervisors and middle managers. Content areas covered include motivation, leadership, employee communication, and other behavioral topics.

The most common reason managers fail after being promoted to management is poor teamwork with subordinates and peers. Other common reasons for management failure include not understanding expectations, failure to meet goals, difficulty in adjusting to management responsibilities, and inability to balance work and home life.

Simulation A development technique that requires participants to analyze a situation and decide the best course of action based on the data given.

Simulations (Business Games) Another development approach uses business games, or simulations which are available commercially. A **simulation** requires participants to analyze a situation and decide the best course of action based on the data given. Some simulations are computer-interactive games in which individuals or teams draw up marketing plans for an organization to determine such factors as the amount of resources to allocate for advertising, product design, selling, and sales effort. The participants make a variety of decisions, and then the computer tells them how well they did in relation to competing individuals or teams. Managers also have used simulations to diagnose organizational problems.[40] When properly done, a simulation can be a useful management development tool. However, the lack of realism can diminish the learning experience. Learning must be the focus, not just "playing the game."[41]

Sabbatical leave Paid time off the job to develop and rejuvenate oneself.

Sabbaticals and Leaves of Absence A **sabbatical leave** is paid time off the job to develop and rejuvenate oneself. Popular for many years in the academic world, sabbaticals have been adopted in the business community as well. About 19% of U.S. corporations offer sabbaticals.[42] Some firms give employees three to six months off with pay to work on "socially desirable" projects. Such projects have included leading training programs in urban ghettos, providing technical assistance in foreign countries, and participating in corporate volunteer programs to aid non-profit organizations.

Companies that offer sabbaticals speak well of the results. They say sabbaticals help prevent employee burnout, offer advantages in recruiting and retention and boost individual employee morale. One obvious disadvantage of paid sabbaticals is the cost. Also, the nature of the learning experience generally falls outside the control of the organization, leaving it somewhat to chance.[43]

Outdoor Training Many organizations, such as General Foods, Xerox, GE, Honeywell, Burger King, AMEX, and Sears, send executives and managers off to ordeals in the wilderness, called outdoor training. As a development tool, the rationale for these wilderness excursions that can last seven days or longer is as follows: For individuals, such experiences can increase self-confidence and help them re-evaluate personal goals and efforts. For individuals in work groups or

Figure 10-10	Advantages and Disadvantages of Major Development Approaches	
Job-Site Methods	**Advantage**	**Disadvantage**
• Coaching	• Natural and job-related	• Difficulty in finding good coaches
• Committee Assignments/Meetings	• Involve participants in critical processes	• Can be time waster
• Job Rotation	• Gives excellent overview of the organization	• Long start-up time
• Assistant-to Positions	• Provides exposure to an excellent manager	• Possible shortage of good assignments
• Online Development	• Flexible	• Niche not yet well defined
• Corporate Universities/ Development Centers	• Can combine academic and real world at work	• May be "university" in name only
• Learning Organization	• Perhaps the ideal mindset for development	• Essentially a theoretical, idealistic notion for most organizations
Off-Site Methods	**Advantage**	**Disadvantage**
• Classroom Courses and Degrees	• Familiar, accepted, status	• Does not always improve performance
• Human Relations Training	• Deals with important management skills	• Difficult to measure effectiveness
• Simulations	• Realism and integration	• Inappropriate "game playing"
• Sabbaticals	• Rejuvenating as well as developmental	• Expensive; employees may lose contact with job
• Outdoor Training	• Increases self-confidence and teamwork through physical challenges	• Not appropriate for all because of physical nature; dangerous

teams, shared risks and challenges outside the office environment can create a sense of teamwork. The challenges may include rock climbing in the California desert, whitewater rafting on a river, backpacking in the Rocky Mountains, handling a longboat off the coast of Maine, or others.

Survival-type management development courses may have more impact than many other management seminars. Companies must consider the inherent perils, however. Some participants have been unable to handle the physical and emotional challenges associated with rappelling down a cliff or climbing a 40-foot tower. The decision to sponsor such programs should depend on the personalities of the employees involved.

To be effective, a development approach must mesh with HR strategies to meet organizational goals. Figure 10-10 summarizes the major advantages and disadvantages of the various on-site and off-site approaches to development.

Management Development

Although development is important for all employees, it is essential for managers. Effective management development imparts the knowledge and judgment needed by managers. Without appropriate development, managers may lack the

capabilities to best deploy and manage resources (including employees) throughout the organization. Necessary capabilities often a focus of management development include leadership, dealing with change, coaching and advising subordinates, controlling operations, and providing performance feedback.

Former U.S. President Dwight D. Eisenhower said leadership is the "art of getting someone else to do something you want done because he wants to do it." An effective leader creates positive change and is important for an organization. But like all development, leadership may be difficult to teach to others.[44]

Experience plays a central role in management development. Indeed, experience often contributes more to the development of senior managers than classroom training does, because much of their experience occurs in varying circumstances on the job over time. Yet, despite a need for effective managers, finding such managers for middle-level jobs is often difficult. At the middle management level, some individuals refuse to take management jobs. "You're a backstop, caught in the middle between upper management and the workforce," a cost account manager (who quit management) noted. "I was told 50 hours a week was not enough and that I had to work my people harder. . . . The few dollars more were not worth the pain." Similarly, few companies seem to take the time to develop their own executive-level managers. Instead executives often are hired from the outside.

Figure 10-11 on the next page shows some lessons and features important in effectively developing both middle- and upper-level managers. Next, the most widely used management development methods are examined individually.

Managerial Modeling

A common adage in management development says that managers tend to manage as they were managed. In other words, managers learn by behavior modeling, or copying someone else's behavior. This tendency is not surprising, because a great deal of human behavior is learned by modeling. Children learn by modeling the behaviors of parents and older children. Management development efforts can take advantage of natural human behavior by matching young or developing managers with appropriate models and then reinforcing the desirable behaviors exhibited. Note that the modeling process involves more than straightforward imitation, or copying; it is considerably more complex. For example, one can learn what not to do by observing a model who does something wrong. Thus, exposure to both positive and negative models can benefit a new manager.

Management Coaching

Coaching combines observation with suggestions. Like modeling, it complements the natural way humans learn. A brief outline of good coaching pointers often includes the following:

- Explaining appropriate behavior
- Making clear why actions were taken
- Accurately stating observations
- Providing possible alternatives/suggestions
- Following up/reinforcing.

Figure 10-11 ▶ *Managerial Lessons and Job Experience*

Job Transitions Individuals forced to deal with entirely new jobs, problems, people, responsibilities, etc.	**Experiences** Starting or changing some major organizational feature, decision-making responsibility, influencing others without formal authority	**Obstacles** Bad job situation, difficult boss, demanding clients, unsupportive peers, negative economic circumstances, etc.

Necessary Lessons to Be Learned

• **Setting Agendas**	Developing technical/business knowledge, taking responsibility, setting goals
• **Handling Relationships**	Dealing successfully with people
• **Management Values**	Understanding successful management behavior
• **Personality Qualities**	Having the temperament necessary to deal with the chaos and ambiguity of executive life
• **Self-Awareness**	Understanding oneself and how one affects others

In the context of management development, coaching involves a relationship between two managers for a period of time as they perform their jobs. Effective coaching requires patience and good communication skills.

Mentoring

Mentoring is a relationship in which experienced managers aid individuals in the earlier stages of their careers. Such a relationship provides an environment for conveying technical, interpersonal, and organizational skills from the more-experienced to the less-experienced person. Not only does the inexperienced employee benefit, but the mentor may enjoy the challenge of sharing his or her wisdom.

However, mentoring is not without its problems. Young minority managers frequently report difficulty finding mentors. Also, men generally show less willingness than women to be mentors. Further, mentors who are dissatisfied with their jobs and those who teach a narrow or distorted view of events may not help a young manager's development. Fortunately, many managers have a series of advisors or mentors during their careers and may find advantages in learning from the different mentors. For example, the unique qualities of individual mentors may help less experienced managers identify key behaviors in management

WEST GROUP
A THOMSON COMPANY

Career Coaching
Describes the nature of employee career coaching by managers and supervisors.
Custom Search:
☑ ANALYSIS
Phrase: Career coaching discussion

Mentoring A relationship in which experienced managers aid individuals in the earlier stages of their careers.

Figure 10-12   **Stages in Mentoring Relationships**

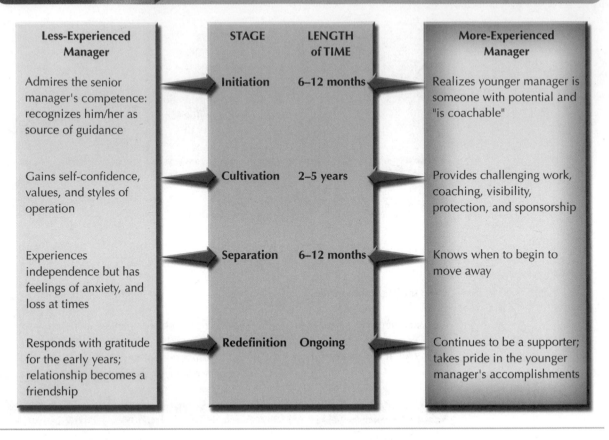

success and failure. Further, those being mentored may find previous mentors to be useful sources for networking.[45] Figure 10-12 describes the four stages in most successful mentoring relationships.

Women and Management Development

In virtually all countries in the world, the proportion of women holding management jobs is lower than the proportion of men holding such jobs. The term *glass ceiling* has been used to describe the situation in which women fail to progress into top management positions. Women are making slow but steady strides into management and the executive suite. Nationally, women hold 49% of managerial/professional positions and 12% of corporate officer positions, and those figures are higher in certain geographical regions.[46]

One approach to breaking through the glass ceiling is mentoring. For example, in some firms women with mentors move up more often than those without mentors. Most of the literature on women and mentoring, based on various narratives of successful women executives, suggests that breaking the glass ceiling requires developing political sophistication, building credibility, refining a management style, and shouldering responsibilities.[47] Research studies have found women generally to rate high in the skills needed for success where teamwork and partnering are important.[48]

Executive Education

Executives in an organization often face difficult jobs due to changing and unknown circumstances. "Churning" at the top of organizations and the stresses of executive jobs contribute to increased turnover in these positions.[49] In an effort to decrease turnover, some organizations are experimenting with a relatively recent phenomenon: special education for executives. This type of training supplements executive education traditionally offered by university business schools and includes strategy formulation, financial models, logistics, alliances, and global issues.[50]

For instance, recently Merck, the large drug company, developed a hybrid model that relies heavily on both the private sector and university input for executive education.[51] Other approaches range from sending executives to successful firms for a visit (to Disney for consumer service, for example) to hiring "executive coaches" who provide one-on-one input.[52]

Problems with Management Development Efforts

Development efforts are subject to certain common mistakes and problems. Most of the management development problems in the United States have resulted from inadequate HR planning and a lack of coordination of HR development efforts. Common problems include the following:

- Inadequate needs analysis
- Trying out fad programs or training methods
- Abdicating responsibility for development to HR staff alone
- Trying to substitute training for selection
- Lack of training among those who lead the development activities
- Using only "courses" as the road to development
- Encapsulated development

Encapsulated development Situation in which an individual learns new methods and ideas in a development course and returns to a work unit that is still bound by old attitudes and methods.

The last item requires some additional explanation. **Encapsulated development** occurs when an individual learns new methods and ideas in a development course and returns to a work unit that is still bound by old attitudes and methods. Therefore, the trainee cannot apply new ways to handle certain situations because of resistance from those having an investment in the *status quo*. The development was "encapsulated" in the classroom and essentially not used on the job.

Summary

- Career planning may focus on organizational needs, individual needs, or both.
- A person chooses a career based on interests, self-image, personality, social background, and other factors.
- A person's life is cyclical, as is his or her career. Putting the two together offers a useful perspective.
- Organizations increasingly are having to deal with individuals who have hit career plateaus.
- Technical employees sometimes may be able to follow dual-career ladders.
- Dual-career couples increasingly require relocation assistance for the partners of transferring employees.
- Development differs from training because it focuses on less tangible aspects of performance, such as attitudes and values.

- Successful development requires top management support and an understanding of the relationship of development to other HR activities.
- Assessment centers provide valid methods of assessing management talent and development needs.
- Succession planning is a process that identifies how key employees are to be replaced.
- On-the-job development methods include coaching, committee assignments, job rotation, and assistant-to positions.
- Off-the-job development methods include classroom courses, human relations training, simulations, sabbatical leaves, and outdoor training.
- Through mentoring and modeling, younger managers can acquire the skills and know-how necessary to be successful. Mentoring follows a four-stage progression in most cases.

Review and Discussion Questions

1. Discuss whether you would prefer organization-centered or individual-centered career planning.
2. List reasons why dual-career paths for professional and technical workers may grow in importance in the future.
3. What is HR development, and why is top management support for it so important?
4. Why have many large organizations used assessment centers?
5. You are the head of a government agency. What two methods of on-the-job development would you use with a promising supervisor? What two off-the-job methods would you use? Why?

Terms to Know

Using the Internet

Development of Management through Coaching

One of the senior managers at your firm has just returned from a management conference. While at the conference, he attended a seminar on management coaching. He has asked you, the HR Director, to put together a presentation for the next senior management meeting to see if management coaching should be considered in each of the firm's major divisions. You have read some research on coaching and believe it is a good concept. Use the Web site *http://www.venturecoach.com* to address the following key issues:

- Issues addressed by coaching
- Different types of coaching
- Benefits of coaching
- Coaching tools

Reverse Mentoring at GE

Lloyd Trotter faced facts: He did not know how to use the Internet. His boss, GE's Jack Welch, proposed a solution to that problem for older GE managers—get a mentor.

The problem is not unique to GE. Older employees in many companies feel uncomfortable with using the Internet. However, today's competitive business world demands that managers adapt to high-tech developments. Most businesses find that Web sites are essential and that the Internet can be used to assess the competition.

Like many companies, GE had used mentors before. This situation was different, however. Instead of the older mentor nurturing the younger protege, in this case the younger person played the mentor role—a sort of reverse mentor. In the pro-

gram GE managers regularly meet with their mentors to critique both their own competitors' Web sites and discuss articles and books assigned as homework. Mr. Trotter noted, "We can share our thoughts and get them on the table and work our way through them." His mentor noted that the sessions made her more comfortable interacting with an executive. Her relationship with Mr. Trotter also exposed her to the skills needed to manage a large operation.[53]

Questions

1. What potential pitfalls might this type of program encounter?
2. Look at the stages in a mentoring relationship and apply them to this situation.

Notes

1. "Career Evolution," *The Economist,* January 29, 2000, 89–92; Carol Hymowitz, "Managers Often Miss the Promising Talent on their Own Staffs," *The Wall Street Journal,* May 9, 2000, B1; Michelle Conlin, "Working Life," *Business Week,* April 24, 2000, 99 104; and Robert Taylor, "Reports of the Career's Death Are Exaggerated," *Financial Times,* May 19, 2000, 11.
2. Scott Thurm, "No Exit Strategies," *The Wall Street Journal,* February 6, 2001, 1A.
3. Adapted from Raymond A. Noe, *Employee Training and Development* (Boston: Irwin/McGraw Hill, 1999), 288–289.
4. John Nunn, "Career Planning: Key to Employee Retention," *Journal of Property Management,* September/October 2000, 20–21.
5. Susan Garland, "When Your Job Doesn't Fit," *Business Week,* October 9, 2000, 206–210.
6. Dave Patel, "Rearranging the Life Cycle," *HR Magazine,* January 2002, 104.

7. Ellen E. Kossek and Richard N. Block, *Managing Human Resources in the 21st Century* (Cincinnati: Thompson Learning, 2000), 24.10.
8. Martin M. Greller and Patricia Simpson, "In Search of Late Career: A Review of Contemporary Social Science Research Applicable to the Understanding of Late Career," *Human Resource Management Review,* 3 (1999), 309–347.
9. "Plateaued Employees," *Bulletin to Management,* March 30, 2000, 103.
10. Carol Hymowitz, "Midlife Career Swaps: An Investment Banker Switches to Preaching," *The Wall Street Journal,* June 12, 2001, B1.
11. Carol Hymowitz, "What Happens When Your Valued Employee Makes a Bad Manager," *The Wall Street Journal,* January 23, 2001, B1.
12. Hal Lancaster, "Managing Your Career," *The Wall Street Journal,* May 15, 1999, B1.
13. Matt Murray, "The Mid-Career Crisis: Am I in This Business to Become a Manager?" *The Wall Street Journal,* September 27, 2000, B1.

14. Sue Shellenbarger, "Many Employers Falter in Helping Families Adjust to Job Transfers," *The Wall Street Journal,* September 27, 2000, B1.
15. Scott E. Seibert, et al., "A Social Capital Theory of Career Success," *The Academy of Management Journal,* 44 (2001), 219–237.
16. Wayne F. Cascio, *Costing Human Resources,* 4th ed. (Cincinnati: South-Western College Publishing, 2000).
17. Belle Wise, "What You Need to Know for Your Tech Career to Grow," *USA Today,* June 26, 2000, 21A.
18. Kevin Sweeney, "Top of the Class," *Employee Benefit News,* March 2001, 33–35; and Harley Frazis, "Correlates of Training," *Industrial and Labor Relations Review,* 53 (2000), 443.
19. Roberta L. Duyff, "The Value of Lifelong Learning: Key Elements in Professional Career Development," *Journal of the American Dietetic Association,* May 1999, 538.
20. Claire Ansberry, "The Gray Team," *The Wall Street Journal,* February 5, 2001, 1A.

21. Dave Marcotte, "Continuing Education, Job Training and the Growth of Earnings," *Industrial and Labor Relations Review,* 53 (2000), 602.

22. "The Boom," *Business Week,* February 14, 2000, 103.

23. Adopted from Scott McCartney, "If the Pitcher Lifts His Pinkie, Odds Are He's a Texas Ranger," *The Wall Street Journal,* March 2, 1998, A1; and Erin While, "Lessons in Shaking Hands, Twirling Spaghetti Await Some Workers," *The Wall Street Journal,* December 7, 1999, B1.

24. Albert R. Karr, "Boot Camp for Job-Hoppers," *The Wall Street Journal,* July 11, 2000, B1; and Brenda Sunoo, "The Hunt for Public Sector IT," *Workforce,* April 2000, 62–70.

25. "Project Leadership," *Human Resource Executive,* September 2000, A16.

26. Al Jones, "Finally a Test for Common Sense," *Training,* November 2000, 30.

27. Based on Albert A. Cannella Jr. and Wei Shen, "So Close and Yet So Far: Promotion vs. Exit for CEO Heirs Apparent," *Academy of Management Journal,* 44 (2001), 252–270.

28. Scott T. Fleischmann, "Succession Management for the Entire Organization," *Employment Relations Today,* Summer 2000, 53–62.

29. "Biggest Problem Facing Small Business? Lack of Succession Planning," *WBHome,* available at www.woodenbenson.com, 2001.

30. For details on developing succession plans, see William J. Rothwell, *Effective Succession Planning* (New York: AMACOM, 2000).

31. Kevin Dobbs, "Training on the Fly," *Sales and Marketing Management,* November 2000, 92.

32. Charles A. O'Reilly III and Jeffrey Pfeffer, "Why Not Cut Training and Development Dollars?" *Workforce,* December 5, 2000, 1–4.

33. Vikas Bajal, "Job Rotations Help Tech Work Force," *Omaha World Herald,* June 18, 2000, 1G.

34. Ruth Palombo Gardner, "Howard Gardner Talks About Technology," *Training and Development,* September 2000, 52.

35. Samuel Greengard, "Going the Distance," *Workforce,* June 2000, 22.

36. Ross Greene and Rick Taylor, "Financial Institutions Look to the Web to Address Training Needs," *Small Business Banker,* November 2000, 30.

37. "Learning Curves for Companies," *Financial Times,* August 2, 1999, 8.

38. Peggy Simonsen, "Keeping Talented Employees Developing," *The Right Communique,* Second Quarter 2000, 3.

39. David Wessel, "How Loyalty Comes by Degrees," *The Wall Street Journal,* May 17, 2001, 1A.

40. George Pfeil, et al., "Visteon's Sterling Plant Uses Simulation-Based Decision Support," *Interfaces,* January/February 2000, 115–133.

41. Pat Rovzer, "May I Help You?" *HR Magazine,* June 1, 2000, 140–146.

42. Toddi Garner, "The Pause that Refreshes," *Business Week,* November 19, 2001, 138; and "Companies Gain Beneficial By-Products from Sabbaticals," *Bulletin to Management,* December 14, 2000, 399.

43. Vicky Uhland, "Sabbatical Is Icing on Cake," *The Denver Rocky Mountain News,* August 20, 2000, J1.

44. Stephanie Overman, "Lackluster Leadership Development Hurts Corporate Performance," *HR News,* December 2001, 9.

45. Monica C. Higgins and Kathy E. Fram, "Reconceptualizing Mentoring at Work: A Developmental Network Perspective," *Academy of Management Review,* 26 (2001), 264.

46. "Women in Management," *Omaha World Herald,* December 3, 2000, 1G.

47. Carol Hymowitz, "In Turbulent Climate, Pioneering Women Face Special Scrutiny," *The Wall Street Journal,* March 3, 2001, B1.

48. Pallavi Gogoi, "As Leaders, Women Rule," *Business Week,* November 20, 2000, 75.

49. "Churning at the Top," *The Economist,* March 17, 2001, 67.

50. Tom Starner, "The Winds of Change," *Human Resource Executive,* December 2001, A2–A5.

51. Louise Axon, "The Private Sector Advantage," *Human Resource Executive,* June 2, 2000, A10.

52. E. DeLisser, "More Entrepreneurs Take Help of Executive Coaches," *The Wall Street Journal,* September 5, 2000, B2.

53. Adapted from Matt Murray, "GE Mentoring Program Turns Underlings into Teachers of the Web," *The Wall Street Journal,* February 15, 2000, B1.

CHAPTER 11

Performance Management and Appraisal

After you have read this chapter, you should be able to:

- Distinguish between job criteria and performance standards.

- Identify the two major uses of performance appraisal.

- Provide examples of several rater errors.

- Describe both the advantages and disadvantages of multisource (360°) appraisals.

- Identify the nature of behavioral approaches to performance appraisal and management by objectives (MBO).

- Discuss several concerns about appraisal feedback interviews.

- Identify the characteristics of a legal and effective performance appraisal system.

Grading on the Curve

"Grading on the Curve" is a phrase college students have all heard. It usually means grades will be *raised* by a certain amount in some difficult classes or if the professor believes grades are "too low." The real concept of "fitting data points to a curve," however, does not necessarily mean higher grades, but rather that each grade level will contain a predetermined percentage: for example, 10% A's, 20% B's, 40% C's, 20% D's, and 10% F's.

Also known as a "forced distribution," the concept is seen in the way managers are required to rate their employees in some firms. Several years ago at Ford Motor Company, 10% of employees got A's, 80% B's, and 10% C's. The lowest grade in the Ford system was a C. If an employee got two in a row, the person's days were numbered. General Electric divides employees into top 20%, middle 70%, and bottom 10%, and there *has to be* 10% rated on the bottom. Another firm used six categories labeled Superior (5%), Excellent (30%), Strong (30%), Satisfactory (20%), and Needs Improvement and "Issues" combined (15%). Cisco Systems and Hewlett-Packard also use forced distributions, which figure into

decisions about layoffs. In fact, an estimated 205 of the *Fortune* 500 companies use such forced ratings or have become tougher with their performance appraisal systems.

Force-fitting a certain percentage into each category is justified for several reasons. These systems require managers to make the tough calls, because if managers rate everyone too high, employees do not receive honest feedback to improve themselves. Companies really do need to know who are high performers and who are low performers for determining promotions and in case layoffs should become necessary. Jack Welch, former CEO of General Electric said, "A company that bets its future on its people must remove the lower 10% and keep removing it every year—always raising the bar of performance and increasing the quality of its workforce."

However, some real problems exist with the forced rating system. One is that such a system frequently compares people against each other, rather than against a standard of job performance. The best person in a poor group might not be as good as

the worst person in an outstanding group. But supervisors trying to fill the percentages may end up giving employees subjective ratings.

Further, trying to distinguish ratings for the majority of employees in the middle is almost impossible. To accurately assign people to grades of A, B, or C or to category 3 or 4 on a 5-point scale may be unrealistic. Also, some elements of performance are difficult to measure objectively—for example "career potential," "teamwork," and "motivation." Finally, (although there are more arguments against forced distribution) a single grade tends to blur the *range* of talents and shortcomings within any employee.

The result of this increased use of forced distribution has been a rash of lawsuits. Suits filed on behalf of older workers, African Americans, and women all allege unfairness in the system. In fact, such a lawsuit caused Ford to stop the "quota system" that assigns ratings in its performance appraisal systems for managers. Nevertheless, one consultant notes, "Companies *do* need something when making pay decisions and downsizing decisions."[1]

> The best person in a poor group might not be as good as the worst person in an outstanding group.

"Maximizing performance is a priority for most organizations today."

—**Bob Cardy**

Performance management system Processes used to identify, encourage, measure, evaluate, improve, and reward employee performance.

All employers want employees who perform their jobs well. However, an effective performance management system increases the likelihood that such performance will occur.[2] A **performance management system** consists of the processes used to identify, encourage, measure, evaluate, improve, and reward employee performance. As shown in Figure 11-1, performance management links organizational strategy to results. The figure lists common performance management practices and outcomes in the strategy-results loop. As identified by HR professionals, a performance management system should do the following:[3]

- Provide information to employees about their performance.
- Clarify what the organization expects.
- Identify development needs.
- Document performance for personnel records.

Figure 11-1 ▶ **Linkage Between Strategy, Outcomes, and Organizational Results**

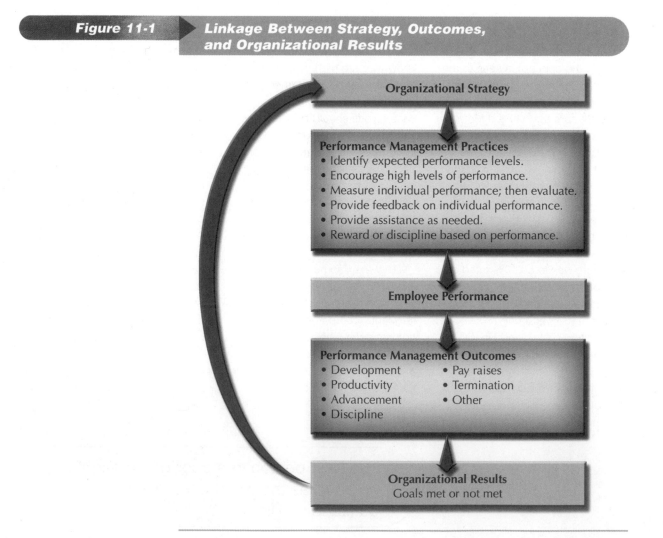

Organizational Strategy

Performance Management Practices
- Identify expected performance levels.
- Encourage high levels of performance.
- Measure individual performance; then evaluate.
- Provide feedback on individual performance.
- Provide assistance as needed.
- Reward or discipline based on performance.

Employee Performance

Performance Management Outcomes
- Development
- Productivity
- Advancement
- Discipline
- Pay raises
- Termination
- Other

Organizational Results
Goals met or not met

Even well-intentioned employees do not always know what is expected or how to improve their performances, which makes some kind of performance management system necessary. Further, if dismissal of an employee becomes necessary, employers risk a negative legal outcome if they cannot show evidence that the employee has been advised of his or her performance problems.

Identifying and Measuring Employee Performance

Performance What an employee does or does not do.

Performance is essentially what an employee does or does not do. Employee performance common to most jobs includes the following elements:

- Quantity of output
- Quality of output
- Timeliness of output
- Presence at work
- Cooperativeness

Job criteria Important elements in a given job.

Other dimensions of performance beyond these general ones apply to various jobs. Specific **job criteria** or dimensions of job performance identify the most important elements in a given job. For example, a college professor's job might include the job criteria of teaching, research, and service. Job criteria are the most important factors people do in their jobs because they define what the organization pays an employee to do; therefore, the performance of individuals on job criteria should be measured and compared against standards, and then the results communicated to the employee.

Most jobs have more than one job criterion or dimension. For example, a baseball outfielder's job criteria might include home runs, batting average, fielding percentage, and on-base performance, to name a few. In sports and many other jobs, multiple job criteria are the rule rather than the exception. Often a given individual might demonstrate better performance on some job criteria than others. Also, some criteria might be more important than others to the organization. Weights can be used to show the relative importance of several job criteria in one job. For example, in a management job at a company that values employee development, that factor might carry more weight than other performance criteria:

Management Job Criteria at Sample Firm	Weight
Employee development	*40%*
Revenue increase	*35%*
Cost control	*25%*
Total Management Performance	*100%*

Types of Performance Information

Managers receive three different types of information about how employees are performing their jobs. *Trait-based* information identifies a subjective character trait of the employee—such as attitude, initiative, or creativity—and may have

little to do with a specific job. Traits tend to be ambiguous, and court decisions generally have held that performance appraisals based on traits such as "adapt-ability" and "general demeanor" are too vague to use when making performance-based HR decisions.

Behavior-based information focuses on specific behaviors that lead to job success. For a salesperson, the behavior of "verbal persuasion" can be observed and used as information on performance. Although more difficult to identify, behavioral information clearly specifies the behaviors management wants to see. A potential problem arises when any of several behaviors can lead to successful performance in a given situation. For example, identifying successful "verbal persuasion" for a salesperson might be difficult because the approach used by one salesperson may not be successful when used by another.

Results-based information considers employee accomplishments. For jobs in which measurement is easy and obvious, a results-based approach works well. However, that which is measured, tends to be emphasized. But this emphasis may leave out equally important but unmeasurable parts of the job. For example, a car sales representative who gets paid *only* for sales may be unwilling to do paperwork or other work not directly related to selling cars. Further, ethical or even legal issues may arise when only results are emphasized and not how the results were achieved.

Relevance of Performance Criteria

Measuring performance requires the use of relevant criteria that focus on the most important aspects of employees' jobs.[4] For example, measuring customer service representatives in an insurance claims center on their "attitude" may be less relevant than measuring the number of calls handled properly. This example stresses that the most important job criteria should be identified and linked to the employees' job descriptions.

Potential Performance Criteria Problems

Performance measures that leave out some important job duties are considered *deficient.* For example, when measuring the performance of an employment interviewer, if only the number of applicants hired and not the quality of those hired is evaluated, performance measurement is likely to be deficient. On the other hand, including some irrelevant criteria *contaminates* the measure. An example of a contaminated criterion might be "appearance" for a telemarketing sales representative whom customers never see. Managers need to guard against using deficient or contaminated criteria in measuring performance.[5]

Performance measures also can be thought of as objective or subjective. *Objective* measures can be directly measured or counted—for example, the number of cars sold or the number of invoices processed. *Subjective* measures require judgment on the part of the evaluator and are more difficult to measure. One example of a subjective measure is a supervisor's ratings of an employee's "attitude" which cannot be seen directly. Unlike subjective measures, objective measures tend to be more narrowly focused, which sometimes leads to them being inadequately defined. However, subjective measures may be prone to contamination or other random errors. Neither is a panacea, and both objective and subjective measures should be used carefully.[6]

Performance Standards

Performance standards
Expected levels of
performance.

To know that an employee produces 10 "photons" per day does not provide a complete basis for judging employee performance as satisfactory or not. A standard against which to compare the information is necessary. Maybe 15 photons is considered a sufficient day's work. **Performance standards** define the expected levels of performance, and are "benchmarks," or "goals," or "targets"—depending on the approach taken. Realistic, measurable, clearly understood performance standards benefit both organizations and employees. In a sense, performance standards define what satisfactory job performance is. And they need to be established *before* the work is performed. Well-defined standards ensure that everyone involved knows the levels of accomplishment expected.

Both numerical and non-numerical standards can be established. Sales quotas and production output standards are familiar numerical performance standards. A standard of performance can also be based on non-numerical criteria. Consider the following performance standards as illustrating both types.

Performance Standards
Discusses what to
consider when identifying
performance standards.
Custom Search:
☑ ANALYSIS
Phrase: Developing
standards

> *Job Criterion.* Keep current on supplier technology.
> *Performance Standards:* 1. Every four months, invite suppliers to make presentation of newest technology. 2. Visit supplier plants twice per year. 3. Attend trade shows quarterly.
> ------
> *Job Criterion.* Do price or cost analysis as appropriate.
> *Performance Standard:* Performance is acceptable when employee follows all requirements of the procedure "Price and Cost Analysis."

How well employees meet established standards is often expressed as either numerical (5, 4, 3, 2, 1) or verbal ratings, for example, "outstanding" or "unsatisfactory." If more than one person is involved in the rating, they may find it difficult to agree on the exact level of performance achieved relative to the standard. Figure 11-2 defines the terms one company uses in evaluating employee performance. Notice that each level specifies performance standards, rather than numbers, in order to minimize variation in interpretations of the standards.

Figure 11-2	Terms Defining Standards at One Company
5	*Outstanding. The person is so successful at this job criterion that special note should be made. Compared with the usual standards and the rest of the department, this performance ranks in the top 10%.*
4	*Very Good. Performance at this level is a better-than-average performance for the unit, given the common standards and unit results.*
3	*Satisfactory. Performance is at or above the minimum standards. This level of performance is what one would expect from most experienced, competent employees.*
2	*Marginal. Performance is somewhat below the minimum-level standard on this job dimension. However, potential to improve the rating within a reasonable time frame is evident.*
1	*Unsatisfactory. Performance on this item in the job is well below standard. Whether the person can improve to meet minimum standards is questionable.*

The following announcement in the *European Report* indicates changes for upper-level government employees in the EU:

"Staff from the level of Director upwards have before now never had the opportunity of having their performance regularly appraised. It will now become possible to set more objective targets for the senior level of the commission hierarchy and assess their performance at least every second year. Human resource utilization and financial management will be considered.

Obviously, these appraisals will play an important role in determining the career prospects of senior-level staff. Positive assessments will affect future assignments and negative assessments may lead to launching a formal procedure for dealing with professional incompetence.

The commission hopes this innovation will also motivate other staff members who are expected to respond well in a professional situation."[7]

Someone external to a given job, such as a supervisor or a quality control inspector, frequently sets the standards for the job. However, standards can be written effectively by employees as well. Experienced employees usually know what constitutes satisfactory performance of tasks in their job descriptions, and so do their supervisors. Therefore, these individuals often can participate in setting standards with their managers.

Uses of Performance Appraisal

Performance appraisal
The process of evaluating how well employees perform their jobs when compared to a set of standards, and then communicating that information to employees.

Performance appraisal is the process of evaluating how well employees perform their jobs when compared to a set of standards, and then communicating that information to those employees. Performance appraisal also is called *employee rating, employee evaluation, performance review, performance evaluation,* and *results appraisal.*

Performance appraisal is widely used for administering wages and salaries, giving performance feedback, and identifying individual employee strengths and weaknesses. Most U.S. employers use performance appraisal systems for office, professional, technical, supervisory, middle management, and nonunion production workers. Globally, these systems provide benefits in a variety of work situations as illustrated in the HR Perspective about the European Union. However, despite their widespread use, not everyone enthusiastically endorses performance appraisals. Criticisms revolve around the way they are done and the results. Those criticisms include:

- With today's emphasis on teamwork, appraisals focus too much on the individual and do too little to develop employees to perform better.[8]
- Most employees who receive reviews and supervisors who give them generally rate the process a resounding failure.[9]
- Most appraisals are inconsistent, short-term oriented, subjective, and valuable only for identifying employees performing extremely well or poorly.[10]

Poorly done performance appraisals lead to disappointing results for all concerned. But to have no formal performance appraisal done may limit an employer's options regarding discipline and dismissal. Performance appraisals

Figure 11-3 ▶ Conflicting Roles for Performance Appraisal

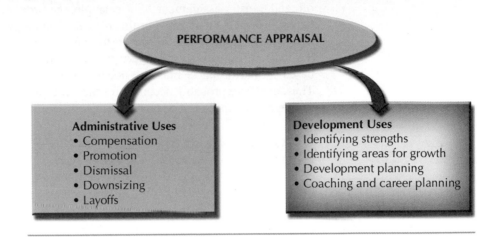

PERFORMANCE APPRAISAL

Administrative Uses
- Compensation
- Promotion
- Dismissal
- Downsizing
- Layoffs

Development Uses
- Identifying strengths
- Identifying areas for growth
- Development planning
- Coaching and career planning

can answer questions about whether the employer acted fairly or how the employer actually knew that the employee's performance did not meet standards.[11] Even though an employer technically may not need a reason to terminate an employee, as a practical matter, appraisals can provide justification for such actions should they become necessary. Employees also benefit if appraisals help them know where they need to improve, even after a positive appraisal.[12]

Organizations generally use performance appraisals in two potentially conflicting roles. One role is to measure performance for the purpose of making pay or other administrative decisions about employees. Promotions or terminations might hinge on these ratings, often creating stress for managers doing the appraisals. The other role focuses on the development of individuals. In that role, the manager acts more as counselor than as judge, which may change the atmosphere of the relationship. The developmental type of performance appraisal emphasizes identifying potential and planning employees' growth opportunities and direction. Figure 11-3 shows the two potentially conflicting roles for performance appraisal.

Administrative Uses

A performance appraisal system is often the link between rewards employees hope to receive and their productivity. The linkage can be thought of as follows:

Productivity → Performance appraisal → Rewards

Performance-based compensation affirms the idea that pay raises should be given for performance accomplishments rather than for seniority. In this system, the manager historically has been the evaluator of a subordinate's performance and also the one who makes compensation recommendations for the employee. If any part of the appraisal process fails, the better performing employees do not receive larger pay increases, resulting in perceived inequity in compensation.

Many U.S. workers say they see little connection between their efforts and the size of their paychecks. However, the use of performance appraisal to determine pay is common. Employees are especially interested in other administrative uses of performance appraisal, such as decisions about promotion, termination, lay-off, and transfer assignments. For example, the order of layoffs can be justified by performance appraisals. For this reason, if an employer claims that the decision was performance-based, the performance appraisals must document clearly the differences in employee performance. Similarly, promotion or demotion based on performance must be documented through performance appraisals. Thus, necessity probably accounts for the widespread administrative use of performance appraisals.

Development Uses

Performance appraisal can be a primary source of information and feedback for employees, which is often key to their future development. In the process of identifying employee strengths, weaknesses, potentials, and training needs through performance appraisal feedback, supervisors can inform employees about their progress, discuss what areas they need to develop, and identify development plans. The manager's role in such a situation parallels that of a coach. A coach rewards good performance with recognition, explains what improvement is necessary, and shows employees how to improve. After all, people do not always know where and how to improve, and managers should not expect improvement if they are unwilling to explain where and how improvement can occur.

The purpose of developmental feedback is to change or reinforce individual behavior, rather than to compare individuals—as in the case of administrative uses of performance appraisal. Positive reinforcement for desired behaviors contributes to both individual and organizational development.[13] The development function of performance appraisal also can identify areas in which the employee might wish to grow. For example, in a performance appraisal interview targeted exclusively to development, an employee found out that the only factor keeping her from being considered for a management job in her firm was a working knowledge of cost accounting. Her supervisor suggested that she consider taking such a course at night at the local college.

The use of teams provides a different set of circumstances for developmental appraisal. The manager may not see all of the employee's work, but team members do. Teams *can* provide developmental feedback. However, it is still an open question whether teams can handle administrative appraisals. When teams are allowed to design appraisal systems, they tend to "get rid of judgment," and avoid differential rewards. Perhaps, then, group appraisal is best suited to developmental purposes.

Informal vs. Systematic Appraisal

Performance appraisal can occur in two ways: informally or systematically. A supervisor conducts *informal appraisal* whenever necessary. The day-to-day working relationship between a manager and an employee offers an opportunity for the employee's performance to be evaluated.[14] A manager communicates this evaluation through conversation on the job, over coffee, or by on-the-spot examination of a particular piece of work. Informal appraisal is especially appropriate when time is an issue, because delays in giving feedback weaken its motivational effect. Frequent informal feedback to employees also can prevent surprises during a formal evaluation. However, informal appraisal can become *too* informal. For example, a senior executive at a large firm so dreaded face-to-face evaluations that he recently delivered one manager's review while both sat in adjoining stalls in the men's room. The boss told the startled subordinate: "I haven't had a chance to give you a performance appraisal this year. Your bonus is going to be 20%. I am really happy with your performance."

A *systematic appraisal* is used when the contact between manager and employee is formal, and a system is in place to report managerial impressions and observations on employee performance. One survey found that almost 90% of employers have a formal performance management system or process.[15] Although informal appraisal is useful, and even necessary, it should not take the place of formal appraisal. Even some Chief Executive Officers receive, and indeed often want, formal appraisal of their performance by Boards of Directors.

Appraisal Responsibilities

The appraisal process can benefit both the organization and the individuals involved, if done properly. As Figure 11-4 shows, the HR unit typically designs a performance appraisal system. The manager then appraises employees using the appraisal system. During development of the formal appraisal system, managers usually offer input as to how the final system will work.

It is important for managers to understand appraisal as *their* responsibility. Through this process, good employees can be developed to be even better, and poor employees' performances are improved or they are removed from the organization.[16] Performance appraisal is not simply an HR requirement; it must also be a management process, because guiding employees' performance is probably the most important responsibility of managers.[17] Although HR does not drive performance management, it assists the individual managers who do.

Timing of Appraisals Most companies require managers to conduct appraisals once or twice a year, most often annually. New employees commonly receive an appraisal 60–90 days after employment, again at six months, and annually thereafter. "Probationary employees" who are new and in a trial period should be informally evaluated often—perhaps weekly for the first month and

Figure 11-4	Typical Division of HR Responsibilities: Performance Appraisal

HR Unit	Managers
• *Designs and maintains formal system*	• *Typically rate performance of employees*
• *Trains raters*	• *Prepare formal appraisal documents*
• *Tracks timely receipt of appraisals*	• *Review appraisals with employees*
• *Reviews completed appraisals for consistency*	• *Identify development areas*

monthly thereafter until the end of the introductory period. After that, annual reviews may be sufficient. Some high-technology employers promise accelerated appraisals—every six months instead of each year—so that employees receive more frequent raises. These companies report a subsequent reduction in turnover among these turnover-prone employees because more feedback has been given.

Systematic appraisals feature a regular time interval, which distinguishes them from informal appraisals. Both employees and managers know that performance will be reviewed on a regular basis, and they can plan for performance discussions. Informal appraisals can be conducted whenever a manager feels they are desirable.[18]

Appraisals and Pay Discussions Many experts argue that performance appraisals and pay discussions should be separate. Two major reasons support this view. One is that employees often focus more on the pay amount received than on the appraisal feedback that identifies what they have done well or need to improve. Second, sometimes managers manipulate performance appraisal ratings to justify the desired pay treatment they wish to give specific individuals.

Who Conducts Appraisals?

Performance appraisal can be conducted by anyone familiar with the performance of individual employees. Possibilities include the following:

- Supervisors who rate their employees
- Employees who rate their superiors
- Team members who rate each other
- Outside sources
- Employees' self-appraisal
- Multisource (360° feedback) appraisal

The rating of employees by their supervisors or managers is the most common method. The immediate superior has the main responsibility for appraisals in most organizations, although often the supervisor's boss may review and approve the appraisals. The growing use of teams and a concern with customer input contribute to the two fast-growing sources of appraisal information: team members and sources outside the organization. Multisource appraisal (or 360° feedback) combines numerous methods and has grown in usage recently.

Dilbert

Figure 11-5 **Traditional Performance Appraisal: Logic and Process**

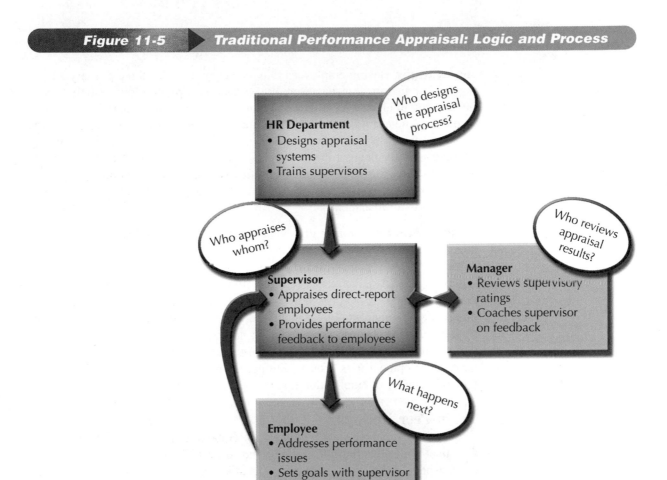

Supervisory Rating of Subordinates

Traditional rating of employees by supervisors is based on the assumption that the immediate supervisor is the person most qualified to evaluate the employee's performance realistically and fairly. Toward this end, some supervisors keep performance logs noting their employees' accomplishments. These logs provide specific examples to use when rating performance. Figure 11-5 shows the traditional review process by which supervisors conduct performance appraisals on employees.

Employee Rating of Managers

A number of organizations today ask employees or group members to rate the performance of supervisors and managers. A prime example of this type of rating takes place in colleges and universities, where students evaluate the performance of professors in the classroom. Industry also uses employee ratings for management development purposes.

An even newer practice evaluates corporate boards of directors. The fundamental responsibility of the board to establish goals and direct their accomplishment justifies evaluation of the performance of board members. In some instances, executives evaluate boards of directors, but board self-review or outside evaluation can be used as well.

Advantages Having employees rate managers provides three primary advantages. First, in critical manager-employee relationships, employee ratings can be quite useful in identifying competent managers. The rating of leaders by combat soldiers is one example. Second, this type of rating program can help make the manager more responsive to employees, though this advantage can quickly become a disadvantage if the manager focuses on being "nice" rather than managing. Nice people without other qualifications may not be good managers in many situations. Finally, employee appraisals can contribute to career development efforts for managers.

Disadvantages A major disadvantage of receiving employee ratings is the negative reaction many superiors have to being evaluated by employees. The "proper" nature of manager-employee relations may be violated by workers rating managers. Also, the fear of reprisals may be too great for employees to give realistic ratings. This approach may prompt workers to rate their managers only on the way the managers treat them and not on critical job requirements. Consequently, the problems associated with having employees rate managers limit the usefulness of this appraisal approach to certain situations, except for managerial development uses. The traditional nature of most organizations restricts the applicability of employee rating to self-improvement purposes.

Team/Peer Ratings

The use of employee peers and team members as raters is another type of appraisal with potential both to help and to hurt. For example, when a group of salespeople meets as a committee to talk about one another's ratings, they may share ideas that could be used to improve the performance of lower-rated individuals. Alternatively, the criticisms could negatively affect future work relationships.

Team and peer ratings are especially useful when supervisors do not have the opportunity to observe each employee's performance, but other work group members do. However, some contend that any performance appraisal, including team/peer ratings, can affect teamwork and participative management efforts negatively.

Team Appraisal and Teamwork Total quality management (TQM) and other participative management approaches emphasize teamwork and team performance rather than individual performance. Effectiveness results from many factors rather than just from individual efforts. In this view, performance appraisals of individuals may hinder the development of teamwork. But even if formal appraisals may seem inappropriate, informal appraisals by peers or team leaders still may occur at times in order to help those whose performance is deficient.

Team Rating Difficulties Although team members have good information on one another's performance, they may not choose to share it. They may unfairly attack or "go easy" to spare feelings. Some organizations attempt to overcome such problems by using anonymous appraisals and/or having a consultant or manager interpret team/peer ratings. However, some evidence indicates that using outsiders to facilitate the rating process does not necessarily result in perceptions of the system being seen as more fair by those being rated. Despite the problems, team/peer performance ratings are probably inevitable, especially where work teams are used extensively.

Self-Ratings

Self-appraisal works in certain situations. As a self-development tool, it forces employees to think about their strengths and weaknesses and set goals for improvement. Employees working in isolation or possessing unique skills may be the only ones qualified to rate themselves. However, employees may not rate themselves as supervisors would rate them; they may use quite different standards. The research is mixed as to whether people tend to be more lenient or more demanding when rating themselves. Still, employee self-ratings can be a valuable and credible source of performance information.[19]

Outside Raters

Rating also may be done by outsiders who may be called in to conduct performance reviews. Examples include a review team evaluating a college president or a panel of division managers evaluating a person's potential for advancement in an organization. However, the outsiders may not know the important demands within the organization.

The customers or clients of an organization are obvious sources for outside appraisals. For salespeople and other service jobs, customers may provide very useful input on the performance behaviors of salespeople. One firm measures customer service satisfaction to determine bonuses for top marketing executives.

Multisource Rating/360° Feedback

Multisource rating, or 360° feedback, has grown in popularity. Figure 11-6 shows graphically some of the parties who may be involved in 360° feedback.

360-Degree Feedback
Discusses design and use of 360° feedback and concerns with it.
Custom Search:
☑ ANALYSIS
Phrase: 360-degree feedback

Figure 11-6 ▶ Multisource Appraisal

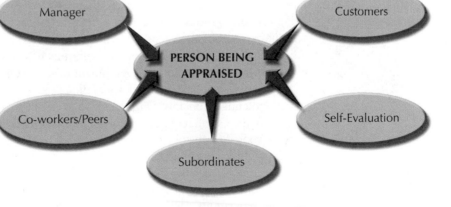

Managing 360° Without Paper

Intermountain Health Care (IMHC), a health-care provider in Salt Lake City, used a Web-based approach to develop a 360° feedback program. The firm's internally developed system can be customized to the person being rated, while at the same time eliminating much of the paperwork and solving data entry problems.

For years, IMHC supervisors evaluated employees in a traditional way. However, it became clear that due to the nature of the work, supervisors were not able to observe workers in enough situations to evaluate them accurately. Therefore, management decided to assemble a team consisting of internal customers, co-workers, and direct reports to appraise employees.

Although this approach proved sound, given the nature of the jobs, it created a serious workflow problem: how to collect and computer-enter each employee's evaluations from as many as 10 other employees of the evaluation team. IMHC tried scanning the paper evaluations into a database, but that solution did not eliminate the paper problem.

The new Web-based system allows employees to select from a database those questions that apply to them and their jobs. For example, a nurse might select different questions than someone in marketing. Once the questions are selected, the supervisor approves them. Then the questions are forwarded via e-mail to a "team" of other evaluators agreed to by the employee and supervisor. Then, each team member e-mails his or her response. The employee and supervisor also answer the evaluation questions. The surveys, kept anonymous, are compiled and returned to both the employee and supervisor, who then meet and discuss the results.[20]

Multisource feedback recognizes that the manager is no longer the sole source of performance appraisal information. (See e-HR: Managing 360° Without Paper.) Instead, various colleagues and constituencies supply feedback about the employee to the manager, thus allowing the manager to obtain input from a variety of sources. However, the manager remains a focal point both to receive the feedback initially and to engage in appropriate follow-up, even in a multisource system. Thus, the manager's perception of an employee's performance still drives the process.

The research on 360° feedback is relatively recent and not large in volume, but the research done thus far suggests that there often is limited agreement among rating sources. It should be remembered that the purpose of 360° feedback is *not* to increase reliability by soliciting like-minded views, but rather to capture the various evaluations of the individual employee's different roles. Although participants generally view multisource feedback as useful, they identify follow-up on the development activities based on the feedback as the most critical factor in the future development of a person.

When using 360° feedback for administrative purposes, managers must anticipate potential problems. Differences among raters can present a challenge, especially in the use of 360° ratings for discipline or pay decisions. Bias can just as easily be rooted in customers, subordinates, and peers as in a boss, and their lack of accountability can affect the ratings.[21] Even though multisource approaches to performance appraisal offer possible solutions to the well-documented dissatisfaction with today's legally necessary administrative performance appraisal, a number of questions arise as multisource appraisals become more common. One concern addresses whether 360° appraisals improve the process or simply multiply the number of problems by the total number of raters. Also, some wonder whether multisource appraisals really create better decisions that offset the additional time and investment required.[22] These issues appear to be less threatening when the 360° feedback is used *only for development.* But those concerns may effectively eliminate multisource appraisals as an administrative tool in many situations.

Methods for Appraising Performance

Performance can be appraised by a number of methods. In Figure 11-7, the various methods are categorized into four groups. In this section, after describing each method, the discussion considers combinations of methods which may occur across different jobs in the same organization and even within the same jobs when appropriate.

The different methods raise the question of whether performance is measured against a valid standard. An employee's performance can be compared to the duties spelled out in the job description or it can be compared to the performance or results of others. Performance can also be rated against expected behaviors that should be made known in advance.

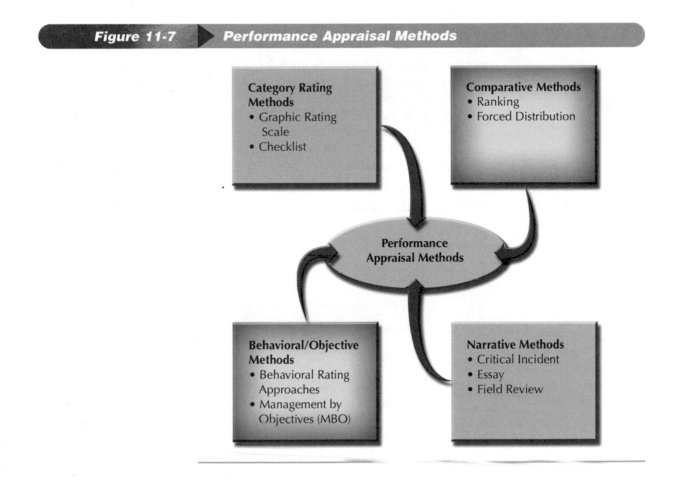

Figure 11-7 ▶ *Performance Appraisal Methods*

Category Rating Methods
• Graphic Rating Scale
• Checklist

Comparative Methods
• Ranking
• Forced Distribution

Performance Appraisal Methods

Behavioral/Objective Methods
• Behavioral Rating Approaches
• Management by Objectives (MBO)

Narrative Methods
• Critical Incident
• Essay
• Field Review

Category Rating Methods

The simplest methods for appraising performance are category rating methods, which require a manager to mark an employee's level of performance on a specific form divided into categories of performance. The graphic rating scale and checklist are common category rating methods.

Graphic Rating Scale The **graphic rating scale** allows the rater to mark an employee's performance on a continuum. Because of its simplicity, this method is used frequently. Figure 11-8 presents a graphic rating scale form used by managers to rate employees. The rater checks the appropriate rating on the scale for each duty listed. More detail can be added in the space for comments following each element.

Two types of graphic rating scales are actually in use today. Sometimes raters use both in rating the same person. The first and most common type lists job criteria such as quantity of work, quality of work, attendance, etc. The second assesses behavioral aspects, such as decision making, developing employees, etc., with specific behaviors listed and the effectiveness of each rated. Regardless of the scales used, either type should focus on the duties and responsibilities identified in the job description.[23]

Some obvious drawbacks to the graphic rating scale can be noted. Often, separate traits or factors are grouped together and the rater is given only one box to check. Another drawback occurs when the descriptive words sometimes used in scales have different meanings to different raters. Terms such as *initiative, dependability,* and *cooperation* are subject to many interpretations, especially if used in conjunction with words such as *outstanding, average,* and *poor.*

Graphic rating scales in many forms are used widely because they are easy to develop; but they encourage errors on the part of the raters, who may depend too heavily on the form to define performance. Both graphic rating scales and the checklist (which follows) tend to emphasize the rating instrument itself and its limitations. If they fit the person and job being rated, the scales work well. However, if the instrument is a poor fit, managers who must use them frequently complain about "the rating form."

Checklist The **checklist** is a performance appraisal tool that uses a list of statements or words. Raters check statements most representative of the characteristics and performance of employees. The following are typical checklist statements:

_____ can be expected to finish work on time

_____ seldom agrees to work overtime

_____ is cooperative and helpful

_____ accepts criticism

_____ strives for self-improvement

The checklist can be modified so that varying weights are assigned to the statements or words. The results can then be quantified. Usually, the rating supervisor does not know weights of the individual list items because they are tabulated by someone else, such as a member of the HR unit.

Figure 11-8 ▶ Sample Performance Appraisal Form

Date Sent	**4/19/00**		Return by	**5/01/00**
Name	**Jane Doe**		Job Title	**Receiving Clerk**
Department	**Receiving**		Supervisor	**Fred Smith**
Full-time	**x**	Part-time ____	Date of Hire	**5/12/00**

Rating Period: From **5/12/02**   To: **5/12/03**

Reason for appraisal (check one): Regular Interval **x**   Introductory ___   Counseling only ___   Discharge ___

Utilizing the following definitions, rate the performance as I, M, or E.

I—Performance is below job requirements and **improvement is needed.**

M—Performance **meets** job requirements and standards.

E—Performance **exceeds** job requirements and standards a **majority** of the time.

SPECIFIC JOB RESPONSIBILITIES: List the principal activities from the job summary, rate the performance on each job duty by placing an "X" on the rating scale at the appropriate location, and make appropriate comments to explain the rating.

```
I ————————————— M ————————————— E
```

Job Duty #1:   Inventory receiving and checking

Explanation: _____

_____

```
I ————————————— M ————————————— E
```

Job Duty #2:   Accuracy of records kept

Explanation: _____

_____

```
I ————————————— M ————————————— E
```

Attendance (including absences and tardies):   Number of absences ___   Number of tardies ___

Explanation: _____

_____

Overall Rating: Based on the total performance, place the letter **I, M, or E** in the box provided that best describes the employee's overall performance.

Explanation: _____

_____

However, several difficulties exist with the checklist: (1) As with the graphic rating scale, the words or statements may have different meanings to different raters. (2) Raters cannot readily discern the rating results if a weighted checklist is used. (3) Raters do not assign the weights to the factors. These difficulties limit the use of the information when a rater discusses the checklist results with the employee, creating a greater barrier to effective developmental counseling.

Comparative Methods

Comparative methods require that managers directly compare the performance of their employees against one another. For example, a data-entry operator's performance would be compared with that of other data-entry operators by the computing supervisor. Comparative techniques include ranking.

Ranking The **ranking** method lists all employees from highest to lowest in performance. The primary drawback of the ranking method is that the size of the differences among individuals is not well defined. For example, the performances of individuals ranked second and third may differ little, but performance between those ranked third and fourth differs a great deal. This drawback can be overcome to some extent by assigning points to indicate the size of the gaps. Ranking also means someone must be last, which ignores the possibility that the last-ranked individual in one group might be equal to the top employee in a different group. Further, the ranking task becomes unwieldy if the group to be ranked is large.

Forced Distribution Forced distribution is a technique for distributing ratings that can be generated with any of the other methods. However, it requires a comparison among people in the work group under consideration.

With the **forced distribution** method, the ratings of employees' performance are distributed along a bell-shaped curve. Using the forced distribution method, for example, a head nurse would rank nursing personnel along a scale, placing a certain percentage of employees at each performance level. Figure 11-9 illustrates a forced distribution scale. This method assumes that the widely known bell-shaped curve of performance exists in a given group. In fact, generally, the distribution of performance appraisal ratings does not approximate the normal distribution of the bell-shaped curve. More commonly, 60% to 70% of the workforce of an organization rates in the top two performance levels. This pattern could reflect outstanding performance by many employees, or it could reflect leniency bias, discussed later in this chapter. As the chapter opening discussion highlighted, General Electric attempts to get around leniency with their 20–70–10 program for managers and professionals. Managers identify the top 20% who they reward richly so few will leave. The bottom 10% are given a chance to improve or leave. Among the 600 highest ranking executives, approximately 60 leave each year for other opportunities or retirement. Among all managers and professionals GE loses about 8,000 each year. Nearly 4,800 of those are forced out in good times or bad.[24]

The forced distribution method suffers from several drawbacks. One problem is that a supervisor may resist placing any individual in the lowest (or the highest) group. Difficulties also arise when the rater must explain to the employee why he or she was placed in one grouping and others were placed in higher groupings. These situations have led to lawsuits. Further, with small

Ranking Listing of all employees from highest to lowest in performance.

Forced distribution Performance appraisal method in which ratings of employees' performance are distributed along a bell-shaped curve.

Figure 11-9 ▸ **Forced Distribution on a Bell-Shaped Curve**

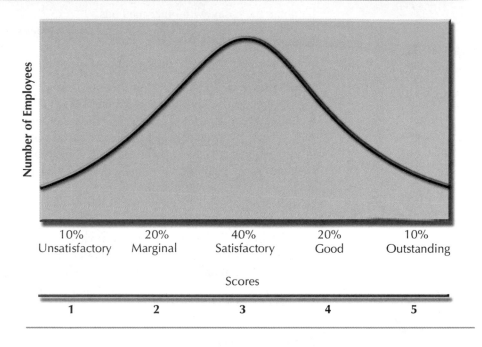

10%	20%	40%	20%	10%
Unsatisfactory	Marginal	Satisfactory	Good	Outstanding

Scores

1	2	3	4	5

groups, the assumption that a bell-shaped or other distribution of performance would apply may be faulty. Finally, in some cases the manager may make distinctions among employees that may not exist.

Narrative Methods

Managers and HR specialists frequently are required to provide written appraisal information. Documentation and description are the essence of the critical incident, the essay, and the field review methods. These methods describe an employee's actions and may indicate an actual rating as well.

Critical Incident In the critical incident method, the manager keeps a written record of both highly favorable and unfavorable actions in an employee's performance during the entire rating period. When a "critical incident" involving an employee occurs, the manager writes it down. The critical incident method can be used with other methods to document the reasons why an employee was rated in a certain way.

The critical incident method also has its unfavorable aspects. First, not all supervisors define what constitutes a critical incident in the same way. Also, producing daily or weekly written remarks about each employee's performance takes considerable time. Further, employees may become overly concerned about what their superiors write and begin to fear the managers' "black books."

Essay The essay, or "free-form," appraisal method requires a manager to write a short essay describing each employee's performance during the rating period. Some essays are "free-form" or without guidelines, while other more structured formats use prepared questions that must be answered. The rater usually categorizes comments under a few general headings. This format allows the rater more flexibility than other methods do. As a result, appraisers often combine the essay with other methods.

The effectiveness of the essay approach depends on the supervisor's ability to write. Some supervisors do not express themselves well in writing, resulting in a poor description of employee performance.

Field Review The field review focuses as much on *who* does the evaluation as the method used. This approach can include the HR department as a reviewer, or a completely independent reviewer outside the organization. In the field review, the outside reviewer becomes an active partner in the rating process. The outsider interviews the manager about each employee's performance, then compiles the notes from each interview into a rating for each employee. Then the rating is reviewed by the supervisor for needed changes. This method assumes that the outsider knows enough about the job setting to help supervisors give more accurate and thorough appraisals.

The major limitation of the field review is the extent of control the outsider exercises over the rating process. Although this control may be desirable from one viewpoint, managers may see it as a challenge to their authority. In addition, the field review can be time-consuming, particularly if a large number of employees are to be rated.

Behavioral/Objectives Methods

In an attempt to overcome some of the difficulties of the methods just described, **behavioral rating approaches** attempt to assess an employee's *behaviors* instead of other characteristics. Some of the different behavioral approaches are *behaviorally anchored rating scales* (BARS), *behavioral observation scales* (BOS), and *behavioral expectation scales* (BES). BARS compare what the employee does with possible behaviors that might be shown on the job. BOS count the number of times certain behaviors are exhibited. BES order behaviors on a continuum to define outstanding, average, and unacceptable performance.

Behavioral rating approaches describe specific examples of employee job behaviors. In BARS, these examples are "anchored" or measured against a scale of performance levels. Figure 11-10 contains a behavioral observation rating scale that rates customer service skills for individuals taking orders for a national catalog retailer. Spelling out the behaviors associated with each level of performance helps minimize some of the problems noted earlier for other approaches.

Constructing Behavioral Scales Identifying important *job dimensions,* which are the most important performance factors in an employee's job description, begins the construction of a behavioral scale. For example, for a college professor, the major job dimensions associated with teaching might be: (a) course organization, (b) attitude toward students, (c) fair treatment, and (d) competence in subject area.

Short statements, similar to critical incidents, describe both desirable and undesirable behaviors (anchors). Then they are "retranslated," or assigned to one of the job dimensions. Development of anchor statements is usually a group

Behavioral rating approach Assesses an employee's behaviors instead of other characteristics.

Figure 11-10 ▸ *Customer Service Skills (BOS)*

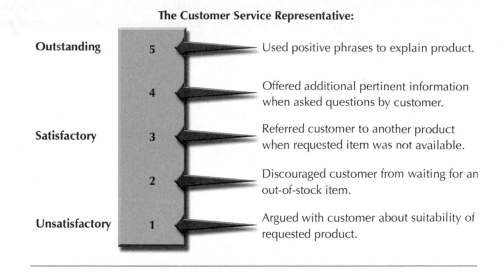

The Customer Service Representative:

Outstanding	5	Used positive phrases to explain product.
	4	Offered additional pertinent information when asked questions by customer.
Satisfactory	3	Referred customer to another product when requested item was not available.
	2	Discouraged customer from waiting for an out-of-stock item.
Unsatisfactory	1	Argued with customer about suitability of requested product.

project, and assignment to a dimension usually requires the agreement of 60% to 70% of the group. The group, consisting of people familiar with the job, then assigns each "anchor" a number that represents how good or bad the behavior is. When numbered, these anchors are fitted to a scale.

Several problems associated with the behavioral approaches must be considered. First, developing and maintaining behaviorally anchored rating scales require extensive time and effort. In addition, various appraisal forms are needed to accommodate different types of jobs in an organization. For instance, because nurses, dietitians, and admission clerks in a hospital all have distinct job descriptions, development of separate BARS forms for each would be necessary.

Management by Objectives

Management by objectives (MBO) specifies the performance goals that an individual and her or his manager agree to try to attain within an appropriate length of time. Each manager sets objectives derived from the overall goals and objectives of the organization; however, MBO should not be a disguised means for a superior to dictate the objectives of individual managers or employees. Although not limited to the appraisal of managers, MBO is most often used for this purpose. Other names for MBO include *appraisal by results, target-coaching, work planning and review, performance objectives,* and *mutual goal setting.*

Key MBO Ideas Three key assumptions underlie an MBO appraisal system. First, an employee who is involved in planning and setting objectives and determining the performance measures tends to show a higher level of commitment and performance. Second, clearly and precisely identified objectives encourage the employee to work effectively toward achieving the desired results. Ambiguity and confusion—and therefore less effective performance—may result when a superior determines the objectives for an individual

Management by objectives (MBO) Specifies the performance goals that an individual and her or his manager agree to try to attain within an appropriate length of time.

Third, performance objectives should be measurable and should define results. Vague generalities such as "initiative" and "cooperation," which are common in many appraisals, should be avoided. Objectives specify actions to be taken or work to be accomplished. Sample objectives might include:

- Submit regional sales report by the fifth of every month.
- Obtain orders from at least five new customers per month.
- Maintain payroll costs at 10% of sales volume.
- Have scrap loss of less than 5%.
- Fill all organizational vacancies within 30 days after openings occur.

The MBO Process Implementing a guided self-appraisal system using MBO is a four-stage process.

1. *Job review and agreement:* The employee and the superior review the job description and the key activities that comprise the employee's job. The idea is to agree on the exact makeup of the job.
2. *Development of performance standards:* Specific standards of performance must be mutually developed. In this phase a satisfactory level of performance that is specific and measurable is determined. For example, a quota of selling five cars per month may be an appropriate performance standard for a salesperson.
3. *Guided objective setting:* Objectives are established by the employee in conjunction with the superior. Objectives should be realistically attainable.
4. *Continuing performance discussions:* The employee and the superior use the objectives as bases for continuing discussions about the employee's performance. Although a formal review session may be scheduled, the employee and the manager do not necessarily wait until the appointed time to discuss performance. Objectives can be mutually modified as warranted.

The MBO process seems to be most useful with managerial personnel and employees who have a fairly wide range of flexibility and control over their jobs. When imposed on a rigid and autocratic management system, MBO often has failed. Emphasizing penalties for not meeting objectives defeats the development and participative nature of MBO.

Combinations of Methods

No single appraisal method is best for all situations. Therefore, a performance measurement system that uses a combination of the preceding methods may be sensible in certain circumstances. Using combinations may offset some of the advantages and disadvantages of individual methods. Category rating methods are easy to develop, but they usually do little to measure strategic accomplishments. Further, they may make inter-rater reliability problems worse. Comparative approaches help reduce leniency, central tendency, and strictness errors, which makes them useful for administrative decisions such as pay raises. But the comparative approaches do a poor job of linking performance to organizational goals, and they do not provide feedback for improvement as well as other methods do.

Narrative methods work best for development because they potentially generate more feedback information. However, without good definitions of criteria or standards, they can be so unstructured as to be of little value. Also, these

methods work poorly for administrative uses. The behavioral/objective approaches work well to link performance to organizational goals, but both can require much more effort and time to define expectations and explain the process to employees. These approaches may not work well for lower-level jobs.

When managers can articulate what they want a performance appraisal system to accomplish, they can choose and/or mix the methods just mentioned to realize the advantages they want. For example, one combination might include a graphic rating scale of performance on major job criteria, a narrative of developmental needs, and an overall ranking of employees in a department. Different categories of employees (e.g., salaried exempt, nonexempt salaried, maintenance) might require different combinations.

Rater Errors

There are many possible sources of error in the performance appraisal process. One of the major sources is mistakes made by the rater. Although completely eliminating these errors is impossible, making raters aware of them through training is helpful. Figure 11-11 lists some of the most common rater errors.

Varying Standards

When appraising employees, a manager should avoid applying different standards and expectations for employees performing similar jobs. Inequities in assessments, whether real or perceived, generally anger employees. Such problems often result from the use of ambiguous criteria and subjective weightings by supervisors.[25]

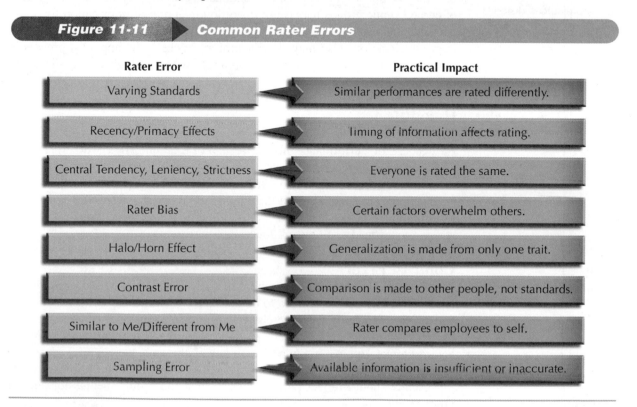

Figure 11-11 ▶ Common Rater Errors

Rater Error	Practical Impact
Varying Standards	Similar performances are rated differently.
Recency/Primacy Effects	Timing of information affects rating.
Central Tendency, Leniency, Strictness	Everyone is rated the same.
Rater Bias	Certain factors overwhelm others.
Halo/Horn Effect	Generalization is made from only one trait.
Contrast Error	Comparison is made to other people, not standards.
Similar to Me/Different from Me	Rater compares employees to self.
Sampling Error	Available information is insufficient or inaccurate.

Recency/Primacy Effect

The **recency effect** occurs when a rater gives greater weight to recent events when appraising an individual's performance. Giving a student a course grade based only on his performance in the last week of class, or giving a drill press operator a high rating even though she made the quota only in the last two weeks of the rating period are examples. The opposite is the **primacy effect**, where information received first gets the most weight.

Central Tendency, Leniency, and Strictness Errors

Ask students, and they will tell you which professors tend to grade easier or harder. A manager also may develop a similar *rating pattern.* Appraisers who rate all employees within a narrow range (i.e., everyone is average) commit a **central tendency error**, where even the poor performers receive an average rating.

Rating patterns also may exhibit leniency or strictness. The *leniency error* occurs when ratings of all employees fall at the high end of the scale. The *strictness error* occurs when a manager uses only the lower part of the scale to rate employees. To avoid conflict, managers often rate employees higher than they should be rated. This "ratings boost" is especially likely when no manager or HR representative reviews the completed appraisals. For related research, see the HR Perspective.

Rater Bias

Rater bias occurs when a rater's values or prejudices distort the rating. Such bias may be unconscious or quite intentional. For example, a manager's dislike of certain ethnic groups may cause distortion in appraisal information for some people. Judgments about age, religion, seniority, sex, appearance, or other arbitrary classifications also may skew appraisal ratings if the appraisal process is not properly designed. A review of appraisal ratings by higher-level managers may help correct this problem.

Halo Effect

The **halo effect** occurs when a manager rates an employee high on all job criteria because of performance in one area. For example, if a worker has few absences, her supervisor might give her a high rating in all other areas of work, including quantity and quality of output, because of her dependability. The manager may not really think about the employee's other characteristics separately, resulting in the halo effect. The "horns" effect is the opposite, where one characteristic may lead to an overall lower rating.

Contrast Error

Rating should be done using established standards. The **contrast error** is the tendency to rate people relative to others rather than against performance standards. For example, if everyone else in a group performs at a mediocre level, a person performing somewhat better may be rated as excellent because of the contrast effect. But in a group performing well, the same person might receive a lower rating. Although it may be appropriate to compare people at times, the rating usually should reflect performance against job requirements, not against other people.

Research on Influence Tactics

Performance ratings are affected by leniency and other errors, but how subordinates attempt to influence their ratings is the subject of research by Wayne and others reported in *Personnel Psychology*. Previous research has suggested that employees are not passive, but actively engage in efforts to improve their work environments. The employees use "upward influence," which is behavior directed at persons higher in the hierarchy in an attempt to favorably influence performance ratings and other outcomes. The researchers considered three such influence attempts and their effects on performance appraisals in their study.

One influence attempt focuses on a manager's perceptions of a subordinate's *skills with other people* that could affect performance ratings. If the subordinate uses interpersonal skill and reasoning in dealing with the man-

ager, the manager may then assume the subordinate treats all people that way and rate him or her higher.

Another possible area for influence occurs when a manager likes the individual because he or she *does favors* for the manager. In turn, the manager appreciates the employee and perhaps feels that employee is "owed" something.

A pervasive effect in social psychology is that people tend to perceive themselves as *being similar* to a person who engages in desirable behavior. The third area for influence could occur if managers view some subordinates as similar to themselves, and allow these perceptions to affect the performance ratings given.

In a large corporation that produces chemicals and machinery, the researchers studied 247 pairs of managers and subordi-

nates. The average age of subordinates was 48, they had been with the company on average more than 16 years, and their average education was a bachelor's degree. Managers had higher levels on all of these items. Researchers mailed a questionnaire designed to cover "career-related issues" to the employees and managers. The questionnaire measured interpersonal skills, similarity, and performance ratings.

The research study found that the managerial perceptions of a subordinate's interpersonal skills and similarity to the manager showed significant positive links with performance ratings. But simply "liking" the subordinate showed no significant linkage. Apparently, some influence attempts *do* affect manager's perceptions of an employee and, in turn, the performance ratings.[26]

WEST GROUP
A THOMSON COMPANY

Performance Appraisal Problems
Identifies typical performance appraisal problems.
Custom Search:
☑ ANALYSIS
Phrase: Sources of rating errors

Similar to/Different from Me

Sometimes raters are influenced by whether people show the same or different characteristics from the rater. Again the error comes in measuring someone against another person rather than on how well the individual fulfills the expectations of the job.

Sampling Error

If the rater has seen only a small sample of the person's work, an appraisal may be subject to sampling error. For example, assume 95% of the work of an employee has been satisfactory, but the boss saw only the 5% that had errors. If the supervisor then rates the person as poor, then a sampling error has occurred. Ideally the work being rated should be a good representative sample of all the work done.

Appraisal Feedback

After completing appraisals, managers need to communicate the results to give employees a clear understanding of how they stand in the eyes of their immediate superiors and the organization. Organizations commonly require managers to discuss appraisals with employees. The appraisal feedback interview provides an opportunity to clear up any misunderstandings on both sides. In this interview, the manager should focus on counseling and development, and not just tell the employee, "Here is how you rate and why." Emphasizing development gives both parties an opportunity to consider the employee's performance as part of appraisal feedback.

The Appraisal Interview

The appraisal interview presents both an opportunity and a danger. It can be an emotional experience for the manager and the employee, because the manager must communicate both praise and constructive criticism. A major concern for managers is how to emphasize the positive aspects of the employee's performance, while still discussing ways to make needed improvements. If the interview is handled poorly, the employee may feel resentment that could lead to conflict, which could be reflected in future work.[27]

Employees usually approach an appraisal interview with some concern. They often feel that discussions about performance are both personal and important to their continued job success. At the same time, they want to know how their managers feel about their performance. Figure 11-12 summarizes hints for an effective appraisal interview for supervisors and managers.

Feedback as a System

The three commonly recognized components of a feedback system include data, evaluation of that data, and some action based on the evaluation. *Data* are factual pieces of information regarding observed actions or consequences. Most often data are facts that report what happened, such as "Charlie broke a photon," or "Mary spoke harshly to an engineer." For instance, when Mary spoke harshly to the engineer, it may have been an instance of poor communications and reflected a lack of sensitivity. However, it also may have been a proper and necessary action. Someone must *evaluate* the meaning or value of the data.

Evaluation is the way the feedback system reacts to the facts, and it requires performance standards. Management might evaluate the same factual information differently than would customers (for example, regarding merchandise

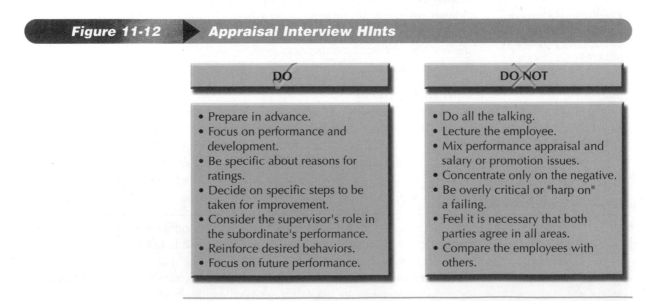

Figure 11-12 ▶ **Appraisal Interview Hints**

DO	DO NOT
• Prepare in advance.	• Do all the talking.
• Focus on performance and development.	• Lecture the employee.
• Be specific about reasons for ratings.	• Mix performance appraisal and salary or promotion issues.
• Decide on specific steps to be taken for improvement.	• Concentrate only on the negative.
• Consider the supervisor's role in the subordinate's performance.	• Be overly critical or "harp on" a failing.
• Reinforce desired behaviors.	• Feel it is necessary that both parties agree in all areas.
• Focus on future performance.	• Compare the employees with others.

Lessons from Two Different Performances: A Supervisor's Story

My employees who do the best work are usually easy to get along with, but not always. I worked with one employee who alienated me and all his colleagues with his fierce competitiveness. He was quick to point out our mistakes, never complimented, and usually whined when someone else had a good project that he thought should have been his instead. I tried praising him and sought out his counsel to ease his obvious insecurities, but he was no fun to be around. However, he *was* productive. He got to work early and left late, was always eager to do more, and frequently worked overtime. He always did good work, could be counted on, and never missed a deadline. When he finally left, I realized I had come to rely on him, even though I did not miss his sour jealousy. He would not change.

Another employee and I shared common interests: good books and movies, the same work values and goals, and other interests. He was generous and willing to help, and his colleagues liked and appreciated him. Early on he was a good producer, but later on he began procrastinating and turned in incomplete work. I dis-cussed it with him, and he promised to do better. But he did not. Project after project either flopped or was not done. Finally, I told him he would have to improve or find another job. The fact that I considered him a friend made it painful, and I put it off longer than I should have. He told me he felt betrayed and quit. Yet when he got a new job, he called to say he had been unhappy but was unable to move until I had pushed.[28]

What conclusions about performance and performance appraisal can you draw from these two real-world examples?

exchange or credit decisions) or co-workers. Evaluation can be done by the person supplying the data, by a supervisor, or by a group.

For feedback to cause change, some decisions must be made regarding subsequent *action*. In traditional appraisal systems, the manager makes specific suggestions regarding future actions the employee might take. Employee input often is encouraged as well. In 360° feedback, those people from whom information was solicited might also suggest actions that the individual may consider. It may be necessary to involve those providing information if the subsequent actions are highly interdependent and require coordination with the information providers. Regardless of the feedback process used, all three components (data, evaluation, and action) are necessary parts of a successful feedback system.[29]

Reactions of Managers

Managers and supervisors who must complete appraisals of their employees often resist the appraisal process. Many managers feel that their role calls on them to assist, encourage, coach, and counsel employees to improve their performance. However, being a judge on the one hand and a coach and counselor on the other may cause internal conflict and confusion for many managers.[30]

The fact that appraisals may affect an employee's future career also may cause raters to alter or bias their ratings. This bias is even more likely when managers know that they will have to communicate and defend their ratings to the employees, their bosses, or HR specialists. From the manager's viewpoint, providing negative feedback to an employee in an appraisal interview can be easily avoided by making the employee's ratings positive, thus avoiding unpleasantness in an interpersonal situation. But avoidance helps no one. A manager owes an employee a well-considered appraisal, as the HR Practice indicates.

Reactions of Appraised Employees

Employees may well see the appraisal process as a threat and feel that the only way to get a higher rating is for someone else to receive a low rating. This win/lose perception is encouraged by comparative methods of rating. However, both parties can win and no one must lose. Emphasis on the self-improvement and developmental aspects of appraisal appears to be the most effective means to reduce zero-sum reactions from those participating in the appraisal process.

Another common employee reaction resembles students' reactions to tests. A professor may prepare a test he or she feels is fair, but it does not necessarily follow that students will feel the test is fair. They simply may see it differently. Likewise, employees being appraised may not necessarily agree with the manager doing the appraising. In most cases, however, employees will view appraisals done well as what they are meant to be—constructive feedback.[31]

Legal and Effective Performance Appraisals

A number of court decisions have focused attention on performance appraisals, particularly on equal employment opportunity (EEO) concerns. The Uniform Guidelines issued by the Equal Employment Opportunity Commission (EEOC) and other federal enforcement agencies make it clear that performance appraisals must be job-related and nondiscriminatory.

Performance Appraisals and the Law

Because appraisals are supposed to measure how well employees are doing their jobs, it may seem unnecessary to emphasize that performance appraisals must be job related. Yet courts have ruled in numerous cases that performance appraisals were discriminatory and not job-related.[32]

The elements of a performance appraisal system that can survive court tests can be determined from existing case law. Various cases have identified the elements of a legally defensible performance appraisal to include the following:

- Performance appraisal criteria based on job analysis
- Absence of disparate impact and evidence of validity
- Formal evaluation criteria that limit managerial discretion
- Formal rating instrument linked to job duties and responsibilities
- Personal knowledge of and contact with appraised individual
- Training of supervisors in conducting appraisals
- Review process that prevents one manager, acting alone, from controlling an employee's career
- Counseling to help poor performers improve

Clearly, employers should have fair and nondiscriminatory performance appraisals. To do this, employers must decide how to design their appraisal systems to satisfy the courts, enforcement agencies, and their employees.[33]

Effective Performance Management

Regardless of the approach used, managers must understand the intended outcome of performance management.[34] When performance management is used to develop employees as resources, it usually works. When management uses one key part of performance management, the performance appraisal, to punish

AHI's Employment Law Resource Center
This Web site offers valuable legal management information on performance appraisals and other HR topics under the problem solver heading.

http://www.ahipubs.com/

employees, or when raters fail to understand its limitations, performance management is less effective. In its simplest form, as part of a performance management process, performance appraisal is a manager's observation: "Here are your strengths and weaknesses, and here is a way to develop for the future." Done well, performance management can lead to higher employee motivation and satisfaction. But in an era of continuous improvement, an ineffective performance management system poses a huge liability. To be effective, a performance management system will be:

- Consistent with the strategic mission of the organization
- Beneficial as a development tool
- Useful as an administrative tool
- Legal and job-related
- Viewed as generally fair by employees
- Effective in documenting employee performance

Most systems can be improved by training supervisors in doing performance appraisals. Because conducting the appraisals is critical in a performance management system, training should center around minimizing rater errors and providing a common frame of reference on how raters observe and recall information.

Organizationally, managers exhibit a tendency to distill performance into a single number that can be used to support pay raises. Systems based on this concept reduce the complexity of each person's contribution in order to satisfy compensation system requirements. Such systems are too simplistic to provide the employees useful feedback or help managers pinpoint training and development needs. In fact, use of a single numerical rating often blocks productive performance discussions, because the system attaches a label to a person's performance, which the manager must then defend.

Summary

- Performance management systems attempt to identify, encourage, measure, evaluate, improve, and reward employee performance.
- Performance provides the critical link between organizational strategies and results.
- Job criteria identify important job dimensions, such as teaching for a college professor, runs batted in for a major-league outfielder, or orders completed by a warehouse shipping worker.
- Relevance, contamination, and deficiency of criteria affect performance measurement.
- Appraising employee performance serves useful development and administrative purposes.
- Performance appraisal can be done either informally or systematically. Systematic appraisals usually are done annually.
- Appraisals can be conducted by superiors, employees, teams, outsiders, or a combination of raters. Employees also can conduct self-appraisals.
- Four types of appraisal methods are available: category rating, comparative, narrative, and behavioral/objective.
- Category rating methods, especially graphic rating scales and checklists, are widely used.
- Comparative methods include ranking and forced distribution.
- Narrative methods include the critical incident technique, the essay approach, and field review.
- Two behavioral/objectives methods of appraisal include behavioral rating approaches and management by objectives (MBO).

- Many performance appraisal problems are caused by rater errors, which can include varying standards, recency effect, rater bias, rating patterns (such as central tendency error), halo effect, contrast error, and others.
- The appraisal feedback interview is a vital part of any appraisal system.
- The reactions of both managers and employees must be considered as performance appraisals are done.
- Federal employment guidelines and numerous court decisions affect the design and use of the performance appraisal process. The absence of specific job-relatedness can create legal problems, as can subjectivity.
- Training appraisers and guarding against the tendency to reduce performance to a single number contribute to the effectiveness of a performance management system.

Review and Discussion Questions

1. Describe the differences between performance standards and job criteria. Why do the criteria problems of contamination and deficiency exist?
2. How might the developmental and administrative uses of performance appraisals conflict?
3. Suppose you are a supervisor. What errors might you make when preparing a performance appraisal on a clerical employee?
4. What sources typically provide information in 360° performance appraisals?
5. Explain the similarities and differences between the behavioral approaches to performance appraisal and management by objectives (MBO).
6. Construct a plan for a post-appraisal interview with an employee who has performed poorly.
7. Discuss the following statement: "Most performance appraisal systems in use today would not pass legal scrutiny."

Terms to Know

performance management systems   338
performance   338
job criteria   338
performance standards   341
performance appraisal   342
graphic rating scale   352
checklist   352
ranking   354
forced distribution   354

behavioral rating approach   356
management by objectives (MBO)   357
recency effect   360
primacy effect   360
central tendency error   360
rater bias   360
halo effect   360
contrast error   360

Using the Internet

360° Feedback for Your Organization

The CEO has recently attended a conference where there was considerable discussion about 360° assessments as development tools. He has asked you, the Director of Human Resources, to research 360° Feedback Assessments as a developmental tool for the middle and front-line supervisors in your organization. He would like you to prepare a report with the following information.

- The uses and benefits of 360° feedback
- Four typical dimensions and one example of each
- Three modes to conduct 360° assessments

Use the following Web site to assist you in this task.
http://www.hr-survey.com

Revising the Performance Appraisal System at St. Luke's Hospital

St. Luke's Hospital, a thoroughly modern hospital in Jacksonville, Florida, discovered a thoroughly modern problem. Its performance appraisal system generated an insurmountable pile of papers; and with 1,325 employees, the HR staff recognized that changes were needed.

Performance appraisal forms in many organizations range from a simple sheet of paper to lengthy and complex packets. At St. Luke's, the performance appraisal system had evolved over the years into a form containing about 20 pages per employee. Although some of the length grew out of concerns about meeting numerous federal, state, and health-care industry requirements, other facets of the system had been developed for administrative purposes.

At St. Luke's the existing performance appraisal system combined job descriptions and a performance appraisal. In addition, health-care accreditation requirements necessitated using a competency management program focusing on employee development and education. To accommodate both, St. Luke's had merged the competency profiles with the job descriptions and performance appraisal forms. To complete an employee appraisal, supervisors and managers scored employee performance on formal weighted criteria and summarized the information by compensation and benefits class. Upper management then reviewed those summaries for consistency. This paper-intensive process required a total of 36 different steps.

Recognizing the need for change, management formed a steering committee to oversee the process of developing a better performance appraisal system. The committee brainstormed to find bottlenecks and identify what a more automated process could be. At this point, the committee understood the current system and what key users wanted. After reviewing literature on performance appraisal systems, surveying other hospitals, and looking at software packages, the committee decided to design its own system.

The option chosen moved the numerical criteria scores from the individual pages of the job description to a summary sheet that contained scores on up to six employees on one form. Then a computer calculated the total scores. Also, written comments were moved to a summary sheet dealing only with exceptions to standards. The most difficult part proved to be designing a database from scratch that interfaced with existing HR systems.

The new performance appraisal process reduced the paperwork from 20 to 7 pages per employee. The new system also offered supervisors and managers the option of using computerized comment sheets. Another time-saver was the ability to use the system to record and document noteworthy employee performance incidents, both positive and negative in nature, as they occurred throughout the year.

To implement the new performance appraisal system, there was training for all 97 supervisors and managers. During the training, attendees received directions for using the on-line performance appraisal forms, along with a timeline and a resource text.

After using the new appraisal system, 90% of the supervisors and managers indicated that the process had indeed been streamlined and was easier to understand. Also, there was a significant reduction in paper, fewer arithmetic errors, and clearer and more concise appraisal information.

In addition, in subsequent years, St. Luke's has implemented minor revisions in the performance appraisal system, updated computer hardware and software, and simplified data screens for management users.[35]

Questions

1. Explain why the new performance appraisal system at St. Luke's Hospital is likely to result in more accurate performance appraisals.
2. Describe some of the advantages and disadvantages of combining job descriptions, performance appraisals, and competency profiles for development as St. Luke's did.

1. Matthew Boyle, "Performance Reviews: Dangerous Curves Ahead," *Fortune,* May 28, 2001, p. 187–188; Carol Hymowitz, "Ranking Systems Gain Popularity, but Have Many Staffers Riled," *The Wall Street Journal,* May 15, 2001, B1; Reed Abelson, "Companies Turn to Grades and Employees Go to Court," *The New York Times,* March 19, 2001, C1; N. Shirouzu, "Ford Stops Using Letter Rankings to Rate Workers," *The Wall Street Journal,* July 11, 2001, B1.
2. "Performance," *Bulletin to Management,* July 13, 2000, p. 5.
3. "SHRM Performance Management Survey," *Society for Human Resource Management Research,"* 2000, 7.
4. "General Motors and Whirlpool: Two Approaches for Developing Performance Benchmarks," *HR Focus,* June 2000, 7–10.
5. Carolyn Pye Sostrom, "Measure Right, Measure Now," *Purchasing Today,* January 2000, 33–40.
6. Mark A. Siders, et. al., "The Relationships of Internal and External Commitment Foci to Objective Job Performance Measures," *Academy of Management Journal,* 44 (2001), 570.
7. "Administrative Reform: Commission to Introduce Regular Appraisal of Senior Officials," *European Report,* January 4, 2001, 101.
8. Dayton Fandray, "The New Thinking in Performance Appraisals," *Workforce,* May 2001, 36–40.
9. "Some Say Evaluations Do More Harm Than Good," *Bulletin to Management,* April 20, 2000, 127.
10. Jon Segal, "86 Your Appraisal Process?" *HR Magazine,* October 2000, 199.
11. Carla Joinson, "Making Sure Employees Measure Up," *HR Magazine,* March 2001, 36–41.
12. Mark Koziel, "Giving and Receiving Performance Evaluations," *The CPA Journal,* December 2000, 22.
13. Carol Hymowitz, "Managers Tell How to Spot 'Gold Talent' in Old and New Hires," *The Wall Street Journal,* March 27, 2001, B1.
14. Don Merit, "Improving Job Performance," *American Printer,* March 2000, 82.
15. "Performance Management Practices," *www.ddi.com.*
16. Michael Scott, "7 Pitfalls for Managers When Handling Poor Performance and How to Overcome Them," *Manage,* February 2000, 12–13.
17. Lin Grensing-Pophal, "Motivate Managers to Review Performance," *HR Magazine,* March 2001, 45.
18. Maria Clapham, "Employee Creativity: The Role of Leadership," *The Academy of Management Executive,* August 2000, 138.
19. Jose Goris, et al., "Effects of Communication Direction on Job Performance and Satisfaction," *The Journal of Business Communication,* October 2000, 348.
20. Based on Larry Stevens, "Rave Reviews," *Human Resource Executive,* January 1998, 41–43; and "Performance Review," *HR Magazine,* May 2001, 169.
21. Alan H. Church, et al., "Since When Is No News Good News?" *Personnel Psychology,* 53 (2000) 435.
22. Joan F. Brett and Leanne E. Atwater, "360 Degree Feedback: Accuracy, Reactions, and Perceptions of Usefulness," *Journal of Applied Psychology* 86 (2001), 930–942.
23. Carol Hymowitz, "Readers Tell Tales of Success and Failure Using Rating Systems," *The Wall Street Journal,* May 29, 2001, B1.
24. Del Jones, "More Firms Cut Workers Ranked at Bottom to Make Way for Talent," *USA Today,* May 30, 2001, B1–2.
25. Yitzhak Fried, et al., "Rater Positive and Negative Mood Predispositions," *Journal of Occupational and Organizational Psychology,* September 2000, 373.
26. Sandy Wayne, et al., "The Role of Upward Influence Tactics in Human Resource Decisions," *Personnel Psychology,* 50 (1997), 979–1005.
27. Winston Fletcher, "Sitting in Judgment on Others," *Management Today,* August 2000, 30.
28. Adapted from Carol Hymowitz, "What to Do When Your Favorite Workers Don't Make the Grade," *The Wall Street Journal,* April 11, 2000, B1.
29. Joshua Freedman, "Feedback for Performance," *Priorities,* 4, (2001), 28.
30. Kathy Simmons, "Ostrich Management," *The Rotarian,* September 2000, 6.
31. Susan Scherreik, "Your Performance Review," *Business Week,* December 17, 2001, 139–140.
32. "Is a Negative Job Evaluation an Adverse Employment Action?" *Bulletin to Management,* September 14, 2000, 115; "EEO Performance Reviews," *Bulletin to Management,* February 24, 2000, 62.
33. Timothy S. Bland, "Anatomy of an Employment Lawsuit," *HR Magazine,* March 2001, 145.
34. Dick Grate, "Performance Appraisal Reappraised," *Harvard Business Review,* January 2000, 21.
35. Based on LaJuan Aderhold, Nancy L. O'Keefe, and Darrell E. Burke, "Critical Care for Review Process," *Personnel Journal,* April 1996, 115–120.

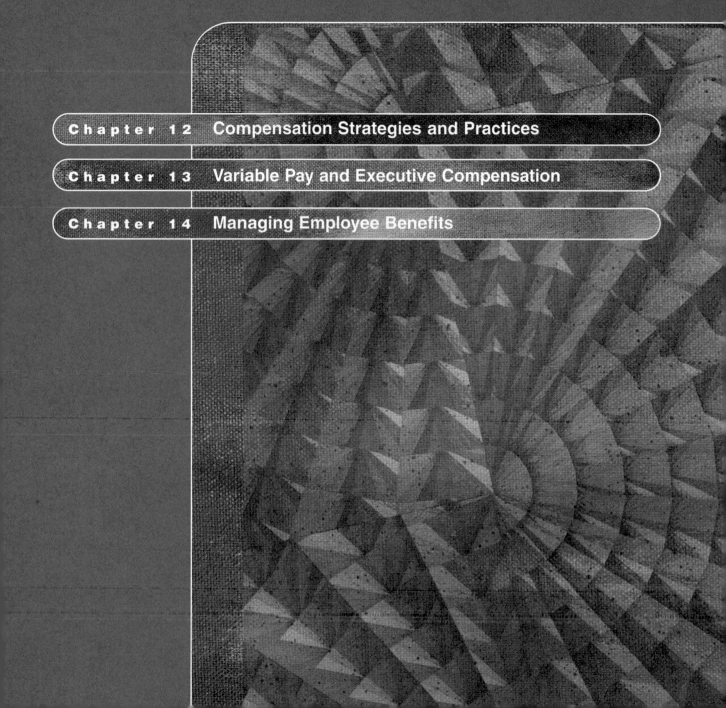

CHAPTER 12

Compensation Strategies and Practices

After you have read this chapter, you should be able to:

- Identify the two general types of compensation and the components of each.

- Give examples of two different compensation philosophies in organizations.

- Discuss four strategic compensation design issues.

- Describe three considerations affecting perceptions of pay fairness.

- Identify the basic provisions of the Fair Labor Standards Act (FLSA).

- Define *job evaluation* and discuss four methods of performing it.

- Outline the process of building a wage and salary administration system.

- Discuss how to establish a pay-for-performance system.

Compensation Rollercoaster

Everyone likes to be paid. Whatever else it does, money still can be turned into items most people want. Of course, the psychological dimensions of the compensation a person receives are important, too.

Compensation frequently is directly tied to the labor market. When certain workers are in short supply, offering higher compensation may increase the number of persons hired. When the economy is slower, more people are just happy to have a paycheck.

At the peak of the last hiring boom, "pay envy" presented a significant problem. Stock options, performance pay, and signing bonuses created ambiguities in pay systems and caused problems. Current employees hired without receiving signing bonuses like those given new employees were envious. Employees with master's degrees making less than new IT hires with no degrees were envious. Some managers who made less than the new hires they supervised were envious too. Employees doing the same job may have had salary differences of $20,000 or more. New hires were paid top dollar just for agreeing to come to work, while current employees had their experience and loyalty rewarded by getting more work instead of more money.

In one survey, more than 50% of workers indicated they believed that they were paid too little, while only 23% expressed satisfaction with their pay. One factor driving the confusion was that wages went up rapidly for those in high demand, but not everyone was in high demand. Also, paying people based on their individual performance often created "winners" and "losers."

All this attention to compensation means that even people who did not worry much about the topic before are tuning into it now. Employers often had no choice but to turn to new and different compensation approaches in order to compete for employees. But many HR professionals and managers now admit these approaches have caused problems. Pay envy dampens morale and teamwork, causes turnover, and creates a "caste system" in the company. One former Apple Vice President recounts how a new hire came in at $115,000 plus a $30,000 hiring bonus right out of college. But star performers in the company made about $80,000 at the time. "If you bring in someone at a big salary and they turn out not to be a good hire it can be catastrophic," he notes. This example illustrates that life is

never fair in a tight labor market, especially when compensation is skewed.

But neither is it fair when the economy turns down. In years 2001–2002 the catered lunches, signing bonuses, free laptops and cell phones, and other generous perks designed to entice and keep many employees during the high times went away. Some workers who liked the amenities willingly gave up such indulgences if it meant their businesses stayed alive and they continued to have paychecks.

Many forms of creative compensation tossed in to attract or keep employees during the "boomtime" seemed frivolous in a weakened economy amid stock market uncertainties. "There is now a very clear distinction between 'nice' and 'necessary' when it comes to perks. We went a little too far," a partner with a big accounting firm noted. Fewer available jobs reduced the need for signing bonuses and other recruiting perks necessary only several years earlier.

All of these changes illustrate that compensation practices must change. But compensation continues to be important, visible, and often a concern in HR management.[1]

> All this attention to compensation means that even people who did not worry about the topic before are tuning into it.

"Organizations need to be fluid to move as markets move. That necessitates a more flexible approach to compensation."

—Kathryn McKee

Compensation systems in organizations must be linked to organizational objectives and strategies. But as the opening discussion illustrates, compensation also requires balancing the interests and costs of the employer with the expectations of employees. An effective compensation program in an organization addresses four objectives:

- Legal compliance with all appropriate laws and regulations
- Cost effectiveness for the organization
- Internal, external, and individual equity for employees
- Performance enhancement for the organization

Employers must balance compensation costs at a level that both ensures organizational competitiveness and provides sufficient rewards to employees for their knowledge, skills, abilities, and performance accomplishments. In order to attract, retain, and reward employees, employers provide several types of compensation.

Nature of Compensation

Compensation is an important factor affecting how and why people choose to work at one organization over others. Employers must be reasonably competitive with several types of compensation to attract and retain competent employees.

Types of Compensation

Rewards can be both intrinsic and extrinsic. *Intrinsic* rewards often include praise for completing a project or meeting performance objectives. Other psychological and social effects of compensation reflect the intrinsic type of rewards.[2] *Extrinsic* rewards are tangible and take both monetary and nonmonetary forms. Tangible components of a compensation program are of two general types (see Figure 12-1). With direct compensation, the employer exchanges

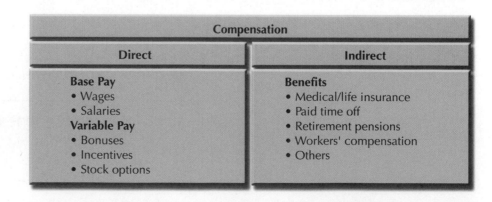

Figure 12-1 ▶ **Components of a Compensation Program**

Compensation	
Direct	**Indirect**
Base Pay • Wages • Salaries **Variable Pay** • Bonuses • Incentives • Stock options	**Benefits** • Medical/life insurance • Paid time off • Retirement pensions • Workers' compensation • Others

monetary rewards for work done. Employers provide indirect compensation—like health insurance—to everyone simply based on membership in the organization. *Base pay* and *variable pay* are the most common forms of direct compensation. Indirect compensation commonly consists of employee *benefits*.

Base Pay The basic compensation that an employee receives, usually as a wage or salary, is called **base pay**. Many organizations use two base pay categories, *hourly* and *salaried,* which are identified according to the way pay is distributed and the nature of the jobs. Hourly pay is the most common means of payment based on time, and employees paid hourly receive **wages**, which are payments directly calculated on the amount of time worked. In contrast, people paid **salaries** receive consistent payments each period regardless of the number of hours worked. Being salaried typically has carried higher status for employees than being paid wages. Some organizations maintain an all-salaried approach with their manufacturing and clerical employees in order to create a greater sense of loyalty and organizational commitment. However, they still must pay overtime to certain employees as defined by federal and state pay laws.

Variable Pay Another type of direct pay is **variable pay**, which is compensation linked directly to individual, team, or organizational performance. The most common types of variable pay for most employees take the form of bonuses and incentive program payments. Executives often receive longer-term rewards such as stock options. Variable pay, including executive compensation, is discussed in Chapter 13.

Benefits Many organizations provide numerous extrinsic rewards in an indirect manner. With indirect compensation, employees receive the tangible value of the rewards without receiving the actual cash. A **benefit** is an indirect reward—health insurance, vacation pay, or retirement pensions—given to an employee or group of employees as a part of organizational membership, regardless of performance.

Compensation Responsibilities

Compensation costs represent significant expenditures in most organizations. For instance, at one large hotel, employee payroll and benefits expenditures comprise about 60% of all costs. Although actual compensation costs can be easily calculated, the value derived by employers and employees proves more difficult to identify. To administer these expenditures wisely, HR specialists and other managers must work together.

A typical division of compensation responsibilities is illustrated in Figure 12-2 on the next page. HR specialists guide the development and administration of an organizational compensation system and conduct job evaluations and wage surveys. Also, because of the technical complexity involved, HR specialists typically assume responsibility for developing base pay programs and salary structures and policies. HR specialists may or may not do actual payroll processing. This labor-intensive responsibility is typically among the first to be outsourced. However, today some companies are retaining in-house processing because of improvements in software and Internet processing.[3] Operating managers evaluate the performance of employees and consider their performance when deciding compensation increases within the policies and guidelines established by the HR unit and upper management.

Base Pay The basic compensation an employee receives, usually as a wage or salary.

Wages Payments directly calculated on the amount of time worked.

Salaries Consistent payments made each period regardless of number of hours worked.

Variable pay Type of compensation linked to individual, team, or organizational performance.

Benefit An indirect reward given to an employee or group of employees as a part of organizational membership.

Figure 12-2 ▶ **Typical Division of HR Responsibilities: Compensation**

HR Unit	Managers
• *Develops and administers the compensation system.* • *Conducts job evaluation and wage surveys.* • *Develops wage/salary structures and policies.*	• *Attempt to match performance and rewards.* • *Recommend pay rates and increases based on guidelines from HR unit.* • *Evaluate employee performance for compensation purposes.*

Compensation System Design Issues

Compensation decisions must be viewed strategically. Because so many organizational funds are spent on compensation-related activities, it is critical for top management and HR executives to match compensation practices with what the organization is trying to accomplish.

Consider the following examples. The compensation practices that typically exist in a new organization may be different from those in a mature, more bureaucratic organization. If a firm wishes to create an innovative, entrepreneurial culture, it may offer bonuses and stock equity programs so that employees can participate in the growth and success of the company, but set its base pay and benefits at relatively modest levels. However, for a large, stable organization, more structured pay and benefit programs may be more common. Or an employer that sees brand identification as a major business objective may want a stable workforce to ensure continuity, so compensation strategy should encourage retention. But for a high tech firm that needs new ideas and a quick trip to market for new products, compensation might be designed to favor recruiting and marketing successes over retention.

Organizations must make a number of important decisions about the nature of a compensation system. Some decisions include the following: What philosophy and approach will be taken? How will the firm react to market pay levels? Is the job to be paid on the person's level of competence? Will pay be individual or team based?

Compensation Philosophies

The two basic compensation philosophies lie on opposite ends of a continuum. At one end of the continuum in Figure 12-3 is the *entitlement* philosophy; at the other end is the *performance-oriented* philosophy.[4] Most compensation systems fall somewhere in between.

Entitlement Orientation Many traditional organizations that give automatic increases to their employees every year practice the entitlement philosophy. Further, most of those employees receive the same or nearly the same percentage increase each year. Employees and managers who subscribe to the entitlement philosophy believe that individuals who have worked another year are *entitled* to a raise in base pay. They also believe all incentives and benefit programs should

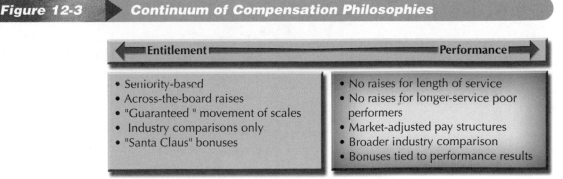

Figure 12-3 ▶ **Continuum of Compensation Philosophies**

◀ Entitlement ▬▬▬▬▬▬▬▬▬▬▬▬▬▬▬▬ Performance ▶

- Seniority-based
- Across-the-board raises
- "Guaranteed" movement of scales
- Industry comparisons only
- "Santa Claus" bonuses

- No raises for length of service
- No raises for longer-service poor performers
- Market-adjusted pay structures
- Broader industry comparison
- Bonuses tied to performance results

continue and be increased, regardless of changing industry or economic conditions. Commonly, in organizations following an entitlement philosophy, pay increases are referred to as *cost-of-living* raises, even if they are not tied specifically to economic indicators. Following an entitlement philosophy ultimately means that as employees continue their employment lives, employer costs increase, regardless of employee performance or organizational competitive pressures. Market comparisons tend to be made within an industry, rather than more broadly considering compensation in firms of all types. Bonuses in many entitlement-oriented organizations are determined in a paternalistic manner that often fails to reflect operating results. Instead, the CEO or owner acts as Santa Claus, passing out year-end bonus checks that generally do not vary from year to year. Therefore employees "expect" the bonus, which becomes another form of entitlement.

Performance Orientation Where a performance-oriented philosophy is followed, organizations do not guarantee additional or increased compensation simply for completing another year of organizational service. Instead, pay and incentives reflect performance differences among employees. Employees who perform well receive larger compensation increases; those who do not perform satisfactorily see little or no increase in compensation. Thus, employees who perform satisfactorily or better maintain or advance in relation to market compensation levels, whereas poor or marginal performers may fall behind. Also, bonuses are determined on the basis of individual, group, and/or organizational performance.

Few organizations follow totally performance-oriented compensation practices. However, in the midst of organizational restructuring occurring throughout many industries, organizations look for compensation systems that break the entitlement mode. Even in the public sector, some organizations have recognized the need to shift toward more performance-oriented re-organized compensation practices. How fast the shift occurs, given the traditions and the strength of public-sector unions, remains to be seen.

A performance orientation requires a variable pay approach in which pay goes up or down based on a measure of performance. Not everyone in the same job will be paid exactly the same, and not everyone will like the approach.

Logging On...

World at Work
Formerly the American Compensation Association, this site lists products, services, and research on compensation and benefits.

http://www.worldatwork.com

Figure 12-4 ▶ *Compensation Approaches*

Traditional Compensation Approach	Total Rewards Approach
Compensation is primarily base pay.	Variable pay is added to base.
Bonuses/perks are for executives only.	Annual/long-term incentives are provided to executives, managers, and employees.
Fixed benefits are tied to long tenure.	Flexible and portable benefits are offered.
Pay grade progression is based on organizational promotions.	Knowledge/skill-based broad bands determine pay grades.
Organization-wide standard pay plan exists.	Multiple plans consider job family, location, and business units.

A Range of Compensation Approaches

Companies regard pay as an important tool for recruiting, motivating, and retaining good people. Indeed, those goals change little over time, but the ways in which some companies approach them differ dramatically from previous approaches. Performance-based pay, tailored to the strategic circumstances of each organization, may consist of base pay, an annual bonus, a profit sharing plan, stock options, and a choice of various other benefits. Such a "total rewards" package would have been uncommon for a worker in 1950, but it is increasingly common today.[5]

The "human capital" within a firm that is performing well is likely to want to split the gains with the owners or shareholders. Variable pay combined with base pay can do that. Variable pay also shifts some of the risk of running a labor-intensive business from the company to the employees when the company is not doing well. Figure 12-4 presents some of the choices organizations must make regarding compensation approaches.

Traditional Compensation Approach

For some organizations a traditional compensation approach makes sense and offers certain advantages in specific competitive situations. It may be more legally defensible, less complex, and viewed as more "fair" by average and below-average employees. However, the total rewards approach helps retain top performers, can be more flexible when the economy goes up or down, and is favored by top-performing companies.[6] It clearly will *not* work in every situation.

Traditional compensation systems have evolved over a period of time to reflect a logical, rational approach to compensating employees. Job descriptions identify tasks and responsibilities and are then used to decide which jobs are more valuable. These systems calculate the value that each job contributes to the organization based on job evaluation. That value then is used to establish a pay range that reflects a person's progression as he or she grows and presumably gets better at the job.

dot.comp

Compensation for employees at the dot.com companies that boomed into the new millenium pushed the total rewards idea to new extremes and created many millionaire employees. Yet in retrospect, it simply reflected a sensible adaptation to unusual strategic conditions. Heavy demand for computer skills, a rapidly changing environment, volatile stock prices, and transparent pay in the industry characterized the unique dot.com market for employees.

Dot.coms, as start-up companies that had Internet-related ideas, needed people to help develop and market the ideas. In some cases these companies made huge amounts of money by selling stock to the public without ever showing any profit at all. Compensation for new employees usually consisted of base pay, often below market, and equity in the form of stock and stock options, which provided the primary reason for highly talented individuals to join these start-up companies. The mix of compensation in this total rewards approach was heavily skewed toward equity.

When individual companies went public during a period of time with wildly rising stock prices, some employees who had acquired stock options as part of their compensation became instant millionaires on paper. However, for those who did not cash out, their stock or options became worth little or nothing when the stock market crashed and many dot.com firms filed for bankruptcy.

A study on compensation in the dot.coms concluded that the opportunity for stock options brought people into risky employment situations. However, the study also revealed that it was not the salary and options that kept people in the company. It was the actual work they were doing, the people with whom they worked, and the way they were managed that kept them around. Thus, "dot.comp" appears to be no different from other attempts to address unique strategic concerns at a specific time and place.[7]

Total Rewards Approach

The total rewards approach tries to place a value on individuals rather than just the jobs. Managers factor in elements such as how much an employee knows or employee competence when determining compensation. The need for such an approach became more evident in trying to pay people with exceptional computer skills who, on the other hand, lacked traditional experience or educational degrees, as the HR Perspectives discusses.

Currently, some organizations incorporate variable pay programs as part of a total rewards approach for all levels of employees. Widespread use of various incentive plans, team bonuses, organizational gainsharing programs, and other designs serves to link growth in compensation to results. However, management must address two main issues when using variable pay systems:

1. Should performance be measured and rewarded based on individual, group, or organizational performance?
2. Should the length of time for measuring performance be short-term (less than one year) or longer-term (more than one year)?

The various types and facets of variable pay are discussed in the next chapter. But it is important to recognize the shift toward compensation being allocated through such plans, rather than the organization relying solely on base pay to reward employees at all levels for attaining strategic organizational objectives.

Figure 12-5 ▶ Compensation Quartile Strategies

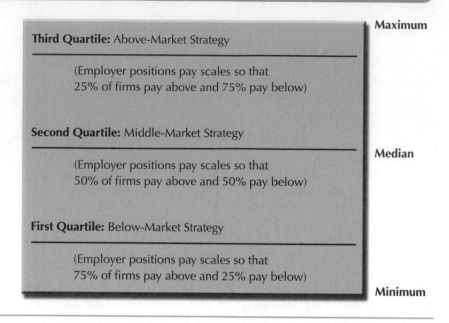

Third Quartile: Above-Market Strategy

(Employer positions pay scales so that
25% of firms pay above and 75% pay below)

Second Quartile: Middle-Market Strategy

(Employer positions pay scales so that
50% of firms pay above and 50% pay below)

First Quartile: Below-Market Strategy

(Employer positions pay scales so that
75% of firms pay above and 25% pay below)

Maximum

Median

Minimum

Decisions about Compensation Levels

Even though a company might wish to pay the top salaries in an industry on philosophical grounds, it may not be possible. Competition that keeps prices of products and services under control forces companies to control the cost of labor too. Especially when competing with lower-wage countries such as China or Mexico, the compensation paid some U.S. workers has become an issue. However, in some industries competition is not as critical a factor. An organization may be able to pay employees more (or less) than other employers.

Some organizations establish specific policies about where they wish to be positioned in the labor market. These policies use a *quartile strategy,* as illustrated in Figure 12-5. Data in pay surveys reveal that the actual dollar difference between quartiles is generally 15% to 20%.

Most employers choose to position themselves in the *second quartile* (median), in the middle of the market, based on pay survey data of other employers' compensation plans. Choosing this level attempts to balance employer cost pressures and the need to attract and retain employees by providing mid-level compensation levels.

An employer using a *first-quartile* approach may choose to pay below market compensation for several reasons. The employer may be experiencing a shortage of funds, making it unable to pay more and still meet objectives. Also, when an abundance of workers is available, particularly those with lower skills, a below-market approach can be used to attract sufficient workers at a lesser cost. The downside of this strategy is that higher turnover of workers is more likely. If the labor market supply tightens, then attracting and retaining workers becomes more difficult.

Logging On...

Economic Research Institute
This institute provides national and geographic salaries for various positions. On this Web site, the database and samples of the product can be viewed.

http://www.erieri.com

A *third-quartile* approach uses an aggressive pay-above-market emphasis. This strategy generally enables a company to attract and retain sufficient workers with the required capabilities and to be more selective when hiring. However, because it is a higher-cost approach, organizations often look for ways to increase the productivity of employees receiving above-market wages.

Competency-Based Pay

The design of most compensation programs rewards employees for carrying out their tasks, duties, and responsibilities. The job requirements determine which employees have higher base rates. Employees receive more for doing jobs that require a greater variety of tasks, more knowledge and skills, greater physical effort, or more demanding working conditions.[8]

However some organizations are emphasizing competencies rather than tasks. A number of organizations are paying employees for the competencies they demonstrate rather than just for the specific tasks performed. Paying for competencies rewards employees who exhibit more versatility and continue to develop their competencies. In knowledge-based pay (KBP) or skill-based pay (SBP) systems, employees start at a base level of pay and receive increases as they learn to do other jobs or gain other skills and therefore become more valuable to the employer. For example, a printing firm operates two-color, four-color, and six-color presses. The more colors, the more skill required of the press operators. Under a KBP or SBP system, press operators increase their pay as they learn how to operate the more complex presses, even though sometimes they may be running only two-color jobs. The success of competency plans requires managerial commitment to a philosophy different from the traditional one in organizations.[9] This approach places far more emphasis on training employees and supervisors. Also, workflow must be adapted to allow workers to move from job to job as needed.

When an organization moves to a competency-based system, considerable time must be spent identifying the required competencies for various jobs. Then each *block* of competencies must be priced using market data. Progression of employees must be possible, and they must be paid appropriately for all of their competencies. Any *limitations* on the numbers of people who can acquire more competencies should be clearly identified. *Training* in the appropriate competencies is particularly critical. Also, a competency-based system needs to acknowledge or certify employees as they acquire certain competencies, and then to verify the maintenance of those *competencies*. In summary, use of a competency-based system requires significant investment of management time and commitment.

Because competency plans focus on the growth and development of employee competencies, employees who continue to develop their competencies also benefit by receiving pay raises. With more organizations recognizing the value of competency-based systems, their usage has doubled in the last five years—16% of organizations now use such systems.[10] Both the organization and employees can benefit from a properly designed and implemented competency-based system. Some possible outcomes are identified in Figure 12-6 on the next page.

Figure 12-6 — Competency-Based Systems Outcomes

Organization-Related Outcomes	Employee-Related Outcomes
• *Greater workforce flexibility* • *Increased effectiveness of work teams* • *Fewer bottlenecks in workflow* • *Increased worker output per hour* • *More career-enhancement opportunities*	• *Enhanced employee understanding of organizational "big picture"* • *Greater employee self-management capabilities* • *Improved employee satisfaction* • *Greater employee commitment*

Individual vs. Team Rewards

As organizations have shifted to using work teams, they face the logical concern of how to develop compensation programs that build on the team concept. At issue is how to compensate the individual whose performance may also be evaluated on the basis of team achievement. Paying everyone on teams the same amount, even though they demonstrate differing competencies and levels of performance, obviously creates equity concerns for many employees.[11]

Many organizations use team rewards as variable pay above base pay. For base pay, individual compensation is based on competency- or skill-based approaches. Variable pay rewards for teams are most frequently distributed annually as a specified dollar amount, not as a percentage of base pay.

Based on experiences in the team-based environment, several factors should be considered when using team-based reward systems:

- Use skill-based pay for the base.
- Make the system simple and understandable.
- Use variable pay based on business entity performance.
- Distribute variable rewards at the team level.
- Maintain a high degree of employee involvement.

But team-based pay does not always succeed easily. At a Frito-Lay facility in Missouri, management implemented a team-based compensation program. "Team behavior" training focused on changing the organizational culture. All went satisfactorily until management announced changes in the pay program. Instead of pay raises being given across-the-board, employees would receive pay-for-performance raises based on team member input. Many workers objected so strongly to their team members influencing pay decisions that the plant management had to defer implementing team-based rewards. In some organizations studies suggest a link between team-based pay and increased turnover.[12]

In summary, the most successful uses of team-based compensation have been as variable pay on top of base pay. Rather than substituting for base pay programs, team-based rewards appear to be useful in rewarding performance of a team beyond the satisfactory level. More discussion on team-based incentives is contained in the next chapter.

Perceptions of Pay Fairness

Most people in organizations work in order to gain rewards for their efforts. Except in volunteer organizations, people expect to receive fair value in the form of tangible compensation for their efforts. Whether considering base pay, variable pay, or benefits, the extent to which employees perceive compensation to be fair often affects their performance and how they view their jobs and employers.

Equity The perceived fairness between what a person does and what the person receives.

This concept of **equity** (covered in Chapter 3) is the perceived fairness of what a person does (inputs) and what the person receives (outcomes). Individuals judge equity in compensation by comparing the effort and performance they give to the effort and performance of others and the subsequent rewards received. These comparisons are personal and based on individual perceptions, not just facts. However, a sense of inequity occurs when the comparison process results in an imbalance between input and outcomes. Figure 12-7 indicates the individual, organizational, and external dimensions of equity.

Procedural and Distributive Justice in Compensation

Internally, equity means that employees receive compensation in relation to the knowledge, skills, and abilities (KSAs) they use in their jobs as well as their responsibilities and accomplishments. Two key issues—procedural justice and distributive justice—relate to internal equity.

Procedural justice The perceived fairness of the process and procedures used to make decisions about employees.

Procedural justice is the perceived fairness of the process and procedures used to make decisions about employees, including their pay. Employees view procedural fairness in terms of the policies, procedures, and actions of supervisors

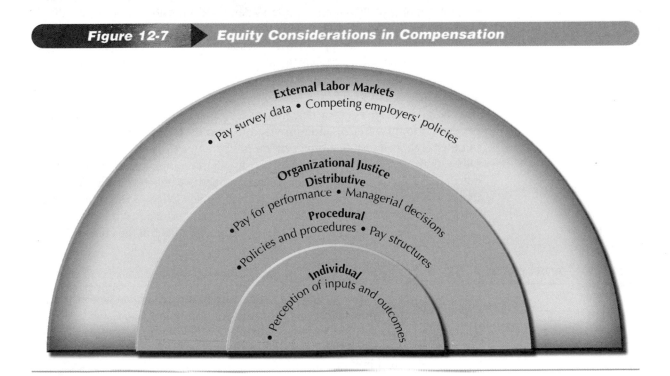

Figure 12-7 **Equity Considerations in Compensation**

External Labor Markets
• Pay survey data • Competing employers' policies

Organizational Justice
Distributive
• Pay for performance • Managerial decisions

Procedural
• Policies and procedures • Pay structures

Individual
• Perception of inputs and outcomes

Distributive justice The perceived fairness in the distribution of outcomes.

and managers who implement the policies and procedures. As it applies to compensation, the process of determining base pay for jobs, allocating pay increases, and measuring performance all must be perceived as fair.

Another related issue that must be considered is **distributive justice**, which refers to the perceived fairness in the distribution of outcomes. This facet of equity examines how pay relates to performance. As one example, if a hard-working employee whose performance is outstanding receives the same across-the-board raise as an employee with attendance problems and mediocre performance, then inequity may be perceived. Likewise, if two employees have similar performance records but one receives a significantly greater pay raise, the other may perceive an inequity due to supervisory favoritism or other factors not related to the job.

To address concerns about both types of justice, some organizations establish compensation appeals procedures. Many types of public-sector organizations formally identify appeals procedures that take more informal forms in private-sector firms. Typically, employees are encouraged to contact the HR department after discussing their concerns with their immediate supervisors and managers.

Pay Openness

Another equity issue concerns the degree of openness or secrecy that organizations allow regarding their pay systems. Pay information kept secret in "closed" systems includes how much others make, what raises others have received, and even what pay grades and ranges exist in the organization.[13]

A growing number of organizations are opening up their pay systems to some degree by informing employees of compensation policies, providing a general description of the compensation system, and indicating where an individual's pay is within a pay grade. Such information allows employees to make more accurate equity comparisons. The crucial element in an open pay system is that managers be able to explain satisfactorily the pay differences that exist.[14]

External Equity

If an employer does not provide compensation that employees view as equitable in relation to the compensation provided to employees performing similar jobs in other organizations, that organization is likely to experience higher turnover. Other drawbacks include greater difficulty in recruiting qualified and high-demand individuals. Also, by not being competitive the employers are more likely to attract and retain individuals with less knowledge, skills, and abilities, resulting in lower overall organizational performance. Organizations track external equity by using pay surveys, which are discussed later in the chapter.

Legal Constraints on Pay Systems

Compensation systems must comply with a myriad of government constraints. Important areas addressed by the laws include minimum wage standards and hours of work. The following discussion examines the laws and regulations affecting base compensation; laws and regulations affecting incentives and benefits are examined in later chapters.

Fair Labor Standards Act (FLSA)

The major federal law affecting compensation is the Fair Labor Standards Act (FLSA), which was passed in 1938. Amended several times to raise minimum wage rates and expand employers covered, the FLSA affects both private- and public-sector employers. Generally, private-sector employers engaged in interstate commerce and retail service firms with two or more employees and gross sales of at least $500,000 per year are covered by the act. Very small, family-owned and -operated entities and family farms generally remain excluded from coverage. Most federal, state, and local government employers also are subject to the provisions of the act, with the exception of military personnel, volunteer workers, and a few other limited groups.

Compliance with FLSA provisions is enforced by the Wage and Hour Division of the U.S. Department of Labor. To meet FLSA requirements employers must keep accurate time records and maintain these records for three years. Inspectors from the Wage and Hour Division investigate complaints filed by individuals who believe they have not received the overtime payments due them. Also, certain industries that historically have had a large number of wage and hour violations can be targeted, and firms in those industries can be investigated.

Penalties for wage and hour violations often include awards of back pay for affected current and former employees for up to two years. For example, The Money Store Inc. (a home equity loan company) was sued by five current and former employees. The employees had been classified as loan officers and assistant managers and the company argued they were exempt from FLSA requirements of overtime for that reason. The court ruled otherwise, and some 600 employees shared in the $4 million settlement.[15]

Some argue that the 60+-year-old law does not reflect today's economy. Its complexity creates great difficulties for employers trying to follow all the requirements of the law. Indeed to end up in court defending an FSLA claim, "all you need is one disgruntled employee." And the burden of proof and record-keeping requirements "falls squarely on the employer" a management attorney notes.[16] However, because little agreement can be reached on to how to change FLSA, it is unlikely to happen. The act focuses on the following three major objectives:

- Establish a minimum wage floor.
- Discourage oppressive use of child labor.
- Encourage limits on the number of weekly hours employees work through overtime provisions (exempt and non-exempt status).

Minimum Wage The FLSA sets a minimum wage to be paid to the broad spectrum of covered employees. The actual minimum wage can be changed only by congressional action. A lower minimum-wage level is set for "tipped" employees, such as restaurant workers, but their compensation must equal or exceed the minimum wage when average tips are included. Minimum wage levels continue to spark significant political discussions and legislative maneuvering. But, as the HR Perspective on the next page indicates, there also is a debate about the use of the minimum wage versus a living wage.

Logging On...

Wage and Hour Division
This government Web site from the Wage and Hour Division of the U.S. Department of Labor provides an overview of the Fair Labor Standards Act and other laws.

http://www.opm.gov/flsa/

WEST GROUP
A THOMSON COMPANY

Child Labor Restrictions
Describes occupational restrictions under child labor regulations.
Custom Search:
☑ ANALYSIS
Phrase: Occupational restrictions

Exempt employees
Employees to whom employers are not required to pay overtime under the Fair Labor Standards Act.

Non-exempt employees
Employees who must be paid overtime under the Fair Labor Standards Act.

Child-Labor Provisions The child-labor provisions of the FLSA set the minimum age for employment with unlimited hours at 16 years. For hazardous occupations (see Chapter 16), the minimum is 18 years of age. Individuals 14 to 15 years old may work outside school hours with certain limitations.

Many employers require age certificates for employees because the FLSA makes the employer responsible for determining an individual's age. A representative of a state labor department, a state education department, or a local school district generally issues such certificates.

Exempt and Non-exempt Status Under the FLSA, employees are classified as exempt or non-exempt. **Exempt employees** hold positions classified as *executive, administrative, professional,* or *outside sales,* to whom employers are not required to pay overtime. **Non-exempt employees** must be paid overtime under the Fair Labor Standards Act.

In base pay programs, employers often categorize jobs into groupings that tie the FLSA status and the method of payment together:

- Hourly
- Salaried non-exempt
- Salaried exempt

Hourly jobs require employers to pay overtime to comply with the FLSA. Employees in positions classified as *salaried non-exempt* are covered by the overtime provisions of the FLSA and therefore must be paid overtime. Salaried non-exempt positions sometimes include secretarial, clerical, and salaried blue-collar positions. *Salaried exempt* employees are not required by the FLSA to be paid overtime, although some organizations have implemented policies to pay a straight rate for extensive hours of overtime. For instance, some electric utilities pay first-line supervisors extra using a special rate for hours worked over 50 per week during storm emergencies. A growing number of salaried-exempt information professionals also receive additional compensation for working extensive hours.

Three major factors determine whether an individual holds an exempt position:

- Discretionary authority for independent action
- Percentage of time spent performing routine, manual, or clerical work
- Earnings level

Figure 12-8 on the next page shows the impact of these factors on each type of exemption. Note that earnings levels are basically meaningless, because they have not changed in years despite increases in the minimum wage. These inconsistencies result from political disagreement among employers, unions, legislators, and federal regulators.

Computer-Related Occupations Due to the growth of information systems and computer jobs, a special category of professionals was added in 1990. For those working in computer-related occupations who are paid at least the equivalent of $27.63 per hour on a salaried basis, the FLSA does not require overtime pay. Because the wage level in this case is set at approximately $58,000 per year, a limited number of jobs and individuals are affected.[18] For all other occupations, the FLSA has no set dollar level above which overtime is not required.

Overtime Provisions The FLSA establishes overtime pay requirements. Its provisions set overtime pay at one and one-half times the regular pay rate for all hours in excess of 40 per week, except for employees who are not covered by the FLSA. Overtime provisions do not apply to farm workers, who also have a lower minimum-wage schedule.

The work week is defined as a consecutive period of 168 hours (24 hours × 7 days) and does not have to be a calendar week. If they wish to do so, hospitals and nursing homes are allowed to use a 14-day period instead of a 7-day week as long as overtime is paid for hours worked beyond 8 in a day or 80 in a 14-day period. No daily number of hours requiring overtime is set, except for special provisions relating to hospitals and other specially designated organizations. Thus, if a manufacturing firm operates on a 4-day/10-hour schedule, no overtime pay is required by the act.

The most difficult part of the act is distinguishing who is and is not exempt. Some recent costly settlements have prompted more white-collar workers to sue for overtime pay. Retail managers, reporters, sales reps, personal bankers, engineers, computer programmers and claims adjusters have sued and in some cases won. For example, Wal-Mart pharmacists were ruled to be non-exempt.[19]

Figure 12-8 ▶ Wage/Hour Status Under Fair Labor Standards Act

Exemption Category	A Discretionary Authority	B Percent of Time	C Earning Levels
Executive	1. Primary duty is managing 2. Regularly directs work of at least two others 3. Authority to hire/fire or recommend these	1. Must spend 20% or less time doing clerical, manual, routine work (less than 40% in retail or service establishments)	2. Paid salary at $155/wk or $250/wk if meets A1-A2
Administrative	1. Primarily responsible for nonmanual or office work related to management policies 2. Regularly exercises discretion and independent judgment and makes important decisions 3. Regularly assists executives and works under general supervision	1. Must spend 20% or less time doing clerical, manual, routine work (less than 40% in retail or service establishments)	1. Paid salary at $155/wk or $250/wk if meets A1-A2
Professional	1. Performs work requiring knowledge of an advanced field *or* creative and original artistic work *or* works as a teacher in educational system 2. Must do work that is predominantly intellectual and varied	1. Must spend 20% or less time doing nonprofessional work	1. Paid salary at least $170/wk or $250/wk if meets A1
Outside Sales	1. Customarily works away from employer site *and* 2. Sells tangible or intangible items *or* 3. Obtains orders or contracts for services	1. Must spend 20% or less time doing work other than outside selling	2. No salary test

NOTE: For more details, see *Executive, Administrative, Professional, and Outside Sales Exemptions Under the Fair Labor Standards Act,* WH Publication no. 1363 (Washington, DC: U.S. Department of Labor, Employment Standards Administration, Wage and Hour Division).

Compensatory Time Off Often called *comp-time,* **compensatory time off** is given in lieu of payment for extra time worked. However, unless it is given to non-exempt employees at the rate of one and one-half time for the hours worked over a 40-hour week, comp-time is illegal in the private sector. Also, comp-time cannot be carried over from one pay period to another.

The only major exception to those provisions is for public-sector employees, such as fire and police employees, and a limited number of other workers. Because they often work 24-hour shifts, these individuals may receive compensatory time off. Police and fire officers can accumulate up to 480 hours; all other covered public-sector employees can accumulate up to 240 hours. When those hours are used, the employees must be paid their normal rates of pay, and the comp-time hours used do not count as hours worked in the paid week. Recently the U.S. Supreme Court ruled that local governments can require employees to take comp-time off rather than pay them overtime up to a certain amount of comp time.[20]

Independent Contractor Regulations

The growing use of contingent workers by many organizations has focused attention on another group of legal regulations—those identifying the criteria that independent contractors must meet. Figure 12-9 illustrates some of the key differences between an employee and an independent contractor.

Classifying someone as an independent contractor rather than an employee offers two primary advantages for the employer. First, the employer does not have to pay Social Security, unemployment, or workers' compensation costs. These additional payroll levies may add 10% or more to the costs of hiring the individual as an employee. Second, if the person is classified as an employee and is doing a job considered non-exempt under the federal Fair Labor Standards

---

Figure 12-9 ▶ **The IRS Test for Employees and Independent Contractors**

An Employee	An Independent Contractor
• *Must comply with instructions about when, where, and how to work*	• *Can hire, supervise, and pay assistants*
• *Renders services personally*	• *Generally can set own hours*
• *Has a continuing relationship with an employer*	• *Usually is paid by the job or on straight commission*
• *Usually works on the premises of the employer*	• *Has made a significant investment in facilities or equipment*
• *Normally is furnished tools, materials, and other equipment by the employer*	• *Can make a profit or suffer a loss*
• *Can be fired by an employer*	• *May provide services to two or more unrelated persons or firms at the same time*
• *Can quit at any time without incurring liability*	• *Makes services available to the public*

Source: U.S. Internal Revenue Service.

Act, then the employer may be responsible for overtime pay at the rate of time-and-a-half for any week in which the person works more than 40 hours. Most other federal and state entities rely on the criteria for independent contractor status identified by the Internal Revenue Service (IRS). The IRS considers 20 factors in making such a determination.[21]

Acts Affecting Government Contractors

Several compensation-related acts apply to firms having contracts with the U.S. government. The first, the *Davis-Bacon Act of 1931,* affects compensation paid by firms engaged in federal construction projects valued in excess of $2,000. It deals only with federal construction projects and requires that the "prevailing" wage rate be paid on all federal construction projects. The *prevailing wage* is determined by a formula that considers the rate paid for a job by a majority of the employers in the appropriate geographic area.

Two other acts require firms with federal supply or service contracts exceeding $10,000 to pay a prevailing wage. Both the *Walsh-Healy Public Contracts Act* and the *Service Contracts Act* apply only to those working directly on a federal government contract or who substantially affect its performance.

Equal Pay and Pay Equity

Various legislative efforts address the issue of wage discrimination on the basis of gender. The Equal Pay Act of 1963 applies to both men and women and prohibits using different wage scales for men and women performing substantially the same jobs. Pay differences can be justified on the basis of merit (better performance), seniority (longer service), quantity or quality of work, or factors other than gender. Similar pay must be given for jobs requiring equal skills, equal effort, or equal responsibility or jobs done under similar working conditions.

Pay equity Similarity in pay for all jobs requiring comparable levels of knowledge, skills, and abilities, even if actual duties and market rates differ significantly.

Pay equity is an issue different from equal pay for equal work. **Pay equity** is the concept (similar to comparable worth) that the pay for all jobs requiring comparable knowledge, skills, and abilities should pay the same even if job duties and market rates differ significantly. States with such laws for public-sector jobs include Hawaii, Iowa, Maine, Michigan, Minnesota, Montana, Ohio, Oregon, Washington, and Wisconsin. Such an approach in Canada has been deemed unsuccessful.[22] However, simply showing the existence of pay differences for jobs that are different has *not been sufficient* to prove discrimination in court in most cases.[23]

State Laws

Many state and municipal government bodies have enacted modified versions of federal compensation laws. If a state has a higher minimum wage than that set under the Fair Labor Standards Act, the higher figure becomes the required minimum wage. On the other end of the spectrum, many states once limited the number of hours women could work. However, these laws generally have been held to be discriminatory in a variety of court cases. Consequently, most states have dropped such laws.

Garnishment Laws

Garnishment A court action in which a portion of an employee's wages is set aside to pay a debt owed a creditor.

Garnishment of an employee's wage occurs when a creditor obtains a court order that directs an employer to set aside a portion of one employee's wages to pay a debt owed a creditor. Regulations passed as a part of the Consumer Credit Protection Act established limitations on the amount of wages that can be garnished and restricted the right of employers to discharge employees whose pay is subject to a single garnishment order. All 50 states have laws applying to wage garnishments.

Development of a Base Pay System

As Figure 12-10 shows, development of a base wage and salary system assumes that accurate job descriptions and job specifications are available. The job descriptions then are used in two activities: *job evaluation* and *pay surveys*. These activities are designed to ensure that the pay system is both internally equitable and externally competitive. The data compiled in these two activities

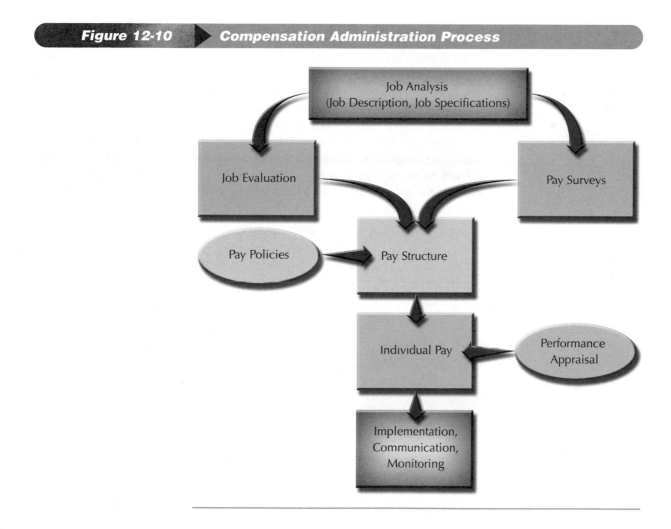

Figure 12-10   Compensation Administration Process

are used to design *pay structures*, including *pay grades* and minimum-to-maximum *pay ranges*. After the development of pay structures, individual jobs must be placed in the appropriate pay grades and employees' pay adjusted based on length of service and performance. Finally, the pay system must be monitored and updated.

Job Evaluation

Job evaluation provides a systematic basis for determining the relative worth of jobs within an organization.[24] It flows from the job analysis process and relies on job descriptions and job specifications. In a job evaluation, every job in an organization is examined and ultimately priced according to the following features:

- Relative importance of the job
- Knowledge, skills, and abilities (KSAs) needed to perform the job
- Difficulty of the job

Employers want their employees to perceive their pay as appropriate in relation to pay for jobs performed by others.[25] Because jobs may vary widely in an organization, it is particularly important to identify **benchmark jobs**—jobs that are found in many other organizations and performed by several individuals who have similar duties that are relatively stable and that require similar KSAs. For example, benchmark jobs commonly used in clerical/office situations are accounts payable processor, word-processing operator, and receptionist. Benchmark jobs are used with the job evaluation methods discussed here because they provide "anchors" against which unique jobs can be evaluated.

Several methods are used to determine internal job worth through job evaluation. All methods have the same general objective, but they differ in complexity and means of measurement. Regardless of the method used, the intent is to develop a usable, measurable, and realistic system to determine compensation in an organization.

Ranking Method The ranking method is one of the simplest methods of job evaluation. It places jobs in order, ranging from highest to lowest in value to the organization. The entire job is considered rather than the individual components. Several different methods of ranking are available, but all present problems.

Ranking methods can be extremely subjective, leaving managers the difficult task of explaining why one job is ranked higher than another to employees whose pay is affected by these rankings. When ranking involves a large number of jobs, the process may become awkward and unwieldy. Therefore, the ranking method generally is more appropriate in a small organization having relatively few jobs.

Classification Method In the classification method of job evaluation, descriptions of each class of jobs are written, and then each job in the organization is put into a grade according to the class description it best matches.

The major difficulty with the classification method is that subjective judgments are needed to develop the class descriptions and to place jobs accurately in them. With a wide variety of jobs and generally written class descriptions, some jobs could easily fall into two or three different grades.

Another problem with the classification method is its reliance on job titles and duties, which assumes that they are similar from one organization to another.

For these reasons, many federal, state, and local government entities, which traditionally used the classification method, have shifted to point systems.

Point Method The point method, the most widely used job evaluation method, is more sophisticated than the ranking and classification methods. It breaks down jobs into various compensable factors and places weights, or *points,* on them. A **compensable factor** identifies a job value commonly present throughout a group of jobs. The factors are derived from the job analysis. For example, for jobs in warehouse and manufacturing settings, *physical demands, hazards encountered,* and *working environment* may be identified as compensable factors and weighted heavily. However, in most office and clerical jobs, those factors are of little importance. Consequently, the compensable factors used and the weights assigned must reflect the nature of the jobs under study.

Figure 12-11 on the next page illustrates how the system works. The individual using the point chart in the figure looks at a job description and identifies the degree to which each element is necessary to perform the job satisfactorily. For example, the points assigned for a payroll clerk for education might be 42 points, third degree. To reduce subjectivity, a group of people familiar with the jobs often makes such determinations. Once points have been identified for all factors, the total points for the payroll clerk job are computed. After point totals have been determined for all jobs, the jobs are grouped together into pay grades.

A special type of point method used by a consulting firm, the Hay Group, has received widespread application, although it is most often used with exempt employees. The *Hay system* uses three factors and numerically measures the degree to which each of these factors is required in each job. The three factors and their subfactors are as follows:

Know-How	**Problem Solving**	**Accountability**
■ Functional expertise	■ Environment	■ Freedom to act
■ Managerial skills	■ Challenge	■ Impact of end results
■ Human relations		■ Magnitude

The point method has been widely used because it is a relatively simple system to use. Also, it considers the components of a job rather than the total job and is much more comprehensive than either the ranking or classification method. Once points are determined and a job evaluation point manual developed, the method can be used easily by people who are not specialists. The system can be understood by managers and employees, which gives it a definite advantage.

Another reason for the widespread use of the point method is that it evaluates the components of a job and determines total points before the current pay structure is considered. In this way, an employer can assess relative worth instead of relying on past patterns of worth.

One major drawback to the point method is the time needed to develop a system. For this reason, employers often use manuals and systems developed by management consultants or other organizations. Point systems have also been criticized for reinforcing traditional organizational structures and job rigidity. Although not perfect, the point method of job evaluation generally is better than the classification and ranking methods because it quantifies job elements.[26]

Figure 12-11 ▶ Job Evaluation Point Chart: Clerical Group

Factor	1st Degree Points	2nd Degree Points	3rd Degree Points	4th Degree Points
1. Education	14	28	42	56
2. Experience	22	44	66	88
3. Initiative and ingenuity	14	28	42	56
4. Contacts with others	14	28	42	56
Responsibility				
5. Supervision received	10	20	35	50
6. Latitude and depth	20	40	70	100
7. Work of others	5	10	15	20
8. Trust imposed	10	20	35	50
9. Performance	7	14	21	28
Other				
10. Work environment	10	25	45	
11. Mental or visual demand	10	20	35	
12. Physical effort	7	14	21	28

Note: The specific degrees and points for **Education** are as follows:

Education is the basic prerequisite knowledge essential to satisfactorily perform the job. This knowledge may have been acquired through formal schooling, as well as correspondence courses, company education programs, or through equivalent experience in allied fields. Analyze the minimum requirements of the job and not the formal education of individuals performing it.

1st Degree–Requires knowledge usually equivalent to a two-year high school education. Requires ability to read, write, and follow simple written or oral instructions and to use simple arithmetic processes involving counting, adding, subtracting, dividing, and multiplying whole numbers. May require basic typing ability.

2nd Degree–Requires knowledge equivalent to a four-year high school education. Requires ability to perform advanced arithmetic processes involving adding, subtracting, dividing, multiplying, or decimals and fractions and ability to maintain or prepare routine correspondence, records, and reports. May require knowledge of advanced typing and/or basic knowledge of bookkeeping, drafting, etc.

3rd Degree–Requires knowledge equivalent to a four-year high school education plus some specialized knowledge/training in a particular field, such as elementary accounting, general design reading, or engineering practices.

4th Degree–Requires knowledge equivalent to two years of college education. Requires ability to understand and perform work involving general engineering or accounting theory. Requires ability to originate and compile statistics and interpretive reports, as well as prepare correspondence of a difficult or technical nature.

Factor Comparison The factor-comparison method is a quantitative and quite complex combination of the ranking and point methods. It involves first determining the benchmark jobs in an organization, selecting compensable factors, and ranking all benchmark jobs factor by factor. Next, a comparison of jobs to market rates for benchmark jobs results in the assignment of monetary values for each factor. The final step is to evaluate all other jobs in the organization by comparing them with the benchmark jobs. A major advantage of the factor-comparison method is that it is tailored specifically to one organization. Each organization must develop its own key jobs and its own factors. For this reason, buying a packaged system may not be appropriate. But the major disadvantages of the factor-comparison method are its difficulty and complexity, and it is time-consuming to establish and develop.

Integrated and Computerized Job Evaluation

Increasingly, organizations are linking the components of wage and salary programs through computerized and statistical techniques. Using a bank of compensable factors, employers can select those factors most relevant for the different job families in the organization. Then these integrated systems can perform the following tasks:

- Create job descriptions that identify the compensable functions for each job.
- Link to pay survey data available on the Internet.
- Use multiple regression and other statistical methods to analyze job evaluation and pay survey relationships.
- Compare current employee pay levels in a database to the job evaluation and pay survey data.
- Develop costing models and budgetary implications of various implementation approaches.

Because of the advanced expertise needed to develop and computerize the integrated systems, management consultants are the primary source for them. These systems really are less a separate method and more an application of information technology and advanced statistics to the process of developing a wage and salary program. Integrated systems, including the consulting expertise necessary to work through and implement them, are relatively expensive to purchase. Therefore they generally are used only by medium- to large-sized employers.

Legal Issues and Job Evaluation

Employers usually view evaluating jobs to determine rates of pay as a separate issue from selecting individuals for those jobs or taking disciplinary action against individuals. Because job evaluation affects the employment relationship, specifically the pay of individuals, it involves legal issues that must be addressed.

Job Evaluation and the Americans with Disabilities Act (ADA) The Americans with Disabilities Act (ADA) requires employers to identify the essential functions of a job. However, all facets of jobs are examined during a job evaluation. For instance, assume a production job requires a punch press operator to drill holes in parts and place them in a bin of finished products. Every three hours the operator must push that bin, which may weigh 200 pounds or more, to the packaging area. The movement of the bin probably is not an essential function. But if job evaluation considers the physical demands associated with pushing the bin, then the points assigned may be different from the points assigned if only the essential functions are considered.

Job Evaluation and Gender Issues Critics have charged that traditional job evaluation programs place less weight on knowledge, skills, and working conditions for many female-dominated jobs in office and clerical areas than on the same factors for male-dominated jobs in craft and manufacturing areas. As discussed earlier, advocates of pay equity view the disparity in pay between

Research on Job Evaluation and Power

Theresa Welbourne and Charles Trevor studied whether the power of a department or the power of the job incumbent affected job evaluation outcomes in a university setting. As described in the *Academy of Management Journal,* the researchers noted that job evaluation attempts to assess the worth of a position (not the person in it) to the organization. The hierarchy of positions that results from job evaluation is then used to allocate pay to positions.

In this study the jobs evaluated were non-academic jobs at a large western university. When a department wanted to upgrade a

job it got approval to proceed and then submitted a job description to the HR unit where the proposed change was officially evaluated. HR specialists used a point system consisting of four main compensable factors: *decision-making responsibility, job complexity, interdepartmental contact,* and *authority.* For jobs each factor was studied then assigned points. Finally, the total points were used to determine the pay grade placement of jobs.

The researchers found that the power of the originating department consistently predicted the numbers of new positions

approved and job upgrades received. Further, the power of the incumbent also affected the results.

This research may call into question one of the hallmarks of job evaluation—its supposed "objectivity" in setting a pay system. However, universities by their nature may be enough different from other organizations that such conclusions may not be valid. In fact, other research has shown that power and politics in universities predict workload, budget allocations, and allocations of other resources too, so the results of this study are not surprising.[27]

men's jobs and women's jobs as evidence of gender discrimination. These advocates also have attacked typical job evaluations as being gender biased. Employers counter that because they base their pay rates heavily on external equity comparisons in the labor market, they are simply reflecting rates the "market economy" sets for jobs and workers rather than engaging in discrimination. Undoubtedly, with further court decisions, government actions, and research, job evaluation activities will face more pressures to address gender differences. As the HR Perspective discusses, recent research suggests that job evaluation has limitations.

Pay Surveys

Pay survey A collection of data on compensation rates for workers performing similar jobs in other organizations.

Another part of building a pay system is surveying the pay that other organizations provide for similar jobs. A **pay survey** is a collection of data on compensation rates for workers performing similar jobs in other organizations. An employer may use surveys conducted by other organizations, or it may decide to conduct its own survey.[28]

Using Prepared Pay Surveys Many different surveys are available from a variety of sources. The Internet provides a large number of pay survey sources and data on-line. However, use of these sources requires caution because their accuracy and completeness may not be verifiable.[29]

Whether available electronically or in printed form, national surveys on many jobs and industries come from the U.S. Department of Labor, Bureau of Labor Statistics, and through national trade associations. In many communities, employers participate in wage surveys sponsored by the local Chamber of Commerce to provide information to new employers interested in locating in the community.

Properly using surveys from other sources requires that certain questions be addressed:

- *Participants:* Is the survey a realistic sample of those employers with whom the organization competes for employees?
- *Broad-based:* Is the survey balanced so that organizations of varying sizes, industries, and locales are included?
- *Timeliness:* How current are the data (determined by the date when the survey was conducted)?
- *Methodology:* How established is the survey, and how qualified are those who conducted it?
- *Job matches:* Does it contain job summaries so that appropriate matches to job descriptions can be made?

Developing a Pay Survey If needed pay information is not already available, the employer can undertake its own pay survey. Employers with comparable jobs should be selected and those employers considered to be "representative" should also be surveyed.

Jobs to be surveyed also must be determined. Because not all jobs in all organizations can be surveyed, those designing the pay survey should select jobs with common job elements that can be easily compared, and that represent a broad range of jobs. Key or benchmark jobs are especially important ones to include. It is also advisable to provide brief job descriptions for jobs surveyed in order to ensure more accurate matches. For executive-level jobs, data on total compensation (base pay and bonuses) is often gathered as well.

In the next phase of designing the pay survey, managers decide what information is needed for various jobs. Information such as starting pay, base pay, overtime rate, vacation and holiday pay policies, and bonuses all can be included in a survey. However, requesting too much information may discourage survey returns.

The results of the pay survey usually are made available to those participating in the survey in order to gain their cooperation. Most surveys specify confidentiality, and data are summarized to assure anonymity. Different job levels often are included, and the pay rates are presented both in overall terms and on a city-by-city basis to reflect regional differences in pay.

Legal Issues and Pay Surveys One reason for employers to use outside consultants to conduct pay surveys is to avoid charges that the employers are attempting "price-fixing" on wages. The federal government has filed suit in the past alleging that by sharing wage data, employers may be attempting to hold wages down artificially in violation of the Sherman Anti-Trust Act.

A key case involved the Utah Society for Healthcare Human Resource Administration and nine hospitals in the Salt Lake City area. The consent decree that resulted prohibits all health-care facilities in Utah from designing, developing, or conducting a wage survey. The hospitals can participate in surveys conducted by independent third-party firms only if privacy safeguards are met. Specifically, only aggregate data that are summarized may be provided, and no data from an individual firm may be identified. As a result, it is likely that fewer firms will conduct their own surveys, and the use of outside consultants to do pay surveys will continue to grow.

Pay Structures

Market line The line on a graph showing the relationship between job value, as determined by job evaluation points and pay survey rates.

Once survey data are gathered, pay structures can be developed by the process depicted in Figure 12-12. As indicated in the figure, tying pay survey information to job evaluation data can be done by plotting a *wage curve,* and *scattergram.* This plotting involves first making a graph that charts job evaluation points and pay survey rates for all surveyed jobs. The graph shows the distribution of pay for surveyed jobs, allowing development of a linear trend line via the *least-squares regression method.* Also, a curvilinear line can be developed by use of multiple regression and other statistical techniques. The end result is the development of a **market line**. This line shows the relationship between job

Figure 12-12 ▶ **Establishing Pay Structures**

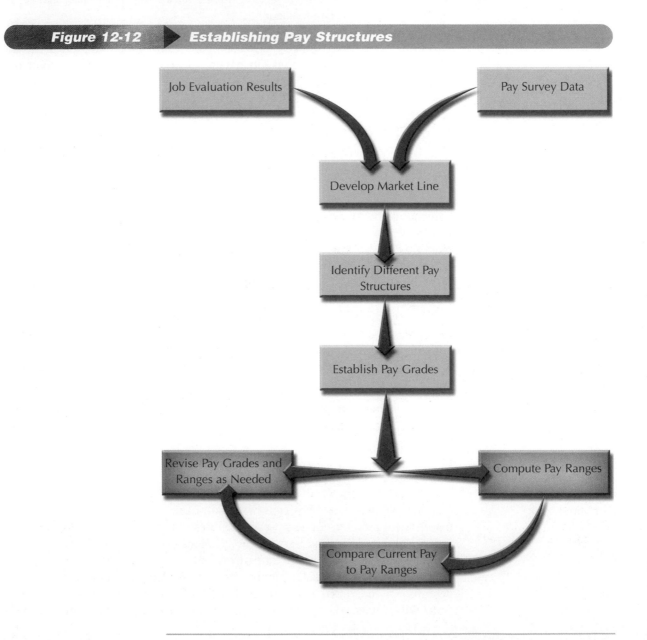

value, as determined by job evaluation points and pay survey rates. (Details on these methods can be found in any basic compensation text.)

Different Pay Structures

In organizations there are a number of different job families. The pay survey data may reveal different levels of pay resulting from market factors that may lead to the establishment of several different pay structures, rather than just one structure. Examples of some common pay structures include: (1) hourly and salaried; (2) office, plant, technical, professional, and managerial; and (3) clerical, information technology, professional, supervisory, management, and executive.

The nature and culture of the organization are considerations for determining how many and which pay structures to have. Another basis is the results of the statistical analysis done when determining market lines, particularly the r^2 levels when the data is analyzed by different job families and groups. Generally, an r^2 of +.85 or higher is desired.

Establishing Pay Grades

Pay grade A grouping of individual jobs having approximately the same job worth.

In the process of establishing a pay structure, organizations use **pay grades** to group individual jobs having approximately the same job worth. Although no set rules govern establishing pay grades, some overall suggestions can be useful. Generally, from 11 to 17 grades are used in small and medium-sized companies with fewer than 500 employees. However, as discussed earlier, a growing number of employers are reducing the number of grades by broadbanding.

Broadbanding

Broadbanding Practice of using fewer pay grades having broader ranges than in traditional compensation systems.

Broadbanding is the practice of using fewer pay grades with much broader ranges than in traditional compensation systems. Combining many grades into these broadbands is designed to encourage horizontal movement and therefore more skill acquisition.[30] Figure 12-13 depicts the difference between traditional pay structures and broadbanding.

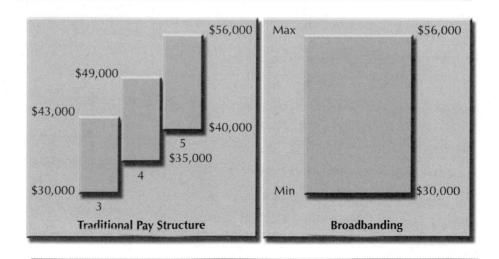

Figure 12-13 ▸ **Traditional Pay Structure vs. Broadbanding**

There are several reasons why it is beneficial to reduce the number of pay grades and broaden pay ranges. First and foremost, broadbanding is more consistent with the flattening of organizational levels and the growing use of jobs that are multidimensional. With fewer bands and broader ranges, employees can shift responsibilities as market conditions and organizational needs change. Traditional questions from employees about when a promotion to a new grade occurs, and what pay adjustments will be made for temporarily performing some new job responsibilities, are unnecessary. The primary reasons for broadbanding are: (1) creating more flexible organizations, (2) encouraging competency development, and (3) emphasizing career development.

However, broadbanding is not appropriate for every organization as seen in survey results that found only about 15 percent of employers use broadbanding.[31] Many organizations operate in a relatively structured manner, and the flexibility associated with broadbanding is not consistent with the traditional culture in many organizations.

A problem with broadbanding is that many employees have become "conditioned" to the idea that a promotion is accompanied by a pay raise and movement to a new pay grade. As a result of removing this grade progression, the organization may be seen as having fewer upward promotion opportunities available.[32] Despite these and other problems, it is likely that broadbanding will continue to grow in usage.

Pay Ranges

The pay range for each pay grade also must be established. Using the market line as a starting point, the employer can determine minimum and maximum pay levels for each pay grade by making the market line the midpoint line of the new pay structure.[33] (See Figure 12-14.) For example, in a particular pay grade, the

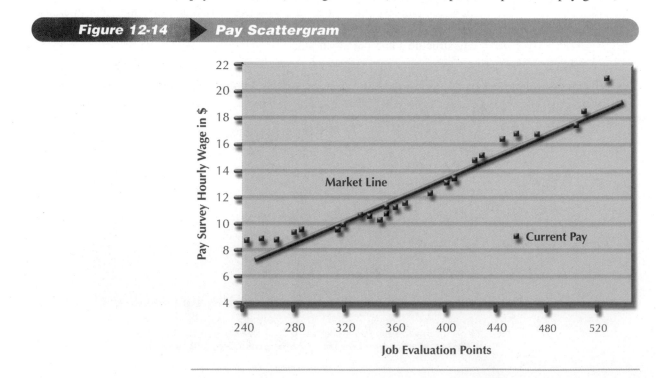

Figure 12-14 ▶ **Pay Scattergram**

Figure 12-15 Typical Pay Range Widths

Types of Jobs	Range Above Minimum	% Around Midpoint
Executives	*50%–70%*	*± 20–25%*
Mid-Management/Professionals	*40%–50%*	*± 16–20%*
Technicians/Skilled Craft & Clerical	*30%–40%*	*± 13–16%*
General Clerical/Others	*25%–35%*	*± 11–15%*

maximum value may be 20% above the midpoint located on the market line and the minimum value 20% below it.

As Figure 12-15 shows, a smaller minimum-to-maximum range should be used for lower-level jobs than for higher-level jobs, primarily because employees in lower-level jobs tend to stay in them for shorter periods of time and have greater promotion possibilities. For example, a clerk-typist might advance to the position of secretary or word-processing operator. In contrast, a design engineer likely would have fewer possibilities for upward movement in an organization. However, using the same percentage range at all levels can make administration of a pay system easier in small firms. If broadbanding is used, then much wider ranges, often exceeding 100%, may be used.

Experts recommend having overlap between grades. This structure means that an experienced employee in a lower grade can be paid more than a less-experienced employee in a job in the next pay grade. With pay grade overlap, an individual in the higher-grade job, for example grade 4, may be paid less than someone in a grade 3 job, but has more room for pay progression. Thus, over time the pay of a person in the grade 4 job may surpass the pay of a person in grade 3, who may "top out" because of the pay grade 3 maximum. Compensation experts have suggested that the same monetary amounts can appear in as many as four different pay grades.

Once pay grades and ranges have been computed, then the current pay of employees must be compared to the draft ranges. If the pay of a significant number of employees falls outside the ranges, then a revision of the pay grades and ranges may be needed. Also, once costing and budgeting scenarios are run in order to assess the financial input of the new pay structures, then pay policy decisions about market positioning may have to be revised, by either lowering or raising the ranges.

Individual Pay

Once managers have determined pay ranges, they can set the pay for specific individuals. Setting a range for each pay grade gives flexibility by allowing individuals to progress within a grade instead of having to be moved to a new grade each time they receive a raise. A pay range also allows managers to reward the better performing employees while maintaining the integrity of the pay system. Each dot in Figure 12-16 on the next page represents an individual employee's current pay in relation to the pay ranges that have been developed.

Figure 12-16 ▶ Example of Pay Grades and Pay Ranges

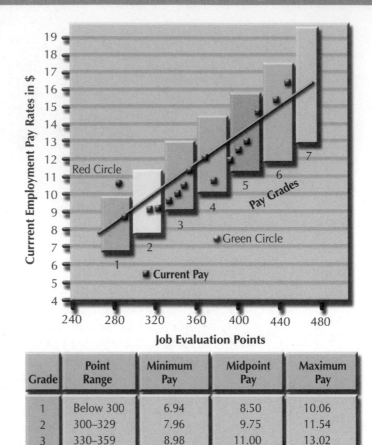

Grade	Point Range	Minimum Pay	Midpoint Pay	Maximum Pay
1	Below 300	6.94	8.50	10.06
2	300–329	7.96	9.75	11.54
3	330–359	8.98	11.00	13.02
4	360–389	10.00	12.25	14.50
5	390–419	11.01	13.49	15.97
6	420–449	11.79	14.74	17.69
7	Over 450	12.79	15.99	19.18

Rates Out of Range

Regardless of how well constructed a pay structure is, there usually are a few individuals whose pay is lower than the minimum or higher than the maximum. These situations occur most frequently when firms that have had an informal pay system develop a new, more formalized one.

Red-circled employee An incumbent who is paid above the range set for the job.

Red-Circled Employees As shown on the graph in Figure 12-16, a **red-circled employee** is an incumbent who is paid above the range set for the job. For example, assume that an employee's current pay is $10.92 per hour but the pay range for that grade is $6.94 to $10.06. The person would be red circled. Over time management would attempt to bring the employee's rate into grade.

Several approaches can be used to bring a red-circled person's pay into line. Although the fastest way would be to cut the employee's pay, that approach is not recommended and is seldom used. Instead, the employee's pay may be frozen until the pay range can be adjusted upward to get the employee's pay rate back into the grade. Another approach is to give the employee a small lump-sum payment but not adjust the pay rate when others are given raises.

Green-Circled Employees An individual whose pay is below the range is a **green-circled employee.** Promotion is a major contributor to this situation. Generally, it is recommended that the green-circled individual receive fairly rapid pay increases to reach the pay grade minimum. More frequent increases can be used if the increase to minimum would be large.

Green-circled employee
An incumbent who is paid below the range set for the job.

Pay Compression

One major problem many employers face is **pay compression,** which occurs when the pay differences among individuals with different levels of experience and performance becomes small. Pay compression occurs for a number of reasons, but the major one involves situations in which labor market pay levels increase more rapidly than current employees' pay adjustments. Such situations are prevalent in many occupational areas, such as the information technology field depending upon specific market conditions.[34]

Pay compression Situation in which pay differences among individuals with different levels of experience and performance in the organization becomes small.

In response to competitive market shortages of particular job skills, managers occasionally may have to deviate from the priced grades to hire people with scarce skills. For example, suppose the worth of a specialized information systems analyst's job is evaluated at $48,000 to $58,000 annual salary in a company, but qualified individuals are in short supply and other employers are paying $70,000. The firm must pay the higher rate. Suppose also that several analysts who have been with the firm for several years started at $48,000 and have received 6% increases each year. These current employees may still be making less than salaries paid to attract and retain new analysts from outside with less experience. One partial solution to pay compression is to have employees follow a step progression based on length of service, assuming performance is satisfactory or better.

Issues Involving Pay Increases

Decisions about pay increases often are critical ones in the relationships among employees, their managers, and the organization. Individuals express expectations about their pay and about how much increase is "fair," especially in comparison with the increases received by other employees. There are several ways to determine pay increases.

Pay Adjustment Matrix

Many employers profess to have a pay system based on performance. But relying on performance appraisal information for making pay adjustments assumes that the appraisals are accurate and done well, which is not always the case. Consequently, some system for integrating appraisals and pay changes must be developed and applied equally. Often, this integration is done through the development of a *pay adjustment matrix,* or *salary guide chart.* Use of pay adjustment matrices

Figure 12-17 ▶ **Pay Adjustment Matrix**

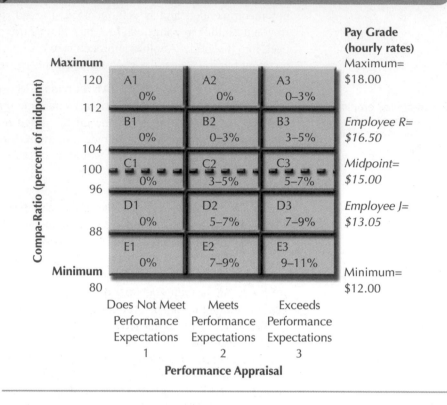

Such charts reflect a person's upward movement in an organization. which often depends on the person's performance, as rated in an appraisal, and on the person's position in the pay range, which has some relation to experience as well. A person's placement on the chart determines what pay raise the person should receive. For example, if employee *J* is rated as exceeding expectations (3) with a compa-ratio of 87, that person is eligible for a raise of 7% to 9% according to the chart in Figure 12-16. Several interesting facets in the sample matrix illustrate the emphasis on paying for performance. First, those individuals whose performance is below expectations receive no raises, not even a so-called cost-of-living raise. This approach sends a strong signal that poor performers will not continue to receive increases just by completing another year of service.

Compa-ratio Pay level divided by the midpoint of the pay range.

bases adjustments in part on a person's **compa-ratio,** which is the pay level divided by the midpoint of the pay range. To illustrate from Figure 12-17, the compa-ratio for two employees would be:

$$\text{Employee } R = \frac{\$16.50 \text{ (current pay)}}{15.00 \text{ (midpoint)}} \times 100 \rightarrow \text{Compa-ratio} = 110$$

$$\text{Employee } J = \frac{\$13.05 \text{ (current pay)}}{15.00 \text{ (midpoint)}} \times 100 \rightarrow \text{Compa-ratio} = 87$$

Second, notice that as employees move up the pay range, they must exhibit higher performance to obtain the same percentage raise as those lower in the range performing at the "meets performance expectations" (2) level. This approach is taken because the firm is paying above the market midpoint but receiving only satisfactory performance rather than above-market performance. Charts can be constructed to reflect the specific pay-for-performance policy and philosophy in an organization.

Seniority

Seniority Time spent in the organization or on a particular job.

Seniority, or time spent in the organization or on a particular job, can be used as the basis for pay increases. Many employers have policies that require a person to be employed for a certain length of time before being eligible for pay increases. Pay adjustments based on seniority often are set as automatic steps once a person has been employed the required length of time, although performance must be at least satisfactory in many non-union systems.

Maturity curve Curve that depicts the relationship between experience and pay rates.

A closely related approach uses a **maturity curve,** which depicts the relationship between experience and pay rates. Pay rises as an employee's experience increases, which is especially useful for professionals and skilled craft employees. Unlike a true seniority system, in which a pay raise occurs automatically once someone has put in the required time, a system using maturity curves is built on the assumption that as experience increases, proficiency and performance also increase, so pay raises are appropriate. If proficiency does not increase, theoretically pay adjustments are reduced, although it seldom happens in practice. Once a person plateaus in proficiency, then the pay progression is limited to the overall movement of the pay structure.

Cost-of-Living Adjustments (COLA)

A common pay-raise practice is the use of a *standard raise* or *cost-of-living adjustment* (COLA). Giving all employees a standard percentage increase enables them to maintain the same real wages in a period of economic inflation. Often, these adjustments are tied to changes in the Consumer Price Index (CPI) or some other general economic measure. However, numerous studies have revealed that the CPI overstates the actual cost of living.

Logging On...

Compensation Link

New information on compensation and economic indicators and trends can be found on this Web site.

http://www.compensationlink. com

Unfortunately, some employers give across-the-board raises and call them *merit raises,* which they are not. If all employees get a pay increase, it is legitimately viewed as a cost-of-living adjustment that has little to do with merit or good performance. For this reason, employers should reserve the term *merit* for any amount above the standard raise, and they should state clearly which amount is for performance and which is the "automatic" COLA adjustment.

Lump-Sum Increases (LSI)

Most employees who receive pay increases, either for merit or seniority, first have their base pay adjusted and then receive an increase in the amount of their regular monthly or weekly paycheck. For example, an employee who makes $12.00 per hour and then receives a 3% increase will move to $12.36 per hour.

Lump-sum increase (LSI) A one-time payment of all or part of a yearly pay increase.

In contrast, **a lump-sum increase (LSI)** is a one-time payment of all or part of a yearly pay increase. The pure LSI approach does not increase the base pay. Therefore, in this example the person's base pay remains at $12.00 per hour. If an LSI of 3% is granted, then the person receives $748.80 (36¢ per hour × 2080 working hours in the year.) However, the base rate remains at $12.00 per hour, which slows down the progression of the base wages. It also allows for the amount of the "lump" to be varied, without having to continually raise the base rate. Some organizations place a limit on how much of a merit increase can be taken as a lump-sum payment. Other organizations split the lump sum into two checks, each representing one-half of the year's pay raise.

As with any plan, LSI offers advantages and disadvantages. The major advantage of an LSI plan is that it heightens employees' awareness of what their performance "merited." A lump-sum check also gives employees some flexibility in their spending patterns so that they can buy big-ticket items without having to take out a loan. In addition, the firm can slow down the increase of base pay, so that the compounding effect of succeeding raises is reduced. Unionized employers, such as Boeing and Ford, have negotiated LSI plans as a way to hold down base wages, which also holds down the rates paid for overtime work. Pension costs and some other benefits, often tied to base wages, can be reduced as well.

One disadvantage of LSI plans is administrative tracking, including a system to handle income tax and Social Security deductions from the lump-sum check. Also, workers who take a lump-sum payment may become discouraged because their base pay has not changed. Unions generally resist LSI programs for this reason and because of the impact on pensions and benefits, unless the total amount paid including the LSI is used in determining pension computations.

Summary

- Compensation provided by an organization can come directly through base pay and variable pay and indirectly through benefits.
- Compensation responsibilities of both HR specialists and managers must be performed well. Compensation practices are closely related to organizational culture, philosophies, strategies, and objectives.
- A continuum of compensation philosophies exists, ranging from an entitlement-oriented philosophy to a performance-oriented philosophy.
- More companies are using competency-based pay, which focuses on individuals' capabilities.
- When designing and administering compensation programs, behavioral aspects must be considered. Equity, organizational justice, pay openness, and external equity are all important.
- The Fair Labor Standards Act (FLSA), as amended, is the major federal law that affects pay systems. It requires most organizations to pay a minimum wage and to comply with overtime provisions, including appropriately classi-

fying employees as exempt or non-exempt and as independent contractors or employees.
- Other laws place restrictions on employers who have federal supply contracts or federal construction contracts, or on those employers who garnish employees' pay.
- Administration of a wage and salary system requires the development of pay policies that incorporate internal and external equity considerations.
- Job evaluation determines the relative worth of jobs. Several different evaluation methods exist, with the point method being the most widely used.
- Once the job evaluation process has been completed, pay survey data must be collected and a pay structure developed. An effective pay system requires that changes continue to be made as needed.
- Developing a pay structure includes grouping jobs into pay grades and establishing a pay range for each grade.

- Broadbanding, which uses fewer pay grades with wider ranges, provides greater career movement possibilities for employees and has grown in popularity.
- Individual pay must take into account employees' placement within pay grades. Problems involving "red circled" jobs, whose rates are above pay range, and "green circled" jobs, that are below pay range, may be addressed in a number of different ways.
- Individual pay increases can be based on performance, cost-of-living adjustments, seniority, or a combination of approaches.
- Many organizations use seniority of employees and provide cost-of-living adjustments, but this negates a pay-for-performance approach.

Review and Discussion Questions

1. Give examples of direct and indirect compensation at a recent job that you have had.
2. Discuss the compensation philosophies that seemed to be used at organizations where you worked. What were the consequences of those philosophies?
3. Why are competency-based compensation, broadbanding, and variable pay all related to changing strategies for compensating employees?
4. Discuss the following statement: "If employees believe that subjectivity and favoritism shape the pay system in an organization, then it does not matter that the system was properly designed and implemented."
5. What factors should be considered to determine if an employee who works over 40 hours in a week is due overtime under the FLSA?
6. Considering all methods, why is the point method the most widely used for job evaluation?
7. You have been named compensation manager for a hospital. How would you establish a pay system?
8. Why are pay-for-performance systems growing in importance?

Terms to Know

base pay   373
wages   373
salaries   373
variable pay   373
benefit   373
equity   381
procedural justice   381
distributive justice   382
exempt employees   384
non-exempt employees   384
compensatory time off   387
pay equity   388
garnishment   389
job evaluation   390

benchmark job   390
compensable factor   391
pay survey   394
market line   396
pay grade   397
broadbanding   397
red-circled employee   400
green-circled employee   401
pay compression   401
compa-ratio   402
seniority   403
maturity curve   403
lump-sum increase (LSI)   403

Researching Salaries Using the Web

As the Compensation Manager for your firm you are charged with making sure base salaries are competitive in all organizational locations across the country. You have recently established a new position, a Compensation Analyst I. This position is intended for new graduates and you plan on hiring four new compensation analysts at four of your locations.

Use the salary wizard on the following website, *http://www/salary.com*, to find geographic pay survey data.

Identify the range of pay for this position at the following locations:

- Omaha, Nebraska
- Las Vegas, Nevada
- Albany, New York
- Los Angeles, California

In your recommendations, include the low, median, and high of each pay range and list them in order from lowest median to highest median pay. Also show the percentage difference for each location between each median data point from lowest to highest.

Implementing a New Compensation Program

The changing nature of jobs in organizations has led to companies redesigning their compensation programs to reflect the changes. As mentioned in the chapter, one approach used by some employers is competency-based pay. One firm has had success with using a knowledge-based program to measure and reward employees.

This medium-sized manufacturing firm has about 5,000 employees in one location, and none are represented by unions. As a result of continuing efforts by the firm's management to examine and apply innovative organization and management practices, the senior managers at the company decided to redesign work processes and compensation in three production departments. A task force of employees analyzed the work in each of the production departments and recommended some changes.

First, individual jobs and job descriptions were changed to using a team-work approach. In the new system, workers were expected to become skilled in several tasks and rotate throughout the different tasks, depending upon the production schedule and workflow. Workers also were expected to perform their own quality control. Finally a pay-for-performance program was developed to encourage workers to broaden their capabilities and to reward them as they did so.

HR specialists and others familiar with the jobs identified a series of "skill blocks," with each skill block containing what a worker is required to know and do. Skill blocks were developed for all processes in the production departments. As employees mastered a skill block, they received pay increases of 20 cents per hour, except for the basic skill block mastery, which provided a 30-cent-per-hour increase. Because pay is based on the number of skill blocks mastered, no maximum pay levels were set. These increases were granted on top of the entry-level pay rate of $9.81 per hour.

Following the communication of the new program, employees could choose to convert to the new program or transfer to other departments still using the traditional job-based pay plan. Only one production worker opted to transfer out of the new production compensation program and the department. HR specialists and production managers spent considerable time meeting with workers on the processes to be used to assess their competencies. Also, extensive training support had to be implemented so that employees could develop additional mastery of other skill blocks. Other coordination and program administration issues had to be addressed as well.

As a result of the changes to the new program, production technicians are rewarded continually for learning more and enhancing their capabilities. Also, greater workforce flexibility has resulted, so that workers can move between jobs and tasks as production needs dictate. Productivity has increased and production employees have become more knowledgeable about the linkage between compensation, their capabilities, and productivity.[35]

Questions

1. Discuss how changing the compensation program was consistent with the strategic shifts occurring in the organization.
2. What difficulties can you identify with shifting to the new compensation program from the traditional ones used in many production settings?

Notes

1. Adapted from Stephanie Armour, "Learning Life Is Not Fair in a Tight Labor Market," *USA Today,* August 16, 2000, B1–B2; and Rachel Beck, "Poof! Go the Perks," *Rocky Mountain News,* August 4, 2001, 1C–14C.
2. Paul W. Mulvey et al., "Rewards of Work," *WorldatWork Journal,* Third Quarter 2000, 6.
3. Bob Acosta, "Internet Payroll Processing," *Workspan,* February 2001, 16.
4. Gerald E. Ledford and Elizabeth J. Hawk, "Compensation Strategy," *ACA Journal,* First Quarter 2000, 28.
5. George T. Milkovich and Jennifer Stevens, "From Pay to Rewards: 100 Years of Change," *ACA Journal,* First Quarter 2000, 6–18.
6. Diane J. Gherson, "Getting the Pay Thing Right," *Workspan,* June, 2000, 47.
7. Mike Wanderer, "Dot-Comp," *Worldat Work Journal,* Fourth Quarter 2000, 15–24.
8. E. Stewart Huckman, "Pay the Person, Not the Job," *Training and Development,* October 2000, 52–57.
9. Jörgen Sandberg, "Understanding Competence at Work," *Harvard Business Review,* March 2001, 24.
10. Dana Rahbar-Daniels et al., "Here To Stay," *WorldatWork,* First Quarter 2001, 70–77.
11. B. L. Kirkman, "Understanding Why Team Members Won't Share," *Small Group Research,* 31, no. 2, n.d. 175–209.
12. James P. Guthrie, "Alternative Pay Practices and Employee Turnover," *Group and Organization Management,* December 2000, 419–439.
13. Talking About Pay," *The Wall Street Journal,* June 27, 2000, A1.
14. Kemba J. Dunham, "Employers Ease Bans on Workers Asking 'What Do They Pay You?'" *The Wall Street Journal,* May 1, 2001, B10.
15. "Wage Lawsuit Settled for $4 Million," *Bulletin to Management,* October 26, 2000, 339.
16. Simon J. Nodel, "Living with FLSA Not Easy," *Bulletin to Management,* June 22, 2000, 199.
17. Carolyn Hirschman, "Paying Up," *HR* Magazine, July 2000, 35–41; Rochelle Sharpe, "What Exactly Is a Living Wage?" *Business Week,* May 28, 2001, 78–79; and "Debating the Minimum Wage," *The Economist,* February 3, 2001, 80.
18. Robert Greenberger, "More Web Workers Claim Unfair Labor Practices," *The Wall Street Journal,* October 17, 2000, B1; and Victoria Roberts, "Think All Computer Workers Are Exempt? Think Again," *Bulletin to Management,* November 30, 2000, 383.
19. Michelle Conlin, "Revenge of the 'Managers,' " *Business Week,* March 12, 2001, 60–61.
20. Richard Willing, "Court Approves Forced Comp Time," *USA Today,* May 2, 2000, 1B.
21. For a more detailed summary, see Noreen McDermott, "Independent Contractors and Employees," *Legal Report* (SHRM), November/December 1999, 1–8.
22. Charles Fay and Howard Risher, "Comparable Worth Redux?" *Workspan,* July 2000, 41.
23. Karen Caldwell, "Comparable Worth Comparisons Called Unfair," *HR News,* May 2001, 23.
24. Deborah M. Figart, "The Role of Job Evaluation in an Evolving Social Norm," *Journal of Economic Issues,* March 2000, 1.
25. Robert McNabb and Keith Whitfield, "Job Evaluation and High Performance Work Practices," *Journal of Management Studies,* March 2001, 293.
26. Robert L. Heneman, "Work Evaluation," *WorldatWork Journal,* Third Quarter 2001, 65–70.
27. Theresa M. Welbourne and Charlie O. Trevor, "The Roles of Departmental and Position Power in Job Evaluation," *Academy of Management Journal,* 43, (2000), 761–771.
28. Charles Trevor and Mary Graham, "Deriving the Market Wage," *World atWork Journal,* Fourth Quarter 2000, 69–76.
29. John A. Menefee, "The Value of Pay Data on the Web," *Workspan,* September 2000, 25–28.
30. Dawne Shand, "Broadbanding the IT Worker," *Computer World,* October 9, 2000, 58.
31. "Broadbanding Pay Structures Do Not Receive Flat-Out Support," *Bulletin to Management,* January 13, 2000, 11.
32. Michael Enos and Greg Limages, "Broadbanding: Is that Your Company's Final Answer?" *WorldatWork Journal,* Fourth Quarter 2000, 61–68.
33. David Westman, "A Story About STEP," *Workspan,* March 2001, 49.
34. Carol Hymowitz, "Managers Face Battle to Keep Salaries Fair in a Tight Job Market," *The Wall Street Journal,* March 21, 2000, B1.
35. Adapted from Gerald D. Klein, "Case Study: A Pay-for-Knowledge Compensation Program That Works," *Compensation & Benefits Review,* March 1998, 69–75.

CHAPTER 13

Variable Pay and Executive Compensation

After you have read this chapter, you should be able to:

- Define variable pay and give examples of three types of variable pay.

- Identify four guidelines for successful incentive programs.

- Discuss three types of individual incentives.

- Explain three different ways that sales employees typically are compensated.

- Identify key factors that must be addressed when using team variable pay plans.

- Discuss why gainsharing, profitsharing, and employee stock ownership plans (ESOPs) have grown as organizational incentive plans.

- Identify the components of executive compensation and discuss criticisms of executive compensation levels.

Incentive System at Discovery

Discovery Communications, headquartered in Bethesda, Maryland, owns the Discovery Channel, Animal Planet, and 31 other cable networks. Due to rapid growth, the firm "outgrew" its compensation system. It was clear that the pay system was not only unfair, it was counterproductive. Some of the firm's top achievers were earning the same amount as office assistants, and people were earning more or less depending on where they were physically located. In addition, an employee doing good work could not get a raise when the market went up unless he or she was also promoted. As a result, managers promoted people before they were ready, just to get them raises.

Like many companies Discovery was concerned about the lack of motivation inherent in its traditional pay system. It wanted a performance-driven design that would reward its best workers without raising total labor costs significantly. Thus, Discovery overhauled its compensation system to include pay-for-performance incentives. The new system allowed both significant raises and bonuses when earned.

More than 50% of U.S. companies now report that they use performance-based incentive systems for *both* management and non-management employees. By linking bonuses to company results, as well as to individual performance, companies can share the wealth in good times, but can cut bonuses (instead of employees) in bad times. The consultant who helped Discovery with its system suggested that every $1 invested in employee incentives might lead to $2 in increased revenue if done correctly.

Discovery now provides two types of incentives. First, all employees are eligible for a performance-based increase in salary. Their base salary and performance appraisal ratings are considered and a minimum and maximum is suggested for a performance raise. Second, each employee is eligible for a year-end bonus that considers both individual and company performance. For example, an executive assistant who had worked at Discovery for a year and one half was eligible for a raise based upon her boss's evaluation of her performance and a bonus up to 10% of her salary. Eighty percent of the bonus was based on employee performance, 10% on the division's performance, and 10% on the company's performance. The executive assistant noted that the lure of higher pay prompted her to take on significantly more and different projects than she might have done otherwise.

The hardest part of compensation redesign at Discovery was deciding how strong a performance message to send. Over-rewarding star performers might cause jealousy. However, some resentment is probably inevitable in any system that differentiates employees by performance levels.

Discovery has found that employee turnover rates are down and complaints about compensation are fewer than before the conversion. Employees seem to feel they are being treated fairly, one executive notes. But whether such a system *is* "fair" is probably a "philosophical decision made by individual employees and managers."[1]

> Some resentment is probably inevitable in any system that differentiates employees by performance levels.

"The new world of work demands employee performance instead of loyalty, creativity instead of compliance, and earned rewards instead of entitlements."

—The Economist

Do people work harder if pay is tied to performance? The answer appears to be: yes, under the right circumstances. People do spend more time working when offered incentives to do so, as opposed to simply receiving base pay for the hours worked.[2]

Employers apparently believe it too, because a growing number are altering their traditional compensation programs to provide some part of employee's pay in a variable fashion. Typically, an employer bases a portion of the pay on how well the individual, group/team, and/or organization performs. Even the compensation plan of the Central Intelligence Agency in the U.S. government ties pay to performance and adds individual bonuses to the compensation mix.[3] The percentages vary somewhat, but roughly two thirds of companies currently offer variable pay through individual incentives, around a third offer group/team incentives, and over half offer organizational performance incentives.[4] Of course, it would be possible to offer all three at once. This chapter examines variable pay, including executive compensation as a special kind of variable pay.

Variable Pay: Incentives for Performance

Variable pay Compensation linked to individual, team, and organizational performance.

Variable pay is compensation linked to individual, team, and organizational performance. Traditionally also known as *incentives,* variable pay plans attempt to provide tangible rewards to employees for performance beyond normal expectations. The philosophical foundation of variable pay rests on several basic assumptions:

- Some jobs contribute more to organizational success than others.
- Some people perform better than others.
- Employees who perform better should receive more compensation.
- A portion of some employees' total compensation should be contingent on performance.

Contrast the assumptions with a pay system based on seniority or length of service:

- Time spent each day is the primary measure of contribution.
- Length of service with the organization is the primary differentiating factor among people.
- Contributions to the organization are recognized through different amounts of base pay.
- Giving rewards to some people but not others is divisive and hampers employees working together.

Types of Variable Pay

Individual incentives are given to reward the effort and performance of individuals. Some of the most common means of providing individuals variable pay includes piece-rate systems, sales commissions, and bonuses. Others include special recognition rewards such as trips or merchandise. Two widely used individual incentives focus on employee safety and attendance. However, individual incentives can present drawbacks. One of the potential difficulties with individual

incentives is that an employee may focus on what is best individually and may block or inhibit performance of other individuals with whom the employee is competing. Competition intensifies if only the top performer or winner receives incentives, which is why *team or group incentives* have been developed.

When an organization rewards an entire work group or *team* for its performance, cooperation among the members usually increases. However, competition among different teams for rewards can lead to decline in overall performance under certain circumstances. The most common *team* or *group incentives* are gainsharing plans, where employee teams that meet certain goals share in the gains measured against performance targets. Often, gainsharing programs focus on quality improvement, cost reduction, and other measurable results.

Organizational incentives reward people based on the performance results of the entire organization. This approach assumes that all employees working together can generate greater organizational results that lead to better financial performance. These programs often share some of the financial gains to the firm with employees through payments calculated as a percentage of each employee's base pay. Also, organizational incentives may be given as a lump-sum amount to all employees, or different amounts may be given to different levels of employees throughout the organization. The most prevalent forms of organization-wide incentives are profit-sharing plans and employee stock plans. For senior managers and executives, variable pay plans often are established to provide stock options and other forms of deferred compensation that minimize the tax liabilities of the recipients. Figure 13-1 shows some of the programs under each type of incentive or variable pay plan.

Successes and Failures of Variable Pay Plans

Even though variable pay has grown in popularity, some attempts to implement it have succeeded and others have not. One study suggests that about 74% of companies have a variable pay plan of some sort. Of those, most feel these plans have been successful in aligning pay with performance for executives (79%), managers (73%), and exempt/professionals (60%). However, only 48% felt variable pay was effective for non-exempt/administrative personnel.[5]

Figure 13-1	Types of Variable Pay Plans

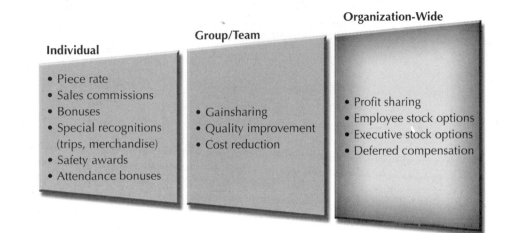

Individual
- Piece rate
- Sales commissions
- Bonuses
- Special recognitions (trips, merchandise)
- Safety awards
- Attendance bonuses

Group/Team
- Gainsharing
- Quality improvement
- Cost reduction

Organization-Wide
- Profit sharing
- Employee stock options
- Executive stock options
- Deferred compensation

Most employees prefer that performance rewards increase their base pay, rather than be given as a one-time, lump-sum payment. Further, employees prefer individual rewards to group/team or organizational incentives. Incentives *do* work, but they are not a panacea. The enthusiasm that many employers have for variable pay is not shared universally by workers. The success of variable pay plans depends upon the circumstances. The next section discusses several factors that affect successful variable pay plans.

Factors Affecting Successful Variable Pay Plans

Most employers adopt variable pay incentives in order to: (1) link individual performance to business goals, and (2) reward superior performance.[6] Other goals might include improving productivity or increasing employee retention. Variable pay plans can be considered successful if they meet the goals the organization had for them when they were initiated. Figure 13-2 shows a number of different elements that can affect the success of a variable pay plan. These factors have been categorized into three areas for discussion:

- Does the plan fit the organization?
- Are the behaviors encouraged by the plan the ones desired?
- Is the plan being administered properly?

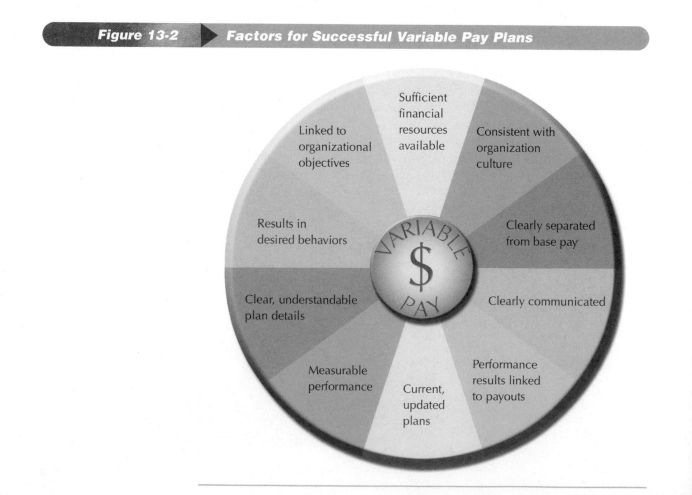

Figure 13-2   *Factors for Successful Variable Pay Plans*

HR Perspectives

Research on the Incentive Effects of Motivators

Alexander Stajkovic and Fred Luthans compared the incentive effects of four approaches on productivity. The four approaches were: (1) money administered contingently, (2) routine pay for performance, (3) social recognition, and (4) performance feedback.

The study, reported in the *Academy of Management Journal,* took place in the operations division of a large company with over 7,000 employees. The organization is an industry leader in objectively measuring the performance of employees. Therefore, good productivity data were available. The study looked at productivity in light of each of the approaches.

The "routine pay for performance" group simply got extra pay for increased performance. The "monetary incentive" group included pay for performance, but supervisors were trained to use the pay as a consequence when critical performance was exhibited. In the "social recognition" group, recognition and attention were used by trained supervisors as rewards. In the "performance feedback" group, individuals received detailed feedback on their performance.

The results of the study found that the "routine pay for performance approach" increased performance over the baseline by 11%, but the "monetary incentive" approach increased performance by 32%. For the two other approaches, the "social recognition" approach increased performance by 24%, and the "performance feedback approach" by 20%. Overall, the results of the study indicate that pay can indeed improve performance, but apparently it works best when presented contingently.[9]

Does the Plan Fit the Organization? In the case of variable pay, one size does not fit all. A plan that has worked well for one company will not necessarily work well for another. Obviously, the plan must be linked to the objectives of the organization. For example, CME Inc. in Irvine, California, wanted reliability, hard work, long hours, and saving money on company projects. Their custom designed variable pay plan rewards those behaviors.[7] Companies must accurately calculate the cost of the incentives to the organization and make sure they are affordable. Ideally, the cost savings or new revenues generated pay for the incentives.

The success of any variable pay program relies on its consistency with the culture of the organization. For example, if an organization is autocratic and adheres to traditional rules and procedures, an incentive system that rewards flexibility and teamwork is likely to fail. The incentive plan is being "planted" in the wrong growing environment.

WEST GROUP

A THOMSON COMPANY

Use of Incentives
Identifies advantages and disadvantages of using incentives.
Custom Search:
☑ ANALYSIS
Phrase: Pros and cons of rewards

Does the Plan Encourage the Desired Behaviors? Variable pay systems should be tied as much as possible to desired performance. Employees must see a direct relationship between their efforts and their financial rewards. Indeed, higher-performing companies give out far more incentive pay to their top performers than do lower-performing companies.[8] The HR Perspective describes a study on incentives and motivation.

Because people tend to produce what is measured and rewarded, organizations must make sure that what is being rewarded ties to meeting organizational objectives. Use of multiple measures helps assure that various performance dimensions are not omitted. For example, assume a hotel reservation center sets incentives for its employees to increase productivity by lowering their time spent per call. That reduction may occur, but customer service and the number of reservations made might drop as employees rush callers to reduce talk time. Therefore, the center should consider talk time, reservations booked, and customer satisfaction survey results.

Indeed, linking pay to performance may not always be appropriate. For instance, if the output cannot be objectively measured, management may not be able to correctly reward the higher performers with more pay. Managers may not even be able to accurately identify the higher performers. Under those circumstances, individual variable pay is inappropriate.

Is the Plan Administered Properly? A variable pay plan may be complex or simple, but it will not be successful if employees do not understand what they have to do to be rewarded. The more complicated a plan is, the more difficult it will be to communicate it meaningfully to employees. Experts generally recommend that a variable pay plan include several performance criteria. However, having two or three areas to focus on should not complicate the calculations necessary for employees to determine their own incentive amounts. Managers also need to be able to explain clearly what future performance targets need to be met.

Successful variable pay plans clearly identify how much is provided to employees separate from their base pay amounts. That separation makes a distinct connection between performance and pay. It also reinforces the notion that part of the employees' pay must be "re-earned" in the next performance period.

An incentive system should consistently reflect current technological and organizational conditions. Offering an incentive for sales representatives to sell older-generation equipment in order to clear it out of stock might be appropriate until that merchandise is gone, but no incentive may be needed to sell high-demand items. Incentive systems should be reviewed continually to determine whether they are operating as designed. Follow-up, through an attitude survey or other means, will determine if the incentive system is actually encouraging employees to perform better. If it is not, then managers should consider changing the system.

Individual Incentives

As noted earlier, individual incentive systems try to relate individual effort to pay. Conditions necessary for the use of individual incentive plans are as follows:

- *Identification of individual performance:* The performance of each individual must be measured and identified because each employee has job responsibilities and tasks that can be separated from those of other employees.
- *Independent work:* Individual contributions result from independent work and effort given by individual employers.
- *Individual competitiveness desired:* Because individuals generally pursue the individual incentives for themselves, competition among employees often occurs. Therefore, independent competition in which some individuals "win" and others do not must be desired.
- *Individualism stressed in organizational culture:* The culture of the organization must be one that emphasizes individual growth, achievements, and rewards. If an organization emphasizes teamwork and cooperation, then individual incentives will be counterproductive.

Piece-Rate Systems

The most basic individual incentive system is the piece-rate system, whether of the straight or differential type. Under the **straight piece-rate system,** wages are determined by multiplying the number of units produced (such as garments sewn or customers contacted) by the piece rate for one unit. The rate per piece does not change regardless of the number of pieces produced. Because the cost is the same for each unit, the wage for each employee is easy to figure, and labor costs can be accurately predicted.

A **differential piece-rate system** pays employees one piece-rate wage for units produced up to a standard output and a higher piece-rate wage for units produced over the standard.

For example, assume that the standard quota for a worker is set at 300 units per day and the standard rate is 14 cents per unit. For all units over the standard, however, the employee receives 20 cents per unit. But the worker producing 400 units in one day will get $62 in wages $(300 \times 14 \text{ cents}) + (100 \times 20 \text{ cents})$. There are many possible combinations of straight and differential piece-rate systems that can be used depending on situational factors.

Despite their incentive value, piece-rate systems are difficult to use because standards for many types of jobs are difficult and costly to determine. In some instances, the cost of determining and maintaining the standards may be greater than the benefits derived. Jobs in which individuals have limited control over output or in which high standards of quality are necessary also may be unsuited to piecework.

Bonuses

Individual employees may receive additional compensation payments in the form of a **bonus,** which is a one-time payment that does not become part of the employee's base pay. Generally, bonuses are less costly to the employer than other pay increases because they do not become part of employees' base wages, upon which future percentage increases are figured. Growing in popularity, individual bonuses often are used at the executive levels in organizations, but bonus usage also has spread to jobs at all levels in some firms.

Bonuses also can be used to reward employees for contributing new ideas, developing skills, or obtaining professional certifications. When the skills or certification requirements are acquired by an employee, a pay increase or a one-time bonus may follow. For example, a financial services firm provides the equivalent of two week's pay to employees who master job-relevant computer skills. Another firm gives one week's pay to members of the HR staff who obtain their professional certifications such as PHR, SPHR, CCP, and others discussed in Chapter 1.

A bonus can recognize performance by an employee, a team, or the organization as a whole. When performance results are good, bonuses go up. When performance results are not met, bonuses go down. Most employers base part of the employee's bonus on individual performance and part on the company if appropriate.

Whatever method of determining bonuses is used, legal experts recommend that bonus plans be described in writing. A number of lawsuits have been filed by employees who leave organizations demanding payment of bonuses

Straight piece-rate system A pay system in which wages are determined by multiplying the number of units produced by the piece rate for one unit.

Differential piece-rate system A system in which employees are paid one piece-rate wage for units produced up to a standard output and a higher piece-rate wage for units produced over the standard.

Bonus A one-time payment that does not become part of the employee's base pay.

Figure 13-3 ▸ **Sources of Bonuses**

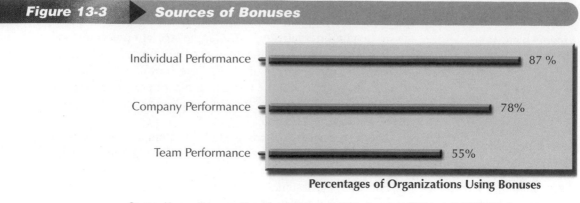

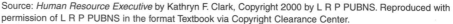

Percentages of Organizations Using Bonuses

Source: *Human Resource Executive* by Kathryn F. Clark, Copyright 2000 by L R P PUBNS. Reproduced with permission of L R P PUBNS in the format Textbook via Copyright Clearance Center.

promised to them. Figure 13-3 shows the bases used to determine bonuses in organizations from one survey.

Special Incentive Programs

Numerous special incentive programs that provide awards to individuals have been used, ranging from one-time contests for meeting performance targets to rewards for performance over time. For instance, safe-driving awards are given to truck drivers with no accidents or violations on their records during a year. Although special programs also can be developed for groups and for entire organizations, these programs often focus on rewarding only high-performing individuals.

Awards Cash merchandise, gift certificates, and travel are the most frequently used incentive rewards. Cash is still highly valued by many employees because they have discretion on how to spend it. However, travel awards, particularly to popular destinations such as Disney World, Las Vegas, Hawaii, and international locations, appeal to many employees. Goodyear Tire & Rubber Company conducted an experiment in which some employees received cash and another set of employees received merchandise and other non-cash rewards. The employees receiving the non-cash incentives outperformed those receiving only cash by 46%. Other similar studies have concluded that many employees like the continuing "trophy" value of merchandise.[10]

Recognition Awards Another type of program recognizes individual employees for their performance or service. For instance, many organizations in service industries such as hotels, restaurants, and retailers have established "employee of the month" and "employee of the year" awards. In the hotel industry more than half of the hotels surveyed use favorable guest comment cards as the basis to provide recognition awards to desk clerks, housekeepers, and other hourly employees.

Recognition awards often work best when given to recognize specific efforts and activities targeted by the organization as important. Even though the criteria for selecting award winners may be subjectively determined in some situations, formally identified criteria provide greater objectivity and are more likely to be seen as rewarding performance, rather than as favoritism. When giving recognition awards, organizations should use specific examples to describe clearly how those receiving the awards were selected.[11]

Service Awards Another common type of reward given to individual employees is the *service award*. Although these awards often may be portrayed as rewarding performance over a number of years, in reality, they are determined by length of service, and performance plays little or no role.

Sales Compensation and Incentives

The compensation paid to employees involved with sales and marketing is partly or entirely tied to individual sales performance. Better-performing salespeople receive more total compensation than those selling less. Sales incentives are perhaps the most widely used individual incentive.

Measuring Sales Performance

Successfully using variable sales compensation requires establishing clear performance criteria and measures. Generally, no more than three sales performance measures should be used in a sales compensation plan. Consultants criticize many sales commission plans as being too complex to motivate sales representatives. Other plans may be too simple, focusing only on the salesperson's pay, not on organizational objectives. Although many companies use an individual's sales revenue compared to established quotas as the primary performance measure, performance could be measured better if these organizations used a variety of criteria, including obtaining new accounts and selling high-value versus low-value items that reflect marketing plans. Figure 13-4 shows the criteria commonly used to determine incentive payments for salespeople based on a number of different surveys and studies.

 **Figure 13-4** ▶ *Different Bases for Sales Incentives, in Order of Use*

Sales relative to quota

Sales relative to other salespeople

Sales from new customers

New product sales

Control of sales expenses

Retaining accounts

Customer satisfaction

Sales Compensation Plans

Sales compensation plans are generally of several different types. The types are based on the degree to which total compensation includes some variable pay tied to sales performance. A look at each type of sales compensation follows next.

Salary Only Some firms pay salespeople only a salary. The salary-only approach is useful when an organization emphasizes serving and retaining existing accounts over generating new sales and accounts. This approach is frequently used to protect the income of new sales representatives for a period of time while they are building up their sales clientele. Generally, the salary-only approach may extend no more than six months, at which point sales plus commission or bonuses are implemented. However, salespeople who want extrinsic rewards function less effectively in salary-only plans because they are less motivated to sell without additional performance-related compensation.[12]

Straight Commission An individual incentive system widely used in sales jobs is the **commission**, which is compensation computed as a percentage of sales in units or dollars. Commissions are integrated into the pay given to sales workers in three common ways: straight commission, salary plus commission, and bonuses.

Commission Compensation computed as a percentage of sales in units or dollars.

In the straight commission system, a sales representative receives a percentage of the value of the sales made. Consider a sales representative working for a consumer products company. She receives no compensation if no sales are made, but for all sales made in her territory, she receives a percentage of the total amount. The advantage of this system is that the sales representative must sell to earn. The disadvantage is that it offers no security for the sales staff.

Draw An amount advanced from and repaid to future commissions earned by the employee.

To offset this insecurity, some employers use a **draw** system, in which sales representatives can draw advance payments against future commissions. The amount drawn then is deducted from future commission checks. However, arrangements must be made for repayment of drawn amounts if individuals leave the organization before earning their draws in commissions.

Salary Plus Commission or Bonuses The most frequently used form of sales compensation is the *salary plus commission,* which combines the stability of a salary with the performance aspect of a commission. Many organizations also pay salespeople salaries and then offer bonuses as a percentage of base pay tied to meeting various levels of sales targets or other criteria. A common split is 70% salary to 30% commission, although the split varies by industry and with other factors.

Sales Compensation Challenges

Sales incentives work well or they would not be so widely used. However, they do present many challenges—from calculating total pay correctly to dealing with sales in e-business, to causing competition among salespeople.[13] Often sales compensation plans become quite complex, and complexity can lead to mistakes. For example, a company miscalculated commissions one year and had to cut commissions 50% the next year to make up. New software can solve that problem; companies can post results weekly or monthly and salespeople can click on an icon to see their results to date.[14]

Balancing Sales Compensation and Ethical Concerns

Sales commission programs can effectively drive the behavior of sales representatives, especially if the sales performance measures are based wholly or mostly on sales volume and revenues. However, some performance-based sales employees may act unethically. For instance, a major retailer paid commissions to employees for generating sales volume and revenue for auto parts in its auto repair centers. Upon closer scrutiny, the retailer discovered that in several cases representatives had convinced customers to buy unnecessary part replacements and pay for unnecessary repairs that were done. By doing so, the sales reps received higher commissions and met corporate performance targets. The resulting investigation received widespread negative press coverage, and the retailer had to revamp its incentive plan.

Other industries have seen similarly shady behavior occur as well. Investigations of several brokerage and insurance firms have looked into misrepresentations of financial products and services that sales representatives marketed to a wide range of customers. A number of cases have resulted in large fines and criminal indictments.

Some legal experts and academics express concerns that performance-driven sales incentives encourage unethical behavior, particularly if compensation of sales representatives is based solely on commissions. These critics charge that sales commission programs align the interest of sales reps with the firm, rather than with those of customers and clients. This criticism applies especially if the customer purchases are likely to be "one-time" purchases, such as a used car or a life insurance policy, where the likelihood of

repeat purchases and a continuing customer relationship are lower.

One solution to address these ethical issues has been to discontinue commission-only plans, so that the basic income of sales reps does not solely depend on what they "hunt and kill." Instead, proponents urge using a mixture of guaranteed base salary and lowered commission rates.

Critics of sales compensation also suggest that other sales-related dimensions be used, such as customer service, repeat business, or customer satisfaction. For instance, sales commissions for investment brokers might be linked to increasing a client's net portfolio value, rather than only to the trading commissions generated. How realistic such changes are in a variety of sales situations may be debated. But clearly ethical issues must be considered when developing and managing sales incentive plans.

Selling over the Internet brings with it incentive compensation challenges. Sophisticated e-commerce sites are forcing companies to develop new incentive compensation approaches to avoid conflict between the traditional sales representative and the new "relationship managers" who work from the Web sites.[15]

The last few years have seen the growth of sales compensation plans that pit one salesperson against another. For example, in the "stack rank plan" the top 20% of sales performers get the highest bonus, the next 30% get the second highest, the next 30% get third highest, and the bottom 20% get nothing. Often, the best salespeople are motivated by incentive plans based on performance measures within their control.[16] But these plans tend to dramatically reduce teamwork and make the climate negative. Sales compensation plans can also lead to ethical issues, as the HR Perspective shows.

Some sales organizations combine both individual and group sales bonus programs. In these programs, a portion of the sales incentive is linked to the attainment of group sales goals. This approach encourages cooperation and teamwork for the salespeople to work together. Team incentives in situations other than sales jobs are discussed next.

Group/Team-Based Variable Pay

A group of employees is not necessarily a "team," but either one can be the basis for variable compensation. The use of work teams in organizations has implications for compensation of the teams and their members. Interestingly, although the use of teams has increased substantially in the past few years, the question of how to equitably compensate the individuals who compose the team remains a significant challenge. As Figure 13-5 notes, organizations establish group or team variable pay plans for a number of reasons. According to several studies about 70% of large firms use work groups or teams in some way. Of those, about 36% say they use group incentives, and 10% say they use team-based pay.[17]

Distributing Team Incentives

Several decisions about methods of distributing and allocating team rewards must be made. The two primary approaches for distributing team rewards are as follows:

1. *Same size reward for each team member:* In this approach, all team members receive the same payout, regardless of job levels, current pay, or seniority.
2. *Different size rewards for each team member:* Using this approach, employers vary individual rewards based upon such factors as contribution to team results, current pay, years of experience, and skill levels of jobs performed.

Generally, more organizations use the first approach as an addition to different levels of individual pay. This method is used to reward team performance by making the team incentive equal, while still recognizing that individual pay differences exist and are important to many employees.[18] The size of the team incentive can be determined either by using a percentage of base pay for the individuals or the team as a whole, or by offering a specific dollar amount. For

Figure 13-5 ▶ **Why Organizations Establish Team Pay Plans**

Team Variable Pay

- Enhances productivity
- Ties earnings to team performance
- Improves quality
- Aids recruiting and retention of employees
- Improves employees morale

example, one firm pays team members individual base rates that reflect years of experience and any additional training that team members have. Additionally, the team reward is distributed to all as a flat dollar amount.

Timing of Team Incentives How often team incentives are paid out is another important consideration. Some of the choices seen in firms with team-based incentives include payment monthly, quarterly, semiannually, or annually. The most common period used is annually. However, the shorter the time period, the more likely it is that employees will see a closer link to their efforts and the performance results that trigger the award payouts. Employers also may limit the team rewards to $1000 or less, allowing them to pay out rewards more frequently. The nature of the teamwork, measurement criteria, and organizational results must all be considered when determining the appropriate time period.

Decision Making About Team Incentive Amounts To reinforce the team concept, some team incentive programs allow group members to make decisions about how to allocate the team rewards to individuals. For example, in one division of Motorola, teams receive a lump-sum amount, which they then decide how to divide among team members. Some teams vote, while others have a team leader decide. In other companies teams divide the team "pot" equally, thus avoiding conflict and recognizing that all members contributed to the team results. However, many companies have found teams unwilling to handle pay decisions for co-workers. In summary, team-based incentives present both opportunities and challenges when they are developed and implemented.[19]

Problems with Team-Based Incentives

The difference between rewarding team members *equally* or *equitably* triggers many of the problems associated with team-based incentives. Rewards distributed equally in amount to all team members may be perceived as "unfair" by employees who work harder, have more capabilities, or perform more difficult jobs. This problem is compounded when a poorly performing individual negatively influences the team results. Also, employees working in teams have shown a relatively low level of satisfaction with rewards that are the same for all, rather than having rewards based on performance, which often may be viewed more equitably.

Generally, managers view the concept of people working in teams as beneficial. But many employees still expect to be paid based on individual performance, to a large extent. Until this individualism is recognized and compensation programs developed that are viewed as more equitable by more "team members," caution should be used in developing and implementing team-based incentives.

Successful Team Incentives

The unique nature of the team and its members figures prominently in the success of establishing team-based rewards. The employer must consider the history of the group and its past performance. Use of incentives generally has proven to be more successful where groups have been used in the past and where those groups have performed well. However, simultaneously introducing the teamwork concept and changing to team-based incentives has not been as successful.[20]

Figure 13-6 ▶ **Conditions for Successful Team Incentives**

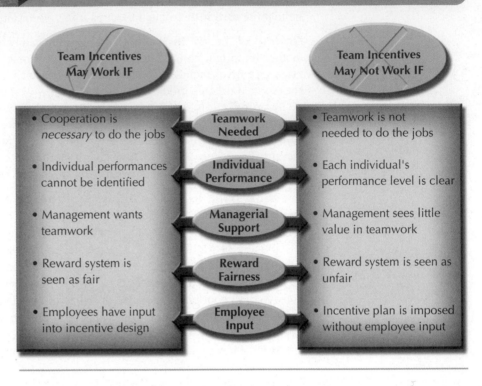

Team Incentives May Work IF		Team Incentives May Not Work IF
• Cooperation is *necessary* to do the jobs	**Teamwork Needed**	• Teamwork is not needed to do the jobs
• Individual performances cannot be identified	**Individual Performance**	• Each individual's performance level is clear
• Management wants teamwork	**Managerial Support**	• Management sees little value in teamwork
• Reward system is seen as fair	**Reward Fairness**	• Reward system is seen as unfair
• Employees have input into incentive design	**Employee Input**	• Incentive plan is imposed without employee input

Another consideration for the success of team-based incentives is the size of the team. If a team becomes too large, employees may feel their individual efforts will have little or no effect on the total performance of the group and the resulting rewards. Team-based incentive plans may encourage teamwork in small groups where interdependence is high. Therefore, in those groups the use of team-based performance measures is recommended. Such plans have been used in many service-oriented industries, where a high degree of contact with customers requires teamwork. Conditions for successful team incentives are shown in Figure 13-6. If these conditions cannot be met, then either individual or organizational incentives may be more appropriate.

Types of Group Incentives

Group/team-based reward systems use various ways of compensating individuals. The components include individual wages and salaries in addition to team-based rewards. Most team-based organizations continue to pay individuals based either on the jobs performed or their competencies and capabilities. The two most frequently used types of group/team incentives situations are work teams and gainsharing.

Work Teams Results Team-based pay plans may reward all members equally on the basis of group output, cost savings, or quality improvement. For example at Alta Distributing, each warehouse employee might receive $20 for each 1% improvement over baseline in the shipping group's rate of on-time delivery each month. The baseline is 90% on-time deliveries. A 93% on-time

Logging On...

HR Guide to the Internet
This Web site discusses incentives and gainsharing in detail.

http://www.hr-guide.com/data/g443.htm

rate for August would mean each group member would receive a $60 bonus based on group performance.

The design of most group incentives is based on a "self-funding" principle, which means that the money to be used as incentive rewards is obtained through improvement of organizational results.[21] A good example is gainsharing, which can be group or plantwide in its incentive scope.

Gainsharing Gainsharing is the sharing with employees of greater-than-expected gains in profits and/or productivity. Gainsharing attempts to increase "discretionary efforts," that is, the difference between the maximum amount of effort a person can exert and the minimum amount of effort necessary to keep from being fired. Workers in many organizations currently are not paid for discretionary efforts, but are paid to meet the minimum acceptable level of effort required. However, when workers demonstrate discretionary efforts, the organization can afford to pay them more than the going rate, because the extra efforts produce financial gains over and above the returns of minimal efforts. To begin a gainsharing program, management must identify the ways in which increased productivity, quality, and financial performance can occur and decide that some of the gains should be shared with employees.

The rewards can be distributed in several ways:

- A flat amount for all employees
- Same percentage of base salary for all employees
- Percentage of the gains by category of employees
- A percentage based on individual performance against measures.

The first two methods generally are preferred because they promote and reward teamwork and cooperation more than the other two methods. Where performance measures are used, only those measures that employees actually can affect should be considered. Often, measures such as labor costs, overtime hours, and quality benchmarks are used. Both organizational measures and departmental measures may be used, with the weights for gainsharing split between the two categories. Naturally, an individual's performance must be satisfactory in order for that individual to receive the gainsharing payments.

Two older approaches similar to gainsharing exist. One, called Improshare, sets group piece rate standards and pays weekly bonuses when the standard is exceeded. The other—the Scanlon plan—uses employee committees and passes on savings to the employees.

Organizational Incentives

An organizational incentive system compensates all employees in the organization based on how well the organization as a whole performs during the year. The basic concept behind organizational incentive plans is that overall results depend on organizational or plant-wide cooperation. The purpose of these plans is to produce better results by rewarding cooperation throughout the organization. For example, conflict between marketing and production can be overcome if management uses an incentive system that emphasizes organization-wide profit and productivity. To be effective, an organizational incentive program should include everyone from non-exempt employees to managers and executives. Common organizational incentive systems include profit sharing, stock options, and employee stock ownership plans (ESOPs).

Profit Sharing

As the name implies, **profit sharing** distributes some portion of organizational profits to employees. The primary objectives of profit-sharing plans include the following:

- Improve productivity
- Recruit or retain employees
- Improve product/service quality
- Improve employee morale

Typically, the percentage of the profits distributed to employees is agreed on by the end of the year before distribution. In some profit-sharing plans, employees receive portions of the profits at the end of the year; in others, the profits are deferred, placed in a fund, and made available to employees on retirement or on their leaving the organization. Figure 13-7 shows how profit-sharing plans can be set up.

Unions sometimes are skeptical of profit-sharing plans.[22] Often, the level of profits is influenced by factors not under the employees' control, such as accounting decisions, marketing efforts, competition, and elements of executive compensation. However, in recent years, some unions have supported profit-sharing plans that tie employees' pay increases to improvements against organizational performance measures, not just the "bottom-line" numbers.

Drawbacks of Profit-Sharing Plans When used throughout an organization, including lower-echelon workers, profit-sharing plans can have some drawbacks. First, management must be willing to disclose financial and profit information to employees. As many people know, both the definition and level of profit can depend on the accounting system used and decisions made. Therefore, to be credible, management must be willing to disclose sufficient financial and profit information to alleviate the skepticism of employees, particularly if profit-sharing levels are reduced from previous years. Second, profits may vary a great deal from year to year, resulting in windfalls and losses beyond the employees' control. Third, payoffs far removed from employees' efforts may fail to strongly link higher rewards with better performance.

Profit-Sharing Plans
Describes advantages and disadvantages of profit-sharing plans.
Custom Search:
☑ ANALYSIS
Phrase: Advantages of profit-sharing plans

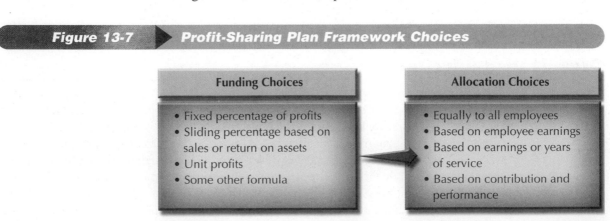

Figure 13-7 ▶ Profit-Sharing Plan Framework Choices

Funding Choices	Allocation Choices
• Fixed percentage of profits • Sliding percentage based on sales or return on assets • Unit profits • Some other formula	• Equally to all employees • Based on employee earnings • Based on earnings or years of service • Based on contribution and performance

Employee Stock Options

Stock options, once the exclusive domain of executive compensation, are now being used throughout some organizations. Employee stock options give employees the right to purchase a fixed number of shares of company stock at a specified price for a limited period of time. If the stock's market price exceeds the exercise price, employees can exercise the option and sell the stock at a profit. If the price falls below the exercise price, the option is worthless. Purchasing and holding company stock is thought to give employees a vested "ownership" in seeing the company do well. However, the incentive value of the stock is reduced whenever employees' stock value declines, as happened in 2000 when the stock market dropped. Obviously, stock prices do not always go up; and when stock values decline, employee anxiety increases. Nevertheless, using stock plans as a means of providing additional compensation to employees appears to help focus employee efforts on increasing organizational performance.[23] Employees tend to like stock-related benefits but do not understand many of the complexities.[24]

One well-known firm that has used stock options effectively is Home Depot. Founded in 1978, Home Depot operates numerous home improvement and building supply stores throughout the United States. Since its early years, Home Depot compensation plans included stock option incentives for management and administrative employees. Additionally, the firm permits virtually all other employees to buy Home Depot stock at a discounted price. At Home Depot the employee stock plans appear to have contributed to the feeling among all employees that they "own" their stores. This feeling has led to higher internal morale and greater attention to customer service. Home Depot employees are also more likely to resist recruiting efforts by other employers because of their stock ownership in the company. The Home Depot stock ownership program benefits employees as well. One share of Home Depot stock bought in 1981 has risen to be worth more than 100 shares today, depending upon stock market variations.

This discussion has highlighted plans that provide employees opportunities to receive stock options or purchase company stock. However, a more extensive approach results in employees actually owning all or significant parts of their employers.

Employee Stock Ownership Plans (ESOPs)

Employee stock ownership plan (ESOP) A plan whereby employees gain stock ownership in the organization for which they work.

An **employee stock ownership plan (ESOP)** is designed to give employees stock ownership in the organization for which they work. According to the National Center for Employee Ownership, an estimated 15,000 firms in the United States offer broad employee-ownership programs. Within these firms, approximately 10,000 have established ESOPs covering about 9 million workers.[25]

Establishing an ESOP An organization establishes an ESOP by using its stock as collateral to borrow capital from a financial institution. Once the loan repayment begins through the use of company profits, the lender releases a certain amount of stock, which the company allocates to an employee stock ownership trust (ESOT). The company then assigns shares of stock kept in the trust to individual employees based on length of service and pay level. On retirement, death, or separation from the organization, employees or their beneficiaries can sell the stock back to the trust or on the open market, if the stock is publicly traded.

Making Stock Ownership Plans Work

Stock ownership plans have grown in recent years, but these programs often fail to reach their potential. Key to success of these programs is the perception of employees of a genuine "ownership culture." In such a culture most employees understand three factors:

1. What drives organizational success
2. How employees impact that success
3. How employees can share in the success financially

According to one study done at Northwestern University, companies with ESOPs outperformed companies of similar size and industry without ownership plans by almost 7%. But another study indicated that most executives in U.S. companies do not believe employees fully understand the link between their actions and company success.

To develop an "ownership culture" where employees see that link requires the following:

• *Shared investment or common stake*—This answers the employees question, "Why should I care?" in the form of ownership equity. The shared investment can be measured by benchmarking the total value of equity delivered to employees.
• *Information*—The extent to which the organization provides useful, understandable business data answers the question, "What should I care *about* it? How well it is answered can be measured by asking employees what they know and want to know about company results.
• *Influence*—The degree to which employees believe they can impact results answers questions about "What should I do differently?" If employees believe they can influence results, then it will be seen in new ideas, innovations, and processes.

Addressing these three areas helps in creating the ownership culture. Merely having an ownership plan does not guarantee its success—measuring and adjusting it can do so.[26]

Advantages and Disadvantages of ESOPs Establishing an ESOP creates several advantages. The major one is that the firm can receive favorable tax treatment of the earnings earmarked for use in the ESOP. Second, an ESOP gives employees a "piece of the action" so that they can share in the growth and profitability of their firm. As a result, employee ownership may be effective in motivating employees to be more productive and focused on organizational performance. In one survey of more than 1,100 ESOP companies, about 60% said productivity had increased, and 68% said financial performance was higher since converting to an ESOP.[27] The HR Practice discusses some factors affecting the success of ESOPs.

Many people approve of the concept of employee ownership as a kind of "people's capitalism." However, the sharing also can be a disadvantage because employees may feel "forced" to join, thus placing their financial future at greater risk. Both their wages/salaries and their retirement benefits depend on the performance of their employer. This concentration poses even greater risk for retirees because the value of pension fund assets also depends on how well the company does.

Another drawback is the use of ESOPs as a management tool to fend off unfriendly takeover attempts. Holders of employee-owned stock often align with management to turn down bids that would benefit outside stockholders but would replace management and restructure operations. Surely, ESOPs were not

WEST GROUP
A THOMSON COMPANY

ESOPs
Provides an overview of ESOPs, including different types and requirements.
Custom Search:
☑ ANALYSIS
Phrase: ESOPs in general

created to entrench inefficient management. Despite these disadvantages, ESOPs continue to grow in popularity.

FASB Rules Employee stock ownership plans are subject to certain tax laws. Perhaps in part because of the increase in popularity of ESOPs, companies have been required to disclose how much they would have earned if the stock options they gave employees had been charged against company income. The Financial Accounting Standards Board (FASB) now requires companies to report the value of the stock options they give employees, but some real controversy has occurred over how to value the options.

Executive Compensation

A history of executive compensation shows that a combination of events have created today's situation in the United States.[28] Strong demand, the tax structure, stock market performance, and pay-for-performance notions have all contributed. Many organizations, especially large ones, administer executive compensation differently from compensation for lower-level employees.

U.S. executives—typically someone in the top two levels of an organization, such as Chief Executive Officer (CEO), President, or Senior Vice-President—do rather well in compensation. Figure 13-8 compares them to executives in the rest of the world. Also, pay for female executives is about 45% less than that of men until adjusted for age and experience, then the gap shrinks to about 5% or less.[29] In real terms, average annual CEO compensation in the U.S. for a recent year was

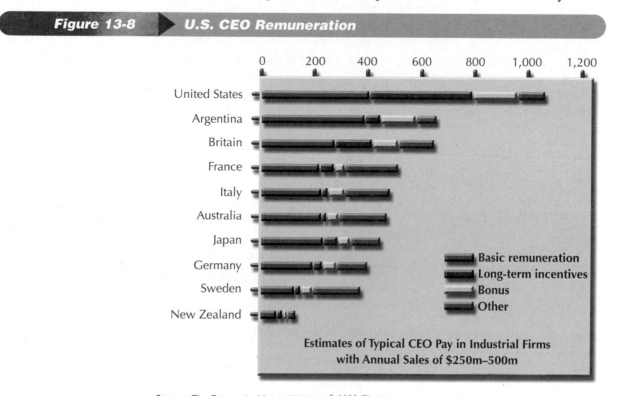

Figure 13-8   U.S. CEO Remuneration

Estimates of Typical CEO Pay in Industrial Firms with Annual Sales of $250m–500m

Source: *The Economist,* May 8, 2000, 16. © 2000. The Economist Newspaper Group, Inc. Reprinted with permission. Further reproduction prohibited. *www.economist.com*

about $13 million. However, the head of Citigroup was paid $293 million, AOL/Time Warner $164 million, and Cisco Systems $157 million.[30]

Of course, those figures, large as they are, provide little meaning unless put into context. If the company is doing well and performing above competitors and expectations, the huge packages might be justifiable to stockholders.[31] Certainly the opposite can be true as well.[32] For example, in the same year the CEO of Applied Micro Circuits guided the company to a return of 4,751%, he earned $4.5 million. However, the Chairman of Walt Disney had a negative 10% return on shareholders' dollars while he earned $699 million.[33] Or consider Lucent Technologies CEO Richard McGinn who was fired after Lucent stock hit an all time low of $6 a share, down from $78. He left Lucent with a $12.5 million severance package.[34]

The absolute amounts of the compensation packages and the questionable tie of pay to performance has made executive compensation a controversial item in some circles. The debate on that issue will be examined shortly. However, in some organizations, it appears that the total level of executive compensation may be unreasonable and not linked closely to organizational performance.

Elements of Executive Compensation

At the heart of most executive compensation plans is the idea that executives should be rewarded if the organization grows in profitability and value over a period of years. Because of the high tax brackets they fall in, most executives want their compensation provided in ways that offer significant tax savings. Therefore, their total compensation packages are more significant than their base pay. Especially when the base salary is $1 million or more, the executive often is interested in the mix of items in the total package, including current and deferred compensation. As Figure 13-9 shows, the common components of

Logging On...

Crystal Report
The Crystal Report evaluates executive compensation levels and issues.

http://www.crystalreport.com

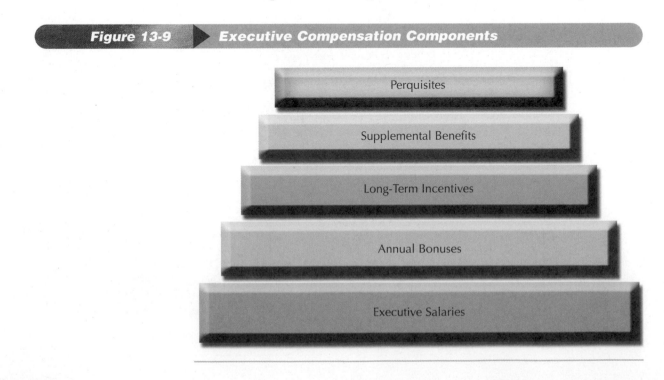

Figure 13-9 — **Executive Compensation Components**

Perquisites

Supplemental Benefits

Long-Term Incentives

Annual Bonuses

Executive Salaries

executive compensation are salaries, annual bonuses, long-term incentives, supplemental benefits, and perquisites.

Executive Salaries Salaries of executives vary by type of job, size of organization, region of the country, and industry. On average, salaries make up about 40% to 60% of the typical top executive's annual compensation total. A provision of a 1993 tax act prohibits a publicly traded company from deducting pay of more than $1 million for each of its top five officers unless that pay is based on performance criteria approved by outside directors and shareholders.

Executive Bonus Plans Executive performance may be difficult to determine, but bonus compensation must reflect some performance measures if it is to be meaningful. To solve the problem, a retail chain with more than 250 stores ties annual bonuses for managers to store profitability. The bonuses have amounted to as much as 35% of a store manager's base salary.

Bonuses for executives can be determined in several ways. A discretionary system whereby bonuses are awarded based on the judgments of the Chief Executive Officer and the Board of Directors is one way. However, the absence of formal, measurable targets detracts significantly from this approach. Also, as noted, bonuses can be tied to specific measures, such as return on investment, earnings per share, or net profits before taxes. More complex systems create bonus pools and thresholds above which bonuses are computed. Whatever method is used, it is important to describe it so that executives trying to earn bonuses understand the plan; otherwise the incentive effect will be diminished.[35]

Performance Incentives: Long Term vs. Short Term Performance-based incentives attempt to tie executive compensation to the long-term growth and success of the organization. However, whether the emphasis is really on the long term or merely represents a series of short-term rewards is controversial. Short-term rewards based on quarterly or annual performance may not result in the kind of long-run-oriented decisions necessary for the company to continue to do well.[36]

Stock option A plan that gives an individual the right to buy stock in a company, usually at a fixed price for a period of time.

As noted earlier, a **stock option** gives an individual the right to buy stock in a company, usually at an advantageous price. The increase in stock options as a component of executive compensation during the past 10 years takes a variety of specialized and technical forms, which are beyond the scope of this discussion. However, the overall trend is toward using stock options as performance-based long-term incentives.

Some firms may grant "stock equivalencies" in the form of *phantom stock* or *share appreciation rights*. These plans pay recipients the increased value of the stock in the future, determined by a base valuation made at the time the phantom stock or share appreciation rights are given. Depending on how these plans are established, the executives may be able to defer taxes or be taxed at lower capital-gains tax rates.

Benefits for Executives As with benefits for non-executive employees, executive benefits may take several forms, including traditional retirement, health insurance, vacations, and others. However, executive benefits may include some items that other employees do not receive. For example, executive health plans with no co-payments and with no limitations on deductibles or physician choice are popular among small and middle-sized businesses. Corporate-owned

Figure 13-10 ▶ **Common Executive Perks**

Transportation	Financial/Legal	Memberships
• Company car or car allowance • First class air travel • Company airplane usage	• Financial planning • Tax planning/tax preparation • No or low interest loans • Legal counseling	• Country club • Health club • Luncheon club

life insurance on the life of the executive is popular and pays both the executive's estate and the company in the event of death. Trusts of various kinds may be designed by the company to help the executive deal with estate issues. Deferred compensation offers another possible means of helping executives with tax liabilities caused by incentive compensation plans.

Executive Perquisites In addition to the regular benefits received by all employees, executives often receive benefits called perquisites. **Perquisites (perks)** are special executive benefits—usually noncash items. Perks help tie executives to organizations and demonstrate their importance to their companies. Many executives value the status enhancement of perks because these visible symbols of status allow executives to be seen as "very important person's (VIP) both inside and outside their organizations. In addition, perks can offer substantial tax savings because many perks are not taxed as income.[37] Figure 13-10 lists some commonly used executive perks.

Executive Compensation and the Board of Directors

In most organizations, the board of directors is the major policy-setting entity. For publicly traded companies covered by federal regulatory agencies, such as the Securities and Exchange Commission (SEC), the board of directors must approve executive compensation packages. Even for many nonprofit organizations, Internal Revenue Service regulations require boards of directors review and approve the compensation for top-level executives. In both family-owned and privately owned firms, boards of directors may have less involvement in establishing and reviewing the compensation packages for key executives.

Compensation Committee of the Board of Directors The **compensation committee** usually is a subgroup of the board composed of directors who are not officers of the firm. Compensation committees generally make recommendations to the board of directors on overall pay policies, salaries for top officers, supplemental compensation such as stock options and bonuses, and additional perquisites ("perks") for executives. However, the independence of board compensation committees increasingly has been criticized.

One major concern voiced by many critics is that the base pay and bonuses of CEOs often are set by board compensation committee members, many of whom are CEOs of other companies with similar compensation packages. Also,

Perquisites (perks)
Special benefits—usually noncash items—for executives.

Compensation committee A subgroup of the board of directors composed of directors who are not officers of the firm.

the compensation advisors and consultants to the CEOs often collect large fees, and critics charge that those fees distort the objectivity of the advice given.

To counter criticism, some corporations have changed the composition of the compensation committee and given it more independence. Some of the changes have included prohibiting "insider" company officers and board members from serving on compensation committees. Also, some firms have empowered the compensation committee to hire and pay compensation consultants without involving executive management.[38]

Debating the "Reasonableness" of Executive Compensation

The notion that monetary incentives tied to performance result in improved performance makes sense to most people. However, how much money does it take? The debate about whether executive compensation in the United States goes too far occurs regularly, with Congress threatening intervention periodically to deal with the astronomical amounts of some compensation packages. Figure 13-11 outlines the arguments in the executive pay debate. The discussion of each point will follow.

Figure 13-11 **Arguments in the Executive Pay Debate**

Criticisms	Counter-Arguments
Boards of Directors give sizable rewards to both high and low performing executives.	The market for executives is tight. Bidding wars and concern over retention drive compensation packages.
Executives should not get rewards and bonuses for laying off much of the workforce.	Executives are paid for making difficult decisions to benefit companies.
Total compensation packages, especially with the "golden parachutes" for failure, are out of line.	Sports and entertainment stars earn as much or more for playing games or acting.
Many people contribute to a company's success, not just the CEO. Others are paid only a fraction of CEOs' salaries.	CEOs earn their money with endless hours, great pressures, and skill sets that few others possess.
Executive compensation frequently is not linked to company performance.	Measuring executive performance is difficult, and stock prices alone are insufficient.

Issue: High and Low Performers Both Get Raises Current pay, such as bonuses or profits on stock options, should be linked with performance for the previous several years. CEO pay remains sensitive to company performance when considered within proper time periods, and poor-performing CEOs indeed may be terminated. On average, a strong statistical correlation exists between CEO pay and company performance.[39] One study found that companies with CEOs who received higher than median total compensation generated five-year annualized returns to shareholders that were 8% higher than companies with CEOs paid below the median compensation.[40] However, the market demand for executives is indeed strong. A shrinking pool of experienced executives commands a powerful position in negotiating exceptional hiring packages. Conseco paid a "golden hello" hiring bonus to a retired GE executive of $45 million.[41] And some truth can be found in the allegation that boards pay a lot of money to some less-than-sterling performers. "These compensation committees are going to approve these packages because they can't find anybody who can do a better job," a shareholder advocate notes.[42]

Issue: Executives Rewarded for Negative Actions It seems contradictory from an employee's perspective to reward executives who often improve corporate results by cutting staff, laying off employees changing pension plans, or increasing the deductible on the health insurance. But sometimes cost-cutting measures are necessary to keep a company afloat. However, a sense of reasonableness may be appropriate too; if rank and file employees suffer, giving bonuses and large payouts to executives appears counterproductive, and even hypocritical.[43]

Issue: Golden Parachutes Are Unreasonably Lavish A special perk available to some executives, a **golden parachute,** provides protection and security to executives in the event that they lose their jobs or their firms are acquired by other firms. Executive employment contracts often include special compensation provided to executives who are negatively affected in an acquisition or merger. Some analysts estimate that more than half of all CEOs and other senior executives in larger major corporations have golden parachutes. A typical golden parachute gives a departing executive a lump-sum amount equal to two to four times the annual salary and bonus, extra pension credits, immediate vesting of stock options, outplacement assistance, and other sweeteners. But the huge size of some parachute packages raises ethical concerns. For example, Michael Ovitz served as the second-highest executive at Walt Disney for about a year. When he quit, he received a golden parachute estimated to be as high as $90 million! The reason for his departure was "incompatibility" with Michael Eisner, CEO of Disney.

Golden parachutes are more noticeable in some executive compensation packages because they seem to offer a safety valve no other employees have. However, with mergers and acquisitions continuing, a golden parachute is often the key to convincing an executive to work for a company that might be acquired. To consider an analogy, shortstop Alex Rodriguez's $250 million contract with the Texas Rangers turned the heads of baseball fans, and $20 million per film payouts are common for top movie stars. How much is an executive worth who can save a multi-billion-dollar company or keep it competing successfully? Competing in the market for such people has led to offering golden parachutes.[44]

Issue: Executive Salaries Compared to Workers' Pay Critics point out that many U.S. corporate CEOs make almost 200 times more than average workers in their firms make, up from 35:1 in the 1970s. Moreover, in Japan the ratio is 15:1 and in Europe 20:1. Also, Japanese CEOs are paid about one-third of what U.S. CEOs in comparable-sized firms are paid. Various organizations opposed to large CEO payments have proposed legislation to cap the tax deductibility of executive compensation at 25 times the amount paid the lowest-paid worker.[45]

Certainly everyone in an organization contributes to its success (or failure). But CEOs do contribute at a different level of complexity. As business has become more global and technology calls for 24/7 performance, executives often move through several time zones each week and communicate with staff around the clock.[46] Not everyone functions successfully under these conditions.

Issue: The Link Between Executive Compensation and Corporate Performance Whether or not executive compensation levels are linked to organizational performance has been the subject of numerous studies. One key aspect of evaluating all of the studies is to examine the performance measures used. In many settings, financial measures such as return on equity, return to shareholders, earnings per share, net income before taxes, and other criteria are used. However, a number of firms also incorporate non-financial organizational measures of performance when determining executive bonuses and incentives. Customer satisfaction, employee satisfaction, market share, productivity, and quality are other areas measured for executive performance rewards.

Measurement of executive performance varies from firm to firm. A short-term focus of one year is used in some executive compensation packages, so performance in a given year may lead to large rewards even though corporate performance over a multi-year period may be mediocre. This difference is especially pronounced if the yearly measures are carefully chosen. Executives can even manipulate earnings per share by selling assets, liquidating inventories, or reducing research and development expenditures. All these actions may make organizational performance look better, but they may impair the long-term growth of the organization.[47]

Determining "Reasonableness" of Executive Compensation

The reasonableness of executive compensation is often justified by comparison to compensation market surveys, but these surveys usually provide a range of compensation data that requires interpretation. Various questions have been suggested for determining if executive pay is "reasonable" in a specific instance, including the following:

- Would another company hire this person as an executive?
- How does the executive's compensation compare with that for executives in similar companies in the industry?
- Is the executive's pay consistent with pay for other employees in the company?
- What would an investor pay for the level of performance of the executive?

Undoubtedly, the criticisms of executive compensation will continue as huge payouts occur, particularly if organizational performance has been weak. Hopefully, boards of directors of more corporations will address the need to better link organizational performance with variable pay rewards for executives and other employees.

Summary

- Variable pay, traditionally called incentives, is additional compensation linked to individual, team (group), and/or organizational performance.
- Effective variable pay plans should recognize organizational culture and resources, be clear and understandable, be kept current, tie incentives to performance, recognize individual differences, and identify plan payments separate from base pay.
- Sales employees may have their compensation tied to their performance on a number of sales-related criteria. Sales compensation can be provided as salary only, commission only, or salary plus commissions or bonuses.
- Design of team (group) variable pay plans must consider how team incentives are to be distributed, the timing of the incentive payments, and how decisions are made about who receives how much of the variable payout.
- To overcome some problems associated with individual incentives, team (group) variable pay plans encourage and reward teamwork and group effort.
- One prominent organization-wide variable pay plan is gainsharing, which provides rewards based on greater-than-expected gains in profits and/or productivity.
- Profit-sharing plans set aside a part of the profits earned by organizations for distribution to employees.
- An employee stock ownership plan (ESOP) enables employees to gain ownership in the firm for which they work.
- Executive compensation must be viewed as a total package composed of salaries, bonuses, long-term performance-based incentives, benefits, and perquisites (perks).
- A compensation committee, which is a subgroup of the board of directors, has authority over executive compensation plans.
- Performance-based incentives often represent a significant portion of an executive's compensation package.

Review and Discussion Questions

1. Identify what variable pay is and discuss why its usage has increased.
2. Describe why incentive plans you have received at work have been successful and/or unsuccessful.
3. Give examples of individual incentives used by an organization in which you were employed.
4. List the positive and negative aspects associated with using salary-only and commission-only sales compensation plans.
5. Describe situations in which team/group incentive plans are likely to be successful and unsuccessful.
6. Why might employees view an employee stock ownership plan (ESOP) as both attractive and risky?
7. Locate a corporate annual report and review it to identify the components of executive compensation discussed in it. How reasonable is the compensation of the CEO compared with the corporate results described in the report?

Terms to Know

variable pay   410
straight piece-rate system   415
differential piece-rate system   415
bonus   415
commission   418
draw   418
gainsharing   423

profit sharing   424
employee stock ownership plan (ESOP)   425
stock option   429
perquisites (perks)   430
compensation committee   430
golden parachute   432

Reviewing Executive Compensation Program

Each year the Board of Directors reviews the executive compensation program in place to evaluate the need for changes. After their review this year the Board Chairman has contacted you as an HR consultant to ask for your assistance with some research. The Board has concluded they do not have a clear compensation strategy for the executive program and want to have you research what issues a compensation strategy should address. Using the following Web site, provide the Board of Directors with a one-page explanation of a compensation strategy and the issues it should address. *http://www.personnelsystems.com/execcomp.htm*

County Governments and Incentive Programs

The spread of incentive programs is not limited to private-sector employers. A number of local and state governmental entities have established incentive programs, including public school districts, state-operated institutions, and county governments. Two county government programs illustrate both the advantages and the reactions to the use of incentives in the public sector.

In Maryland several years ago, Baltimore County employee morale was very low, and for good reason. Over the last five years, employees had received raises in only one of the years, the number of employees had declined, and some layoffs had occurred. During the same period of time the population in Baltimore County had increased significantly, which meant more work for fewer workers who had received limited pay increases. Also, the quality of the services delivered by the county employees had declined somewhat.

Then changes began to be made when a new county executive, Dutch Ruppensberger, took office. Ruppensberger, who previously had served on the council, recruited outside consultants to help design an employee gainsharing program. Ruppensberger saw this program as a way to improve quality and productivity in delivering county services while also rewarding employees for their efforts. The program began by gathering employee ideas and obtaining employee input through some employee teams. Then Ruppensberger initiated a pilot program in two different divisions, Dietary Services and Recreational and Parks Maintenance. Employees in the two divisions participated in training on teamwork and resolving conflicts. Then the teams met to draft program objectives and action plans. The Dietary Services Division, which provided meals to prisoners in the county jails, identified potential savings of $88,000 that could be made. The Recreation and Parks Maintenance employees estimated that savings of $126,000 could be reached. Both divisions submitted their plans to county management and then the County Council.

With approvals granted, the gainsharing program was implemented. Under the plan half of the estimated savings in each division goes to the county, while the other half of the savings is divided equally among participating division employees up to an identified maximum amount. The first year of the plan yielded significant savings for these two divisions, and participating employees received their appropriate payments. The success of programs at Baltimore County appears to result from its focus on rewarding employees directly involved in delivering county services.

However, a bonus incentive plan for executive-level managers in San Diego County in California created a firestorm of controversy. Under the San Diego County plan, executive-level, across-the-board pay increases were eliminated. Performance bonuses were paid only to executives who attained established performance objectives. A total of 180 executives and administrators received bonus payments totaling $1.34 million; but one-third of all executives received no bonus, and several had their base pay cut because of missing performance objectives.

When the amounts of the bonuses were made public, a furor resulted. The local union representing lower-paid county employees protested that executives—including the top county executive, who got a $45,000 bonus—were getting huge sums, while lower-level employees got only a 3% raise. Further, the union noted that some of the bonuses amounted to more than the annual income of many lower-level county employees. Also, the bonus pro-gram for executives cost $500,00 more than if 3% across-the-board raises had been given to those executives. As a result of the controversy, the county board directed that the program be revised.[48]

Questions

1. What factors determined the success and failure of the two programs described in the case?
2. Given the strength of public-sector unions, some experts believe that incentive programs in public-sector organizations will never become widespread. Comment on this view and discuss why it may or may not prevail.

Notes

1. Adapted from Jonathan D. Glater, "Seasoning Compensation Stew," *The New York Times,* March 7, 2001, C1.
2. G. A. Matthews and Alyce M. Dickinson, "Effects of Alternative Activities on Time Allocated to Task Performance Under Different Percentages of Incentive Pay," *Journal of Organizational Behavior Management,* 20, (2000), 3.
3. Ward Mannering, "Mission Possible," *WorldatWork Journal,* Third Quarter 2001, 33–41.
4. "SHRM Examines Success of Incentive Pay Plans," *IOMA's Report on Hourly Compensation,* March 1, 2000, 1.
5. "Study Questions If Incentive Pay Is Really Hitting It's Mark," *IOMA Report on Salary Surveys,* February 2000, 13.
6. "Short-Term Incentives Considered Ineffective, Survey Reveals," *HR News,* January 2000, 5.
7. Claire Ginther, "Incentive Programs That Really Work," *HR Magazine,* August 2000, 118.
8. "Towers Perrin Reveals How to Design the Most Effective Incentive Plans," *IOMA's Report on Salary Surveys,* March 2000, 14.
9. Alexander D. Stajkovic and Fred Luthans, "Differential Effects of Incentive Motivators on Work Per-formance," *Academy of Management Journal,* 43 (2001) 580–590.
10. Marlene A. Prost, "New Worth," *Human Resource Executive,* February 2001, 78.
11. Paul A. Gilseter, "Online Incentives Sizzle—and You Shine," *Workforce,* January 2001, 44.
12. Lisa J. Riley and Arthur Anderson, "Little Things Make a Big Difference," *Workspan,* May 2001, 57.
13. Bill Weeks, "Running On Empty?" *Workspan,* January 2002, 20–24.
14. William M. Bulkeley, "Incentives System Fine-Tunes Pay/Bonus Plans," *The Wall Street Journal,* August 16, 2001, B4.
15. Nina McIntyre, "Rewards in the E-Business World," *Workspan,* July 2000, 31.
16. Chad Albrecht and Mike O'Hara, "Its Not All Relative," *WorldatWork Journal,* Third Quarter 2001, 59–64.
17. "Four Studies Track What Alternative Pay Plans Work Best," *IOMA's Report on Salary Surveys,* January 2000, 10.
18. Todd Manas, and M. H. L. Vuitton, "Combining Reward Elements to Create the Right Team Chemistry," *Workspan,* November 12, 2000, 46–52.
19. Todd Zenger and C. R. Marshall, "Determinants of Incentive Intensity in Group-Based Rewards," *Academy of Management Journal,* 43, (2000), 149–163.
20. Jerry McAdams and Elizabeth J. Hawk, "Making Group Incentive Plans Work," *WorldatWork Journal,* Third Quarter 2000, 28–34.
21. Edilberto F. Montemayer, "Pay and Incentive Systems," in *Managing Human Resources in the 21st Century* (Cincinnati: South-Western Publishing, 2000, 17.7.
22. Jeanie Casison and Tina Benetiz, "Division of Labor," *Incentive,* September 2001, 52–57.
23. Ruth Simon, "Options Overdose," *The Wall Street Journal,* June 4, 2001, C1.
24. Barbara Estes et al., "Stock Options: Are They Still the Brass Ring?" *Workspan,* May 2001, 24.
25. Corey Rosen, NCEO, "A Brief Introduction to Employee Ownership," available at *www. NCEO.org.*
26. Based on Mike Butler and Dianne Eberlein, "Measuring the Ownership Dynamics," *WorldatWork Journal,* Third Quarter 2000: 57–63.
27. "More Companies See Value in Employee Stock Plans," *Omaha World-Herald,* January 26, 1997, 46R.
28. Bruce Ellig, "CEO Pay: A 20th Century Review," *WorldatWork Journal,* Third Quarter 2000, 71–78.

29. Michael McKee, "History, Age Push at Ceiling," *The Denver Post,* October 21, 2000, C1.

30. Louis Lavelle, "Executive Pay," *Business Week,* April 16, 2001, 77–108.

31. Erik Stern, "A Good Way to Put the Boss's Achievements into Context," *Financial Times,* March 6, 2001, 12.

32. Joann S. Lublin, "Hedging their Bets," *The Wall Street Journal,* April 12, 2001, R1.

33. Lavelle, "Executive Pay," 78.

34. Al Lewis, "Something Out There Is Bugging Big Companies," *Denver Post,* August 19, 2001, K1.

35. M. C. Struman and J. C. Short, "Lump-Sum Bonus Satisfaction: Testing the Construct Validity of a New Pay Satisfaction Dimension," *Personnel Psychology,* 53 (2000) 673–700.

36. "Organizations Are Diversifying Executive Incentive Pay Plans," *Bulletin to Management,* October 19, 2000, 332.

37. "Benefits Policies," *Bulletin to Management,* June 22, 2000, 196.

38. James Reda, "The Compensation Committee," *ACA Journal,* First Quarter 2000, 39–45.

39. Ira T. Kay and Steven E. Rushbrook, "The U.S. Executive Pay Model," *WorldatWork Journal,* First Quarter 2001, 8–16.

40. Ira T. Kay, "CEOs Are a Good Investment," *Rocky Mountain News,* July 14, 2001, 2C.

41. Gary Strauss, "Forget Brass Rings—Execs Grab for Gold," *USA Today,* March 20, 2001, 1B.

42. Louis Lavelle, "CEO Pay: The More Things Change . . . ," *Business Week,* October 6, 2000, 106–108.

43. Kathy Kristof, "Executive Pay for Performance Has Its Critics," *The Denver Post,* August 13, 2001, 2C.

44. Gary Strauss, "CEO Paychecks: Fair or Foul?" *USA Today,* April 16, 2001, B1.

45. Louis Aguilar, "Exec–Worker Pay Gap Widens to Gulf," *The Denver Post,* July 8, 2001, 16A.

46. Carol Hymowitz, "How CEOs Get the Energy to Work Those Endless Days," *The Wall Street Journal,* March 20, 2001, B1.

47. Jack Dolmat, "Executive Pay for Performance," *WorldatWork Journal,* First Quarter 2001, 19–27.

48. Based on James Fox and Bruce Lawson, "Gainsharing Lifts Baltimore Employees' Morale," *American City & County,* September 1997, 93; and Ellen Perlman, "Bonus Bucks Cause a Ruckus," *Governing,* December 1997, 82.

CHAPTER 14

Managing Employee Benefits

After you have read this chapter, you should be able to:

- Define a benefit and identify two strategic reasons why employers provide benefits.

- Distinguish between mandated and voluntary benefits and list three examples of each.

- Describe two security benefits.

- List and define at least six pension-related terms.

- Explain the importance of health-care cost management and identify some methods of achieving it.

- Discuss the growth of family-oriented and time-off benefits and their importance to many employees.

- Summarize benefits communication and flexible benefits as considerations in benefits administration.

Changing Benefits

When the term *employee benefits* is used, most people think of paid vacation, sick leave, or health insurance. However, during the long economic boom that resulted in a tight market for employees, employers invented "creative" employee benefits to help recruiting and retention. Many no longer exist, but they stand as a monument to employers' creativity.

- At Netscape Communications, a dental van came to the office complex twice a week and dentists performed root canals, teeth cleaning, and other general dental services.
- At some locations of Barnett Banks in Florida, employees could arrange for car washes.
- On his or her birthday, each employee at Mary Kay Cosmetics in Dallas, Texas, received a birthday card and a coupon for a free lunch or movie tickets for two. After five years with the company, employees received a $100 U.S. savings bond.
- At ConAgra's frozen food division in Omaha, Nebraska, employees with a sick child could request that a trained baby-sitter go to the employee's house so that the employee could go to work. ConAgra paid 75% of the cost for the "sick kid" sitter.

An employer that provided a more attractive benefits package often enjoyed an advantage over other employers in hiring and retaining qualified employees when the competing firms offered similar base pay. In fact, such benefits may create "golden handcuffs," making employees more reticent to move to other employers.

Many employees with family responsibilities value both child-care and elder-care benefits. On-site child-care centers, elder-care referral networks, alternative work schedules, and telecommuting are just some of the benefits options available to assist employees attempting to balance work and family demands.

Other off-beat "benefits" were used at Microstrategy, where every year the *entire* company went on a cruise paid for by the company. One year the firm rented an entire ship. However, such unusual benefits have been affected by economic pressures since then.

Concierge benefits and services have been offered to help employees with life's distractions from work—finding tickets, selecting gifts, scheduling car repair and picking up dry cleaning. Even pet insurance is provided as an optional benefit by Lenox Hill Hospital.

In another benefit area corporate housing does not resemble the "company town" of yesteryear. Today, some organizations offer accommodations to employees on temporary assignment, searching for more permanent housing, or waiting for a home to be built. "When you are relocating a family, they're generally relocating with a spouse and a dog and cat. They are used to living in a nice home and don't want to be in a hotel for months," the president of a corporate housing firm observes.

Times change with benefits, as with other areas of HR Management. One observer notes that the rising costs of health care and the governmental mandates on employer-offered health plans are likely to force many employers to reduce or drop health-care coverage altogether.

Large companies are moving toward defined contribution programs, whereby employees receive an amount to be used toward the costs of their own health insurance policies. However, some portion of the costs may exceed the amount given by employers, thus employees may have to pay for more benefits costs from their own pockets. Many employers also are already developing exit strategies from their current plans that provide a wide range of health benefits at virtually no costs to employees. All of these illustrations make it clear that employee benefits are indeed changing.[1]

> Times change with benefits, as with other areas of HR management.

"In this era of greater personal responsibility and demographic changes, government, employers, and individuals are changing their approaches to financial security and how it can be maintained through employee benefits."

—**Anna M. Rappaport**

Benefit Indirect compensation given to an employee or group of employees as a part of organizational membership.

Logging On...

Benefit News.com
This Web site consists of surveys, archived articles, and the latest trends and information regarding employee benefits.

http://www.benefitnews.com

Employers provide employee benefits to their workers for being part of the organization. A **benefit** is a form of indirect compensation. Benefits often include retirement plans, vacations with pay, health insurance, educational assistance, and many more programs.

Employers in the United States often fill the role of major provider of benefits for citizens. However, in many other nations, citizens and employers are taxed to pay for government-provided benefits, such as health care and retirement programs managed through government social programs. Although federal regulations require U.S. employers to provide certain benefits, U.S. employers voluntarily provide many others.

Benefits influence employees' decisions about which particular employer to work for, whether to stay or leave employment, and when they might retire. However, the unique characteristics of benefits sometimes make them difficult to administer. For example, government involvement in benefits continues to expand. The federal and state governments *require* that certain benefits be offered (Social Security, worker's compensation, unemployment insurance, etc.), and they regulate many of the non-required benefits as well (retirement, family leave, flexible benefits, etc.).

Further, employees tend to take benefits for granted. For instance, so many organizations offer health insurance, that employees expect it. However, benefits are also very complex, and as a result, employees may not understand them, or in many cases may not even know what benefits exist. Yet benefits are costly to the employer, averaging about 40% of payroll costs over the past several years (for required and voluntary benefits together). These characteristics of benefits suggest that HR managers should carefully consider the strategic role of benefits in their organizations.

Strategic Perspectives on Benefits

From the employers' perspective, employee benefits represent a double-edged sword. On one side, employers know that in order to attract and retain employees with the necessary capabilities they must offer appropriate benefits.[2] On the other side, they know the importance of controlling or even cutting costs. Benefits comprise a significant part of the total compensation package offered to employees. Total compensation includes money paid directly (such as wages and salaries) and money paid indirectly (such as benefits). Too often, both managers and employees think of only wages and salaries as compensation and fail to consider the additional costs associated with benefits expenditures.

Total compensation costs for labor amounts to more than half of total operating costs in many organizations, even more in some service operations. For example, about 80% of the U.S. Post Office budget is labor cost. Because of their sizable proportion of organizational costs, the compensation components of base pay, variable pay, and benefits require serious and realistic assessment and planning. Figure 14-1 shows where each benefit dollar typically is spent, on average, based on various surveys conducted regularly.

Figure 14-1 ► **How the Benefit Dollar Is Spent**

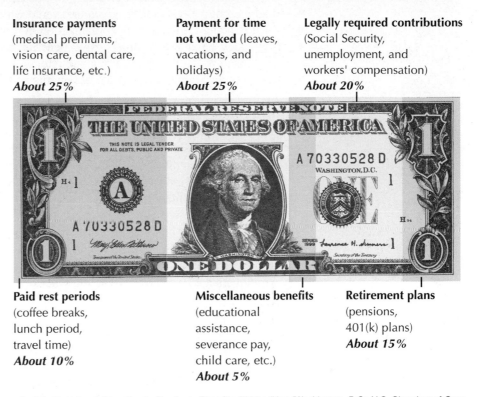

Insurance payments
(medical premiums,
vision care, dental care,
life insurance, etc.)
About 25%

**Payment for time
not worked** (leaves,
vacations, and
holidays)
About 25%

Legally required contributions
(Social Security,
unemployment, and
workers' compensation)
About 20%

Paid rest periods
(coffee breaks,
lunch period,
travel time)
About 10%

Miscellaneous benefits
(educational
assistance,
severance pay,
child care, etc.)
About 5%

Retirement plans
(pensions,
401(k) plans)
About 15%

Source: Based on information in *Employee Benefits*, 2000 edition (Washington, D.C.: U.S. Chamber of Commerce, 2000).

Goals for Benefits

Benefits should be looked at as part of the overall compensation strategy of the organization. For instance, an organization can choose to compete for employees by providing base compensation, variable pay, or benefits, or perhaps all three. Which approach is chosen depends on many factors, such as the competition, organizational life cycle, and corporate strategy.[3] For example, a new firm may choose to have lower base pay, and use high variable incentives to attract new employees, but keep the cost of benefits as low as possible for awhile. Or an organization that hires predominately younger female employees might choose a family-friendly set of benefits including on-site child care to attract good employees.[4]

Benefits Needs Analysis

Benefits needs analysis
A comprehensive look at all aspects of benefits.

A **benefits needs analysis** includes a comprehensive look at all aspects of benefits in a firm. Done periodically, such an analysis is more than simply deciding what benefits employees might want. A benefits needs analysis to make certain the mix of benefits is doing what it should might consider the following issues:

■ How much total compensation, including benefits, should be provided?

■ What part should benefits comprise of the total compensation of individuals?

- What expense levels are acceptable for each benefit offered?
- Why is each type of benefit offered?
- Which employees should be given or offered which benefits?
- What is being received by the organization in return for each benefit?
- How does having a comprehensive benefits package aid in minimizing turnover or maximizing recruiting and retention of employees?
- How flexible should the package of benefits be?

Funding Benefits

Total benefits costs can be funded both by contributions made by the employer and contributions made by the employee. If the employer fully subsidizes a benefit, the cost to the employee would be zero. But if an employer chooses to pay $400 per month toward an employee's health insurance premium while the employee pays $150, then the employee contributes to covering benefits costs.

Benefit plans can be funded by purchasing insurance from an insurance provider. Premiums to be paid reflect the predicted claims and will be adjusted based on actual claims. Some large employers choose to "self-fund" and be their own insurers by setting aside moneys to cover benefits costs. Self-funding by large employers has been effective in a number of situations.

The Nature and Types of Benefits

Employers offer some benefits to aid recruiting and retention, some because they are required to do so, and some simply because doing so reinforces the company philosophy.[5] For example, insurance can be purchased at a better rate if the purchaser is a large employer that qualifies for a group rate. Further, tax laws provide beneficial tax treatment of some benefits for employees that they would not get if purchased by individuals.

Benefits generally are not taxed as income to employees. For this reason, they represent a somewhat more valuable reward to employees than an equivalent cash payment. For example, assume that employee Henry Gomez is in a 25% tax bracket. If Henry earns an extra $400, he must pay $100 in taxes on this amount (disregarding exemptions). But if his employer provides prescription drug coverage in a benefit plan, and he receives the $400 as payments for prescription drugs, he is not taxed on the amount; he receives the value of the entire $400. This feature makes benefits a desirable form of compensation to employees.

Types of Benefits

There are a wide range of benefits offered. Figure 14-2 shows the many different benefits classified by type.

Mandated benefits Ones that employers in the United States must provide to employees by law.

Government-Mandated Benefits There are many **mandated benefits** that employers in the United States must provide to employees by law. Social Security and unemployment insurance are funded through a tax paid by the employer based on the employee's compensation. Workers' compensation laws exist in all states. In addition, under the Family and Medical Leave Act (FMLA), employers must offer unpaid leaves to employees with certain medical or family difficulties. Other mandated benefits are available through Medicare, which provides health care for those age 65 and over. It is funded in part by an employer tax

Figure 14-2 ▶ Types of Benefits

░░ Government Mandated   **░░ Employer Voluntary**

Security

Workers' compensation
Unemployment compensation

Supplemental unemployment
  benefits (SUB)
Severance pay

Retirement Security

Social Security

Early Retirement options
Pre-retirement counseling
Disability retirement benefits
Health care for retirees
Pension plans
Individual retirement accounts
  (IRAs)
401(k) and 403(b) plans

Health Care

COBRA and HIPAA provisions

Medical and dental
HMO or PPO health-care plans
Long-term care
Vision care
Prescription drugs
Psychiatric counseling
Wellness programs

Financial, Insurance and Related

Life insurance
Legal insurance
Disability insurance
Financial counseling
Credit unions
Company-provided car and
  expense account
Life insurance
Educational assistance

Family-Oriented

Family and Medical Leave Act

Dependent care
Alternative work arrangements

Time Off

Military reserve time off
Election and jury leaves

Lunch and rest breaks
Holidays and vacations
Funeral and bereavement leaves
Sick leave and paid time off

Social and Recreational

Tennis courts
Bowling leagues
Service awards
Sponsored events (athletic and
  social)
Cafeteria and food services
Recreation programs

---

through Social Security. The Consolidated Omnibus Budget Reconciliation Act (COBRA) and the Health Insurance Portability and Accountability Act (HIPAA) mandate that an employer continue health-care coverage paid for by the employees after they leave the organization, and that most employees be able to obtain coverage if they were previously covered in a health plan.

Additional mandated benefits have been *proposed* for many other areas, but as yet none of the proposals have been adopted. Areas in which coverage has been proposed are as follows:

- Universal health-care benefits for all workers
- Child-care assistance
- Pension plan coverage that can be transferred by workers who change jobs
- Core benefits for part-time employees working at least 500 hours per year.

A major reason for these proposals is that federal and state governments want to shift many of the social costs for health care and other expenditures to employers. This shift would relieve some of the budgetary pressures facing governments who otherwise might have to raise taxes and cut spending.

Logging On...

**Employee Benefit
Research Institute**
This Web site provides the
latest legislative and research
information affecting benefits.

http://www.ebri.com

Voluntary Benefits Employers voluntarily offer other types of benefits in order to compete for and retain employees. By offering additional benefits, organizations are recognizing the need to provide greater security and benefit support to workers with widely varied personal circumstances. By offering more benefits, employers hope to strengthen the ties with their employees as valuable human resources. Also, as the workforce ages and more individuals retire, financial security in retirement becomes an issue that employees want to address. In addition, as work and jobs change to emphasize flexibility and choice, both workers and employers are realizing that choices among benefits are necessary, as evidenced by the growth in flexible benefits and cafeteria benefit plans. The following sections describe the different types of benefits that were shown in Figure 14-2.

Security Benefits

A number of benefits provide employee security. These benefits include some mandated by laws and others offered by employers voluntarily. The primary benefits found in most organizations include workers' compensation, unemployment compensation, and severance pay.

Workers' Compensation

Workers' compensation
Benefits provided to persons injured on the job.

Workers' compensation provides benefits to persons injured on the job. State laws require most employers to provide workers' compensation coverage by purchasing insurance from a private carrier or state insurance fund or by providing self-insurance. U.S. government employees are covered under the Federal Employees' Liability Act, administered by the U.S. Department of Labor.

The workers' compensation system requires employers to give cash benefits, medical care, and rehabilitation services to employees for injuries or illnesses occurring within the scope of their employment.[6] In exchange, employees give up the right of legal actions and awards. However, it is in the interests of both employers and employees to reduce workers' comp costs through safety and health programs.[7] More discussion on workers' compensation occurs in Chapter 15.

Unemployment Compensation

Another benefit required by law is unemployment compensation, established as part of the Social Security Act of 1935. Because each U.S. state operates its own unemployment compensation system, provisions differ significantly from state to state. Employers finance this benefit by paying a tax on the first $7,000 (or more, in 37 states) of annual earnings for each employee. The tax is paid to state and federal unemployment compensation funds. The percentage paid by individual employers is based on "experience rates," which reflect the number of claims filed by workers who leave.

An employee who is out of work and is actively looking for employment normally receives up to 26 weeks of pay, at the rate of 50% to 80% of normal pay. Most employees are eligible. However, workers fired for misconduct or those not actively seeking employment generally are ineligible. Only about 40% of eligible people use the unemployment compensation system. This underutilization may be due both to the stigma of receiving unemployment and the complexity of the system, which some feel is simply not worth the effort.[8]

Criticisms of Unemployment Insurance Two reasons explain changes in unemployment insurance laws proposed at both state and federal levels: (1) abuses are estimated to cost billions each year; and (2) many state unemployment funds are exhausted during economic slowdowns. Some states allow striking union workers to collect unemployment benefits despite strike fund payments from the union, a provision bitterly opposed by many employers.

Supplemental Unemployment Benefits (SUB) Supplemental unemployment benefits (SUB) are closely related to unemployment compensation, but they are *not required by law*. First obtained by the United Steelworkers in 1955, a SUB program is a benefit provision negotiated by a union with an employer as part of a collective bargaining agreement. The provision requires organizations to contribute to a fund that supplements the unemployment compensation available to employees from federal and/or state sources.

Severance Pay

Severance pay A security benefit voluntarily offered by employers to employees who lose their jobs.

Severance pay is a security benefit voluntarily offered by employers to employees who lose their jobs. Severed employees may receive lump-sum severance payments if their employment is terminated by the employer. For example, if a facility closes because it is outmoded and no longer economically profitable to operate, the employees who lose their jobs may receive lump-sum payments based on their years of service. Severance pay provisions often provide higher severance payments corresponding to an employee's level within the organization and the person's years of employment. Figure 14-3 shows features typically included in severance services.

Figure 14-3 ▶ **Services During Severance**

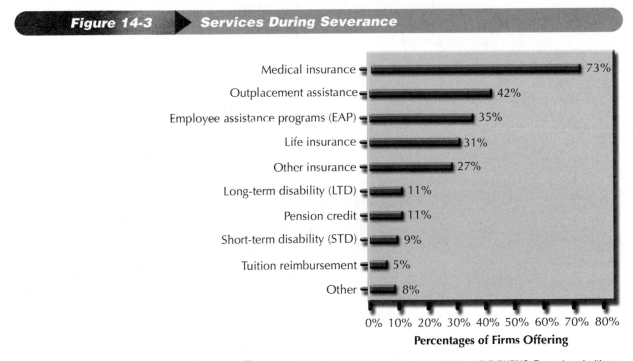

Percentages of Firms Offering

Some employers have offered reduced amounts of cash severance and replaced some of the severance value by offering continued health insurance and outplacement assistance. Through *outplacement* assistance ex-employees receive resume writing instruction, interviewing skills workshops, and career counseling.

The Worker Adjustment and Retraining Notification Act (WARN) of 1988 requires that many employers give 60 days' notice if a mass layoff or facility closing is to occur. The act does not require employers to give severance pay. Regardless, a written severance policy is a good idea.[9]

Retirement Security Benefits

Few people set aside sufficient financial reserves to use when they retire, so employer retirement benefits attempt to provide income for retired employees. Except for some employers with fewer than 100 employees, most employers offer some kind of retirement plan. Generally, private pensions make up a critical portion of income for people after retirement. With the baby boomer generation in the U.S. closing in on retirement, pressures on such funds are likely to grow. As Figure 14-4 indicates the median age of retirement has dropped significantly over the past 50 years. With more people retiring earlier, but living longer, retirement benefits are becoming a greater concern for employers, employees, and retired employees.

Retirement Benefits and Age Discrimination

As a result of a 1986 amendment to the Age Discrimination in Employment Act (ADEA), most employees cannot be forced to retire at a specific age. As a result, employers have had to develop different policies to comply with these regulations. In many employer pension plans, "normal retirement" is the age at which employees can retire and collect full pension benefits. Employers must decide whether individuals who continue to work past normal retirement age (perhaps age 65) should receive the full benefits package, especially pension credits. As

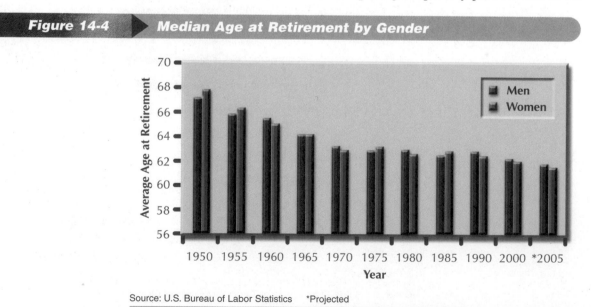

Figure 14-4 ▶ Median Age at Retirement by Gender

Source: U.S. Bureau of Labor Statistics   *Projected

possible future changes in Social Security may increase the age for full benefits past 65, modifications in policies are likely. Despite removal of mandatory retirement provisions, the age at which individuals retire has continued to decline in the United States. About 75% of all workers retire before the age of 65 years.

Early Retirement In many pension plans provisions for early retirement can be found in order to give workers opportunities to leave their jobs. After spending 25 to 30 years working for the same employer, individuals may wish to use their talents in other areas. Phased-in and part-time retirements offer an alternative to individuals and firms.

Some employers use early retirement buyout programs to cut back their workforces and reduce costs. Employers must take care to make these early retirement programs truly voluntary. Forcing workers to take advantage of an early retirement buyout program led to the passage of a federal law entitled the Older Workers Benefit Protection Act (OWBPA).

Older Workers Benefit Protection Act Passed in 1990, the Older Workers Benefit Protection Act (OWBPA) amended the ADEA and overturned a decision by the U.S. Supreme Court in *Public Employees Retirement System of Ohio v. Betts*.[10] This act requires equal treatment for older workers in early retirement or severance situations. It also sets forth some specific criteria that must be met when older workers sign waivers promising not to sue for age discrimination.

Retiree Benefits Some employers choose to offer their retirees benefits, which may be paid for by the retirees, the company, or both. These benefits are usually available until the retiree is eligible for Medicare. The costs of such coverage have risen dramatically, and to ensure that firms adequately reflect the liabilities for retiree health benefits, the Financial Accounting Standards Board (FASB) issued Rule 106 that requires employers to establish accounting reserves for funding retiree health-care benefits.

FASB Rule 106 has affected many firms, because the retiree benefits liabilities on their financial statements may reduce their current earnings each year. Huge write-offs against earnings have been taken by many firms in order to comply with FASB 106. As another way to respond to FASB 106, some employers have changed or discontinued some retiree benefits.[11] Other reactions to Rule 106 include the use of trust funds, "creative" accounting, and other "not necessarily legal" solutions.[12]

Social Security

The Social Security Act of 1935, with its later amendments, established a system providing *old age, survivor's, disability,* and *retirement benefits.* Administered by the federal government through the Social Security Administration, this program provides benefits to previously employed individuals. Employees and employers share in the cost of Social Security through a tax on employees' wages or salaries.

Social Security Changes Since the system's inception, Social Security payroll taxes have risen to 15.3% currently, with employees and employers each paying 7.65% up to an established maximum. In addition, Medicare taxes have more than doubled, to 2.9%. But benefits also became increasingly generous during the 1960s and 1970s.[13]

China's Pension Plan

China's long-bankrupt pension system has become a major source of social unrest for the populous nation. When the communist party came to power in 1949, it promised cradle-to-grave support for its workers. But now the much-diluted promise to support its elderly presents its biggest single liability.

The policy of the Chinese government to penalize citizens who had more than one child, another current social trend, combined with longer life expectancy, means the number of retired workers is growing much faster than new workers in the Chinese workforce who are paying into the pension system. Indeed, the retired population will triple to one-fourth of the population in the next 30 years.

At the same time, economic reforms are pushing millions of Chinese out of work and into early retirement. Some estimates put China's current pension liabilities at *half* the country's national economic output. To make matters worse, traditionally close Chinese family relationships are diminishing somewhat, leaving some older Chinese people without family support in their old age.

Eventually China wants to establish U.S.-style stock market retirement accounts, and perhaps invest pension funds in overseas markets. However, prior ineptitude and corruption make just getting some money to retirees a significant problem in the short run.[14]

Because the Social Security system affects a large number of individuals and is government operated, it is a politically sensitive program. Congress responded to popular pressure by raising payments and introducing cost-of-living adjustments. Now, Congress must respond to criticisms that the system is not financially sound and that changes are needed to ensure the future viability of the Social Security system. The problems with a national pension plan are not limited to the United States, as the HR Perspective shows.

Pension Plans

Pension plans Retirement benefits established and funded by employers and employees.

Pension plans are retirement benefits established and funded by employers and employees. Organizations are not required to offer pension plans to employees, and only 40% to 50% of U.S. workers are covered by them. Smaller firms offer them less often than large ones.

Traditional Pension Plans "Traditional" pension plans, where the employer makes the contributions and the employee gets a defined amount each month upon retirement, are no longer the norm in the private sector. In these **defined-benefit plans** the employees' contributions are based on actuarial calculations that focus on the *benefits* to be received by employees after retirement and the *methods* used to determine such benefits. A defined-benefit plan gives the employee greater assurance of benefits and greater predictability in the amount of benefits that will be available for retirement. Older workers often prefer defined-benefit plans.[15]

Defined-benefit plan One in which an employee is promised a pension amount based on age and service.

If the funding in a defined-benefit plan is insufficient, the employers may have to make up the shortfall. Therefore, a growing number of employers are dropping defined-benefit plans in favor of defined-contribution plans so that their contribution liabilities are known.

Defined-contribution plan One in which the employer makes an annual payment to an employee's pension account.

In a **defined-contribution plan**, the employer makes an annual payment to an employee's pension account. The key to this plan is the *contribution rate;*

employee retirement benefits depend on fixed contributions and employee earnings levels. Profit-sharing plans, employee stock ownership plans (ESOPs), and thrift plans are common defined-contribution plans. Because these plans hinge on the investment returns on the previous contributions, which can vary according to profitability or other factors, employees' retirement benefits are somewhat less secure and predictable. But because of their structure, these plans sometimes are preferred by younger, shorter-service employees.

Cash Balance Plans Employers are increasingly changing traditional pension plans to "cash balance plans," a hybrid based on ideas from both defined benefit and defined contribution plans. Cash balance plans define retirement benefits for each employee not on years of service and salary, but by reference to a hypothetical account balance. Cash balance plans began in 1985 after ERISA regulations for defined benefit plans made them a greater source of liability for many employers.[16]

Conversions to cash balance caused a flurry of discontent and even rebellion among older employees at AT&T, Electronic Data Systems, and most notably at IBM. At IBM workers in their 40's would have lost a significant amount of retirement under the new plan. Their vocal protests and agitation caused IBM to change its initial plans for the new pension system. Cash balance plans spread funding across a worker's entire career, making them better for mobile younger workers. About 20% of the *Fortune* 1000 firms use cash balance plans, and the number is growing.[17]

Many employers do not offer pension plans for a number of reasons. The primary reason, in addition to their cost, is the administrative burdens imposed by government legislation, such as the law discussed next.

Employee Retirement Income Security Act (ERISA) The widespread criticism of many pension plans led to the passage of the Employee Retirement Income Security Act (ERISA) in 1974. The purpose of this law is to regulate private pension plans in order to assure that employees who put money into them or depend on a pension for retirement funds actually receive the money when they retire.

ERISA essentially requires many companies to offer retirement plans to all employees if they are offered to any employees. Accrued benefits must be given to employees when they retire or leave. The act also sets minimum funding requirements and plans not meeting these requirements are subject to IRS financial penalties. Additional regulations require that employers pay plan termination insurance to ensure payment of employee pensions should the employers go out of business. To spread out the cost of pension administration and overhead costs, some employers use plans funded by multiple employers.[18]

Pension Terms and Concepts

Contributory plan
Pension plan in which the money for pension benefits is paid in by both employees and employers.

Non-contributory plan
Pension plan in which all the funds for pension benefits are provided by the employer.

Pension plans can be either contributory or non-contributory. In a **contributory plan**, money for pension benefits is paid in by both the employee and the employer. In a **non-contributory plan**, the employer provides all the funds for pension benefits. As would be expected, the noncontributory plans are generally preferred by employees and labor unions.

Certain rights are attached to employee pension plans. Various laws and provisions have been passed to address the right of employees to receive benefits from

Vesting The right of employees to receive benefits from their pension plans.

Portability A pension plan feature that allows employees to move their pension benefits from one employer to another.

their pension plans. Called **vesting,** it assures employees of a certain pension, provided they work a minimum number of years. If employees resign or are terminated before they have been employed for the required time, no pension rights accrue to them except the funds they have contributed. If employees stay the allotted time, they retain their pension rights and receive the funds contributed by both the employer and themselves.

Another feature of some employee pensions is **portability**. In a portable plan, employees can move their pension benefits from one employer to another. A growing number of firms offer portable pension plans. Instead of requiring workers to wait until they retire to move their traditional pension plan benefits, the portable plan takes a different approach. Once workers have vested in a plan for a period of time, such as five years, they can transfer their fund balances to other retirement plans if they change jobs.

Because statistics show that women generally live longer than men, women received lower benefits than men for the same contributions before 1983. However, a U.S. Supreme Court decision made this kind of discrimination illegal. The *Arizona Governing Committee v. Norris* ruling forced pension plan administrators to use "unisex" mortality tables that do not reflect the gender differential in mortality.[19] To bring legislation in line with this decision, Congress passed the Retirement Equity Act in 1984 as an amendment to ERISA and the Internal Revenue Code. It liberalized pension regulations that affect women, guaranteed access to benefits, prohibited pension-related penalties owing to absences from work such as maternity leave, and lowered the vesting age.

Individual Retirement Options

The availability of several retirement benefit options makes the pension area more complex. The most prominent options are individual retirement accounts (IRAs), 401(k) and 403(b) plans, and Keogh plans. These plans may be available in addition to company-provided pension plans.

Individual retirement account (IRA) A special account in which an employee can set aside funds that will not be taxed until the employee retires.

Keogh plan A type of individualized pension plan for self-employed individuals.

Individual Retirement Accounts (IRAs) An **individual retirement account (IRA)** is a special account in which an employee can set aside funds that will not be taxed until the employee retires. The major advantages of an IRA are the ability to accumulate extra retirement funds and the shifting of taxable income to later years, when total income—and therefore taxable income—is likely to be lower. Federal law changes in 1997 authorized a special type of IRA, called the Roth IRA, which likely will increase the usage of IRAs.

Keogh Plans A **Keogh plan** is a special type of individualized pension plan for self-employed persons. These individuals can set aside a percentage of their incomes in pension accounts. Keogh plans can be either defined-contribution or defined-benefit plans. Because of the complexity of Keogh plans and the special regulations covering them, many self-employed individuals seek advice from tax specialists before establishing one.

401(k) and 403(b) Plans Both the 401(k) and 403(b) plans allow employees to elect to reduce their current pay by a certain percentage, which is then paid into a retirement plan. The 403(b) plan is available to non-profit employers, while 401(k) plans are available to those in the private sector. Therefore, for discussion purposes, the focus will be on 401(k) plans due to their greater prominence.

Logging On...

401K-Site.com
This Web site provides investors with information on 401(k) plans.

http:www.401k-site.com

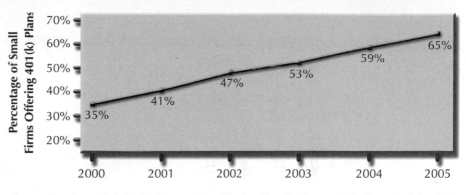

Source: Based on data in Virginia Munger Kahn, "Pension Plans for Everyone," *Business Week Small Biz,* July 10, 2001, 22.

401(k) plan An agreement in which a percentage of an employee's pay is withheld and invested in a tax-deferred account.

The **401(k) plan** gets its name from Section 401(k) of the federal tax code and is an agreement in which a percentage of an employee's pay is withheld and invested in a tax-deferred account. It allows employees to choose whether to receive cash or have employer contributions from profit-sharing and stock-bonus plans placed into tax-deferred accounts. See Figure 14-5 for a projection of the continued growth of 401(K) plans in small businesses.

The use of 401(k) plans and the assets in them have grown significantly in the past few years.[20] The advantage to employees is that they can save approximately $10,000 per year (as a ceiling) of pretax income toward their retirement. However, as the Enron and other situations have shown, employees with major stock holdings in their employer in their 401(k) is rather risky. Federal regulations to address these concerns have been proposed.

Health-Care Benefits

Employers provide a variety of health-care and medical benefits, usually through insurance coverage. The most common plans cover medical, dental, prescription drug, and vision care expenses for employees and their dependents. Basic health-care insurance to cover both normal and major medical expenses is also desired and expected by most employees. Dental insurance is also important to many employees. Some dental plans include orthodontic coverage, which is a major expense for some families. Some employer medical insurance plans also cover psychiatric counseling, but many do not.

The costs of health-care insurance have continued to escalate at a rate well in excess of inflation for several decades. By the 1990s, the rise in health-care costs forced many employers to make concerted efforts to control medical premium increases and other health-care costs. Estimates are that the average health-care cost per employee is over $5,500 per year.[21] Although successful for a while, the rate of increases in health-benefits costs has turned up again, as Figure 14-6 on the next page indicates.

Figure 14-6 ▶ *Increases in Health-Care Benefits Costs to Employers*

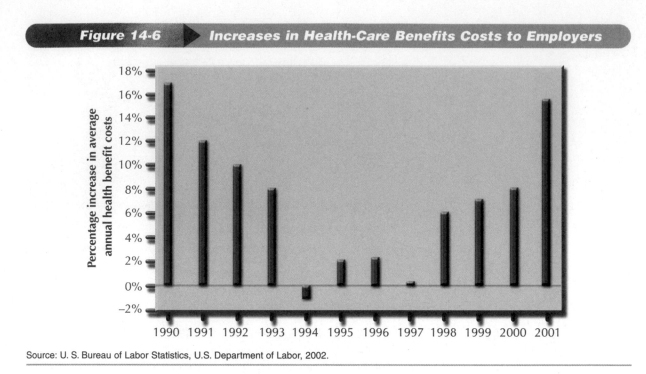

Source: U. S. Bureau of Labor Statistics, U.S. Department of Labor, 2002.

As a result of these large increases, many employers find that dealing with health-care benefits is time-consuming and expensive. This is especially frustrating for employers who have found that many employees seem to take their health benefits for granted. Consequently, a growing number of firms, particularly smaller ones, have asked, "Why are we offering these benefits anyway?" and have answered the question by discontinuing health benefits altogether.[22]

Controlling Health-Care Benefits Costs

For employers who do not drop health benefits altogether, there are a number of different approaches that can be used to control their costs. Two approaches that focus specifically on what employers pay are increasing co-payments and using deferred contribution plans.

Co-Payment In the past, many employers offered *first-dollar coverage*. With this type of coverage, all expenses, from the first dollar of health-care costs, were paid by the employee's insurance. Experts claim that when first-dollar coverage is included in a basic health plan, many employees see a doctor for every slight illness, which results in an escalation of the benefits costs.

Co-Payment Employee's payment of a portion of the cost of both insurance premiums and medical care.

As health insurance costs rise, employers have tried to shift some of those costs to employees. The **co-payment** strategy requires employees to pay a portion of the cost of both insurance premiums and medical care. Employers who have raised the deductible per person, from $50 to $250 have realized significant savings in health-care expenses due to decreased employee usage of health-care services.[23]

Defined Contribution Plans for Health Benefits Rather than dropping health benefits altogether or continuing to raise co-payments, some employers have implemented *defined contribution plans.* In this type of plan an employer makes a defined contribution of a set amount into each employee's "account." Then individual employees decide what type of health-care coverage they want to select and pay for from the alternatives identified by the employer. For instance, assume the employer provides $250 per month, to employees. One employee may choose an HMO costing $230 per month, and use the remaining money for additional life insurance. Another employee may choose a family plan costing $480 per month, and the additional $230 is deducted from the employee's paycheck. Coupled with flexible spending accounts (discussed later), employees become the ones deciding how much they will pay for health benefits, rather than the employer deciding for everyone.

The advantage of such plans for employers is shifting more of the increases in health-care benefits to be paid by employees.[24] However, as would be expected, negative reactions from employees may result. Therefore, implementing a defined contribution plan for health benefits requires extensive planning and educational efforts with employees.[25] Nevertheless, one survey of companies found that 45% of them were interested in or actively considering switching to defined contribution plans for health benefits.[26]

Managed Care

Several other types of programs attempt to reduce health-care costs paid by employers. **Managed care** consists of approaches that monitor and reduce medical costs through restrictions and market system alternatives. These managed care plans emphasize primary and preventative care, the use of specific providers who will charge lower prices, restrictions on certain kinds of treatment, and prices negotiated with hospitals and physicians. The most prevalent types of managed care are Preferred Provider Organizations (PPOs) and Health Maintenance Organizations (HMOs).

Managed care
Approaches that monitor and reduce medical costs using restrictions and market system alternatives.

Preferred Provider Organizations (PPOs) One type of managed care plan is the **preferred provider organization (PPO)**, a health-care provider that contracts with an employer or an employer group to provide health-care services to employees at a competitive rate. Employees have the freedom to go to other providers if they want to pay the difference in costs. Point-of-service plans are somewhat similar and offer financial incentives to encourage employees to use designated medical providers.

Preferred provider organization (PPO) A health-care provider that contracts with an employer group to provide health-care services to employees at a competitive rate.

Health Maintenance Organizations A **health maintenance organization (HMO)** provides services for a fixed period on a prepaid basis. The HMO emphasizes both prevention and correction. An employer contracts with an HMO and its staff of physicians and medical personnel to furnish complete medical care, except for hospitalization. The employer pays a flat rate per enrolled employee or per family. The covered individuals may then go to the HMO for health care as often as they need to. Supplemental policies for hospitalization also are provided.

Health maintenance organization (HMO) Managed care plan that provides services for a fixed period on a prepaid basis.

HMO organizations continue to experience mergers, alliances, and acquisitions. Critics contend that, in some cases, competing HMOs spend millions of dollars on business matters such as destructive price wars and acquiring other businesses instead of focusing on innovation in health care. As an alternative, employers in some areas have chosen to negotiate with smaller groups of doctors

On-line auctions in which health providers compete against each other are now a reality. Two companies currently are helping employers use the Web to lower benefit costs through the direct competition of an auction. "The purpose of the auction is to stimulate more direct competition among plans, thereby improving HMO negotiation results for companies," notes one of the participants.

The usual HMO bidding and negotiation process is time-consuming, often taking four to six weeks. With the auction process, time is greatly reduced. Employers carefully select which plans they invite to participate in the auction to make sure they meet minimum standards of access and quality.

The plan providers gain as well as the buyers. HMOs get a real-time view of market-price information and they learn where they stand with rates, design features, quality scores, and member satisfaction. The Web, as the main technological driver, allows central posting, viewing, and communication. It is expected that the value of the auction for those participating in it will increase as the number of users on both sides increases.[27]

and hospitals, provide employees with information and vouchers, and let them shop among competing medical groups. The e-HR describes how the Internet is being used as part of negotiation. Even with some customizing, managed care, particularly HMOs, face a mounting backlash.[28] Some critics argue that the cost savings associated with managed care and HMOs have already been realized.[29] That is why other means have been used to contain health-care costs, including utilization reviews and wellness programs.

Utilization Review Many employers have found that some of the health care provided by doctors and hospitals is unnecessary, incorrectly billed, or deliberately overcharged. Consequently, both employers and insurance firms often require that medical work and charges be audited through a **utilization review**. This process may require a second opinion, review of procedures used, and review of charges for procedures done.

Utilization review An audit and review of the services and costs billed by health-care providers.

Wellness Programs Wellness programs encourage employees to lead more healthy lifestyles. Often wellness programs include activities such as smoking cessation classes, diet and nutrition counseling, exercise and physical fitness centers and programs, and health education. Chapter 15 provides a more in-depth discussion of wellness programs.

Many employers also share programs to educate employees about health-care costs and how to reduce them. Newsletters, formal classes, and many other approaches are all designed to help employees understand why health-care costs are increasing and what they can do to control them. Some employers even are offering financial incentives to improve health habits. These programs reward employees who stop smoking, lose weight, and participate in exercise programs, among other activities.[30]

Health-Care Legislation
The importance of health-care benefits to employers and employees has led to a variety of federal and state laws. Some laws have been enacted to provide

COBRA
Displays a sample
COBRA election letter.
Custom Search:
☑ ANALYSIS
Phrase: COBRA election
letter

HIPAA Certificate
Depicts sample HIPAA
certificate of health plan
coverage.
Custom Search:
☑ ANALYSIS
Phrase: HIPAA certificate

protection for employees who leave their employers, either voluntarily or involuntarily. To date, the two most important ones are COBRA and HIPAA.

COBRA Provisions Legal requirements in the Consolidated Omnibus Budget Reconciliation Act (COBRA) require that most employers (except churches and the federal government) with 20 or more employees offer extended health-care coverage to the following groups:

- Employees who voluntarily quit, except those terminated for "gross misconduct"
- Widowed or divorced spouses and dependent children of former or current employees
- Retirees and their spouses whose health-care coverage ends.

Employers must notify eligible employees and/or their spouses and qualified dependents within 60 days after the employees quit, die, get divorced, or otherwise change their status. The coverage must be offered for 18 to 36 months, depending on the qualifying circumstances. The individual no longer employed by the organization must pay the premiums, but the employer may charge this individual no more than 102% of the premium costs to insure a similarly covered employee.

For most employers the COBRA requirements mean additional paperwork and related costs. For example, firms must not only track the former employees but also notify their qualified dependents. The 2% premium addition generally does not cover all relevant costs; the costs often run several percentage points more. Consequently, management efforts to reduce overall health benefits costs have become concerns to employee as well.

HIPAA Provisions The Health Insurance Portability and Accountability Act (HIPAA) of 1996 allows employees to switch their health insurance plan from one company to another to get new health coverage, regardless of pre-existing health conditions. The legislation also prohibits group insurance plans from dropping coverage for a sick employee, and requires them to make individual coverage available to people who leave group plans.[31]

"Before I forget, Detrick, here's the dental plan."

Figure 14-7 ▶ **U.S. Population Lacking Health Insurance**

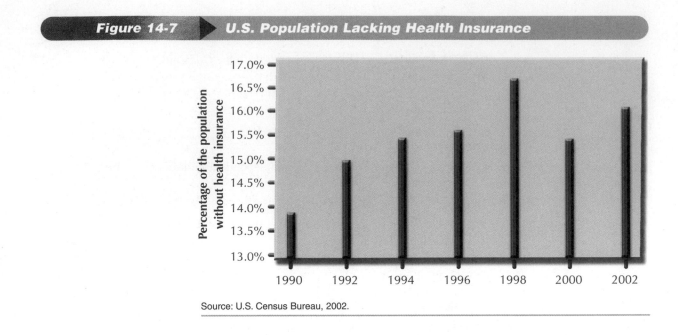

Source: U.S. Census Bureau, 2002.

Some of the governmental pressure is due to concerns about the rising number of individuals in the U.S. without health insurance coverage. As Figure 14-7 indicates, about 16% of the U.S. population lacks health coverage.

Financial and Other Benefits

Employers may offer workers a wide range of special benefits: financial benefits, insurance benefits (in addition to health-related insurance), educational benefits, social benefits, and recreational benefits. From the point of view of the employer, such benefits can be useful in attracting and retaining employees. Workers like receiving special benefits, which often are not taxed as income.

Financial Benefits

Financial benefits include a wide variety of items. A *credit union* sponsored by the employer provides saving and lending services for employees. *Purchase discounts* allow employees to buy goods or services from their employers at reduced rates. For example, a furniture manufacturer may allow employees to buy furniture at wholesale cost plus 10%, or a bank may allow use of a safe deposit box and free checking for its employees.

Employee *thrift, savings,* or *stock investment plans* may be made available. Some employers match a portion of the employee's contribution. To illustrate, in a stock purchase plan, the corporation provides matching funds equal to the amount invested by the employee to purchase stock in the company. In this way, employees benefit from the future growth of the corporation. Also, the intent is to develop greater employee loyalty and interest in the organization and its success.

Financial planning and counseling are especially valuable services for executives many of whom may need information on investments, tax shelters, and comprehensive financial counseling because of their higher levels of compensation. The importance of these financial planning benefits likely will grow as a greater percentage of workers approach retirement age.

Relocation Benefits

Relocation benefits are offered by 60% of respondents according to one survey. In addition, 39% of the surveyed employers offered temporary relocation benefits, and almost 20% provided assistance in finding a job for the spouse of a transferred employee.[32] Numerous other financial-related benefits may be offered as well, including the use of a company car, company expense accounts and assistance in buying or selling a house when employees are transferred.[33]

Insurance Benefits

In addition to health-related insurance, some employers provide other types of insurance. These benefits offer major advantages for employees because many employers pay some or all of the costs. Even when employers do not pay any of the costs, employees still benefit because of the lower rates available through group programs.

Life Insurance It is common for employers to provide *life insurance* for employees. Life insurance is bought as a group policy, and the employer pays all or some of the premiums, but the level of coverage is usually low and is tied to the employee's base pay. A typical level of coverage is one-and-a-half or two times an employee's annual salary. Some executives may get higher coverage as part of executive compensation packages.

Disability Insurance Other insurance benefits frequently tied to employee pay levels are *short-term* and *long-term disability insurance.* This type of insurance provides continuing income protection for employees who become disabled and unable to work. Long-term disability insurance is much more common because many employers cover short-term disability situations by allowing employees to accrue the sick leave granted annually. A growing number of employers are integrating their disability insurance programs with efforts to reduce workers' compensation claims. There are a number of reasons to have **integrated disability management programs,** such as cost savings and better coordination.[34]

Legal Insurance Legal insurance is offered as a benefit through some employers, often as part of cafeteria benefit plans, which let workers choose from many different benefits. Legal insurance plans operate in much the same way health maintenance organizations do. Employees (or employers) pay a flat fee or a set amount each month. In return, they have the right to use the service of a network of lawyers to handle their legal problems.

Educational Benefits

Another benefit used by employees comes in the form of *educational assistance* to pay for some or all costs associated with formal education courses and degree programs, including the costs of books and laboratory materials. Some employers

Integrated disability management programs
A benefit that combines disability insurance programs and efforts to reduce workers' compensation claims.

Strategic Decisions about Educational Benefits

Employers have found that educational and tuition aid assistance benefits are highly desired by employees. These programs have been found to aid employee retention and recruitment. When establishing and managing such benefits, the following suggestions can make programs more successful:

- Encourage employees to take specific courses or degrees to *change careers* or develop *entirely new skills.* Section 127 of the IRS Code now allows study not related to the current job. For example, a firm might send an IT employee to learn accounting.
- Offer the benefits to *part-time employees* as well. When they finish their degrees, they might become full-time employees in a field for which employees are difficult to hire.
- Help by providing *flexible scheduling.* Allow employees to adjust their work schedules around their classes, given work considerations.
- Provide *mentors.* For example, if an employee is interested in accounting have her meet with the accounting department manager to discuss what skills are needed, and follow up while in school.
- Recognize employee *achievements.* When someone finishes a degree recognize it, which shows that the company values the time and effort put in by the employee.

pay for schooling on a proportional schedule, depending on the grades received; others simply require a passing grade of C or above. The HR Practice highlights some ideas for educational benefits.

Unless the education paid for by the employer meets certain conditions, the cost of educational aid must be counted as taxable income by employees. Section 127 of the Internal Revenue Code received favorable treatment in recent federal tax legislation and now includes graduate education for the first time.[35]

Social and Recreational Benefits

Some benefits and services are social and recreational in nature, such as bowling leagues, picnics, parties, employer-sponsored athletic teams, organizationally owned recreational lodges, and other sponsored activities and interest groups. As interest in employee wellness has increased, more firms provide recreational facilities and activities. But employers should retain control of all events associated with their organizations because of possible legal responsibility.

The idea behind social and recreational programs is to promote employee happiness and team spirit. Employees may appreciate this type of benefit, but managers should not necessarily expect increased job productivity or job satisfaction as a result. Other such benefits too numerous to detail are made available by various employers as well.

Family-Oriented Benefits

The composition of families in the United States has changed significantly in the past few decades. The number of traditional families, in which the man went to work and the woman stayed home to raise children, has declined significantly, while the percentage of two-worker families has more than doubled. The growth in dual-career couples, single-parent households, and increasing work demands on many workers has increased the emphasis some employers are placing on family-oriented benefits. As mentioned in Chapter 1, balancing family and work demands presents a major challenge to many workers at all levels of organizations. To provide assistance, employers have established a variety of family-oriented benefits, and the federal government passed the Family and Medical Leave Act.

Family and Medical Leave Act (FMLA)

Passed in 1993, the Family and Medical Leave Act (FMLA) covers all employers with 50 or more employees who live within 75 miles of the workplace and includes federal, state, and private employers. Only employees who have worked at least 12 months and 1,250 hours in the previous year are eligible for leaves under FMLA.

FMLA Eligibility The law requires that employers allow eligible employees to take a total of 12 weeks' leave during any 12-month period for one or more of the following situations:

- Birth, adoption, or foster care placement of a child
- Caring for a spouse, child, or parent with a serious health condition
- Serious health condition of the employee

Serious health condition
A health condition requiring inpatient, hospital, hospice, or residential medical care or continuing physician care.

A **serious health condition** is one requiring inpatient, hospital, hospice, or residential medical care or continuing physician care. An employer may require an employee to provide a certificate from a doctor verifying such an illness. FMLA provides for the following guidelines regarding employee leaves:

- Employees taking family and medical leave must be able to return to the same job or a job of equivalent status or pay.
- Health benefits must be continued during the leave at the same level and conditions. If, for a reason other than serious health problems, the employee does not return to work, the employer may collect the employer-paid portion of the premiums from the non-returning employee.
- The leave taken may be intermittent rather than in one block, subject to employee and employer agreements, when birth, adoption, or foster child care is the cause. For serious health conditions, employer approval is not necessary.
- Employees can be required to use all paid-up vacation and personal leave before taking unpaid leave.
- Employees are required to give 30-day notice, where practical.

Employer Reactions to FMLA Since the passage of the act, several factors have become apparent. First, many employers have not paid enough attention to the law. Some employers are denying leaves or failing to reinstate workers after leaves are completed. However, the law does not protect one from layoff during or after leave. In fact, cutbacks are legitimate reasons for layoff regardless of FMLA, and courts have decided against employees in 74% of cases involving layoffs and job security.[36]

Employers also encounter problems with the FMLA, because of the many different circumstances in which employees may request and use family leave. Many employers have difficulty in interpreting when and how the provisions are to be applied. Also, the need to arrange work coverage for employees on FMLA

WEST GROUP
A THOMSON COMPANY

FMLA Policy
Contains sample FMLA policy statements.
Custom Search:
☑ ANALYSIS
Phrase: Model family and medical leaves

leaves can be particularly challenging for smaller employers. This difficulty is compounded because the law requires that workers on these leaves be offered similar jobs at similar levels of pay when they return to work. A recent study of FMLA results for employers found that:

- Many employers still find complying with the law to be difficult.
- Sixty-five percent of employers make exceptions to provide more flexibility for employees than the law requires.
- Sixty percent of employees do not schedule leave in advance.
- More than half of the employers reported experiences where they felt the FMLA request was not legitimate but granted it anyway.
- Almost two-thirds of the employers felt they had retained some employees because of FMLA who would have been dismissed for attendance problems if the law had not existed.[37]

Family-Care Benefits

The growing emphasis on family issues is important in many organizations and for many workers. But those employees without families may feel some resentment against those who seem to get special privileges because they have families. Two-thirds of employees do *not* have children under the age of 18 and are offered fewer opportunities to use personal days off, telecommuting, etc. Further, they are more frequently asked to travel or put in overtime because they "don't have a family."[38]

Adoption Benefits Many employers provide maternity and paternity benefits to employees who give birth to children. In comparison to those giving birth, a relatively small number of employees adopt children, but in the interest of fairness, a growing number of organizations provide benefits for employees who adopt children. For example, Microsoft gives a $5,000 cash benefit and four weeks of paid leave to employees who adopt children. Wendy's provides $4,000 cash payments to cover adoption expenses and up to six weeks of paid leave for employee adoptions.[39]

Child Care Balancing work and family responsibilities is a major challenge for many workers. Whether single parents or dual-career couples, these employees often experience difficulty in obtaining high-quality, affordable child care. Employers are addressing the child-care issue in several ways. Some organizations provide on-site day-care facilities. Relatively few such facilities have been established, primarily because of costs and concerns about liability and attracting sufficient employee use. However for a number of firms, providing on-site child care has had a positive impact on employees who use the service. Having on-site child care also has been an advantage in recruiting workers in tight labor markets.[40] Other options for child-care assistance include the following:

- Providing referral services to aid parents in locating child-care providers
- Establishing discounts at day-care centers, which may be subsidized by the employer
- Arranging with hospitals to offer sick-child programs partially paid for by the employer
- Developing after-school programs for older school-age children, often in conjunction with local public and private school systems.

Logging On...

Work and Family Connection

This Web site provides organizations with information on work and family issues such as child care and elder care for employees.

http://www.workfamily.com

Elder Care Another family-related issue of growing importance is caring for elderly relatives. Various organizations have surveyed their employees and found that as many as 30% of them have had to miss work to care for an aging relative. The responsibilities associated with caring for elderly family members have resulted in reduced work performance, increased absenteeism, and more personal stress for the affected employees. Lost productivity and absenteeism by workers caring for elders cost employers $29 billion per year. Some responses by employers have included conducting needs surveys, providing resources, and giving referrals to elder-care providers. Some employers provide eldercare assistance through contracts with firms that arrange for elder care for an employee's relatives located in other geographic locales.[41]

Benefits for Domestic Partners and Spousal Equivalents

As lifestyles change in the United States, employers are being confronted with requests for benefits by employees who are not married but have close personal relationships with others. The terminology often used to refer to individuals with such living arrangements are *domestic partners* and *spousal equivalents*. The employees who are submitting these requests are:

- unmarried employees who have living arrangements with individuals of the opposite sex,
- gay and lesbian employees requesting benefits for their partners.

The argument made by these employees is that if an employer provides benefits for the spouses of married employees, then benefits should be provided for employees without spouses but with alternative lifestyles and relationships. This view is reinforced by: (1) data showing that a significant percentage of heterosexual couples live together before or instead of formally marrying; and (2) the fact that more gays and lesbians are being open about their lifestyles.

The proportion of couples fitting the "traditional" definition of a family, including husband, wife, and children, is only 25% today. The number of Americans living in unmarried partner households is growing much more rapidly than those living in married households. The latest census found about 600,000 same-sex couple homes, or about 0.5% of the total of the nation's households.[42] Several studies have show that employers who offer this coverage will experience enrollment in the 1% to 2% range. If coverage is offered to opposite sex couples, enrollment rates will be closer to the 2%. About 22% of companies surveyed now offer such benefits and two-thirds of the employers who offer the benefits cover both same- and opposite-sex couples who are not married.[43]

At some firms, both the employee and the "eligible partner" must sign an "Affidavit of Spousal Equivalence." In this affidavit, the employee and the partner are asked to affirm the following:

- Each is the other's only spousal equivalent.
- They are of the same sex and/or not blood relatives.
- They are living together and jointly share responsibility for their common welfare and financial obligations.

Decisions to extend benefits to domestic partners have come under attacks from certain religious leaders opposed to homosexual lifestyles. However, it

WEST GROUP
A THOMSON COMPANY
Domestic Partner Benefits
Discusses issues and laws on domestic partner benefits.
Custom Search:
☑ ANALYSIS
Phrase: Recognizing domestic partners

must be noted that most employees using the domestic partner benefits are of the opposite sex and are involved in heterosexual relationships.

Time-Off Benefits

Employers give employees paid time off in a variety of circumstances. Paid lunch breaks and rest periods, holidays, and vacations are common. But leaves are given for a number of other purposes as well. Time-off benefits represent an estimated 5% to 13% of total compensation. Typical time-off benefits include holiday pay, vacation pay, and leaves of absence.

Holiday Pay

Most, if not all, employers provide pay for a variety of holidays, as Figure 14-8 shows. Other holidays are offered to some employees through laws or union contracts. As an abuse-control measure, employers commonly require employees to work the last scheduled day before a holiday and the first scheduled workday after a holiday to be eligible for holiday pay. Some employers pay time-and-a-half to hourly employees who must work holidays.

Vacation Pay

Paid vacations are a common benefit. Employers often use graduated vacation-time scales based on employees' length of service. Some organizations allow

Figure 14-8 ▶ *Most Common Paid Holidays in the U.S.*

January	February	March	April
New Year's Day Martin Luther King Jr. Day	President's Day	Good Friday Easter	
May	**June**	**July**	**August**
Memorial Day		Independence Day	
September	**October**	**November**	**December**
Labor Day	Columbus Day	Veteran's Day Thanksgiving Day Day after Thanksgiving	Christmas Eve Christmas Day New Year's Eve

| Figure 14-9 | Companies Offering Different Types of Paid Time Off |

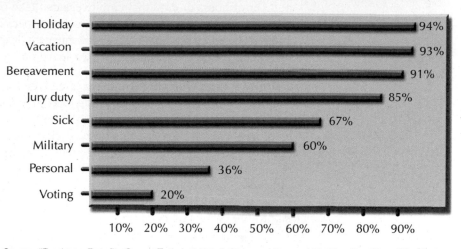

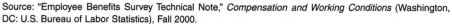

Source: "Employee Benefits Survey Technical Note," *Compensation and Working Conditions* (Washington, DC: U.S. Bureau of Labor Statistics), Fall 2000.

employees to accumulate unused vacation. A growing number of companies allow employees to "buy" additional vacation or let them sell unused vacation back to employers. About 25% of all firms permit such options.[44] As with holidays, employees often are required to work the day before and the day after a vacation. Figure 14-9 shows the percent of companies offering different types of paid time-off.

Leaves of Absence

Employers grant *leaves of absence,* taken as time off with or without pay, for a variety of reasons. All of the leaves discussed here add to employer costs even if unpaid, because the missing employee's work must be covered, either by other employees working additionally or by temporary employees working under contract.

Family Leave As mentioned earlier in the chapter, the passage of the Family and Medical Leave Act (FMLA) clarified the rights of employees and the responsibilities of most employers. Even though *paternity leave* for male workers is available under FMLA, a relatively low percentage of men take it. The primary reason for the low usage is a perception that it is not as socially acceptable for men to stay home for child-related reasons. That view likely will change as the number of dual-career couples in the workforce increases.

Medical and Sick Leave Medical and sick leave are closely related. Many employers allow employees to miss a limited number of days because of illness without losing pay. Some employers allow employees to accumulate unused sick leave, which may be used in case of catastrophic illnesses. Others pay employees for unused sick leave. Some organizations have shifted emphasis to reward people who do not use sick leave by giving them **well-pay**—extra pay for not taking sick leave.

Well-pay Extra pay for not taking sick leave.

Paid time-off plan Plan that combines all sick leave, vacation time, and holidays into a total number of hours or days that employees can take off with pay.

Paid Time-Off (PTO) Plans Other employers have made use of the **paid time-off plan**, which combines sick leave, vacations, and holidays into a total number of hours or days that employees can take off with pay.[45] One organization found that when it stopped designating a specific number of sick-leave days and a PTO plan was implemented, absenteeism dropped, time off was scheduled better, and employee acceptance of the leave policy improved.

Other Leaves Other types of leaves are given for a variety of purposes. Some, such as *military leave, election leave,* and *jury leave,* are required by various state and federal laws. Employers commonly pay the difference between the employee's regular pay and the military, election, or jury pay. Some firms grant employees military time off and give them regular pay while the employees also receive military pay. Federal law prohibits taking discriminatory action against military reservists by requiring them to take vacation time to attend summer camp or other training sessions. However, the leave request must be reasonable and truly required by the military.

Funeral or *bereavement leave* is another common leave offered. Leave of up to three days for immediate family members is usually given, as specified in many employers' policy manuals and employee handbooks. Some policies also give unpaid time off for the death of more distant relatives or friends.

Benefits Administration

With the myriad of benefits and regulations, it is easy to see why many organizations must make coordinated efforts to administer benefits programs. Figure 14-10 shows how benefits administration responsibilities can be split between HR specialists and other managers. HR specialists play the more significant role, but managers must assume responsibility for some of the communication aspects of benefits administration.

Benefits Communication

Employees generally do not know much about the values and costs associated with the benefits they receive from employers. Yet benefits communication and benefits satisfaction are linked. Many employers have instituted special benefits communication systems to inform employees about the value of the benefits they provide.

Benefits Statements Some employers also give each employee an annual "personal statement of benefits" that translates benefits into dollar amounts. Federal regulations under ERISA require that employees receive an annual pension-reporting statement, which also can be included in the personal statements. By having a personalized statement, each employee can see how much his or her own benefits are worth. Employers hope that by educating employees about benefit costs, they can manage expenditures better and can give employees a better appreciation for the employers' payments.

HRIS and Benefits Communication The advent of HRIS options linked to intranets provides additional links to communicate benefits to employees. The use of employee self-service kiosks allows employees to obtain benefits information on-line. These kiosks and other information technology also allow

Logging On...

My Benefits.com
This Web site is for an organization that specializes in administering employee benefits for organizations using the Internet.

http://www.mybenefits.com

Figure 14-10

Typical Division of HR Responsibilities: Benefits Administration

HR Unit	Managers
• *Develops and administers benefit systems.* • *Answers employees' technical questions on benefits.* • *Assists employees in filing benefit claims.* • *Coordinates special prerequirement programs.*	• *Answer simple questions on benefits.* • *Maintain liaison with HR specialists on benefits.* • *Maintain good communications with employees near retirement.* • *Coordinate use of time-off benefits*

employees to change their benefits choices, track their benefits balances, and submit questions to HR staff members and external benefits providers. HR professionals are utilizing information systems to communicate benefits information, conduct employee benefit surveys, and provide other benefits communications.

Flexible Benefits

Flexible benefits plan
One that allows employees to select the benefits they prefer from groups of benefits established by the employer.

A **flexible benefits plan**, sometimes called a *flex* or *cafeteria* plan, allows employees to select the benefits they prefer from groups of benefits established by the employer. By making a variety of "dishes" or benefits available, the organization allows each employee to select an individual combination of benefits within some overall limits. As a result of the changing composition of the workforce, flexible benefits plans have grown in popularity.

Larger employers use flexible benefits plans more often than smaller ones do. Because benefits vendors require a sufficient number of employees to make providing the choices worthwhile, they generally recommend that at least 100 employees be covered to make a flexible benefits plan feasible.

Flexible benefits systems recognize that individual employee situations differ because of age, family status, and lifestyle. For instance, individuals in dual-career couples may not want the same benefits from two different employers. Under a flex plan, one of them can forego some benefits available in the partner's plan and take other benefits instead.

Flexible spending account Account that allows employees to contribute pretax dollars to buy additional benefits.

Flexible Spending Accounts Under current tax laws (Section 125 of the IRS Code), employees can divert some income before taxes into accounts to fund certain benefits. These **flexible spending accounts** allow employees to contribute pretax dollars to buy additional benefits. An example illustrates the advantage of these accounts to employees. Assume an employee earns $3,000 per month and has $100 per month deducted to put into a flexible spending account. That $100 does not count as gross income for tax purposes, so the employee's taxable income is reduced. The employee uses the money in the account to purchase additional benefits.

Under tax laws at the time of this writing, the funds in the account can be used only to purchase the following: (1) additional health care (including offsetting deductibles), (2) life insurance, (3) disability insurance, and (4) dependent-care benefits. Furthermore, tax regulations require that if employees do not spend all of the money in their accounts by the end of the year, they forfeit it. Therefore, it is important that employees carefully estimate the additional benefits they will use.

Flexible spending accounts have grown in popularity as more flexible benefits plans have been adopted by more employers. Of course, such plans and their tax advantages can be changed as Congress passes future health-care and tax-related legislation.

Problems with Flexible Plans

A problem with flexibility in benefit choice is that an *inappropriate benefits package* may be chosen by an employee. A young construction worker may not choose a disability benefit; however, if he or she is injured, the family may suffer financial hardship. Part of this problem can be overcome by requiring employees to select a core set of benefits (life, health, and disability insurance) and then offering options on other benefits.

Another problem can be **adverse selection**, whereby only higher-risk employees select and use certain benefits. Because many insurance plans are based on a group rate, the employer may face higher rates if insufficient numbers of employees select an insurance option.

Despite these disadvantages, it is likely that flex plans will continue to grow in popularity. The ability to match benefits to differing employee needs, while also controlling some costs, is so attractive that employers will try to find ways to overcome the disadvantages that exist in their benefits plans.

Benefits in the Future

Benefits are indeed changing and those changes and the IRS have made them increasingly complex. As a result, benefit functions are among the most outsourced in HR. Whether pension plan, health plan administration, or COBRA tracking, benefit outsourcing is a wave of the present and future. Benefits administration, service, financial reporting and accounting, and compliance and reporting can all be outsourced.

Many employees also have access to Internet-based benefits support systems. For instance, use of the Internet allows employees in a growing number of organizations to check their retirement fund balances and move funds among various financial options. The range of functions is shown in Figure 14-11.

Benefits and Different Generations Individuals in generations X and Y frequently express different needs and wants from those of the baby boomer generation in many job-related areas. However, that is not so in benefits, as new college graduates often are looking for the following (in order) in their first jobs.[46]

- Medical insurance
- 401(k) plan
- Annual raises
- Life insurance
- Dental insurance

Of course, most employers already offer those benefits because their baby boomer employees want them too.

Adverse selection Situation in which only higher-risk employees select and use certain benefits.

Figure 14-11 ▶ **Pension and Retirement Functions on the Internet**

- Access account balances
- Adjust asset allocation
- View quarterly reports/fund performance
- Tax saving calculators
- Transfers between funds
- Change contributions
- View frequently asked questions
- Enrollment forms
- View summary plan descriptions
- Links to retirement sites

Temporary and Part-Time Employee Benefits Workers who are not regular full-time employees sometimes do not receive benefits, but that is changing. In one survey, 49% of employers said they offer health insurance to part-timers. The contribution is half the amount provided for full-timers.[47] For instance, 7-Eleven is a company that has been a leader in offering part-time benefits because it hires many part-timers.[48] Even temporary workers who are employed by a temp agency might be legally entitled to benefits unless they are properly excluded, as held in the Microsoft "Perma-temp" case.[49]

Summary

- Benefits provide additional compensation to employees as a reward for organizational membership.
- Because benefits generally are not taxed, they are highly desired by employees. The average employee now receives an amount equal to about 40% of his/her pay in benefit compensation.
- Strategic reasons for offering benefits include attracting and retaining employees, improving the company's image, and enhancing job satisfaction

- The general types of benefits include security, retirement, health-care, financial, social and recreational, family-oriented, and time-off.
- An important distinction is made between mandated and voluntary benefits. Mandatory benefits are required by law.
- Three prominent security benefits are workers' compensation, unemployment compensation, and severance pay.
- Organizations that provide retirement-related benefits should develop policies on how to integrate Social Security benefits into employees' benefit plans.
- The pension area is a complex one, and it is governed by the Employee Retirement Income Security Act (ERISA) and other laws.
- Individual retirement accounts (IRAs), 401(k) plans, and Keogh plans are important individual options available for supplementing retirement benefits.

- Because health-care benefits are the most costly insurance-related benefits, employers are managing their health-care costs more aggressively.
- Various types of insurance, financial planning assistance, tuition aid, and other benefits that employers may offer enhance the appeal of the organization to employees.
- Family-related benefits include complying with the Family and Medical Leave Act (FMLA) of 1993 and offering both child-care and elder-care assistance.
- Holiday pay, vacation pay, and various leaves of absence are means of providing time-off benefits to employees.
- Because of the variety of benefit options available and the costs involved, employers need to develop systems to communicate these options and costs to their employees.
- Flexible benefits systems, which can be tailored to individual needs and situations, are increasing in popularity.

Review and Discussion Questions

1. Why are benefits strategically important to employers?
2. Discuss the following statement: "Employers should expect that more benefits will become mandatory and more varied."
3. Why are workers' compensation, unemployment compensation, and severance pay appropriately classified as security-oriented benefits?
4. Define the following terms: (a) *contributory plan,* (b) *defined-benefit plan,* (c) *portability,* (d) *vesting.*

5. Discuss the following statement: "Health-care costs are out of control in the United States, and it is up to employers to put pressure on the medical system to reduce costs."
6. Some experts have forecast an expansion of family-oriented and time-off benefits in the future. Why?
7. Why are benefits communications and flexible benefits systems so intertwined?

Terms to Know

benefit   440
benefits needs analysis   441
mandated benefits   442
workers' compensation   444
severance pay   445
pension plans   448
defined-benefit plan   448

defined-contribution plan   448
contributory plan   449
non-contributory plan   449
vesting   450
portability   450
individual retirement account (IRA)   450
Keogh plan   450

Using the Internet

OWBPA and Early Retirement Plans

As the HR manager of your organization, you are in charge of all benefits and compliance with the laws. Senior management is considering offering a voluntary early retirement plan for employees who are age 55 or older and have at least 10 years of service.

Before making the final decision to proceed with the early retirement option, the executives have asked you to investigate and report back about the effects of the Older Workers Benefit Protection Act (OWBPA) and the conditions that must be met. Using the following website from the Employment Law Resource Center, write your report. *http://www.ahipubs.com/FAQ/benefits/older.html*

CASE

Merging 401(k) Plans

Many employees get a sinking feeling when their company is acquired. They worry that something awful will happen, and the most common concerns are about compensation and benefits, notes Nancy Lazgin, Director of Corporate Benefits for Staples, an office supply retailer. Staples has acquired a number of companies, giving it a lot of experience in what happens when companies merge. When Staples bought Claricom, the pension plans from each of the firms used different vesting schedules. Because vesting is a protected benefit under ERISA, meaning features of the plan must be retained under merger, Staples had to be careful when merging the plans.

Staples tends to hire younger shorter-service employees and had designed a vesting schedule to reward longer-service employees. It had a graded five-year schedule; after one year employees are 20% vested, and every year they gain another 20%. Even short-term employees get some of the com-

pany match when they leave, but longer service means receiving more of the matching funds. The decision was made to keep Staples' five-year schedule for the merged companies.

The Claricom plan was similar, but it used a four-year graded vesting schedule. Three groups of former Claricom employees had to be considered: employees who were vested at Claricom, those who were not yet vested with Claricom, and new employees with less than one year.[50]

Questions

1. What are some possible options for Staples dealing with the vested employees?
2. How should Staples approach the issue with the longer-term unvested employees?
3. For those employees with less than one year of service, what should Staples have done?

1. Belle Wise, "Not Your Father's Pension Plan," *USA Today*, March 29, 2000, 11A; Karla Taylor, "May I Help You Please?" *HR Magazine*, August 2000, 90–96; "Tom's of Maine: Small Company, Big Ideas," *Bulletin to Management*, September 21, 2000, 297; Karen Matthews, "Pet Perks Join Benefits List," *Sunday World-Herald*, April 9, 2000, 1G; Kristi Areliano, "New Perk: Corporate Housing," *The Denver Post*, December 20, 2000; K. Carol Patton, "Brave New Benefits," *HR Executive*, November 2000, 41–44.

2. Daniel Moskowitz, "Care Package," *Human Resource Executive*, May 1, 2001, 1.

3. "Baby Boomers Need Attention Too," *Bulletin to Management*, July 13, 2000, 5–6.

4. Margaret M. Clark, "Employers Cater to Changing Benefit Needs, Survey Finds," *HR-News*, May 2001, 17; and Lore Lawrence, "Companies Still Offering Perks, but HR's Taking Another Look," *HR-News*, June 2001, 4.

5. Rodney K. Platt, "Value of Benefits Remains Constant," *Workspan*, June 2000, 34–39.

6. William Atkinson, "Is Worker's Comp Changing?" *HR Magazine*, July 2000, 50–61.

7. John Pikiell, "An RX for Detection and Prevention of Worker's Comp Fraud," *Employee Benefit News*, November 1, 2000, 34.

8. "Unemployed Workers Turn Down Paltry Job Benefits, a Study Says," *The Wall Street Journal*, August 21, 2001, A1.

9. Carolyn Hirschman, "The Kindest Cut," *HR Magazine*, April 2001, 48–53.

10. *Public Employees Retirement System of Ohio v. Betts*, 109 S. Ct. 256 (1989).

11. Ellen E. Schultz, "Pension Cuts 101," *The Wall Street Journal*, July 27, 2000, 1A.

12. Ellen E. Schultz, "Using a Trust Fund to Help Pay Retiree Benefits," *The Wall Street Journal*, October 25, 2000, C1; Ellen E. Schultz, "This Won't Hurt," *The Wall Street Journal*, October 26, 2000, A1; and Ellen E. Schultz, "Retirees Found Variety Untruthful," *The Wall Street Journal*, November 6, 2000, C1.

13. The Hay Group, *Social Security Summary 2000* (Philadelphia: Hay Group, 2000).

14. Karby Leggett, "China Pension System Is Cause for Increased Agitation," *The Wall Street Journal*, October 20, 2000, A24.

15. James H. Dulebohn, et al., "Selection Among Employer-Sponsored Pension Plans: The Role of Individual Differences," *Personnel Psychology*, 53, (2000), 405.

16. "Cash Balance Conversions Are Raising Age Bias Specter," *Bulletin to Management*, October 19, 2000, 334.

17. Stephen Tarnoff, "Balancing Act," *Human Resource Executive*, May 1, 2001, 37.

18. Harvey Kurtz and Isabelle A. Côté, "Multiple Employer Plans," *Journal of Pension Benefits*, 7, Winter 2000, 4–9.

19. *Arizona Governing Committee v. Norris*, 103 S. Ct. 3492, 32 FEP Cases 233 (1983).

20. "Survey Says Labor Market Drives 401(k) Plan Strategies," *Bulletin to Management*, December 7, 2000, 388.

21. Julie Appleby, "Health Insurance Prices to Soar," *USA Today*, August 27, 2001, 1A-2A; and Steve Jordan, "Health Insurance Costs Set to Soar," *Omaha World-Herald*, November 4, 2001, 1D.

22. Jack Bruner, "Value of Health Coverage," *ACA Journal*, First Quarter 2000, 57.

23. Mary S. Case, "A New Model for Controlling Health-Care Costs," *Workforce*, July 2000, 44.

24. Robert J. Chitadore, "Defined Contribution," *WorldatWork Journal*, Third Quarter 2001, 11–17.

25. Carolyn Hirschman, "More Choices, Less Cost?" *HR Magazine*, January 2002, 36–41.

26. "Defined Contributions Remain on Horizon of Health Benefits," *Bulletin to Management*, November 16, 2000, 364.

27. Tom Starner, "Going, Going," *Human Resource Executive*, March 1, 2001, 74.

28. Laura Cohn and Phoebe Eliopoulos, "What Comes After Managed Care?" *Business Week*, October 23, 2000, 149–156.

29. Yochi Dreazen, "Rise in Benefits Costs Takes on Urgency," *The Wall Street Journal*, June 2, 2000, A2.

30. Steve Jordon, "Wellness Is Insurer's 'Watchword,'" *Omaha World Herald*, January 21, 2001, 1B.

31. Alex M. (Kelly) Clarke, "The New HIPPA Regulations," *13th Annual Baird Holm Labor Law Forum 2001*, 57.

32. "Benefit Policies," *Bulletin to Management*, May 11, 2000, 148.

33. Sarah Fister Gale, "Discovering Relocation Home Loans," *Workforce*, April 2001, 44–48

34. Miriam Basch Scott, "Disability Management," *Employee Benefits Plan Review*, March 2000, 16.

35. "Nine in 10 Employers Offer Educational Benefit Programs," *Bulletin to Management*, August 3, 2000, 244.

36. Sue Shellerbarger, "Work and Family," *The Wall Street Journal*, August 22, 2001, B1.

37. "Family Leave," *Bulletin to Management*, January 18, 2001, 18.

38. "Working Parents Are Still Singled Out for Benefits, Critics Say," *Bulletin to Management*, October 19, 2000, 335; and Bill Briggs, "Pampered Parents," *The Denver Post*, July 9, 2000, F1.

39. Nancy Woodward, "Benefiting from Adoption," *HR Magazine*, December 2000, 119; and Amy Dunkin, "Adopting? You Deserve Benefits Too," *Business Week*, February 21, 2000, 160.

40. Bob Calandra, "Kids at Work," *Human Resource Executive*, March 15, 2001, 49.

41. Ellen Neuborne, "Elder Care: High Tech Makes for Low Anxiety," *Business Week*, November 20, 2000, 170 EG; and Gary Roberts, "Business Gives Careers a Break," *Financial Times*, December 1, 2000, 9; and Kelly Green, "Firms Try Again to Help with Elder Care," *The Wall Street Journal*, March 29, 2001, B1.

42. Genaro C. Aramas, "Gay Couples Lead 549,391 Households," *The Denver Post*, August 22, 2001, 7A.

43. Kim Mills, "Domestic Partner Benefits," *Workspan,* August 2000, 32–35; and "Benefits Policies," *Bulletin to Management,* December 21, 2000, 404.

44. Sue Shellengarger, "Work and Family," *The Wall Street Journal,* April 11, 2001, B1; and Michael Greve, "Buying Time Off," *Benefits Link,* available at *www.benefitslink. com.*

45. Jackie Reinberg, "It's About Time: PTOs Gain Popularity," *Workspan,* February 2002, 53–55.

46. "New Grads, Employers See Eye to Eye," *Bulletin to Management,* March 8, 2001, 75.

47. Robert Schwab, "Employers Forced to Expand Benefits," *The Denver Post,* September 3, 2000, GL.

48. Carol Patton, "Recipes for Part-time Benefits, *HR Magazine,* April 2000, 56.

49. Gilbert Nicholoson, "Get Your Benefit Ducks in a Row," *Workforce,* September 2000, 78–84.

50. Adapted from J. Bradnitzki and S. Schochet, "Merging 401(k) Plans," *Workforce,* May 2000, 40–44.

Employee Relations and Global HR

CHAPTER 15

Health, Safety, and Security

After you have read this chapter, you should be able to:

- Define *health, safety,* and *security* and explain their importance in organizations.

- Discuss several legal requirements affecting health and safety.

- Identify the basic provisions of the Occupational Safety and Health Act of 1970.

- Describe the Occupational Safety and Health Administration (OSHA) inspection and record-keeping requirements.

- Discuss the activities that comprise effective safety management.

- Discuss three different workplace health issues and how employers are responding to them.

- Explain the three levels of health promotion in organizations.

- Discuss workplace violence as a security issue and describe some components of an effective security program.

Health and Safety Pays Off

Employers in a variety of industries have found that placing emphasis on health and safety pays off in a number of ways. Lower employee benefits costs for health care, fewer work-related accidents, lower workers' compensation costs, and more productive employees are all results of employers emphasizing health and safety. Some examples include Applied Materials, Harley-Davidson, and UtiliCorp United.

At Applied Materials, a semiconductor equipment manufacturer based in Santa Clara, California, a company fitness center is used heavily by employees as part of the firm's corporate wellness program. Programs for employees of all ages and athleticism are available. According to company data, employees participating in the fitness center programs had worker compensation claim costs 79% lower than non-users of the fitness center. Users also had 70% fewer hospital admissions and 20% less in medical payments. In addition, Applied Materials allows two different five-minute stretching breaks each work shift for manufacturing workers, which has reduced muscle strains and sprains by 65%.

A different well-known manufacturer, Harley-Davidson, has a Safety Point program at its Franklin, Wisconsin, distribution center. In each work group one individual is identified as the Safety Point. That person assists the HR staff with safety training, accident prevention, and work team safety and health. Once a month all Safety Point employees meet to discuss workplace health and safety issues. Particularly noteworthy is that no safety incident injuries or accidents have been reported in the loading docks in several years due to both the Safety Point program and equipment and engineering efforts on the loading docks. Because the greatest safety risks are on the loading docks, this result testifies to the importance of emphasizing safety at Harley-Davidson.

UtiliCorp United, based in Kansas City, Missouri, is an international electric and natural gas utility operating in the U.S., Canada, United Kingdom, New Zealand, and Australia. However, this widely diverse firm did not have a coordinated safety effort. UtiliCorp managers decided to focus on the employees most at risk, including the field employees such as line workers, meter readers, and other service workers. A review of three years of records showed that these workers had 98% of all company accidents.

To develop a more coordinated program, safety committees throughout the firm were formed or reinvigorated. Also, a Think Safety program was established. Accident and injury rates were tracked, and individuals who had a vehicle accident or recordable injury had to work safely for three months to re-establish eligibility for safety rewards. Company-wide programs and recognition efforts were used and quarterly bonuses were paid for achieving safety performance over previous years' results. Participants receive "Utilibucks" for meeting safety goals, which can be used for ordering items from various catalogs.

The success of Utilicorp's renewed emphasis on safety is shown by data whereby workers' compensation claims decreased by about 40% over the first few years. Additionally, better safety practices continue to produce positive results for UtiliCorp.

These three examples illustrate that managerial commitment and attention to employee health and safety pays off. Other firms have found similar payoffs as well.[1]

> Managerial commitment and attention to employee health and safety pays off.

"If only it weren't for the people always getting tangled up with the machinery . . . Earth would be an engineer's paradise."

—Kurt Vonnegut

Today employees expect their employers to provide work environments that are safe, secure, and healthy. However, many employers once viewed accidents and occupational diseases as unavoidable by-products of work. This idea may still be prevalent in many industrial settings in underdeveloped countries. Fortunately in the United States and most developed nations, this idea has been replaced with the concept of using prevention and control to minimize or eliminate risks in workplaces.

Health, Safety, and Security

A number of laws and regulations have been enacted that establish requirements for U.S. employers. As highlighted by Applied Materials, Harley-Davidson, and UtiliCorp, employers have recognized that addressing health, safety, and security issues is part of effective HR management.

Nature of Health, Safety, and Security

Health A general state of physical, mental, and emotional well-being.

The terms *health, safety,* and *security* are closely related. The broader and somewhat more nebulous term is **health,** which refers to a general state of physical, mental, and emotional well-being. A healthy person is free of illness, injury, or mental and emotional problems that impair normal human activity. Health management practices in organizations strive to maintain the overall well-being of individuals.

Safety Condition in which the physical well-being of people is protected.

Typically, **safety** refers to protecting the physical well-being of people. The main purpose of effective safety programs in organizations is to prevent work-related injuries and accidents. The purpose of **security** is protecting employees and organizational facilities. With the growth of workplace violence, security at work has become an even greater concern for employers and employees alike.

Security Protection of employees and organizational facilities.

Health, Safety, and Security Responsibilities

The general goal of providing a safe, secure, and healthy workplace is reached by operating managers and HR staff members working together. As Figure 15-1 indicates, the primary health, safety, and security responsibilities in an organization usually fall on supervisors and managers. An HR manager or safety specialist can help coordinate health and safety programs, investigate accidents, produce safety program materials, and conduct formal safety training. However, department supervisors and managers play key roles in maintaining safe working conditions and a healthy workforce. For example, a supervisor in a warehouse has several health and safety responsibilities: reminding employees to wear safety hats; checking on the cleanliness of the work area; observing employees for any alcohol, drug, or emotional problems that may affect their work behavior; and recommending equipment changes (such as screens, railings, or other safety devices) to engineering specialists in the organization.

A position becoming more common in many companies is that of safety/environmental officer. This combination may make sense in situations where danger results from chemical or other sources of pollution that may be

Figure 15-1 ▶ Typical Division of HR Responsibilities: Health, Safety, and Security

HR Unit	Managers
• Coordinates health and safety programs • Develops safety reporting system • Provides accident investigation expertise • Provides technical expertise on accident prevention • Develops restricted-access procedures and employee identification systems • Trains managers to recognize and handle difficult employee situations	• Monitor health and safety of employees daily • Coach employees to be safety conscious • Investigate accidents • Observe health and safety behavior of employees • Monitor workplace for security problems • Communicate with employees to identify potentially difficult employees • Follow security procedures and recommend changes as needed

hazardous to both employees and the public or the environment. Because both safety and environmental responsibilities require working with governmental agencies (OSHA and/or EPA), putting someone in the job with the skills to deal with governmental agencies and ensure compliance with a wide range of regulatory issues is a good choice.[2]

Regarding security, HR managers and specialists can coordinate their efforts with those in other operating areas to develop access restrictions and employee identification procedures, contract or manage organizational security services such as guards, and train all managers and supervisors to handle potentially volatile situations. Managers and supervisors can observe work premises to identify potential security problems and communicate with employees exhibiting signs of stress that could lead to workplace violence.

Legal Requirements for Safety and Health

Employers must comply with a variety of federal and state laws as part of their efforts when developing and maintaining healthy, safe, and secure workforces and working environments. A look at some major legal areas follows next.

Workers' Compensation

First passed in the early 1900s, currently all states have workers' compensation laws in some form. Under these laws, employers contribute to an insurance fund to compensate employees for injuries received while on the job. Premiums paid reflect the accident rates at each employer, with those employers with higher incident rates being assessed higher workers' comprehensive premiums. Also, these laws usually provide payments to injured workers for wage replacements, dependent on the amount of lost time and wage levels.[3] Workers' compensation payments also cover costs for medical bills, and for retraining if a worker cannot

Figure 15-2 ► *Workers' Compensation Injuries*

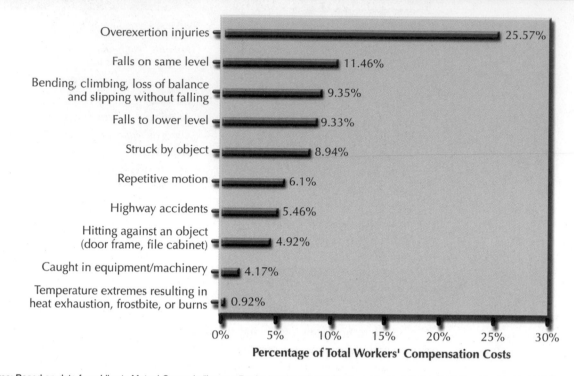

Source: Based on data from Liberty Mutual Group, in "Insurer Ranks Leading Workers' Comp Injuries," *National Underwriter*, March 19, 2001, 7.

go back to the current job. Figure 15-2 shows the top ten types of workers' compensation injuries, which make up 80% of all these costs paid by employers.

Expanded Scope of Workers' Compensation Workers' compensation coverage has been expanded in many states to include emotional impairment that may have resulted from physical injury, as well as job-related strain, stress, anxiety, and pressure.[4] Some cases of suicide also have been ruled to be job-related, with payments due under workers' compensation.

A new twist on workers' compensation coverage relates to the increasing use of telecommuting by employees. An attempt by the U.S. Department of Labor to set regulations for employers with employees who work at home was widely disparaged by legislators and business representatives, so there are limited federal regulations in this area. However, it is not widely known that in most situations while working at home for an employer, individuals are covered under workers' compensation laws. Therefore, if an employee is injured while doing employer-related work at home, the employer likely is liable for the injury.

Controlling Workers' Compensation Costs Workers' compensation costs have increased for many employers and have become a major issue in many states. These costs represent from 2% to 10% of payroll for most employers. Major contributors to the increases have been higher litigation expenses and medical costs.

Employers must continually monitor their workers' compensation expenditures. Efforts to reduce workplace injuries and illnesses can reduce workers' compensation premiums and claims costs. Many of the safety and health management suggestions discussed later contribute to reducing workers' compensation costs.

FMLA and Workers' Compensation The Family Medical Leave Act (FMLA), discussed in the previous chapter, affects workers' compensation as well. Because the FMLA allows eligible employees to take up to 12 weeks of leave for their serious health conditions, injured employees may request additional leave time, even if it is unpaid. Some employers have policies that state that FMLA runs concurrently with any workers' comp leave.[5]

Americans with Disabilities Act and Safety

The Americans with Disabilities Act (ADA) is another law affecting health and safety policies and practices of employers. Problems arising from ADA include employers who sometimes try to return injured workers to "light-duty" work in order to reduce workers' compensation costs. However, under the ADA, in making accommodations for injured employees through light-duty work, employers may undercut what really are essential job functions. Making such accommodations for injured employees for a period of time also may require an employer to make accommodations for job applicants with disabilities.[6]

Health and safety record-keeping practices also have been affected by the following provision in the ADA:

Information from all medical examinations and inquiries must be kept apart from general personnel files as a separate confidential medical record available only under limited conditions specified in the ADA.

As interpreted by attorneys and HR practitioners, this provision requires that all medical-related information be maintained separately from all other confidential files. Also, specific access restrictions and security procedures must be adopted for medical records of all types, including employee medical benefit claims and treatment records.

Child Labor Laws

Another area of safety concern is reflected in restrictions affecting younger workers, especially those under the age of 18. Child labor laws, found in Section XII of the Fair Labor Standards Act (FLSA), set the minimum age for most employment at 16 years. For "hazardous" occupations, 18 years is the minimum. Figure 15-3 on the next page lists 17 occupations that the federal government considers hazardous for children who work while attending school.

Two examples illustrate violations of these provisions. At a fast-food restaurant specializing in roast beef sandwiches, a teenage worker operated a meat slicer, which is a hazard covered by the FLSA. At a national discount retailer, teenage workers were found to have operated the mechanical box crushers. Both situations resulted in enforcement actions and fines for violating the FLSA.

In addition to complying with workers' compensation, ADA, and child labor laws, most employers must comply with the Occupational Health and Safety Act of 1970. This act has had a tremendous impact on the workplace. Therefore, any

Figure 15-3

Selected Child Labor Hazardous Occupations (minimum age: 18 years)

Hazardous Work

1. Manufacturing or storing explosives
2. Driving a motor vehicle and being an outside helper
3. Coal mining
4. Logging and saw milling
5. Using power-driven woodworking machines*
6. Exposure to radioactive substances and to ionizing radiations
7. Operating power-driven hoisting apparatus
8. Operating power-driven, metal-forming, punching, and shearing machines*
9. Mining, other than coal mining
10. Slaughtering or meat packing, or rendering
11. Using power-driven bakery machines
12. Operating power-driven paper products machines*
13. Manufacturing brick, tile, and related products
14. Using power-driven circular saws, and guillotine shears*
15. Wrecking, demolition, and ship-breaking operations
16. Roofing operations*
17. Excavation operations*

* In certain cases the law provides exemptions for apprentices and student learners in these occupation

person interested in HR management must develop a knowledge of the provisions and implications of the act, which is administered by the Occupational Safety and Health Administration (OSHA).

Occupational Safety and Health Act

The Occupational Safety and Health Act of 1970 was passed "to assure so far as possible every working man or woman in the Nation safe and healthful working conditions and to preserve our human resources." Every employer engaged in commerce who has one or more employees is covered by the act.[7] Farmers having fewer than 10 employees are exempt. Employers in specific industries, such as coal mining, are covered under other health and safety acts. Federal, state, and local government employees also are covered by separate provisions or statutes.

The Occupational Safety and Health Act of 1970 established the Occupational Safety and Health Administration, known as OSHA, to administer its pro-

Figure 15-4 ▶ **Private Industry Injury Rate**

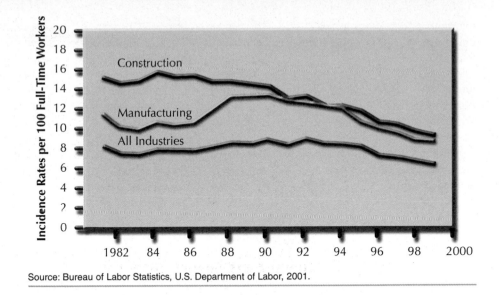

Source: Bureau of Labor Statistics, U.S. Department of Labor, 2001.

visions. The act also established the National Institute of Occupational Safety and Health (NIOSH) as a supporting body to do research and develop standards. In addition, the Occupational Safety and Health Review Commission (OSHRC) has been established to review OSHA enforcement actions and address disputes between OSHA and employers who have been cited by OSHA inspectors.

By making employers and employees more aware of safety and health considerations, OSHA has significantly affected organizations.[8] It does appear that OSHA regulations have contributed to reductions in the number of accidents and injuries in some cases. But even though some studies have shown that OSHA has had a positive impact in some industries, in other industries studies show no impact at all.

If one examines a 20-year history of private industry accident rates (see Figure 15-4), declines in accidents in the construction industry are noticeable. In manufacturing, accident rates per 100 full-time workers actually rose in the early 1990s, but have declined since then. Because safety issues in all other industries are much less significant, the all-industry rates are significantly below those in the construction and manufacturing industries.

OSHA Enforcement Standards

To implement OSHA, specific standards were established regulating equipment and working environments. National standards developed by engineering and quality control groups are often used. OSHA rules and standards are frequently complicated and technical. Small-business owners and managers who do not have specialists on their staffs may find the standards difficult to read and understand. In addition, the presence of many minor standards has hurt OSHA's credibility.

Material Safety Data Sheets Online

Information technology allows employers to use the Internet and intranets for a number of safety-related purposes. Because many firms must maintain material safety data sheets (MSDS) on chemicals and workplace substances, numerous pages of information must be made available to employees and managers throughout work facilities.

However, using MSDS software, firms can update the MSDS regularly rather than having to reissue printed manuals regularly. An employer can place all MSDS on an intranet, through an Internet link, or access manufacturer's information sheets. Many MSDS can be found on Web sites such as *www.MSDS provider.net, www.siri.org, www.MSDSpro.com,* and *www.MSDSonline.com.* At

specific work locations, the necessary MSDS can be printed out and saved in binders; otherwise if Internet access exists at work sites, the entire MSDS data base can be available on-line. Employers also can subscribe to MSDS service providers and receive automatic updates of individual chemicals and substances used regularly.[9]

A number of provisions have been recognized as key to OSHA compliance efforts by employers. Two of the most basic ones are as follows:

- *General duty:* The act requires that the employer has a "general duty" to provide safe and healthy working conditions, even in areas where OSHA standards have not been set. Employers who know or reasonably should know of unsafe or unhealthy conditions can be cited for violating the general duty clause.
- *Notification and posters:* Employers are required to inform their employees of safety and health standards established by OSHA. Also, OSHA posters must be displayed in prominent locations in workplaces.

Hazard Communication OSHA has enforcement responsibilities for the federal Hazard Communication Standard, which requires manufacturers, importers, distributors, and users of hazardous chemicals to evaluate, classify, and label these substances. Employers also must make available to employees, their representatives, and health professionals information about hazardous substances. This information is contained in material safety data sheets (MSDSs), which must be kept readily accessible to those who work with chemicals and other substances. The MSDSs also indicate antidotes or actions to be taken should someone come in contact with the substances. The e-HR describes how employers can provide MSDS information online.

It should be noted that if there are numbers of workers for whom English is not their primary language, then the MSDS should be available in other languages. Also, workers should be trained on how to access and use the MSDS information.

Lock out/tag out regulations Requirements that locks and tags be used to make equipment inoperative for repair or adjustment.

As part of hazard communications, OSHA has established **lock out/ tag out regulations.** To comply, locks and tags are provided to mechanics and tradespersons for use when they make equipment inoperative for repair or adjustment to prevent accidental start-up of defective machinery. These safety locks and tags must be removed only by the person whose name is printed on the tag or engraved on the lock.

Bloodborne Pathogens OSHA issued a standard "to eliminate or minimize occupational exposure to hepatitis B virus (HBV), human immunodeficiency virus (HIV), and other bloodborne pathogens." This regulation was developed to protect employees who regularly are exposed to blood and other such substances from AIDS. Obviously, health-care laboratory workers, nurses, and medical technicians are at greatest risk. However, all employers covered by OSHA regulations must comply in workplaces where cuts and abrasions are common. Regulations require employers with the most pronounced risks to have written control and response plans and to train workers in following the proper procedures.

Personal Protective Equipment (PPE) One goal of OSHA has been to develop standards for personal protective equipment. These standards require that employers conduct analyses of job hazards, provide adequate PPE to employees in those jobs, and train employees in the use of PPE items. Common PPE items include safety glasses, hard hats, and safety shoes. If the work environment presents hazards or if employees might have work contact with hazardous chemicals and substances, then employers are required to provide PPE to employees.

Ergonomics and OSHA

Ergonomics The study and design of the work environment to address physiological and physical demands on individuals.

Ergonomics is the study and design of the work environment to address physiological and physical demands on individuals. In a work setting, ergonomic studies look at such factors as fatigue, lighting, tools, equipment layout, and placement of controls. Human factors engineering is a related field.

For a number of years OSHA focused on the large number of work-related injuries due to repetitive stress, repetitive motion, cumulative trauma disorders, carpal tunnel syndrome, and other injuries in workplaces. **Cumulative trauma disorders (CTDs)** occur when workers repetitively use the same muscles to perform tasks, resulting in muscle and skeletal injuries.

Cumulative trauma disorders (CTDs) Muscle and skeletal injuries that occur when workers repetitively use the same muscles to perform tasks.

Carpal tunnel syndrome, one of the frequent cumulative trauma disorders, is an injury common to people who put their hands through repetitive motions such as typing, playing certain musical instruments, cutting, or sewing. The motion irritates the tendons in the carpal tunnel area of the wrist. As the tendons swell, they squeeze the median nerve. The result is pain and numbness in the thumb, index finger, and middle finger. The hands of victims become clumsy and weak. Pain at night increases, and at advanced stages not even surgery can cure the problem. Victims eventually lose feeling in their hands if they do not receive timely treatment.

These problems occur in a variety of work settings. The meat-packing industry has the highest level of CTDs. Grocery cashiers also have experienced CTDs from repetitively twisting their wrists when they scan bar codes on canned goods. But office workers experience CTDs too, primarily from extensive typing and data entry on computers and computer-related equipment. Most recently, attention has focused on the application of ergonomic principles to the design of workstations where computer operators work with personal computers (PCs) and video display terminals (VDTs) for extended periods of time.

OSHA Standards To address such concerns, OSHA in 2000 developed some ergonomics standards to address *muscoloskeletal disorders* that affect muscles, nerves, tendons, ligaments, joints, cartilage, blood vessels, or spinal discs affecting

the neck, shoulder, elbow, forearm, wrist, hand, abdomen (hernia only), back, knee, ankle, and foot. Excluded are injuries arising from slips, trips, falls, motor vehicle accidents, or blunt trauma. Estimates are that 600,000 workers each year suffer such muscoloskeletal injuries.[10]

Reaction to the OSHA standards was negative by employers and other groups who thought the standards were onerous and too costly. As a result, in 2001, the U.S. Congress repealed the standards. The U.S. Secretary of Labor was directed to develop new ergonomics standards that would not be as costly for employers to meet.[11] Those revised standards have been proposed in 2002, and developments in this area can be monitored at the OSHA Web site.

Effective Ergonomics Programs Despite the repeal of the original OSHA regulations, many employers have recognized that efforts to reduce CDT and other injuries are important. For example, Ultra Tool & Plastics in Amherst, New York, implemented an ergonomics program that cut back injuries by 70% and reduced associated lost workdays by 80%. Some solutions included ergonomic chairs, pallet jacks, robot presses, and back safety training. At Enid Memorial Hospital in Enid, Oklahoma, the rate of workplace injuries was cut by 75% and lost workdays were reduced more than 85% over three years through an ergonomics program that stressed safe biomechanical lifting of patients.[12]

There are several components of a successful ergonomics program. First, there must be managerial commitment to reducing those types of injuries, including providing both financial and other resources to support the efforts. Involvement of employees also is key in order to get their support. Other actions should include reviewing jobs where CTD problems could exist and ensuring that proper equipment, seating, lighting, and other engineering solutions are utilized. Supervisors and managers also should be trained to observe signs of CTD and how to respond to employee complaints about musculoskeletal and repetitive motion problems.[13]

Work Assignments and OSHA
The rights of employees regarding certain work assignments have been addressed as part of OSHA regulations. Two prominent areas where work assignments and concerns about safety and health meet are described next.

Work Assignments and Reproductive Health Related to unsafe work is the issue of assigning employees to work in areas where their ability to have children may be affected by exposure to chemical hazards. Women who are able to bear children or who are pregnant have presented the primary concerns, but in some situations, the possibility that men might become sterile also has been a concern.

In a court case involving reproductive health, the Supreme Court held that Johnson Controls' policy of keeping women of childbearing capacity out of jobs that might involve lead exposure violated the Civil Rights Act and the Pregnancy Discrimination Act.[14] Even though employers have established these policies to protect the health of women, employers also need to protect themselves from liability for the effects of workers' exposure to threats to the reproductive health of women.

Although employers have no *absolute* protection from liability, the following actions are suggested:

- Maintain a safe workplace for all by seeking the safest methods.
- Comply with all state and federal safety laws.
- Inform employees of any known risks.
- Document employee acceptance of any risks.

Refusing Unsafe Work Both union and non-union workers have refused to work when they considered the work unsafe. In many cases that refusal has been found to be justified.[15] Based upon several U.S. Supreme Court decisions, legal conditions for refusing work because of safety concerns are:

- The employee's fear is objectively reasonable.
- The employee has tried to have the dangerous condition corrected.
- Using normal procedures to solve the problem has not worked.

Record-Keeping Requirements

OSHA has established a standard national system for recording occupational injuries, accidents, and fatalities. Employers are generally required to maintain a detailed annual record of the various types of accidents for inspection by OSHA representatives and for submission to the agency. Employers that have had good safety records in previous years and those with fewer than 10 employees are not required to keep detailed records. Because of revisions effective in 2002, many organizations must complete OSHA Form 300 to report workshop accidents and injuries. Organizations required to complete OSHA 300 reports include firms having frequent hospitalizations, injuries, illnesses, or work-related deaths, and firms in OSHA's annual labor statistics survey.

No one knows how many industrial accidents go unreported. It may be many more than anyone suspects, despite the fact that OSHA has increased its surveillance of accident-reporting records. OSHA guidelines state that facilities whose accident records are below the national average rarely need inspecting.

Reporting Injuries and Illnesses Four types of injuries or illnesses have been defined by the Occupational Safety and Health Act of 1970:

- *Injury- or illness-related deaths*
- *Lost-time or disability injuries:* These include job-related injuries or disabling occurrences that cause an employee to miss his or her regularly scheduled work on the day following the accident.
- *Medical care injuries:* These injuries require treatment by a physician but do not cause an employee to miss a regularly scheduled work turn.
- *Minor injuries:* These injuries require first-aid treatment and do not cause an employee to miss the next regularly scheduled work turn.

The record-keeping requirements for these injuries and illnesses are summarized in Figure 15-5 on the next page. Notice that only very minor injuries do not have to be recorded for OSHA. Managers may attempt to avoid reporting lost-time or medical care injuries. For example, if several managers are trained in first aid, some minor injuries can be treated at the work site. Effective 2002, OSHA adopted some revised definitions of what constitutes medical treatment, first aid, and restricted work.[16]

Figure 15-5

Guide to Recordability of Cases Under the Occupational Safety and Health Act

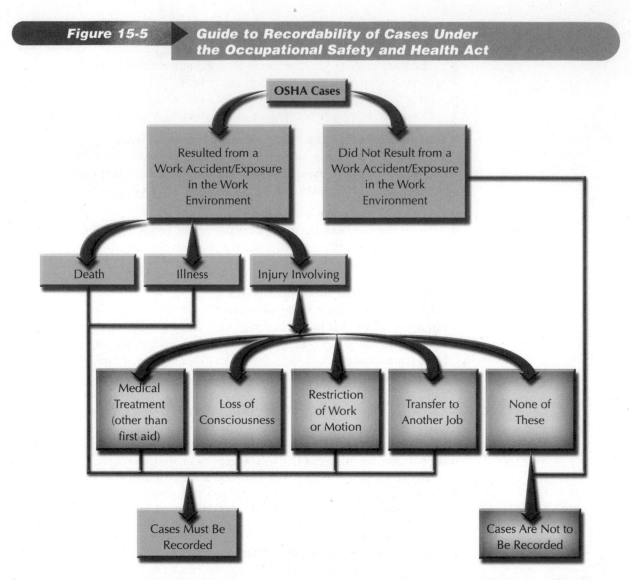

Source: U.S. Department of Labor Statistics, *What Every Employer Needs to Know About OSHA Record Keeping* (Washington, DC: U.S. Government Printing Office).

OSHA Inspections

The Occupational Safety and Health Act provides for on-the-spot inspections by OSHA representatives, called compliance officers or inspectors. Under the original act, an employer could not refuse entry to an OSHA inspector. It also prohibited a compliance officer from notifying an organization before an inspection. Instead of allowing an employer to "tidy up," this no-knock provision permits inspection of normal operations. The U.S. Supreme Court ruled on the issue in the case of *Marshall v. Barlow's, Inc.* and rejected the government's arguments, holding that safety inspectors must produce a search warrant if an employer refuses to allow an inspector into the plant voluntarily. However, the Court ruled that an inspector does not have to show probable cause to obtain a search warrant. A warrant can easily be obtained if a search is part of a general enforcement plan.[17]

1. Hazard communication program, training, labeling, and warnings
2. Inadequate machine guarding, including at point of operation
3. Lock out/tag out energy control program and procedures
4. Head protection: hardhats
5. Record-keeping violation: unsatisfactory OSHA log of illnesses and injuries
6. Inadequate emergency drenching facilities
7. Noncomplying guardrails or handrails on stairs or work platforms
8. Guard adjustment on abrasive wheel machinery
9. Noncomplying electrical wire cabinet boxes
10. Pulley guards on power transmission belts

Source: U.S. Department of Labor, Occupational Safety and Health Administration, 2001. Available at *www.osha.gov*.

Dealing with an Inspection When an OSHA compliance officer arrives, managers should ask to see the inspector's credentials. Next, the HR representative for the employer should insist on an opening conference with the compliance officer. The compliance officer may request that a union representative, an employee, and a company representative be present while the inspection is conducted. In the inspection, the officer checks organizational records to see if they are being maintained and to determine the number of accidents that have occurred. Following this review of the safety records, the officer conducts an on-the-spot inspection and may use a wide variety of equipment to test compliance with standards. After the inspection, the compliance officer can issue citations for any violations of standards and provisions of the act.

Citations and Violations Although OSHA inspectors can issue citations for violations of the provisions of the act, whether or not a citation is issued depends on the severity and extent of the problems, and on the employer's knowledge of them. In addition, depending on the nature and number of violations, penalties can be assessed against employers. The nature and extent of the penalties depend on the type and severity of the violations as determined by OSHA officials. Figure 15-6 shows the most frequently cited violations for a recent year. Notice that a mixture of workplace and administrative violations are among those cited most often.

The five types of violations ranging from the most severe to minimal, including a special category for repeated violations, follow:

- *Imminent danger:* When there is reasonable certainty that the condition will cause death or serious physical harm if it is not corrected immediately, an imminent-danger citation is issued and a notice posted by an inspector. Imminent-danger situations are handled on the highest-priority basis. They are reviewed by a regional OSHA director and must be corrected immediately. If the condition is serious enough and the employer does not cooperate, a representative of OSHA may obtain a federal injunction to close the company until the condition is corrected. The absence of guard railings to prevent employees from falling into heavy machinery is one example.
- *Serious:* When a condition could probably cause death or serious physical harm, and the employer should know of the condition, OSHA issues a serious-violation citation. Examples are the absence of a protective screen on a lathe or the lack of a blade guard on an electric saw.
- *Other than serious:* These types of violations could have an impact on employees' health or safety but probably would not cause death or serious harm. Having loose ropes in a work area might be classified as an other-than-serious violation.
- *De minimis:* A de minimis condition is one not directly and immediately related to employees' safety or health. No citation is issued, but the condition is mentioned to the employer. Lack of doors on toilet stalls is a common example of a de minimis violation.
- *Willful and repeated:* Citations for willful and repeated violations are issued to employers who have been previously cited for violations. If an employer knows about a safety violation or has been warned of a violation and does not correct the problem, a second citation is issued. The penalty for a willful and repeated violation can be high. For example, if death results from an accident that involves such a safety violation, a jail term of six months can be imposed on responsible executives or managers.

Critique of OSHA Inspection Efforts

OSHA has been criticized on several fronts. Because the agency has so many work sites to inspect, many employers have only a relatively small chance of being inspected. Some suggest that many employers pay little attention to OSHA enforcement efforts for this reason. Labor unions and others have criticized OSHA and Congress for not providing enough inspectors. For instance, it is common to find that many of the work sites at which workers suffered severe injuries or deaths had not been inspected in the previous five years.

Employers, especially smaller ones, continue to complain about the complexity of complying with OSHA standards and the costs associated with penalties and with making changes required to remedy problem areas. Very small employers point out that according to statistics from OSHA (see Figure 15-7), their businesses already have significantly lower work-related injury and illness rates than larger ones. Larger firms can afford to hire safety and health specialists and establish more proactive programs. To counter some of the criticism OSHA has established several programs.

Figure 15-7 ▸ **Workplace Injuries by Employment Size**

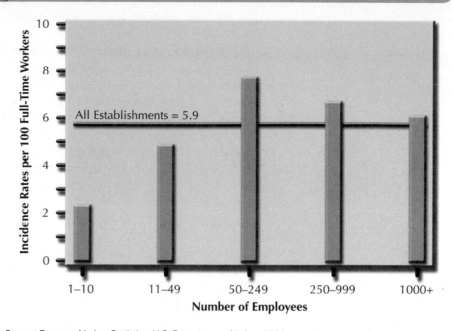

Source: Bureau of Labor Statistics, U.S. Department of Labor, 2001.

Strategic Partnership Program Under this voluntary program OSHA brings together employer groups and labor unions to address worker safety health issues. There are over 70 partnerships in existence. For example, the Maine Safe Logging partnership covers 3,000 employees and 300 employers, while in St. Louis, Missouri, the PRIDE program covers 25,000 employees and 1,000 employers in construction and other high incident industries.[18]

Voluntary Protection Programs (VPP) Companies with Voluntary Protection Programs (VPP) go beyond regulations by having exemplary safety and health practices at work. Most participating companies are award winners, with safety records two-thirds better than industry averages. These companies often establish "best practices" benchmarks in safety and health that can be shared with other employers by OSHA as demonstration programs. OSHA also offers some voluntary consultation programs in which employers may voluntarily—and without penalty—request OSHA consultations to identify hazards and violations so that the problems can be corrected.

Safety Management

Effective safety management requires an organizational commitment to safe working conditions. But more importantly, well-designed and managed safety programs can pay dividends in reduced accidents and the associated costs, such as workers' compensation and possible fines. Further, accidents and other safety concerns usually decline as a result of management efforts emphasizing safety.

There is a difference between firms with good safety performance and those OSHA has targeted as being well below the industry average. Often the difference is an effective safety management program.

Organizational Commitment and Safety Culture

At the heart of safety management is an organizational commitment to a comprehensive safety effort. This effort should be coordinated from the top level of management to include all members of the organization. It also should be reflected in managerial actions.[19] If the president of a small electrical manufacturing firm does not wear a hard hat in the manufacturing shop, he can hardly expect to enforce a requirement that all employees wear hard hats in the shop. Unfortunately, sincere support by top management often is missing from safety programs.

One result of a strong commitment to safety is that a "safety culture" pervades the organization. Firms such as Johnson & Johnson, Dupont Chemical, and Frito-Lay are well-known for emphasizing safety as part of their organizational cultures.[20] There are three different approaches that employers such as these use in managing safety. Figure 15-8 shows the organizational, engineering, and individual approaches and their components. Successful programs may use all three in dealing with safety issues.

The value of a comprehensive focus on safety is seen in the results at Chevron Products. Significant safety problems and frequent accidents and injuries occurred with Chevron's fuel truck drivers. But by using a multifaceted effort, the firm's injury and accident rates declined 60% to 70% over a multiyear period.[21]

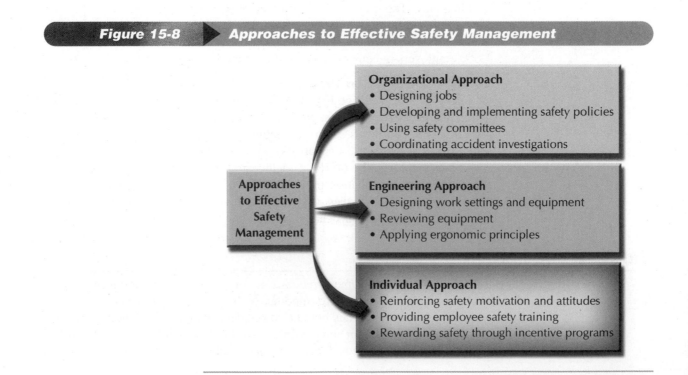

Figure 15-8 ▶ **Approaches to Effective Safety Management**

Safety and Engineering Employers can prevent some accidents by having machines, equipment, and work areas so that workers who daydream periodically or who perform potentially dangerous jobs cannot injure themselves and others. Providing safety equipment and guards on machinery, installing emergency switches, installing safety rails, keeping aisles clear, and installing adequate ventilation, lighting, heating, and air conditioning can all help make work environments safer.

Designing jobs properly requires consideration of the physical setting of a job. The way the work space surrounding a job is utilized can influence the worker's performance of the job itself. Several factors that affect safety have been identified, including size of work area, kinds of materials used, sensory conditions, distance between work areas, and interference from noise and traffic flow.

Individual Considerations and Safety Engineers approach safety from the perspective of redesigning the machinery or the work area. On the other hand, industrial psychologists and "human factors" experts see safety differently. They address the proper match of individuals to jobs and emphasize employee training in safety methods, fatigue reduction, and health awareness. Numerous field studies with thousands of employees, conducted by experts, have looked at the human factors in accidents. The results have found a definite relationship between emotional factors, such as stress, and accidents. Other studies point to the importance of individual differences, motivation, attitudes, and learning as key factors in controlling the human element in safety.

Attitudinal variables are among the individual factors that affect accident rates because careless employees cause more problems than do machines or employer negligence. At one time, workers dissatisfied with their jobs were thought to have higher accident rates. However, this assumption has been questioned in recent years. Although employees' personalities, attitudes, and individual characteristics apparently have some influence on accidents, exact cause-and-effect relationships are difficult to establish.

Work schedules can be another cause for accidents. The relationship between work schedules and accidents can be explained as follows: Fatigue based on physical exertion sometimes exists in today's industrial workplace. But boredom, which occurs when a person is required to do the same tasks for a long period of time, is rather common. As fatigue of this kind increases, motivation is reduced; along with decreased motivation, workers' attention wanders, and the likelihood of accidents increases. A particular area of concern is *overtime* in work scheduling. Overtime work has been consistently related to accident incidence. Further, the more overtime worked, the more severe accidents appear to be.

Another area of concern is the relationship of accident rates to different shifts, particularly late-night shifts. Because there tend to be fewer supervisors and managers working the "graveyard" shifts, workers tend to receive less training and supervision. Both of these factors lead to higher accident rates.

Safety Policies and Discipline

Designing safety policies and rules and disciplining violators are important components of safety efforts. Frequently reinforcing the need for safe behavior and supplying feedback on positive safety practices also are effective in improving worker safety.[22] Such efforts must involve employees, supervisors, managers,

Cellular Phones, Safety, and Individual Rights

The explosive growth and use of cellular phones has created both safety and ethical issues for HR professionals to address. As background, many individuals have personal cell phones that they use while operating company vehicles. Also, employers provide cell phones for business uses for employees such as top executives, delivery drivers, repair technicians, and information technology specialists. Because of several local and state laws that restrict cell phone usage while driving, many employers have developed policies on cell phone use while driving during work.

One illustration of the importance of the issues is that of a stockbroker for Saloman Smith Barney who was traveling to lunch while using his cell phone. The broker ran a red light and hit a motorcyclist who was killed by the impact. Ultimately, sued by the family of the motorcyclist, Saloman Smith Barney settled the lawsuit by paying $500,000.

To deal with such concerns, a growing number of employers have established policies prohibiting employees from using cell phones when using company-provided vehicles or when using personal vehicles for business purposes. Other firms such as Apache Corporation (Houston) and Coca-Cola Bottling (Atlanta) do not have a specific policy prohibiting driving and use of cell phones. However, these firms have conducted safety training that suggests that drivers pull over when using cell phones.

Some employers, such as the pharmaceutical firm Merck, Verizon Wireless, and others provide hands-free kits or headsets for employees who travel and are likely to use cell phones regularly. A New York City ordinance requires that taxi companies prohibit use of cell phones by cab drivers while carrying passengers.

Although a questionable practice, some firms even track employees' cell phone use while they are likely to be driving for work-related reasons. These individuals then receive "reminders" about cell phone usage while driving. A more controversial use is tracking who is called, when called, and for how long if the employer pays for the cell phone.

At this point, some concerns about infringing on individual rights begin to arise. Regardless of how far an employer goes, the growing use of cell phones, personal data assistants, and other wireless devices should be addressed by employers.[23]

---

safety specialists, and HR staff members. One of the newest areas where safety policies have been needed is described in the HR Perspective.

Safety Committees

Employees frequently participate in safety planning through safety committees, often composed of workers from a variety of levels and departments. A safety committee generally meets at regularly scheduled times has specific responsibilities for conducting safety reviews, and makes recommendations for changes necessary to avoid future accidents. Usually, at least one member of the committee comes from the HR department.

Companies must take care to ensure that managers do not compose a majority on their safety committees. Otherwise, the employer may be in violation of some provisions of the National Labor Relations Act. That act, as explained in detail in Chapter 17, prohibits employers from dominating a labor organization. Some safety committees have been ruled to be labor organizations because they deal with working conditions.

In approximately 32 states, all but the smallest employers may be required to establish safety committees. From time to time, legislation has been introduced at

WEST GROUP
A THOMSON COMPANY

Safety Committees
Discusses different types of safety committees and how they operate.
Custom Search:
☑ ANALYSIS
Phrase: Safety steering committee

the federal level to require joint management/employee safety committees. But as yet, no federal provisions have been enacted.

Safety Training and Communications

One way to encourage employee safety is to involve all employees at various times in safety training. Safety training can be done in various ways. Regular sessions with supervisors, managers, and employees often are coordinated by HR staff members. Showing videos, television broadcasts, and Internet-based resources all are means used to conduct safety training.

To reinforce safety training, continuous communication to develop safety consciousness is necessary. Merely sending safety memos is not enough. Producing newsletters, changing safety posters, continually updating bulletin boards, and posting safety information in visible areas also are recommended.

Employee Safety Motivation and Incentives

To encourage employees to work safely, many organizations have used safety contests and have given employees incentives for safe work behavior. Jewelry, clocks, watches, and even vacation trips have been given as rewards for good safety records. Unfortunately, some evidence indicates that incentives tend to reinforce underreporting and "creative" classifying of accidents. This concern about safety incentives, raised by OSHA, is that employees and managers do not report accidents and injuries so that they may collect the incentive rewards.[24]

Inspection, Accident Investigation, and Evaluation

It is not necessary to wait for an OSHA inspector to inspect the work area for safety hazards. Inspections may be done by a safety committee or by a safety coordinator. They should be done on a regular basis, because OSHA may inspect organizations with above-average lost workday rates more frequently.

When accidents occur, they should be investigated by the employer's safety committee or safety coordinator. The phases of accident investigation are depicted in Figure 15-9. In investigating the scene of an accident, the inspector needs to determine which physical and environmental conditions contributed to the accident. Investigation at the scene should be done as soon as possible after an accident to ensure that the conditions under which the accident occurred have not changed significantly.

The second phase of the investigation is the interview of the injured employee, his or her supervisor, and witnesses to the accident. The interviewer

Figure 15-9   *Phases of Accident Investigation*

Accident → Review the Scene → Interview Employees/Others → Prepare Report → Identify Recommendations

attempts to determine what happened and the cause of the accident. These interviews may also generate some suggestions on how to prevent similar accidents in the future. In the third phase, based on observations of the scene and interviews, investigators complete an accident investigation report. This report form provides the data required by OSHA.

Finally, recommendations should be made on how the accident could have been prevented, and on what changes are needed to avoid similar accidents. Identifying why an accident occurred is useful, but taking steps to prevent similar accidents from occurring also is important.

Closely related to accident investigation is research to determine ways of preventing accidents. Employing safety engineers or having outside experts evaluate the safety of working conditions is useful. If many similar accidents seem to occur in an organizational unit, a safety education training program may be necessary to emphasize safe working practices. As an example, a publishing company reported a greater-than-average number of back injuries among employees who lifted heavy boxes. Safety training on the proper way to lift heavy objects was initiated to reduce the number of back injuries.

Organizations should monitor and evaluate their safety efforts.[25] Just as organizational accounting records are audited, a firm's safety efforts should be audited periodically as well. Accident and injury statistics should be compared with previous accident patterns to identify any significant changes. This analysis should be designed to measure progress in safety management.

Health

Employee health problems are varied—and somewhat inevitable. They can range from minor illnesses such as colds to serious illnesses related to the jobs performed. Some employees have emotional health problems; others have alcohol or drug problems. Some problems are chronic; others are transitory. But all may affect organizational operations and individual employee productivity.

Workplace Health Issues

Employers face a variety of workplace health issues. Previously in this chapter cumulative trauma injuries and exposure to hazardous chemicals have been discussed because OSHA has addressed these concerns through regulations or standards. There are a number of concerns associated with employee substance abuse, workplace air quality and smoking.

Substance abuse The use of illicit substances or the misuse of controlled substances, alcohol, or other drugs.

Substance Abuse **Substance abuse** is defined as the use of illicit substances or the misuse of controlled substances, alcohol, or other drugs. The millions of substance abusers in the workforce, cost global employers billions of dollars annually. In the U.S. the incidence of substance abuse is greatest among white men aged 19 to 23. At work it is higher among men than women and higher among whites than other groups. Also, blue-collar workers are more likely than white-collar workers to abuse substances.

Employers' concerns about substance abuse stem from the ways it alters work behaviors: tardiness, increased absenteeism, slower work pace, higher rate of mistakes, and less time spent at the workstation. Substance abuse also can cause altered behaviors at work. The increase in withdrawal (physical and psychological) and antagonistic behaviors may lead to workplace violence.

Figure 15-10 ▶ **Common Signs of Substance Abuse**

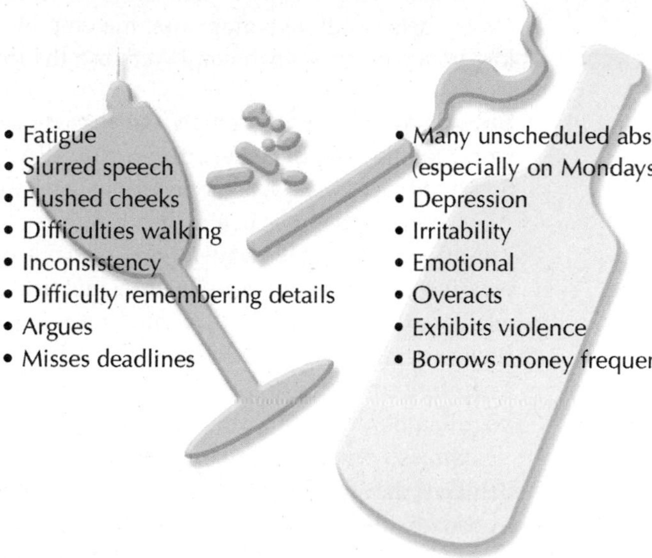

- Fatigue
- Slurred speech
- Flushed cheeks
- Difficulties walking
- Inconsistency
- Difficulty remembering details
- Argues
- Misses deadlines

- Many unscheduled absences (especially on Mondays and Fridays)
- Depression
- Irritability
- Emotional
- Overacts
- Exhibits violence
- Borrows money frequently

Figure 15-10 shows common signs of substance abuse. However, not all signs are present in any one case. A pattern that includes some of these behaviors should be a reason to pay closer attention.

The Americans with Disabilities Act (ADA) affects how management can handle substance abuse cases. Current illegal drug users are specifically excluded from the definition of disabled under the act. However, those addicted to legal substances (alcohol, for example) and prescription drugs are considered disabled under the ADA. Also, recovering substance abusers are considered disabled under the ADA.

Alcohol and drug testing is used by many employers, especially following an accident or some other reasonable cause. Some employers also institute a random testing program. Additional discussion on substance abuse testing is contained in Chapter 16.

Some firms use fitness-for-duty tests, also called impairment testing, to detect work performance safety problems before putting a person behind dangerous equipment. As an example, when a crew of delivery truck drivers comes to work, they are asked to "play" a video game—with serious consequences. Unless the machine presents a receipt saying they passed the test, they are not allowed to drive their trucks that day. The computer has already established a baseline for each employee. Subsequent testing measures the employees against these baselines. Interestingly, most test failures are not drug- or alcohol-related. Rather, fatigue, illness, and personal problems more frequently render a person unfit to perform a sensitive job.[26]

To encourage employees to seek help for their substance abuse problems, a *firm-choice option* is usually recommended and has been endorsed legally. In this procedure, the employee is privately confronted by a supervisor or manager about unsatisfactory work-related behaviors. Then, in keeping with the disciplinary system, the employee is offered a choice between help and discipline. Treatment options and consequences of further unsatisfactory performance are clearly discussed, including what the employer will do. Confidentiality and follow-up are critical when employers use the firm-choice option.

Emotional/Mental Health Concerns Many individuals today are facing work, family, and personal life pressures. Although most people manage these pressures successfully, some individuals have difficulties handling the demands. Also, specific events, such as death of a spouse, divorce, or medical problems, can affect individuals who otherwise have been coping successfully with life pressures. A variety of emotional/mental health issues arise at work that must be addressed by employers. It is important to note that emotional/mental illnesses such as schizophrenia and depression are considered disabilities under the ADA. Therefore employers should be cautious when using disciplinary policies if diagnosed employees have work-related problems.

Stress, whereby individuals cannot successfully handle the multiple demands they face, is one concern. All people encounter stress, but when "stress overload" hits, work-related consequences can result. HR professionals, managers, and supervisors all must be prepared to handle employee stress; otherwise employees may "burn out" or exhibit unhealthy behaviors, such as excess drinking of alcohol, misusing prescription drugs, having outbursts of anger, or other symptoms. Beyond efforts at communications and relieving some workload pressures, it is generally recommended that supervisors and managers contact the HR staff who may intervene and may refer affected employees to outside resources through employee assistance programs.[27]

Depression is another common emotional/mental health concern. Estimates are that 20% of individuals in workplaces suffer from depression. One indicator of the extent of clinical depression is that the sales of prescription drugs, such as Prozac and Zoloft, covered by employee benefits plans have risen significantly in the past several years.[28]

The effects of depression are seen at all levels, from warehouses and accounting offices to executive suites. Carried to extreme, depression can result in an employee suicide. The subsequent guilt and sorrow felt by those who worked with the dead individuals becomes an issue for HR staff, who may be aided by crisis counselors. To deal with depression, it is recommended that HR professionals, managers, and supervisors be trained on the symptoms of depression and what to do when symptoms are noticed. Often, employees then are guided to employee assistance programs and aided with obtaining medical treatment.[29]

Workplace Air Quality An increasing number of employees work in settings where air quality is a health issue.[30] Poor air quality may occur in "sealed" buildings where windows cannot be opened and when air flows are reduced to save energy and cut operating costs. Also, inadequate ventilation, as well as airborne contamination from carpets, molds, copy machines, adhesives, and fungi, can cause poor air quality and employee illnesses.[31] In industrial settings the presence of various chemicals and substances can lead to poor air quality.

Air quality concerns prompted the U.S. Environmental Protection Agency (EPA) to define *sick building syndrome* as a situation in which occupants experience acute health problems and discomfort that appear to be linked to time spent in a building. Also, OSHA has investigated workplace illnesses due to poor air quality. One major contributor to air quality problems is smoking in workplaces.

Smoking at Work Arguments and rebuttals characterize the smoking-at-work controversy, and statistics abound. A multitude of state and local laws deal with smoking in the workplace and public places. As a result of health studies, complaints by nonsmokers, and state laws, many employers have no-smoking policies throughout their workplaces. Although employees who smoke tend to complain initially when a smoking ban is instituted, they seem to have little difficulty adjusting within a few weeks, and many quit smoking or reduce the number of cigarettes they use each workday. Some employers also offer smoking cessation workshops as part of health promotion efforts.

Health Promotion

Employers concerned about maintaining a healthy workforce must move beyond simply providing healthy working conditions and begin promoting employee health and wellness in other ways. **Health promotion** is a supportive approach to facilitate and encourage employees to enhance healthy actions and lifestyles. Health promotion efforts can range from providing information and enhancing employee awareness of health issues to creating an organizational culture supportive of employee health enhancements, as Figure 15-11 indicates. Going beyond just compliance with workplace safety and health regulations, organizations engage in health promotion by encouraging employees to make physiological, mental, and social choices that improve their health.[32]

The first level is useful and may have some impact on individuals, but much is left to individual initiatives to follow through and make changes in actions and behaviors. Employers provide information on such topics as weight control,

Health promotion A supportive approach to facilitate and encourage employees to enhance healthy actions and lifestyles.

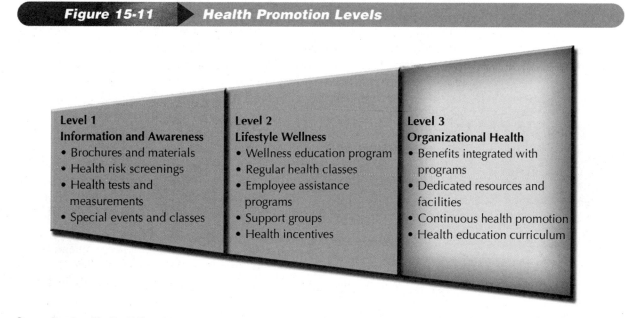

Figure 15-11 **Health Promotion Levels**

Level 1
Information and Awareness
- Brochures and materials
- Health risk screenings
- Health tests and measurements
- Special events and classes

Level 2
Lifestyle Wellness
- Wellness education program
- Regular health classes
- Employee assistance programs
- Support groups
- Health incentives

Level 3
Organizational Health
- Benefits integrated with programs
- Dedicated resources and facilities
- Continuous health promotion
- Health education curriculum

Source: Developed by Kay F. Ryan (Nebraska Methodist College) and Robert L. Mathis (University of Nebraska at Omaha). May not be reproduced without permission.

stress management, nutrition, exercise, and smoking cessation. One indicator that many employers have limited their efforts to the first level is that 93% of surveyed employers have some type of health promotion program and 72% of them offer health education and training programs. However, only 27% of the firms conducted health risk screenings and appraisals.[33] Even though such efforts may be beneficial for some employees, employers who wish to impact employees' health must offer second-level efforts through more comprehensive programs and efforts that focus on the lifestyle "wellness" of employees.

Wellness Programs Employers' desires to improve productivity, decrease absenteeism, and control health-care costs have come together in the "wellness" movement. **Wellness programs** are designed to maintain or improve employee health before problems arise. Wellness programs encourage self-directed lifestyle changes. Early wellness programs were aimed primarily at reducing the cost and risk of disease. Newer programs emphasize healthy lifestyles and environment, including reducing cholesterol and heart disease risks and individualized exercise programs and follow-up. Employer-sponsored support groups have been established for individuals dealing with health issues such as weight loss, nutrition, or smoking cessation.

Organizations can assess the effectiveness of their wellness programs in a number of ways. Participation rates by employees is one way and the rates vary by type of activity, but generally 20% to 40% of employees participate in the different activities in a wellness program. Although more participation would be beneficial, the programs have resulted in healthier lifestyles for more employees. Cost/benefit analyses by organizations also tend to support the continuation of wellness programs as well.[34]

Employee Assistance Programs (EAPs) One method organizations use as a broad-based response to health issues is the **employee assistance program (EAP),** which provides counseling and other help to employees having emotional, physical, or other personal problems. In such a program, an employer contracts with a counseling agency. Employees who have problems may then contact the agency, either voluntarily or by employer referral, for assistance with a broad range of problems. Counseling costs are paid for by the employer, either in total or up to a pre-established limit.

EAPs help employees with a variety of problems. One survey of EAP counselors found that the most common employee issues dealt with were: (1) depression and anxiety, (2) marital and relationship problems, (3) legal difficulties, and (4) family and children concerns.[35] Other areas commonly addressed as part of an EAP include substance abuse, financial counseling, and career advice. Critical to employee usage of an EAP is preserving confidentiality. For that reason, employers outsource EAPs to trained professionals, who usually report only the numbers of employees and services provided, rather than details on individuals using an EAP.

The effectiveness of EAPs depends upon how well employers integrate and support them in the workplace. One study of EAPs found that such support results in five times more supervisory referrals of employees to EAPs, and three

Wellness programs Programs designed to maintain or improve employee health before problems arise.

Employee assistance program One that provides counseling and other help to employees having emotional, physical, or other personal problems.

EAP Policy
Contains a sample employee assistance plan policy.
Custom Search:
☑ ANALYSIS
Phrase: Sample employee assistance program

Research on Financial Impact of Health Promotion

Many organizations have found that health promotion efforts produce financial savings. Various reports by both individual firms and research studies have revealed that such savings exist. But to provide an overall view, Steven Aldana conducted a comprehensive review of the literature and studies on the links between lifestyle behaviors, organizational health promotion programs, and financial results attributed to those programs.

Conducting a meta-analysis, which is a review of other research and then summarizing the results, Aldana examined 72 different studies. As reported in the *American Journal of Health Promotion*, Aldana's research revealed strong support that health promotion efforts produce significant financial returns for employers. The researcher found that average health-care cost savings per dollar spent on health promotion

programs was $3.48. Also, average absenteeism savings per dollar spent on health promotion programs was significant. When all costs and savings were combined, Aldana concluded that for every dollar spent on health promotion, employers received a return of $4.30. While the results may vary from one employer to another, it is evident that health promotion provides significant financial returns for investing in employee health.[36]

times the numbers of employees with substance abuse problems who receive assistance than those firms that do not support EAPs.[37]

Organizational Health Culture Employers both large and small may recognize that an organizational culture that emphasizes and supports health efforts is beneficial. Common to these employers is an integrative, broad-based effort supported both financially and managerially. Development of policies and procedures supporting health efforts, establishing on-site exercise facilities, and consistently promoting health programs all contribute to creating a health promotion environment throughout the organization. The benefits of health promotion efforts have been documented by individual firms and research studies, as the HR Perspective describes.

Two examples of firms that illustrate such a culture and commitment are Coors, the Colorado-based brewing firm, and 3Com, the network communications firm based in Santa Clara, California. At Coors, a 25,000-square-foot Wellness Center is located at the Golden, Colorado, plant and office complex and used extensively by Coors employees. Coors also provides on-site breast cancer screening, cardiac rehabilitation groups, complementary medicine assistance, wellness at work educational sessions, and work conditioning programs. 3Com has 40% of its 4,200 employees in Santa Clara as members of its WellCom program. A large fitness center is open 24 hours a day, seven days a week. At that center and other locations at facilities in Illinois, Massachusetts, and England, classes, seminars, support programs, and other efforts reinforce that a healthy workforce contributes to reduced health-care costs and aids employee recruiting and retention.[38]

Logging On...

Healthy Culture
This Web site describes services and programs that support organizational health cultures.

www.healthyculture.com

Traditionally, when employers have addressed worker health, safety, and security, they have been concerned about reducing workplace accidents, improving workers' safety practices, and reducing health hazards at work. However, over the past decade providing security for employees has grown in importance. A survey of security professionals at companies identified the top eight security concerns at work, in order, as follows:[39]

1. Workplace violence
2. Internet/intranet security
3. Business interruption/disaster recovery
4. Fraud/white-collar crime
5. Employee selection/screening concerns
6. General employee theft
7. Unethical business conduct
8. Computer hardware/software theft

Notice that virtually all of these areas have significant HR implications. Heading the list of security concerns is workplace violence.

Workplace Violence

Estimates by the National Institute for Occupational Safety and Health (NIOSH) indicate that 10–15 workplace homicides occur every week. Annually, NIOSH estimates that an additional million people are attacked at work.[40] About 70% of the workplace fatalities involved attacks against workers such as police officers, taxi drivers, and convenience store clerks. Often, these deaths occur during armed robbery attempts. But what has shocked many employers in a variety of industries has been the number of disgruntled employees or former employees who have resorted to homicide in the workplace to deal with their anger and grievances.

Figure 15-12 shows the warning signs and characteristics of a potentially violent person at work. Research on individuals who have committed the most violent acts shows the relatively common profile depicted in Figure 15-12. A person with some of these signs may cope for years until a trauma pushes him or her over the edge. A profound humiliation or rejection, the end of a marriage, or the loss of a lawsuit or job may make a difficult employee turn violent.

Management of Workplace Violence The increase in workplace violence has led many employers to develop workplace violence prevention and response policies and practices. As recommended by the American Society of Safety Engineers (ASSE), employers need to conduct a risk assessment of the organization and its employees. Unfortunately, according to ASSE, only 16% of surveyed employers have conducted such a study.[41] After completing such a study, an organization can establishing HR policies to identify how workplace violence is to be dealt with in conjunction with disciplinary actions and referrals to employee assistance programs.

One aspect of these policies is a violence response team. Composed of security personnel, key managers, HR staff members, and selected employees, these

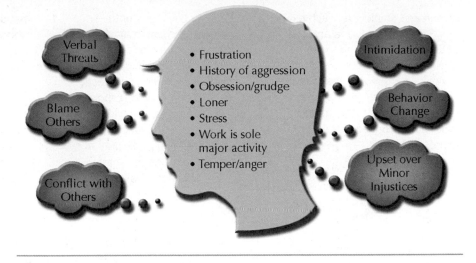

- Frustration
- History of aggression
- Obsession/grudge
- Loner
- Stress
- Work is sole major activity
- Temper/anger

Verbal Threats

Blame Others

Conflict with Others

Intimidation

Behavior Change

Upset over Minor Injustices

WEST GROUP

A THOMSON COMPANY

Workplace Violence
Identifies steps to take to minimize workplace violence and gives a sample policy.
Custom Search:
☑ ANALYSIS
Phrase: Causes of workplace violence

individuals function much like a safety committee, but with a different focus. At firms such as Motorola and Blue Shield of California the teams conduct analyses, respond and investigate employee threats, and may even aid in calming angry, volatile employees.

However, employers must be careful, because they may face legal action for discrimination if they discharge employees for behaviors that often precede violent acts. For example, in several cases, employees who were terminated or suspended for making threats or even engaging in physical actions against their co-workers have sued their employers, claiming they had mental disabilities under the Americans with Disabilities Act (ADA).

Post-violence response is another part of managing workplace violence. Whether the violence results in physical injuries or deaths, or just intense interpersonal conflicts, it is important that employers have plans to respond afterwards. That response must reassure employees who may be fearful of returning to work or who experience anxiety and sleeplessness, among other reactions. Providing referrals to EAP resources, allowing employees time to meet with HR staff, and arranging for trained counselors on-site are all part of post-violence response efforts.[42]

Domestic Causes of Workplace Violence Women are much more likely than men to experience violence committed as a result of a personal relationship. Too often, violence that begins at home with family or "friends" can spill over to the workplace. One in five homicides of women at work is perpetrated by current or former husbands or boyfriends. Also, many abused women report being harassed frequently at work, by telephone, or in person by abusing partners.

The worse reaction by employers is to ignore obvious signs of domestic violence. In fact, some employers have been sued and found liable for ignoring pleas for help from employees, who later are victims of domestic violence in

HR Practices

Handling Domestic Violence in Workplaces

Enlightened employers, such as Blue Shield of California and the State of North Carolina, have active programs to combat domestic violence. Based on their experiences, some suggestions have been identified for handling the work-related consequences of domestic violence.

- *Organizational policies:* Employers should establish policies stating that employees suffering from domestic abuse will be assisted. Also, any instances of workplace harassment by family abusers will be handled by local law enforcement and other outside agencies. Additionally, employee benefits and time-off policies should allow employees to take time for court appearances, to relocate to shelters, or meet with counselors, attorneys, and law officers.

- *Training:* Two types of training are needed. First, managers, supervisors, and HR staff members should be trained to recognize symptoms of domestic violence and how to respond to those situations. Second, all employees, but especially women, should participate in training sessions on what domestic violence is, how they should handle it, and who in the organization to contact. Training materials and resources are available from the Family Violence Prevention Fund (*www.fvpf.org*) and other organizations and agencies.
- *Security:* Physical security arrangements should be reviewed. This review often includes maintaining limited or controlled access to work areas, providing security lighting and services in company

parking lots, and offering escort services and special parking for employees requesting assistance.
- *EAP referrals and counseling:* Employees facing domestic problems should be encouraged to contact trained professionals using the employer's employee assistance program (EAP). For smaller employers without EAPs, individuals can be referred to community agencies and non-profit organizations providing domestic violence assistance.

Taking steps such as these reassures employees who are victims of domestic violence that they have a place of safety and support at work. It also signals employer commitment to managing the workplace consequences of domestic violence.[43]

---

company parking lots or on employer premises. The HR Practice contains some suggestions for HR staff and managers for dealing with domestic violence.

Training on Workplace Violence Managers, HR staff members, supervisors, and employees should be trained on how to recognize the signs of a potentially violent employee and what to do when violence occurs. During training at many firms, participants learn the typical profile of potentially violent employees and are trained to notify the HR department and to refer employees to outside counseling professionals. Specific suggestions addressed in training for dealing with potentially violent employees include the following:

- Notice verbal and nonverbal reactions by individuals that may indicate anger or hostility.
- Listen to the individual and pay attention to the words, actions, and unspoken "messages."
- Ask questions that require explanations and longer answers that allow the individual to "vent."

Security audit A comprehensive review of organizational security.

- Respond calmly and nonthreatingly to the individual's emotions and acknowledge concerns and understanding about how the individual feels.
- Get assistance from others, particularly HR staff or another manager not directly affected by the situation being discussed.
- Indicate the need to be able to have time to respond to the concerns voiced and set up another time for follow-up.
- Notify security personnel and HR staff members whenever employees' behaviors change dramatically or when job disciplinary action may provoke significant reactions by employees.

Security Management

An overall approach to security management is needed to address a wide range of issues including workplace violence. Often HR managers have responsibility for security programs, or they work closely with security mangers or consultants to address employee security issues.

Security Audit In a **security audit,** HR staff conducts a comprehensive review of organizational security. Sometimes called a *vulnerability analysis,* such an audit uses managers inside the organization—such as the HR manager and facilities manager—and outsiders, such as security consultants, police officers, fire officials, and computer security experts to assess security issues.

Typically, a security audit begins with a survey of the area around the facility. Such factors as lighting in parking lots, traffic flow, location of emergency response services, crime in the surrounding neighborhood, and the layout of the buildings and grounds are evaluated.[44] The audit also may include a review of the security available within the firm, including the capabilities of guards. Another part of the security audit reviews disaster plans, which address how to deal with events such as earthquakes, floods, tornados, hurricanes, and fires. Such efforts have become even more prominent since the New York events of September 2001.

Controlled Access A key part of security involves controlling access to the physical facilities of the organization. As mentioned earlier, many workplace homicides occur during robberies. Therefore, those employees most vulnerable, such as taxi drivers and convenience store clerks, must be provided secure areas to which access is limited. For instance, providing plexiglass partitions and requiring use of cash trays have reduced deaths at some convenience store locations.

Many organizations limit access to facilities and work areas by using electronic access or keycard systems. Although not foolproof, these systems can make it more difficult for an unauthorized person, such as an estranged husband or a disgruntled ex-employee, to enter the premises. Access controls also can be used in elevators and stairwells to prevent unauthorized persons from entering certain areas within a facility.

Computer Security Yet another part of security centers on controlling access to computer systems. With so many transactions and records being handled by computers, adequate security provisions are crucial to prevent unauthorized access to computer systems, including human resource information systems (HRIS). The growth of the Internet and e-mail systems has made computer security issues an even greater concern. This concern is magnified when individuals are terminated or leave an organization. HR staff must coordinate with information technology staff to change passwords, delete access codes, and otherwise protect company information systems.

Employee Screening and Selection

A key facet of providing security is to screen job applicants. Regulations somewhat limit what can be done, particularly regarding the use of psychological tests and checking of references. However, firms that do not screen employees adequately may be subject to liability if an employee commits crimes later. For instance, an individual with a criminal record for assault was hired by a firm to perform interior maintenance of sound equipment. The employee used a passkey to enter a home and assault the owner, and the employer was ruled liable. Of course, employers must be careful when selecting employees to use only valid, job-related screening means and to avoid violating federal EEO laws and the Americans with Disabilities Act.

Security Personnel

Adequately trained security personnel in sufficient numbers is another critical part of security management. Many employers contract for this service with firms specializing in security. If security is handled in-house, those employees must be selected and trained to handle a variety of workplace security problems, ranging from dealing with violent behavior by an employee to taking charge in natural disasters.

Summary

- Health is a general state of physical, mental, and emotional well-being, while safety involves protecting the physical well-being of people.
- Security involves protection of employees and organizational facilities.
- Workers' compensation coverage is provided by employers to protect employees who suffer job-related injuries and illnesses.
- Both the Family Medical Leave Act (FMLA) and the Americans with Disabilities Act (ADA) affect employer health and safety policies and practices.
- The Fair Labor Standards Act (FLSA) limits the types of work that employees under the age of 18 can perform.
- The Occupational Safety and Health Act states that employers have a general duty to provide safe and healthy working conditions.
- Occupational Safety and Health Administration (OSHA) enforcement standards have been established to aid in a number of areas, including hazard communications and others.

- Ergonomics looks at the physiological and physical demands of work and has grown in importance.
- OSHA requires employers to keep records on occupational illnesses and injuries, conducts inspections of workplaces, and can issue citations for several different levels of violations.
- Effective safety management requires integrating three different approaches: organizational, engineering, and individual.
- Developing safety policies, establishing safety committees, conducting safety training, and evaluating work areas for safety concerns are all part of comprehensive safety management efforts.
- Substance abuse, emotional/mental health concerns, workplace air quality, and smoking at work, among other common health issues, are growing concerns for organizations and employees.
- Health promotion efforts by employers are important and can occur at several levels.

- Employers have responded to health problems by establishing and supporting wellness programs and employee assistance programs (EAPs).
- Establishing and maintaining an organizational health culture continues to pay off for a number of employers.

- Security of workplaces has grown in importance, particularly in light of the increasing frequency in which workplace violence occurs.
- Employers can enhance security by conducting a security audit, controlling access to workplaces and computer systems, screening employees adequately, and providing security personnel.

Review and Discussion Questions

1. Identify the purpose of health, safety, and security as HR activities, and discuss how they are interrelated.
2. Discuss how controlling workers' compensation costs is related to effective health, safety, and security practices.
3. Describe the Occupational Safety and Health Act and some of its key provisions, including current issues and standards.
4. What should an employer do when faced with an OSHA inspection, and what records should be available?

5. Why must safety management contain a number of activities to be effective?
6. Discuss the following statement by a supervisor: "I feel it is my duty to get involved with my employees and their personal problems to show that I truly care about them."
7. Evaluate the health promotion activities and their effectiveness at a current or former employer.
8. Describe some security issues that might be identified during a security audit at a firm where you have worked.

Terms to Know

health   476
safety   476
security   476
lock out/tag out regulations   482
ergonomics   483
cumulative trauma disorders (CTDs)   483

substance abuse   494
health promotion   497
wellness programs   498
employee assistance program   498
security audit   503

Using the Internet

Developing a Wellness Program

As the HR manager of a distribution and warehouse firm with 250 employees, you recognize the need for a broader corporate emphasis on employee health. Although the current safety management program has been effective, you know that developing a com-

pany wellness program may be beneficial for employees and your company. Therefore at a meeting with the company executives next week you plan to discuss what a wellness program is, what can be included, how it will be beneficial, and the process for establishing it. To develop your presentation, consult the following Web site: *www.welcoa.org.*

CASE

Anheuser-Busch Brews Employee Wellness

Anheuser-Busch (A-B) is best known for its Budweiser, Bud Lite, and Michelob beers. To get those products brewed and to market takes a large number of employees in a number of brewing plants in the U.S. In addition to producing beer, A-B has also worked to produce healthy employees. One prime example of the health and wellness efforts at A-B can be seen at its Jacksonville, Florida, brewery. Many of the workers at the Jacksonville plant have considerable years of experience with the average age of the workforce being 48 years. As the workforce has grown older, employee health and wellness has become a higher priority.

Beginning several years ago an annual health appraisal on employees was conducted by occupational nurses. This extensive appraisal obtained employees' details on personal and family health history, nutrition habits, blood pressure, cholesterol, and other health measures. Once all of the data on each employee were compiled, "health report cards" were provided to the employees and their primary care physicians.

Then employees were encouraged to participate in wellness programs relevant to their individual needs. Also, an employee wellness committee met regularly to plan wellness programs and events, including a month-long wellness fair. The fair invited spouses, children, and family members as well as employees to participate.

These efforts have resulted in healthier employees for A-B, fewer medical care costs for employees and their dependents, and fewer workplace illnesses and injuries. Because of all of these health initiatives, the Jacksonville plant has been awarded a "gold star" designation by the Wellness Council of America. While brewing beer, Anheuser-Busch has also produced employee wellness.[45]

Questions

1. Identify how A-B has incorporated elements from each of the levels of health promotion described in the chapter.
2. How could wellness and health promotion efforts be justified to senior managers at A-B corporate headquarters?

Notes

1. Based on Marilyn Chase, "Healthy Assets," *The Wall Street Journal,* May 1, 2000, R9, R15; Kyle Nelson, "Serious About Safety," *Occupational Health & Safety,* December 2000, 34–38; and Jerry Laws, "A Solid Utility Plan," *Occupational Health & Safety,* June 2001, 67–69.
2. "Business Challenged to Demonstrate Corporate Citizenship," *Business and the Environment,* May 2001, 9.
3. Jon Grice, "The Cost of Comp," *Occupational Health & Safety,* February 2001, 59–60.
4. William Atkinson, "Is Workers' Comp Changing?" *HR Magazine,* July 2000, 50–61.

5. Susan H. Abeln, "FMLA and Workers' Comp," at *www.quinlan.com.*
6. Christopher G. Bell, "The ADA, FMLA, and Workers' Compensation," SHRM White Paper, May 2001, available at *www.shrm.org.*
7. Richard A. Stempniak, "Administering a Safety Program," *Purchasing Today,* April 2001, 16–18.
8. "OSHA at 30: Three Decades of Progress in Occupational Safety and Health," *Job Safety & Health Quarterly,* Spring 2001, 23–32.
9. Based on Randy White, "Weighing MSDS Management Programs," *Occupational Health & Safety,* October 2000, 200–203.

10. Susan Hall Fleming, "Ergonomics: Preventing Injury and Preserving Health," *Job Safety & Health Quarterly,* Winter 2000, 22–25.
11. For a discussion of the standards and criticisms, see Timothy S. Bland and Pedro R. Forment, "Navigating OSHA's Ergonomic Rules," *HR Magazine,* February 2001, 61; and Yochi J. Dreazen and Phil Kuntz, "New OSHA Proposal Enrages Businesses," *The Wall Street Journal,* November 8, 2000, A2, A6.
12. "Ergonomics: Snapshots of Success," *Job Safety & Health Quarterly,* Winter 2000, 26.

13. Robert J. Grossman, "Make Ergonomics Go," *HR Magazine,* April 2000, 36–42.

14. *United Autoworkers v. Johnson Controls, Inc.,* 111 S. Ct. 1196 (1991).

15. Mark Harcourt and Sandra Harcourt, "When Can an Employee Refuse Unsafe Work and Expect to be Protected from Discipline?" *Industrial & Labor Relations Review* 53 (2000), 684–704.

16. Steve Bates, "OSHA Has New Record Keeping Rules, Forms," *HR News,* December 2001, 2. Also available at *www.osha.gov.*

17. *Marshall v. Barlow's Inc.,* 98 S. Ct. 1816 (1978).

18. Judith Weinberg, Christopher Warren, and Audie Woolsey, "OSHA's Strategic Partnership Program: Protecting Workers, Transforming Relationships," *Job Safety & Health Quarterly,* Summer 2000, 18–27.

19. James G. Grant, "Involving the Total Organization," *Occupational Health & Safety,* September 2000, 64–65.

20. Valerie Overheul, "20 Years of Safety," *Occupational Health & Safety,* June 2001, 70–74.

21. "Employer Curtails Accidents with Holistic Safety Program," *Bulletin to Management,* September 21, 2000, 302.

22. Earl Blair and E. Scott Geller, "Behavior-Based Safety," *Occupational Health & Safety,* September 2000, 61–63.

23. Based on Julie Cook, "Fatal Distractions," *Human Resource Executive,* April 2001, 98–100; and "Cellular Phones and Driver Safety: What Every Employer Should Know," *Bulletin to Management,* November 23, 2000, S1–S4.

24. Jeanie Casison, "Safety Dance: OSHA Weighs in Heavily on Incentive Programs," *Incentive,* May 2000, 9.

25. Robert A. Menard, "Talking Dollars and Sense," *Occupational Health & Safety,* February 2001, 62–65.

26. Evelyn Beck, "Is the Time Right for Impairment Testing?" *Workforce,* February 2001, 69–71.

27. William Atkinson, "When Stress Won't Go Away," *HR Magazine,* December 2000, 105–110.

28. Elyse Tanouye, "Mental Illness: A Rising Workplace Cost," *The Wall Street Journal,* June 13, 2001, B1+ .

29. Joseph Kline, Jr., and Lyle Sussman, "An Executive Guide to Workplace Depression," *Academy of Management Executive,* August 2000, 103–114.

30. Robert J. Grossman, "Out With the Bad Air," *HR Magazine,* October 2000, 37–45.

31. Michelle Conlin, "Is Your Office Killing You?" *Business Week,* June 5, 2000, 114–128.

32. Angela Downey, "Promoting Health on the Job," *CMA Management,* May 2001, 24–28.

33. "Employers Use Education, Incentives, Screenings to Reduce Health Care Costs," *Employee Benefit Plan Review,* August 2000, 18.

34. Bill Gillette, "Promoting Wellness Programs Results in a Healthier Bottom Line," *Managed Healthcare Executive,* February 2001, 45.

35. "Psychological Issues Most Often Addressed by EAPs," July 5, 2000, available at *www.worldatwork.org.*

36. Based on Steven G. Aldana, "Financial Impact of Health Promotion Programs: Comprehensive Review of the Literature," *American Journal of Health Promotion,* 15(2001), 296–320.

37. Kenneth Collins, "HR Must Find New Ways to Battle Substance Abuse in the Workplace," *HR News,* April 2001, 11.

38. Marilyn Chase, "Healthy Assets," R9.

39. "Corporate Threats," *Human Resource Executive,* June 2, 2000, 98.

40. Marlene Piturro, "Workplace Violence," *Strategic Finance,* May 2001, 35–38.

41. "Workplace Survey and White Paper," February 5, 2001, available at *www.asse.org.*

42. "After the Shooting Stops," *Business Week,* March 12, 2001, 98–100.

43. Andrew R. McIlvaine, "Hidden Victims," *Human Resource Executive,* March 15, 2001; Family Violence Prevention Fund, available at *www.fvpf.org;* and "Employers Aim to Protect Victims, Prevent Abuse," *Bulletin to Management,* September 14, 2000, 295.

44. Barbara A. Nadel, "Better Safe: Planning Secure Environments," *Area Development,* May 2001, 24–27.

45. Based on "Brewery's Aging Workforce Is Given a Shot of Wellness," *Bulletin to Management,* May 4, 2000, 147.

CHAPTER 16

Employee Rights and Discipline

After you have read this chapter, you should be able to:

- Explain the difference between statutory rights and contractual rights.

- Define employment-at-will and identify three exceptions to it.

- Describe what due process is and explain some means of alternative dispute resolution.

- Identify employee rights associated with access to employee records and free speech.

- Discuss issues associated with workplace monitoring, surveillance, investigations, and drug testing.

- List elements to consider when developing an employee handbook.

- Differentiate between the positive approach and progressive approach to discipline.

E-Mail and Privacy

Employees and employers both are searching for definitions and boundaries when it comes to personal use of office computers. Technology has blurred the line between company time and private time, and many employees feel it is acceptable to use their company's computer for personal matters.

Employees often forget that they leave an electronic record of what they do, and it has created problems for both employees and employers. For example, an insurance company fired a worker for gross misconduct, accusing her of charging personal expenses to her corporate credit card. After the termination, corporate officials sent an e-mail to seven managers outlining her discharge. The e-mail was transmitted to some additional managers, one of whom forwarded it to five other employees. With all those people receiving e-mails about her dismissal, which was recorded in their computers, the employee sued for defamation of character and won $1.3 million.

Even before the Internet, employees had sued employers for secret searches of their desks and voice mails. A few regulations have been established providing minimal guidelines. For example, an employer cannot listen to personal telephone conversations unless employees have been told that their calls may be monitored. A number of states require signed general permission forms.

But laws on e-mail monitoring are largely nonexistent, although the same sort of notice is probably appropriate for e-mails. Many employers have specialized software that can retrieve deleted e-mail, and even record each keystroke made. For instance, if disgruntled employees draft complaints to their boss, then change their minds and delete the message, it's too late. All the keystrokes likely have been stored on their hard drives where an IT manager can retrieve a record of them.

Monitoring workers' communication and performance has become more prevalent, with about 78% of larger organizations doing so. Of surveyed employers sixty-three percent monitor Internet activities, and 47% store and review e-mails. These figures show a dramatic increase over the past four years ago. Surveys of employees indicate that most individuals receive one to five non-work related e-mails per day, and less than half say they never receive "sexually explicit" or otherwise improper e-mail.

Just because employers can legally monitor employees' e-mails, should they do so? It depends. If monitoring e-mail is only for *productivity concerns,* better measures of productivity are available for that purpose. However, if the fear is legal liability, that fact should be made clear to everyone. Employers do have legitimate concerns about liability issues when employees have access to inappropriate Web sites or can offend colleagues with inappropriate e-mails. Clear policies on employee monitoring and e-mail use are important. Also, addressing the subject in orientation and training programs is needed in order to inform all employees and managers of the policies.[1]

Technology has blurred the line between company time and private time . . .

This chapter considers three related and important issues in managing human resources: employee rights, HR policies and rules, and discipline. These areas may seem separate, but they definitely are not. The policies and rules that an organization enacts define employee rights at that employer to a certain extent, as well as constrain those rights (sometimes inappropriately or illegally). Similarly, discipline for those who fail to follow policies and rules often is seen as a fundamental right of employers. Employees who feel that their employers have taken inappropriate actions can challenge those actions—both inside and outside the organization—using an internal dispute resolution process or through external legal means.

Employees join organizations with certain rights established by the U.S. Constitution, including *freedom of speech, due process, protection against unreasonable search and seizure,* and others. Although the U.S. Constitution grants these and other rights to citizens, over the years laws and court decisions have identified limits on those rights in the workplaces. For example, an employee who voices threats against other employees may face disciplinary action by the employer without the employee's freedom of speech being threatened. However, today management rights have been restrained as employee rights have been expanded.

Rights and Responsibilities Issues

Rights That which belongs to a person by law, nature, or tradition.

Generally, rights do not exist in the abstract. Instead they exist only when someone is successful in demanding their application. **Rights** belong to a person by law, nature, or tradition. Of course, defining a right presents considerable potential for disagreement. For example, does an employee have a right to privacy of communication in personal matters when using the employer's computer on company time? (The opening HR Insights in this chapter provides a good example). Moreover, *legal* rights may or may not correspond to certain *moral* rights, and the reverse is true as well, which opens up "rights" to controversy and lawsuits.

Responsibilities Obligations to be accountable for actions.

Rights are offset by **responsibilities**, which are obligations to be accountable for actions. Employment is a reciprocal relationship (both sides have rights and obligations). For example, if an employee has the right to a safe working environment, then the employer must have an obligation to provide a safe workplace. If the employer has a right to expect uninterrupted, high-quality work from the employee, then the worker has the responsibility to be on the job and meet job performance standards. The reciprocal nature of rights and responsibilities suggests that both parties to an employment relationship should regard the other as having equal rights and should treat the other with respect.

Statutory Rights

Statutory rights Rights based on laws.

Employees' **statutory rights** are the result of specific laws or statutes passed by federal, state, or local governments. Various federal, state, and local laws have granted employees certain rights at work, such as equal employment opporttunity, collective bargaining, and workplace safety. These laws and their interpretations also have been the subjects of a considerable number of court cases.

Contractual Rights

Contractual rights Rights based on a specific contractual agreement between employer and employee.

An employee's **contractual rights** are based on a specific contract agreement with an employer. For instance, a union and an employer may agree on a labor contract that specifies certain terms, conditions, and rights that employees have with the employer.

Contracts formalize the employment relationship. For instance, when hiring an independent contractor or consultant, the employer would use a contract to spell out the work to be performed, expected time lines, parameters, and costs and fees to be incurred. Formal contracts are also used in a **separation agreement**, when employees who are being terminated agree not to sue the employer in exchange for specified benefits, such as additional severance pay or other considerations. Contractual rights can be spelled out formally in written employment contracts or implied in employer handbooks and policies disseminated to employees.

Separation agreement Agreement in which a terminated employee agrees not to sue the employer in exchange for specified benefits.

Employment contract Agreement that formally outlines the details of employment.

Employment Contracts A formal **employment contract** outlines the details of an employment agreement. These written contracts often are very detailed. Traditionally, employment contracts have been used mostly for executives and senior managers, but the use of employment contracts is filtering down the organization to include scarce-skilled, highly specialized professionals and technical employees.

Figure 16-1 depicts common employment contract provisions. Typically an identification section lists the parties to the contract, and the general nature of

Figure 16-1   *Typical Employment Contract Provisions*

Employment Contract

- Terms and conditions of employment
- General job duties and expectations
- Compensation and benefits
- Confidentiality and secrecy
- Non-piracy and non-compete agreements
- Non-solicitation of current employees upon departure
- Termination/Resignation

Date: _____
Employee's signature: _____
Company respresentative's signature: _____

Seal

Non-compete agreement
Agreement that prohibits an individual who leaves the organization from competing with the employer in the same line of business for a specified period of time.

the employee's job duties. The level of compensation and types of benefits often are addressed including any special compensation, benefits, incentives, or perquisites to be provided by the employer. The employment contract also may note whether the employment relationship is to be for an indeterminate time, or whether it can be renewed automatically after a specified period of time. Typically, employment contracts indicate that employment can be terminated at the will of either the employer or employee, or for just cause. The contract also may spell out the severance agreement, continuation of benefits, and other factors related to employees leaving the employer.

Typical Employment Contract Provisions Depending upon the organization and individuals involved, employment agreements may contain a number of different provisions including the key ones highlighted next.

Under common law employers have legal rights to protect their *intellectual property* and *trade secrets* from leaving with employees. In fact, a 1996 federal law made the theft of trade secrets a federal crime punishable by fines up to $5,000,000 and 15 years in jail. Employer rights include the following:[2]

- The right to keep trade secrets confidential
- The right to have employees bring business opportunities to the employer first before pursuing them elsewhere
- A common law copyright for works prepared by employees for their employers

Common as a separate contract or as a clause in an employment contract are **non-compete agreements** that prohibit individuals who leave the organization from competing with the employer in the same line of business for a specified period of time. Sometimes these agreements may be written to be so restrictive that they prohibit an individual from earning a living, which affects how enforceable they are in state courts.[3] Non-compete agreements may present both legal and ethical drawbacks for the employer as discussed in the HR Perspective. Consequently some employers have considered other alternatives.[4]

Employment contracts also may contain *non-piracy agreements* that bar former employees from soliciting business from former customers and clients for a specified period of time. Also, clauses requiring *non-solicitation of current employees* can be incorporated into employment agreements, in order to prevent a former employee from contacting or encouraging co-workers at the former firm to join a different company.

Implied Contracts

The idea that a contract (even an implied or unwritten one) exists between individuals and their employers affects the employment relationship. The rights and responsibilities of the employee may be spelled out in a job description, in an employment contract, in HR policies or a handbook, but often are not. The rights and responsibilities of the employee may also exist *only* as unwritten employer expectations about what is acceptable behavior or performance on the part of the employee. For instance, a number of court decisions have held that if an employer hires someone for an indefinite period or promises job security, the employer has created an implied contract. Such promises establish employee expectations. When the employer fails to follow up on the implied promises, the employee may pursue remedies in court. Numerous federal and state court deci-

Ethics, Intellectual Property, and Noncompetes

Does an employer own what employees know? In an increasingly cut-throat business environment, more employers are restricting for whom former employees can work, how they can use their new ideas, and even with whom they can associate.

Employers have long sought to keep their intellectual property secret from competitors, information theft continues to rise. It is not just at high-tech firms either. For example, Starbucks employees may be required to sign confidentiality and/or non-compete agreements. Wal-Mart sued Amazon.com saying the online retailer lured away specific employees who knew strategic information about Wal-Mart. Monster.com sued 18 workers, accusing them of conspiring to steal confidential marketing information. The company later dropped the suit, paid a $71,000 settlement, and denied that the purpose had been to intimidate workers.

The high-tech industry in particular has struggled with the issues of proprietary information and the protection of it, because information or ideas can be the key to innovative products and services. For example, Lucent Technologies sued 10 former employees who left to work for Cisco Systems. The engineers who left had information on Lucent's optical networking business.

Problems arise when non-compete agreements severely limit an employee or ex-employee's job opportunities. Some even bar laid-off workers from calling their colleagues at work to meet for lunch. Employees often must sign such agreements to get severance pay when they have been laid off or have chosen to resign. But, critics say the agreements can keep laid-off workers from finding other jobs.

Albert Erisman suggests that technology has made the ethical issues more difficult. It is easy enough to reject the idea of robbing the company's cash box as being unethical (and illegal), but what about using the company's laptop computer to surf the Web at home? The intangibility of some corporate assets blurs the distinction at times of what belongs to the employee and what belongs to the company. Intangibles like "knowledge" present special difficulties.

Both companies and employees face the dilemma of determining the ethical limits of declaring "work time" when an employee returns a client's phone call on the way to a child's soccer game in the employee's own car or reads company e-mail from home at night. Whose time is it and how should it be compensated?

Erisman notes that old-fashioned ethics still apply. The principles of right and wrong still exist. But now more subtle ways of violating trust, privacy, and misusing assets has made knowing what is ethical more difficult.[5]

sions have held that such implied promises, especially when contained in an employee handbook, constitute a contract between an employer and its employees, even without a signed document.

Employment Practices Liability Insurance (EPLI)

Workplace litigation has reached epidemic proportion as employees who feel that their rights have been violated sue their employers. Contracts alone do not guarantee an employer will not be sued and lose. On one side, advocates for expanding employee rights warn that management policies abridging free speech, privacy, or due process will lead to further national legislation to regulate the employer-employee relationship. On the other, HR professionals argue that they must protect management's traditional prerogatives to hire, promote, transfer, or terminate employees as they see fit, or the effectiveness of the organization may be affected.

As a result, some employers have purchased insurance to try and cover their risks from numerous lawsuits. Employment practices liability insurance (EPLI) is purchased by employers for amounts ranging from $5,000 to hundreds of thousands of dollars, depending on the industry of the employer and the size of an employer's workforce.[6] The EPLI policies typically cover employer costs for legal fees, settlements, and judgments associated with employment-related actions. Insurance carriers provide coverage for some or all of the following employment-related lawsuits:

- Discrimination
- Sexual harassment
- Wrongful termination
- Breach of employment contract
- Negligent evaluation
- Failure to employ or promote

- Wrongful discipline
- Deprivation of career opportunity
- Infliction of emotional distress
- Improper management of employee benefits

To determine the level of risk and premiums to be charged to employers wanting EPLI, most insurance carriers conduct reviews of employers' HR policies and practices. This review may include a detailed look at an employer's HR policy manuals, employee handbooks, employment forms, and other items. Also, the employer's history of employment-related charges and complaints over the past three to five years is reviewed.[7]

As employees increasingly regard themselves as free agents in the workplace—and as the power of unions declines—the struggle between individual employee and employer "rights" is heightening. Employers frequently do not fare well in court. Further, it is not only the employer that is liable in many cases. Individual managers and supervisors have been found liable when hiring or promotion decisions have been based on discriminatory factors, or when they have had knowledge of such conduct and have not taken steps to stop it.

Rights Affecting the Employment Relationship

Several other legal concepts often influence the employment relationship: employment-at-will, due process, dismissal for just cause, and dispute resolution.

Employment-at-Will

Employment-at-will (EAW)
A common law doctrine stating that employers have the right to hire, fire, demote, or promote whomever they choose, unless there is a law or contract to the contrary.

Employment-at-will (EAW) is a common law doctrine stating that employers have the right to hire, fire, demote, or promote whomever they choose, unless there is a law or contract to the contrary. Conversely, employees can quit whenever they want and go to another job under the same constraints. Figure 16-2 presents a sample employment-at-will statement. Employers often defend EAW based on one or more of the following reasons:

- The rights of private ownership of a business guarantees EAW.
- EAW defends employees' rights to change jobs, as well as employers' rights to hire and fire.
- Interfering with EAW reduces productivity in a firm and in the economy.

In the past three decades numerous state courts have questioned the *fairness* of an employer's decision to fire an employee without just cause and due process. Many suits have stressed that employees' job rights must be balanced against EAW.[8]

Figure 16-2 ▶ Sample Employment-at-Will Statement

EMPLOYMENT AT WILL

The policies stated in this handbook are guidelines only and with the exception of our policy on at-will employment, as described below, are subject to change at the sole discretion of the Employer, as are all other policies, procedures, benefits, or other programs of the Employer. This handbook is not a contract, express or implied, guaranteeing employment for any specific duration. Although we hope that your employment relationship with us will be long term, either you or the Employer may terminate this relationship at any time, for any reason, with or without cause or notice.

Please understand that no supervisor, manager, or representative of the Employer other than the [e.g., president] has the authority to enter into any agreement with you for employment for any specified period of time or to make any promises or commitments contrary to the foregoing. Further, any employment agreement entered into by the [e.g., president] shall not be enforceable unless it is in a formal written agreement and signed by you and the [e.g., president]. Please also understand, that no supervisor, manager, or other representative of the Employer, has the authority to make any verbal promises, commitments, or statements of any kind regarding the Employer's policies, procedures, or any other issues that are legally binding on the Employer.

EAW and the Courts In general, the courts have recognized three different rationales for hearing EAW cases.

- *Public policy exception:* This exception to EAW holds that an employee can sue if he or she was fired for a reason that violates public policy. For example, if an employee refused to commit perjury and was fired, he or she could sue.
- *Implied employment contract:* This approach holds that the employee will not be fired as long as he or she does the job. Long service, promises of continued employment, and lack of criticism of job performance imply continuing employment.
- *Good faith and fair dealing:* This approach suggests that a covenant of good faith and fair dealing exists between the employer and at-will employees. If the employer breaks this covenant by unreasonable behavior, the employee may seek legal recourse.

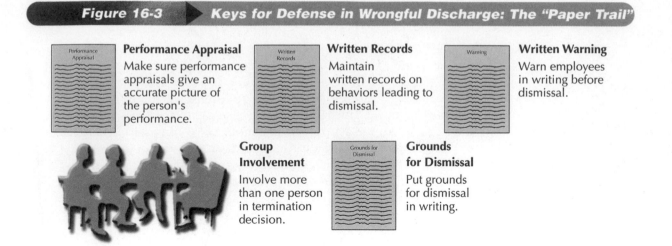

Figure 16-3 ▶ **Keys for Defense in Wrongful Discharge: The "Paper Trail"**

Performance Appraisal
Make sure performance appraisals give an accurate picture of the person's performance.

Written Records
Maintain written records on behaviors leading to dismissal.

Written Warning
Warn employees in writing before dismissal.

Group Involvement
Involve more than one person in termination decision.

Grounds for Dismissal
Put grounds for dismissal in writing.

Nearly all states have enacted one or more statutes to limit an employer's right to discharge employees. The national restrictions include the use of race, age, sex, national origin, religion, and disabilities. Restrictions on other areas vary from state to state.

Wrongful discharge
Occurs when an employer terminates an individual's employment for reasons that are improper or illegal.

Wrongful Discharge Employers who run afoul of EAW restrictions may be found guilty of **wrongful discharge,** which occurs when an employer terminates an individual's employment for reasons that are illegal or improper. Some state courts have recognized certain nonstatutory grounds for wrongful-discharge suits. Additionally, courts generally have held that unionized workers cannot pursue EAW actions as at-will employees because they are covered by the grievance arbitration process. The lesson of wrongful discharge suits is that employers should take care to see that dismissals are handled properly, that all HR management systems are in order, and that due process and fair play are observed.[9] Figure 16-3 offers suggestions for preparing a defense against any such lawsuits.

A landmark court case in wrongful discharge was *Fortune v. National Cash Register Company.* The case involved the firing of a salesperson (Fortune) who had been with National Cash Register (NCR) for 25 years.[10] Fortune's termination came shortly after he won a large order that would have earned him a big commission. From the evidence, the court concluded that he was wrongfully discharged because NCR wanted to avoid paying him the commission, which violated the covenant of good faith and fair dealings.

Wrongful discharge lawsuits have become a major concern for many firms. Compensatory awards for wrongful termination cases lost by employers can run more than $200,000 and employers are as likely to lose the lawsuits as to win them.

Just Cause

Just cause Reasonable justification for taking employment-related actions.

What constitutes a "good reason" or **just cause** for disciplinary actions such as dismissal can usually be found in union contracts, but not in at-will situations. Even though definitions of *just cause* vary, the courts use well-defined criteria as shown in Figure 16-4.

Just cause is about fairness. To be viewed by others as being *just,* any disciplinary action must be based on facts in each individual case.

Generally *not* viewed as just cause is the act of **constructive discharge,** which occurs when an employer deliberately makes conditions intolerable in an attempt to get an employee to quit. Under normal circumstances, an employee who resigns rather than being dismissed cannot later collect damages for violation of legal rights. An exception to this rule occurs when the courts find that the working conditions were made so intolerable as to *force* a reasonable employee to resign. Then, the resignation is considered a discharge. For example, an employee was told he should resign but refused. He was then given lesser assignments, publicly ridiculed by his supervisor, and threatened each day with dismissal. He finally resigned and sued his employer. The judge in the case held that the employee had been "constructively discharged" and ordered his employer to pay damages because it forced him to resign. Figure 16-4 shows legal criteria used for just cause, as well as due process.

Constructive discharge Occurs when an employer deliberately makes conditions intolerable in an attempt to get an employee to quit.

Due Process

Due process, like just cause, is also about fairness.[11] **Due process** addresses the fairness of means used to determine employee wrongdoing and/or disciplinary measures, and includes the opportunity for individuals to explain and defend their actions. Figure 16-4 shows some factors to be considered when evaluating whether an individual received due process. How HR managers and their employers address these factors of just cause and due process figures prominently in whether the courts perceive employers' actions as fair.[12]

Due process Means used for individuals to explain and defend their actions against charges or discipline.

Distributive Justice and Procedural Justice Employees' perceptions of fairness or justice in their treatment depend on at least two other factors. First, people prefer *favorable outcomes* for themselves. They decide the favorability of their outcomes by comparing them with the outcomes of others, given their relative situations. This decision involves the concept of **distributive justice**, which deals with the question: Were outcomes distributed fairly? Fairness would not include disciplinary action being based on favoritism or the punishment being seen as inappropriate for the offense.

Distributive justice Perceived fairness in the distribution of outcomes.

Figure 16-4 ▶ *Criteria for Just Cause and Due Process*

Just Cause Determinants
- Was the employee warned of the consequences of the conduct?
- Was the employer's rule reasonable?
- Did management investigate before disciplining?
- Was the investigation fair and impartial?
- Was there evidence of guilt?
- Were the rules and penalties applied in an evenhanded fashion?
- Was the penalty reasonable, given the offense?

Due Process Considerations
- How have precedents been handled?
- Is a complaint process available?
- Was the complaint process used?
- Was retaliation used against the employee?
- Was a decision made based on facts?
- Were the actions and processes viewed as "fair" by outside entities?

Procedural justice Perceived fairness of the process used to make decisions about employees.

The other factor, **procedural justice**, focuses on whether the *procedures* that led to an action were appropriate, clear and provided opportunity for employee input. It deals with the question: Was the decision-making process fair? If organizations provide procedural justice, employees tend to respond with positive behaviors that benefit the organization in return.[13]

Complaints and Due Process For unionized employees, due process usually refers to the right to use the grievance procedure specified in the union contract. Due process may involve including specific steps in the grievance process, imposing time limits, following arbitration procedures, and providing knowledge of disciplinary penalties. More discussion of the grievance process and procedures in unions can be found in Chapter 17.

Compared with due process procedures specified in union contracts, procedures for at-will employees are more varied and may address a broader range of issues. Non-union organizations generally benefit by having formal complaint procedures that provide due process for their employees. Just the presence of such a formal complaint mechanism provides one indicator that an employee has been given due process. Further, if employees view a due process procedure as fair and available for use, they may be less likely to sue their employer.

Alternative Dispute Resolutions (ADR) as Due Process

Disputes between management and employees over different work issues are normal and inevitable. How they resolve their disputes becomes important. Formal grievance procedures or lawsuits provide two methods to resolve disputes. However, more and more companies look to alternative means of ensuring that due process occurs in cases involving employee rights. Dissatisfaction with the expense and delays common in the court system when lawsuits are filed explains the growth in alternative dispute resolution (ADR) methods such as arbitration, peer review panels, and ombudsmen.

Arbitration Process that uses a neutral third party to make a decision.

Arbitration Because employers and employees do not always agree, disagreements often mean lawsuits and large legal bills to determine settlement. One alternative, **arbitration,** uses a neutral third party to make a decision, thereby eliminating the necessity of using the court system. While arbitration has been a common feature of union contracts, a growing number of employers are requiring that arbitration be used to settle non-union employment-related disputes.

Many firms use *compulsory arbitration,* which requires employees to sign a pre-employment agreement stating that all disputes will be submitted to arbitration, and that employees waive their rights to pursue legal action until the completion of the arbitration process. However, because employers often select the arbitrators, and because arbitrators may not be required to issue written decisions and opinions, many critics see the use of arbitration in employment-related situations as unfair.[14] For instance, a stockbroker who was fired was unable to pursue her sex discrimination claim because she had signed a mandatory arbitration clause when joining the brokerage firm 13 years earlier.

Continuing pressure from state courts, federal employment regulatory commissions, and additional cases have challenged the fairness of compulsory arbitration in some situations. However, a U.S. Supreme Court decision in *Circuit City v. Adams* held that requiring arbitration as a condition of employment is

Logging On...

American Arbitration Association
Information and resources on arbitration can be found at this Web site.

www.adr.org

Figure 16-5 ▶ Examples of Four-Step ADR Approaches

Paine-Webber Approach	Science Applications International Corporation Approach
1. *"Open-door":* Employee is encouraged to work dispute out with supervisor.	1. **Management review committee:** *Supervisor, division manager, operations manager, and group manager convene early on in dispute.*
2. **Toll Free "hotline":** *An in-house issues resolution office is staffed by people who act as "ombudsmen."*	2. **Appeals committee:** *Composed of peers chosen by the employee, VP HR, and Operations Manager, the committee provides remedies except punitive damages.*
3. **Mediation:** *Outside neutral mediator is hired and the company pays all costs except attorney fees.*	3. **Mediation:** *Company and employee agree on mediator. Company pays all but $50.*
4. **Binding arbitration:** *Arbitrator uses AAA employment dispute rules and company pays up to 75% of costs.*	4. **Binding arbitration:** *Arbitrator is chosen from AAA list, who has final and binding judgment. Employee pays $150 and company pays the rest.*

Source: Adapted from "HR Shop Talk," *Bulletin to Management,* May 25, 2000, 166; and "Alternative Dispute Resolution," *Bulletin to Management,* August 3, 2001, 247.

legal, but the option remains unpopular with lawyers who earn fees bringing employment lawsuits.[15]

Arbitration must be set up carefully if an employer wants to use it.[16] Often employers utilize the resources from the American Arbitration Association (AAA). Two different approaches to arbitration used by different employers are shown in Figure 16-5.

Peer Review Panels Some employers allow employees to appeal disciplinary actions to an internal committee of employees. A **peer review panel** composed of employees hears appeals from disciplined employees and makes recommendations or decisions. Peer review panels provide review by a jury of peers at work. Panel members, a specially trained group of volunteers, sign confidentiality agreements, after which the company empowers them to hear appeals.

Such bodies can serve as the last stage of a formal complaint process for non-union employees, and their use has reduced the likelihood of unhappy employees filing lawsuits. Also, if an employee files a lawsuit, the employer presents a stronger case if a peer group of employees previously reviewed the employer's decision and found it to be appropriate. In general, these panels reverse management decisions much less often than might be expected.

Organizational Ombudsman Some organizations ensure process fairness through use of an **ombudsman,** who is a person outside the normal chain of command who acts as a problem solver for both management and employees. Many universities and private firms use ombudsmen to address employees' complaints.

Peer review panel A panel of employees hear appeals from disciplined employees and make recommendations or decisions.

Ombudsman Person outside the normal chain of command who acts as a problem solver for both management and employees.

Balancing Employer Security Concerns and Employee Rights

Privacy and American Business
This nonprofit organization is a leading resource for information on new and existing business privacy issues.

http://www.pandab.org

An individual's **right to privacy** is defined in legal terms as the freedom from unauthorized and unreasonable intrusion into their personal affairs. Although the right to privacy is not specifically identified in the U.S. Constitution, a number of past Supreme Court cases have established that such a right must be considered. Also, several states have enacted right-to-privacy statutes. Additionally, federal acts related to privacy have been passed, some of which affect HR policies and priorities in organizations.[17]

The growing use of technology in organizations is making it more difficult to balance employer security rights with employee privacy concerns. Although computers, cameras, and telecommunications systems are transforming many workplaces, the usage of these items by employers to monitor employee actions is raising concerns that the privacy rights of employees are being threatened.[18]

On one side, employers have a legitimate need to ensure that employees are performing their jobs properly in a secure environment. On the other side, employees have expectations that the rights to privacy that they have outside of work also exist at work. Even though these two views may seem clear, balancing them becomes more difficult when addressing such issues as access to employee records, employees' freedom of speech, workplace performance monitoring and surveillance, employer investigations, and substance abuse and drug testing.

Chief Privacy Officer

Privacy issues present a sufficient concern that has led some organizations to appoint someone with responsibility for watching over the privacy of both customers and employees. Often called a chief privacy officer (CPO), the position can be found at MasterCard, IBM, Citigroup, Sony, and many others. Today such positions number about 300. But some detractors have called a CPO a public relations ploy. The privacy concerns of consumers especially lead to a need to supervise these issues, and employee privacy issues find their way into the mix as well.[19]

Rights Issues and Employee Records

As a result of concerns about protecting individual privacy rights, the Privacy Act of 1974 was passed. It includes provisions affecting HR record-keeping systems. This law applies *only* to federal agencies and organizations supplying services to the federal government; but similar state laws, somewhat broader in scope, also have been passed. For the most part, state rather than federal law regulates private employers on this issue. Public-sector employees are permitted greater access to their files in most states than private-sector employees. The following legal issues concern employee rights to privacy and HR records:

- Access personal information
- Respond to unfavorable information
- Correct erroneous information
- Know when information is given to a third party

Figure 16-6 ▶ *Employee Record Files*

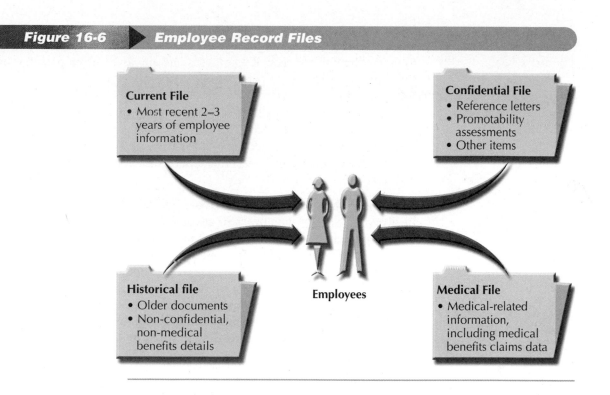

Americans with Disabilities Act (ADA) and Employee Medical Records Record-keeping and retention practices have been affected by the following provisions in the Americans with Disabilities Act (ADA):

> *Information from all medical examinations and inquiries must be kept apart from general personnel files as a separate confidential medical record available only under limited conditions specified in the ADA.*

As interpreted by attorneys and HR practitioners, this provision requires that all medical-related information be maintained separately from all other confidential files. As a result of all the legal restrictions, many employers have established several separate files on each employee, as illustrated in Figure 16-6.

Security of Employee Records The following guidelines are offered regarding employer access and storage of employee records:

- Restrict access to records to a limited number of individuals.
- Utilize confidential passwords for accessing employee records in an HRIS database.
- Set up separate files and restricted databases for especially sensitive employee information.
- Inform employees of types of data retained.
- Purge employee records of outdated data.
- Release employee information only with employee's consent.

It is important that specific access restrictions and security procedures for employee records be established. These restrictions and procedures are designed to protect both the privacy of employees and employers from potential liability for improper disclosure of personal information.

Employees' Free Speech Rights

The right of individuals to have freedom of speech is protected by the U.S. Constitution. However, that freedom is *not* an unrestricted one in the workplace. Three areas in which employees' freedom of speech have collided with employers' restrictions are discussed next.

Employee Advocacy of Controversial Views One area of free speech involves the right of employees to advocate controversial viewpoints at work. Numerous examples can be cited. For instance, can an employee of a tobacco company join in antismoking demonstrations outside of work, or can a disgruntled employee at a non-union employer wear a union badge on his cap at work? In situations such as these, employers must follow due process procedures and demonstrate that disciplinary actions taken against employees can be justified for job-related reasons. These precautions become especially important when dealing with whistle-blowing situations.

Whistle-blowers Individuals who report real or perceived wrongs committed by their employers.

Whistle-Blowing Individuals who report real or perceived wrongs committed by their employers are called **whistle-blowers.** Employers need to address two key questions in regard to whistle-blowing: (1) When do employees have the right to speak out with protection from retribution? (2) When do employees violate the confidentiality of their jobs by speaking out? Even though the answers maybe difficult to determine, retaliation against whistle-blowers clearly is not allowed, based on a number of court decisions.

Whistle-blowers are less likely to lose their jobs in public employment than in private employment, because most civil service systems follow rules protecting whistle-blowers. However, no comprehensive whistle-blowing law fully protects the right to free speech of both public and private employees. Many whistle-blowing incidents occur annually.[20]

Monitoring of E-Mail and Voice Mail Both e-mail and voice-mail systems increasingly are seen by employers as areas where employers have a right to monitor what is said and transmitted. Information and telecommunications technological advances have become a major issue for employers regarding employee privacy. The use of e-mail and voice mail increases every day, also raising each employer's liability if they improperly monitor or inspect employee electronic communications.

To address the various concerns regarding monitoring of e-mail and voice mail, many employers have established policies with the following elements:

- Voice mail, e-mail, and computer files are provided by the employer and are for business use only.
- Use of these media for personal reasons is restricted and subject to employer review.
- All computer passwords and codes must be available to the employer.
- The employer reserves the right to monitor or search any of the media, without notice, for business purposes.

WEST GROUP
A THOMSON COMPANY
E-Mail Communications Policy
Provides sample e-mail and electronic communications policy.
Custom Search:
☑ POLICIES
Phrase: E-mail and communications

Figure 16-7 ▸ **Keeping Tabs on Employees Online**

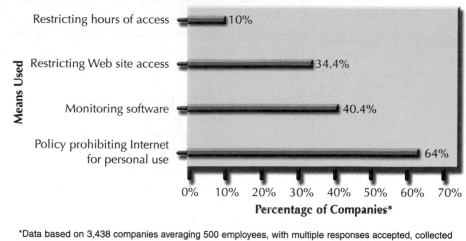

*Data based on 3,438 companies averaging 500 employees, with multiple responses accepted, collected by Data Management Recruiters International.
Source: Based on data in "Keeping Tabs on Employees Online," *Business Week,* February 19, 2001, 16.

One of the problems with e-mail includes the way most people express themselves in e-mail, which is closer to conversation than formal memos. This tendency can create sloppy, racist, sexist, or otherwise defamatory messages. Further, messages can be sent rapidly to multiple (sometimes incorrect) recipients. Also, e-mail can be stored, and a growing number of legal cases hinge on e-mails that can be retrieved.[21]

The most important actions that every employer can take to decrease potential exposure to lawsuits include: (1) creating an *electronic communications policy;* (2) informing employees and having them *sign an acknowledgment;* (3) *strictly enforcing* every portion of the policy, and (4) *monitoring usage* for business purposes only.

Tracking Employee Internet Usage About 90% of employees admit to visiting non-work Web sites during work hours and many companies are watching them do it. The numbers vary, but as many as 74% of firms always or sometimes monitor employees' Internet usage.[22] Through this monitoring, employers attempt to guard against some employees accessing pornographic or other Web sites that could create problems for employers. If law enforcement investigations are conducted, the employer could be accused of aiding and abetting illegal behavior. Therefore, many employers have purchased software that tracks the Web sites accessed by employees. Also, some employers use software programs for blocking certain categories and Web sites inappropriate for business use. Figure 16-7 shows some of the steps that businesses take.

Another concern about Internet usage is the common practice of composing and/or forwarding personal messages to and from others outside the company. For instance, individuals may receive jokes or other items clearly not business related, and then may forward them to co-workers and friends both inside and outside the organization. At one financial services firm, some African-American employees filed race discrimination charges against their employer because of racist jokes forwarded to them and others in the firm. Ultimately the firm resolved the complaint by firing the two executives transmitting the jokes.

A growing number of employers have developed and disseminated Internet usage policies. Communicating these policies to employees, enforcing them by monitoring employee Internet usage, and disciplining offenders are the ways employers ensure that appropriate usage of the Internet access occurs.[23]

Workplace Performance Monitoring and Surveillance

Federal constitutional rights, such as the right to protection from unreasonable search and seizure, protect an individual only against the activities of the government. Thus, employees of both private-sector and governmental employers can be monitored, observed, and searched at work by representatives of the employer. Several court decisions reaffirmed this principle, which held that both private-sector and government employers may search desks and files without search warrants if they believe that work rules were violated.[24] Often, employers use workplace searches and surveillance as part of employee performance monitoring. Employers also conduct workplace investigations for theft and other illegal behavior.

Employee Performance Monitoring Employee performance may be monitored to measure performance, ensure performance quality and customer service, check for theft, or enforce company rules or laws. Performance monitoring occurs with truck drivers, nurses, teleservice customer service representatives, and many other jobs.[25] The common concern in a monitored workplace usually does not center on whether monitoring should be used, but how it should be conducted, how the information should be used, and how feedback should be communicated to employees.

"Oh, can't complain."

At a minimum, employers should obtain a signed employee consent form that indicates performance monitoring and taping of phone calls will occur regularly.

Also, it is recommended that employers provide feedback to employees on monitoring results to help employees improve their performance and to commend them for good performance. For example, one major catalog retailer allows employees to listen to their customer service calls and rate their own performance. Then the employees meet with their supervisors to discuss both positive and negative performance issues.

Video Surveillance at Work Numerous employers have installed video surveillance systems in workplaces. Sometimes these video systems are used to ensure employee security, such as in parking lots, garages, and dimly lit exterior areas. Other employers have installed them in retail sales floors, production areas, parts and inventory rooms, and lobbies. But it is when video surveillance is extended into employee restrooms, changing rooms, and other more private areas, that employer rights and employee privacy collide. As with other forms of surveillance, it is important that employers develop a video surveillance policy, inform employees about it, do it only for legitimate business purposes, and strictly limit those who view the video surveillance results.

Investigating Misconduct
Provides guidelines for investigating charges of employee misconduct.
Custom Search:
☑ ANALYSIS
Phrase: Investigating employee misconduct

Employer Investigations

Another area of concern regarding employee rights involves workplace investigations. The U.S. Constitution protects public-sector employees in the areas of due process, search and seizure, and privacy, but employees in the private sector are not protected. Whether at work or off the job, unethical or illegal employee behavior is becoming an increasingly serious problem for organizations. Employee misconduct may include theft, illegal drug use, falsification of documents, misuse of company funds, disclosure of organizational secrets, workplace violence, employment discrimination, workers compensation misuse and much more.

Investigations may be conducted by outside investigators—the police or a private investigator. But sometimes management becomes involved, such as the case in which a female employee downloaded the company's client list to a disk and put it in her purse. She was confronted and asked to submit to a search. With this type of situation, experts recommend the following:[26]

- Do not touch the person.
- Have two managers witness the search (one the same sex as the suspect).
- If the employee refuses the search, make it clear the person will be immediately terminated.
- Call the police about the suspected theft if time permits.

Employee Theft

An increasing problem faced by employers is theft of employer property and vital company secrets. According to one study, workplace theft and fraud have resulted in a 6% increase in the prices charged by employers to consumers, and employee theft has now reached higher dollar amounts than shoplifting loss.[27] For instance, employee theft is estimated to cost retailers over $12 billion per year. Some major retailers have even joined forces to create a Theftnet database of workers who have confessed to theft, and all job applicants are checked to see if

Figure 16-8 ▶ **Methods of Dealing with Workplace Theft**

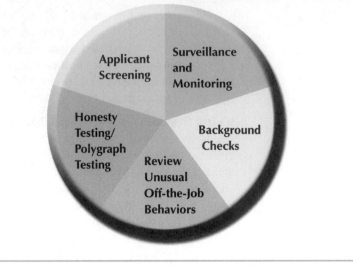

they appear in Theftnet. Any person appearing in Theftnet is not hired. Other methods provide ways to deal with employee theft and other misconduct. Figure 16-8 shows some of the most common ones.

Polygraph and Honesty Testing The theory behind a polygraph is that the act of lying produces stress, which in turn causes observable physical changes. An examiner can thus interpret the physical responses to specific questions and make a judgment as to whether the person being tested is practicing deception. However, the Polygraph Protection Act prohibits the use of polygraphs for most preemployment screening and for judging a person's honesty while employed.

"Pencil-and-paper" honesty tests show recent gains in popularity. The tests do not fall within the restrictions of the Polygraph Protection Act or the laws of most states. Many organizations use this alternative to polygraph testing, with more than two dozen variations of such tests available. But as discussed in Chapter 8, there are problems with using these tests, and their use has been challenged successfully in some court decisions.

Behavior Off the Job Employers encounter special difficulty in establishing "just cause" for disciplining employees for their off-the-job behavior. Most people believe an employer should not control the lives of its employees off the job except in the case of clear job-related consequences. However, in general, disciplinary action for off-the-job behavior of employees unsettles both employers and employees. Further, the general public remains leery of employers' investigating the off-the-job behavior of their workers. Many workers believe that their employers have no right to monitor or question employees' private lives, lifestyles, and off-work activities.

Employee Substance Abuse and Employer Drug Testing

The issues of substance abuse and drug testing at work has received a great deal of attention.[28] The importance of the problem to HR management is clear as

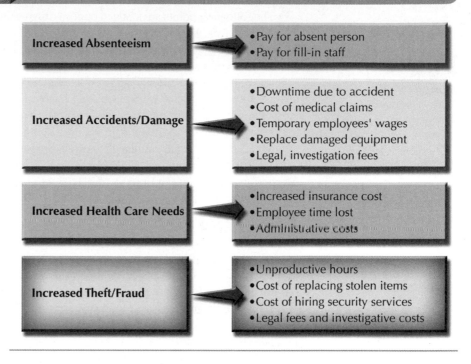

Figure 16-9 **Financial Impact of Substance Abuse on Employers**

Increased Absenteeism
- Pay for absent person
- Pay for fill-in staff

Increased Accidents/Damage
- Downtime due to accident
- Cost of medical claims
- Temporary employees' wages
- Replace damaged equipment
- Legal, investigation fees

Increased Health Care Needs
- Increased insurance cost
- Employee time lost
- Administrative costs

Increased Theft/Fraud
- Unproductive hours
- Cost of replacing stolen items
- Cost of hiring security services
- Legal fees and investigative costs

Figure 16-9 indicates. Concern about substance abuse at work also is appropriate, given that accident rates, absenteeism, and workers' compensation costs are higher for workers using illegal substances. The extent of substance abuse problems is seen in U.S. Department of Labor estimates that 70% of all users of illegal drugs are employed, totaling over 10 million people. However, among workers, the rate of drug usage has declined from 18% a decade ago to about 5.5% currently, according to data from a major pharmaceutical firm.[29] Many experts believe that the decline is due to increased usage of workplace drug testing by employers.

WEST GROUP
A THOMSON COMPANY
Drug Free Workplace Act
Contains commentary on the act and a sample drug use policy.
Custom Search:
☑ ANALYSIS
Phrase: DFWA

Drug-Free Workplace Act of 1988 The U.S. Supreme Court has ruled that certain drug-testing plans do not violate the Constitution. Private employer programs are governed mainly by state laws, which can currently be called a confusing hodgepodge. The Drug-Free Workplace Act requires government contractors to take steps to eliminate employee drug usage. Failure to do so can lead to contract termination. Tobacco and alcohol do not qualify as controlled substances under the act, and off-the-job drug use is not included. Additionally, the U.S. Department of Transportation (DOT) requires regular testing of truck and bus drivers, train crews, mass-transit employees, airline pilots and mechanics, pipeline workers, and licensed sailors.[30]

Drug Testing and Employee Rights Disciplinary action of an employee because of substance-abuse problems must be done only in keeping with the due process described in an employer's policy. Unless state or local law prohibits testing, employers have a right to require applicants or employees to submit to a

drug test. Random drug testing of current employees may be more controversial, and public agencies must show "probable cause" to conduct drug tests.

The following points are made to oppose drug testing: (1) It violates employees' rights. (2) Drugs may not affect job performance in every case. (3) Employers may abuse the results of tests. (4) Drug tests may be inaccurate. (5) The results can be misinterpreted.

It is interesting to note the apparent change in employee attitudes toward drug testing. Experience with workplace drug problems tends to make managers and employees less tolerant of drug users. Drug testing appears to be most acceptable to employees when they see the procedures being used as fair, and when characteristics of the job (such as danger to other people) require that the employee be alert and fully functioning. *Procedural justice* becomes an important issue in perceptions of fairness of drug testing, but drug testing raises less concern about employee rights than it once did.

Types of Drug Tests The most common tests for drug use are urinalysis, radio immunoassay of hair, and fitness-for-duty testing. Urinalysis is the test used most frequently. It requires a urine sample that must be tested at a lab. Despite concerns about sample switching and the test's ability to detect drug use only over the past few days, urinalysis is generally accurate and well accepted.

Hair radioimmunoassay requires a strand of an employee's hair, which is analyzed for traces of illegal substances. These tests, based on scientific studies, indicate that a relationship exists between drug dosage and the concentration of drugs detected in the hair. A 1.6-inch hair sample provides a 90-day profile. Sample swapping generally proves more difficult than in urinalysis, and the longer time period covered offers testing advantages. However, the testing remains somewhat controversial and is not recommended following accidents, because it cannot detect how recent the drug usage was.[31]

The fitness-for-duty tests discussed in Chapter 15 can be used alone or in conjunction with drug testing. These tests can also distinguish individuals under the influence of alcohol or prescription drugs to the extent their abilities to perform their jobs are impaired.

Conducting Drug Tests Employers who conduct drug tests can do so for both applicants and employees. Pre-employment drug testing is widely used and many believe its use by more employers has contributed to the decline in employee drug use. Employers in some areas report that word spreads among applicants about which employers test and which do not test. Therefore, substance abusers do not even apply to employers who conduct pre-employment drug tests. The rights of those testing positive but not yet employed differ from the rights of employees, according to various court rulings.

Where drug testing is done, employers use one of three different policies: (1) random testing of everyone at periodic intervals; (2) testing only in cases of probable cause; or (3) testing after accidents. Each method raises its own set of problems.

If testing is done for probable-cause reasons, it is important that managers be trained on how to handle such situations. It is important that the actions taken by managers and supervisors be based on performance-related consequences, such as excessive absenteeism or reduced productivity, not just the substance usage itself.[32]

From a policy standpoint, it is most appropriate to test for drugs when the following conditions exist:

- Job consequences of abuse are so severe that they outweigh privacy concerns.
- Accurate test procedures are available.
- Written consent of the employee is obtained.
- Results are treated confidentially, as with any medical record.
- Employers have a complete drug program, including an EAP.

HR Policies, Procedures, and Rules

Policies General guidelines that focus organizational actions.

It is useful at this point to consider some guidelines for HR policies, procedures, and rules. They greatly affect employee rights (just discussed) and discipline (discussed next). Where there is a choice among actions, **policies** act as general guidelines that focus organizational actions. Policies are general in nature, while procedures and rules are specific to the situation. The important role of policies in guiding organizational decision making requires that they be reviewed regularly, because obsolete policies can result in poor decisions. Policy proliferation also must be carefully monitored. Failure to review, add to, or delete policies as situations change may lead to problems.

Procedures Customary methods of handling activities.

Procedures provide for customary methods of handling activities and are more specific than policies. For example, a policy may state that employees will be given vacations. Procedures establish a specific method for authorizing vacation time without disrupting work.

Rules Specific guidelines that regulate and restrict the behavior of individuals.

Rules are specific guidelines that regulate and restrict the behavior of individuals. They are similar to procedures in that they guide action and typically allow no discretion in their application. Rules reflect a management decision that action be taken—or not taken—in a given situation, and they provide more specific behavioral guidelines than policies. For example, see the HR Practice on organizational holiday parties on the next page.

HR Policy Coordination Responsibilities

For policies, procedures, and rules to be effective, coordination between the HR unit and other managers is vital. As Figure 16-10 shows, managers are the main

Figure 16-10	Typical Division of HR Responsibilities: Policies and Rules

HR Unit	Managers
• *Designs formal mechanisms for coordinating HR policies*	• *Help in developing HR policies and rules*
• *Provides advice in development of organization-wide HR policies, procedures, and rules*	• *Review policies and rules with all employees*
• *Provides information on application of HR policies, procedures, and rules*	• *Apply HR policies, procedures, and rules*
• *Explains HR rules to managers*	• *Explain rules and policies to all employees*
• *Trains managers to administer policies, procedures, and rules*	• *Gives feedback on effectiveness of policies and rules*

Rules and Holiday Parties

Who would think that such a common employer practice as holiday parties would require rules? But HR issues arise, and organizations must address them. Companies like to have holiday parties as a way to promote interaction and camaraderie and to say thanks with good food and drink.

However, concern about sexual harassment or other liability claims have resulted in employers establishing party rules. These rules cover everything from how much to drink, to a kiss under the mistletoe.

For example, some employers have issued party guidelines for second- and third-shift workers who go to work after the party. Others limit the number of drinks each person can have, designate drivers, and pull problem partiers aside to make sure they understand the limits of good taste.

The problem usually begins with alcohol usage, but one survey found that 90% of holiday parties serve alcohol anyway; it is apparently expected by employees. Because alcohol reduces inhibitions in some people, an incident at a party (usually coupled with

other events in a chain) can lead to allegations of sexual harassment. Also, a general expansion of "social host liability" over the past years forces organizations to be aware of not letting guests drive after too many drinks, which can lead to lawsuits.

Some employers react to these issues by moving the party away from the office to reduce liability. Other companies handle the problem by doing away with the party all together if the rules do not work. Happy holidays, but follow the rules![33]

users and enforcers of rules, procedures, and policies; and they should receive some training and explanation in how to carry them out. The HR unit supports managers, reviews disciplinary rules, and trains managers to use them. It is critical that any conflict between the two entities be resolved so that employees receive appropriate treatment. Well-designed HR policies should be consistent, necessary, applicable, understandable, reasonable, distributed, and clearly communicated. Often they are provided in employee handbooks.

Employee Handbooks

Employee handbooks give employees a reference source for company policies and rules and can be a positive tool for effective management of human resources. Even smaller organizations can prepare handbooks relatively easily using available computer software. However, management should consider several factors when preparing handbooks.

Legal Review of Language As mentioned earlier, there is a current legal trend to use employee handbooks against employers in lawsuits charging a broken "implied" contract.[34] But the tendency should not eliminate employee handbooks as a way to communicate policies to employees. Not having an employee handbook with HR policies spelled out can also leave an organization open to costly litigation and out-of-court settlements.

Logging On...

SHRM Policy Handbooks
This Web site contains sample policies, procedures and handbooks collected by the Society for Human Resource Management.

http://www.shrm.org/hrlinks/policy/html.

A more sensible approach is first to develop sound HR policies and employee handbooks to communicate them and then have legal counsel review the language contained in them. Recommendations include the following:

- *Eliminate controversial phrases.* For example, "permanent employee" as a phrase often is used to describe those people who have passed a probationary period. This wording can lead to disagreement over what the parties meant by permanent. A more appropriate phrase is "regular employee."

- *Use disclaimers.* Courts generally uphold disclaimers, but only if they are prominently shown in the handbook.[35] However, a trade-off between disclaimers and the image presented by the handbook mean that disclaimers should not be overused. A disclaimer also should appear on application forms. A disclaimer in the handbook can read as follows:

  "This employee handbook is not intended to be a contract or any part of a contractual agreement between the employer and the employee. The employer reserves the right to modify, delete, or add to any policies set forth herein without notice and reserves the right to terminate an employee at any time with or without cause."

- *Keep the handbook current.* Many employers simply add new material to handbooks rather than deleting old, inapplicable rules. Those old rules can become the bases for new lawsuits. Consequently, handbooks and HR policies should be reviewed periodically and revised every few years.

Readability The HR specialists who prepare employee handbooks sometimes fail to write at an appropriate reading level. One review of the reading level of some company handbooks revealed that on average they were written at the third-year college level, which is much higher than the typical reading level of employees in most organizations. One solution is to test the readability of the handbook on a sample of employees before it is published.

WEST GROUP
A THOMSON COMPANY

Employee Handbooks
Discusses reasons for and problems with having employee handbooks.
Custom Search:
☑ ANALYSIS
Phrase: Employee handbooks: pros and cons

Use Another important factor to be considered in preparing an employee handbook is its method of use. Simply giving an employee a handbook and saying, "Here's all the information you need to know," is not sufficient. To communicate and discuss HR information, a growing number of firms are distributing employee handbooks electronically using an intranet, which enables employees to access policies in employee handbooks at any time. Also, changes in policies in the handbook can be made electronically, rather than having to distribute correction pages and memos that must be filed with every handbook. In addition to distributing policies and rules in an employee handbook, it is important that communication about HR issues, policies, rules, and organizational information be disseminated widely.

Communicating HR Information

HR communication focuses on the receipt and dissemination of HR data and information throughout the organization. *Downward communication* flows from top management to the rest of the organization, informing employees about what is and will be happening in the organization, and what top management expectations and goals are. *Upward communication* enables managers to know about the ideas, concerns, and information needs of employees. Various methods are used.

HR Publications and Media Organizations communicate with employees through internal publications and media, including newspapers, company magazines, organizational newsletters, videotapes, Internet postings, and computer technology. Whatever the formal means used, managers should make an honest attempt to communicate information employees need to know. Communication should not be solely a public relations tool to build the image of the organization. Bad news, as well as good news, should be reported objectively in readable style. For example, an airline publication distributed to employees contains a question-and-answer section in which employees anonymously can submit tough questions to management. Management's answers are printed with the questions in every issue. Because every effort is made to give completely honest answers, this section has been very useful. The same idea fizzled in another large company because management answered the questions with "the company line," and employees soon lost interest in the less-than-candid replies.

Some employers produce *audiotapes* or *videotapes* to explain benefit programs, corporate reorganizations, and revised HR policies and programs to employees, especially those in organizational branches. At those locations, employees in groups view the tapes and ask questions of a manager or someone from headquarters. The spread of electronic communications allows for more timely and widespread dissemination of HR information.

Electronic Communication: E-Mail and Teleconferencing As electronic and telecommunications technologies have developed, many employers are adding more technologically based methods of communicating with employees. The growth of information systems in organizations has led to the widespread use of electronic mail. With the advent of e-mail systems, communication through organizations can be almost immediate. E-mail systems can operate worldwide through networks. Replies can be returned at once rather than in a week or more. E-mail systems often result in the bypassing of formal organizational structure and channels. Some organizations also communicate through *teleconferencing,* in which satellite technology links facilities and groups in various locations. In this way, the same message can be delivered simultaneously to various audiences.

Some companies use electronic "message boards" on the company's Web site.[36] Message boards allow communication among management, employees, and others on issues of concern. They can be useful but sometimes problematic as Northwest Airlines discovered when the medium was used to promote a "sick out" and the whole matter ended up in court.[37]

Suggestion system A formal method of obtaining employee input and upward communication.

Suggestion Systems A **suggestion system** is a formal method of obtaining employee input and upward communication. Such programs give employees the opportunity to suggest changes or ways in which operations could be improved, which may encourage loyalty and commitment to the organization. Often, an employee in the work unit knows more about how waste can be eliminated, how hazards can be controlled, or how improvements can be made than do managers. Many suggestion systems give financial rewards to employees for cost-saving suggestions, and payments to employees may be tied to a percentage of savings, up to some maximum level. Often a committee of employees and managers review and evaluate suggestions.

One study found that about 15% of managers in the United States are unwilling to listen to employees' suggestions. But 38% were very willing to listen.[38] In Japan, Toyota during a seven-year period averaged 2 million suggestions annually from its workforce.[39]

Employee Discipline

Discipline Form of training that enforces organizational rules.

The earlier discussion about employee rights provides an appropriate introduction to the topic of employee discipline, because employee rights often are a key issue in disciplinary cases. **Discipline** is a form of training that enforces organizational rules. Those most often affected by the discipline systems in an organization are problem employees. Fortunately, problem employees comprise a small number of employees, but they often are the ones who cause the most disciplinary situations. If employers fail to deal with problem employees, negative effects on other employees and work groups often result.[40] Common disciplinary issues caused by problem employees include absenteeism, tardiness, productivity deficiencies, alcoholism, and insubordination.

Figure 16-11 shows a possible division of responsibilities for discipline between the HR unit and managers. Notice that managers and supervisors are the ones to make disciplinary decisions and administer the discipline. HR specialists often are consulted prior to disciplinary action being instituted, and they may assist managers in administering the disciplinary action.

Approaches to Discipline

The disciplinary system can be viewed as an application of behavior modification to problem or unproductive employees. The best discipline is clearly self-discipline; when most people understand what is required at work, they can usually be counted on to do their jobs effectively. Yet some find that the prospect of external discipline helps their self-discipline. This philosophy has led to the development of the positive discipline approach.

Figure 16-11 ▶	**Typical Division of HR Responsibilities: Discipline**
HR Unit	**Managers**
• *Designs HR procedures that consider employees' rights* • *Designs progressive discipline process if nonunion* • *Trains managers on the use of discipline process* • *Assists managers with administration of discipline*	• *Are knowledgeable about organizational HR policies and rules* • *Make disciplinary decisions* • *Notify employees who violate policies and rules* • *Discuss discipline follow-up with employees*

Positive Discipline Approach The positive discipline approach builds on the philosophy that violations are actions that usually can be constructively corrected without penalty. In this approach, managers focus on fact-finding and guidance to encourage desirable behaviors, rather than using penalties to discourage undesirable behaviors. The four steps to positive discipline are as follows:

1. *Counseling.* The goal of this phase is to heighten employee awareness of organizational policies and rules. Often, people simply need to be made aware of rules, and knowledge of disciplinary actions may prevent violations. Counseling by a supervisor in the work unit also can have positive effects.

2. *Written documentation.* If the employee fails to correct his or her behavior, then a second conference becomes necessary. Whereas the first stage took place as a conversation between supervisor and employee, this stage is documented in written form. As part of this phase, the employee and the supervisor develop written solutions to prevent further problems from occurring.

3. *Final warning.* When the employee does not follow the written solutions noted in the second step, a final warning conference is held. In that conference the supervisor emphasizes to the employee the importance of correcting the inappropriate actions. Some firms incorporate a decision day-off, in which the employee is given a day off with pay to develop a firm, written action plan to remedy the problem behaviors. The decision day-off is used to emphasize the seriousness of the problem and the manager's determination to see that the behavior is changed.

4. *Discharge.* If the employee fails to follow the action plan that was developed and further problems exist, then the supervisor discharges the employee.

The advantage of this positive approach to discipline is that it focuses on problem solving. The greatest difficulty with the positive approach to discipline is the extensive amount of training required for supervisors and managers to become effective counselors, and it takes more supervisory time than the progressive discipline approach discussed next.

Progressive Discipline Approach As another approach, progressive discipline incorporates a sequence of steps, each of which becomes progressively more stringent and are designed to change the employee's inappropriate behavior. Figure 16-12 shows a typical progressive discipline system, and most progressive discipline procedures use verbal and written reprimands and suspension before resorting to dismissal. At one manufacturing firm, failure to call in when an employee will be absent from work may lead to a suspension after the third offense in a year. Suspension sends a strong message to an employee that undesirable job behavior must change, or termination is likely to follow.[41]

The progressive approach provides opportunities for an employee to correct deficiencies before being dismissed. Following the progressive sequence ensures that both the nature and seriousness of the problem are clearly communicated to the employee. Not all steps in the progressive discipline procedure are followed in every case. Certain serious offenses are exempted from the progressive pro-

Figure 16-12 ▸ **Progressive Discipline Procedure**

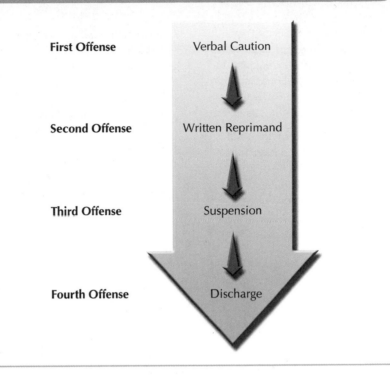

First Offense — Verbal Caution

Second Offense — Written Reprimand

Third Offense — Suspension

Fourth Offense — Discharge

cedure and may result in immediate termination. Typical offenses leading to immediate termination include the following:

- Intoxication at work
- Possession of weapons
- Alcohol or drug use at work
- Fighting
- Theft
- Falsifying employment application

Reasons Why Discipline Might Not Be Used

For a number of reasons, managers may be reluctant to use discipline. Some of the main ones include the following:

- *Organizational culture regarding discipline.* One factor affecting the use of discipline is the culture of the organization and managerial willingness to use discipline. If the organizational "norm" is to avoid penalizing problem employees, then managers are more likely not to use discipline. This reluctance to discipline extends even to dismissal of problem employees.
- *Lack of support.* Many managers do not want to use discipline, because they fear that their decisions will not be supported by higher management. The degree of support also is a function of the organizational culture.
- *Guilt.* Some managers feel that before they become managers, they committed the same violations as their employees, and they cannot discipline others for doing something they used to do.

The Hot Stove Rule

For many years, the "Hot Stove Rule" has been a part of successful training programs designed to teach supervisors about discipline.

The Hot Stove Rule: Good discipline is like a hot stove in that

- *It provides a warning.* A hot stove sends a warning in that you can feel the heat, and you know if you touch it you will be burned. Employees need a warning too before discipline occurs.
- *It is consistent.* A hot stove burns every time. Good discipline addresses the same offense under the same circumstances every time it occurs.
- *It is immediate.* The hot stove burns immediately if it is touched. The longer after an offense the discipline occurs, the less effective it is in changing behavior.
- *It is impersonal.* The hot stove burns anyone who touches it. Good discipline is not emotional or random, and it affects each violator the same.

The rule presents an analogy to help remember discipline basics.

- *Loss of friendship.* Managers who allow themselves to become too friendly with employees may fear losing those friendships if discipline is used.
- *Time loss.* Discipline, when applied properly, requires considerable time and effort. Sometimes it is easier for managers to avoid taking the time required for disciplining, especially if their actions may be overturned on review by higher management.
- *Fear of lawsuits.* Managers are increasingly concerned about being sued for disciplining someone, particularly for taking the ultimate disciplinary step of dismissal.[42]

Effective Discipline

Because of legal concerns, managers must understand discipline and know how to administer it properly. Effective discipline should be aimed at the behavior, not at the employee personally, because the reason for discipline is to improve performance. Discipline can be positively related to performance, which surprises those who feel that discipline can only harm behavior. Distributive and procedural justice suggest that if a manager tolerates unacceptable behavior, the group may resent the unfairness of it. The HR Practice relates an old management analogy about effective discipline. It offers a helpful way to remember the essentials.

Training of Supervisors Training supervisors and managers on when and how discipline should be used is crucial. Research has found that training supervisors in procedural justice as a basis for discipline results in both their employees and others seeing disciplinary action as more fair than discipline done by untrained supervisors. Regardless of the disciplinary approach used, training on counseling and communicating skills provides supervisors and managers with the tools necessary to deal with employee performance problems.

Discharge: The Final Disciplinary Step

The final stage in the disciplinary process is termination. A manager may feel guilty when dismissing an employee, and sometimes guilt is justified. If an employee fails, perhaps the manager failed to create an appropriate work environment. Perhaps the employee lacked adequate training, or perhaps management neglected to establish effective policies. Managers are responsible for their employees, and to an extent, they share the blame for failures.

Both the positive and progressive approaches to discipline clearly provide warnings to employees about the seriousness of their performance problems before dismissal occurs. Terminating workers because they do not keep their own promises is more likely to appear equitable and defensible to a jury. When dismissal occurs, the reasons for the termination should be clearly stated. Any effort to "sugar-coat" the reason ultimately confuses the employee, and it could undermine the employer's legal case should the termination decision be challenged. Many employers provide a specific letter or memo, which can provide evidence that the employee was notified of the termination decision.[43]

Often, both an HR representative and the employee's supervisor or manager attend the termination meeting to provide an additional witness to what occurs. Also, any severance benefits or other HR-related issues can be described. Some HR-related items include COBRA notification rights, any continuance of other employee benefits, and payments for unused vacation or sick leave. Finally, throughout the termination discussion the supervisor and others need to remain professional and calm, rather than becoming emotional, apologetic, or making sarcastic or demeaning remarks.[44]

Summary

- The employment relationship is a reciprocal one in which both employers and employees have rights.
- The two primary types of rights are statutory rights and contractual rights.
- Contractual rights can be spelled out in an employment contract or be implied as a result of employer promises.
- Rights affecting the employment relationship include employment-at-will, due process, and dismissal for just cause.
- Employment-at-will allows employers the right to hire or terminate employees with or without notice or cause.
- Courts are changing aspects of employment-at-will relationships based on exceptions for public policy, implied contract, and reasons related to good-faith/fair-dealing.
- Although due process is not guaranteed for at-will employees, the courts expect to see evidence of due process in employment-related cases.
- Wrongful discharge occurs when an employer improperly or illegally terminates an individual's employment.

- Just cause for employment-related actions should exist. When just cause is absent, constructive discharge may occur, in which the employee is forced to "voluntarily" quit the job.
- Due process is important for both unionized and non-union employees. In non-union situations, alternative dispute resolution (ADR) offers a means to insure due process.
- Balancing employer security concerns and employee rights becomes an issue when dealing with access to employee records, free speech, workplace monitoring, employer investigations, and employee substance abuse.
- Employers increasingly are facing free speech issues in areas such as whistle-blowing, monitoring of e-mail, and voice mail, and Internet usage.
- Drug testing provides a widely used and legal method for employers in dealing with increasing drug problems at work.
- To be effective, HR policies and rules should be consistent, necessary, applicable, understandable, reasonable, and communicated.
- Courts sometimes view employee handbooks as implied contracts, which presents few problems

as long as the handbook conforms to appropriate standards. Issues to be considered in preparing an employee handbook include reliability, use, and legal review of language.
- Discipline is best thought of as a form of training. Although self-discipline is the goal, some-

times positive or progressive discipline is necessary to encourage self-discipline.
- Managers may fail to discipline for a variety of reasons. However, effective discipline can have positive effects on the productivity of employees.

Review and Discussion Questions

1. Assume you are assigned to develop an employment contract for a key research manager. What provisions would you include?
2. Give some examples to illustrate the public policy exception to employment-at-will.
3. Discuss the differences and similarities between the issues of due process and just cause.
4. Discuss the following statement: "Even though efforts to restrict employees' free speech at work may be permissible, such efforts raise troubling questions affecting individual rights."
5. Identify some advantages and disadvantages associated with employers monitoring employee e-mail and work performance using technological and electronic means.
6. Examine an employee handbook from a local employer and identify problems and issues with its content.
7. Why has the positive approach to discipline been useful in reducing employee lawsuits?

Terms to Know

rights   510
responsibilities   510
statutory rights   510
contractual rights   511
separation agreement   511
employment contract   511
non-compete agreement   512
employment-at-will (EAW)   514
wrongful discharge   516
just cause   516
constructive discharge   517
due process   517

distributive justice   517
procedural justice   518
arbitration   518
peer review panel   519
ombudsman   519
right to privacy   520
whistle-blowers   522
policies   529
procedures   529
rules   529
suggestion system   532
discipline   533

Using the Internet

Progressive Discipline in the Workplace

One of the difficult situations facing new supervisors is employee discipline. These situations have to be handled correctly or they can become employee relations or even employee legal issues. Because of the importance of this area, as the Human Resources Manager, you have decided to prepare some guidelines for supervisors to use when they have to

discipline employees to make sure it is being done correctly. Using the following Web site, prepare an information guide for supervisors on employee progressive discipline. Include the steps in the process and explain how each of the steps should be completed. Click on *Staffing—Tools,* then click on *Discipline and Termination—Progressive Counseling Form* to gather the information needed from the Web site: *http://www. thesauce.com/*

Managers on Camera

A retail store was losing cash, but *only* when the surveillance system was turned off. The surveillance system could only be turned off from the manager's office. When the manager went on vacation a video camera with no audio pickup was placed in his office to see how the system was being deactivated. When he returned from vacation he noticed the camera and discussed the additional camera with the HR department but made no effort to have it removed.

The employer decided to transfer the manager to the same position at a nearby store because he had risen quickly through the ranks at the current store and was experiencing difficulty managing his former co-workers. The employer explained to the manager that the transfer decision was made to provide him with opportunity to develop further with the company. The employer offered to give the manager its standard relocation package or a raise to offset the increased commuting costs.

The manager rejected the transfer and resigned. Then he sued the employer claiming it had wrongfully monitored his communications and that the transfer was in retaliation for his having raised the issue of his right to privacy. The employer argued that the firm's surveillance practices *were* legal and that the transfer was in no way an adverse employment action against the manager.

Both the federal and state wiretap laws in this case are clear. They block the secret interception of the transfer of a human voice.[45]

You be the judge.

Questions

1. Do you believe the company guilty of an "illegal wiretap"?
2. Was the company guilty of violating the manager's rights? Why or why not?

(Your instructor can give you the actual decision.)

Notes

1. Adapted from Ann Carrns, "Prying Times," *The Wall Street Journal*, February 4, 2000, A1; "E-Mail Message about Fired Employee Spurs Lawsuit," *Bulletin to Management*, March 8, 2001, 80; Doug Bedell, "E-Mail and Worker Privacy," *Omaha World Herald*, May 21, 2000, 1G; M. J. McCarthy, "Thinking Out Loud," *The Wall Street Journal*, March 7, 2000, A1; Gene Koretz, "Big Bro Is Eyeing Your E-Mail," *Business Week*, June 4, 2001, 30; Jeffrey Seglin, "Attention, E-Mail Snoops," *Fortune*, May 14, 2001, 254; "You've Got Nailed!" *Bulletin to Management*, October 5, 2000, 314.

2. James O. Castagnera, "Dealing with Departing Employees Who 'Know Too Much,'" *HR Policies and Practices Update*, March 18, 2000, 5.

3. Carol Kleiman, "Noncompete Clauses Can Lead to Limited Career Possibilities," *Omaha World Herald*, February 25, 2001, C9.

4. Adapted from "Policy Guide: Intellectual Property," *Bulletin to Management*, April 6, 2000, 111.

5. Diane Stafford, "Technology Creates New Ethical Issues," *Omaha World Herald*, October 22, 2000, 19G; Stephanie Armour, "Laid-Off Workers Face Fallout from Legal Agreements," *USA Today*, June 6, 2001, 1B; Deborah Solomon, "Lucent Files Suit to Keep Ex-Employees from Cisco," *The Wall Street Journal*, June 21, 2000, B5; Stephanie Armour, "Does Your Company Own What You Know?" *USA Today*, January 19, 2000, 1A.

6. Sally Roberts, "More Employers Putting EPL Coverage to Work," *Business Insurance*, November 6, 2000, 3.

7. David Schaffer and Ron Schmidt, "The HR Manager's Guide to Employment Practices Liability Insurance," *Legal Report (SHRM)*, May–June 2000, 1–12.

8. "Working with People: At-Will Employment," *Bulletin to Management*, October 19, 2000, 336.

9. David C. Marin et. al., "The Legal Ramifications of Performance Appraisal," *Public Personnel Management*, Fall 2000, 379.

10. *Fortune v. National Cash Register Co.*, 373 Mass. 96, 36NE 2d 1251, 1977.

11. Peter Brimelow, "The Death of Due Process," *Forbes*, December 11, 2000, 98.

12. Steve Janosik and Jerry Riehl, "Stakeholder Support for Due Process in Campus Disciplinary Hearings," *NASPA Journal,* Winter 2000, 444–453.

13. Mary A. Konovsky, "Understanding Procedural Justice and Its Impact on Business Organizations," *Journal of Management,* 26 (2000), 489–511.

14. Stephanie Armour, "Arbitration's Rise Raises Fairness Issue," *USA Today,* June 12, 2001, B1.

15. Robert S. Greenberger, "Justices Back Arbitration Use in Work Arena," *The Wall Street Journal,* March 22, 2001, A3; and Margaret M. Clark, "Alternative Dispute Resolution Goes Mainstream," *HR News,* August 2001, 5.

16. Andrew McIlvaine, "Arbitration Plans Are Still Tricky," *HR Executive,* March 30, 2001, 18; "Supreme Court Gives Employers Green Light," *Bulletin to Management,* March 29, 2001, 97–104.

17. "Privacy: HR's New Minefield," *HR Focus,* April 2001, 1+.

18. Maureen Minehan, "The HR Balancing Act: Privacy vs. Protection," *HR Policies and Practices* (West Group), January 20, 2001.

19. Jared Sandberg, "The Privacy Officer," *The Wall Street Journal,* July 16, 2001, R10.

20. "Whistleblower to Collect $250,000," *Bulletin to Management,* November 9, 2000, 355; Ryan Morgan, "Mapmaker Gets $75,000 in Whistle-Blower Case," *The Denver Post,* May 4, 2001, 3C.

21. "Electronic Communication," *Bulletin to Management,* July 13, 2000, 54.

22. "HR Professionals and Privacy Issues," *Workplace Visions,* 1 (2001), 2.

23. Michelle Conlin, "Workers Surf at Your Own Risk," *Business Week,* June 12, 2000, 105; Michael J. McCarthy, "Web Surfers Beware: The Company Tech May Be a Secret Agent," *The Wall Street Journal,* January 10, 2000, 1A.

24. Marcia Stepanek, "Privacy," *Business Week,* September 25, 2000, 188.

25. Anna Mathews, "For Truckers Electronic Monitors Rev Up Fears of Privacy Invasion," *The Wall Street Journal,* February 25, 2000, B1.

26. "Investigations and Workplace Privacy," *Bulletin to Management,* July 13, 2000, S1–S8.

27. Calmeta Coleman, "Sticky Fingers," *The Wall Street Journal,* September 18, 2000, A1.

28. Employer Tip Sheet #9. The National Clearinghouse for Alcohol and Drug Information, available at *www.health.org/govpubs/workit/ts9.htm.*

29. Jane Easter Bahls, "Drugs in the Workplace," *HR Magazine,* February 1998, 81–87.

30. Michael A. Gips, "Industry Comment Shapes Drug Testing Rule," *Security Management,* March 2001, 18.

31. A. McBay, "Legal Challenges to Testing Hair for Drugs: A Review," *The International Journal of Drug Testing,* 1 (2000), 75.

32. Dominic Taurone, "What to Do When an Employee Tests Positive for Drugs," *Employee Benefit News,* October 1, 2000, 19.

33. Based on Diane Lewis, "Party Rules Designed to Head Off Liability," *Omaha World-Herald,* December 24, 2000, 3G.

34. "Many Well-Intentioned HR Policies Sow Legal Headaches," *Bulletin to Management,* February 17, 2000, 49–56.

35. "Did Disclaimer Create a Handbook Without Binding?" *Bulletin to Management,* August 30, 2001, 280.

36. Jodi S. Arthur, "Look Who's Talking," *HR Executive,* May 15, 2001, 79–82.

37. Mike France, "Free Speech on the Net? Not Quite," *Business Week,* February 28, 2000, 93.

38. "Most Surveyed Employees Find Managers Less than Enthusiastic About Worker's Ideas," *Bulletin to Management,* July 13, 2000, 219.

39. Daniel Gross, "Power of Suggestion," *Attaché,* October 2000, 1b.

40. M. T. Miklave and J. A. Trafimon, "Measuring Discipline," *Workforce,* September 2000, 124–126.

41. "HR Must Teach Supervisors New Tricks of Discipline," *Bulletin to Management,* July 27, 2000, 233–240.

42. Edward Lee Isler et al., "Personal Liability and Employee Discipline," *SHRM Legal Report* September–October 2000, 1–8.

43. "Firing with Finesse," *Bulletin to Management,* March 29, 2001, 51–54.

44. Sarah Breckenridge and Michele Marchetti, "The Fire Drill." *Smart Money,* October 2001, 141–142.

45. Based on "Life in Front of Camera Does Not Suit Manager," *Bulletin to Management,* July 6, 2000, 216.

CHAPTER 17

Union-Management Relationship

After you have read this chapter, you should be able to:

- Describe what a union is and explain why employees join unions.

- Identify several reasons for the decline in union membership.

- Explain the acts that compose the "National Labor Code."

- Identify and discuss the stages of the unionization process.

- Describe the typical collective bargaining process.

- Define *grievance* and explain why a grievance procedure is important for employers.

Unions and Wal-Mart

The difficulties unions have in getting more members in the service sector are seen at Wal-Mart, the giant retailer. Worldwide, Wal-Mart has over 3,200 stores, with about 2,500 located in the U.S., employing nearly 900,000 workers. Yet none of the U.S. workers are unionized, and only one store in Canada has any unionized workers.

Wal-Mart says the absence of unions is because it takes care of its employees. The company conducts regular employee surveys, and many workers have been promoted from cashiers and stockers to management jobs. A company-wide stock ownership program has generated significant returns for employees when a long-term view is used.

Unions counter that Wal-Mart uses aggressive and even unfair labor practices to prevent unionization. Where a union has tried to organize workers, the company often reacts with a coordinated "union prevention" program. Mandatory employee meetings are held in stores, where managers and supervisors read prepared scripts explaining the consequences of unionizing and show videos emphasizing the negatives of unionization. Even external surveillance cameras are used to record activities of individuals picketing a store. The company also aggressively enforces requirements to keep union organizers away from the entrances to stores. In some situations Wal-Mart has gotten court orders against union representatives for trespassing on company property.

The United Food and Commercial Workers (UFCW), has targeted Wal-Mart because it represents 1 million supermarket workers, who face Wal-Mart competition in the supermarkets industry. If Wal-Mart remains non-union and has lower labor costs, then some of its competitors may have to reduce staff and are more likely to resist UFCW efforts to obtain higher wages and benefits for members during contract negotiations.

Despite Wal-Mart's resistance, the UFCW was able to win a union election with 11 meat-department workers in Jacksonville, Texas. The UFCW cheered this result as the first crack in the non-union workforce at Wal-Mart. However, the union's victory was short-lived. As it had a right to do, Wal-Mart decided to shut down meat cutting operations in 180 stores, including the one in Jacksonville. The company ultimately switched to using pre-packaged meat from suppliers so that butchers and meat cutters were not needed. The employees losing their jobs were offered other jobs at Wal-Mart, but these jobs were not union and part of different possible bargaining units.

The example of Wal-Mart illustrates the difficulties facing unions in the U.S. The fastest growing sector of the economy is the service industry, where unions have traditionally had limited membership. Also, when unionization efforts are made, employers increasingly are responding aggressively to prevent those efforts from succeeding. Situations such as this one raise questions if unions in the U.S. will be able to slow or reverse their declining membership and influence in U.S. workplaces.[1]

> The fastest growing sector of the economy is the service industry, where unions have traditionally had limited membership.

*"Unions have a place, and as long as management
doesn't manage well, you are going to have unions."*

—**Steve Darien**

Union A formal association of workers that promotes the interests of its members through collective action.

A **union** is a formal association of workers that promotes the interests of its members through collective action. The state and nature of union-management relations varies among countries. In the United States, a complex system of laws, regulations, court decisions, and administrative rulings have identified that workers may join unions when they wish to do so. Although fewer workers choose to do so today than before, the mechanisms remain for a union resurgence if employees feel they need formal representation to deal with management.

Nature of Unions

Employers usually would rather not have to deal with unions because they constrain what managers can and cannot do in a number of areas. Generally, the union workers receive higher wages and benefits than do non-union workers.[2] However, unions *can* be associated with higher productivity, although management must find labor-saving ways of doing work to offset the higher labor costs.

Some employers pursue a strategy of good relations with the unions. Others may choose an aggressive, adversarial approach. Regardless of the type of employer, several common factors explain why employees unionize.

Why Employees Unionize

Whether a union targets a group of employees or the employees themselves request union assistance, the union still must win sufficient support from the employees in order to become their legal representative. Research consistently shows that employees join unions for two primary reasons: They are dissatisfied with how they are treated by their employers and they believe that unions can improve their work situations. If the employees do not receive organizational justice from their employers, they turn to unions for assistance in obtaining what they believe is equitable. As Figure 17-1 shows, the major factors that can trigger unionization are compensation, working environment, management style, and organizational treatment issues.

The primary determinant of whether employees unionize is management. If management treats employees as valuable human resources, then employees generally feel no need for outside representation. Reasonably competitive compensation, good working environments, effective management and supervision, and fair and responsive treatment of workers all act as antidotes to unionization efforts. For example, a survey of nurses revealed that unionization results when employees feel disrespected, unsafe, underpaid, and unappreciated.[3] If such conditions exist, then unions offer a viable option to employees. Once unionization occurs, the union's ability to foster commitment from members and to remain as their bargaining agent apparently depends on how well the union succeeds in providing services that its members want. To prevent unionization, as well as to work effectively with unions already representing employees, both HR professionals and operating managers must be attentive and responsive.

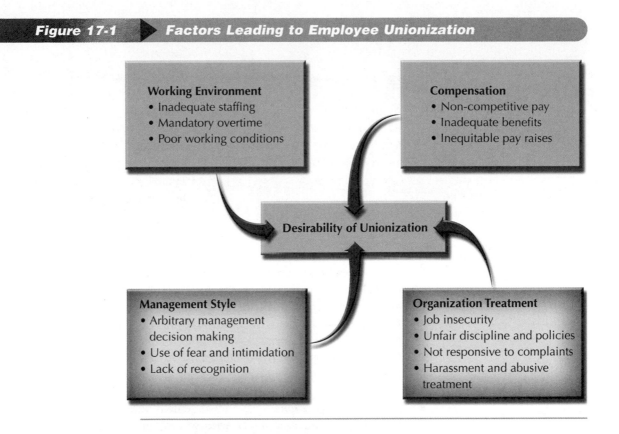

Figure 17-1 ▶ *Factors Leading to Employee Unionization*

Working Environment
- Inadequate staffing
- Mandatory overtime
- Poor working conditions

Compensation
- Non-competitive pay
- Inadequate benefits
- Inequitable pay raises

Desirability of Unionization

Management Style
- Arbitrary management decision making
- Use of fear and intimidation
- Lack of recognition

Organization Treatment
- Job insecurity
- Unfair discipline and policies
- Not responsive to complaints
- Harassment and abusive treatment

HR Responsibilities with Unions

The pattern of dealing with unionized employees varies among organizations. In some organizations, operating management handles labor relations and HR's involvement is minimal. In other organizations, the HR unit takes primary responsibility for labor relations. The typical division of responsibilities between the HR unit and operating managers in dealing with unions falls somewhere between these extremes, as shown in Figure 17-2 on the next page.

State of U.S. Unions

The union movement in the United States has been characterized by approaches different from those used in some other countries. In the United States the key emphases have been:

- *Focus on economic issues.* Unions typically have focused on improving the "bread and butter" issues for their members—wages, benefits, job security and working conditions. In some other countries political power and activism are equal concerns along with economic issues.
- *Organized by kind of job and employer.* In the United States, carpenters often belong to the carpenters' union, truck drivers to the Teamsters, and teachers to the American Federation of Teachers or the National Education

Figure 17-2 ▶ **Typical Division of HR Responsibilities: Labor Relations**

HR Unit	Managers
• *Deals with union organizing attempts at the company level* • *Monitors "climate" for unionization and union relationships* • *Helps negotiate labor agreements* • *Provides detailed knowledge of labor legislation as needed*	• *Promote conditions conducive to positive relationships with employees* • *Avoid unfair labor practices during organizing efforts* • *Administer the labor agreement on a daily basis* • *Resolve grievances and problems between management and employees*

Association. Also, unionization can be done on a company-by-company basis. In other countries there are national unions that bargain with the government or nationally with employer groups.

■ *Collective agreements as "contracts."* Collective bargaining contracts usually spell out compensation, work rules, and the conditions of employment for several years. In other countries the agreements are made with the government and employers, sometimes for only one year because of political and social concerns.

■ *Competitive relations.* U.S. management and labor traditionally take the roles of competing adversaries who often "clash" to reach agreement. However, in many other countries "tri-parte" bargaining occurs among the national government, employers' associations, and national labor federations.

Union Structure

Craft union One whose members do one type of work, often using specialized skills and training.

Industrial union One that includes many persons working in the same industry or company, regardless of jobs held.

Federation Group of autonomous national and international unions.

American labor is represented by many different kinds of unions. But regardless of size and geographical scope, two basic types of unions developed over time. In a **craft union**, members do one type of work, often using specialized skills and training. Examples include the International Association of Bridge, Structural, and Ornamental Iron Workers, and the American Federation of Television and Radio Artists. An **industrial union** includes many persons working in the same industry or company, regardless of jobs held. The United Food and Commercial Workers, the United Auto Workers, and the American Federation of State, County, and Municipal Employees are examples of industrial unions.

Labor organizations have developed complex organizational structures with multiple levels. The broadest level is the **federation**, which is a group of autonomous national and international unions. A federation allows individual unions to work together and present a more unified front to the public, legislators, and members. The most prominent federation in the United States is the AFL-CIO, which is a confederation of national and international unions.

National Unions National or international unions are not governed by the federation even if they are affiliated with it. They collect dues and have their own boards, specialized publications, and separate constitutions and bylaws. Such national-international unions as the United Steel Workers and the American Federation of State, County, and Municipal Employees determine broad union policy and offer services to local union units. They also help maintain financial records and provide a base from which additional organizing drives may take place. Political infighting and corruption sometimes pose problems for national unions, as when the federal government stepped in and overturned the results of an election held by the Teamsters Union.

Local Unions Local unions may be centered around a particular employer organization or around a particular geographic location. The membership of local unions elect officers who are subject to removal if they do not perform satisfactorily. For this reason, local union officers tend to be concerned with how they are perceived by the union members. They often react to situations as politicians do because their positions depend on obtaining votes.

Local unions typically have business agents and union stewards. A **business agent** is a full-time union official who operates the union office and assists union members. The agent runs the local headquarters, helps negotiate contracts with management, and becomes involved in attempts to unionize employees in other organizations. A **union steward** is an employee of a firm who is elected to serve as the first-line representative of unionized workers. Stewards address grievances with supervisors and generally represent employees at the worksite.

Business agent A full-time union official who operates the union office and assists union members.

Union steward An employee elected to serve as the first-line representative of unionized workers.

Mergers of Unions

Like companies, unions find strength in size. In the past decade about 40 mergers of unions have occurred, with a number of other unions considering doing the same. For smaller unions these mergers provide financial and union-organizing resources in the merged unions. Larger unions can add new members to cover managerial and administrative costs without spending funds to organize non-union workers to become members.[4]

Union Membership in the United States

The statistics on union membership tell a disheartening story for organized labor in the United States over the past several decades. As shown in Figure 17-3 on the next page, unions represented over 30% of the workforce from 1945 through 1960. But by 2002, unions in the United States represented less than 14% of all civilian workers. When unionized government employees are excluded, unions represent only 9.5% of the private-sector workforce. Even more disheartening for the unions, the actual number of members has declined in most years even though more people are employed than previously. Of the approximately 120 million U.S. workers, only about 16 million belong to a union.[5]

Public-Sector Unionism

An area where unions have had some measure of success is with public-sector employees, particularly with state and local government workers. The government sector (federal, state, and local) is the most highly unionized part of the U.S. workforce.

Figure 17-3 ▶ **Union Membership as a Percentage of U.S. Workforce**

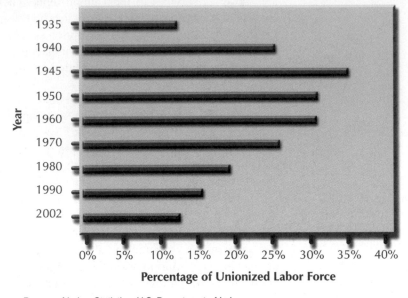

Percentage of Unionized Labor Force

Source: Bureau of Labor Statistics, U.S. Department of Labor.

Unionization of state and local government employees presents some unique problems and challenges. First, some employees work in critical service areas. Allowing police officers, firefighters, and sanitation workers to strike endangers public health and safety. Consequently, more than 30 states have laws prohibiting public employee work stoppages. These laws also identify a variety of ways to resolve negotiation impasses, including arbitration. But unions still give employees in these areas greater security and better ability to influence decisions on wages and benefits.

Although unions in the federal government hold the same basic philosophy as unions in the private sector, they do differ somewhat. Previous Executive Orders and laws established methods of labor-management relations that consider the special circumstances present in the federal government. In the United States, the government sector is the only one to see recent growth and strengthening of unions.

Reasons for Union Decline in the U.S.

It is speculated that several issues have contributed to the decline of unions: deregulation, foreign competition, a larger number of people looking for jobs, and a general perception by firms that dealing with unions is expensive compared with the non-union alternative. Also, management at many employers has taken a much more activist stance against unions than during the previous years of union growth.

To some extent, unions may be a victim of their own successes. Because unions have emphasized helping workers obtain higher wages, shorter working hours, job security, and safe-working conditions from their employers, some believe that one cause for the decline of unions has been their success in getting their important issues passed into law for everyone. Therefore, unions are not as necessary for many workers, even though they enjoy the results of past union efforts to influence legislation.

Geographic Changes Over the past decade, job growth in the United States has been the greatest in states located in the South, Southwest, and Rocky Mountains. Most of these states have "employer-friendly" laws, and they have relatively small percentages of unionized workers.

Another issue involves the movement of many lower-skill jobs outside the United States. Primarily because of cheaper labor, many manufacturers with heavily unionized U.S. workforces have moved a significant number of low-skill jobs to the Philippines, China, Thailand, and Mexico. The passage of the North American Free Trade Agreement (NAFTA) provided a major impetus for moving low-skill, low-wage jobs to Mexico. It removed tariffs and restrictions affecting the flow of goods and services among the United States, Canada, and Mexico. Because of significantly lower wage rates in Mexico, a number of jobs previously susceptible to unionization have been moved there.

Workforce Changes Many of the workforce and economic changes discussed in Chapter 1 have contributed to the decline in union representation of the labor force.[6] The primary growth in jobs in the U.S. economy has been in technology, financial, and other service industries with large numbers of white-collar jobs including clerical workers, insurance claims representative, data input processors, nurses, teachers, mental health aides, computer technicians, loan officers, auditors, and retail sales workers. The increase in efforts by unions to organize white-collar workers has come as advances in technology have boosted their numbers in the workforce. However, unions face a major difficulty in organizing these workers. Many white-collar workers see unions as resistant to change and not in touch with the concerns of the more educated workers in technical and professional jobs. In addition, many white-collar workers exhibit a mentality and set of preferences quite different from those held by blue-collar union members.

The growing percentage of women in the U.S. workforce presents another challenge to unions. In the past, unions have not been as successful in organizing women workers as they have in organizing men. There are some indications that unions are trying to focus on recruiting women members. Unions have been in the forefront in the push for legislation on such family-related goals as child care, maternity and paternity leave, pay equity, and flexible work arrangements. Women in "pink-collar" lower-skilled, service jobs have been somewhat more likely to join unions than women working in other white-collar jobs.

Industrial Changes Another cause for the decline of unions is the shift in U.S. jobs from industries such as manufacturing, construction, and mining to service industries. There is a small percentage of union members in the financial services and wholesale/retail industries, the sectors in which many new jobs have been added, whereas the number of industrial jobs continues to shrink. In summary, union membership is primarily concentrated in the shrinking part of the economy and unions are not making in-roads into the fastest growing segments of the U.S.[7]

Figure 17-4 ▸ **Union Membership by Industry**

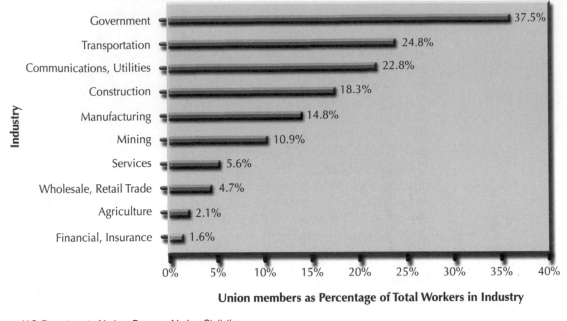

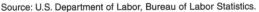

Source: U.S. Department of Labor, Bureau of Labor Statistics.

A look at Figure 17-4 reveals that non-governmental union members are heavily concentrated in transportation, utilities, and other "industrial" jobs. Unions also have targeted workers in the technology industry, specifically those in the "dot.coms" such as Amazon.com, Webvan, and other firms. However, the collapse of many dot.coms in 2000–2001 made unionization less likely.[8]

Union Targets for Membership Growth

To attempt to counteract the overall decline in union membership, unions are targeting a number of industries and types of workers. Some of the most frequently discussed groups are highlighted next.

Professional Unions Traditionally, professionals in many occupations have been skeptical of the advantages of unionization. However, some professionals who have turned to unionization include engineers, physicians, nurses, and others. The health-care industry has been a specific focus for unionization, and over 50,000 doctors have joined unions. As the number of physicians who are salaried employees (perhaps with HMOs) increases from less than 25% to almost 50%, these professionals are joining unions. Also, one of the fastest growing areas of union growth in the past few years is nursing.[9] The primary cause for health-care employees considering unions is the growth of managed care and HMOs. As a result of managed care, a frequent complaint of health-care professionals is that they have lost control of patient-care decisions as the drive to reduce health-care costs has spread.

Contingent and Part-Time Workers As many employers have added "contract workers" instead of full-time employees, unions have tried to unionize part-time, temporary, and other employees. An NLRB decision allows temporary workers to be included in firms to be represented by unions.[10] In another field, teaching assistants (future professors) at several universities are unionized. Time will tell if the efforts to unionize part-time workers and other groups will halt the decline of union membership in the United States.

Low-Skilled Workers On the other end of the labor scale, unions have targeted low-skilled workers, many of whom have lower-paying, less desirable jobs. Janitors and building cleaners, nursing home aides, and meat packing workers are examples of groups targeted by unions. For instance, in the health-care industry, workers in nursing homes dealing with the elderly are a fast-growing segment of the workforce. However, many employees in this industry are relatively dissatisfied. The industry is often noted for its low pay and hard work, and many employees are women who work as nurse's aides, cooks, launderers, and in other low-wage jobs. Many of these individuals also are immigrants, and unions are targeting immigrant workers in low-skill jobs. Although these efforts are not always successful, unions are likely to continue pursuing industries and employers with numerous low-skilled jobs and workers.

The History of American Unions

The evolution of the union movement in the United States began with early collective efforts by workers to address job concerns and counteract management power. As early as 1794, shoemakers organized a union, picketed, and conducted strikes. However, in those days, unions in the United States received very little support from the courts. In 1806, when the shoemaker's union struck for higher wages, a Philadelphia court found union members guilty of engaging in a "criminal conspiracy" to raise wages.

The AFL-CIO

In 1886, the *American Federation of Labor (AFL)* united a number of independent national unions. Its aims were to organize skilled craft workers and to emphasize economic issues and working conditions.

As industrialization increased in the U.S., many factories used semiskilled and unskilled workers. However, it was not until 1938 when the Congress of Industrial Organizations (CIO) was founded, that a labor union organization focused on semiskilled and unskilled workers. Years later, the AFL and the CIO merged to form one coordinating federation, the AFL-CIO. That federation is now the major organization coordinating union efforts in the United States today.

Early Labor Legislation

The right to organize workers and engage in collective bargaining offers little value if workers cannot freely exercise it. Historical evidence shows that management consistently has developed practices calculated to prevent workers from using this right. Over a period of many years the federal government has taken action to both hamper unions and protect them.

Logging On...

AFL-CIO
The AFL-CIO's homepage provides union movement information.

http://www.aflcio.org

Labor Conflicts in the Airline Industry

Over the past seven years no other industry has seen as many labor conflicts as the U.S. airline industry. Hostility, work slowdowns, and/or strikes have occurred at United, American, Delta, Midwest Express, U.S. Air, and Northwest Airlines, among others. Even commuter airlines such as Comair and Air Wisconsin have had labor strikes.

Why the airline industry has had many problems is multifaceted. But one broad cause is that the airlines are covered by the Railway Labor Act (RLA), rather than the other laws covering most other industries. Under the RLA, a complex and cumbersome dispute resolution process is mandated. This process allows either the unions or management to use the National Relations Board, a multistage dispute resolution process, and even the ability of the President of the U.S. to appoint an emergency board. The act also prohibits strikes/lockouts until 30 days after that emergency board submits its reports.

The end result of having both a prolonged process and one subject to political interference has been unions working for two or more years after the expiration of their old contracts because the process has taken so long. For instance, a union representing some employees at American Airlines went over four years without a settlement. Such delays often create hostility and resentment within the unionized employees, which makes the contract negotiations even more difficult.

Probably the most prolonged strike occurred at Comair, where pilots went on strike for almost two months, resulting in thousands of other Comair employees being laid off or losing their jobs. Ultimately, the strike was settled, with the pilots getting raises of 40% or more over several years and additional benefits. However, shortly afterward Comair reduced the number of flights and cities served, cutting the number of Comair jobs.

On top of this labor chaos, the terrorist attacks on September 11, 2001, resulted in cuts in airline flights and staff of 20% to 30%. Many union employees who previously won large contract settlements saw their jobs eliminated, but those remaining still received the higher wages and benefits negotiated prior to the fall-off in airline revenues and profits, leading to further financial instability at many of the airlines.

What the future holds for airlines and their unionized employees is uncertain, but without significant changes in the legal processes and the bargaining behaviors of airline management and union employees, labor strife is likely to continue in the U.S. airline industry.

Railway Labor Act The Railway Labor Act (1926) represented a shift in government regulation of unions. As a result of a joint effort between railroad management and unions to reduce transportation strikes, this act gave railroad employees "the right to organize and bargain collectively through representatives of their own choosing." In 1936, airlines and their employees were added to those covered by the act. Both of these industries are still covered by this act rather than by others passed later. Some experts believe that some of the labor relations problems in the airline industry stem from the provisions of this act, which would be more easily resolved if these unions fell within the labor laws covering most other industries, as the HR Perspective describes.

Norris-LaGuardia Act The crash of the stock market and the onset of the Great Depression in 1929 led to massive cutbacks by employers. In some industries, resistance by employees led to strikes and violence. Under the laws at that time, employers could go to court and have a federal judge issue injunctions ordering workers to return to work. In 1932, Congress passed the Norris-LaGuardia Act, which guaranteed workers some rights to organize and restricted the issuance of court injunctions in labor disputes.

Basic Labor Law: "National Labor Code"

The economic crises of the early 1930s and the restrictions on workers' ability to organize into unions led to the passage of landmark labor legislation. Later acts reflected other pressures and issues that required legislative attention. Together, the following three acts, passed over a period of almost 25 years, comprise what has been labeled the "National Labor Code": (1) the Wagner Act, (2) the Taft-Hartley Act, and (3) the Landrum-Griffin Act. Each act was passed to focus on some facet of the relationships between unions and management. Figure 17-5 indicates the primary focus of each act.

Wagner Act (National Labor Relations Act)

The National Labor Relations Act, more commonly referred to as the Wagner Act, has been called the Magna Carta of labor and was, by anyone's standards, pro-union. Passed in 1935, the Wagner Act was an outgrowth of the Great Depression. With employers having to close or cut back their operations, workers were left with little job security. Unions stepped in to provide a feeling of solidarity and strength for many workers. The Wagner Act declared, in effect, that the official policy of the U.S. government was to encourage collective bargaining. Specifically, it established workers' right to organize unhampered by management interference.

Unfair Labor Practices To protect union rights, the act prohibited employers from undertaking the following five unfair labor practices:

- Interfering with, restraining, or coercing employees in the exercise of their right to organize or to bargain collectively.
- Dominating or interfering with the formation or administration of any labor organization.
- Encouraging or discouraging membership in any labor organization by discriminating with regard to hiring, tenure, or conditions of employment.
- Discharging or otherwise discriminating against an employee because he or she filed charges or gave testimony under the act.
- Refusing to bargain collectively with representatives of the employees.

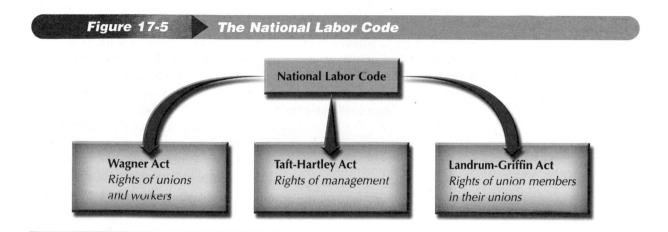

Figure 17-5 ▶ **The National Labor Code**

National Labor Code

Wagner Act
Rights of unions and workers

Taft-Hartley Act
Rights of management

Landrum-Griffin Act
Rights of union members in their unions

National Labor Relations Board (NLRB) Another key part of the Wagner Act established the National Labor Relations Board (NLRB) as an independent entity to enforce the provisions of the Act. The NLRB administers all provisions of the Wagner Act and subsequent labor relations acts. Primary functions of the NLRB include conducting unionization elections, investigating complaints by employers or unions through its fact-finding process, issuing opinions on its findings, and prosecuting violations in court. The five members of the NLRB serve staggered terms; they are appointed by the President of the United States and confirmed by the U.S. Senate.[11]

Taft-Hartley Act (Labor-Management Relations Act)

The passage in 1947 of the Labor-Management Relations Act, better known as the Taft-Hartley Act, addressed the concerns of many who felt that unions had become too strong. As an attempt to balance the collective bargaining equation, this act was designed to offset the pro-union Wagner Act by limiting union actions; therefore, it was considered to be pro-management and became the second part of the National Labor Code.

The new law amended or qualified in some respect all of the major provisions of the Wagner Act and established an entirely new code of conduct for unions. The Taft-Hartley Act forbade unions from a series of unfair labor practices, much like those prohibited by management. Coercion, discrimination against non-members, refusing to bargain, excessive membership fees, and other practices were not allowed by unions. A 1974 amendment extended coverage of the Taft-Hartley Act to private, non-profit hospitals and nursing homes.

The Taft-Hartley Act also established the Federal Mediation and Conciliation Service (FMCS) as an agency to help management and labor settle labor contract disputes. The act also required that FMCS be notified of disputes over contract renewals or modifications if not settled within 30 days after the designated date. More on the role of FMCS is discussed later in the chapter.

National Emergency Strikes The Taft-Hartley Act also allows the president of the United States to declare that a strike presents a national emergency. A **national emergency strike** is one that would impact an industry or a major part of it in such a way that the national economy would be significantly affected.

National emergency strike A strike that would impact the national economy significantly.

Right-to-Work Provision One specific provision of the Taft-Hartley Act, Section 14(b), deserves special explanation. This section allows states to pass laws that restrict compulsory union membership. Accordingly, some states have passed **right-to-work laws,** which prohibit requiring employees to join unions as a condition of obtaining or continuing employment. The laws were so named because they allow a person the right to work without having to join a union. The states that have enacted these laws are shown in Figure 17-6.

Right-to-work laws State laws that prohibit requiring employees to join unions as a condition of obtaining or continuing employment.

The nature of union-management relationships are affected by the right-to-work provisions. Specifically, the Taft-Hartley Act prohibits the **closed shop**, which requires individuals to join a union before they can be hired. Because of concerns that a closed shop allows a union to "control" who may be considered for employment and who must be hired by an employer, Section 14(b) prohibits the closed shop except in construction-related occupations.

Closed shop A firm that requires individuals to join a union before they can be hired.

Figure 17-6 ▶ **Right-to-Work States**

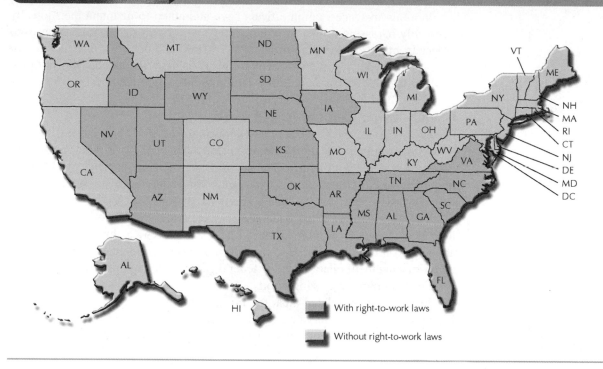

With right-to-work laws

Without right-to-work laws

Open shop Workers are not required to join or pay dues to unions.

Logging On...

Right-to-Work
This Web site contains information from the National Right to Work Legal Defense Foundation

www.nrtw.org

In states with right-to-work laws, **open shops** exist, which means workers cannot be required to join or pay dues to unions. In states that do not have right-to-work laws, the following types of arrangements exist.

- *Union shop.* Requires that individuals join the union, usually 30 to 60 days after being hired.
- *Agency shop.* Requires employees who refuse to join the union to pay amounts equal to union dues and fees in return for the union's representation services.
- *Maintenance-of-membership shop.* Requires workers to remain members of the union for the period of the labor contract.

Landrum-Griffin Act (Labor-Management Reporting and Disclosure Act)

The third segment of the National Labor Code, the Landrum-Griffin Act, was passed in 1959. A congressional committee investigating the Teamsters Union found corruption in the union. The law was passed to protect the rights of individual union members against such practices. Under the Landrum-Griffin Act, unions are required to have bylaws, make financial reports, and provide union members with a bill of rights. It also appointed the Secretary of Labor to act as a watchdog of union conduct. Because a union is supposed to be a democratic institution in which union members vote on and elect officers and approve labor contracts, the Landrum-Griffin Act was passed in part to ensure that the federal government protects those democratic rights.

In a few instances, union officers have attempted to maintain their jobs by physically harassing or attacking individuals who have tried to oust them from office. In other cases, union officials have "milked" pension fund monies for their own use. Such instances are not typical of most unions, but illustrate the need for legislative oversight to protect individual union members.

Civil Service Reform Act of 1978

Passed as part of the Civil Service Reform Act of 1978, the Federal Service Labor-Management Relations statute made major changes in how the federal government deals with unions. The act also identified areas subject to bargaining. For example, as a result of the law, wages and benefits are not subject to bargaining. Instead, they are set by congressional actions.

The act established the Federal Labor Relations Authority (FLRA) as an independent agency similar to the NLRB. The FLRA, a three-member body appointed on a bipartisan basis, was given authority to oversee and administer union-management relations in the federal government and to investigate unfair practices in union organizing efforts.

In a somewhat related area, the Postal Reorganization Act of 1970 established the U.S. Postal Service as an independent entity. Part of the 1970 act prohibited postal workers from striking and established a dispute resolution process.

The Process of Unionizing

The process of unionizing an employer may begin in one of two primary ways: (1) union targeting of an industry or company, or (2) employees requesting union representation. In the former case, the local or national union identifies a firm or industry in which it believes unionization can succeed. The logic for targeting is that if the union succeeds in one firm or a portion of the industry, then many other workers in the industry will be more willing to consider unionizing.

The second impetus for union organizing occurs when individual workers in an employer contact a union and express a desire to unionize. The employees themselves—or the union—then may begin to campaign to win support among the other employees.

Employers may make strategic decisions and take aggressive steps to remain non-union. Such a choice is perfectly rational, but may require some specific HR policies and philosophies to accomplish. "Preventative" employee relations may emphasize good morale and loyalty based on concern for employees, competitive wages and benefits, a fair system for dealing with employee complaints, and safe working conditions. Other issues may also play a part in employees' decisions to stay non-union, but if employers adequately address the points just listed, fewer workers are likely to feel the need for a union to represent them.[12]

Once unionizing efforts begin, all activities must conform to the requirements established by applicable labor laws. Both management and the unions must adhere to those requirements, or the results of the effort can be appealed to the NLRB and overturned. With those requirements in mind, the union can embark on the typical union organizing process, as outlined in Figure 17-7.

Figure 17-7 ▶ **Typical Unionization Process**

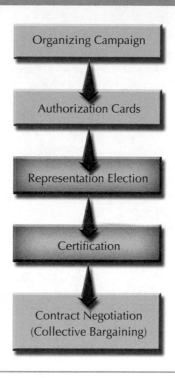

Organizing Campaign

Like other entities seeking members, a union usually mounts an organized campaign to persuade individuals to support its efforts. This persuasion takes many forms, including personally contacting employees outside of work, mailing materials to employees' homes, inviting employees to attend special meetings away from the company, and publicizing the advantages of union membership. Brochures, leaflets, and circulars can be passed out to employees as they leave work, mailed to their homes, or even attached to their vehicles, as long as they comply with the rules established by laws and the NLRB. The purpose of all of this publicity is to encourage employees to sign authorization cards. The e-HR on the next page describes how unions use electronic communications in their organizing efforts.

"Salting" Unions sometimes use paid organizers to infiltrate a targeted employer for the purpose of trying to organize other workers. In this practice, known as **salting,** the unions hire and pay people to apply for jobs at certain companies; when the people are hired, they begin organizing efforts. The U.S. Supreme Court has ruled that refusing to hire otherwise qualified applicants, even if they also are paid by a union, violates the Wagner Act. However, employers may refuse to hire "salts" if they were denied job offers for job-related and non-discriminatory reasons.[13]

Salting Practice in which unions hire and pay people to apply for jobs at certain companies.

The Internet is changing many facets of HR, including union organizing efforts. Unions are using e-mail and the Internet in several ways to try to gain new members. Some unions have established Web sites where interested workers can check the benefits of unionization. For instance, the Service Employees International Union (SEIU) has Web sites and chat rooms for nurses at non-union hospitals to exchange information with unionized nurses. The American Federation of Teachers links its publications on educational topics to an online wire service for teachers, and provides union information.

E-mail has changed union organizing efforts also. The United Food and Commercial Workers (UFCW) union receives over 100 e-mails in a typical day from workers wanting information on unionization and their rights to union representation. Other unions have gathered the home e-mail addresses for workers who are targets for unionization and sends them union solicitation information.

It should be noted that employers with e-mail restrictions and usage may enforce them when union solicitation e-mails are received, sent, or forwarded using employer-provided systems. But if employers are restricting some union-related messages, they must also exclude all personal, non-business messages. For instance, if employees can send a blanket e-mail offering a free dog or a car for sale, then restrictions on employees soliciting other employees for union support cannot be imposed, according to employment law experts. Thus, e-mail is protected by the NLRB as a "concerted activity."

This concept means that employees using e-mail to protest or comment on employers' actions or the desirability of unionization may be protected unless employers have clear, established, and enforced policies.[14]

Authorization Cards

Union authorization card
Card signed by an employee to designate a union as his or her collective bargaining agent.

A **union authorization card** is signed by an employee to designate a union as his or her collective bargaining agent. At least 30% of the employees in the targeted group must sign authorization cards before an election can be called.

In reality, the fact that an employee signs an authorization card does not mean that the employee is in favor of a union; it means only that he or she would like the opportunity to vote on having one. Employees who do not want a union still might sign authorization cards because they want management to know they are disgruntled.

Representation Election

An election to determine if a union will represent the employees is supervised by the NLRB for private-sector organizations and by other legal bodies for public-sector organizations. If two unions are attempting to represent employees, the employees will have three choices: union A, union B, or no union.

Bargaining unit Employees eligible to select a single union to represent and bargain collectively for them.

Bargaining Unit Prior to any election, the appropriate bargaining unit must be determined. A **bargaining unit** is composed of all employees eligible to select a single union to represent and bargain collectively for them. If management and the union do not agree on who is and who is not included in the unit, the regional office of the NLRB must make the determination. A major criterion in deciding the composition of a bargaining unit is what the NLRB calls a "community of interest." A community of interest likely would not exist at a warehouse distribution firm if delivery drivers, accounting clerks, computer programmers, and mechanics were to be included in the same "unit." These employees have widely varying jobs, areas of work, physical locations, and other differences likely to negate a community of interest.

This concept means that the employees have mutual interests in the following areas:

- Wages, hours, and working conditions
- Traditional industry groupings for bargaining purposes
- Physical location of employees and the amount of interaction and working relationships among employee groups
- Supervision by similar levels of management

Supervisors and Bargaining Units Determination Who is in the bargaining unit is affected by provisions of the National Labor Relations Act that excludes supervisors from protection when attempting to vote for or join unions. As a result, supervisors cannot be included in bargaining units for unionization purposes, except for industries covered by the Railway Labor Act.

But who qualifies as a supervisor is not always clear. The NLRB uses a detailed definition that identifies a supervisor as any individual with authority to hire, transfer, discharge, discipline, and use independent judgment with employees.[15] Numerous NLRB and court decisions have been rendered on specific situations. A major case decided by the U.S. Supreme Court found that charge nurses with RN degrees were supervisors because they exercised independent judgment.[16] This case and others have provided some guidance to employers and unions about who should be considered supervisors, thus excluding these individuals from bargaining units.

Unfair Labor Practices Employers and unions engage in a number of activities before an election. Both the Wagner Act and the Taft-Hartley Act place restrictions on these activities.

Various tactics may be used by management representatives in attempting to defeat a unionization effort. Such tactics often begin when union publicity appears or during the distribution of authorization cards. Some employers hire experts who specialize in combating unionization efforts. Using these "union busters," as they are called by unions, appears to enhance employers' chances of winning the representation election. Certainly Wal-Mart uses aggressive tactics to avoid unionization by employees, as the chapter opening discussion illustrates.

Election Process Assuming an election is held, the union need receive only the votes of a *majority of those voting* in the election. For example, if a group of 200 employees is the identified unit, and only 50 people vote, only 50% of the employees voting plus one (in this case, 26) would need to vote yes in order for the union to be named as the representative of all 200 employees. Over the past few years, unions have won representation elections about 50% of the time.[17] Also, the smaller the number of employees in the bargaining unit, the higher the percentage of elections typically are won by the unions.[18] In the past few years, unions have won slightly more elections than they have lost.

If either side believes unfair labor practices were used by the other side, the election results can be appealed to the NLRB. If the NLRB finds evidence of unfair practices, it can order a new election. Assuming that no unfair practices were used and the union obtains a majority in the election, the union then

DO (LEGAL)	DON'T (ILLEGAL)
• Tell employees about current wages and benefits and how they compare with those in other firms • Tell employees that the employer opposes unionization • Tell employees the disadvantages of having a union (especially cost of dues, assessments, and requirements of membership) • Show employees articles about unions and relate negative experiences elsewhere • Explain the unionization process to employees accurately • Forbid distribution of union literature during work hours in work areas • Enforce disciplinary policies and rules consistently and appropriately	• Promise employees pay increases or promotions if they vote against the union • Threaten employees with termination or discriminate when disciplining employees • Threaten to close down or move the company if a union is voted in • Spy on or have someone spy on union meetings • Make a speech to employees or groups at work within 24 hours of the election (before that, it is allowed) • Ask employees how they plan to vote or if they have signed authorization cards • Encourage employees to persuade others to vote against the union (such a vote must be initiated solely by the employee)

petitions the NLRB for certification. Figure 17-8 lists some common tactics management can use legally and some tactics it cannot use.

Certification and Decertification

Official certification of a union as the legal representative for employees is given by the NLRB (or by the equivalent body for public-sector organizations). Once certified, the union attempts to negotiate a contract with the employer. The employer *must* bargain, because refusing to bargain with a certified union constitutes an unfair labor practice. Newly certified unions are given up to a year before decertification can be attempted by workers in the bargaining unit.

When members no longer wish to be represented by the union, they can use the election process also. Similar to the unionization process, **decertification** is a process whereby a union is removed as the representative of a group of employees. Employees attempting to oust a union must obtain decertification authorization cards signed by at least 30% of the employees in the bargaining unit before an election may be called. If a majority of those voting in the election want to remove the union, the decertification effort succeeds. Some reasons that employees decide to vote out a union include better treatment by employers, the inability of some unions to address the changing needs of a firm's workforce, and the declining image of unions. However, current regulations prohibit employers from initiating or supporting decertification efforts.

Figure 17-9 ▶ **Collective Bargaining Relationship Continuum**

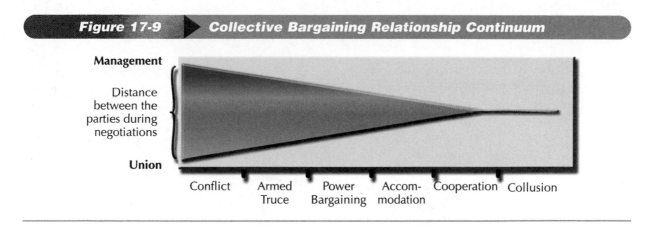

Management

Distance
between the
parties during
negotiations

Union

| Conflict | Armed Truce | Power Bargaining | Accom- modation | Cooperation | Collusion |

Contract Negotiation (Collective Bargaining)

Collective bargaining
Process whereby representatives of management and workers negotiate over wages, hours, and other terms and conditions of employment.

Collective bargaining, the last step in unionization, is the process whereby representatives of management and workers negotiate over wages, hours, and other terms and conditions of employment. This give-and-take process between representatives of two organizations attempts to establish conditions beneficial to both. It is also a relationship based on relative power.

The power relationship in collective bargaining involves conflict, and the threat of conflict seems necessary to maintain the relationship. But perhaps the most significant aspect of collective bargaining is that it is a continuing relationship that does not end immediately after agreement is reached. Instead, it continues for the life of the labor agreement and beyond. Therefore, the more cooperative the attitude that management takes, the less hostility and conflict with unionized employees carries over to the workplace.[19] However, this cooperation does not mean that the employer gives in to all union demands.

Management-union relationships in collective bargaining can follow one of several patterns. Figure 17-9 depicts the relationship as a continuum, ranging from conflict to collusion. On the left side of the continuum, management and the union see each other as enemies. On the right side, the two entities join together in collusion, which is relatively rare in U.S. labor history and is illegal. Most positions fall between these two extremes.

Logging On...

LABORNET
This site describes unions, news, legislation, and upcoming union events.

www.labornet.org

Collective Bargaining Issues

A number of different issues can be addressed during collective bargaining. Although not often listed as such in the contract, management rights and union security are two important issues subject to collective bargaining.

Management Rights

Management rights
Those rights reserved to the employer to manage, direct, and control its business.

Virtually all labor contracts include **management rights**, which are those rights reserved so the employer can manage, direct, and control its business. Such a provision might reads as follows:

The employer retains all rights to manage, direct, and control its business in all particulars, except as such rights are expressly and specifically modified by the terms of this or any subsequent agreement.

By including such a provision, management attempts to preserve its unilateral right to make changes in areas not identified in a labor contract.

Union Security

A major concern of union representatives when bargaining is the negotiation of **union security provisions,** which are contract clauses to aid the union in obtaining and retaining members. One union security provision is the *dues checkoff,* which provides for the automatic deduction of union dues from the payroll checks of union members. The dues checkoff makes it much easier for the union to collect its funds; otherwise it must collect dues by billing each member separately.

Another form of security involves *requiring union membership* of all employees, subject to state right-to-work laws. As mentioned earlier, the closed shop is illegal except in limited construction industry situations. But other types of arrangements can be developed, including *union shops, maintenance-of-membership, and agency shops.*

A growing facet of union security in labor contracts is the *no-layoff* policy, or *job security* guarantee. Such provisions are important to many union workers, especially in light of all the mergers, downsizings, and job reductions taking place in many industries.

Classification of Bargaining Issues

A number of issues can be addressed during collective bargaining. The NLRB has defined bargaining issues in three ways: mandatory, permissive, and illegal. A discussion of each follows.

Mandatory Issues Those issues identified specifically by labor laws or court decisions as subject to bargaining are **mandatory issues**. If either party demands that issues in this category be subject to bargaining, then that must occur. Generally, mandatory issues relate to wages, benefits, nature of jobs, and other work-related subjects. Mandatory subjects for bargaining include the following:

- Discharge of employees
- Grievances
- Work schedules
- Union security and dues checkoff
- Retirement and pension coverage
- Vacations
- Christmas bonuses
- Rest- and lunch-break rules
- Safety rules
- Profit-sharing plans
- Required physical exam

Permissive Issues Those issues that are not mandatory but relate to certain jobs are **permissive issues**. For example, the following issues can be bargained over if both parties agree:

- Benefits for retired employees
- Product prices for employees
- Performance bonds

Illegal Issues A final category, **illegal issues**, includes those issues that would require either party to take illegal action, such as giving preference to union members when hiring employees. If one side wants to bargain over an illegal issue, the other can refuse.

Union security provision
Contract clauses to aid the union in obtaining and retaining members.

WEST GROUP
A THOMSON COMPANY
Dues Checkoff
Discusses typical dues checkoff provisions used by unionized employers.
Custom Search:
☑ ANALYSIS
Phrase: Checkoff authorization cards

Mandatory issues Collective bargaining issues identified specifically by labor laws or court decisions as subject to bargaining.

Permissive issues Collective bargaining issues that are not mandatory but relate to certain jobs.

Illegal issues Collective bargaining issues that would require either party to take illegal action.

The Bargaining Process

The collective bargaining process consists of a number of stages: preparation, initial demands, negotiations, settlement or impasse, and strikes or lockouts.

Preparation and Initial Demands

Both labor and management representatives spend much time preparing for negotiations. Employer and industry data concerning wages, benefits, working conditions, management and union rights, productivity, and absenteeism are gathered. If the organization argues that it cannot afford to pay what the union is asking, the employer's financial situation and accompanying data become all the more relevant. However, the union must request such information before the employer is obligated to provide it. Typical bargaining includes initial proposals of expectations by both sides. The amount of rancor or calmness exhibited may set the tone for future negotiations between the parties.

Refusal to Bargain
Describes conditions relating to refusal to bargain as an unfair labor practice.
Custom Search:
☑ ANALYSIS
Phrase: Refusing to recognize

Continuing Negotiations

After taking initial positions, each side attempts to determine what the other side values highly so the best bargain can be struck. For example, the union may be asking the employer to pay for dental benefits as part of a package that also includes wage increases and retirement benefits. However, the union may be most interested in the retirement benefits, and may be willing to trade the dental payments for more better retirement benefits. Management must determine which the union wants more and decide exactly what to give up.

Good Faith Provisions in federal law require that both employers and union bargaining representatives negotiate in good faith. In good-faith negotiations, the parties agree to send negotiators who can bargain and make decisions, rather than people who do not have the authority to commit either group to a decision. Meetings between the parties cannot be scheduled at absurdly inconvenient hours. Some give-and-take discussions also must occur.

Settlement and Contract Agreement

After reaching an initial agreement, the bargaining parties usually return to their respective constituencies to determine if the informal agreement is acceptable. A particularly crucial stage is **ratification** of the labor agreement, which occurs when union members vote to accept the terms of a negotiated agreement. Prior to the ratification vote, the union negotiating team explains the agreement to the union members and presents it for a vote. If the members approve the agreement, it is then formalized into a contract. Figure 17-10 on the next page lists typical items in labor agreements.

Ratification Process by which union members vote to accept the terms of a negotiated labor agreement.

Bargaining Impasse

Regardless of the structure of the bargaining process, labor and management do not always reach agreement on the issues. If impasse occurs, then the disputes can be taken to conciliation, mediation, or arbitration.

Conciliation Process by which a third party attempts to keep union and management negotiators talking so that they can reach a voluntary settlement.

★**Conciliation and Mediation** When an impasse occurs, an outside party such as the Federal Mediation and Conciliation Service may aid the two deadlocked parties to continue negotiations and arrive at a solution. In **conciliation,** the third

Figure 17-10 ▶ **Typical Items in a Labor Agreement**

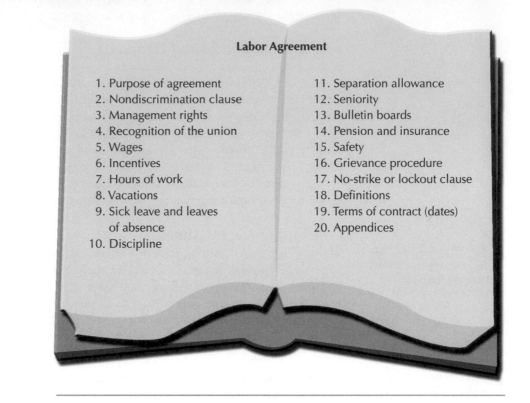

Labor Agreement

1. Purpose of agreement
2. Nondiscrimination clause
3. Management rights
4. Recognition of the union
5. Wages
6. Incentives
7. Hours of work
8. Vacations
9. Sick leave and leaves of absence
10. Discipline
11. Separation allowance
12. Seniority
13. Bulletin boards
14. Pension and insurance
15. Safety
16. Grievance procedure
17. No-strike or lockout clause
18. Definitions
19. Terms of contract (dates)
20. Appendices

Mediation Process by which a third party assists negotiators in reaching a settlement.

party attempts to keep union and management negotiators talking so that they can reach a voluntary settlement, but makes no proposals for solutions. In **mediation,** the third party assists the negotiators in reaching a settlement. In neither conciliation nor mediation does the third party attempt to impose a solution. Sometimes *fact-finding* helps to clarify the issues of disagreement as an intermediate step between mediation and arbitration.

Arbitration Process that uses a neutral third party to make a decision.

Arbitration The process of **arbitration** uses a neutral third party to make a decision. It can be conducted by either an individual or a panel of individuals. Arbitration attempts to solve bargaining impasses, primarily in the public sector. This "interest" arbitration is not frequently used in the private sector, because companies generally do not want an outside party making decisions about their rights, wages, benefits, and other issues. However, grievance, or "rights" arbitration is used extensively in the private sector. Arbitration is discussed in more detail along with the grievance procedures described later in this chapter. Fortunately, in many situations agreements are reached through negotiations without the need for arbitration. However, when disagreements continue, strikes or lockouts may occur.

Strikes and Lockouts

Strike Work stoppage in which union members refuse to work in order to put pressure on an employer.

If a deadlock cannot be resolved, then an employer may revert to a lockout—or a union may revert to a strike. During a **strike,** union members refuse to work in order to put pressure on an employer. Often, the striking union members picket or demonstrate against the employer outside the place of business by carrying placards and signs. In a **lockout,** management shuts down company operations to prevent union members from working. This action may avert possible damage or sabotage to company facilities or injury to employees who continue to work. It also provides leverage to managers.

Lockout Shutdown of company operations undertaken by management to prevent union members from working.

Types of Strikes The following types of strikes can occur:

- *Economic strikes* happen when the parties fail to reach agreement during collective bargaining.
- *Unfair labor practice strikes* occur when union members walk away from their jobs over what they feel are illegal employer actions, such as refusal to bargain.
- *Wildcat strikes* occur during the life of the collective bargaining agreement without approval of union leadership and violate a no-strike clause in a labor contract. Strikers can be discharged or disciplined.
- *Jurisdictional strikes* exist when one union's members walk out to force the employer to assign work to them instead of to another union.
- *Sympathy strikes* express one union's support for another union involved in a dispute, even though the first union has no disagreement with the employer.

The Communications Workers of American (CWA) demonstrated the effective use of a strike by a union when it struck Verizon Communications. More than 90,000 workers walked off jobs primarily because of the mandatory overtime policy at Verizon. Many workers were putting in 15–20 overtime hours every week, and the CWA members finally said, "No more." The union charged that the company was using extensive overtime to avoid hiring additional employees. Ultimately, Verizon and the CWA settled their dispute: Employees received a 12% pay increase over three years and, just as important to the CWA, an eight-hour cap on weekly overtime.[20]

As a result of the decline in union power, work stoppages due to strikes and lockouts are relatively rare. Thus, many unions are reluctant to go on strike because of the financial losses their members would incur, or the fear that the strike would cause the employer to go bankrupt. In addition, management has shown its willingness to hire replacements, and some strikes have ended with union workers losing their jobs.

Replacement of Workers on Strike Management retains and sometimes uses its ability to simply replace workers who strike. Workers' rights vary depending on the type of strike that occurs. For example, in an economic strike, an employer is free to replace the striking workers. But with an unfair labor practices strike, workers who want their jobs back at the end of the strike must be reinstated.

The Strike Page
This Web site contains a listing of all current strikes in the United States and other major countries.

www.igc.apc.org/strike

Union-Management Cooperation

The adversarial relationship that naturally exists between unions and management may lead to strikes and lockouts. However such conflicts are relatively rare. Even more encouraging is the growing recognition on the part of union leaders and employer representatives that cooperation between management and labor unions

▼ Union-Management Cooperation in Workplace Restructuring

Over the past decade numerous firms have engaged in organizational and workplace restructuring in response to industry competitive pressures, mergers, and acquisitions, or other reasons. For organizations with unions, restructurings have had significant effects, such as lost jobs, changed work rules, and altered job responsibilities. When such restructurings occur, unions can take different approaches, ranging from resistance to cooperation.

Ann C. Frost conducted research on the effect of different union approaches when confronted with restructurings, the results of which were published in *Industrial & Labor Relations Review.* The study examined four different restructuring situations in the steel industry. The author

looked at four dimensions of union abilities to: (1) access information, (2) educate and mobilize union members, (3) communicate with management at multiple levels, and (4) access decision making at multiple points.

Access to information considered the ability of local unions to locate, process, and share information with their members. Closely related, for unions to be participants in restructurings, they had to be able to educate their members and mobilize them to take action in order to reinforce their concerns with management. Communication with management occurred at different levels, when in some of the situations union stewards were not included in discussions and others where they were. Finally, involvement of the

local unions in decision making throughout the restructuring process, not just at the beginning, was seen in some situations but not others.

Frost's analyses revealed that some unions were more successful and involved than others. Specifically, when unions were able to obtain information and share that information with their members in order to work constructively with the company managers at various levels, then the organizational restructurings were handled more successfully. This research seems to support the idea that union-management cooperation can reduce problems when work and organizational restructurings have been necessary.[21]

offers the most sensible route if organizations are going to compete effectively in a global economy. The HR Perspective describes a study on cooperative efforts between management and unions when work restructuring becomes necessary.

Cooperation and Joint Efforts

There are a number of notable examples of successful union-management cooperation. One of the most frequently cited examples is at Saturn Corporation, a part of General Motors. There union-management cooperation was established when the Tennessee plant was built, and it has survived a number of challenges and changes for more than a decade.[22] Other firms with successful union-management cooperation include Ford Motor and Boeing, although conflicts in these relationships occasionally arise.

Employee Involvement Program

Suggesting that union-management cooperation or involving employees in making suggestions and decisions could be bad seems a little illogical. Yet some decisions by the NLRB appear to have done just that. Some historical perspective is required to understand the issues that surrounded the decisions.

In the 1930s, when the Wagner Act was written, certain employers would form sham "company unions," coercing workers into joining them in order to keep legitimate unions from organizing the employees. As a result, the Wagner Act contained prohibitions against employer-dominated labor organizations. These prohibitions were enforced, and company unions disappeared. But the growing use of employee involvement programs in organizations today have raised new concerns.

Because of the Wagner Act, many employee involvement programs set up in recent years may be illegal, according to an NLRB decision dealing with Electromation, an Elkhart, Indiana, firm. Electromation used teams of employees to solicit other employees' views about such issues as wages and working conditions. The NLRB labeled them as "labor organizations," according to the Wagner Act in 1935. It further found that the teams were "dominated" by management, which had formed the teams, set their goals, and decided how they would operate. The result of this and other decisions forced many employers to rethink and restructure their employee involvement efforts.

In some cases, federal court decisions have upheld the NLRB position and in others reversed it. The key to decisions allowing employee involvement committees and programs seems to be that these entities do not deal directly with traditional collective bargaining issues such as wages, hours, and working conditions.[23] Also, the composition of the committees and the authority of the groups to make operational suggestions and decisions appear to be permissible, according to several NLRB and court decisions. For instance, at Crown Cork & Seal, the employee "teams" include just one member of management, and the teams address production, safety, training, and attendance issues. Recommendations from the teams are rarely, if ever, ignored by the plant manager.[24]

Unions and Employee Ownership

Unions in some situations have encouraged workers to become partial or complete owners of the companies that employ them. These efforts were spurred by concerns that firms were preparing to shut down, merge, or be bought out, resulting in a cut in the number of union jobs and workers.

Unions have been active in assisting members in putting together employee stock ownership plans (ESOPs) to purchase all or part of some firms. Such programs have been successful in some situations, but have caused problems in others. Some in the labor movement fear that such programs may undermine union support by creating a closer identification with the concerns and goals of employers, instead of "union solidarity."

Grievance Management

Unions know that employee dissatisfaction is a potential source of trouble for employers, whether it is expressed or not. Hidden dissatisfaction grows and creates reactions that may be completely out of proportion to the original concerns. Therefore, it is important that dissatisfaction be given an outlet. A **complaint,** which is merely an indication of employee dissatisfaction, is one outlet.

Complaint Indication of employee dissatisfaction.

If the employee is represented by a union, and the employee says, "I should have received the job transfer because I have more seniority, which is what the union contract states," and she submits it in writing, then that complaint becomes a grievance. A **grievance** is a complaint formally stated in writing. Management

Grievance Complaint formally stated in writing.

should be concerned with both complaints and grievances, because both indicate potential problems within the workforce. Without a grievance procedure, management may be unable to respond to employee concerns because managers are unaware of them. Therefore, a formal grievance procedure provides a valuable communication tool for the organization.

Grievance Responsibilities

The typical division of responsibilities between the HR unit and line managers for handling grievances is shown in Figure 17-11. These responsibilities vary considerably from one organization to another, even between unionized firms. But the HR unit usually has more general responsibilities. Managers must accept the grievance procedure as a possible constraint on some of their decisions.

Grievance Procedures

Grievance procedures

Formal channels of communications used to resolve grievances.

Grievance procedures are formal communications channels designed to settle grievances as soon as possible after the problem arises. First-line supervisors are usually closest to a problem, however, the supervisor is concerned with many other matters besides one employee's grievance, and may even be the subject of an employee's grievance. So, to receive the appropriate attention, grievances go through a specific process for resolution.

Union Representation in Grievances A unionized employee generally has a right to union representation if he or she is being questioned by management and if discipline may result. If these so-called *Weingarten rights* (named after the court case that established them) are violated and the employee is dismissed, he or she usually will be reinstated with back pay. A recent case concerns an NLRB decision to extend these rights to non-union employees involved in disciplinary grievance situations. A lower court decision ruled that non-union employees may request a co-worker to be present during disciplinary meetings.[25] However, that decision has been appealed to higher courts and will likely be decided ultimately by the U.S. Supreme Court.

Figure 17-11 ▶ **Typical HR Responsibilities: Grievance Management**

HR Unit	Managers
• *Assists in designing the grievance procedure*	• *Operate within provisions of the grievance procedure*
• *Monitors trends in grievance rates for the organization*	• *Attempt to resolve grievances where possible*
• *May assist in preparing grievance cases for arbitration*	• *Document grievance cases for the grievance procedure*
• *May have responsibility for settling grievances*	• *Engage in grievance prevention efforts*

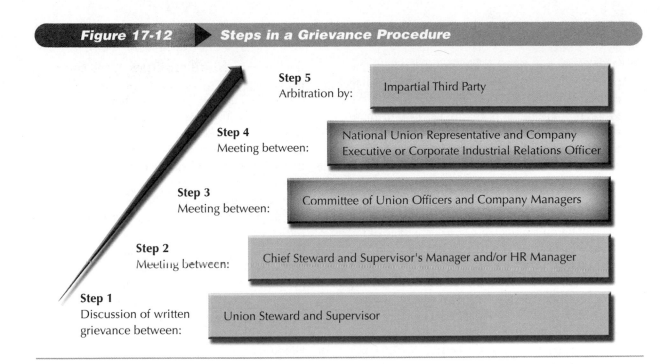

Figure 17-12 ▶ *Steps in a Grievance Procedure*

Step 5
Arbitration by:
Impartial Third Party

Step 4
Meeting between:
National Union Representative and Company Executive or Corporate Industrial Relations Officer

Step 3
Meeting between:
Committee of Union Officers and Company Managers

Step 2
Meeting between:
Chief Steward and Supervisor's Manager and/or HR Manager

Step 1
Discussion of written grievance between:
Union Steward and Supervisor

Grievance Procedures
Discusses how grievance procedures typically operate.
Custom Search:
☑ ANALYSIS
Phrase: Good grievance procedures

Steps in a Grievance Procedure

Grievance procedures can vary in the number of steps they include. Figure 17-12 shows a typical grievance procedure, which includes the following steps:

1. The employee discusses the grievance with the union steward (the union's representative on the job) and the supervisor.
2. The union steward discusses the grievance with the supervisor's manager.
3. The union grievance committee discusses the grievance with appropriate company managers.
4. The representative of the national union discusses the grievance with designated company executives.
5. The final step may be to use an impartial third party for ultimate disposition of the grievance.

If the grievance remains unsettled, representatives for both sides would continue to meet to resolve the conflict. On rare occasions, a representative from the national union might join the process. Or, a corporate executive from headquarters (if the firm is a large corporation) might be called in to help resolve the grievance. If not solved at this stage, the grievance goes to arbitration.

Grievance arbitration
Means by which a third party settles disputes arising from different interpretations of a labor contract.

Grievance arbitration is a means by which a third party settles disputes arising from different interpretations of a labor contract. This process should not be confused with contract or issues arbitration, discussed earlier, in which arbitration is used to determine how a contract will be written. The U.S. Supreme Court has ruled that grievance arbitration decisions issued under labor contract provisions are enforceable.[26] The subjects of grievance arbitration include more than 50 different topic areas, with discipline and discharge, safety and health, and security issues being more prevalent.[27]

Summary

- A union is a formal association of workers that promotes the interests of its members through collective action.
- Workers join unions primarily because of management's failure to address organizational and job-related concerns.
- The structural levels of unions include federations, national or international unions, and local unions. Business agents and union stewards work at local levels.
- Current union membership as a percentage of the workforce is down dramatically to 13.5% of the civilian workforce.
- While public sector unions have grown, decline in union membership has resulted due to geographic, workforce, and industrial changes.
- To grow, unions are targeting professionals, contingent, and low-skilled workers.
- The "National Labor Code" is composed of three laws that provide the legal basis for labor relations today: the Wagner Act, the Taft-Hartley Act, and the Landrum-Griffin Act.
- The Wagner Act was designed to protect unions and workers; the Taft-Hartley Act restored some powers to management; and the Landrum-Griffin Act was passed to protect individual union members.
- The process of unionizing includes an organizing campaign, authorization cards, a representation election, NLRB certification, and collective bargaining.
- Collective bargaining occurs when management negotiates with representatives of workers over wages, hours, and working conditions.
- The issues subject to collective bargaining fall into three categories: mandatory, permissive, and illegal.
- The collective bargaining process includes preparation, initial demands, negotiations, and settlement.
- Once an agreement (contract) is signed between labor and management, it becomes the document governing what each party can and cannot do.
- When impasse occurs, work stoppages through strikes or lockouts can be used to pressure the other party.
- Union-management cooperation has been beneficial in a number of situations, although care must be taken to avoid violations of NLRB provisions.
- Grievances express workers' written dissatisfactions or differences in contract interpretations. Grievances usually follow a formal process to resolution.
- A grievance procedure begins with the first-level supervisor and may end—if the grievance is not resolved along the way—with arbitration.

Review and Discussion Questions

1. Discuss the following statement: "Usually management gets the union it deserves."
2. How realistic is it to think that unions will reverse their decline in membership during the next five years?
3. Identify the three parts of the "National Labor Code" and the key elements of each.
4. A co-worker just brought you a union leaflet that urges each employee to sign an authorization card. What events would you expect to occur from this point on?
5. What are the stages in typical union-management negotiations that usually lead to agreements, rather than strikes or lockouts?
6. Why is it important to resolve grievances at the lowest possible level of the grievance process?

Using the Internet

Responding to Unionization Activity

Some supervisors in your organization have approached you, the HR manager, about union activity. They have heard some rumors and have asked you to give them a list of activities, behaviors, or actions to look for as they supervise their employees. Their intent is to recognize union activity before the union movement has spread throughout the plant. Use the following Web site to develop a set of guidelines for the supervisors:
www. genelevine. com/Papers/66.htm.

CASE

Misfiring the Furnace, Firing the Employee

An employee who had been a vocal supporter of unionizing the workers at a metal casting plant and a union together filed an unfair labor practices charge with the NLRB. The filing charged that the employee had been fired because of his unionization activities. Management responded that the employee was fired for deliberately destroying plant property.

Consider the following facts: A chief electrician at a metal casting plant in Ohio was told to perform a regularly scheduled "rebuild" of a furnace used to melt scrap iron and other raw materials. The employee had performed the job numerous times in the past and was the logical choice for the job.

As was plant policy, the electrician who performed the rebuild also was required to restart the furnace. This time, however, the employee refused to come in for the start-up, indicating that doing so would violate the company's new policy against overtime. When a different electrician started up the furnace, sparks and fire came from the wires. An investigation found loose wires, disconnected fuses, and a cracked coil in the furnace. Ultimately, every wire on one side of the furnace needed to be replaced.

The company fired the employee for sabotaging the rebuild of the furnace and for "shoddy work-manship resulting in the very real possibility of melt furnace loss and resultant production loss." The employee defended his work and filed a case with the National Labor Relations Board. He claimed that he had been ordered to use faulty wires, and made no protest out of fear of retaliation.[28]

Questions

1. Identify which facts would be the most important in deciding for the employee or the company.

2. How would you rule in the case?

(Your instructor can give you the actual decision.)

Notes

1. Based on Wendy Zellner and Aaron Bernstein, "Up Against Wal-Mart," *Business Week,* March 13, 2000; and Ann Zimmerman, "Pro-Union Butchers at Wal-Mart Win a Battle, Lose War," *The Wall Street Journal,* April 11, 2000, A1+.

2. Barry T. Hirsch and David A. MacPherson, *Union Membership and Earnings Data Book,* (Washington, DC: BNA Plus, 2001).

3. Melissa Fitzpatrick, "Collective Bargaining Vulnerability Assessment," *Nursing Management,* February 2001, 40–42.

4. Yochi Dreazen, "Labor Unions Turn to Mergers in Pursuit of Growth," *The Wall Street Journal,* September 1, 2000, A2.

5. U.S. Department of Labor, Bureau of Labor Statistics, 2002.

6. Edward E. Potter, "Labor's Love Lost?" *Journal of Labor Research,* 22 (2001), 321–334.

7. Henry S. Farber and Bruce Western, "Accounting for the Decline of Unions . . . ," *Journal of Labor Research,* 22 (2001), 459–485.

8. Katherine Pflegler, "Unions Striking Out in High-Tech Sector," *Omaha World-Herald,* February 4, 2001, 1G; and Nick Wingfield and Yochi J. Dreazen, "Dot.Com Rout Is a Mixed Blessing for Unionizers," *The Wall Street Journal,* January 2, 2001, A9.

9. U.S. Department of Labor, Bureau of Labor Statistics, 2002.

10. "Temps Join In," *The Wall Street Journal,* October 30, 2001, A1; and Margaret A. Bryant and Roger P. Gilson, "Unions Can Organize Temporary Employees. . . ." *Legal Report,* November–December 2000, 7–8.

11. Susan J. McGolrick, "Current State, Future of NLRB. . . . ," *HR News,* June 2001, 17.

12. Bob Calandra, "Besting the Unions," *Human Resource Executive,* October 16, 2000, 72–75.

13. Diane Hatch and James E. Hall, "Salting Cases Clarified by NLRB," *Workforce,* August 2000, 92; and *NLRB v. Town & Country Electric, Inc. and Ameristaff Contractors, Ltd.,* 115 U.S. S. Ct. 450 (1995).

14. Based on John E. Lyncheski and Leslie D. Heller, "Cyber Speech Cops," *HR Magazine,* January 2001, 145–150; Greg Toppo, " 'Net Revolutionizes Union Organizing," *The Denver Post,* September 4, 2000, 6A; and Carlos Tejado, "Union Hopes 'Barney' Shows It Is No Dinosaur," *The Wall Street Journal,* January 2, 2000, B1.

15. John E. Lyncheski and Ronald J. Andrykovitch, "Who's a Supervisor?" *HR Magazine,* September 2001, 159–167.

16. *NLRB v. Kentucky River Community Care, Inc.,* 121 S. Ct. 1861 (2001).

17. "Union Organizing," *Bulletin to Management,* December 21, 2000, 405.

18. Henry S. Farber, "Union Success in Representation Elections: Why Does Unit Size Matter?" *Industrial & Labor Relations Review,* 54 (2001), 329–348.

19. Gillian Flynn, "When the Unions Come Calling," *Workforce,* November 2000, 82–87.

20. Ellene Zimmerman, "HR Lessons from a Strike," *Workforce,* November 2000, 36–42.

21. Based on Ann C. Frost, "Explaining Variation in Workplace Restructuring," *Industrial & Labor Relations Review,* 53 (2000), 559–578.

22. Saul R. Rubinstein, "A Different Kind of Union: Balancing Co-Management and Representation," *Industrial Relations,* 40 (2001), 163–203.

23. G. Roger King, "New Guidelines from the NLRB on Participative Management Initiatives and Employee Committees," *Legal Report,* November–December, 2001, 1–4.

24. *Crown Cork & Seal Co.,* 334 NLRB 92, July 20, 2001.

25. *Epilepsy Foundation of Northeast Ohio v. NLRB,* DC 00-1332, November 2, 2001.

26. *Eastern Associated Coal Co. vs. United Mine Workers of America,* U.S. S. Ct. 99-1038, November 28, 2000.

27. For a review of grievance arbitration decisions by topic areas, see *Grievance Guide* (Washington, DC: BNA Books, 2000).

28. Reprinted with permission from *Bulletin to Management (BNA Policy and Practice Series)* vol. 51, No. 13, p. 104 (March 30, 2000). Copyright 2000 by The Bureau of National Affairs, Inc. (800-372-1033) *http:// www.bna.com.*

CHAPTER 18

Globalization of HR Management

After you have read this chapter, you should be able to:

- Identify key forces driving globalization of management and organizations.

- Describe how political, legal, economic, and cultural factors affect global HR management.

- List and define three types of international employees.

- Discuss the five factors considered necessary to select successful global employees.

- Explain the activities needed to increase expatriate completion rates.

- Identify basic international compensation practices.

- Describe several international health, safety, and security concerns.

HR Concerns and the Backlash Against Globalization

The globalization of business has provided tremendous opportunities for both global employers and individuals in lesser-developed countries. Through globalization jobs have been created in areas where unemployment traditionally has been high and living conditions primitive. However, a growing concern has been voiced about the effects of globalization on people in other countries. Protesters have demonstrated both peacefully and violently at meetings of world economic ministers over the past few years. Many of the concerns raised focused on the HR practices in less-developed countries. Several reasons for these concerns exist.

U.S. labor unions are joining these protest efforts, because jobs of unionized U.S. workers in a number of industries are lost when plants close and operations shift to lower-wage countries like China, Mexico, and Thailand. Global employers counter that even though the wages in the countries are low, they pay higher wages and provide better working conditions than exist in the local countries. Also, many host-country employees now have jobs, which allows them to improve their living standards. But activists counter by citing numerous examples of abuse by global firms.

Specifically relating to HR management, one concern is the use of child labor and prison labor. According to one estimate, more than 80 million children under age 18 are working in factories and fields for international companies. In some countries, people convicted of "political crimes" are forced to work in factories that manufacture goods to be sold to U.S. and European firms. In those countries, prison labor also competes with other labor sources at lower wage rates.

Critics of globalization practices of employers also cite the extremely low wage rates paid by the international firms. *Global Exchange,* an advocacy group, cites examples whereby Cambodian garment workers make $40 per month sewing garments for U.S. retailers, and many Chinese toy manufacturing firms pay their workers $1 per day. Nike, the Gap, and other global firms, have been accused of being "sweatshop employers" by students at over 170 colleges through United Students Against Sweatshops (USAS). International campaigns have been mounted using customer boycotts, unfavorable news media coverage, and group protests.

To deal with these concerns and protests, firms such as Levi Strauss, Starbuck's, Nike, and others have established minimum standards that are supposed to be met by all operations of their subsidiaries, suppliers, and subcontractors throughout the world. The firms established the Fair Labor Association, and that association has published standards for compliance with its guidelines.

Other firms have used independent auditing organizations to inspect and monitor their factories, sometimes including representatives of the globalization critics in the monitoring efforts. For instance, Reebok had a social research group inspect factories employing 10,000 workers and identify problems and remedies. Liz Claiborne has used outside entities to investigate worker conditions at its factories in Guatemala and other countries in order to provide candid reports and recommendations.

Disagreements continue about whether these efforts are sincere and are sufficient to address significant HR problems in global operations, or if they are just "window dressing" to try and counter the protests and prevent consumer boycotts. Regardless of which viewpoint is considered, it is evident that the globalization of business presents significant HR implications and issues to be managed.[1]

> A growing concern has been voiced about the effects of globalization on people in other countries.

"Globalization continues to bring the people of the world closer together."

The internationalization of business has proceeded at a rapid pace. A compilation of the world's largest companies found that 59 are based in the U.S., 31 in Europe, and 7 in Japan.[2] Many U.S. firms large and small receive a substantial portion of their profits and sales from outside the United States. Firms such as Coca-Cola, Exxon, Mobil, Microsoft, Ford Motor, General Electric, and others derive half or more of total sales and profits outside the United States. The globalization of business has shifted from trade and investment to integrating global operations, management, and strategic alliances worldwide.

Globalization of Business and HR

There are a number of forces that together have led to world trade increasing over 60% in the past decade. Some of the more prominent ones are highlighted next.

Global Population Changes

Throughout the world in the developed, industrialized countries such as those in the European Union (EU), Japan, and the United States, population growth has slowed significantly. In those areas an aging population and declining birth rates have contributed to slower growth in the number of workers and consumers. However, population in China, India, Africa, Latin America, and other countries and regions continues to grow significantly.

To take advantage of this growth, firms throughout the world have established operations, formed joint ventures, or merged with firms in these countries. The prospect of billions of new consumers in the faster-growing countries is driving global investments and operations. Consumer demands for products from other countries is also driving globalization. As examples, German and Japanese cars, French cosmetics, U.S. fast food, Mexican beer, and Korean electronics are all available globally and desired by consumers in many countries.

Global Economic Interdependence

Economic experts estimate that by 2020 the six largest economies will be the U.S., China, Japan, Indonesia, India, and Korea.[3] Firms based in many countries are responding to these opportunities. Thus the economic future of organizations throughout the world is linked to growth of the world economy. An example of this linkage is unrest, as has occurred in Indonesia, Turkey, Argentina, and some other countries. This unnrest has affected stock markets throughout the world. Other examples of the global economy can be seen by the effects of the economic stagnation in Japan, the fall of the U.S. stock market, and results of international terrorist acts at the U.S. World Trade Center. These examples indicate the high level of interdependence among the economies of individual countries.

Regional Alliances

The development of a number of regional trade and political alliances also has contributed to globalization. The two most well-known alliances are discussed next.

Section 5   Employee Relations and Global HR

North American Free Trade Agreement (NAFTA) The United States, Canada, and Mexico recognized the importance of world trade by eliminating barriers and working more closely together by signing the North American Free Trade Agreement (NAFTA). But NAFTA also has placed restrictions on employers to ensure that their HR practices in Mexico met certain standards. The Commission on Labor Cooperation (CLC), established as part of NAFTA, reviews complaints filed in the U. S., Canada, or Mexico regarding occupational safety and health, child labor, benefits, and labor-management relations. Discussions have been held about expanding NAFTA to include other Latin American countries also.

European Union (EU) In Western Europe, efforts over several decades led to the creation of the European Union. The economic integration of the countries in the EU received a major push in 2002 with the introduction of the Euro currency. The EU also has established labor and other standards, adopted by individual EU countries, which has led to greater similarity of HR practices in EU-based firms. Foreign firms operating in the EU have had to comply with the requirements.

Global Communications

Another major contributor to globalization is the development and evolution of telecommunications and technology that aids the rapid transfer of information. Satellite technology has brought television and wireless telephone services to remote villages in Africa, India, China, and Latin America. The explosive worldwide growth in use of the Internet has meant that peoples and firms can easily communicate and have access to huge amounts of information and data.

Much of the communication on the Internet is in English.[4] As the global language of business, English allows easier communications and information flow. In many countries students learn English as their second language, and many foreign firms train their employees in English. For instance, Telecom Italia provides English courses for its employees, and several large Japanese global firms use English as their "business language."[5]

Types of Global Organizations

A growing number of organizations that operate within only one country have recognized the need to develop more global operations. Organizations may pass through three stages as they broaden their operations worldwide as shown in Figure 18-1 on the next page. A discussion of each stage follows.

Importing and Exporting The first phase of international interaction consists of **importing and exporting**. Here, an organization begins selling and buying goods and services with organizations in other countries. Most of the international contacts are made by the sales and marketing staff and a limited number of other executives who negotiate contracts. Generally, HR activities are not affected except for travel policies for those going abroad.

Multinational Enterprises As firms develop and expand, they identify opportunities to begin operating in other countries. A **multinational enterprise (MNE)** is one in which an organization has operating units located in foreign countries. Typically these units provide goods and services for the geographic

Importing and exporting
Selling and buying goods and services with organizations in other countries.

Multinational enterprise (MNE) An organization with operating units located in foreign countries.

areas surrounding the countries where operations exist. Key management positions in the foreign operations are filled with employees from the home country of the corporation. As the MNE expands, it hires workers from the countries in which it has operations.

One critical area for MNEs is to have HR practices for employees sent from corporate headquarters so that these employees and their dependents may continue their economic lifestyles while stationed outside the home country. Ways to link these individuals to the parent company are also critical, especially if the international job assignment is two-three years long. Because laws and regulations likely differ from those in the home country, the HR professionals in the parent organization must become knowledgeable about each country in which the MNE operates and know how staffing, training, compensation, health and safety, and labor relations must be adapted.

Global Organization The MNE can be thought of as an international firm, in that it operates in various countries, but each foreign business unit is operated

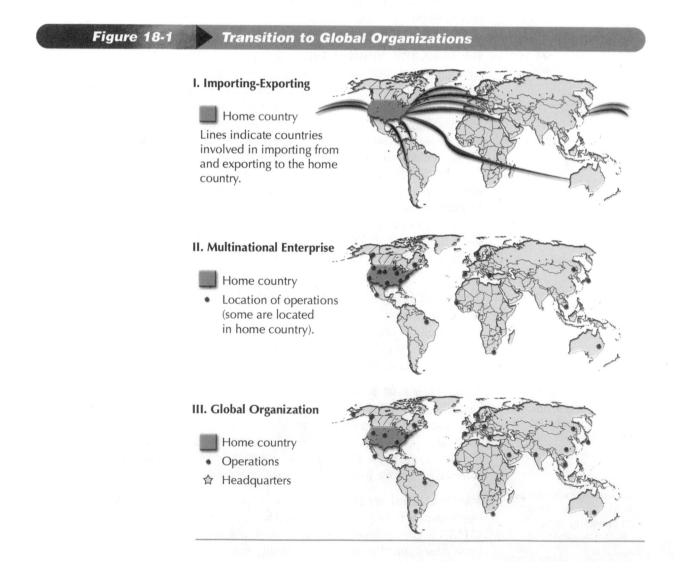

Figure 18-1 ▶ **Transition to Global Organizations**

I. Importing-Exporting

■ Home country

Lines indicate countries involved in importing from and exporting to the home country.

II. Multinational Enterprise

■ Home country
• Location of operations (some are located in home country).

III. Global Organization

■ Home country
• Operations
☆ Headquarters

Global organization One having corporate units in a number of countries integrated to operate worldwide.

separately. In contrast, a **global organization** has corporate units in a number of countries that are integrated to operate as one organization worldwide. An MNE may evolve into a global organization as operations in various countries become more integrated.

HR management in truly global organizations moves people, especially key managers and professionals, throughout the world. Individuals who speak several languages fluently are highly valued, and they will move among divisions and countries as they assume more responsibilities and experience career growth. As much as possible, international HR management must be viewed strategically in these organizations. Global HR policies and activities are developed, but decentralization of decision making to subsidiary units and operations in other countries is necessary in order for country-specific adjustments to be made.

Factors Affecting Global HR Management

Managing human resources in different cultures, economies, and legal systems presents some challenges. However, when done well, global HR management pays dividends. Doing business globally requires consideration of four general factors. Each of the four depicted in Figure 18-2 is discussed next.

Legal and Political Factors

The nature and stability of political systems vary from country to country. Firms in the U.S. are accustomed to a relatively stable political system, and the same is true in many of the other developed countries in Europe. Although presidents, prime ministers, premiers, governors, senators, and representatives may change,

Figure 18-2 ▶ **Factors Affecting Global HR Management**

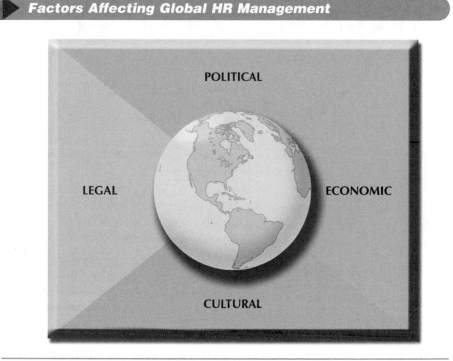

Ethics and Global Differences

Because of differences in legal, political, and culture values and practices in different countries, global employers often face ethical issues. But these employers must comply with home-country laws also. To illustrate, the U.S. and some Western European countries have laws regarding the conduct of firms based in their countries. For example, the Foreign Corrupt Practices Act (FCPA) prohibits U.S. firms from engaging in bribery and other practices in foreign countries that would be illegal in the United States. However, competing firms from certain other countries are not bound by similar restrictions, which may create competitive disadvantages for U.S. and European firms.

The impact of the FCPA and similar laws often requires global managers to draw some fine distinctions between paying "special fees," which is legal, and bribery, which is illegal. Several examples illustrate how ethical dilemmas may conflict with business practices in other countries.

- Many global firms have found that establishing or expanding business operations in some African and Latin American countries is much easier if the children of key government officials are provided "educational assistance." This means the global firm arranges for these students to get admitted to and receive scholarships to attend colleges and universities in the U.S. or the United Kingdom. Without this "sponsorship," the global firm often faces endless delays in obtaining the necessary government agency approvals for its operations.
- In one Eastern European country, obtaining a new telephone line in less than three months requires making a cash payment, referred to as an "expediting charge" to the local manager of the telephone office. All parties to the deal know that the manager personally will retain the cash, but a tele-

phone is essential for doing business internationally.
- Foreign firms wishing to do business in one Asian Pacific country must hire a "business representative" in order to obtain appropriate licenses and operating permits. In this country, it is well known that the best representatives are friends and relatives of the head of the country. It also is expected to offer the representative 10% to 20% ownership in the business as an "agent fee" for promptly completing the licensing process.

These and other situations reflect how different legal, political, and cultural factors in other countries can lead to ethical conflicts for global managers. Some global firms have established guidelines and policies to reduce the payments of bribes, but even these efforts do not provide detailed guidance on handling the situations that can arise.

the well-established legal systems offer continuity and consistency on which global firms can depend.

However, many other nations function under turbulent legal and political systems. Some governments regularly are overthrown by military coups. Dictators and despots in other countries use their power to require international firms to buy goods and services from host-country firms owned or controlled by the rulers or the rulers' families. In some parts of the world, the number of political parties and factions causes constant change in governments. In other countries, one-party rule or a ruling "political elite" has led to pervasive corruption.[6] As the HR Perspective illustrates, ethical considerations for global managers arise in many situations.

From country to country, legal systems vary in character and stability, with business contracts sometimes becoming unenforceable because of internal political factors. International firms may have to decide strategically when to comply with certain host-country laws and regulations and when to ignore them because of operational or political reasons.

For example, in many Western European countries, laws on labor unions and employment make it difficult to reduce the number of workers because required payments to former employees can be very high. Equal employment legislation exists to varying degrees in various countries, but in others because of religious or ethical differences, employment discrimination may be an accepted practice. As a result, it is crucial for HR professionals to conduct a comprehensive review of the political environment and employment-related laws before beginning operations in a country. The role and nature of labor unions should be a part of that review also.

Economic Factors

Economic factors are linked to political, legal, and cultural issues, and different countries have different economic systems. Some even still operate with a modified version of communism, which has essentially failed. For example, in China communism is the official economic approach. But as the government attempts to move to a more mixed model, it is using unemployment and layoffs to reduce government enterprises bloated with too many workers.

In many developed countries, especially in Europe, employment restrictions and wage levels are high. Consequently, many European firms are transferring jobs to lower-wage countries, such as Romania, China, Thailand, and others. U.S.-based firms also have shifted a significant number of manufacturing jobs to Mexico using *maquiladora* plants along the U.S.–Mexican border. Estimates are that there are over 4,000 such plants employing several hundred thousand workers whose average wage rate is $90 to $100 per week, considerably cheaper than in the U.S.[7]

In addition, nations with weak economies may not be able to invest in maintaining and upgrading the necessary elements of their infrastructures, such as roads, electric power, schools, and telecommunications. The absence of good infrastructures may make it more difficult to convince managers from the United States, EU countries, or Japan to take assignments overseas.

Cultural Factors

Cultural forces represent another important concern affecting international HR management. The culture of organizations was discussed earlier in the text, and of course, national cultures also exist. **Culture** is composed of the societal forces affecting the values, beliefs, and actions of a distinct group of people. Cultural differences certainly exist between nations, but significant cultural differences exist within countries also. One only has to look at the conflicts caused by religion or ethnicity in Central Europe and other parts of the world to see the importance of culture in international organizations. Convincing individuals from different ethnic or tribal backgrounds to work together may be difficult in some parts of the world.

One widely used way to classify and compare cultures was developed by Geert Hofstede, a Dutch scholar and researcher. Hofstede conducted research on more than 100,000 IBM employees in 53 countries, and he defined five dimensions

Culture Societal forces affecting the values, beliefs, and actions of a distinct group of people.

	Country	Power Distance	Individualism	Masculinity/ Femininity	Uncertainty Avoidance	Long-Term Orientation*
	Brazil	14	26	27	21	6
	Canada	39	4	24	41	20
	France	15	10	35	10	N/A
	Great Britain	42	3	9	47	18
	India	10	21	20	45	7
	Israel	52	19	29	19	N/A
	Japan	33	22	1	7	4
	Mexico	5	32	6	18	N/A
	Netherlands	40	4	51	35	10
	South Africa	35	16	13	39	N/A
	South Korea	27	43	41	16	5
	United States	38	1	15	43	17

Figure 18-3 ▶ **Selected Countries on Hofstede's Culture Dimensions**

Note: The scores indicate a rank among 53 countries.   *Rankings based on only 22 countries as part of later study.

Source: Based on data contained in Geert Hofstede, *Cultures and Organizations* (London: McGraw-Hill Book Co., 1991).

useful in identifying and comparing culture. Figure 18-3 shows the results of Hofstede's studies on selected countries. A review of each of those dimensions follows.[8]

Power distance Dimension of culture that refers to the inequality among the people of a nation.

Power Distance The dimension of **power distance** refers to the inequality among the people of a nation. In countries such as Canada, the Netherlands, and the United States, there is less inequality than in such countries as France, Mexico, and Brazil. As power distance scores increase, there is less status and authority difference between superiors and subordinates.

One way in which differences on this dimension affect HR activities is that the reactions to management authority differ among cultures. A more autocratic approach to managing is more common in many countries, while in the Netherlands and the United States there may be more use of employee participation in decision-making.

Individualism Another dimension of culture identified by Hofstede is **individualism**, which is the extent to which people in a country prefer to act as individuals instead of members of groups. On this dimension, people in some Asian countries tend to be less individualistic and more group-oriented, whereas those in the United States are more individualistic. An implication of these differences is that more collective action and less individual competition is likely in those countries that de-emphasize individualism.

Individualism Dimension of culture that refers to the extent to which people in a country prefer to act as individuals instead of members of groups.

Masculinity/Femininity The cultural dimension **masculinity/femininity** refers to the degree to which "masculine" values prevail over "feminine" values. Masculine values identified by Hofstede were assertiveness, performance orientation, success, and competitiveness, whereas feminine values included quality of life, close personal relationships, and caring. Respondents from Japan had the most masculinity, while those from the Netherlands had more femininity-oriented values. Differences on this dimension may be tied to the role of women in the culture. Considering the different roles of women and what is "acceptable" for women in the United States, Saudi Arabia, Japan, and Mexico suggests how this dimension might affect the assignment of women expatriates to managerial jobs in the various countries.[9]

Masculinity/femininity Dimension of cultures that refers to the degree to which "masculine" values prevail over "feminine" values.

Uncertainty Avoidance The dimension of **uncertainty avoidance** refers to the preference of people in a country for structured rather than unstructured situations. A structured situation is one in which rules can be established and there are clear guides on how people are expected to act. Nations focusing on avoiding uncertainty, such as Japan and France, tend to be more resistant to change. In contrast, people in places such as the United States and Great Britain tend to have more "business energy" and to be more flexible.

A logical use of differences in this factor is to anticipate how people in different countries will react to changes instituted in organizations. In more flexible cultures, what is less certain may be more intriguing and challenging, which may lead to greater entrepreneurship and risk taking than in the more "rigid" countries.

Uncertainty avoidance Dimension of culture that refers to the preference of people in a country for structured rather than unstructured situations.

Long-Term Orientation The dimension of **long-term orientation** refers to values people hold that emphasize the future, as opposed to short-term values, which focus on the present and the past. Long-term values include thrift and persistence, while short-term values include respecting tradition and fulfilling social obligations. Hofstede developed this dimension a decade after his original studies on dimension. A long-term orientation was more present in Japan and India, while people in the United States and France tended to have more short-term orientations.

Differences in many other facets of culture could be discussed. But it is enough to recognize that international HR managers and professionals must recognize that cultural dimensions differ from country to country and even within

Long-term orientation Dimension of culture that refers to values people hold that emphasize the future, as opposed to short-term values focusing on the present and the past.

countries. Therefore, the HR activities appropriate in one culture or country may have to be altered to fit appropriately into another culture or country.

Staffing Global Assignments

Staffing global assignments involves selecting, placing, and locating employees in other countries. The need for individuals who can provide leadership in global organizations emphasizes the importance of global staffing. According to several different surveys of large multinational corporations, about 85% of the firms indicated a shortage of global leaders with the capabilities required for success.[10]

When staffing global assignments, cost is a major factor to be considered. The cost of establishing a manager or professional in another country can run as high as $1 million for a three-year job assignment. The actual costs for placing a key manager outside the United States often are twice the manager's annual salary. For instance, if the manager is going to Japan, the costs may be even higher when housing costs, schooling subsidies, and tax equalization payment are calculated. Further, if a manager, professional, or executive quits an international assignment prematurely or insists on a transfer home, associated costs can equal or exceed the annual salary. "Failure" rates for managers sent to other countries may run as high as 40% to 50% in some firms or countries, and the reasons for this failure are explored later in the chapter.

Types of Global Employees

Global organizations can be staffed in a number of different ways. Each staffing option presents some unique HR management challenges. For instance, when staffing with citizens of different countries, different tax laws and other factors apply. HR professionals need to be knowledgeable about the laws and customs

"Grab some lederhosen, Sutfin. We're about to climb aboard the globalization bandwagon."

© The New Yorker Collection 2001 Robert Weber from cartoonbank.com. All Rights Reserved.

Research on Staffing Foreign Subsidiaries

The different ways that foreign subsidiaries can be staffed was the subject of a research study by Anne-Wil Harzing published in *Human Resource Management*. The purpose of her research was to learn about the staffing policies and practices of global firms for the top managers in their global subsidiaries. Specifically, the study examined the extent Parent-Country Nationals or Host-Country Nationals are selected and why those choices occur.

To conduct her research, Harzing obtained data from a directory of about 2,700 global subsidiaries of over 200 Multinational Enterprises (MNEs) operating in 48 different countries and 23 different industries. Additionally,

surveys mailed to 104 different MNEs were used to obtain additional data. However, the study did not include any U.S.-based MNEs.

The results of her study found that about 40% of the executives in the global subsidiaries were Parent-Country Nationals. The remaining executives came from host-country and third-country nationals. One interesting finding was that Japanese MNEs were much more likely to place Japanese as top executives than were European-based firms to use Europeans. Also, almost all of the HR directors in the global subsidiaries came from the host countries, probably due to the cultural and local knowledge and contacts needed.

Reinforcing other studies and experiences of global firms, it appears that having the top executive (or managing director in global terms) as a Parent-Country National is done to ensure that global subsidiaries and their operations are tied in with overall global strategies and operations. Use of more host-country and third-country nationals in functions such as finance, marketing, and HR provides local linkages and understanding important to success in the individual countries. However, generalizing about staffing patterns of all MNEs, including U.S.-based ones, must be done cautiously because the study did not include U.S. MNEs.[11]

---

of each country. They must establish appropriate payroll and record-keeping procedures, among other activities, to ensure compliance with varying regulations and requirements. International employees typically are placed in three different classifications, as discussed next.

Expatriate An employee, working in an operation, who is not a citizen of the country in which the operation is located, but is a citizen of the country of the headquarters organization.

Expatriates An **expatriate** is an employee, working in an operation, who is not a citizen of the country in which the operation is located, but is a citizen of the country of the headquarters organization. Also referred to as *parent-country nationals (PCN),* expatriates are used to ensure that foreign operations are linked effectively with the parent corporations. Generally, expatriates also are used to develop global capabilities within an organization. Experienced expatriates can provide a pool of talent that can be tapped as the organization expands its operations more broadly into even more countries. For example, Japanese-owned firms with operations in the United States have rotated Japanese managers through U.S. operations in order to expand the knowledge of U.S. business practices in the Japanese firms. The HR Perspective describes a research study on use of expatriates who are parent-country nationals and host-country nationals to staff global subsidiaries.

Host-country national An employee working for a firm in an operation who is a citizen of the country where the operation is located, but where the headquarters for the firm are in another country.

Host-Country Nationals A **host-country national** is an employee working for a firm in an operation who is a citizen of the country where the operation is located, but where the headquarters for the firm are in another country. Using host-country nationals is important for several reasons. One reason is that the organization wants to establish clearly that it is making a commitment to the host country and not just setting up a foreign operation. Host-country nationals often know the culture, politics, laws, and business customs better than an outsider would. Tapping into the informal "power" network may be important. Another reason to use host-country nationals is to provide employment in the country. As the chapter opening discussion indicates, in many lesser-developed countries, compensation levels are significantly lower than in the United States, so U.S. firms can gain cost advantages by using host-country nationals to staff many jobs.

Third-country national A citizen of one country, working in a second country, and employed by an organization headquartered in a third country.

Third-Country Nationals A **third-country national** is a citizen of one country, working in a second country, and employed by an organization headquartered in a third country. For example, a U.S. citizen working for a British oil company as a manager in Norway is a third-country national. Staffing with use of third-country nationals shows a truly global approach. Often, these individuals handle responsibilities throughout a continent or region. For instance, a major U.S.-based electronics company has its European headquarters in Brussels, Belgium. Although most employees on the clerical staff are Belgians, only about 20% of the professionals and managers are from Belgium. Most of the rest, except for five U.S. expatriates, come from other Western European countries.

Possible Global Assignments

Decisions about how to staff global assignments vary based on the nature, purpose, and length of the assignment. As shown in Figure 18-4, there are four different types of global assignments requiring intercultural capabilities:[12]

- For *technical assignments,* individuals are sent to do limited jobs then return, which requires limited cultural skills.
- In *functional assignments,* individuals are sent for extended projects or jobs but return upon completion, and some intercultural skills are needed.
- For *developmental assignments,* individuals are sent to develop and broaden their understanding of global operations, and intercultural understanding and skills are important.

Figure 18-4 ▶ **Types of Global Assignments**

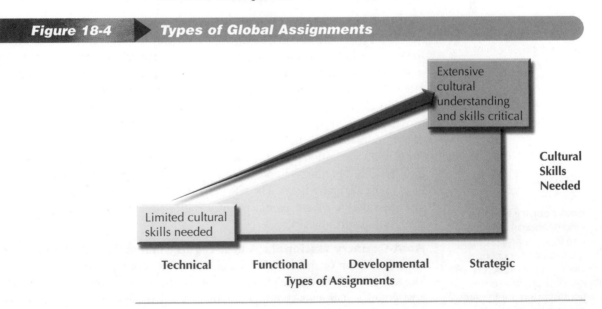

Section 5   Employee Relations and Global HR

- On *strategic assignments,* individuals are sent to fill critical strategic jobs, requiring extended efforts, and intercultural understanding and skills are critical to success.

The importance of intercultural capabilities increases as assignments progress from technical to strategic. Also, the higher the level of responsibility and the longer the assignment, the more intercultural capabilities are needed. Rather than making assignments three years long or more, global employers now find that shorter-term assignments can be effective in reducing the "resistance" of assignees and their failure rates. Short-term assignments of several months at a time create different personal and family stresses than relocation for several years. Also, the assignments provide global development experiences for employees without disrupting the individuals' careers. Different compensation and lodging issues arise with shorter-term assignment. But success with shorter assignments requires planning to address such issues as housing, travel, return trips, compensation, and health and safety concerns.[13]

Another means of providing global experience is through the use of multi-cultural or *transnational* teams. These teams may be temporary or somewhat permanent, formed to solve a specific problem or to handle ongoing activities. They often include headquarters representatives, host-country nationals, and third-country nationals. They are useful not only as potentially valuable business units, but also as development vehicles for leaders.[14]

Recruiting for Global Assignments

Recruiting employees for global assignments requires approaches and understanding different from the typical recruiting efforts in a home-country setting. The recruiting processes must consider cultural differences, laws, and language considerations. For instance, in Eastern Europe potential recruits like to work for European and U.S. firms, so recruiters emphasize the "western" image. In Hong Kong recruiting ads often stress success factors by showing "typical employees" of a firm wearing expensive watches and stylish clothes.[15]

The growth of the Internet has made global recruiting much more accessible, particularly for individuals in search of professional management jobs. Those individuals and more technologically knowledgeable candidates can be reached using Internet advertising. Global search firms also can be used to locate specialized global managerial talent.

Selection for Global Assignments

The selection process for an international assignment should provide a realistic picture of the life, work, and culture to which the employee may be sent. HR managers start by preparing a comprehensive description of the job to be done. This description notes responsibilities that would be unusual in the home nation, including negotiating with public officials; interpreting local work codes; and responding to ethical, moral, and personal issues such as religious prohibitions and personal freedoms. Figure 18-5 on the next page shows the most frequently cited key competencies for successful global employees. A look at each of the areas follows next.

Figure 18-5 | **Global Employee Selection Factors**

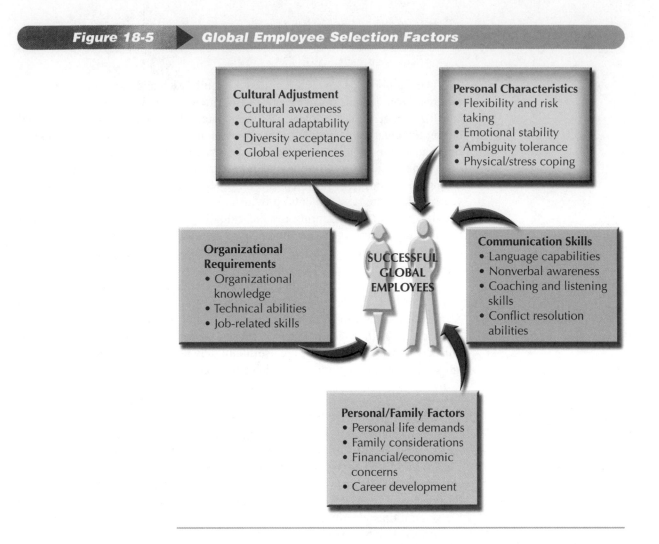

Cultural Adjustment
- Cultural awareness
- Cultural adaptability
- Diversity acceptance
- Global experiences

Personal Characteristics
- Flexibility and risk taking
- Emotional stability
- Ambiguity tolerance
- Physical/stress coping

Organizational Requirements
- Organizational knowledge
- Technical abilities
- Job-related skills

SUCCESSFUL GLOBAL EMPLOYEES

Communication Skills
- Language capabilities
- Nonverbal awareness
- Coaching and listening skills
- Conflict resolution abilities

Personal/Family Factors
- Personal life demands
- Family considerations
- Financial/economic concerns
- Career development

Logging On...

Etiquette International

This professional firm works with organizations to make their employees more effective and professional when working with other cultures.

http://www.etiquetteintl.com/

Cultural Adjustment Crucial to global success for individuals is how they adjust to the culture differences in their foreign assignments. Prior global experiences, even foreign vacation travel, can be explored as part of the selection process to gain insights on how culturally adaptable individuals are. Awareness of cultural issues and differences and acceptance of diverse cultural demands and customs are important areas to explore. For example, in Nigeria the local telephone system is so inefficient that overseas calls can be made more easily than crosstown calls, especially in Lagos, the capital city. A U.S. citizen accustomed to the convenience and reliability of the U.S. telephone system may become impatient and angry when confronted with such delays. Throughout the selection process, especially in the selection interviews, it is crucial to assess the potential employee's ability to accept and adapt to different customs, management practices, laws, religious values, and infrastructure conditions.

However, individuals with different cultural backgrounds must be considered as well.[16] For instance, the U.S. emphasis on assertiveness, individualism, and independence may lead U.S. interviewers to expect applicants to exhibit those characteristics. But in some Asian cultures deference to authority and conflict avoidance may result in Asian candidates not displaying the "American characteristics" in selection interviews.[17] Therefore, if candidates are to be placed in China or Japan, the interviewers' styles and expectations may need to be altered.

Organizational Requirements Many global employers find that knowledge of the organization and how it operates is as important as cultural adjustment factors in determining global assignment success.[18] Interacting with managers in the home country, representing the firm in the foreign locations, and managing foreign employees all require some understanding of the firm's products, services, organizational "politics," and policies.

As with any job, the individuals must have the needed technical abilities and meet the job-related KSAs to be successful. However, simply meeting organizational requirements may not be sufficient for ensuring global assignment success. For this reason, the selection process for someone from inside the company must also assess the other factors shown in Figure 18-5. For candidates from outside the organization, industry knowledge may be helpful, but a realistic preview of the organization is essential in order to determine person-organization fit.

Personal Characteristics The experiences of many global firms demonstrate that the best employees in the home country may not be the best employees in a global assignment, primarily because of personal charactcristics of individuals.[19] A number of identified personal characteristics contribute to the success of global employees. The stress of living and working in foreign countries requires people who exhibit emotional stability, are flexible, tolerate ambiguity well, see adjusting to different cultures as challenges, and enjoy the risks associated with those challenges. Also, the physical demands of travel, jet lag, time zone changes, long work hours, and frequent business meetings and dinners place significant stress on global employees.

During the selection process many global employers use personality tests and other assessment means in order to assess candidates' suitability for global assignments. For example, Motorola uses intelligence and personality tests, as well as assessment centers and role-playing exercises, to assess potential candidates for global assignments.[20] The importance of assessing personality characteristics was underscored by a study that found that extroversion, agreeableness, and emotional stability increased the desire of expatriates to complete their global assignments.[21]

Communication Skills One of the most basic skills needed by expatriate employees is the ability to communicate orally and in writing in the host-country language. Inability to communicate adequately in the language may significantly inhibit the success of an expatriate. Numerous firms with international operations select individuals based on their technical and managerial capabilities and then have the selected individuals take foreign language training. Intensive 10-day courses offered by Berlitz and other schools teach basic foreign language skills.

But in any language, communication includes far more than simple vocabulary. Nonverbal communications through greetings, gestures, pace, and proximity all vary in different countries. Interacting with other people through coaching and

Logging On...

Berlitz International
Language and culture adjustment training and information is provided by this well-known firm.

www.Berlitz.com

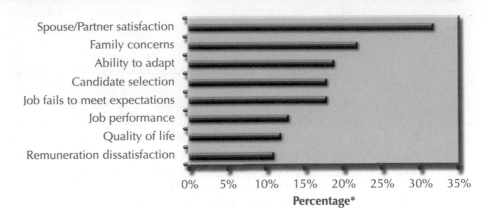

Figure 18-6 ▶ *Causes of Expatriate Assignment Failure*

*Percentages reflect "often caused failure" responses only. More than one answer could be given.

Source: Based on data from the GMAC Global Relocation Services *Global Relocation Trends 2000 Survey Report* (New York: GMAC GRS/Windham International, 2000), 48. Used with permission.

listening skills is at least as important as speaking the language. Conflict resolution abilities are essential, particularly given different cultural values regarding conflict. For example, in some Western European countries, the individual parties address conflicts directly and forcefully; in many other cultures conflicts go unstated, and conflict resolution often requires more time and extensive communications sensitivities.

WEST GROUP
A THOMSON COMPANY
Foreign Assignments
Discusses ways to reduce foreign assignment failure.
Custom Search:
☑ ANALYSIS
Phrase: Foreign assignment failures

Personal/Family Factors The preferences and attitudes of spouses and other family members also present major staffing considerations. Two of the most common reasons for turning down international assignments are family considerations and spouses' careers. Many expatriates are married, and three-fourths of the married expatriates are accompanied on overseas assignments by their spouses, and 60% bring children with them.[22] Also, the growth in dual-career couples complicates the transfer of international employees, particularly on light of the work-permit restrictions common in many countries. Figure 18-6 shows the most common reasons why global assignments fail or are terminated early. Notice that person/family concerns top the list, followed by factors related to candidate selection and the job not meeting individuals' expectations.

Because personal/family factors play such a large role in the success of global employees, the selection process commonly may include interviews of spouses, partners, and even children. If significant resistance or opposition to accepting a global relocation and adapting to different cultures will create family conflicts, then there is a greater likelihood that the global employee will not complete the assignment or will not be as successful.

Legal Issues in Selecting Global Employees

Employment regulations in some countries have government-controlled employment processes that require foreign employers to obtain government approval to

Women Employees, EEO, and Global Staffing

The extent to which U.S. Equal Employment regulations apply to U.S. employees working for U.S. firms internationally was finally decided when the Civil Rights Act of 1991 extended coverage of EEO laws and regulations to U.S. citizens working internationally for U.S.-controlled companies. However, the act states that if laws in a foreign country require actions in conflict with U.S. EEO laws, the foreign laws will apply. If no laws exist, but only customs or cultural considerations are used, then the U.S. EEO laws will apply.

Despite these regulations, women comprise only 14% of U.S. citizens working abroad for U.S. firms, even though they comprise about 50% of all middle managers in U.S. firms. A number of reasons explain why relatively few U.S. women professionals and managers serve in international positions for U.S. firms.

A study by Catalyst, a U.S. women's advocate organization, focused on why the gap exists. One finding of the study shows that women rejected foreign assignments about as often as men. However, the major problem identified was that a large number of supervisors and managers, many of whom are men, believed that women would not want foreign assignments or would not succeed in such assignments if they were offered. Interestingly, managers and supervisors assumed the opposite for men.

Concerns about the safety of women working in certain locales was another reason for not offering women international assignments. Also, concerns about family issues and spouse employment were cited as reasons for not considering women, even though these same issues exist for many male international managers. On top of these reasons, concerns about the acceptance of women in certain foreign cultures have also resulted in limiting the opportunities to U.S. women to work internationally.[23]

hire local employees. Many countries, including the U.S., Australia, and others, require foreign workers to apply for work permits or visas.

Employment discrimination legislation also varies from country to country. For instance, in Great Britain the Data Protection Act and Human Rights Acts restrict the type of information employers can request on application forms.[24] Also, European Union countries have implemented laws relating to privacy of information provided by applicants. For U.S.-based firms, the assignment of women and members of racial/ethnic minorities to international posts involves complying with U.S. EEO regulations and laws. The HR Perspective describes some of the issues associated with global staffing and women employees.

In a related area, some foreign firms in the United States, particularly those owned by Japanese firms, "reserve" top-level positions for those from the home country, resulting EEO charges being brought against these firms. However, U.S. court decisions have ruled that because of a treaty between Japan and the United States, Japanese subsidiaries can give preference to Japanese over U.S. citizens.

Most other EEO regulations and laws do apply to foreign-owned firms operating in the U.S. For example, some women have brought sexual harassment charges against foreign managers, and other protected-class individuals have brought EEO charges against foreign-owned firms with U.S. operations for refusal to hire or promote them. In those cases, courts have treated the foreign-owned firms just as they would U.S.-owned employers, and in well-known cases involving Mitsubishi and other foreign firms, courts have found them guilty of violating U.S. EEO laws.

Global Assignment Management

Expatriation Preparing and sending global employees to their foreign assignments.

Repatriation Planning, training, and reassignment of global employees to their home countries.

Once employees have been selected for international assignments, continuing organizational support for the employees is crucial. The intention of expatriates to quit and their commitment to their organizations are affected by how they view the support given to them by their employers. That is why management of global assignments is so important. As Figure 18-7 indicates, there are two major phases in the cycle of global assignment management. The first phase is **expatriation,** in which an organization prepares and sends global employees to their foreign assignments. Once there, employees need continuing support and development, as discussed later in the chapter. Upon completion of the assignment **repatriation** occurs. Repatriation involves planning, training, and reassignment of global employees to their home countries. It should also be noted that if the global employee is being sent to a third-country, then expatriation must begin as part of repatriation actions.

Pre-Departure Orientation and Training

The orientation and training that expatriates and their families receive before departure significantly affect the success of the overseas assignment. Unfortunately, various surveys have found that only 50% to 60% of global employers provide formal training programs for expatriates and their families. When offered, most expatriates participate in this training, which generally produces a positive effect on cross-cultural adjustment.

The most common topics covered in pre-departure training are:

- Daily living conditions
- Cultural customs
- Business issues
- Country history

Figure 18-7   Global Assignment Management Cycle

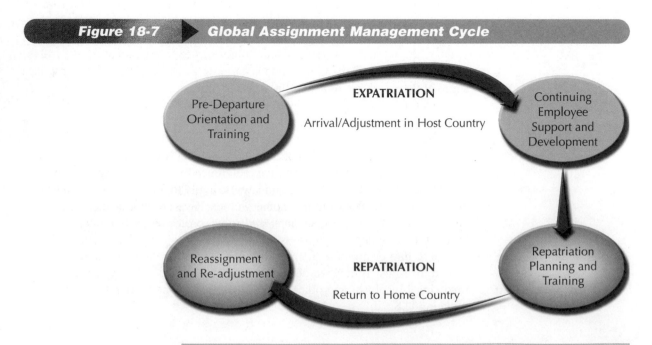

Figure 18-8 ▷ *Intercultural Competency Training*

Component	Possible Training
Cognitive	• *Culture-specific training (traditions, history, culture customs, etc.)* • *Language course*
Emotional	• *Uneasiness: social skills training focusing on new/unclear and intercultural situations* • *Prejudices: coaching may be clarifying* • *Sensitivity: communication skills course (active listening, verbal/nonverbal cues, empathy)*
Behavioral	• *Culture Assimilator* • *International projects* • *Social skills training focusing on intercultural situations*

Source: Developed by Andrea Graf, Ph.D., Technical University of Braunschweig, Germany, and Robert L. Mathis, Ph.D., SPHR.

■ Geographical climate
■ Transportation and communication systems

Individuals selected to work outside their home countries need answers to many specific questions about their host countries. Training in various areas aids the adjustment of expatriates and their families to deal with host-country counterparts. Training in customs and practices can be especially valuable to individuals who will not live outside the home country but will travel to other countries for business purposes.[25]

A related issue is the promotion and transfer of foreign citizens to positions in the United States. As more global organizations start or expand U.S. operations, more cross-cultural training will be necessary for international employees relocated to the United States.[26] For example, many Japanese firms operating in the United States conduct training programs to prepare Japanese for U.S. food, customs, labor and HR practices, and other facets of working and living in the U.S.[27] The acceptance of a foreign boss by U.S. workers is another concern. These issues underscore the importance of training and development for international adjustment.

Global Training
Describes nature and importance of multinational and global training.
Custom Search:
☑ ANALYSIS
Phrase: Matching training to business needs

Intercultural Competence Training Growing numbers of global employers are providing intercultural competence training for their global employees. Intercultural competence incorporates a wide range of human social skills and personality characteristics. As noted in Figure 18-8, three components of intercultural competence require attention when training expatriates for global assignments:

■ *Cognitive:* What does the person know about other cultures?
■ *Emotional:* How does the person view other cultures and how much sensitivity exists to cultural customs and issues?
■ *Behavioral:* How does the person act in intercultural situations?

But knowing about the country and one's abilities may not be sufficient. A growing number of global employers are using training methods that allow individuals to behave in international situations and then receive feedback. One of the most popular methods is the Culture Assimilator. Used worldwide, especially by European-based firms, the Culture Assimilator is a programmed training and learning method consisting of short case studies and critical incidents. The case studies describe intercultural interactions and potential misunderstandings on the part of expatriates and host-country nationals. Each case study centers around some situation or difficulties experienced by an expatriate, a host national, or both. The incidents are analyzed after the answers are given and they are discussed and evaluated from two viewpoints: the original home-country culture and the target host-country culture. The assumption behind Culture Assimilator training is that as the trainees receive feedback on their responses, they begin to understand both the cognitive and emotional facets of the target culture. This understanding allows them to subsequently select more appropriate behavioral responses during their global assignments.[28]

Expatriate Support and Development

There are several areas that affect the cross cultural adjustment process.[29] To get global employees to their new assignments requires planning relocation efforts including moving their possessions, selling their existing homes, obtaining new housing, and other activities.[30] Once global employees arrive in the host country, they need assistance in "settling in." Arrangements should include someone to meet them and assist them. Basics such as obtaining housing, establishing bank accounts, obtaining driver's licenses, arranging for admissions to schools for dependent children, and establishing a medical provider relationship need to be part of international relocation. But differences in culture, language, and laws may complicate these activities in a foreign country. The sooner the expatriates and their families can establish a "normal" life, the better the adjustment will be, and the less likely that expatriate failure will occur. Figure 18-9 on the next page illustrates the typical adjustment process that expatriates experience.

Continuing Employee Communications and Support Continuing home-office support helps to reduce premature assignment departure.[31] One of the greatest deterrents to accepting foreign assignments comes from employees' concerns that they will be "out of sight, out of mind."[32] If they do not have direct and regular contact with others at the corporate headquarters, expatriates can feel isolated and left out of important company activities. The growth of the Internet and company intranets helps alleviate some of the communication concerns. Personal contact through phone conversations also is important, but may be difficult due to time zone differences and the quality of telecommunications services in some lesser-developed countries. For instance, a 15-hour time difference between headquarters in the United States and operations in Malaysia and Indonesia makes scheduling conference calls a challenge.

Continuing Career Development Many expatriates experience anxiety about their continued career progression. Therefore, the international experiences of expatriates must offer benefits to the employer and to the expatriate's career.[33] Firms sometimes address this issue by inviting the expatriates back for development programs and through regular interaction with other company managers and professionals. Another useful approach is to establish a mentoring system which matches an expatriate with a corporate executive in the headquarters.

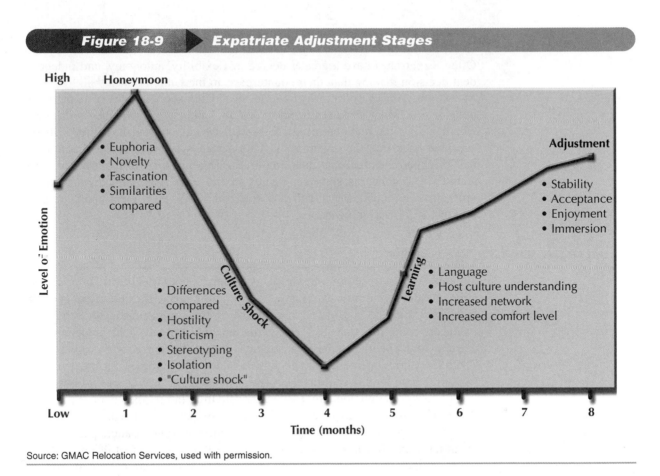

Figure 18-9 ▶ Expatriate Adjustment Stages

High   Honeymoon

- Euphoria
- Novelty
- Fascination
- Similarities compared

Level of Emotion

Culture Shock

- Differences compared
- Hostility
- Criticism
- Stereotyping
- Isolation
- "Culture shock"

Learning

- Language
- Host culture understanding
- Increased network
- Increased comfort level

Adjustment

- Stability
- Acceptance
- Enjoyment
- Immersion

Low   1   2   3   4   5   6   7   8

Time (months)

Source: GMAC Relocation Services, used with permission.

This executive talks with the expatriate frequently, ensures that the expatriate's name is submitted during promotion and development discussions at the headquarters, and resolves any headquarters-based problems experienced by the expatriate.

Repatriation

The process of repatriation, whereby expatriates are brought home or moved to other global assignments, must address potential difficulties that can arise when it is time to bring expatriates home. For example, expatriates no longer receive the special compensation packages often available to them during their assignments, which means that the expatriates experience a net decrease in total income, even if they receive promotions and pay increases.

In addition to concerns about personal finances, expatriates often must reacclimate themselves to U.S. lifestyles, transportation services, and other cultural practices, especially if they have been living in less-developed countries. For example, the wife of a U.S. expatriate was accustomed to bargaining for lower prices when she shopped in the foreign country. During the first week after her return to the United States, she tried to bargain with the checkout cashier at a supermarket before she realized that she was back in a place where this practice was not normal.

WEST GROUP
A THOMSON COMPANY

Repatriate Career Planning
Emphasizes the importance of career planning for repatriates.
Custom Search:
☑ ANALYSIS
Phrase: Managing repatriates

Back in the home organization, repatriated employees must readjust to a closer working and reporting relationship with other corporate employees. Often, expatriates have a greater degree of flexibility, autonomy, and independent decision making than their counterparts in the United States.[34]

Another major concern focuses on the organizational status of expatriates upon return. Many expatriates have concerns about what jobs they will have, whether their international experiences will be valued, and how they will be accepted back into the organization. Unfortunately, surveys reveal that almost half of expatriates feel that their employers do a poor job of repatriation.[35] To counter these concerns, some companies provide career planning, the mentoring programs mentioned earlier, and even guarantees of employment upon completion of foreign assignments.

International Compensation

Organizations with employees in many different countries face some special compensation pressures. Variations in laws, living costs, tax policies, and other factors all must be considered in establishing the compensation for expatriate managers and professionals. Even fluctuations in the value of the home-country currency must be tracked and adjustments made as the currency rises or falls in relation to currency rates in other countries. Add to all of these concerns the need to compensate employees for the costs of housing, schooling of children, and yearly transportation home for themselves and their family members. With all of these different issues involved, international compensation becomes extremely complex. Typical components of an international compensation package for expatriates are shown in Figure 18-10. Notice that a number of different items often are included. The two primary approaches to international compensation are discussed next.

Balance-Sheet Approach

Balance-sheet approach
Compensation package that equalizes cost differences between international assignments and those in the home country.

Many multinational firms have compensation programs for international employees using the **balance-sheet approach,** which equalizes cost differences between the international assignment and the same assignment in the home country of the individual or the corporation. The balance-sheet approach is based on some key assumptions, discussed next.

Home-Country Reference Point An appropriate compensation package keeps corporate global employees at a level appropriate to their jobs in relation to similar jobs in the home country. Various indices can be obtained.[36] Based on the calculations made using those indices, special benefits or allowances can be provided so that global employees can maintain a standard of living at least equivalent to what they would have in the home country.[37]

Some global employers use a *headquarters approach* whereby an individual's pay does not vary regardless of differences in international location. But in reality, firms frequently have to make adjustments and allowances to account for significant living cost differences. This approach may be more successfully used for shorter-term global assignments.

Compensation and Assignment Duration Generally, the balance-sheet approach bases expatriate employee compensation on the assumption that inter-

Figure 18-10 ▶ **Typical Expatriate Compensation Components**

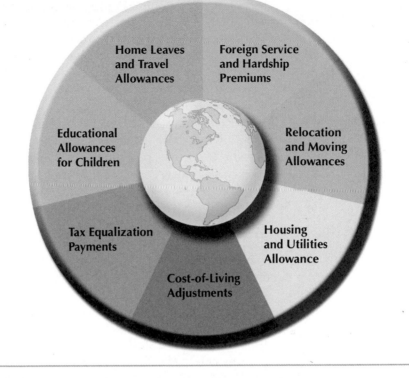

national assignments last two to three years. International compensation packages are designed to keep the expatriates "whole" for a few years until they can be reintegrated into the home-country compensation program. Thus, the "temporary" compensation package for the international assignment must be structured to make it easy for the repatriated employee to reenter the domestic compensation and benefits programs. Also, it is assumed that the international employee will retire in the home country, so pension and other retirement benefits will be home-country-based.

Global Market Approach

Increasingly, global organizations have recognized that compensating global employees requires taking a broad perspective. In many large multinational enterprises, key executives have worked in several countries during their careers and may be of many different nationalities. These executives are moved from one part of the world to another and to corporate headquarters, wherever the firms are based. Because of a high demand for these global managers, they almost form their own "global market" for compensation purposes.[38]

Unlike the balance-sheet approach, a global market approach views international assignments as continual, not just temporary, where the assignments may take global employees to different countries for differing lengths of time. This approach attempts to be more comprehensive in providing core components such as insurance benefits and relocation expenses regardless of the country to which the employee is assigned. But pegging the appropriate pay level by considering rates in the host country, home country, and/or headquarters country becomes more complex. Further, the acceptability of incentives and distributing compensation unequally based on performance varies from country to country.[39] Therefore, the global market approach to compensation requires greater flexibility, more detailed analyses, and significant administrative effort.

Tax Concerns

Tax equalization plan
Compensation plan used to protect expatriates from negative tax consequences.

Many international compensation plans attempt to protect expatriates from negative tax consequences by using a **tax equalization plan.** Under such a plan, the company adjusts an employee's base income downward by the amount of estimated U.S. tax to be paid for the year. Thus, the employee pays only the foreign-country tax. The tax equalization plan helps ensure that expatriates will not pay any more or less in taxes than if they had stayed in the United States. Because of the variation in tax laws and rates from country to country, tax equalization is very complex to determine.[40]

Global Benefits

Benefits vary from county to country. For example, the amount of leave and vacation time varies significantly. Of 130 countries, only the United States, Australia, and Ethiopia do not provide paid leave for new parents.[41] The annual leave/vacation in European countries averages 36 days per year, whereas the United States and Canada average the lowest amounts of annual vacation leave of many developed countries.[42]

Health-care benefits also differ significantly worldwide. Many countries, including Great Britain and Canada, have national health services. Some global firms require employees to use host-country medical services, while other global employers provide special coverage allowing the expatriates to receive health care from private providers. Arranging quality private coverage becomes an especially important issue for global employees located in underdeveloped countries where the availability and quality of medical facilities and treatment varies widely.[43]

Global Employee Relations Issues

Employee relations often raise concerns in international situations for several reasons. Employers must comply with a wide range of employment and labor laws that differ by region and country.

Global Labor-Management Relations

In some countries, unions either do not exist at all or are relatively weak. Such is the case in China and a number of African countries. In other countries, unions are extremely strong and are closely tied to political parties. For instance, in Italy national strikes occur regularly to protest proposed government policy changes on retirement, pension programs, and regulations regarding dismissal of employees. The strength and nature of unions differ from country to country as Figure 18-11 indicates.

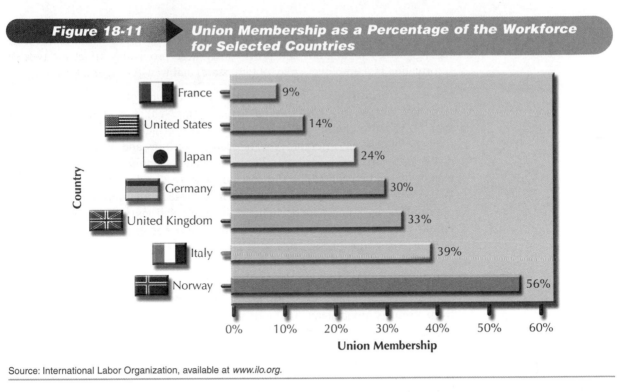

Figure 18-11 **Union Membership as a Percentage of the Workforce for Selected Countries**

Source: International Labor Organization, available at *www.ilo.org*.

Co-determination A practice whereby union or worker representatives are given positions on a company's board of directors.

Some countries require that firms have union or worker representatives on their boards of directors. This practice, called **co-determination,** is common in European countries. Differences from country to country in how collective bargaining occurs also are quite noticeable. In the United States, local unions bargain with individual employers to set wages and working conditions. In Australia, unions argue their cases before arbitration tribunals. In Scandinavia, national agreements with associations of employers are the norm. In France and Germany, industry-wide or regional agreements are common. In Japan, local unions bargain but combine at some point to determine national wage patterns.

Global labor relations standards are being addressed by several organizations. The International Labour Organization, based in Switzerland, serves as a forum for labor unions worldwide to coordinate their efforts and has issued some principles and rights at work.[44] Such coordination is increasingly occurring as unions deal with multinational firms with operations in multiple countries.

Sexual Harassment Regulations Globally

Throughout the world, employment regulations are changing. Laws and regulations prohibiting employment discrimination exist in various places in the world, and often include sexual harassment regulations. For instance, even though the United States enacted sexual harassment regulations several decades ago, only recently have regulations prohibiting sexual harassment been enacted in Japan and Thailand. Since the introduction of Japanese regulations, relatively few sexual harassment incidents have been reported, even though a survey found that about 70% of female workers for the Japanese government report being sexually harassed at work.[45] Employers and countries in the EU must comply with the Equal Treatment Revision Directive. Also, the EU has been a leader in establishing privacy regulations and provisions. These provisions affect the type of information that employers may obtain, store, and transfer on employees.[46]

Worker Consultation Regulations Another type of employment regulations involves *worker consultation* requirements. The EU requires that firms with 50 or more employees consult with workers (and their union representatives) before laying off employees, relocating facilities and operations, or other corporate restructuring actions. These regulations apply in all EU countries except the United Kingdom and Ireland, who received exemptions for seven years. While social advocates have supported these regulations, employers have opposed them. Some experts believe these regulations will result in greater employer costs, and ultimately lead to more European employers closing down or transferring jobs to countries with less restrictive regulations.

Global Health, Safety, and Security
Safety and health laws and regulations vary from country to country, ranging from virtually nonexistent to more stringent than in the United States. The importance placed on workplace safety relates somewhat to the level of regulation in different countries.[47]

International Emergency Health Services With more and more expatriates working internationally, especially in some of the less-developed countries, significant health and safety issues require attention. Addressing these issues is part of the HR role. One consideration is provision of emergency evacuation services. For instance, how to evacuate and care for an expatriate employee who sustains internal injuries in a car accident in the Ukraine or Sierra Leone may be a major issue. Many global firms purchase coverage for their international employees from an organization that provides emergency services, such as International SOS, Global Assistance Network, or U.S. Assist. If an emergency arises, the emergency services company dispatches physicians or even transports employees by chartered aircraft. If adequate medical assistance can be obtained locally, the emergency services company maintains a referral list and makes arrangements for the expatriate to receive treatment. Emergency services firms also may provide legal counsel in foreign countries, emergency cash for medical expenses, and assistance in reissuing lost documents.

International Security and Terrorism As more U.S. firms operate internationally, the threat of terrorist actions against those firms and the employees working for them increases. The extent to which employees are likely to experience security problems and violence depends upon the country. It is crucial that the HR staff regularly check the security conditions in countries where expatriates are traveling and working.

Global firms take a variety of actions to address security concerns. Firms themselves are taking other actions. For example, one U.S. firm removed signs identifying its offices and facilities in a Latin American country in order to reduce the visibility of the firm and thus reduce its potential as a target for terrorist acts. Many international firms screen entry by all employees, and many use metal detectors to scan all packages, briefcases, and other items. Firms com-

Logging On...

Travel Warnings
Current travel warnings and consular advisories by country are available from the U.S. State Department.

http://travel.state.gov

monly use physical barriers, such as iron security fences, concrete barricades, bulletproof glass, and electronic surveillance devices in offices as part of their security efforts.

Kidnapping and Terrorism Concerns It should be noted that not all violence occurs at work. Kidnapping, murder, home invasion, robberies, and carjackings happen relatively frequently in some cities, such as Mexico City, and a number of countries throughout the world. U.S. citizens are especially vulnerable to extortions, kidnapping, bombing, physical harassment, and other terrorist activities. In a recent year, one-third of the 1,800 kidnapping and terrorist incidents were directed against U.S. citizens and employees of U.S. firms, and terrorists killed or injured almost 200 Americans working outside of the United States.[48]

To counter such threats, many global firms have *kidnap and ransom (KR) insurance.* This insurance covers the costs of paying ransoms to obtain releases of kidnapped employees and family members, pay for bodily injuries suffered by kidnap victims, and deal with negotiation and other expenses.[49]

Individual employees and their family members working and living abroad must constantly be aware of security concerns. Both pre-departure and on-going security training should be given to all expatriates, their dependents, and employees of global firms working internationally, especially if located in high-risk areas. Some of the training includes telling employees and their children to avoid wearing sweatshirts with U.S. logos and to be discreet when meeting friends. In a number of countries schools for children of U.S. expatriates have instituted tight security measures, including sign-in procedures for visitors, guards for the grounds, and improved security fences and surveillance equipment.

These problems and others associated with global assignments have been noted throughout the chapter. Although well-documented, the problems do not always get enough attention by employers who send employees internationally. Organizations must help their global employees deal with the risks. Those that choose the right people for these very challenging assignments benefit by having successful employees.

Summary

- Globalization of business continues to grow because of forces such as population changes, economic interdependence, regional alliances, and global communications capabilities.
- Organizations doing business internationally may evolve from organizations engaged in importing and exporting activities, to multinational enterprises, to global organizations.
- Legal, political, economic, and cultural factors influence global HR management.
- Culture consists of the societal forces that affect the values, beliefs, and actions of a distinct group of people.
- One scheme for classifying national cultures considers power distance, individualism, masculinity/femininity, uncertainty avoidance, and long-term orientation.
- Staffing global jobs can be done using expatriates, host-country nationals, and third-country nationals.

- Global assignments can be used for a number of reasons and for varying durations.
- The selection of global employees should consider cultural adjustment, organizational requirements, personal characteristics, communications skills, and personal/family factors.
- Once selected, the assignments of global employees must be managed through both effective expatriation and repatriation.
- Training and development for international employees focus on pre-departure orientation and training, continued employee development, and readjustment training for repatriates.
- Compensation practices for international employees are much more complex than those for domestic employees because many more factors must be considered.
- Global organizations must be concerned about the health, safety, and security of their employees.
- Labor-management relations vary from country to country.

Review and Discussion Questions

1. Discuss the following statement: "Shifts in the types of jobs and the industries in which jobs are gained or lost reflect global and economic competition that is occurring in the many countries."
2. What are some advantages and disadvantages associated with using expatriate managers instead of host-country nationals?
3. Select a foreign country and identify how you believe it would stand on Hofstede's five dimensions of culture.
4. If you were the HR person responsible for selecting someone to be director of sales and marketing for your firm's subsidiary in China, what criteria would you use to determine which person to select?
5. Assume you have been asked to consider a job in Italy with a U.S.-based corporation. Develop a list of questions and issues that the corporation should address before you decide.
6. Discuss the following statement: "Global compensation packages should keep expatriates even with what they would receive at home, but not allow them to get rich."
7. Suppose an expatriate employee is to work in Russia for two years. What health, safety, and security issues should be addressed?

Terms to Know

importing and exporting   577
multinational enterprise (MNE)   577
global organization   579
culture   581
power distance   582
individualism   583
masculinity/femininity   583
uncertainty avoidance   583
long-term orientation   583

expatriate   585
host-country national   585
third-country national   586
expatriation   592
repatriation   592
balance-sheet approach   596
tax equalization plan   598
co-determination   599

Setting International Compensation

The Vice President of International Marketing has asked you to do some research on international exchange rates for base compensation and other living expenses for foreign-based expatriates. Your organization is considering opening several new offices and this is part of the assessment process. Utilize the Web site below to identify the categories of data that can be gathered and should be considered. Then prepare a report listing all of the relevant items to be considered and provide an example of a city containing such information.
http://www. runzheimer.com

McDonald's Global HR

One of the best-known companies worldwide is McDonald's Corporation. The fast-food chain, with its symbol of the golden arches, has spread from the United States into 91 countries. With more than 18,000 restaurants worldwide, McDonald's serves 33 million people each day. International sales represent an important part of McDonald's business, and more than 50% of the company's operating income comes from sales outside the United States. To generate these sales, McDonald's employs more than 2 million people.

Operating in so many different countries means that McDonald's has had to adapt its products, services, and HR practices to legal, political, economic, and cultural factors in each one of those countries. A few examples illustrate how adaptations have been made. In some countries, such as India, beef is not acceptable as a food to a major part of the population, so McDonald's uses lamb or mutton. To appeal to Japanese customers, McDonald's developed teriyaki burgers. Separate dining rooms for men and women are constructed in McDonald's restaurants in some Middle Eastern countries.

HR practices must adapt to different cultures. Before beginning operations in a different country, HR professionals at McDonald's research the country and determine how HR activities must be adjusted. One method of obtaining information is to contact HR professionals from other U.S. firms operating in the country and ask them questions about laws, political factors, and cultural issues. In addition, the firm conducts an analysis using a detailed outline to ensure that all relevant information has been gathered. Data gathered might include what employment restrictions exist on ages of employees and hours of work, what benefits must be offered to full-time and part-time employees (if part-time work is allowed), and other operational requirements. For instance, in some of the former communist countries in Eastern Europe, employers provide locker rooms and showers for their employees. These facilities are necessary because shower facilities, and even consistent water supplies, are unavailable in many homes, particularly in more rural areas around major cities. Also, public transportation must be checked to ensure employees have adequate means to travel to work.

Once a decision has been made to begin operations in a new country, the employment process must begin. Often, McDonald's is seen as a desirable employer, particularly when its first restaurant is being opened in a country. For instance, in Russia, 27,000 people initially applied to work at the first McDonald's in Moscow. Because customer service is so important to McDonald's, recruiting and selection activities focus on obtaining employees with customer service skills. For worker positions such as counter representative and cashier, the focus is to identify individuals who will be friendly, customer service-oriented employees. A "trial" process whereby some applicants work for a few days on a conditional basis may be used to ensure that these individuals will represent McDonald's appropriately and will work well with other employees.

For store managers, the company uses a selection profile emphasizing leadership skills, high work expectations, and management abilities appropriate to a fast-paced restaurant environment. Once applicant screening and interviews have been completed, individuals are asked to work for up to a week in a restaurant. During that time, both the applicants and the company representatives evaluate one another to see if the job "fit" is appropriate. After the first group of store managers and assistant managers are selected, future managers and assistant managers are chosen using internal promotions based on job performance.

Once the restaurants are staffed, training becomes crucial to acquaint new employees with their jobs and the McDonald's philosophy of customer service and quality. McDonald's has taken its Hamburger University curriculum from the United States and translated it into 22 different languages to use in training centers throughout the world. Once trainers and managers complete the training, they then conduct training for all employees selected to work at McDonald's locations in the foreign countries.[50]

Questions

1. Identify cultural factors that might be important in a training program for food handlers at McDonald's in Saudi Arabia.
2. Rather than focusing on the differences, what similarities do you expect to exist among McDonald's customers and employees in both the United States and abroad?

Notes

1. Based on "Profits Over People," *The Economist,* September 29, 2001, S5–9. Robert Kuttner, "Globalization and Its Critics," *The American Prospect,* July 2001, S1; Dennis R. Briscoe, "Global Ethics, Labor Standards, and International HRM," *International Focus,* Winter 2000; "Sweating for Nothing," available at *www.globalexchange.org;* Clay Chandler and Frank Swoboda, "In Chinese Wages, a U.S. Bump," *The Washington Post,* May 23, 2000, E1; and Mary Beth Marklein, "Making Them Sweat," *USA Today,* April 13, 2000, D1+.

2. "The Global 100," *The Wall Street Journal,* September 25, 2000, R24–25; and "The Global 100," *Business Week,* July 9, 2001, 73–90.

3. "Globalization and the Human Resource Profession," *Workplace Visions,* 5 (2000), 2–7.

4. Julie Schmit, "No English, No Job," *USA Today,* July 21, 2000, 1B+.

5. Linda Solon, "Global Business," *SHRM Global,* December 2000, 13–14.

6. John Parrish, "Coming Clean," *Global HR,* May 2001, 32–35.

7. Elizabeth Malkin "Is the Magic Starting to Fade?" *Business Week,* August 6, 2001, 42–43.

8. Based on Geert Hofstede, "Difference and Danger: Cultural Profiles of Nations and Limits to Tolerance," in Maryann H. Albrecht, ed. *International HRM* (Malden, MA: Blackwell Publishers, 2001), 9–23.

9. Paula Caligiuri and Wayne F. Cascio, "Sending Women on Global Assignments," *WorldatWork Journal,"* Second Quarter 2000, 34–41.

10. Ruth E. Thaler-Carter, "Whither Global Leaders?" *HR Magazine,* May 2000, 83–88.

11. Based on Anne-Wil Harzing, "Who's In Charge? An Empirical Study of Executive Staffing Practices in Foreign Subsidiaries," *Human Resource Management,* 40 (2001), 139–158.

12. Adapted from Hara Marks, "International Assignments: Fine-Tuning the Selection Process," *Global HR,* available at *www.hr-esource,* April 16, 2001.

13. Eric Lekus, "Employers Shorten Assignments of Workers Abroad," *Bulletin to Management,* January 4, 2001, 7.

14. Martha L. Maznevski and Joseph J. DiStefano, "Global Leaders Are Team Players," *Human Resource Management,* 39 (2000), 195–208.

15. Kate Dale, "I'd Search the Whole World Over," *HR World,* January/February 2000, 23–26.

16. Laura J. Spence and Joseph A. Patrick, "Multinational Interview Decisions: Integrity Capacity and Competing Values," *Human Resource Management Journal,* 10 (2000), 49–67.

17. Phooi-Chiung Lai and Irene Wong, "The Clash of Cultures in the Job Interview," *The Journal of Language for International Business,* 11 (2000), 31–40.

18. "Fishing in International Waters," *PersonnelToday,* available at *www.shrmglobal.org/publications,* (no date).

19. Ed Silverman, "Precarious Liaisons," *Human Resource Executive,* February 2001, 60–65.

20. David Woodruff, "Distractions Make Global Manager a Difficult Role," *The Wall Street Journal,* November 21, 2000, B1.

21. Paula M. Caliguri, "The Big Five Personality Characteristics as Predictors of Expatriate's Desire to Terminate the Assignment and Supervisor-Rated Performance," *Personnel Psychology,* 43 (2000), 67–88.

22. *Global Relocation Trends Survey Report* (New York: GMAC GRS/ Windham International, 2001).

23. "Survey Says Women Want to be Expats . . . ," *Bulletin to Management,* February 8, 2001, 43; Alison Maitland, "U.S. Gender Gap Travels Abroad," *The Financial Times,* October 20, 2000, 14; and Kathryn Tyler, "Don't Fence Her In," *HR Magazine,* March 2001, 70–73.

24. Patricia Leighton, "Don't Ask, Don't Tell," *People Management,* May 11, 2000, 42–45.

25. Elizabeth Chazottes, "International Training: It's Smart Business," *Area Development,* August 2001, 83–85.

26. Carroll Lachnit, "Low-Cost Tips for Successful Inpatriation," *Workforce,* August 2001, 42–47.

27. May Markuda, "Global Leaders Wanted, Apply Within," *Workspan,* April 2001, 36–41.

28. K. Cushner and R. W. Brislin, *Intercultural Interactions: A Practical Guide* (Thousand Oaks, CA: Sage Publishing, 2000).

29. Maria L. Kraimer, Sandy J. Wayne, and Renata A. Jaworski, "Sources of Support and Expatriate Performance," *Personnel Psychology,* 54 (2001), 71–99.

30. Lin Grensing-Pophal, "Transferring Employees Smoothly Takes Time," *HR Magazine,* September 2001, 113–120.

31. Ron Garonzik, Joel Brockner, and Phyllis A. Siegel, "Identifying International Assignees at Risk for Premature Departure," *Journal of Applied Psychology,* 55 (2000), 13–20.

32. Jeremy Handel, "Out of Sight, Out of Mind," *Workspan,* June 2001, 55–58.

33. Jo Ann S. Lublin, "How to Know Whether Another Overseas Stint Will Help Your Career," *The Wall Street Journal,* July 3, 2001, B1.

34. Andreas C. Poe, "Welcome Back," *HR Magazine,* March 2000, 94–105.

35. "Study Says Employers Ignore Expatriates' Personal Issues," *Bulletin to Management,* May 10, 2001, 146.

36. Virginia Morrow, "Why Your Employer Might Be Using Different Indexes," *Expatriate Observer,* Summer 2001, 1–4.

37. Geoffrey W. Latta, "For Richer, For Poorer," *Workspan,* August 2000, 22–25.

38. Maureen Minehan, "The New Face of Global Compensation," *Global Supplement,* December 2000, 1–4.

39. Stephanie Overman, "In Sync," *HR Magazine,* March 2000, 87–92.

40. Rob Outram, "The Taxman Cometh," *Global HR,* February/ March 2001, 22–25.

41. Based on data from the National Partnership for Women and Families, 2000.

42. Data obtained from Bert Roughton, "Europeans Receive a Wealth of Vacation Time," *Omaha World-Herald,* May 27, 2001, 9G; and William Mercer, Inc., 2001.

43. Stephanie Overman, "Check the Vitality of Health Care Abroad," *HR Magazine,* March 2000, 77–84.

44. Roy J. Adams, "Human Rights: Indications of the International Consensus for Management Training and Practice," *Journal of Comparative International Management,* 4 (2001), 22–32.

45. "Sexual Harassment Defined," *SHRM Global Perspectives,* 2 (2001), 5.

46. Jon F. Doyle, "FYI: EU Privacy Directive Impacts Global HR and Benefits," *Workspan,* January 2002, 48–51.

47. Jessica Dresler, "Ready Reminders," *Occupational Health & Safety,* May 2001, 102–105.

48. "Kidnapped," *SHRM Global Perspectives,* 3 (2001), 3–5.

49. Karyn-Siobhan Robinson, "Violence Abroad Prompts Review of Insurance Needs," *HR News,* April 2001, 5.

50. Adapted from "Where's the Beef?" *The Economist,* November 3, 2001, 20; Robert Grossman, "HR in Asia," *HR Magazine,* July 1997, 104; and Charlene M. Solomon, "Big Mac's McGlobal HR Secrets," *Personnel Journal* (April 1996), 47–54; and Chuck Hutchcraft, "Cultural Considerations," *Restaurants & Institutions,* September 1, 2001, 21.

Appendix A

Human Resource Certification Institute Test Specifications*

There are two levels of certification, the Professional in Human Resources (PHR) and the Senior Professional in Human Resources (SPHR). Two different exams are used for certification testing. PHR questions tend to be at an operational/technical level, whereas SPHR questions tend to be more at the strategic and/or policy level.

Examination questions for both levels cover a wide range of topics. Each multiple choice exam consists of 200 scored questions plus 25 pretest questions for a total of 225 questions. Pretest questions are not counted in the scoring of the examination and are used for statistical purposes only. Each question lists *four possible answers,* only one of which is correct.

Item Classification Scheme

The test specifications identify six functional areas. After each major functional area are the weightings for that area. **The first number in the parentheses is the PHR percentage weighting and the second number is the SPHR percentage weighting.** Within each area *responsibilities* and *knowledge* topics are specified. To aid readers of this book, the authors have identified text locations for the **KNOWLEDGE** items, as follows:

- [page numbers] Content discussed on specific pages is noted this way.

- [—] For the few instances where content does not appear in the text, it is noted this way.

- [★] Broad concepts and multiple topics discussed in several places throughout the text are noted this way. Consult the Subject Index following the appendices to locate specific content areas.

FUNCTIONAL AREA:

01 STRATEGIC MANAGEMENT (12%, 26%)

The processes and activities used to formulate HR objectives, practices, and policies to meet the short- and long-range organizational needs and opportunities, to guide and lead the change process, and to evaluate HR's contributions to organizational effectiveness.

Responsibilities:

Interpret information related to the organization's operations from internal sources, including financial/accounting, marketing, operations, information technology, and individual employees, in order to participate in strategic planning and policy making.

01 Interpret information related to the general business environment, industry practices and developments, and technological developments from external sources (for example, publications, government documents, media, and trade organizations), in order to participate in strategic planning and policy making.

03 Participate as a partner in the organization's strategic planning process.

04 Establish strategic relationships with individuals in the organization, to influence organizational decision-making.

05 Establish relationships/alliances with key individuals in the community and in professional capacities to assist in meeting the organization's strategic needs.

06 Evaluate HR's contribution to organizational effectiveness, including assessment, design, implementation, and evaluation of activities with respect to strategic and organizational measurement in HR objectives.
*(** 06 refers to participation in change management)*

07 Provide direction and guidance during changes in organizational processes, operations, planning, intervention, leadership training and

culture that balances the expectations and needs of the organization, its employees, and other stakeholders (including customers). *(** 07 refers to participation in change management)*

08 Develop and shape organizational policy related to the organization's management of its human resources.

09 Cultivate leadership and ethical values in self and others through modeling and teaching.

10 Provide information for the organizational budgeting process, including budget development and review.

11 Monitor legislative environment for proposed changes in law and take appropriate action to support, modify, or stop the proposed action (for example, write to a member of Congress, provide expert testimony at a public hearing, lobby legislators).

Knowledge Of:

01 lawmaking and administrative regulatory processes [★; 38–39; 102–131; 137–161; 477–484]

02 internal and external environmental scanning techniques [6–8; 38–47]

03 strategic planning process and implementation [19–20; 21; 30–57]

04 organizational social responsibility (for example, welfare to work, philanthropy, alliances with community-based organizations) [203; 575]

05 management functions, including planning, organizing, directing, and controlling [★; 6–8; 35–38]

06 techniques to sustain creativity and innovation [170–177; 255; 374; 415]

FUNCTIONAL AREA:

02 WORKFORCE PLANNING AND EMPLOYMENT (26%, 16%)

The processes of planning, developing, implementing, administering, and performing ongoing evaluation of recruiting, hiring, orientation, and organizational exit to ensure that the workforce will meet the organization's goals and objectives.

Responsibilities:

01 Identify staffing requirements to meet the goals and objectives of the organization.

02 Conduct job analyses to write job descriptions and develop job competencies.

03 Identify and document the essential job functions for positions.

04 Establish hiring criteria based on the competencies needed.

05 Assess internal workforce, labor market, and recruitment agencies to determine the availability of qualified applicants.

06 Identify internal and external recruitment methods and implement them within the context of the organization's goals and objectives.

07 Develop strategies to market the organization to potential applicants.

08 Establish selection procedures, including interviewing, testing, and reference and background checking.

09 Implement selection procedures, including interviewing, testing, and reference and background checking.

10 Develop and/or extend employment offers.

11 Perform or administerpost-offer employment activities (for example, employment agreements, completion of I-9 verification form, relocation agreements, and medical examinations).

12 Facilitate and/or administer the process by which non-US citizens can legally work in the United States.

13 Design, facilitate, and/or conduct the orientation process, including review of performance standards for new hires and transfers.

14 Evaluate selection and employment processes for effectiveness and implement changes if indicated (for example, employee retention).

15 Develop a succession planning process.

16 Develop and implement the organizational exit process, including unemployment insurance claim responses. *(includes severance, turnover and outplacement)*

17 Develop, implement, manage, and evaluate affirmative action program(s), as may be required.

Knowledge of:

07 federal/state/local employment-related laws (for example, Title VII, ADA, ADEA, Vietnam Veterans, WARN) and regulations (for example, EEOC Uniform Guidelines on Employee Selection Procedures) [★]

08 immigration law (for example, visas, I-9) [115; 244]

09 quantitative analyses required to assess past and future staffing (for example, cost benefit analysis, costs-per-hire, selection ratios, adverse impact) [224–227]

10 recruitment methods and sources [205–224]

11 staffing alternatives (for example, telecommuting, outsourcing) [178; 208–210]

12 planning techniques (for example, succession planning, forecasting) [43–47; 321–323]

13 reliability and validity of selection tests/tools/methods [123–127; 237–239]

14 use and interpretation of selection tests (for example, psychological/personality, cognitive, and motor/physical assessments) [247–252]

15 interviewing techniques [252–260]

16 relocation practices [264]

17 impact of compensation and benefits plans on recruitment and retention [80; 84–86]

18 international HR and implications of international workforce for workforce planning and employment [8–10; 576–579; 584–591]

19 downsizing and outplacement [48–51]

20 internal workforce planning and employment policies, practices, and procedures [205–208]

FUNCTIONAL AREA:

03 HUMAN RESOURCE DEVELOPMENT (15%, 13%)

The processes of ensuring that the skills, knowledge, abilities, and performance of the workforce meet the current and future organizational and individual needs through developing, implementing, and evaluating activities and programs addressing employee training and development, change and performance management, and the unique needs of particular employee groups.

Responsibilities:

01 Conduct needs analyses to identify and establish priorities regarding human resource development activities.

02 Develop training programs.

03 Implement training programs.

04 Evaluate training programs.

05 Develop programs to assess employees' potential for growth and development in the organization.

06 Implement programs to assess employees' potential for growth and development in the organization.

07 Evaluate programs to assess employees' potential for growth and development in the organization.

08 Develop change management programs and activities.

09 Implement change management programs and activities.

10 Evaluate change management programs and activities.

11 Develop performance management programs and procedures.

12 Implement performance management programs and procedures.

13 Evaluate performance management programs and procedures.

14 Develop programs to meet the unique needs of particular employees (for example, work-family programs, diversity programs, outplacement programs, repatriation programs, and fast-track programs).

15 Implement programs to meet the unique needs of particular employees (for example, work-family programs, diversity programs, outplacement programs, repatriation programs, and fast-track programs).

16 Evaluate programs to meet the unique needs of particular employees (for example, work-family programs, diversity programs, outplacement programs, repatriation programs, and fast-track programs).

Knowledge of:

21 applicable international, federal, state, and local laws and regulations regarding copyrights and patents [—]

22 human resource development theories and applications (including career development and leadership development) [83; 306–368]

23 organizational development theories and applications [30–32; 306–368]

24 training methods, programs, and techniques *(design, objectives, methods, etc.)* [271–302]

25 employee involvement strategies [51; 72–75; 425–427]

26 task/process analysis [168–178]

27 performance appraisal and performance management methods [337–368]

28 applicable international issues (for example, culture, local management approaches/ practices, societal norms) [29; 575–604]

29 instructional methods and program delivery *(content, building modules of program, selection of presentation/delivery mechanism)* [271–302; 306–368]

30 techniques to assess HRD program effectiveness (for example, satisfaction, learning and job performance of program participants, and organizational outcomes such as turnover and productivity) [19–21; 23–25; 30–35; 52–60; 75–79; 141–143; 271–302; 306–368]

FUNCTIONAL AREA:

04 COMPENSATION AND BENEFITS (20%, 16%)

The processes of analyzing, developing, implementing, administering, and performing ongoing evaluation of a total compensation and benefits system for all employee groups consistent with human resource management goals.

Responsibilities:

01 Ensure the compliance of compensation and benefits with applicable federal, state, and local laws. *(includes IRS Rulings, strict definitions of which tend to go more with K-31; applications/calculations/ interpretations of those rulings tend to go more with K-32)*

02 Analyze, develop, implement, and maintain compensation policies and a pay structure consistent with the organization's strategic objectives. *(includes broad definitions and designs)*

03 Analyze and evaluate pay rates based on internal worth and external market conditions. *(includes wage and salary surveys)*

04 Develop/select and implement a payroll system.

05 Administer payroll functions.

06 Evaluate compensation policies to ensure that they are positioning the organization internally and externally according to the organization's strategic objectives. *(0406 refers to 'tweaking,' 'refinement,' or 'alterations;' turnover issues related to compensation also belong under this responsibility)*

07 Conduct a benefit plan needs assessment and determine/select the plans to be offered, considering the organization's strategic objectives. *(0407 addresses more specific definitions and plan design issues; includes 401K; tends to go more with K-38)*

08 Implement and administer benefit plans. *(addresses more the carrying out the objectives of the benefit plan; tends to go more with K-39)*

09 Evaluate benefits program to ensure that it is positioning the organization internally and externally according to the organization's strategic objectives. *(refers more to evaluation and tweaking of the benefit plan; tends to go more with K-38)*

10 Analyze, select, implement, maintain, and administer executive compensation, stock purchase, stock options, and incentive, and bonus programs. *(includes profit-sharing)*

11 Analyze, develop, select, maintain, and implement expatriate and foreign national compensation and benefit programs.

12 Communicate the compensation and benefits plan and policies to the workforce.

Knowledge of:

31 federal, state, and local compensation and benefit laws (for example, FLSA, ERISA, COBRA) [370–405]

32 accounting practices related to compensation and benefits (for example, excess group term life, compensatory time) [★; 306–368; 370–405; 427; 447]

33 job evaluation methods [390–394]

34 job pricing and pay structures [84–86]

35 incentive and variable pay methods [408–437]

36 executive compensation [408–437]

37 non-cash compensation methods (for example, stock option plans) [416–418; 425–427]

38 benefits needs analysis [441–442]

39 benefit plans (for example, health insurance, life insurance, pension, education, health club) [440–470]

40 international compensation laws and practices (for example, expatriate compensation, socialized medicine, mandated retirement) [575–602]

FUNCTIONAL AREA:

05 EMPLOYEE AND LABOR RELATIONS (21%, 24%)

The processes of analyzing, developing, implementing, administering, and performing ongoing evaluation of the workplace relationship between employer and employee (including the collective bargaining process and union relations), in order to maintain effective relationships and working conditions that balance the employer's needs with the employees' rights in support of the organization's strategic objectives.

Responsibilities:

01 Ensure compliance with all applicable federal, state, and local laws and regulations. *(catch-all responsibility, including NLRB, ADA, FMLA)*

02 Develop and implement employee relations programs that will create a positive organizational culture. *(most of the legal definitions and general definitions)*

03 Promote, monitor, and measure the effectiveness of employee relations activities.

04 Assist in establishing work rules and monitor their application and enforcement to ensure fairness and consistency (for union and non-union environments).

05 Communicate and ensure understanding by employees of laws, regulations, and organizational policies.

06 Resolve employee complaints filed with federal, state, and local agencies involving employment practices. *(formal, legal complaints)*

07 Develop grievance and disciplinary policies and procedures to ensure fairness and consistency.

08 Implement and monitor grievance and disciplinary policies and procedures to ensure fairness and consistency. *(includes investigation)*

09 Respond to union organizing activity.

10 Participate in collective bargaining activities, including contract negotiation and administration.

Knowledge of:

41 applicable federal, state, and local laws affecting employment in union and non-union environments, such as anti-discrimination laws, sexual harassment, labor relations, and privacy [★]

42 techniques for facilitating positive employee relations (for example, small group facilitation, dispute resolution, and labor/management cooperative strategies and programs) [518–519; 565–566]

43 employee involvement strategies (for example, alternate work schedules, work teams) [174–179; 566–567]

44 individual employment rights issues and practices (for example, employment at will, negligent hiring, defamation, employees' rights to bargain collectively) [262–263; 514–519]

45 workplace behavior issues/practices (for example, absenteeism, discipline) [75–78; 533–537]

46 methods for assessment of employee attitudes, opinions, and satisfaction (for example, opinion surveys, attitude surveys, focus panels) [91–93]

47 unfair labor practices [553–554; 559–560]

48 the collective bargaining process, strategies, and concepts *(up to and after contract)* [561–565]

49 public sector labor relations issues and practices [547–548]
50 expatriation and repatriation issues and practices [584–596]
51 employee and labor relations for local nationals (i.e., labor relations in other countries) [598–600]

FUNCTIONAL AREA:

06 OCCUPATIONAL HEALTH, SAFETY, AND SECURITY (6%, 5%)

The processes of analyzing, developing, implementing, administering, and performing ongoing evaluation of programs, practices, and services to promote the physical and mental well-being of individuals in the workplace, and to protect individuals and the workplace from unsafe acts, unsafe working conditions, and violence.

Responsibilities:

01 Ensure compliance with all applicable federal, state, and local workplace health and safety laws and regulations.
02 Determine safety programs needed for the organization.
03 Develop and/or select injury/occupational illness prevention programs.
04 Implement injury/occupational illness prevention programs.
05 Develop and/or select safety training and incentive programs
06 Implement safety training and incentive programs.
07 Evaluate the effectiveness of safety prevention, training, and incentive programs.
08 Implement workplace injury/occupational illness procedures (for example, worker's compensation, OSHA).
09 Determine health and wellness programs needed for the organization.
10 Develop/select, implement, and evaluate (or make available) health and wellness programs.
11 Develop/select, implement, and evaluate security plans to protect the company from liability.
12 Develop/select, implement, and evaluate security plans to protect employees (for example, injuries resulting from workplace violence).
13 Develop/select, implement, and evaluate incident and emergency response plans (for example, natural disasters, workplace safety threats, evacuation).

Knowledge of:

52 federal, state, and local workplace health and safety laws and regulations (for example, OSHA, Drug-Free Workplace Act, ADA) [476–497]
53 workplace injury and occupational illness compensation laws and programs (for example, worker's compensation) [480–494]

54 investigation procedures of workplace safety, health, and security enforcement agencies (for example, OSHA) [486–494]
55 workplace safety risks [476–494]
56 workplace security risks (for example, theft, corporate espionage, information systems/technology, and vandalism) [503–504; 525–526]
57 potential violent behavior and workplace violence conditions [500–503]
58 general health and safety practices (for example, fire evacuation, HAZCOM, ergonomic evaluations) [481–484]
59 incident and emergency response plans [503]
60 internal investigation and surveillance techniques [522–525]
61 Employee Assistance Programs [498–499]
62 employee wellness programs [497–499]
63 issues related to chemical use and dependency (for example, identification of symptoms, drug testing, discipline) [494–496; 526–529]

CORE Knowledge Required by HR Professionals

64 needs assessment and analysis [278–281]
65 third-party contract management, including development of requests for proposals (RFPs) [—]
66 communication strategies [331–333]
67 documentation requirements [★]
68 adult learning processes [283–284]
69 motivation concepts and applications [68–72]
70 training methods [285–295]
71 leadership concepts and applications [—]
72 project management concepts and applications [—]
73 diversity concepts and applications [138–161]
74 human relations concepts and applications (for example, interpersonal and organizational behavior) [—]
75 HR ethics and professional standards [21–26; 116; 419; 513; 580]
76 technology and human resource information systems (HRIS) to support HR activities [41–42; 57–60]
77 qualitative and quantitative methods and tools for analysis, interpretation, and decision-making purposes [43–47; 55–57; 278–281]
78 change management [14–15; 73–75; 362–364]
79 liability and risk management [237; 513–514; 500–504; 513–514; 520–522]
80 job analysis and job description methods [170–196]
81 employee records management (for example, retention, disposal) [52–60; 127–128; 244; 520–522]
82 the interrelationships among HR activities and programs across functional areas [★; 6–8; 16–21; 52–60; 205–206; 235; 491–492]

Appendix B

Current Literature in HR Management*

Students are expected to be familiar with the professional resources and literature in their fields of study. Five groups of resources are listed below.

A. Research-Oriented Journals

In HR management the professional journals are the most immediate and direct communication link between researchers and the practicing managers. These journals contain articles that report on original research. Normally these journals contain either sophisticated writing and quantitative verifications of the author's findings, or conceptual models and literature reviews of previous research.

Academy of Management Journal
Academy of Management Review
Administrative Science Quarterly
American Behavioral Scientist
American Journal of Health Promotion
American Journal of Psychology
American Journal of Sociology
American Psychological Measurement
American Psychologist
American Sociological Review
Annual Review of Psychology
Applied Psychology: An International Review
Behavioral Science
British Journal of Industrial Relations
British Journal of Management
Business Ethics
Cognitive Studies
Decision Sciences
Dispute Resolution Quarterly
Entrepreneurship Theory and Practice
Ethics and Critical Thinking Journal
Group and Organization Studies
Human Organization
Human Relations

Human Resource Development Review
Human Resource Management Journal
Human Resource Management Review
Industrial & Labor Relations Review
Industrial Relations
Industrial Relations Journal
Industrial Relations Law Journal
Interfaces
International Journal of Human Resource
    Management Education
International Journal of Management Reviews
International Journal of Training and
    Development
International Journal of Selection and Assessment
Journal of Abnormal Psychology
Journal of Applied Behavioral Science
Journal of Applied Business Research
Journal of Applied Psychology
Journal of Business
Journal of Business Communications
Journal of Business and Industrial Marketing
Journal of Business and Psychology
Journal of Business Research
Journal of Collective Negotiations
Journal of Communication
Journal of Comparative International Management
Journal of Compensation & Benefits
Journal of Counseling Psychology
Journal of Experimental Social Psychology
Journal of Human Resources
Journal of Individual Employment Rights
Journal of Industrial Relations
Journal of International Business Studies
Journal of International Management
Journal of Knowledge Management
Journal of Labor Economics
Journal of Management
Journal of Management Development

*Special thanks to Professor Gundars Kaupins, Boise State University, for his input into this appendix.

Journal of Management Education
Journal of Management Studies
Journal of Managerial Psychology
Journal of Occupation and Organization
   Psychology
Journal of Organizational Behavior
Journal of Organizational Change Management
Journal of Personality and Social Psychology
Journal of Quality Management
Journal of Quality & Participation
Journal of Social Issues
Journal of Social Psychology
Journal of Social Policy
Journal of Social Psychology
Journal of Vocational Behavior
Labor History
Labor Relations Yearbook
Labour
Management Science
New Technology, Work, and Employment
Occupational Psychology
Organization Behavior and Human Decision
   Processes
Personnel Monographs
Personnel Psychology
Personnel Review
Psychological Bulletin
Psychological Review
Public Personnel Management
Quarterly Review of Distance Education
Social Forces
Social Science Research
Sociology Perspective
Sociometry
Work and Occupations

B. Selected Professional/Managerial Journals

These journals generally cover a wide range of subjects. Articles in these publications normally are aimed at HR professionals and managers. Most articles in these publications are written to interpret, summarize, or discuss the implications of research. They also provide operational and administrative ideas.

Academy of Management Executive
Across the Board
Administrative Management
Arbitration Journal
Australian Journal of Management
Benefits and Compensation Solutions
Business
Business Horizons
Business Management
Business Monthly
Business Quarterly
Business and Social Review
Business Week
California Management Review
Canadian Manager
Columbia Journal of World Business
Compensation and Benefits Management
Compensation and Benefits Review
Corporate Governance
Directors and Boards
Economist
Employee Benefit Plan Review
Employee Benefits News
Employee Relations Law Journal
Employment Practices Decisions
Employment Relations
Employment Relations Today
Forbes
Fortune
Global HR
Harvard Business Review
Hospital and Health Services Administration
HR Magazine
Human Behavior
Human Resource Executive
Human Resource Management
Human Resource Planning
IHRIM Link
INC.

Incentive
Industrial Management
Industry Week
International Management
Journal of Business Strategy
Journal of Pension Planning
Journal of Systems Management
Labor Law Journal
Long Range Planning
Manage
Management Consulting
Management Planning
Management Review
Management Solutions
Management Today
Management World
Managers Magazine
Michigan State University Business Topics
Monthly Labor Review
Nation's Business
Next Frontier
Occupational Health & Safety
Occupational Outlook Quarterly
Organizational Dynamics
Pension World
Personnel
Personnel Journal
Personnel Management
Personnel Management Abstracts
Psychology Today
Public Administration Review
Public Manager
Public Opinion Quarterly
Recruiting Today
Research Management
SAM Advanced Management Journal
Security Management
Sloan Management Review
Supervision
Supervisory Management
Training
Training and Development
Workforce
Working Woman
Workplace Ergonomics
Workspan
WorldatWork Journal

C. Selected HR-Related Internet Links

American Arbitration Association
  http://www.adr.org
Academy of Management
  http://www.aom.pace.edu
American Federation of Labor/Congress of
  Industrial Organizations (AFL-CIO)
  http://www.aflcio.org
American Institute for Managing Diversity
  http://www.aimd.org
American Psychological Association
  http://www.apa.org
American Society for Industrial Security
  http://www.asisonline.org
American Society for Payroll Management
  http://www.aspm.org
American Society for Training and Development
  http://www.astd.org
Australian Human Resource Institute
  http://www.ahri.com.au
CPR Institute for Dispute Resolution
  http://www.cpradr.org
Employee Benefit Research Institute
  http://www.ebri.org
Employment Management Association
  http://www.shrm.org/ema
Foundation for Enterprise Development
  http://www.fed.org
Hong Kong Institute of Human Resource
  Management
  http://www.hkihrm.org
Human Resource Certification Institute
  http://www.hrci.org
Industrial Relations Research Association
  http://www.ilr.cornell.edu/irra
Institute for International Human Resources
  http://www.shrm.org/docs/IIHR.html
Institute of Personnel and Development (UK)
  http://www.ipd.co.uk
International Association for Human Resource
  Information Management
  http://ihrim.org
International Association of Industrial Accident
  Boards and Commissions
  http://www.iaiabc.org
International Foundation of Employee Benefit
  Plans (IFEBP)
  http://www.ifebp.org

International Personnel Management Association
http://www.ipma~hr.org
International Personnel Management Association
 Assessment Council
http://ipmaac.org
National Center for Employee Ownership
http://www.nceo.org
National Health Information Research Center
http://www.nhirc.org
Society for Human Resource Management
http://www.shrm.org
Union Resource Network
http://www.unions.org
World at Work
http://www.worldatwork.org

D. Selected Government Internet Links

Bureau of Labor Statistics
http://stats.bls.gov
Census Bureau
http://www.census.gov
Department of Labor
http://www.dol.gov
Economic Statistics Briefing Room
http://www.whitehouse.gov/fsbr/esbr.html
Employment and Training Administration
http://www.do/eta.gov
Equal Employment Opportunity Commission
http://www.eeoc.gov
FedStats
http://www.fedstats.gov
National Institute of Environmental Health Sciences
http://www.niehs.nih.gov
National Institute for Safety and Health (NIOSH)
http://www.cdc.gov/niosh/homepage.html
National Labor Relations Board
http://www.nlrb.gov
Occupational Safety and Health Administration
http://www.osha.gov
Office of Personnel Management
http://www.opm.gov
Pension Benefit Guaranty Corporation
http://www.pbgc.gov
Pension and Welfare Benefits Administration
http://www.dol.gov/dol/pwba
Small Business Administration
http://www.sba.gov

Social Security Administration
http://www.ssa.gov
Training Technology Resource Center
http://www.ttrc.doleta.gov
U. S. House of Representatives
http://www.house.gov
U. S. Senate
http://www.senate.gov

E. Abstracts, Indices, and Databases

ABI Inform Global
ACM Digital
ArticleFirst
Arts & Humanities Search
Book Review Digest
Books in Print
Business and Company ASAP
ComAbstracts
ContentsFirst
Criminal Justice Abstracts
Dissertation Abstracts
Ebsco Masterfile Premier
Ebsco Online Citations
ECO: Electronic Collections Online
EconLit
Education
ERIC
Essay and General Literature Index
Expanded Academic Index
Government Periodicals
GPO Monthly Catalog
Health Reference Center
HRAF: Human Relations Area
Human Resource Abstracts
Index to Legal Periodicals and Books
Internet and Personal Computing Abstracts
NCJRS Justice Information Center
NetFirst
Newspaper Source from Ebsco
PAIS: Public Affairs Information Service
PapersFirst
PsycInfo
Readers Guide Abstracts
Sociological Abstracts

Appendix C

Major Federal Equal Employment Opportunity Laws and Regulations

Act	Year	Key Provisions
Broad-Based Discrimination		
Title VII, Civil Rights Act of 1964	*1964*	*Prohibits discrimination in employment on basis of race, color, religion, sex or national origin.*
Executives Orders 11246 and 11375	*1965* *1967*	*Require federal contractors and subcontractors to eliminate employment discrimination and prior discrimination through affirmative action.*
Executive Order 11478	*1969*	*Prohibits discrimination in the U.S. Postal Service and in the various government agencies on the basis of race, color, religion, sex, national origin, handicap, or age.*
Vietnam-Era Veterans Readjustment Act	*1974*	*Prohibits discriminations against Vietnam-era veterans by federal contractors and the U.S. government and requires affirmative action.*
Civil Rights Act of 1991	*1991*	*Overturns several past Supreme Court decisions and changes damage claims provisions.*
Congressional Accountability Act	*1995*	*Extends EEO and Civil Rights Act provisions to U.S. congressional staff.*
Race/National Origin Discrimination		
Immigration Reform and Control Act	*1986* *1990* *1996*	*Establishes penalties for employers who knowingly hire illegal aliens; prohibits employment discrimination on the basis of national origin or citizenship.*
Gender/Sex Discrimination		
Equal Pay Act	*1963*	*Requires equal pay for men and women performing substantially the same work.*
Pregnancy Discrimination Act	*1978*	*Prohibits discrimination against women affected by pregnancy, childbirth, or related medical conditions; requires that they be treated as all other employees for employment-related purposes, including benefits.*
Age Discrimination		
Age Discrimination in Employment Act (as amended in 1978 and 1986)	*1967*	*Prohibits discrimination against persons over age 40 and restricts mandatory retirement requirements, except where age is a bona fide occupational qualification.*
Older Workers Benefit Protection Act of 1990	*1990*	*Prohibits age-based discrimination in early retirement and other benefits plans.*
Disability Discrimination		
Vocational Rehabilitation Act *Rehabilitation Act of 1974*	*1973* *1974*	*Prohibit employers with federal contracts over $2,500 from discriminating against individuals with disabilities.*
Americans with Disabilities Act	*1990*	*Requires employer accommodations for individuals with disabilities.*

Starting A Career*

Individuals completing college degrees usually should think about their careers and getting jobs about a year before graduation. The concerns for younger students with limited experience may be somewhat different from those of older students who have five, ten, or more years of work experience, but are completing degrees as part of career enhancement efforts. While some of the concerns may differ, all individuals considering starting or expanding their careers have questions about job search, resume preparation, and interviewing. The purpose of this appendix is to provide some tips that may aid your chance of success in the job market. Many other resources are available to you, and you are encouraged to make use of as many of these as possible.

Beginning the Job Search

As you begin preparing for a job search, or to change jobs either internally or externally if you are currently employed, you should have two primary considerations: (a) what jobs are of interest and available, and (b) what your capabilities and interests might be.

Checking out Job Opportunities There are many sources that can be used to check out the availability of job opportunities. Newspapers and business magazines often carry headlines regarding employment trends and career issues. One valuable source is the placement/career center at your college/university for information on career opportunities and on which industries and fields are in high demand or are crowded with applicants. Campus career fairs featuring employers hiring for different areas provide opportunities to collect information on available jobs and preferred skills for a variety of employers. Also, most states have employment information through the Department of Labor or Job Service. The federal government publishes the Occupational Outlook Handbook, and America's Job Bank, available at *www.ajb,* is an excellent source to check.

A major source for checking out job opportunities is the Internet. There are many Web sites, both general ones and specific ones in designated fields. Also, many professional associations have employment listings for their members. In addition, accessing specific employer Web sites can provide information on job possibilities.

Know your Interests and Capabilities The other key preparation step is to know your interests and capabilities. First, sit down and determine your abilities, skills, work values, interests, strengths, and weaknesses. Next, go back to

*The authors thank Nealy A. Vicker for her assistance with this appendix and the sample resumes in it.

your list and determine what your job focus should be. For example, if you have good analytical skills, like understanding and explaining how systems or processes work, and enjoy solving problems, you may want to consider jobs that use these capabilities. However, if you like dealing with people, problems, and variety in your job responsibilities, certain other career areas may be appropriate.

What you are willing and able to do will begin to shape your job search. You will use this information in determining types of positions that are of interest and employers you want to contact. You must be honest with yourself and know your strengths and weaknesses. Only then will you head down a career path to landing a job that fits you as a person. Once you have identified your interests and capabilities, you should prepare or update your resume.

The Resume

Many individuals put off constructing a resume for fear that they do not have enough information to put on the page or because of a lack of personal focus. If you have completed the key step of the job search process—knowing who you are—it will be easier to construct your resume. The resume is important because it is the first impression the employer will have of you as a candidate. Unfortunately, employers often spend less than a minute looking at this document; therefore, you must make it an effective marketing document for you.

Some general guidelines for resume construction are as follows:

1. *Usually keep it to one page.* Be aware that employers may look at your resume initially for only about a minute. Keep it to the point and on one page. Only those individuals who have significant work experience, such as more experienced adult students, should have two-page resumes.
2. *No mistakes!* Lack of attention to the details on your resume will speak a thousand words to the employer. Have three knowledgeable people proofread it, and then correct any mistakes in spelling, punctuation, and grammar.
3. *No personal information.* Employers can't legally ask about your marital and family status, weight, health, height, or age, and the resume is not the place to provide this information.
4. *Provide contact information.* Be sure to include your name, address, phone number, and e-mail address. Use contact information that will remain current if you are nearing graduation.
5. *Keep your resume uncluttered.* Use a readable type style, no smaller than 10–12 points, and avoid the use of graphics that can distract from your text. Many resumes today are being submitted electronically, so be sure yours will be easy to read and will transmit clearly. For printed resumes use a good-quality printer and good-quality bond paper of a conservative color.
6. *Place your most important information close to the top.* Include your name, contact details, career objective, education, skills, and related work experience. Make it easy for the employer to find items of importance.
7. *Use action verbs, and avoid using "I."* Your resume should include statements stressing your accomplishments, not just listing your job duties.
8. *Do not put your references on the resume.* Indicate that references are available upon request. Be sure you compile a list of references should it be requested.

Resume Format A variety of resume formats can be used. Some of them can be seen on various career-oriented websites, which allow you to construct your resume using format templates. For college graduates with limited work experience, the chronological format is used most often. However, for adult students with significant professional experience, either the chronological or functional format may be used. Figure D-1 on page 618 shows an example of a chronological resume. Notice that the experience listed contains details on accomplishments, not just a listing of tasks performed on the jobs. Figure D-2 on page 619 is a functional resume that focuses on capabilities and accomplishments. Both resumes contain key words. The inclusion of key words aids employers in sorting and locating resumes in electronic scanning databases. A similar version also can be used for submitting your resume electronically over the Internet or World Wide Web.

Cover Letter

The purpose of the cover letter is to tell employers why you are writing, and to persuade them to consider you for an interview if an opening exists, or to consider you for future openings. Submission of electronic resumes may not require a cover letter, depending on the parameters identified by employers. Some employers accept electronic cover letters, while others specify that the resume only should be sent electronically. When submitting printed resumes, you should always send a cover letter.

The cover letter must be specific to the company and demonstrate you know what the firm does and how you might fit into the organization. It should be directed to a specific person, or to a title if a person's name is not available. The cover letter must be error-free and one page in length, whether submitted electronically or by mail. It must be specific to the company and to the position of interest. The letter ends with a closing, such as "Sincerely," and signature followed by your typed name. Proofread carefully and make sure you sign it before you send it.

Applications

Some employers will ask you to complete an application before being considered for employment. Make sure you are thorough and complete all sections to the best of your ability. On occasion you may encounter what may be illegal questions on the application form. Questions pertaining to age, gender, marital status, race, national origin, religion, and mental and physical limitations are usually not allowed. It is best if you, as the applicant, leave these questions blank or put a dash (——) in the blank. Employers asking questions for the purpose of EEO compliance should provide these questions on a separate form or after you have been hired.

The Interview

The purpose of the cover letter and resume is to generate an interview. Once you know you have an interview, you must begin to prepare for it. The key to a successful interview is to know yourself, to know the employer and the position for which you are being interviewed, and to be professional and enthusiastic in your approach.

Dana B. Olson
187 Sunnyridge Lane
Villa Park, CA 92861
714-283-6469
DanaOlson@vpcamail.com

Career Objective
A position in Human Resource Management using my capabilities to enhance the growth and profitability of a company.

Education

MidCoast University, Orange, CA	Graduated 2001
B.S. Business Administration	GPA—3.4 of 4.0
Concentration: Human Resource Management	

Work Experience

Human Resource Specialist—Continental Bank, Orange, CA
2001–Present
- Answers employee questions regarding payroll/benefits
- Advises departmental managers on time-off policies
- Explains benefit materials to newly hired workers
- Administers employee bonus incentive plans

Human Resource Assistant—Victoria Entertainment, Woodland Hills, CA
1998–2001
- Developed and conducted interviews for all clerical applicants
- Conducted background and reference checks on applicants
- Developed new system for processing employment paperwork

Customer Service Clerk—Rockwood Health Services, Thousand Oaks, CA
1996–1998
- Resolved various customer-related concerns
- Scheduled clients for appointments in various departments
- Coordinated front desk and reception services for clients
- Prepared weekly and monthly cash balance reports

Activities
Volunteer Coordinator, Big Sisters of Los Angeles—Developed volunteer orientation program, new employee handbook, and intramural athletics program.

Computer Skills
Windows and Microsoft Office: Word, Excel, and PowerPoint

Key Words

* Customer Service	* Payroll
* Human Resource Management	* Computer Skills

Jean M. DeSola

608 Rochester Drive   540-864-9927
Alexandria, VA 22303   DeSola@alxva.com

Seeking a Management position utilizing my strong organizational, managerial, and communications skills.

Education

Maryville University, Reston, Virginia   May 2003
B.S. Business Administration   Concentration: Management
GPA 3.8/4.0

Relevant Skills

Supervisor:
- Increased departmental revenues by 16% by developing and implementing a motivational program for sales staff.
- Implemented and enforced departmental company policies and procedures, which aided in the retention of key employees and the training of new employees.
- Reduced employee turnover by 32% in one year through increased retention and training efforts.

Trainer:
- Improved efficiency and overall sales performance through training 40–50 employees on sales skills and techniques.
- Led and implemented on-the-job training and new employee orientations, which improved new employee productivity and decreased formal training time.
- Increased company and departmental performance through developing and implementing sales training programs.

Finance:
- Managed and monitored large corporate accounts up to $500,000 during high volume and seasonal promotions.
- Managed $400,000 monthly departmental budgets.

Work Experience

Supervisor, Trainer & Outbound Representative   1994–Present
Maxim Industries, Inc., Alexandria, VA

Activities
- Planned and conducted presentations to multi-state sorority conferences.
- Volunteered at the Brigman Shelter tutoring adults on job skills.

Computer Skills: Microsoft Windows, Office (Word, Excel, PowerPoint)

Key Words

* Trainer	* Supervisor
* Budgets	* Computer Skills

Research the Employer You should know what the employer does, where the organization is located, and the requirements and descriptions of the jobs under consideration. With the growth of the Internet, research on many employers can be found on-line. After reviewing the employer information, identify how your capabilities and experiences may match the employer's needs, so that you can give specific examples in the interview and show that you have done your homework. It is also recommended that you prepare a list of questions to ask the interviewer. Remember this is a two-way street, and you will also be making a decision on where will be the best place to begin your career. However, it is not appropriate during a screening interview to ask about your salary or benefits.

Being Prepared for the Interview It is strongly suggested that you participate in a practice interview prior to the real one. Either with friends, family, or others, practice answering typical questions. Many career centers offer video-taped practice interviews. By doing this, you will increase your confidence and comfort level.

You need to make sure that you present a professional appearance. A suit and tie for men and a skirted suit for women are the most appropriate attire, even if the employer has a "business casual" dress code. You should be conservative with accessories, jewelry, makeup, and cologne or perfume. Your hair should be clean and off the face. This is your first step into the professional world, and you need to look the part. Take the time to make sure everything is clean and pressed, because first impressions last the longest. Also, make sure that you reflect enthusiasm about your future.

During the Interview On the day of the interview, plan to arrive about 10 minutes early, which will give you time to locate the proper office. If you are headed to an unfamiliar site, map your route ahead of time and plan for the unexpected. While being lost and having flat tires make funny stories later, your potential employer will not be impressed. Do not smoke before you walk in the door, and remember to get rid of your gum. It is acceptable to have a leather portfolio with extra resumes and a writing portfolio that you take into the interview.

You may initially be greeted by a receptionist or secretary. Be polite and patient if you have to wait. When the person with whom you will be interviewing comes to get you, stand, smile, and shake hands firmly. The person is already forming an impression of you based on this initial interaction.

During the interview, sit straight but be comfortable and maintain an acceptable amount of eye contact with the employer. It is important that you listen to each question in its entirety, because it may contain more than one part. Answer the questions to the best of your ability. When appropriate, use an example to personalize your answer, which allows you to demonstrate your research on the company. It is appropriate to ask for clarification if you do not understand a question, but do not do it often. If you should be given the opportunity to ask some questions, ask two or three questions that are focused on the job and the employer. At the end of the interview, the interviewer should indicate the next step in the selection process and tell you when that will occur. If the interviewer does not give this information, it is acceptable to ask for it.

The employer may invite you back for a second, more extensive interview. This second interview may include managers, co-workers, and other HR professionals. It also may include meeting with employer representatives at breakfast or lunch. Many students do not think about the meal until it is about to occur. Proper etiquette is very important, especially if you will be placed in situations where you will be dining with clients or customers. Brush up on your dining etiquette before the interview. For example, do not order foods that are difficult to eat or that may spill easily (such as spaghetti), do not order an alcoholic drink even if the employer does, and learn which utensils are appropriate for each course.

Interview Follow-Up Soon after leaving the interview, make notes about the questions asked, areas where you answered well and poorly, and other details. These notes will help you later in preparing for additional interviews and in making your employment decision.

It is important to take time to send a thank-you note or e-mail. If you interviewed with several people in the company, send a thank-you note or e-mail to all appropriate individuals. In the note, thank them for their time, and again express your interest in the position. If you are no longer interested in the position, send a thank-you note indicating that as well.

Accepting a Position

This step is the one you hope to get to quickly! Before accepting a position, make sure you have in writing the starting salary and start date, the benefit package, and the location. Once you have accepted a position, you should cease your job search. It is unethical to continue to interview once you have accepted a position, and it could have long-term ramifications for your career.

Concluding Thoughts

You have worked long and hard to get to this point. With preparation, determination, and persistence, you will be able to reach your goal. The main points are to know yourself and what you are looking for, to know the employers and what they are looking for, and to be able to communicate these things in writing and in person. The easier you can make it for employers to see that the qualifications you offer fit what they need, the more successful you will be.

Good luck!

Glossary

Active practice The performance of job-related tasks and duties by trainees during training.

Adverse selection Situation in which only higher-risk employees select and use certain benefits.

Affirmative action Process in which employers identify problem areas, set goals, and take positive steps to enhance opportunities for protected-class members.

Affirmative Action Plan (AAP) Formal document that an employer compiles annually for submission to enforcement agencies.

Applicant pool All persons who are actually evaluated for selection.

Applicant population A subset of the labor force population that is available for selection using a particular recruiting approach.

Arbitration Process that uses a neutral third party to make a decision.

Assessment center A collection of instruments and exercises designed to diagnose individuals' development needs.

Attitude survey One that focuses on employees' feelings and beliefs about their jobs and the organization.

Autonomy The extent of individual freedom and discretion in the work and its scheduling.

Availability analysis An analysis that identifies the number of protected-class members available to work in the appropriate labor markets in given jobs.

Balance-sheet approach Compensation package that equalizes cost differences between international assignments and those in the home country.

Bargaining unit Employees eligible to select a single union to represent and bargain collectively for them.

Base Pay The basic compensation an employee receives, usually as a wage or salary.

Behavior modeling Copying someone else's behavior.

Behavioral interview Interview in which applicants give specific examples of how they have performed a certain task or handled a problem in the past.

Behavioral rating approach Assesses an employee's behaviors instead of other characteristics.

Benchmark job Job found in many organizations and performed by several individuals who have similar duties that are relatively stable and require similar KSAs.

Benchmarking Comparing specific measures of performance against data on those measures in other "best practice" organizations.

Benefit Indirect compensation given to an employee or group of employees as a part of organizational membership.

Benefits needs analysis A comprehensive look at all aspects of benefits.

Bona fide occupational qualification (BFOQ) Characteristic providing a legitimate reason why an employer can exclude persons on otherwise illegal bases of consideration.

Bonus A one-time payment that does not become part of the employee's base pay.

Broadbanding Practice of using fewer pay grades having broader ranges than in traditional compensation systems.

Business agent A full-time union official who operates the union office and assists union members.

Business necessity A practice necessary for safe and efficient organizational operations.

Career The series of work-related positions a person occupies throughout life.

Central tendency error Rating all employees in a narrow range in the middle of the rating scale.

Checklist Performance appraisal tool that uses a list of statements or words that are checked by raters.

Closed shop A firm that requires individuals to join a union before they can be hired.

Coaching Training and feedback given to employees by immediate supervisors.

Co-determination A practice whereby union or worker representatives are given positions on a company's board of directors.

Cognitive ability tests Tests that measure an individual's thinking, memory, reasoning, and verbal and mathematical abilities.

Collective bargaining Process whereby representatives of management and workers negotiate over wages, hours, and other terms and conditions of employment.

Commission Compensation computed as a percentage of sales in units or dollars.

Compa-ratio Pay level divided by the midpoint of the pay range.

Compensable factor Identifies a job value commonly present throughout a group of jobs.

Compensation committee A subgroup of the board of directors composed of directors who are not officers of the firm.

Compensatory time off Hours given in lieu of payment for extra time worked.

Competencies Basic characteristics that can be linked to enhanced performance by individuals or teams.

Complaint Indication of employee dissatisfaction.

Compressed workweek One in which a full week's work is accomplished in fewer than five days.

Conciliation Process by which a third party attempts to keep union and management negotiators talking so that they can reach a voluntary settlement.

Concurrent validity Measured when an employer tests current employees and correlates the scores with their performance ratings.

Construct validity Validity showing a relationship between an abstract characteristic and job performance.

Constructive discharge Occurs when an employer deliberately makes conditions intolerable in an attempt to get an employee to quit.

Content validity Validity measured by use of a logical, nonstatistical method to identify the KSAs and other characteristics necessary to perform a job.

Contractual rights Rights based on a specific contractual agreement between employer and employee.

Contrast error Tendency to rate people relative to others rather than against performance standards.

Contributory plan Pension plan in which the money for pension benefits is paid in by both employees and employers.

Co-payment Employee's payment of a portion of the cost of both insurance premiums and medical care.

Core competency A unique capability that creates high value and that differentiates the organization from its competition.

Correlation coefficient Index number giving the relationship between a predictor and a criterion variable.

Cost-benefit analysis Comparison of costs and benefits associated with training.

Craft union One whose members do one type of work, often using specialized skills and training.

Criterion-related validity Validity measured by a procedure that uses a test as the predictor of how well an individual will perform on the job.

Culture Societal forces affecting the values, beliefs, and actions of a distinct group of people.

Cumulative trauma disorders (CTDs) Muscle and skeletal injuries that occur when workers repetitively use the same muscles to perform tasks.

Decertification Process whereby a union is removed as the representative of a group of employees.

Defined-benefit plan One in which an employee is promised a pension amount based on age and service.

Defined-contribution plan One in which the employer makes an annual payment to an employee's pension account.

Development Efforts to improve employees' ability to handle a variety of assignments.

Differential piece-rate system A system in which employees are paid one piece-rate wage for units produced up to a standard output and a higher piece-rate wage for units produced over the standard.

Disabled person Someone who has a physical or mental impairment that substantially limits life activities, who has a record of such an impairment, or who is regarded as having such an impairment.

Discipline Form of training that enforces organizational rules.

Disparate impact Occurs when substantial underrepresentation of protected-class members results from employment decisions that work to their disadvantage.

Disparate treatment Situation that exists when protected-class members are treated differently from others.

Distributive justice Perceived fairness in the distribution of outcomes.

Diversity The differences among people.

Draw An amount advanced from and repaid to future commissions earned by the employee.

Due process Means used for individuals to explain and defend their actions against charges or discipline.

Duty A larger work segment composed of several tasks that are performed by an individual.

Economic value added (EVA) A firm's net operating profit after the cost of capital is deducted.

e-learning The use of the Internet or an organizational intranet to conduct training on-line.

Employee assistance program One program that provides counseling and other help to employees having emotional, physical, or other personal problems.

Employee stock ownership plan (ESOP) A plan whereby employees gain stock ownership in the organization for which they work.

Employment-at-will (EAW) A common law doctrine stating that employers have the right to hire, fire, demote, or promote whomever they choose, unless there is a law or contract to the contrary.

Employment contract Agreement that formally outlines the details of employment.

Employment "test" Any employment procedure used as the basis for making an employment-related decision.

Environmental scanning Process of studying the environment of the organization to pinpoint opportunities and threats.

Encapsulated development Situation in which an individual learns new methods and ideas in a development course and returns to a work unit that is still bound by old attitudes and methods.

Equal employment opportunity (EEO) Individuals should have equal treatment in all employment-related actions.

Equity The perceived fairness of what the person does compared with what the person receives.

Ergonomics The study and design of the work environment to address physiological and physical demands on individuals.

Essential job functions Fundamental duties of a job.

Exempt employees Employees to whom employers are not required to pay overtime under the Fair Labor Standards Act.

Exit interview An interview in which individuals are asked to identify reasons for leaving the organization.

Expatriate An employee, working in an operation, who is not a citizen of the country in which the operation is located, but is a citizen of the country of the headquarters organization.

Expatriation Preparing and sending global employees to their foreign assignments.

Extranet An Internet-linked network that allows employees access to information provided by external entities.

Federation Group of autonomous national and international unions.

Feedback The amount of information received about how well or how poorly one has performed.

Flexible benefits plan One that allows employees to select the benefits they prefer from groups of benefits established by the employer.

Flexible spending account Account that allows employees to contribute pretax dollars to buy additional benefits.

Flexible staffing Use of recruiting sources and workers who are not traditional employees.

Flextime Scheduling arrangement in which employees work a set number of hours per day but vary starting and ending times.

Forced distribution Performance appraisal method in which ratings of employees' performance are distributed along a bell-shaped curve.

Forecasting Use of information from the past and present to identify expected future conditions.

401(k) plan An agreement in which a percentage of an employee's pay is withheld and invested in a tax-deferred account.

4/5ths Rule Rule stating that discrimination generally is considered to occur if the selection rate for a protected group is less than 80% (4/5ths) of the selection rate for the majority group or less than 80% of the group's representation in the relevant labor market.

Gainsharing The sharing with employees of greater-than-expected gains in profits and/or productivity.

Garnishment A court action in which a portion of an employee's wages is set aside to pay a debt owed a creditor.

Glass ceiling Discriminatory practices that have prevented women and other protected-class members from advancing to executive-level jobs.

Global organization One having corporate units in a number of countries integrated to operate worldwide.

Golden parachute A severance benefit that provides protection and security to executives in the event that they lose their jobs or their firms are acquired by other firms.

Graphic rating scale A scale that allows the rater to mark an employee's performance on a continuum.

Green-circled employee An incumbent who is paid below the range set for the job.

Grievance Complaint formally stated in writing.

Grievance arbitration Means by which a third party settles disputes arising from different interpretations of a labor contract.

Grievance procedures Formal channels of communications used to resolve grievances.

Halo effect Rating a person high on all items because of performance in one area.

Health A general state of physical, mental, and emotional well-being.

Health maintenance organization (HMO) Managed care plan that provides services for a fixed period on a prepaid basis.

Health promotion A supportive approach to facilitate and encourage employees to enhance healthy actions and lifestyles.

Host-country national An employee working for a firm in an operation who is a citizen of the country where the operation is located, but where the headquarters for the firm are in another country.

Hostile environment Sexual harassment where an individual's work performance or psychological well-being is unreasonably affected by intimidating or offensive working conditions.

HR audit A formal research effort that evaluates the current state of HR management in an organization.

HR generalist A person with responsibility for performing a variety of HR activities.

HR research The analysis of data from HR records to determine the effectiveness of past and present HR practices.

HR specialist A person with in-depth knowledge and expertise in a limited area of HR.

HR strategies Means used to anticipate and manage the supply of and demand for human resources.

Human resource information system (HRIS) An integrated system designed providing information used in HR decision making.

Human resource (HR) management The design of formal systems in an organization to ensure effective and efficient use of human talent to accomplish organizational goals.

Human resource (HR) planning Process of analyzing and identifying the need for and availability of human resources so that the organization can meet its objectives.

Illegal issues Collective bargaining issues that would require either party to take illegal action.

Immediate confirmation The concept that people learn best if reinforcement and feedback is given after training.

Importing and exporting Selling and buying goods and services with organizations in other countries.

Independent contractors Workers who perform specific services on a contract basis.

Individual-centered career planning Career planning that focuses on individuals' careers rather than on organizational needs.

Individualism Dimension of culture that refers to the extent to which people in a country prefer to act as individuals instead of members of groups.

Individual retirement account (IRA) A special account in which an employee can set aside funds that will not be taxed until the employee retires.

Industrial union One that includes many persons working in the same industry or company, regardless of jobs held.

Informal training Training that occurs through interactions and feedback among employees.

Integrated disability management programs A benefit that combines disability insurance programs and efforts to reduce workers' compensation claims.

Intranet An organizational network that operates over the Internet.

Job Grouping of tasks, duties, and responsibilities that constitutes the total work assignment for employees.

Job analysis Systematic way to gather and analyze information about the content, context, and the human requirements of jobs.

Job criteria Important elements in a given job.

Job description Identification of the tasks, duties, and responsibilities of a job.

Job design Organizing tasks, duties, and responsibilities into a productive unit of work.

Job enlargement Broadening the scope of a job by expanding the number of different tasks to be performed.

Job enrichment Increasing the depth of a job by adding the responsibility for planning, organizing, controlling, and evaluating the job.

Job evaluation The systematic determination of the relative worth of jobs within an organization.

Job posting A system in which the employer provides notices of job openings and employees respond to apply.

Job rotation The process of shifting an employee from job to job.

Job satisfaction A positive emotional state resulting from evaluating one's job experience.

Job specifications The knowledge, skills, and abilities (KSAs) an individual needs to perform a job satisfactorily.

Just cause Reasonable justification for taking employment-related actions.

Keogh plan A type of individualized pension plan for self-employed individuals.

Labor force population All individuals who are available for selection if all possible recruitment strategies are used.

Labor markets The external supply pool from which organizations attract employees.

Lockout Shutdown of company operations undertaken by management to prevent union members from working.

Lock out/tag out regulations Requirements that locks and tags be used to make equipment inoperative for repair or adjustment.

Long-term orientation Dimension of culture that refers to values people hold that emphasize the future, as opposed to short-term values focusing on the present and the past.

Lump-sum increase (LSI) A one-time payment of all or part of a yearly pay increase.

Managed care Approaches that monitor and reduce medical costs using restrictions and market system alternatives.

Marginal functions Duties that are part of a job but are incidental or ancillary to the purpose and nature of a job.

Management by objectives (MBO) Specifies the performance goals that an individual and her or his manager agree to try to attain within an appropriate length of time.

Management rights Those rights reserved to the employer to manage, direct, and control its business.

Mandated benefits Ones that employers in the United States must provide to employees by law.

Mandatory issues Collective bargaining issues identified specifically by labor laws or court decisions as subject to bargaining.

Market line The line on a graph showing the relationship between job value, as determined by job evaluation points and pay survey rates.

Masculinity/femininity Dimension of cultures that refers to the degree to which "masculine" values prevail over "feminine" values.

Massed practice The performance of all of the practice at once.

Maturity curve Curve that depicts the relationship between experience and pay rates.

Mediation Process by which a third party assists negotiators in reaching a settlement.

Mentoring A relationship in which experienced managers aid individuals in the earlier stages of their careers.

Motivation The desire within a person causing that person to act.

Multinational enterprise (MNE) An organization with operating units located in foreign countries.

National emergency strike A strike that would impact the national economy significantly.

Non-compete agreement Agreement that prohibits an individual who leaves the organization from competing with the employer in the same line of business for a specified period of time.

Non-contributory plan Pension plan in which all the funds for pension benefits are provided by the employer.

Nondirective interview Interview that uses questions that are developed from the answers to previous questions.

Non-exempt employees Employees who must be paid overtime under the Fair Labor Standards Act.

Ombudsman Person outside the normal chain of command who acts as a problem solver for both management and employees.

Open shop Workers are not required to join or pay dues to unions.

Organization-centered career planning Career planning that focuses on jobs and on identifying career paths that provide for the logical progression of people between jobs in an organization.

Organizational commitment The degree to which employees believe in and accept organizational goals and desire to remain with the organization.

Organizational culture The shared values and beliefs of a workforce.

Orientation The planned introduction of new employees to their jobs, co-workers, and the organization.

Paid time-off plan Plan that combines all sick leave, vacation time, and holidays into a total number of hours or days that employees can take off with pay.

Panel interview Interview in which several interviewers interview the candidate at the same time.

Pay compression Situation in which pay differences among individuals with different levels of experience and performance in the organization becomes small.

Pay equity Similarity in pay for all jobs requiring comparable levels of knowledge, skill, and ability, even if actual duties and market rates differ significantly.

Pay grade A grouping of individual jobs having approximately the same job worth.

Pay survey A collection of data on compensation rates for workers performing similar jobs in other organizations.

Peer review panel A panel of employees hear appeals from disciplined employees and make recommendations or decisions.

Pension plans Retirement benefits established and funded by employers and employees.

Performance What an employee does or does not do.

Performance appraisal The process of evaluating how well employees perform their jobs when compared to a set of standards, and then communicating that information to employees.

Performance consulting A process in which a trainer and the organizational client work together to boost workplace performance in support of business goals.

Performance management system Processes used to identify, encourage, measure, evaluate, improve, and reward employee performance.

Performance standards Expected levels of performance.

Permissive issues Collective bargaining issues that are not mandatory but relate to certain jobs.

Perquisites (perks) Special benefits—usually noncash items—for executives.

Person-job fit Matching the KSAs of people with the characteristics of jobs.

Person-organization fit The congruence between individuals and organizational factors.

Phased retirement Approach in which employees reduce their workloads and pay.

Physical ability tests Tests that measure individual abilities such as strength, endurance, and muscular movement.

Placement Fitting a person to the right job.

Policies General guidelines that focus organizational actions.

Portability A pension plan feature that allows employees to move their pension benefits from one employer to another.

Power distance Dimension of culture that refers to the inequality among the people of a nation.

Predictive validity Measured when test results of applicants are compared with subsequent job performance.

Preferred provider organization (PPO) A health-care provider that contracts with an employer group to provide health-care services to employees at a competitive rate.

Primacy effect Information received first gets the most weight

Primary research Research method in which data are gathered firsthand for the specific project being conducted.

Procedural justice Perceived fairness of the process used to make decisions about employees.

Procedures Customary methods of handling activities.

Production cells Groupings of workers who produce entire products or components.

Productivity A measure of the quantity and quality of work done, considering the cost of the resources used.

Profit sharing A system to distribute a portion of the profits of the organization to employees.

Protected class Individuals within a group identified for protection under equal employment laws and regulations.

Psychological contract The unwritten expectations employees and employers have about the nature of their work relationships.

Psychomotor tests Tests that measure dexterity, hand-eye coordination, arm-hand steadiness, and other factors.

Quality circle Small group of employees who monitor productivity and quality and suggest solutions to problems.

Quid pro quo Sexual harassment in which employment outcomes are linked to the individual's granting sexual favors.

Ranking Listing of all employees from highest to lowest in performance.

Rater bias Error that occurs when a rater's values or prejudices distort the rating.

Ratification Process by which union members vote to accept the terms of a negotiated labor agreement.

Realistic job preview (RJP) The process through which a job applicant receives an accurate picture of a job.

Recency effect Error in which the rater gives greater weight to recent events when appraising an individual's performance.

Reasonable accommodation A modification or adjustment to a job or work environment for a qualified individual with a disability.

Recruiting The process of generating a pool of qualified applicants for organizational jobs.

Red-circled employee An incumbent who is paid above the range set for the job.

Reinforcement People tend to repeat responses that give them some type of positive reward and avoid actions associated with negative consequences.

Reliability Consistency with which a test measures an item.

Repatriation Planning, training, and reassignment of global employees to their home countries.

Responsibilities Obligations to perform certain tasks and duties.

Retaliation Punitive actions taken by employers against individuals who exercise their legal rights.

Return on investment (ROI) Calculation showing the value of expenditures for HR activities.

Reverse discrimination When a person is denied an opportunity because of preferences given to protected-class individuals who may be less qualified.

Right to privacy Defined for individuals as the freedom from unauthorized and unreasonable intrusion into their personal affairs.

Rights That which belongs to a person by law, nature, or tradition.

Right-to-sue letter A letter issued by the EEOC that notifies a complainant that he or she has 90 days in which to file a personal suit in federal court.

Right-to-work laws State laws that prohibit requiring employees to join unions as a condition of obtaining or continuing employment.

Rules Specific guidelines that regulate and restrict the behavior of individuals.

Sabbatical leave Paid time off the job to develop and rejuvenate oneself.

Safety Condition in which the physical well-being of people is protected.

Salaries Consistent payments made each period regardless of number of hours worked.

Salting Practice in which unions hire and pay people to apply for jobs at certain companies.

Secondary research Research method using data already gathered by others and reported in books, articles in professional journals, or other sources.

Security Protection of employees and organizational facilities.

Security audit A comprehensive review of organizational security.

Selection Process of choosing individuals who have needed qualifications to fill jobs in an organization.

Selection criterion Characteristic that a person must have to do a job successfully.

Selection rate The percentage hired form a given group of candidates.

Self-directed work team One composed of individuals assigned a cluster of tasks, duties, and responsibilities to be accomplished.

Self-efficacy A person's belief that he/she can successfully learn the training program content.

Seniority Time spent in the organization or on a particular job.

Separation agreement Agreement in which a terminated employee agrees not to sue the employer in exchange for specified benefits.

Serious health condition A health condition requiring inpatient, hospital, hospice, or residential medical care or continuing physician care.

Severance pay A security benefit voluntarily offered by employers to employees who lose their jobs.

Sexual harassment Actions that are sexually directed, are unwanted, and subject the worker to adverse employment conditions or create a hostile work environment.

Shamrock team One composed of a core of members, resource experts who join the team as appropriate, and part-time/temporary members as needed.

Simulation A development technique that requires participants to analyze a situation and decide the best course of action based on the data given.

Situational interview A structured interview composed of questions about how applicants might handle specific job situations.

Skill variety The extent to which the work requires several different activities for successful completion.

Spaced practice Several practice sessions spaced over a period of hours or days.

Special-purpose team Organizational team formed to address specific problems, improve work processes, and enhance product and service quality.

Statutory rights Rights based on laws.

Stock option A plan that gives an individual the right to buy stock in a company, usually at a fixed price for a period of time.

Straight piece-rate system A pay system in which wages are determined by multiplying the number of units produced by the piece rate for one unit.

Strategic human resource management Organizational use of employees to gain or keep a competitive advantage against competitors.

Stress interview Interview designed to create anxiety and put pressure on an applicant to see how the person responds.

Strike Work stoppage in which union members refuse to work in order to put pressure on an employer.

Structured interview Interview that uses a set of standardized questions asked of all job applicants.

Substance abuse The use of illicit substances or the misuse of controlled substances, alcohol, or other drugs.

Succession planning Process of identifying a longer-term plan for the orderly replacement of key employees.

Suggestion system A formal method of obtaining employee input and upward communication.

Task A distinct, identifiable work activity composed of motions.

Task identity The extent to which the job includes a "whole" identifiable unit of work that is carried out from start to finish and that results in a visible outcome.

Task significance The impact the job has on other people.

Tax equalization plan Compensation plan used to protect expatriates from negative tax consequences.

Team interview Interview in which applicants are interviewed by the team members with whom they will work.

Telecommuting Process of going to work via electronic computing and telecommunications equipment.

Third-country national A citizen of one country, working in a second country, and employed by an organization headquartered in a third country.

Training A process whereby people acquire capabilities to aid in the achievement of organizational goals.

Transition stay bonus Extra payment for employees whose jobs are being eliminated, thereby motivating them to remain with the organization for a period of time.

Turnover Process in which employees leave the organization and have to be replaced.

Uncertainty avoidance Dimension of culture that refers to the preference of people in a country for structured rather than unstructured situations.

Undue hardship Significant difficulty or expense imposed on an employer when making an accommodation for individuals with disabilities.

Union A formal association of workers that promotes the interests of its members through collective action.

Union authorization card Card signed by an employee to designate a union as his or her collective bargaining agent.

Union security provision Contract clauses to aid the union in obtaining and retaining members.

Union steward An employee elected to serve as the first-line representative of unionized workers.

Unit labor cost Computed by dividing the average cost of workers by their average levels of output.

Utility analysis Analysis in which economic or other statistical models are built to identify the costs and benefits associated with specific HR activities.

Utilization analysis An analysis that identifies the number of protected-class members employed and the types of jobs they hold in an organization.

Utilization review An audit and review of the services and costs billed by health-care providers.

Validity Extent to which a test actually measures what it says it measures

Variable pay Type of compensation linked to individual, team, or organizational performance.

Vesting The right of employees to receive benefits from their pension plans.

Wages Payments directly calculated on the amount of time worked.

Wellness programs Programs designed to maintain or improve employee health before problems arise.

Well-pay Extra pay for not taking sick leave.

Whistle-blowers Individuals who report real or perceived wrongs committed by their employers.

Work Effort directed toward producing or accomplishing results.

Workflow analysis A study of the way work (inputs, activities, and outputs) moves through an organization.

Work sample tests Tests that require an applicant to perform a simulated job task.

Workers' compensation Benefits provided to persons injured on the job.

Wrongful discharge Occurs when an employer terminates an individual's employment for reasons that are improper or illegal.

Yield ratios A comparison of the number of applicants at one stage of the recruiting process to the number at the next stage.

Name Index

Container Store, 96–97
county governments and
    incentive programs, 435–436
implementing a new
    compensation program,
    406–407
McDonald's, 603–604
merging 401(k) plans, 469
merging incompatible
    organizational cultures, 62
performance appraisal revision
    at St. Luke's Hospital, 367
recruiting for the
    Ritz-Carlton, 229
reverse mentoring at GE, 333
selection improvement in
    smaller companies, 266
training and customer service,
    300–301
unions, 571–572
Cash balance plans, 449
CBP. *See* Certified Benefits
    Professional
CBS Broadcasting, 101
CCP. *See* Certified Compensation
    Professional
CEBS. *See* Certified Employee
    Benefits Specialist
Central Intelligence Agency, 410
Central tendency error, 360
Ceridian, 273
Certification, 24–25, 560
Certified Benefits Professional
    (CBP), 25
Certified Compensation
    Professional (CCP), 24
Certified Employee Benefits
    Specialist (CEBS), 24
Certified Safety Professional
    (CSP), 25
Charles Schwab & Co., 49, 140, 243
Checklists, for performance
    appraisals, 352, 354
Chief executive officers'
    compensation, 427–428
Chief knowledge officers
    (CKO), 276
Chief learning officers (CLO), 276
Chief privacy officer, 520
Child care, 460
Child labor, 383
Child labor laws, 479–480
    hazardous occupations
        minimum age: 18 years, 480
Child-care assistance, 443
Chrysler, 49

Churning, 331
Circuit City v. Adams, 518
Cisco Systems, 15, 49, 67, 272, 273
    and e-learning, 271
Civil Rights Act of 1964, Title VII,
    105–107, 146, 210
Civil Rights Act of 1991, 107–108,
    151, 484
Classification method, 390–391
Classroom courses and training,
    294, 325–326
Closed shop, 554
CME Inc., 413
Co-determination, 599
Co-payment strategy, 452
Co-worker relations, 88
Coaching, 323
    management, 328–329, 332
COBRA. *See* Consolidated Omnibus
    Budget Reconciliation Act
Coca-Cola, 576
    and race discrimination, 133
Cognitive ability tests, 247–248
COLA. *See* Cost-of-living
    adjustments
Collective bargaining (contract
    negotiation), 561–564
College and university recruiting, 219
Combination jobs, 171
Committee assignments/meetings,
    323–324
Communications Workers of
    America (CWA), 565
Compa-ratio, 402
Comparable worth, 110, 388
Compensable factor, 391
Compensation, 8, 370–407
    base pay, 372–373
    benefits, 372–373
    child labor, 384
    compensatory time off (comp-
        time), 387
    competency-based pay, 379–380
    components chart, 372
    computer-related
        occupations, 385
    Davis-Bacon Act of, 1931, 388
    distributive justice in, 382
    entitlement orientation, 374–375
    Equal Pay Act of, 1963, 388
    equity considerations, 381–382
    exempt and non-exempt status,
        384–386
    external openness, 382
    Fair Labor Standards Act
        (FLSA), 383–387

garnishment laws, 389
    implementing a new program,
        406–407
    independent contractors,
        387–388
    individual vs. team rewards, 380
    integrated and computerized job
        evaluation, 393
    international, 596–598, 603
    IRS test for employees and
        independent contractors, 387
    job evaluation, 390–393
    minimum wage, 383–384
    objectives of, 372
    overtime, 385
    pay equity, 110, 111, 388
    pay openness, 382
    and performance, 85–86
    performance orientation, 375
    procedural justice in, 381–382
    quartile strategies, 378–379
    responsibilities of, 373–374
    salaries, 373
    Service Contracts Act, 388
    state laws, 388
    total rewards approach to, 377
    traditional approach to, 376
    variable pay, 372–373
    wages, 373
    Walsh-Healy Public Contracts
        Act, 388
    see also Benefits; Executive
        compensation; Incentives;
        Organizational incentives;
        Pay; Sales compensation;
        Variable pay
Compensation committee, 430–431
Compensation Link, 403
Compensatory approach, 239
Compensatory damages, 107
Compensatory time off
    (comp-time), 387
Competencies, 193, 195–196
Competency-based pay, 379–380
Competition, and labor supply,
    39–40
Competitive advantage, 30
    linking HR planning and
        strategy for, 33–35
Competitive relations, 546
Complaints, 518, 567
Compliance, 54
Compressed workweek, 177
Compulsory arbitration, 518
Computer security, 503–504
Computer-related occupations, 385